CIMA

KU-520-357

STRATEGIC

PAPER E3

ENTERPRISE STRATEGY

Our text is designed to help you study **effectively** and **efficiently**.

In this edition we:

- **Highlight** the **most important elements** in the syllabus and the **key skills** you will need

- **Signpost** how each chapter links to the syllabus and the learning outcomes

- **Provide** lots of **exam alerts** explaining how what you're learning may be tested

- **Include examples** and **questions** to help you apply what you've learnt

- **Emphasise key points** in **section summaries**

- **Test your knowledge** of what you've studied in **quick quizzes**

- **Examine your understanding** in our **exam question bank**

- **Reference all the important topics** in the **full index**

FOR EXAMS UP TO SEPTEMBER 2013

BPP
LEARNING MEDIA

First edition May 2009
Fourth edition June 2012

ISBN 9781 4453 9604 0

(Previous ISBN 9780 7517 9477 9)

e-ISBN 9781 4453 9261 5

British Library Cataloguing-in-Publication Data
A catalogue record for this book
is available from the British Library

Published by

BPP Learning Media Ltd
BPP House, Aldine Place
London W12 8AA

www.bpp.com/learningmedia

Printed in the United Kingdom

We are grateful to the Chartered Institute of
Management Accountants for permission to
reproduce past examination questions. The
suggested solutions in the exam answer bank have
been prepared by BPP Learning Media Ltd.

Contents

Page

How our Study Text can help you pass

Streamlined studying	• We show you the best ways to study efficiently
	• Our Text has been designed to ensure you can easily and quickly navigate through it
	• The different features in our Text emphasise important knowledge and techniques
Exam expertise	• **Studying E3** (on page xi) introduces the key themes of the syllabus and summarises how to pass
	• We highlight throughout our Text how topics may be tested and what you'll have to do in the exam
	• We help you see the complete picture of the syllabus, so that you can answer questions that range across the whole syllabus
	• Our Text covers the syllabus content – no more, no less
Regular review	• We frequently summarise the key knowledge you need
	• We test what you've learnt by providing questions and quizzes throughout our Text

Our other products

BPP Learning Media also offers these products for the E3 exam:

Practice and Revision Kit	Providing lots more question practice and helpful guidance on how to pass the exam
Passcards	Summarising what you should know, in visual, easy to remember, form
Success CDs	Covering the vital elements of the E3 syllabus in less than 90 minutes and also containing exam hints to help you fine tune your strategy
i-Pass	Providing computer-based testing in a variety of formats, ideal for self-assessment
Interactive Passcards	Allowing you to learn actively with a clear visual format summarising what you must know
Strategic case study kit	Providing question practice with specially written questions, based on the preseen case study material issued by CIMA

You can purchase these products by visiting www.bpp.com/cimamaterials

CIMA Distance Learning

BPP's distance learning packages provide flexibility and convenience, allowing you to study effectively, at a pace that suits you, where and when you choose. There are four great distance learning packages available.

Online classroom	Through live interactive online sessions it provides you with the traditional structure and support of classroom learning, but with the convenience of attending classes wherever you are
Online classroom live	Through pre-recorded online lectures it provides you with the classroom experience via the web with the tutor guidance & support you'd expect from a face to face classroom
Basics Plus	A guided self study package containing a wealth of rich e-learning & physical content
Basics Online	A guided self study package containing a wealth of rich e-learning content

You can find out more about these packages by visiting www.bpp.com/cimadistancelearning

BPP LEARNING MEDIA

Features in our Study Text

 Section Introductions explain how the section fits into the chapter

 Key Terms are the core vocabulary you need to learn

KEY TERM

 Key Points are points that you have to know, ideas or calculations that will be the foundations of your answers

KEY POINT

 Exam Alerts show you how subjects are likely to be tested

 Exam Skills are the key skills you will need to demonstrate in the exam, linked to question requirements

 Examples show how theory is put into practice

 Questions give you the practice you need to test your understanding of what you've learnt

 Case Studies link what you've learnt with the real-world business environment

CASE STUDY

 Links show how the syllabus overlaps with other parts of the qualification, including Knowledge Brought Forward that you need to remember from previous exams

 Website References link to material that will enhance your understanding of what you're studying

 Further Reading will give you a wider perspective on the subjects you're covering

 Section Summaries allow you to review each section

Streamlined studying

What you should do	In order to
Read the Chapter and Section Introductions	See why topics need to be studied and map your way through the chapter
Go quickly through the explanations	Gain the depth of knowledge and understanding that you'll need
Highlight the Key Points and Key Terms	Make sure you know the basics that you can't do without in the exam
Focus on the Exam Skills and Exam Alerts	Know how you'll be tested and what you'll have to do
Work through the Examples and Case Studies	See how what you've learnt applies in practice
Prepare Answers to the Questions	See if you can apply what you've learnt in practice
Revisit the Section Summaries in the Chapter Roundup	Remind you of, and reinforce, what you've learnt
Answer the Quick Quiz	Find out if there are any gaps in your knowledge
Answer the Question(s) in the Exam Question Bank	Practise what you've learnt in depth

Should I take notes?

Brief notes may help you remember what you're learning. You should use the notes format that's most helpful to you (lists, diagrams, mindmaps).

Further help

BPP Learning Media's *Learning to Learn Accountancy* provides lots more helpful guidance on studying. It is designed to be used both at the outset of your CIMA studies and throughout the process of learning accountancy. It can help you **focus your studies on the subject and exam**, enabling you to **acquire knowledge, practise and revise efficiently and effectively.**

Syllabus and learning outcomes

Paper E3 Enterprise Strategy

The syllabus comprises:

Topic and Study Weighting

Interacting with the Competitive Environment	20%
Change Management	20%
Evaluation of Strategic Options	30%
Implementation of Strategic Plans	30%

Learning Outcomes		
Lead	**Component**	**Indicative syllabus content**
Interacting with the Competitive Environment		
1 Evaluate the key external factors affecting an organisation's strategy	(a) Evaluate the impact and influence of the external environment on an organisation and its strategy	(i) Non-market strategy and forms of corporate political activity
	(b) Recommend approaches to business/government relations and to relations with civil society	(ii) External demands for responsible business practices and ways to respond to these
	(c) Discuss the drivers of external demands for corporate social responsibility and the organisation's response	(iii) Stakeholder management (stakeholders to include government and regulatory agencies, non-governmental organisations and civil society, industry associations, customers and suppliers)
	(d) Recommend how to manage relationships with stakeholders	(iv) The customer portfolio: Customer analysis and behaviour, including the marketing audit and customer profitability analysis as well as customer retention and loyalty
	(e) Recommend how to interact with suppliers and customers	(v) Strategic supply chain management
		(iii) Implications of these interactions Chartered Management Accountants and the management accounting system.
2 Evaluate the impact of information systems on an organisation	(a) Evaluate the impact of the internet on an organisation and its strategy	(i) The impact of IT (including the internet) on an organisation (utilising frameworks such as Porter's Five Forces, the Value Chain)
	(b) Evaluate the strategic and competitive impact of information systems	(ii) Competing through exploiting information (rather than technology), eg use of databases to identify potential customers or market segments, and the management of data (warehousing and mining)
		(iii) Contemporary developments in the commercial use of the internet (eg Web 2.0)

Change Management

1	Advise on important elements in the change process	(a)	Discuss the concept of organisational change	(i)	External and internal change triggers (eg environmental factors, mergers and acquisitions, re-organisation and rationalisation)	
		(b)	Recommend techniques to manage resistance to change	(ii)	Stage models of change	
				(iii)	Problem identification as a precursor to change	
				(iv)	Cultural processes of change, ie change within the context of the whole firm	
2	Evaluate tools and methods for successfully implementing a change programme	(a)	Evaluate approaches to managing change	(i)	The importance of managing critical periods of discontinuous change	
		(b)	Compare and contrast continuous and discontinuous change	(ii)	Tools, techniques and models associated with organisational change	
		(c)	Evaluate tools, techniques and strategies for managing the change process	(iii)	Approaches, styles and strategies of change management	
		(d)	Evaluate the role of leadership in managing the change process	(iv)	Importance of adaptation and continuous change	
				(v)	Leading change	
3	Recommend change management processes in support of strategy implementation	(a)	Evaluate the role of change management in the context of strategy implementation	(i)	Change management and its role in the successful implementation of strategy	
		(b)	Evaluate ethical issues and their resolution in the context of organisational change	(ii)	The advantages and disadvantages of different styles of management on the successful implementation of strategy	
				(iii)	Group formation within organisations and its impact on change processes within organisations	
				(iv)	Business ethics in general and the CIMA Code of Ethics for Professional Accountants (Parts A and B) in the context of the implementation of strategic plans	

BPP LEARNING MEDIA

Evaluation of Strategic Position and Strategic Options

1	Evaluate the process of strategy development	(a)	Evaluate the process of strategy formulation	(i)	Mission statements and their use in orientating the organisation's strategy
		(b)	Evaluate strategic options	(ii)	The process of strategy formulation
		(c)	Evaluate different organisational structures	(iii)	The identification and evaluation of strategic options
		(d)	Discuss the role and responsibilities of directors in the strategy development process	(iv)	Strategic options generation (eg using Ansoff's product/market matrix and Porter's generic strategies).
				(v)	Real Options as a tool for strategic analysis. (Note: Complex numerical questions will not be set).
				(vi)	Scenario planning and long range planning as tools in strategic decision-making.
				(vii)	Game theoretic approaches to strategic planning and decision-making. (Note: Complex numerical questions will not be set).
				(viii)	Acquisition, divestment, rationalisation and relocations strategies and their place in the strategic plan.
				(ix)	The relationship between strategy and organisational structure.
				(x)	The role and responsibilities of directors in making strategic decisions (including issues of due diligence, fiduciary responsibilities).
2	Evaluate tools and techniques used in strategy formulation	(a)	Evaluate strategic analysis tools	(i)	Audit of resources and the analysis of this for use in strategic decision making
		(b)	Recommend appropriate changes to the product portfolio of an organisation to support the organisation's strategic goals	(ii)	Forecasting and the various techniques used: trend analysis, system modelling, in-depth consultation with experts (Delphi method)
		(c)	Produce an organisation's value chain	(iii)	Management of the product portfolio
				(iv)	Value chain analysis
		(d)	Discuss both qualitative and quantitative techniques in the support of the strategic decision making function	(v)	Strategic decision-making processes.

Implementation of Strategic Plans and Performance Evaluation

1	Evaluate the tools and processes of strategy implementation	(a)	Recommend appropriate control measures	(i)	Alternative models of performance measurement (eg the balanced scorecard)
		(b)	Evaluate alternative models of performance measurement	(ii)	Business unit performance and appraisal, including transfer pricing, reward systems and incentives
		(c)	Recommend solutions to problems in performance measurement	(iii)	Project management: monitoring the implementation of plans
				(iv)	The implementation of lean systems across an organisation
		(d)	Advise managers on the development of strategies for knowledge management and information systems that support the organisation's strategic requirements	(v)	Theories of control within organisations and types of organisational structure (eg matrix, divisional, network)
				(vi)	Assessing strategic performance (ie the use an development of appropriate measures that are sensitive to industry characteristics and environmental factors)
		(e)	Recommend changes to information systems appropriate to the organisation's strategic requirements	(vii)	Non-financial measures and their interaction with financial ones (Note: candidates will be expected to use both qualitative and quantitative techniques)
				(viii)	The purpose and contents of information systems strategies, and the need for strategy complementary to the corporate and individual business strategies.
				(ix)	Critical success factors: links to performance indicators and corporate strategy, and their use as a basis for defining an organisation's information needs.

Studying E3

1 What's E3 about

1.1 Business Strategy

Strategy reflects an organisation's goals and the way it seeks to organise its resources in the long term, to achieve competitive advantage in its environment, and to meet market and stakeholder expectations.

E3 looks at how organisations **design** and **implement** strategy. In Chapter 1 we look at how business strategies are developed, and we identify the different approaches to strategy development.

In Chapter 2 we look at the **goals and objectives** of organisations, and how **stakeholders** affect them. Strategy is developed in a situational context, so it is important to understand how an organisation's external environment and its stakeholders can affect strategy development. It is also important to recognise the range of objectives an organisation may have, and we reflect this by looking at themes of **corporate social responsibility** and sustainability.

Although strategy development is a process, it is one which is affected by a significant degree of **uncertainty**. In Chapter 3 we look at some of the ways businesses can address this uncertainty in their **strategic decision making process**.

1.2 Internal capabilities

Alongside the external context in which it operates, the internal resources and capabilities of an organisation also help shape the strategic options which are available to it. In Chapter 4 we look at some of the key aspects of an organisation's current position – including its **resources**, **value chain** and **product portfolio**.

1.3 Strategic options

By drawing together external and internal factors, organisations can identify appropriate strategies which they can pursue to exploit their core competences and achieve their strategic objectives.

Chapters 5 and 6 of this book are concerned with the **strategic choices** organisations make. The most important issues here are how they **compete**, and what methods they employ to **grow**. With respect to growth, we consider both the **directions** (products and markets) and the **method** of growth – acquisition, organic growth or strategic alliances.

In Chapter 7 we highlight that an organisation should make strategic choices on the basis of three key factors: suitability, feasibility and acceptability. In this context, we also look at the way management accountants can apply decision techniques to assist strategic decision making.

1.4 Strategic marketing

Technology and the use of databases can help organisations compete by identifying potentially profitable customers and market segments. In Chapter 8 we turn to look more specifically at the way organisations **attract and retain customers**, and we highlight the importance of organisations analysing the profitability of their customers (**customer profitability analysis**).

1.5 Information systems

Information and **information systems** play a major part in business strategies. On the one hand, **information** and **knowledge** are crucial in supporting business strategies, and enabling organisations to

plan and control activities. On the other hand, technological developments are increasingly influencing business strategies in their own right, most notably through the growth of **e-commerce**.

Chapter 9 looks both at how organisations can manage data, information and knowledge to help them compete, and also at how information systems and the internet can directly affect an organisation and its strategy.

1.6 Change management

We have already identified the importance of options and choices in business strategy, however, once an organisation has made a strategic choice it will have to implement that strategy. Implementing strategy involves a number of tools and techniques associated with change management, and we look at these in Chapters 11 and 12.

We begin Chapter 11 by looking at some of the factors that may **trigger change**, before turning to look at the **process of change** itself.

However, we also need to recognise that there organisations can face different **types of change**, and the styles needed to manage change will vary according to the type of change, and the **context** in which the change is taking place. We look at the different **styles and strategies for managing change** in Chapter 12, and we also highlight the need for **leadership** in shaping the change process.

1.7 Implementing strategy

The final part of this book covers issues which require strategic management attention. In Chapter 10 we look at project management, lean systems, business process re-engineering and organisational structure.

However, for an organisation to know whether its strategy has been successful it also needs to be able to **measure performance** and **manage performance**. (Chapters 13 and 14). These are areas where the management accountant's role will be vital, although it is important that non-financial performance is considered as well as purely financial performance. Frameworks such as the balanced scorecard illustrate how financial and non-financial measures can be combined.

2   What's required

At the heart of E3 is the ability to **apply your knowledge** to **analyse and resolve practical problems**. The examiner is not simply looking for you to display your knowledge of the syllabus, but to be able to apply it to a specific context given in the question scenario.

Key skills which will be tested are your ability to **analyse** information, **evaluate** it and make **sensible recommendations** based on that analysis and evaluation.

The aspects of business strategy you discuss in your answer must follow from the **content and context** of the scenario. You may also have to use appropriate numerical techniques to quantify a strategic choice or an issue facing an organisation.

Any advice you give, or recommendations you make, must not only be **relevant** to deal with the issues identified in the question, but must also be **appropriate** for the organisation described in the scenario. For example, a strategy which may be appropriate for a small, not-for-profit organisation may not be appropriate for a large, multinational corporation.

2.1 What the examiner means

The table below has been prepared by CIMA to help you interpret the syllabus and learning outcomes and the meaning of exam questions.

You will see that there are 5 levels of Learning objective, ranging from Knowledge to Evaluation, reflecting the level of skill you will be expected to demonstrate. CIMA Certificate subjects were constrained to levels 1 to 3, but in CIMA's Professional qualification the entire hierarchy will be used.

At the start of each chapter in your study text is a topic list relating the coverage in the chapter to the level of skill you may be called on to demonstrate in the exam.

Learning objectives	Verbs used	Definition
1 Knowledge What are you expected to know	• List • State • Define	• Make a list of • Express, fully or clearly, the details of/facts of • Give the exact meaning of
2 Comprehension What you are expected to understand	• Describe • Distinguish • Explain • Identify • Illustrate	• Communicate the key features of • Highlight the differences between • Make clear or intelligible/state the meaning of • Recognise, establish or select after consideration • Use an example to describe or explain something
3 Application How you are expected to apply your knowledge	• Apply • Calculate/compute • Demonstrate • Prepare • Reconcile • Solve • Tabulate	• Put to practical use • Ascertain or reckon mathematically • Prove with certainty or to exhibit by practical means • Make or get ready for use • Make or prove consistent/compatible • Find an answer to • Arrange in a table
4 Analysis How you are expected to analyse the detail of what you have learned	• Analyse • Categorise • Compare and contrast • Construct • Discuss • Interpret • Prioritise • Produce	• Examine in detail the structure of • Place into a defined class or division • Show the similarities and/or differences between • Build up or compile • Examine in detail by argument • Translate into intelligible or familiar terms • Place in order of priority or sequence for action • Create or bring into existence
5 Evaluation How you are expected to use your learning to evaluate, make decisions or recommendations	• Advise • Evaluate • Recommend	• Counsel, inform or notify • Appraise or assess the value of • Propose a course of action

3 How to pass

3.1 Study the whole syllabus

You need to be comfortable with **all areas of the syllabus**, as questions, particularly compulsory Question 1, will often span a number of syllabus areas. **Wider reading** – particularly of a good quality daily newspaper such as the *Financial Times* – will help you understand the strategic issues businesses face today. *The Economist* and the *Harvard Business Review* can also provide you with useful background information about topical business issues.

3.2 Lots of question practice

You can **develop application skills** by attempting questions in the Exam Question Bank, and later on by attempting the questions in the BPP Practice and Revision Kit.

3.3 Analysing questions

For E3 it is particularly important to **consider the question requirements carefully** to:

*   Make sure you understand exactly what the question is asking, and whether there is more than one part to a requirement

*   See whether each question part has to be answered in the context of the scenario or whether it is more general.

Also, make sure you **read the scenario carefully to** pick up all the details given so that your answer is practical in the context (for example, how easy will it be to the organisation to raise funds to make an acquisition?)

3.4 Answering questions

Relevant points and **sensible recommendations** grounded in the scenario will always score well, as markers for this paper have a wide remit to reward good answers. You need to be **selective** though. The examiners have stated that lists of points memorised from texts and reproduced without any thought won't score well. Similarly scenario details should only be used if they support the points you're making.

3.5 Exam technique

The following points of exam technique are particularly relevant to this paper.

*   Analyse questions during the 20 minute reading time – for example by putting notes in the question margin

*   Be aware of the verbs used in exam questions – for example, if you are asked to 'evaluate' a course of action you have to appraise and assess the value of that course of action, indicating whether it is beneficial or not.

*   Identify all the question's requirements in your answer plan. The requirements of a question often contain a number of sub-requirements. Candidates often fail to answer the whole question because they do not address these sub-requirements. Read the question very carefully.

*   Knowledge alone is not enough to pass E3 - you have to be able to **apply** your knowledge to the scenario given in the question. A mistake which a lot of students make is to over-emphasise the theories in this paper, but fail to apply their knowledge as required. Remember, the vast majority of the marks available in this paper are for your ability to **provide practical solutions** to problems.

*   Within each question in Paper E3 you will be presented with scenarios that detail the problems that organisations face. As such, the examiners want you to provide practical advice to these

organisations as to how their problems can be overcome. Consequently your answer must relate to the organisation in question and its specific issues. General discussions with little or no application to the scenario will earn few marks. **Refer to the person or organisation in the question by name** in each point that you make in your answer.

4 Brought forward knowledge

The examiner may test knowledge or techniques you've learnt at Certificate or Managerial level. As E3 is at the top of the Enterprise pillar, the content of Papers E1 and E2 will be significant.

A number of areas of material from other Managerial level papers are relevant as well, including

- Product and pricing decisions (P2)
- Managing costs for competitive advantage (P2)
- Budgeting and management control (P2)
- Organisational structure in management control (P2)
- Performance management and control (P2)

Remember, however, that brought forward knowledge will only be useful if it is **applied at a strategic level**. Hence for example you are unlikely to be asked to prepare a budget in E3, but you may have to discuss how effective budgets are as control mechanisms.

Equally, although the E3 paper is likely to include some calculations and numerical analysis, these will be tested in the context of what the calculations tell you about a possible strategy, for example, rather than simply as calculations for their own sake.

5 Links with other Strategic level papers

CIMA expects you to make links between the various papers and not see the three subjects (E3, F3 and P3) in isolation.

- **Enterprise strategy decisions** will **impact** upon the financial objectives, sources of finance chosen, the investment decisions, the risks the organisation faces and the controls necessary to counter those risks.

- Enterprise strategy decisions will also be constrained by an **organisation's risk management strategy** and its attitude to risk.

- Enterprise strategy can have an impact on the information systems in an organisation, and so the **risks and controls associated with information systems** need to be considered.

- At the same time, **investment choices** will be **constrained** by the finance available and the financial objectives of an organisation. Equally, the possible **costs**, **benefits** and **risks** attached to a strategic choice all need to be subject to a **financial evaluation**. Investment decisions and project control are covered in detail in the Financial Strategy paper (F3).

- **Performance measurement** techniques such as ratio analysis may be useful in any paper. The **effectiveness of management accounting systems**, particularly the information provided and how useful they are as control mechanisms, could also be relevant to any of the strategic level papers.

The exam paper

Format of the paper

		Number of marks
Section A:	A maximum of 4 compulsory questions, totalling 50 marks, all relating to a pre-seen study* and further new un-seen case material	50
Section B:	2 out of 3 questions, 25 marks each	50
		100

Time allowed: 3 hours, plus 20 minutes reading time

* The pre-seen is shared between all three strategic level papers (E3, F3 & P3) and will be published six weeks before the exams. The pre-seen material relates to Section A only.

An example Section A question is included at the back of this Study Text.

CIMA guidance

CIMA has indicated that, as a general principle, there will only be a very small number of marks available for knowledge itself. Instead, marks will be given for applying the correct theories or knowledge and for making practical evaluations and recommendations in a variety of different business scenarios.

A likely weakness of answers is that they are too general, and do not relate closely enough to the scenario given in the question.

Plausible alternative answers could be given to many questions, so the model answers in the Answer Bank should not be regarded as all-inclusive.

Numerical content

There will be small number of marks (up to about 15) available for computations and the analysis of numerical data. These are likely to be in the compulsory Section A question, but the examiner is under no obligation to restrict numerical elements to Section A.

Breadth of question coverage

Questions in *both* sections of the paper may cover more than one syllabus area.

Again, this reinforces the importance of reading the question requirements for each question carefully, to make sure you are fully aware of all the syllabus areas being tested before you start to answer a question.

Knowledge from other syllabuses

Where relevant, candidates should use their knowledge from other Strategic level papers. One aim of this paper is to prepare candidates for the T4 – Part B (TOPCIMA) exam, which brings together ideas from across all three strategic level examinations.

May 2012 examination

Section A

1   The scenario focuses on a supermarket group which operates four different types of store and aims to employ different generic strategies for the different market segments in which it trades. The group practises sustainable investment and seeks to promote an ethical and environmentally responsible culture. The group is looking to expand its business into a new country through a franchising agreement with local entrepreneurs.

Question requirements are:

(a)   **Calculate** the number of franchises needed to earn the income the group requires.

(b)   **Advise** the factors which are likely to influence local entrepreneurs in relation to the desirability of investing in the franchise

(c)   **Evaluate** how the new business could assist the group in achieving sustainable investment

(d)   **Advise** the advantages and disadvantages of changing the group's planning and management control system.

Section B

2   **Identify** two models a company (a pesticide manufacturer) could use to form an understanding of its external environment.

Discuss whether a proposal for the company to abandon its mission statement is consistent with corporate social responsibility.

Recommend strategies for dealing with different types of stakeholder in relation to the suggestion to abandon the mission statement.

3   **Explain** the circumstances in which different types of change are appropriate.

Evaluate three potential solutions for changing an organisation's marketing information system.

Advise how resistance to change (in relation to introducing the new marketing information system) could be overcome.

4   **Advise** how a Balanced Scorecard could assist a company in delivering its vision and strategy

Recommend an objective, a measure, a target and an initiative for the different perspectives in the Scorecard.

Briefly **discuss** two drawbacks of the Scorecard.

March 2012 re-sit exam

Section A

(The pre-seen material for Section A was the same as for November 2011.)

1   The scenario focuses on a newspaper company which is considering whether it should offer its newspapers free of charge rather than making customers pay for them.

Question requirements are:

(a)   **Calculate** the number of pages of advertising the free paper needs in order for it to break even, and then **discuss** the factors which could affect the paper's ability to achieve this level of advertising.

Advise the managing director about the extent to which the proposed free paper fits with the company's strategic and financial objectives, and **advise** whether changes associated with the free paper fit with the company's corporate social responsibility principles.

(b)   Using Porter's generic strategies, **evaluate** the likelihood that the proposed free paper will deliver a sustainable competitive advantage.

(c)   **Advise** how Lewin's three-step model of change could be used to help staff make the change to the new working environment associated with the free paper.

Section B

2   **Advise** whether the aspects of an ethical business policy could cause concerns for a company's shareholders.

Advise how a company's ethical business policy will affect its relationships with different stakeholder groups.

3   **Advise** how the 'SMART' model could be used to help an organisation achieve a new set of control objectives.

Advise the organisation of the activities it must undertake to manage the process of changing its culture and introducing a new structure. Then **discuss** the role that a change agent could play in the change process.

4   **Advise** what additional information a company's board needs to support its planning and decision-making, and **recommend** improvements to the current information provided to the board.

Advise how the company could benefit from benchmarking.

November 2011 examination

Section A

1   The scenario focuses on a news media company which is considering whether it should charge users a subscription for viewing its online news sites or whether it should offer them free of charge. The company is also looking to reduce the number of people it currently employs.

Question requirements are:

(b)   **Calculate** the impact that different pricing strategies will have on the company's income, but then also **advise** of the other factors the company should consider before deciding to change to a subscription-only service.

(b)   **Advise** the extent to which changing to a subscription-only service represents a conflict with the company's strategic and financial objectives.

(c)   **Advise** how the BCG matrix could be used to help decide which websites to continue and which to discontinue.

(d)   **Recommend** ways the current headcount reduction programme could be improved, and **advise** how management could deal with resistance to the programme.

Section B

2   Use Porter's Five Forces model to **evaluate** a company's potential to earn future profits in a country. Then **advise** the company whether it should continue to operate in that country.

Advise the company how it could use Porter's Diamond when considering future investments in foreign countries.

3   **Recommend** changes a company should make to improve its performance across three different aspects of its business.

Recommend three principles which the company should include within its ethical code.

4   **Evaluate** the effectiveness of a company's performance management system, and then **recommend** improvements the company could make to its current performance management system.

Recommend performance measures which could be used to assess the company's progress towards achieving one of its strategic objectives.

September 2011 re-sit examination

Section A

(The pre-seen material for Section A was the same as for May 2011.)

1   The scenario focuses on a food manufacturer, with three divisions, which is committed to finding ways to increase its returns to investors by expanding its share of both its domestic and overseas markets, whilst still acting in a socially responsible manner. The Desserts division has been investigating 'Freezer deals' under which it would supply ice cream freezers to independent retailers.

Question requirements are:

(a)   **Recommend** which of three possible Freezer deals the Desserts division should offer the retailers.

(b)   **Advise** the Board whether: (i) it should have a strategic aim dealing with Corporate Social Responsibility (CSR); and (ii) it should include its internal CSR report in its annual report.

(c)   **Advise** the Board how it could use Information Systems to help manage the company's CSR performance.

Section B

2   **Evaluate** the strengths and weaknesses of a company's current control system.

Advise how the Balanced Scorecard could be used within the company, and suggest one appropriate measure for each of the scorecard perspectives.

Advise the company's managing director of the potential problems he might face if he introduced the Scorecard.

3   Using Ansoff's matrix, **advise** a company of the future strategic directions available to it.

Discuss the potential advantages and disadvantages of a potential acquisition the company is considering.

Recommend things the company should plan for if the acquisition goes ahead.

4   Using Mendelow's matrix, classify a company's stakeholders and then rank their needs.

Discuss the purpose of, and advantages from, having a mission statement.

Advise the benefits of using a change agent to help in the relocation of a company's corporate headquarters.

Advise whether the suggestion to move the headquarters represents a breach of the Code of Ethics.

May 2011 examination

Section A

1   The scenario focuses on a food manufacturer, with three divisions, which is committed to seek ways to increase its return to investors by expanding its share of both its domestic and overseas markets.

Question requirements are:

(a)   **Advise** the Board whether or not to approve the relocation of one of the divisions

(b)   **Advise** how resistance to change could be overcome in relation to proposals to improve performance in one of the divisions.

(c)   **Recommend** improvements which could be made in that division to improve performance.

Section B

2   **Identify** two models a hotel could use to analyse its external environment and **explain** how they could be used to help it develop its strategy.

Explain how Porter's generic strategies could help the hotel design its strategy, and then **advise** how information systems could support the generic strategies.

3   **Evaluate** the appropriateness of an organisation's control systems.

Recommend, and justify, two critical success factors which could allow a company which designs kitchens to achieve future success.

Advise the company of the changes it will need to make to achieve improved performance and improved control.

4   **Evaluate** (using Mendelow's matrix) the power and interests of a company's shareholders, and **advise** the company's Board of other stakeholders with an interest in a key strategic decision.

Advise the Board about responsible business practice.

March 2011 re-sit examination

Section A

(The pre-seen material for Section A was the same as for November 2010).

1   The scenario focuses on a European airport which seeks to offer its customers high quality services and to be a good corporate citizen in everything it does.

Question requirements are:

(a)   **Explain** the alternative approaches to managing stakeholders' conflicting objectives.

Discuss how the airport's mission statement might change if a local investment bank (focused on cost-cutting) becomes a shareholder in the airport.

(b)   **Advise** the airport's board whether the acquisition of an American cargo handling company is an appropriate strategic option, taking account of: (i) the company's financial performance and (ii) its corporate social responsibility.

(c) **Recommend** future strategies for the airport's current and potential business segments. (The question suggests using the BCG matrix as a framework for your answer.)

Section B

2 **Advise** a chemical manufacturer of the benefits of a CSR policy, and then recommend the contents of a suitable policy for the company.

Advise the company how it could use Lewin's stage model of change to implement a CSR policy.

3 **Discussion** of using financial ratio analysis to exercise financial control and helping to achieve return on investment targets.

Recommend how a government department could implement a knowledge management strategy.

4 **Advise** the Board of a company with different divisions why it should have an overall strategy for IS and IT.

Advise what the strategy should include, and then **recommend** how the company should implement the strategy.

November 2010 examination

Section A

1 The scenario focuses on a European airport which seeks to offer its customers high quality services and to be a good corporate citizen in everything it does.

Question requirements are:

(a) Using Porter's generic strategies (of cost leadership, differentiation and focus) **advise** the Board how the airport could achieve sustainable competitive advantage.

(b) **Advise** the Board how the airport's approach to strategic formation and its mission might be challenged if a local investment bank (which is focused on cost-cutting and short-term profitability) becomes a shareholder.

Advise which of the airport's current objectives the investment bank might oppose, and how the bank becoming a shareholder might affect the airport's future operations.

(c) Using financial projections provided, **recommend** whether the airport should start offering cargo handling services.

Section B

2 **Discuss** the uses and limitations of a control system which only looks at financial performance, in particular ROCE and actual expenditure compared to budget.

Advise how non-financial measures could assist in evaluating performance against key success factors.

Evaluate how Customer Profitability Analysis could assist in achieving a company's strategic aims (of continued expansion, and secure well-paid jobs for employees).

3 **Discuss** the respective advantages and disadvantages of organic growth and acquisition as international expansion strategies for a small company.

Recommend how the company can avoid the difficulties it experienced in a previous, failed acquisition.

Discuss how a change agent could assist in making the acquisition successful.

4   **Advise** the proprietor of a small business which is about to expand the purpose and benefits of using IS, IT and IM strategies in the business.

Recommend the actions needed to implement each of the strategies.

September 2010 re-sit examination

Section A

(The pre-seen material for Section A was the same as for May 2010).

1   The scenario focuses on an electronic components company which is looking to expand internationally.

Question requirements are:

(a)   **Discuss** whether it is appropriate for the company to continue using its current style of strategy for its new international markets, and **recommend** two alternative approaches to strategy that could be appropriate for the company to use.

Advise the company the factors it should consider before withdrawing from an overseas trading company.

(b)   **Advise**: (i) how strategic management accounting can contribute to strategic success, and (ii) how scenario planning could be used to help make the decision about whether or not to withdraw from the overseas company.

(c)   **Evaluate** a bullish profit forecast for a new international market.

(d)   **Explain** the threats faced by a management accountant, and **recommend** the safeguards which could eliminate or reduce those threats.

Section B

2   **Advise** how control measures assist in the successful implementation of strategy; then **recommend** controls a university could use to improve areas of its performance.

Advise how information systems could support the successful implementation of the university's new strategic plan.

3   **Categorise** stakeholder groups according to Mendelow's matrix, and **explain** what the different groups' power and interests are. Then **advise** a company how to resolve the problem of its stakeholders' competing objectives.

Discuss the potential conflicts in a mission statement which states that a company exists to maximise the possible profits for its shareholders while minimising environmental damage and being a good corporate citizen.

4   **Advise** why the staff of a successful, family-run business might be resistant to a change of ownership, and then **advise** how this resistance might be overcome.

Advise how the balanced scorecard can be used to manage strategic performance, and how targets in a staff incentive scheme could be set to support the balanced scorecard.

May 2010 examination

Section A

1   The scenario focuses on an electronic components company which is looking to expand internationally.

Question requirements are:

(a)   Discuss the relevance of the company's current style of strategy for developing its target market, and advise two alternative approaches to strategy which it could use.

(b)   Evaluate the company's current organisational structure in respect of the proposed expansion.

(c)   Explain two control problems with using agents as a means of achieving international growth, and advise what control measures the company could use to deal with these problems.

(d)   Construct an incremental profit forecast for the proposed expansion, and discuss the consequences of this forecast for the shareholders.

Evaluate the ethical issues presented by the Director of Operations' attitude to preparing the forecast.

Section B

2   Use the value chain to analyse the strengths and weaknesses of a business.

Advise on practical issues for implementing an e-commerce solution, evaluate how e-commerce could affect the business' value chain.

3   Strategy as analysis, choice and implementation; Identify CSFs for an organisation; then recommend KPIs to support each of the CSFs identified.

4   Evaluate strategic options using Ansoff's product-market matrix.

Advise of the difficulties in changing organisational structure and reducing employee numbers, and recommend how the process of changing the organisational structure could be managed.

Specimen examination paper

Section A

1   The scenario focuses on an electricity supply company which has recently been taken over.

Question requirements are:

(a)   Compare and contrast different approaches to strategic planning and advise the directors on a suitable strategic planning process for the organisation following the takeover

(b)   Financial analysis of different ways of servicing customers, and a discussion of the consequences of choosing either method

(c)   Evaluate the ethical issues presented by a director's approach to customer service

(d)   (i)   Recommend CSFs that might be appropriate for the company

(ii)   Discuss the attributes of an effective Information System for the company

Section B

2   Advise how stakeholder mapping can assist in making strategic choices. Construct a stakeholder analysis; evaluate the strategic options a company faces, and recommend the preferred option.

3   Explain the perspectives of the balances scorecard. Discuss and recommend two measures for each of the four perspectives for an architectural practice to use. Recommend how that firm could use the scorecard to achieve changes in strategy and culture.

4   Advise how Porter's generic strategies could improve the profitability of a restaurant chain. Advise how the chain could use information systems to support its strategy.

KEY STRATEGIC MODELS

xxviii

KEY STRATEGIC MODELS

 Paper E3 builds on knowledge acquired during your CIMA studies to date, in particular drawing on materials from Paper E2.

The syllabus for E2 refers to a number of models which can be used in strategic management and assessing the competitive environment. These models (such as Porter's Five Forces model) are not specifically referred to in the E3 syllabus, but they are **assumed knowledge** for E3, and could therefore be re-tested in a question in your exam.

Therefore, it is very important that you re-familiarise yourself with these models, to allow you to use your knowledge of them as a basis for tackling questions in the E3 exam.

This section aims to provide you with some basic revision of the models, but is in no way intended as a comprehensive guide. It is recommended that you consult the E2 Study Text if you require more detailed information in these areas.

Also, it is important to note that in E3 you will be expected to demonstrate your knowledge in the context of a scenario, and in relation to advising an organisation about its strategy or the strategic decisions it has to make. You are extremely unlikely to be asked simply to describe the models in their own right.

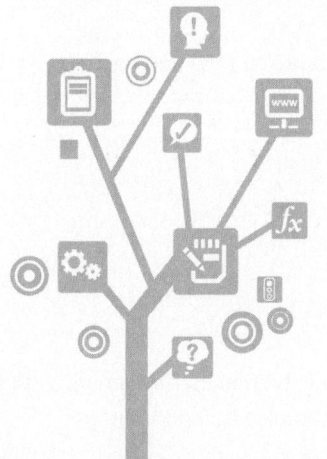

topic list	learning outcomes	syllabus references	ability required
1 PEST	A1 (a)	A1 (i)	Evaluate
2 SWOT Analysis	–	–	–
3 Stakeholder mapping	A1 (a)	A1 (i)	Evaluate
4 Porter's Diamond	A1 (a)	A1 (i)	Evaluate
5 Porter's Five Forces	A1 (a)	A1 (i)	Evaluate
6 Competitor analysis	A1 (a)	A1 (i)	Evaluate
7 Competitive strategies	–	–	–

1 PEST   (Examined in May '12 exam)

Introduction

The environment exists outside an organisation's boundaries. To secure environmental fit, an analysis of the environment is required.

KEY POINT

PEST is a framework that can be used to analyse the macro-environment in which an organisation operates by identifying the Political, Economic, Social and Technological factors that make up the environment.

Management can use the PEST framework to identify factors affecting the organisation. Be aware that not all factors will fit neatly into a group: they interact and take effect in complex ways. For example, government policy affects economic factors.

Political/Legal – many areas of the business are subject to government policy and legal regulation, such as:

- Data Protection
- Health and Safety
- Tax
- Trade regulations

Political stability in a country can also affect the macroeconomic environment in which a business operates. For example, a change of government in a country might prove to be a significant factor in an organisation's decision about whether or not to do business in that country.

Economic – a business can be affected by national and international economic factors, such as:

- Inflation
- Interest rates
- Exchange rates
- Tax levels
- Unemployment levels
- Business cycles and trends in national income
- International trade (and balance of payments)

Social factors – demographics (eg birth and death rates, average age, ethnicity) and culture are important for understanding the market, and developing marketing strategies. They can also be important in developing HR policies.

Other important social factors include:

- Income distribution
- Levels of education
- Attitudes to work and leisure
- Attitudes to consumption, and lifestyle choices

Technological – developments in technology affect all aspects of business. Technological developments can result in new:

- Products and services
- Methods of production and service provision
- Sales channels (such as e-commerce) and media for communication (eg Internet)
- Organisation structures to exploit technology

The level of government spending on research, and government attitudes to research, can affect the level of new product development in a country.

Technological factors are also important to the extent that they encourage innovation in a country or an industry.

Sometimes PEST is extended to **PESTEL**, with the categories being: Political, Economic, Social, Technological, Environmental and Legal. The 'environmental' category highlights the importance of considering issues such as sustainability and corporate social responsibility in strategic decisions.

The 'legal' category highlights issues such as employment law, anti-discrimination policies, consumer protection, and health and safety.

Exam skills

The **E2** syllabus required you to be able to **discuss** different competitive environments and the key external characteristics of those environments.

However, in **E3**, the focus will be on your ability to **apply** different models in order to **evaluate** the impact of the external environment on strategic decisions.

So, for example, in E3 you shouldn't expect to be asked to describe or discuss PEST analysis in its own right. Instead, you might be asked to use it to analyse the extent to which political, economic, social or technological factors represent opportunities or threats to an organisation, and therefore how they might shape its strategic decisions.

Analysing PEST (or PESTEL) factors could also be a useful way of identifying drivers for change in an organisation's external environment. Bear this in mind later in this Study Text (Chapter 11) when we look at organisational change.

2 SWOT analysis

Introduction

Having gathered information about an organisation and its environment, strategic planners can go on to make a corporate appraisal.

KEY POINT

SWOT analysis or corporate appraisal is a quantitative and qualitative review of internal strengths and weaknesses and their relationship with external threats and opportunities.

Strengths and **weaknesses** relate to the organisation itself – its resources and its products/services. They are internal matters, and are specific to the individual organisation.

Opportunities and **threats** exist in the business market in which the organisation operates. They are external matters. Given this, SWOT analysis should be undertaken in conjunction with environmental analysis (PEST).

An appraisal of strengths, weaknesses, opportunities and threats will help an organisation understand its current strategic position before preparing its long-term plan.

Strategies should be developed to remove weaknesses or develop strengths and to exploit opportunities and counter threats. SWOT analysis can help indicate the types of strategies that appear to be available, for example a firm might identify the following:

Strengths	Weaknesses
• $100 million of capital available • Production expertise and appropriate marketing skills	• Heavy reliance on a small number of customers • Limited product range, with no new products and expected market decline • Small marketing organisation
Opportunities	**Threats**
• Government tax incentives for new investment • Growing demand in a new market, although customers so far relatively small in number	• Major competitor has already entered the new market

In this example, it might be possible to identify that the company is in imminent danger of losing its existing markets and must diversify. The new market opportunity exists to be exploited and since the number of customers is currently few, the relatively small size of the existing marketing force would not be an immediate hindrance.

SWOT analysis can be used to guide strategy formulation, through applying S, W, O and T to the **TOWS matrix**.

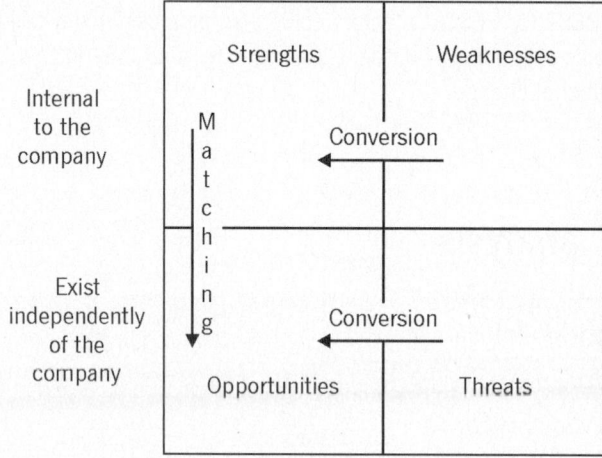

The organisation should try to **match** its strengths to the opportunities presented by the market.

It should also look to **convert** weaknesses into strengths in order to take advantage of some particular opportunity.

A third possible option is to attempt to **remedy weaknesses** so as to reduce exposure to threats and increase the ability to grasp opportunities. However, this course does not in itself lead to a sustainable strategy and is best regarded as a preliminary phase to matching or conversion.

3 Stakeholder mapping   (Examined in May '12 exam)

Introduction

Stakeholders are groups or individuals that have an interest in an organisation's strategy. Different stakeholder groups have different levels of power and interest, and management must respond to each in a different way.

There are three broad types of stakeholder in an organisation:

- **Internal** stakeholders (employees, management)
- **Connected** stakeholders (shareholders, customers, suppliers, financiers)
- **External** stakeholders (the community, government, pressure groups)

Stakeholders who have a contractual relationship with the organisation are called primary stakeholders, while those who do not are known as secondary stakeholders. The primary stakeholder category thus includes internal and connected stakeholders, while the secondary stakeholders category equates to external stakeholder status.

Stakeholder interests are likely to conflict. For example, shareholders will want high profits, but at the same time customers want high quality and low prices, while employees want higher pay and better working conditions.

Mendelow's stakeholder mapping helps the organisation to establish its priorities and manage stakeholder expectations, by looking at the relative levels of **interest** and **power** different stakeholder groups have in relation to the organisation.

Stakeholder power can come from a number of different sources. For example, **position** power within an organisation (eg directors); **resource** power (eg a supplier may have high power if it supplies a vital input into a manufacturing process; and **expert** power (eg skilled staff may have a high level of power if their skills are critical to a business and difficult to replace.)

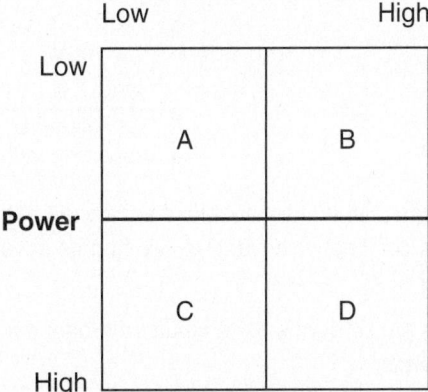

A   Stakeholders in this quadrant of Mendelow's matrix have low interest and low power, therefore only **minimal effort** should be given to their needs.

B   Stakeholders in this quadrant have important views, but little ability to influence strategy, therefore they should be **kept informed** only.

C   An organisation should treat stakeholders in this quadrant with care because while they are often passive they are capable of moving to segment D. Therefore it is important to **keep them satisfied**.

D   These are **key players**, eg a major customer, so the strategy must be **acceptable** to them at least. Equally, powerful stakeholder groups must have confidence in the management team of an

organisation. **Regular communication** with the stakeholder groups can be a good way to help achieve this.

A single stakeholder map is unlikely to be appropriate for all circumstances. Stakeholders may move from quadrant to quadrant when different potential future strategies are concerned; for example, because different groups may have different degrees of power over different potential strategies. As a result, and stakeholder analysis has to be carried out in the context of each specific strategic decision being considered.

4 Porter's diamond   (Examined in Nov '11 exam)

Introduction

Porter identifies four main determinants of national competitive advantage on an industry basis: factor conditions, demand conditions, related and supporting industries, and firm strategy, structure and rivalry.

Porter refers to this as the 'diamond'.

When an organisation is looking to expand internationally, one of the choices it has to make is which country to invest in. But what factors allow some countries to produce more successful international firms than others?

Porter's diamond identifies four key factors which determine the relative attractiveness of different countries, and which also determine why some industries within countries are more successful than others.

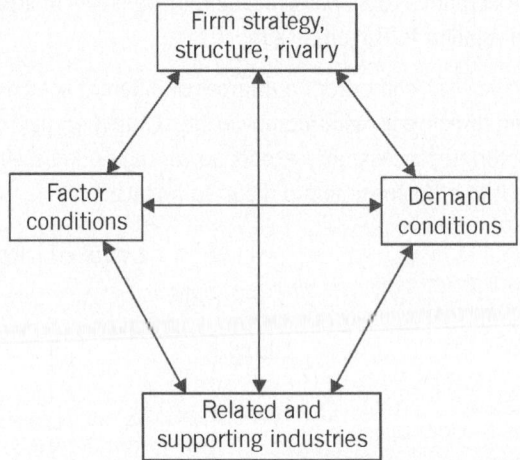

Each element of the diamond is capable of enhancing national competitive advantage. Conversely, a nation that enjoys competitive advantage will find its advantage diminishes if the elements cease to work positively.

Factor conditions are endowments to inputs of production (in effect, supply side factors). Porter distinguishes between:

(a)   **Basic factors**: natural resources, climate, unskilled labour – these are basic requirements, but will not, by themselves, confer a sustainable competitive advantage

(b)   **Advanced factors**: infrastructure and communications, technical and higher education, high tech industries – promote competitive advantage

Demand conditions: The domestic market determines how firms perceive, interpret and respond to buyer needs. A tough domestic market is likely to encourage competitiveness as firms have to produce high quality, innovative goods to meet the requirements of their domestic customers. The experience which the firm gets from supplying domestic customers will allow it to compete successfully on a global scale.

Related and supporting industries: Competitive success in one industry is linked to success in related industries. (Notice there is a potential link here to ideas of value chains and value systems, which we will look at further in Chapter 4 of this Study Text.)

Strong home suppliers make the industry more robust. Rivalry creates supplier specialisations. Clusters of related industries derive strength from their links.

Firm strategy, structure and rivalry: The way firms are created, organised and managed can affect a foreign company's decision to invest in a country.

Equally, cultural factors could be important – management structures, management styles and work ethics in the country need to fit with those of the investing company. Rivalry among existing firms leads to competitive strength, and spurs innovation.

Government policy. Porter also points out the importance of government policy in nurturing all four of the diamond factors by means of investing in infrastructure, and higher education. The tax regime and attitudes to foreign investors could also affect an investment decision.

Chance events can also change the factors in the diamond unexpectedly. For example, civil unrest can make a country a much less attractive location.

The factors in the diamond are interrelated. Competitive advantage rarely rests on only one element of the diamond.

Porter also highlights that successful firms tend to have **linkages** between them, and this leads to **clustering**. Clustering helps to reinforce the factors in the diamond – for example, by providing a concentration of advanced factor conditions, and related/supporting industries (as with the high-tech electronics industry in Silicon Valley, California).

However, remember that the individual factors which determine the attractiveness of different locations change over time. So, for example, if a country fails to maintain its skill base or invest in new technologies and infrastructure, it will lose its competitive advantage over time.

Be aware, also, that Porter's diamond model is not without its critics. For example, some critics argue that ultimately it is **companies, not countries, which deliver international success**, and companies deliver success by virtue of their strategies and their management, rather then being located in a specific country. This might be particularly true in relation to **multinational companies**.

Other critics have argued that the analysis on which Porter based his model was too narrow. Porter only looked at a narrow range of manufacturers, banks and management consultancy firms in ten developed countries. Therefore, critics argue, the model may not apply so well to less developing countries, or to companies in other sectors (for example, fast food restaurants.)

5 Porter's five forces   (Examined in Nov '11 exam)

Introduction

Porter suggested that for any industry, **five forces** determine its profitability: 'threat of new entrants, substitute products, bargaining power of customers, bargaining power of suppliers and the intensity of competition'.

If the forces are, collectively, strong in an industry, this is likely to reduce the overall level of profitability which can be sustained in that industry.

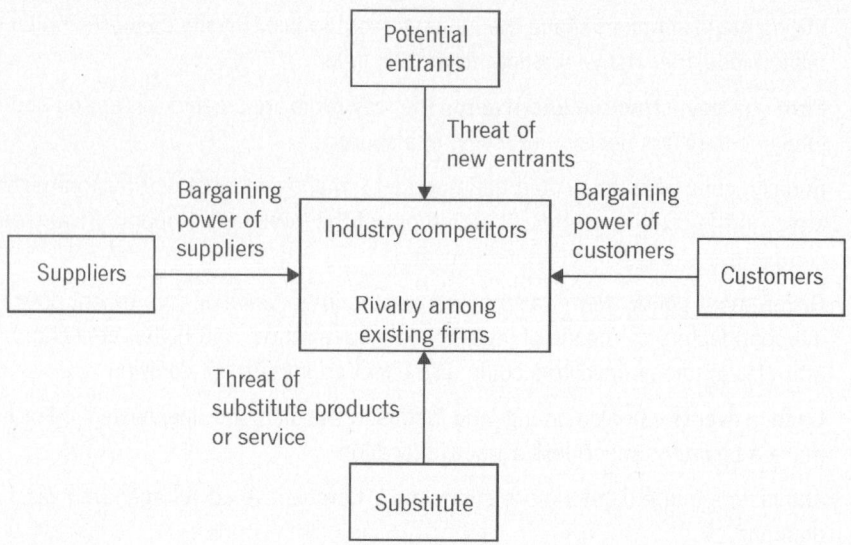

Source: adapted from Porter (Competitive Strategy)

Threat of new entrants

The threat of new entrants is limited by **barriers to entry**:

- **Economies of scale**. Increased scale leads to lower costs. New entrants must also start on large scale or they will suffer cost disadvantage compared to established producers.

- **Product differentiation.** Existing brand images and customer loyalty make it difficult for new competitors to enter the market.

- **Capital requirements**. High or risky capital investment requirements create strong barriers to entry.

- **Switching costs.** Costs incurred by a customer when switching from one supplier's product to another's. High switching costs are likely to make a customer more loyal to their existing supplier.

- **Access to distribution channels.** These carry the manufacturer's product to the end-buyer. New distribution channels are hard to set up and existing channels hard to gain access to.

- **Access to resources** eg patent rights, experience and know-how, and government subsidies.

- **Expected retaliation** eg through a price war, which in turn reduces profit margins. If a potential entrant expects the existing competitors to retaliate fiercely to its entry, this may act as a deterrent from entering the market at all.

Substitute products

A substitute product is a good/service provided by **another industry** which satisfies the same customer needs. An industry which has few substitutes will be more able to sustain a high profit than an industry with many substitutes.

Bargaining power of customers

The bargaining power of customers depends on:

- How much the **customer buys**
- How **critical** the product is to the customer's own business
- Whether the products are **standard items** (easily copied) or specialised
- The **customer's own profitability**
- Customer's **ability to bypass** the supplier or take over the supplier
- The **skills** of the customer's **purchasing staff**, or price-awareness of customers
- The importance of **product quality** to the customer

If customers have high bargaining power this will restrict the industry's ability to sustain high profits.

Bargaining power of suppliers

The bargaining power of suppliers depends on:

- The **number** of **suppliers** (one or two dominant can charge monopoly or oligopoly prices)
- The threat of **new entrants** or substitute products to the **supplier's industry**
- The **number** of **customers** in the industry
- The scope for **substitution**
- Whether **switching costs** for customers would be high
- Whether the supplier has a **differentiated product** which buyers need to obtain

Competitive rivalry among existing firms

The intensity of competitive rivalry within an industry will affect the profitability of the industry as a whole. Rivalry levels are affected by:

- **Market growth** – rivalry is intensified in markets where growth is low

- Ability of customers to **switch** (eg Coke and Pepsi)

- **Market structure** – Markets in which a number of competitors are roughly the same size are likely to have more intensive rivalry than, for example, a monopoly market.

- Level of output **capacity** required to obtain reductions in unit costs

- **Cost structure**. If fixed costs are high, firms may be tempted to compete on price. In the short term, any contribution to profit (to help cover fixed costs) is better than none at all

- **Uncertainty** about competitor's strategy. There is a tendency to respond to uncertainty by formulating a more competitive strategy

- **Exit barriers** which make it difficult to leave the industry. If it is hard for existing suppliers to leave the industry, they will stay and compete, thereby intensifying competition

High levels of rivalry are likely to suppress the level of sustainable profits in the industry.

Importantly, however, an **individual firm** can earn better margins that its competitors in an industry if it can deal more effectively with key forces, or if it can develop some distinctive competences which provide it with a sustainable competitive advantage in relation to its competitors.

Equally, it is important to note that Porter's model assumes that firms operate independently and so are looking to **compete** against, rather than **collaborate** with, other firms in an industry. However, this may not always be the case; for example, with joint ventures or strategic alliances.

Role of government

Although Porter only identified five forces which he felt determine the level of profitability in an industry, some commentators suggest that the role of **government needs to be added as a sixth force**. For example, if governments offer subsidies to certain firms or industries, this could allow them to reduce the price of their goods or services yet still earn a sustainable profit.

6 Competitor analysis

Introduction

Firms should **analyse their competitors** and build models of how they might react based on their future goals, assumptions, capability and current situation.

KEY TERM

COMPETITIVE POSITION is the market share, costs, prices, quality and accumulated experience of an entity or a product relative to the competition.

COMPETITOR ANALYSIS is the 'identification and quantification of the relative strengths and weaknesses (compared with competitors or potential competitors), which could be of significance in the development of a successful competitive strategy.'

(CIMA OfficialTerminology)

An organisation should look at the following key factors when undertaking competitor analysis

- **Objectives**: What are the competitor's current goals? How well is it achieving them? Are its goals likely to change in the future?

- **Strategy**. How is the competitor firm competing (eg cost leadership)? In what markets is the firm competing?

- **Assumptions**. What assumptions does the competitor hold about the industry and its own performance?

- **Resources and competences**. What are the competitor's key strengths and weaknesses? What resources, competences and capabilities does it have, or not have?

- **Response profile.** How is the competitor likely to respond to any strategic initiatives the organisation introduces? Will its response be the same across all products/markets, or might it react more aggressively in some markets than others? What strategic changes might the competitor initiate itself?

Competitor analysis helps an organisation understand its **competitive advantages/disadvantages compared to its competitors**. It can also provide an organisation with **insights into its competitors' strategies**. In doing so, competitor analysis helps the organisation **develop its own strategies** to achieve (or sustain) competitive advantage over its competitors.

However, as well as looking at competitors' current strategies and objectives, competitor analysis can also help a firm try to **forecast competitors' future strategies and decisions**. Again, such insight might be useful to the firm in **shaping its own strategies** for the future.

The role of the management accountant in competitor analysis is to analyse relative costs, market share, cost structure and behaviour.

However, there is a very wide range of information organisations can gather on their competitors as part of competitor analysis. This may include:

- Products and services (eg range of current products, new products, market share)
- Marketing (segmentation, branding, promotions, key customers)
- Customer types and numbers (and what customers want, eg quality, service, price)
- Operations and processes
- Technology
- Organisational structure
- Management profiles and management capabilities
- Financial performance
- Corporate reputation

Sources of information that may assist in competitor analysis include:

- Financial statements
- Customers and suppliers
- Products
- Former employees
- Job advertisements

7 Competitive strategies

Introduction

Porter suggests that, in order to be successful and outperform the other firms in an industry, a firm must follow one of three generic strategies: **cost leadership, differentiation** and **focus**. For Porter, if a firm doesn't follow only one of these strategies it risks being 'stuck in the middle'.

Cost leadership

Cost leadership means being the **lowest cost producer** in the industry as a whole. It can be achieved by:

- Establishing economies of scale
- Using the newest (most efficient) production technologies
- Exploiting the learning curve effect
- Improving productivity
- Minimising overheads
- Relocating to cheaper areas

(Note: cost leadership is about costs not selling price. A cost leader may not necessarily have the lowest selling price in the industry.)

Differentiation

Differentiation aims to exploit a product or service which is perceived to be unique within the industry as a whole. Such products may be categorised as:

- Breakthrough products – products which offer radical performance advantage compared to existing products

- Improved products – more cost-effective alternatives to existing products

- Competitive products – products which offer a unique combination of features.

Differentiation can be achieved by:

- Developing a strong brand image
- Giving the product special features to make it stand out
- Exploiting other activities of the **value chain** such as marketing and sales or service.

Advantages and disadvantages of industry-wide strategies

Competitive Force	Advantages		Disadvantages	
	Cost leadership	Differentiation	Cost leadership	Differentiation
New entrants	Economies of scale raise entry barriers	Brand loyalty and perceived uniqueness are entry barriers		
Substitutes	Firm is not as vulnerable to the threat of substitutes as its less cost effective competitors	Customer loyalty is a weapon against substitutes		
Customers	Customers cannot drive down prices further than the next most efficient competitor	Customers have no comparable alternative Brand loyalty should lower price sensitivity		Customers may no longer need the differentiation factor Differentiation may be more appropriate to products in the early stages of their product life cycle than to more mature products Sooner or later, customers become price sensitive
Suppliers	Flexibility to deal with cost increases	Higher margins can offset vulnerability to supplier price rises	Increase in input costs can reduce price advantages	
Industry rivalry	Firm remains profitable when rivals collapse due to excessive price competition	Unique features reduce direct competition	Technological change will require capital investment, or make production cheaper for competitors Competitors learn via imitation Cost concerns ignore product design or marketing issues	Imitation narrows differentiation

Cost leadership and differentiation strategies look at how a firm positions its product or service across the industry as a whole. However, rather than competing across the industry as a whole, a firm can concentrate on a more narrowly defined segment.

Focus strategy

Focus (niche) strategy is where a firm concentrates its activity on one or more particular segments of the market, and does not try to serve the entire market with a single product. Either cost leadership or differentiation is then pursued. Such concentrated effort can be more effective, but the segment may be attacked by a larger firm.

INTERACTING WITH THE COMPETITIVE ENVIRONMENT

Part A

2

BUSINESS STRATEGY & STRATEGY DEVELOPMENT

 This chapter provides an overview of the key approaches to corporate strategy theory, and the way organisations develop their corporate strategies.

We will begin by looking at some of the general principles and practice of business strategy, before comparing some different approaches to strategic planning.

The chapter finishes with a discussion of the role of directors in the strategic process.

This Chapter builds on knowledge gained in paper E2 where you first saw different approaches to strategy (for example, prescriptive versus emergent approaches).

Although we can identify these different generic approaches to strategy, there are still a number of interpretations about how an organisation can best implement its strategy. Ultimately, an organisation's strategy needs to be seen in the context of its history and culture, its competitive environment and its resources.

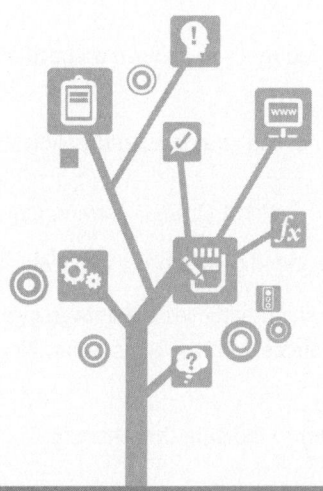

topic list	learning outcomes	syllabus references	ability required
1 Strategic planning	C 1 (a)	C 1 (ii)	Evaluate
2 Strategic planning: the rational model	C 1 (a)	C 1 (ii)	Evaluate
3 Less formal strategic planning	C 1 (a)	C 1 (ii)	Evaluate
4 Strategy lenses	C 1 (a)	C 1 (ii)	Evaluate
5 Environmental complexity and organisations	C 1 (a)	C 1 (ii)	Evaluate
6 Resource-based strategy	C 1 (a)	C 1 (ii)	Evaluate
7 Management accounting and business strategy	–	A 1 (vi)	Recommend
8 Directors' strategic roles and responsibilities	C 1 (d)	C 1 (x)	Evaluate

1 Strategic planning

Introduction

The E3 syllabus explores the ways in which organisations design and implement their strategies, and looks at the factors which affect those strategies. However, before we move on to look at these issues, we will look at why organisations need to develop strategies.

All organisations need to plan if they going to maintain their direction and scope over the long term. If they do not plan, they are liable to drift and lose their competitive advantage in a changing environment.

KEY POINT

Strategic decisions relate to the scope of a firm's activities, the long-term direction of the organisation, and allocation of resources.

Managing business strategy involves the entire cycle of **planning and control**, at a **strategic** level.

- Strategic analysis
- Strategic choice
- Implementation of chosen strategies
- Review and control

KEY TERM

PLANNING is the 'establishment of objectives and the formulation, evaluation and selection of the policies, strategies, tactics and action required to achieve them. Planning comprises long-term/strategic planning, and short-term/operational planning'.
(CIMA Official Terminology)

How does this relate to the management of business strategy?

KEY TERMS

A STRATEGY is a 'course of action, including the specification of resources required, to achieve a specific objective'.

A STRATEGIC PLAN is a 'statement of long-term goals along with a definition of the strategies and policies which will ensure achievement of these goals'.

(CIMA Official Terminology)

Johnson, Scholes and Whittington in their text *Exploring Corporate Strategy* define strategy as follows:

'**Strategy** is the **direction** and **scope** of an organisation over the **long term** which achieves **advantage** in a **changing environment**, through its configuration of **resources** and **competences** with the aims of fulfilling **stakeholder expectations**.'

We can take the highlighted phrases out of this definition, and expand them to indicate that there is general agreement on what constitutes the key elements of strategy.

Phase	Comment
Direction and scope	Strategy gives at least an **initial deliberate direction**, range of **activities** and **future** for the company to aim at, even if environmental circumstances conspire to send it off course and demand management action.
Long term	Most organisations are 'in it' for the **achievement of objectives** that will go beyond short-term profit targets. What constitutes 'long term' in business strategy is open to debate; it has been claimed that the average lifespan of commercial organisations in Western countries is about 40 years. Bear in mind that: • Time horizons are culturally determined; the 'long-term' means different things in different cultures. • The 'long-term' varies from industry to industry: compare fashion retailing with mining. A turnaround strategy for a fashion retailer depends on success in one or two seasons.

Phase	Comment
Achieves advantage	Strategy affects the overall **welfare** of the organisation and its **position against competitors**.
Changing environment	It is a tenet of business strategy that an organisation is inextricably linked with its environment, and strategy can help the organisation to cope with **changes** and **complexity**. An organisation needs to match its activities to its **capabilities** and the **environment** in which it operates.
Configuration of resources and competences	Strategies require **processes** to guide the **effective utilisation** of resources and competences in order to achieve competitive advantage. Strategies also require integration across functional and operational boundaries.
Stakeholder expectations	Stakeholders (in particular **shareholders**) have their own interests in the organisation. Should the pursuit of shareholder wealth be the main concern of management? What about customer expectations and satisfying market demand?

A strategic thinker should have a **vision** of:

- What the business is now
- What the ideal world would be like
- What it could be in an ideal world

To develop a business strategy, an organisation has to decide the following.

- What it is **good at**
- How the market might **change**
- How **customer satisfaction** can be delivered
- What might **constrain** realisation of the plan
- What should be done to **minimise risk**
- What **actions** should be put in place

We will return to look at this point in more detail in Chapter 5 (in relation to choosing a generic strategy), but another way of defining 'strategy' might be:

- Deciding **how** to compete (eg in terms of cost, or quality)
- Deciding **where** to complete (which geographical markets to compete in, and which market segments to compete in)

Exam skills

There is often no single 'right' or 'wrong' strategy an organisation can use in a situation, although some strategies will be more suitable than others. A good strategy will enable an organisation to use its resources and capabilities successfully in circumstances it cannot confidently predict.

Remember this as you tackle the case study scenarios in the exam – and always make sure that any strategies you suggest address the circumstances and **context** highlighted by the scenario.

The context of strategy is very important. For example, **small businesses** tend to have limited resources and face strong competition. **Large multinationals** will have more resources, but have to make decisions about structure, resource allocation, and which markets to compete in.

Public sector and **not-for-profit organisations** are influenced by ideology, politics and a range of stakeholders.

It is also important to recognise that firms can take different **approaches to strategic planning**. There are three main approaches:

- **Accounting-led**: An organisation starts by looking at its key stakeholders and their objectives (eg to increase pre-tax profits by x% per year, and earnings per share (EPS) by y% per year). Then the organisation develops plans which are designed to achieve those objectives.

  However, critics argue that such an approach to strategic planning is flawed. because it doesn't take sufficient account of market conditions and the external environment.

- **Position-based approach**: An organisation analyses its environment (eg PEST factors; competitors' actions and strategies etc) before setting its objectives and strategy. Its strategic plans are then designed to try to ensure a good 'fit' with the environment.

  The rational model of strategic planning follows this kind of approach.

- **Resource-based approach**: Critics of the position-based approach argue that the extent of the changes in the environment make it very difficult for organisations to predict the future. Therefore, rather than trying to focus on a 'fit' with the environment, organisations should focus their strategy on their own core competences, and what they are good at.

  However, the potential flaw with this approach is that it is too inward-looking. For example, it would be little use an organisation being good at something if there is no longer a market demand for it. Equally, environmental changes may mean that the organisation's core competences are no longer a source of competitive advantage (for example, due to the emergence of new technologies or substitute products.)

Section summary

Organisations need strategies to establish their direction and scope in the long term, and to determine the resources and competences needed to achieve their desired courses of action.

2 Strategic planning: the rational model   5/10, 9/10

Introduction

The **rational model** is a comprehensive approach to strategy. It suggests a logical sequence which involves analysing the current situation, generating choices (relating to competitors, products and markets) and implementing the chosen strategies.

2.1 Stages of the rational model

Strategic planning can be divided into three related stages: strategic **analysis**, strategic **choice** and strategic **implementation**.

Exam skills

The examiner has indicated that the 'analysis – choice – implementation' model of the strategic management process can be used as an overview of many of the requirements of the E3 syllabus, and so may feature regularly in the exams.

Note, however, that whilst the rational model adopts a linear approach to strategic management, *Johnson, Scholes and Whittington* (in Exploring Corporate Strategy) argue that strategy is not a linear process. For *Johnson, Scholes and Whittington*, the three stages of 'analysis, choice and implementation' do not necessarily have to follow each other in sequence. For example, when an organisation implements a strategy, in doing so it may discover things about its environment or capabilities that may in turn help it with future strategic analysis and choices.

In this respect, *Johnson, Scholes and Whittington* stress the **interdependence** and **integration** of the three elements of analysis, choice and implementation in strategic management.

2.1.1 Strategic analysis

Strategic analysis can be viewed as understanding the **strategic position** of any organisation. Michael Porter, one of the key writers on business strategy, highlights the importance of understanding the strategic position of an organisation when he argues that 'the essence of formulating competitive strategy is relating a company to its environment'.

We can break down the strategic analysis stage of strategic planning into a series of steps:

	Stage	Comment	Key tools, models, techniques
Step 1	Mission and/or vision	Mission denotes values, the business's rationale for existing; vision refers to where the organisation intends to be in a few years time	• Mission statement
Step 2	Goals	Interpret the mission to different stakeholders	• Stakeholder analysis
Step 3	Objectives	Quantified embodiments of mission	• Measures such as profitability, time scale, deadlines
Step 4	Environmental analysis	Identify opportunities and threats	• PEST analysis • Porter's 5 force analysis; 'diamond' (competitive advantage of nations) • Scenario building
Step 5	Position audit or situation analysis	Identify strengths and weaknesses Firm's current resources, products, customers, systems, structure, results, efficiency, effectiveness	• Resource audit • Distinctive competence • Value chain • Product life cycle • BCG matrix • Marketing audit
Step 6	Corporate appraisal	Combines Steps 4 and 5	• SWOT analysis charts
Step 7	Gap analysis	Compares outcomes of Step 6 with Step 3	• Gap analysis

2.1.2 Strategic choice

Stage	Comment	Key tools, models, techniques
Strategic options generation	Come up with new ideas: • How to compete (competitive advantage) • Where to compete • Method of growth	• Value chain analysis • Scenario building • Porter's generic strategic choices • Ansoff's growth vector matrix • Acquisition vs organic growth
Strategic options evaluation	Normally, each strategy has to be evaluated on the basis of • Suitability • Acceptability • Feasibility	• Stakeholder analysis • Risk analysis • Decision-making tools such as decision trees, matrices, ranking and scoring methods • Financial measures (eg ROCE, DCF)

Strategy selection involves choosing between the alternative strategies.

The **competitive strategies** are the generic strategies for competitive advantage an organisation will pursue. They determine **how an organisation generates competitive advantage**: for example, by cost leadership or differentiation.

Product-market strategies (which markets you should enter or leave) determine **where you compete** and the direction of growth.

Institutional strategies (ie relationships with other organisations) determine the **method of growth**.

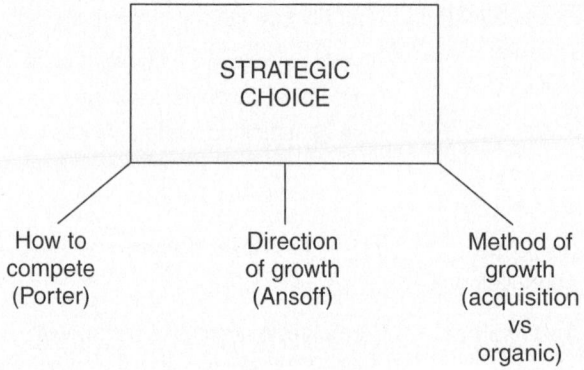

2.1.3 Strategy implementation

Strategy implementation is the **conversion** of the strategy into detailed plans or objectives for operating units. In this respect, strategic implementation is a vital part of the strategic planning process, because a strategy can only start delivering benefit to an organisation once it has been put into practice.

The planning of implementation has several aspects.

• **Resource** planning
• **Operations** planning
• **Organisation** structure and control systems

Change is often a critical component of strategy implementation, because organisations have to change in order to achieve their chosen strategies.

Importance of interdependency – However, remember the point we made earlier that *Johnson, Scholes and Whittington* emphasise the strategic management process should not be seen as a linear model.

Whilst strategic implementation is shown as the final stage of the rational model (after strategic analysis and strategic choice) it is important to recognise that implementation is still inter-linked with these other two elements of the strategic management process. When an organisation actually starts to implement a strategy, it may discover things about its resources and structure which lead to it to re-evaluate its assessment of strategic position and strategic choice.

2.2 Types of strategy

Corporate strategy is the most general level of strategy in an organisation, identifying the strategy for the business as a whole. For example, this might include goal setting and objectives, and identifying corporate values, or the decision to enter a new industry or to leave an existing industry.

Business strategy. This relates to how an organisation approaches a particular market, or the activity of a particular business unit. For example, this might include the way a business unit adapts to customer requirements or competitor's actions, and how it manages unique competences to compete successfully in specific markets.

Operational and functional strategies involve decisions which are made at operational level and affect the day-to-day operation of the business. These decisions include product pricing, marketing strategy, HR strategy, IT strategy and so forth. The contributions of these different functions determine the success of the strategy. This again reinforces the importance of **strategy implementation** within strategic management. A strategic plan is ultimately only likely to be successful if it is delivered effectively at an operational level.

We will look at organisational structures and control later in this Study Text, but the existence of these different levels of strategy also illustrates that a business may need to decide whether it treats strategy as a top-down process (imposed by the corporate centre) or whether it is a divisional (business unit) responsibility.

 The idea of different levels of strategy can be represented by the Anthony hierarchy. We look at the Anthony hierarchy in relation to performance measurement and control in Chapter 13 of this text.

 ### Section summary

The **rational model** describes a highly structured approach to strategic planning. An organisation identifies its objectives, analyses its current position, develops its strategic options and then selects a strategy to implement.

3 Less formal strategic planning   5/10, 9/10

 ### Introduction

The rational model can be seen as a formal approach to strategy. This approach has identifiable advantages, but it has problems also. In an attempt to address these problems, alternative models of strategic planning have been developed, including **freewheeling opportunism, incrementalism** and **emergent strategies**. The management accountant's role differs in each case.

3.1 Advantages of formal planning

These are the advantages of a formal system of strategic planning.

Advantages	Comments
Identifies risks	Strategic planning helps in managing these risks.
Forces managers to think	Strategic planning can encourage creativity and initiative by tapping the ideas of the management team.
Forces decision-making	Companies cannot remain static – they have to cope with changes in the environment. A strategic plan draws attention to the need to change and adapt, not just to 'stand still' and survive.
Better control	Management control can be better exercised if targets are explicit.
Enforces consistency at all levels	Long-term, medium-term and short-term objectives, plans and controls can be made consistent with one another. Otherwise, strategies can be rendered ineffective by budgeting systems and performance measures which have no strategic content.
Identifies risks	The management writer, Peter Drucker, has argued that an entrepreneur who builds a long-lasting business has 'a theory of the business' which informs his or her business decisions. In large organisations, that theory of the business has to become public knowledge, as decisions cannot be taken only by one person.

3.2 Criticisms of strategic planning in practice (Mintzberg)

The idea that strategy-making can be reduced to planning processes has come under attack from Henry Mintzberg, in his book *The Rise and Fall of Strategic Planning.* Mintzberg argues there are a number of problems with formal planning processes.

Problem	Comments
Practical failure	Empirical studies have not proved that formal planning processes contribute to success. Companies which adopt long-range views and planning techniques do not consistenly out-perform those which do not.
Routine and regular	Strategic planning occurs often in an annual cycle. But a firm cannot allow itself to wait every year for the budget planning process to address its problems.
Reduces initiative	Formal planning discourages strategic thinking. Once a plan is locked in place, people are unwilling to question it, or to take alternative actions to improve a situation, because they feel that, if they do, they will have to defend themselves for acting 'outside the plan' – regardless of any benefits which result from their actions.
Internal politics	The assumption of 'objectivity' in evaluation ignores political battles between different managers and departments.
Exaggerates power	Managers are not all-knowing, and there are limits to the extent to which they can control the behaviour of the organisation.

3.3 General limitations of planning models

Plans are made so that sensible attempts may be made to guide and control future developments. All planning methods are limited in their ability to help in doing this, simply because of the **difficulty in trying to predict the future** with any degree of certainty.

(a)   It is very common to assume that **the future will resemble the past**. Unfortunately, discontinuities or shocks occur and these are, by definition, impossible to predict with accuracy.

(b)   All models require **assumptions** to be made. This has two important implications:

    (i)   The assumptions used should be tailored to the industry and organisation in question. For example, industry price inflation rates may be different from the national rate.

    (ii)   The further into the future one looks, the less likely it is that assumptions will **remain valid**. Predictions of more distant future events become less reliable. For some industries with extremely distant time horizons, forecasting on any basis may be quite impractical. However, one of the characteristics of strategic planning is that it looks at the **long-term** direction an organisation might take.

3.3.1 Difficulties with long term planning

One of the key difficulties in strategic (long term) planning comes from trying to accurately forecast what will happen in the long term.

The fact that they are dealing with a long time period could, in itself, be a problem for strategic planners.

However, their difficulties are likely to be increased further by the **complexity and dynamism of the environment**, and **the rapidity of change** within the environment.

Equally, it can be difficult to predict how the relationships between different variables in the environment will develop.

Long term planning versus **short term pressures**. Although managers might set long term plans, they will also be under pressure to deliver short tem results (particularly in listed companies). One of the criticisms of long term plans is that they are too rigid, and do not give companies the flexibility to react to unforeseen **short-term** opportunities or unexpected short-term crises.

Exam skills

One of the difficulties which strategic planners face is the pressure to deliver strategies which are acceptable to different stakeholder groups with different (possibly contradictory) objectives.

This highlights the importance of **stakeholder management**, which we will look at in more detail in Chapter 2 of this Study Text. Stakeholder management is a key theme throughout the E3 syllabus, and when discussing or recommending a proposed strategy it is important that you consider how acceptable that strategy might be to different stakeholder groups.

3.4 Structural determinism

KEY TERM

STRUCTURAL DETERMINISM is the notion that an organisation's response to an environmental shock or influence will depend on what type of structure it [the organisation] is.

We also need to acknowledge the concept of structural determinism when considering the relationships between an organisation and its environment.

We have already noted that one of the potential problems of prescriptive approaches to strategy is that they cannot predict or control external environmental factors. However, this problem is complicated further by the fact that an **organisation's response to an environmental shock will depend on what type of structure the organisation is**.

As an analogy, if you put clay into a hot oven, the clay will harden. But if you put ice into a hot oven, the ice will melt. Although the environmental conditions are the same in both cases, they generate very different responses. The same is true for organisations: where the same environmental conditions can

generate different strategic responses in different organisations, depending on the internal characteristics of the organisations.

For example, in the UK the recession in 2009 forced Marks & Spencer to make job cuts and close some of its food stores. However, at the same time, low cost food retailers such as Aldi and Lidl were reporting increasing sales as cash-conscience customers looked to buy their groceries as cheaply as possible.

Structural determinism has two important implications for strategy makers.

- For all organisations to pursue a single approach for strategic success is inappropriate because organisations are different. A strategy needs to be adapted to the specific circumstances of the organisation.

- Strategists need to look inside the organisation as well as at the environment. They need to understand the behaviour of the organisation as much as the environment.

Exam skills

The first bullet point about structural determinism also has important implications for your exam. The fact that 'A strategy needs to be adapted to the specific circumstances of the organisation' is crucial advice for the E3 exam. Make sure that any strategies you recommend are appropriate to the organisation and context described in the scenario.

3.5 No strategic planning: 'freewheeling opportunism'

The **freewheeling opportunism approach** suggests firms should not bother with strategic plans and should exploit opportunities as they arise.

The opportunist approach means that an organisation can **seize opportunities** quickly as they arise (rather than getting slowed down by formal planning processes), but the lack of planning may also mean the organisation **fails to identify possible opportunities** which might be available.

Advantages

(a) Good opportunities are not lost through spending time completing formal planning processes.

(b) A freewheeling opportunistic approach would **adapt to change** more quickly (eg, if there were a very steep rise in the price of a key material input, the opportunist firm would look to find any alternative material as quickly as possible).

(c) It might encourage a more **flexible, creative attitude**.

Disadvantages

(a) **No co-ordinating framework** for the organisation, so that some potentially valuable opportunities get missed

(b) It emphasises the **profit motive** to the exclusion of all other considerations.

(c) The firm ends up **reacting** all the time rather than acting purposively.

3.5.1 Management accounting and freewheeling opportunism

A freewheeling opportunism approach abandons the careful routine of planning, and instead seizes such opportunities that arise. Not all 'opportunities' will work out, and there may be problems sustaining this policy.

The management accountant's role will be **investigative**.

(a) What are the financial characteristics of the proposed strategy? For example, in an acquisition, what is the effect on **cash flow**?

(b)   How does the proposed strategy affect the firm's **risk profile**?

(c)   What **new markets** will the firm be entering by pursuing this strategy? If so, what is the likely response of competitors?

3.6 Incrementalism

Herbert Simon suggested that managers often have to adopt a solution which is reasonable, if not ideal. Managers are limited by **time**, by the **information** they have and by their own skills, habits and perceptions of reality.

This has the following implications:

(a)   Strategic managers do not evaluate all the possible options but choose between relatively few alternatives. Managers can only handle a limited number of options at any one time. (This restriction in the number of options managers are able to choose from is known as **bounded rationality**.)

(b)   Strategy making tends to involve small scale extensions of past policy – **incrementalism** – rather than radical shifts.

KEY POINT

Incrementalism is an approach to strategy and decision making highlighting small and slow changes rather than one-off changes in direction. The danger is that such small scale adjustments may not be enough to move with customers and their needs, leading to **strategic drift**.

We look at issues around the speed and extent of change in more detail later in the chapters on change management.

Quinn coined the term **logical incrementalism** to mean that strategies might not be formulated by planning, but using an incremental process with an underlying logic. Top managers guide internal activities (as with the rational approach) while at the same time responding to external events, and develop their conscious strategies this way.

CASE STUDY

Tesco.com and Webvan

Tesco.com, the online shopping operation set up by the UK supermarket giant is an excellent example of successful incrementalism. In 1996, Tesco decided to test the potential for online grocery shopping with a website based on a single store at Osterley in West London. Over the next two years the business model was refined and the crucial decision to impose a delivery charge was made. This had the beneficial effect of leading customers to place fewer, larger orders so as to obtain the greatest benefit from the flat-rate charge. Tesco.com has grown successfully each year since its launch, partly because costs have been held down by making deliveries from existing stores. By 2007, Tesco.com had 850,000 customers worldwide, and completed more than 250,000 online orders each week. In the same year (2007), Tesco.com generated more than £1 billion revenue in the UK alone.

By 2010, over 15,000 products were available online. As well as offering an online grocery shopping service, Tesco.com also offers a wide range of other products, including electronic goods, entertainment and books, clothing, and homewares.

Tesco's approach was markedly different from that of Webvan which set out to completely remodel the US grocery retailing industry in 1997. It aimed to create a chain of highly automated warehouses in order to increase worker productivity, and it offered free delivery regardless of location. Unfortunately, Webvan was never really in control of its costs and it was estimated that the company lost US$130 on every order. By July 2001, the company was declared insolvent after losing US$1.2bn.

Herbert Simon's ideas about the constraints which affect managers' decisions highlight that ultimately it is the actions of the **people** in an organisation (the directors, managers, and employees) that actually

deliver a strategy. This contrasts with ideas in prescriptive strategy which treat strategy as if it is something objective, imposed upon an organisation.

Critics of the prescriptive approach are very damning in this respect. They argue it is quite inappropriate to simply think of an organisation's behaviour as being a set of deliberate choices from a menu of alternatives. Instead the strategies an organisation chooses, and the ways they are implemented, will be guided by the people and processes already working at that organisation.

Therefore it is important to consider the human resource based implications of strategy, and to highlight the importance of **motivation**, **politics** and **culture** in organisations. As we will discuss later in this study text, it also important to consider the **impact of change and uncertainty** as new strategies are introduced.

3.7 Emergent strategies

Whereas the rational model describes a top-down process which is clearly defined from the outset, *Henry Mintzberg* argues that strategy is better viewed as an emergent process.

An emergent strategy is one whose **final objective is unclear** at the outset, and whose **elements develop** during its life as the strategy proceeds.

Moreover, emergent strategies can emerge 'bottom up'; they can result from a number of **ad hoc choices** within an organisation, possibly made lower down the organisation, not just by senior management.

KEY POINT

An **emergent strategy** is one developed out of a pattern of behaviour rather than being consciously imposed in advance by senior management. There is a high degree of experimentation to find the most productive route.

Timescale: Emergent strategies usually **take longer to develop than planned strategies**, because they evolve rather than being formally planned in one go.

Emergent strategies can sometimes be seen as **survival-based theories of strategy**. In order to survive and prosper in an environment which is shifting and changing an organisation has to be 'fitter' than in its competitors: only the fittest will survive.

In which case, there is little point having a prescriptive strategy which has to be regularly changed; it is better for an organisation to change and develop as the market changes, letting its strategy emerge in the process.

The diagram below should help to explain the contrast between prescriptive (planned) and emergent strategy.

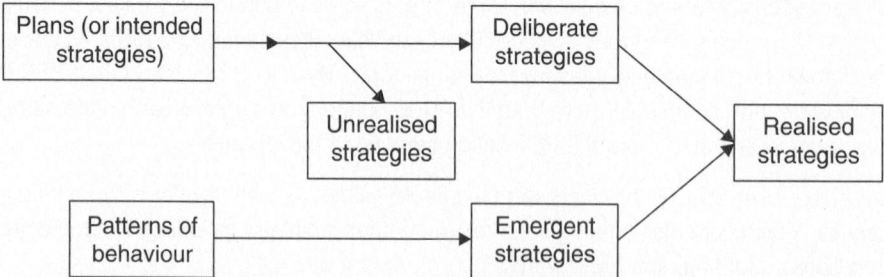

There are dangers in following an emergent strategy. It may involve **risks**, or it may **interfere** with other strategies. It will need to be **managed** if it commits the organisation to using resources.

The diagram above also highlights the important distinction between **realised** and **unrealised** strategies. Plans may be unworkable for a variety of reasons: resources may be inadequate, important stakeholders may oppose them, and so on.

You have probably encountered examples in everyday life where an intended strategy is not realised. For example, how many times have organisations promised you 'excellent customer service' or 'first rate service'? Has the service you have actually received matched those promises?

The intended plan may have been to offer 'excellent customer service', but what is realised often falls short of what is intended.

3.7.1 Crafting strategy

Mintzberg uses the metaphor of **crafting strategy** to help understand the idea.

CASE STUDY

Honda

Honda is now one of the leading manufacturers of motorbikes. The company is credited with identifying and targeting an untapped market for small 50cc bikes in the US, which enabled it to expand, trounce European competition and severely damage indigenous US bike manufacturers. By 1965, Honda had 63% of the US market. But this occurred by accident.

On entering the US market, Honda had wanted to compete with the larger European and US bikes of 250ccs and over. These bikes had a defined market, and were sold through dedicated motorbike dealerships. Disaster struck when Honda's larger machines developed faults – they had not been designed for the hard wear and tear imposed by US motorcyclists. Honda had to recall the larger machines.

Honda had made little effort to sell its small 50 cc motorbikes – its staff rode them on errands around Los Angeles. Sports goods' shops, ordinary bicycle and department stores had expressed an interest, but Honda did not want to confuse its image in its 'target' market of men who bought the larger bikes.

The faults in Honda's larger machines meant that reluctantly, Honda had to sell the small 50cc bikes just to raise money. They proved very popular with people who would never have bought motorbikes before. Eventually the company adopted this new market with enthusiasm with the slogan: 'You meet the nicest people on a Honda'. The strategy had emerged, against managers' conscious intentions, but they eventually responded to the new situation.

How to craft strategy

Mintzberg mentions the following essential activities in strategic management.

(a)   Manage stability.

(b)   Detect discontinuity. Environments do not change regularly, nor are they always turbulent. Some changes are more important than others.

(c)   Know the business. This has to include an awareness and understanding of operations.

(d)   Manage patterns. Detect emerging patterns and help them take shape if appropriate.

(e)   Reconcile change and continuity. Avoid concentrating on one or the other.

Following these, **crafting strategy** might involve the following roles for the management accountant.

(a)   **Managing stability.** Standard management accounting information in stable environments enables the business to **control its activities** and use its resources effectively.

(b)   **Detecting discontinuity.** Management accountants are probably not the best source of information for detecting **environmental change.** Concerns such as the failure of a major customer may be picked up through receivables' age analysis.

(c)   **Know the business**

(i)   Management accounting information can model the operations of the business in financial terms.

(ii)   Many of a business's **critical success factors,** such as customer confidence, are not easily susceptible to management accounting analysis.

BPP
LEARNING MEDIA

(d)   **Managing patterns**. The management accounting system must enable 'patterns' to be detected. All this would suggest an aggregation of financial and non-financial information in a **relational database**, with a variety of tools and techniques (eg graphical systems).

(e)   **Reconciling change and continuity**. The inflexibility of management accounting information makes it inappropriate for this purpose.

3.8 Learning in strategy

Another important aspect of emergent strategy is the value of learning strategy development. Proponents of learning-based strategy, such as *Senge*, emphasise that managers should be prepared to use **trial and error**, and to **learn from mistakes** on the way to developing their optimal strategy.

Some advocates of the emergent approach also argue that the **creation and dissipation of new ideas** throughout an organisation are the most important aspects of strategy development.

This learning approach to strategy is very different to the focus of the prescriptive model: rather than being clearly defined in advance, an organisation's strategy emerges as a result of **trial and error**, and **experimentation.** Here again, the rational model and the prescriptive approach do not fully reflect the strategic process.

However, while emergent strategies highlight some weaknesses in prescriptive strategies, we must not overlook the fact that there are also some concerns about the emergent strategic process. Emergent strategies seem to overlook the **role of the corporate centre**.

This is unrealistic though. Directors and board members will not simply let companies operate without any targets or direction. Management *will* have a vision of where they want the organisation to be, and they are likely to have some plans for how to get there, what resources are required and so on.

3.9 Is a compromise approach needed?

While critics of the rational model and its prescriptive approach to strategy argue that there is no room for flexibility or learning in the strategy formulation process, critics of the emergent approach argue that letting a strategy evolve means there is no overall control over the strategy. Therefore, perhaps the best way to develop strategy is through a way that combines elements of both approaches.

So far we have presented the prescriptive and emergent approaches to strategy as two conflicting approaches. However, in his classic text *The Mind of the Strategist,* Kenichi Ohmae argues that what is important is not what approach to strategy an organisation takes, but that everyone in the organisation shares the same vision and goals, and pulls in the same direction to achieve those goals.

Ohmae makes an analogy with an orchestra making music. The score (the printed music on the page) is equivalent to the strategic plan. It sets out what the composer intended, plus any subsequent arrangements or edits that have been made to it.

The conductor represents the senior management of the organisation; controlling speeds, dynamics and phrasing, and making sure that the orchestra's playing is co-ordinated.

The orchestra represent the organisation itself. Each musician in the orchestra has their own role to play, (as indicated by the score), guided by the conductor and playing in harmony with their fellow musicians.

Finally there is an element of the unexpected. Even though orchestras rehearse in advance of a performance, they can never know how a performance will turn out until it happens. Moreover, some truly great performances have come about when everything did not go exactly as planned, but everyone pulled together and adapted or improvised successfully.

This analogy illustrates that both formal, rational strategy and emergent strategy have a role to play in an organisation's success. An organisation needs a plan to act underpin its success. But the real strategic story lies in how the strategy unfolds on top of that plan, how the organisation reacts and adapts to what is going on around it and within it.

Exam skills

In this text, we have compared and contrasted the rational approach to strategy and the less formal, emergent approaches. The E3 syllabus expects you to be able to 'Evaluate the process of strategy formation' so you may need to assess whether an organisation would be better served by a rational approach or an emergent approach given the context provided in a case study scenario. It is imporatant that you understand the advantages and disadvantages of each approach so that you can assess which circumstances they would be most appropriate for.

Section summary

There is a basic distinction to be made between **prescriptive** and **emergent** theories of strategy. The emergent process does not identify final strategic objectives in advance, and so is more adaptable than a prescriptive approach. It also recognises the important role people play in actually designing and delivering strategies, and the importance of learning and innovation as outputs from strategy.

4 Strategy lenses

Introduction

We have already seen that opinions about the best approach to business strategy are divided. However, rather than thinking only in terms of prescriptive or emergent theories, we can analysis the different approaches to strategy into three different 'lenses': strategy as design, strategy as experience, and strategy as ideas.

Johnson, Scholes and Whittington in their text *'Exploring Corporate Strategy'* suggest that the rational approach to strategic planning and the less formal approaches can both offer some understanding of what strategy is, and what it is for.

Johnson, Scholes and Whittington suggest that approaches to strategy can be summarised into three lenses through which strategy can be examined.

* Strategy as design
* Strategy as experience
* Strategy as ideas

Strategy as design

The strategy as design approach follows the view of strategy as a **rational, top-down process** by which senior managers analyse and evaluate strategic constraints and forces in order to establish a clear and rational course of strategic action.

This view appeals to senior managers, because it is logical and also supports the role of management in an organisation. It can also appeal to stakeholders such as shareholders and banks because it suggests an organisation has a **clear vision** of what it wants to achieve.

The view of strategy as design is also useful since it leads to the use of a number of strategic tools and techniques that are logical and practical.

However, the assumptions that strategic problems can always be solved by rational analysis, and that an organisation is a rational system that can always implement management's plans do not describe the complexity of strategic management.

Strategy as experience

This view sees strategy as an **adaptation and extension of what has worked in the past**. It is based on the experience and assumptions of influential figures in an organisation, and the ways of doing things that **fit with the organisation's culture**.

The 'strategy as experience' view appreciates that managers tend to **simplify the complexity** they face in order to be able to deal with it, selecting and using the elements of their knowledge and understanding that seem most relevant or important.

However, this simplification may pose a risk to the organisation. For example, if an organisation has identified a key competitor, this competitor may come to represent competition in general. The problem is that this may blind managers to the actions of emerging competitors that have the potential to disrupt the existing market structure.

Where there are choices or disputes about strategic choices, these are resolved by negotiation and bargaining. The result is decisions that **satisfice rather than optimise**, and strategies that develop in an incremental and adaptive way. So the strategy as experience lens aligns with the emergent view of strategy.

Strategy as ideas

This approach to strategy emphasises **innovation and the need for diversity of ideas** in an organisation. Strategy can emerge from the way the people within the organisation handle and respond to the changing forces present in the organisation and the environment.

The role of senior managers is to **create the context and conditions in which new ideas can emerge**, and that the best ones survive and thrive. An important feature of this role is to avoid relying on either the design approach or the experience approach. Relying too much on the design approach tends to lead to over-emphasis on control, while relying too much on the experience approach encourages the organisation to only move incrementally.

In either case, innovation is unlikely and so the organisation is likely to be **susceptible to strategic drift**.

However, there is still a need for some degree of control in an organisation. The aim must be for managers to create an '**adaptive tension**' that keeps the organisation functioning without resorting to machine-like procedures, or descending into unproductive disarray. This can be achieved by the use of simple rules, which are general principles rather than detailed procedures.

Section summary

Rather than looking at strategy as being either prescriptive or emergent we could look at it in terms of design, experience or ideas, using the notion of the **three strategic lenses**. The design lens shows strategy as a rational, top-down process operating under careful controls. This contrasts with the experience lens which presents strategy as an extension of what has worked in the past. The ideas lens suggests that strategy is formed by diversity of ideas, leading to innovation.

5 Environmental complexity and organisations

Introduction

A business can be seen as a self-organising, complex entity that responds to its dynamic and complex environment in ways determined and promoted by its pattern of human relationships.

The classical, rational view of strategy treats organisations as being as **automatic and machine-like** as possible, but alternative (and more recent) views recognise the challenge presented to this approach by a **dynamic and complex environment**.

Ralph Stacey discerns a further layer of complication in the way that organisations work, which he explores in terms of **chaos theory**. He proposes a radical theory of how strategy emerges, based on a view of the organisation as a **self-organising complex process.**

Stacey suggests that modern thinking about complexity can offer us a useful insight into the way organisations actually work, and how they move towards learning, innovation and adaptation in a complex and unstable global environment.

The interaction between an organisation and its environment has the potential for significant disruption. *Stacey* argues that the complexity and instability of the business environment means that organisations are operating in unpredictable circumstances. Consequently, there is no value in setting a prescriptive strategy. The reality is so complex that the **linear assumptions** between **cause** and **effect** cannot be justified.

The classical approach to theory – for example, the world of models such as *Porter*'s Five Forces - assumes that the environment is in a stable equilibrium, and so works in a regular, orderly and predictable way. But *Stacey* argues this is too simplistic, and to understand how companies actually work we need to understand complexity in a way which the classical, rational model does not allow. Given this, strategy should be allowed to emerge and adapt to the changes in the environment, rather than being prescribed.

Uncertainty-based theories of strategy ultimately derive from **chaos theory** and mathematical modelling, which are most obviously used in weather forecasting. The key point behind chaos theory is that although a system - the weather (or the business environment) - is not completely random and does follow some patterns, it is not totally predictable either.

The sheer number of influences in the environment as a whole mean that small 'triggers' can sometimes lead to major changes later on – changes which could not have been predicted when the initial 'trigger' occurred.

The importance of this for business strategists is that, because organisations are **operating in an unpredictable environment**, strategy becomes virtually impossible to model because the future can not be known with any certainty.

One other characteristic of chaotic systems is that they **oscillate between steady states and states of flux**, and at the end of a period of turbulence a new order will emerge. The combination of these periods of turbulence and the inherent complexity of the environment have led *Stacey* to suggest that many businesses – particularly those in rapidly growing industries, or those where innovation is vital to success – are inherently unstable. They are operating in the chaotic region between stability and instability. Consequently, their business strategies have to emerge, rather than being subjected to the constraints of prescriptive strategy.

5.1 Complex adaptive systems

Below the level of the collective response, it should be remembered that organisations rely heavily on the individual **people** they contain. Those people interact according to common rules that are laid down in various ways.

- The formal organisation structure
- The organisation's culture
- The informal organisation
- Legal presumptions
- Cultural norms of the industry/national origin

Stacey sees the behaviour of the organisation as taking place both at the level of its people, and the collective level, simultaneously. He suggests that organisations that are capable of learning and adapting do so because, as systems, they are operating in the chaotic region between stability and instability.

Importance of management

Stacey pays considerable attention to the **position of the manager** in all this, and particularly the manager or managers at the **strategic apex**. Management has a very important role to play. Managers are in a position to see how things are going and to interact with many more other agents than most members of the organisation.

In this context, *Stacey* highlights the difference between **ordinary management** and **extraordinary management**.

Ordinary management is just what most of us would mean by that term: it is bureaucratic, procedural, hierarchical, rational and largely consists of controlling resources and operations in order to achieve the objects of a stated plan.

Extraordinary management, on the other hand, is about the emergence of new paradigms from a free-form process of persuasion, intuition and group-based organisational learning. It exists alongside ordinary management and is the means by which the problems and anomalies that ordinary management finds it difficult to deal with are integrated and resolved.

Section summary

Stacey argues that organisations operate in the chaotic region between **stability** and **instability**. This makes it difficult to predict the future with any certainty, but also highlights the importance of the strategic manager role in guiding organisations through **states of flux**.

6 Resource-based strategy

Introduction

All the approaches to strategy we have looked at so far show how organisations respond to their competitive environment (the position-based approach to strategy). However, organisations can base their strategy around exploiting their own resources and competences: the resource-based approach to strategy.

All the approaches to strategy we have discussed so far are examples of the **position-based approach** to strategy. This is because they seek to develop competitive advantage in a way that responds to the **nature of the competitive environment**: the firm positions its offering in response to the opportunities or threats it discerns.

Resource-based approaches to strategy offer a fundamentally different approach. In the resource-based approach, rather than being developed in response to the external competitive environment, strategy is developed by looking at what makes a firm unique, and using an understanding of these unique competences to determine what to produce and what markets to produce for.

Resource-based strategy was developed in response to two problems with the positioning method.

(a)   Many environments are too complex and dynamic to permit continuing effective analysis and response.

(b)   Once an opportunity is discerned and an offering made, it is very easy for competitors to make similar offerings, thus rapidly eroding competitive advantage.

The resource-based view is that sustainable competitive advantage is only attained as a result of the possession of distinctive resources. These may be physical **assets or resources**, such as the effective monopolisation of diamonds by *De Beers*, or, more typically in today's service economies, they may be capabilities or **competences**.

Competences develop in a variety of ways. Here are some examples:

- **Experience** in making and marketing a product or service
- The talents and potential of **individuals** in the organisation
- The **quality of co-ordination.**

6.1 Resources and competences

Johnson, Scholes and Whittington in *Exploring Corporate Strategy* provide a clear and specific set of terms which you can use when discussing resources and competences.

KEY TERMS

STRATEGIC CAPABILITY is the adequacy and suitability of the resources and competences of an organisation for it to survive and prosper.

TANGIBLE RESOURCES are the physical assets of an organisation, such as plant, labour and finance.

INTANGIBLE RESOURCES are non-physical assets such as information, reputation and knowledge.

COMPETENCES are the activities and processes through which an organisation deploys its resources effectively.

THRESHOLD CAPABILITIES are essential for the organisation to be able to compete in a given market.

THRESHOLD RESOURCES and THRESHOLD COMPETENCES are needed to meet customers' minimum requirements and therefore for the organisation to continue to exist.

UNIQUE RESOURCES and CORE COMPETENCES underpin competitive advantage and are difficult for competitors to imitate or obtain.

This analysis requires some discussion.

(a)   Note the way that *Johnson, Scholes and Whittington* use the word **capabilities** to denote a useful overall category that contains both resources and competences.

(b)   Look carefully at the definitions of **tangible** and **intangible resources**. These are not the tangible and intangible *assets* you are familiar with as an accountant: the inclusion of labour and finance under tangible resources, for example, demonstrates this.

(c)   **Competences**. A connected point is the definition of **competences;** make sure you appreciate the difference between a **competence** and an **intangible resource**. We might say that the relationship between the two is that a competence might well create, use or exploit an intangible resource (or a tangible one, for that matter). Thus, information is an **intangible resource**; the ability to make good use of it is a **competence**.

(d)   **Capabilities**. We have said that capabilities consist of **resources** and **competences**. As you can see, this means that Johnson, Scholes and Whittington effectively give a choice of definition for **threshold resources** and **threshold competences**. Each has its own specific definition, but since each qualifies as a **threshold capability**, we could, presumably, also use that definition.

(e)   *Johnson, Scholes and Whittington* do not provide a term to mean **unique resources** and **core competences** taken together as a class: we might speculate that **unique capabilities** or **core capabilities** could be used in this way, but it would probably be unwise to do this in your exam.

An important point to note here is that **resources are not productive on their own**. Therefore organisational capability – an organisation's capacity to successfully deploy its resources to achieve a desired end result – is vital as a basis for achieving competitive advantage. These organisational capabilities could be in a range of different areas:

- Corporate functions (financial control; multi-national co-ordination)
- Research and development
- Product design
- Operations (operational efficiency; continuous improvement; flexibility)
- Marketing
- Sales and distribution

GlaxoSmithKline and capabilities

Since the 1950s, a key resource for large pharmaceutical companies has been patented drugs with regulatory approval. This resource stock has been continually refreshed through research and development (R&D) activity which has involved testing large numbers of prototype drugs for their effectiveness in treating different illnesses.

Pharmaceutical companies built up learning dynamic capabilities through establishing and developing teams of specialist researchers, and other groups who were skilled in the extensive phases of testing required to gain regulatory approval for new drugs.

At the end of the 20th century, a series of mergers and acquisitions led to consolidation in the industry, for example with GlaxoWellcome merging with SmithKline (which had previously merged with Beecham) to form GSK in 2000.

However, GSK has also acquired some much smaller firms, many of whom have never sold any products, and who operate with quite different technologies and sciences bases; for example, biotechnology firms. This is because biotechnology is now seen as the main driver of innovation in the pharma sector, and the big pharmaceutical companies are seeking closer relations with the highly innovative biotech industry.

For example, GSK's acquisition of Corixa in 2005, despite being partially driven by the financial potential of Corixa's Monophosphoryl Lipid A (MPL) (which was contained in many of GSK's candidate vaccines including its potential blockbuster Cervarix), also dramatically expanded GSK's already lucrative vaccine platform, providing it with much needed additional expertise in the field.

Similarly, in 2007, GSK bolstered its biopharmaceuticals portfolio with the purchase of the UK-based speciality antibody company, Domantis. The acquisition cost £230 million, but Domantis has become a key part of GSK's Biopharmaceuticals Centre of Excellence for Drug Discovery (CEDD), and helped catapult GSK into the arena of next-generation antibody drugs by more than doubling the number of projects it has in this area.

More recently, GSK has also divested (or outsourced) activities traditionally performed in house. Pharmaceutical giants have not been immune to the global economic downturn, and they have been forced to adopt cost-saving strategies like organisations across other industries. However, GSK has looked towards more sophisticated approaches than simply cutting jobs and shelving expensive projects.

GSK has assigned a group of its scientists and patents to a standalone company dealing specifically with pain relief. 14 of GSK's leading researchers, along with the rights to a number of patents for experimental analgesic medicines, have been moved into a start-up company formed in October 2010: Convergence Pharmaceuticals.

This arrangement has been specifically engineered to reduce the overhead costs involved with research and development, while simultaneously allowing GSK to benefit from any breakthroughs that Convergence might develop and go on to market.

So, Glaxo's original learning processes of R&D have subsequently been augmented by three different phases of reconfiguring its capabilities. The first phase (of mega-mergers) involved similar firms combining; the second phase consisted of the acquisition of innovative biotech companies; and the third, most recent, phase consisted of restructuring and outsourcing activities.

This sequence of phases is evidence of GSK's regenerative dynamic capabilities, triggered by performance problems caused by the declining value of the existing resource base as the patents on existing products expired. GSK's existing R&D capabilities were insufficient in themselves to maintain, or expand, the stock of resources. The move into biotechnology acquisitions was triggered by the realisation that the pipeline of new drugs was drying up, as well as the fact that pharmaceutical companies are operating in an increasingly challenging environment, with high competitive rivalry, price sensitivity among health care providers, and stricter ethical standards.

6.2 Hamel and Prahalad

Hamel and Prahalad suggest that an important aspect of strategic management is the determination of the competences the company will require **in the future** in order to be able to provide new benefits to customers. They say a **core competence** must have the following qualities.

- It must make a **disproportionate** contribution to the **value** the customer perceives, or to the efficiency with which that value is delivered

- It must be '**competitively unique**', which means one of three things: actually unique; superior to competitors; or capable of dramatic improvement

- It must be **extendable**, in that it must allow for the development of an array of new products and services

In many cases, a company might choose to combine competences.

Bear in mind that **relying on a competence is no substitute for a strategy**. However, a core competence can form a basis for a strategy. Here it is important to reiterate that a core competence must be difficult to imitate if it is to confer lasting competitive advantage. In particular, skills that can be bought in are unlikely to form the basis of core competences, since competitors would be able to buy them in just as easily. Core competences are more about what the organisation is than about what it does. So it is possible to regard a strong brand as a kind of core competence: it is a unique resource that confers a distinct competitive advantage.

Section summary

In essence, approaches to strategy can either be **position-based** or **resource-based**. The resource-based approach to strategy starts from a consideration of strengths and weaknesses and highlights the importance of developing core competences as a basis of competitive advantage.

7 Management accounting and business strategy

Introduction

Although we have focused on the process of developing strategy, it is important to think how a management accountant can contribute to this process; for example, by providing information which is relevant for strategic decision making.

7.1 Management accounting and planned strategies

The role of the **management accountant in strategic planning** is to provide management information in order that strategic planning and control decisions can be made. Particular examples of the role of the management accountant are found throughout this text.

KEY TERM

MANAGEMENT ACCOUNTING is 'the application of the principles of accounting and financial management to create, protect, preserve and increase value for the stakeholders of for profit and not-for-profit enterprises in the public and private sectors.

Management accounting is an integral part of management. It requires the identification, generation, presentation, interpretation and use of information relevant to:

- Inform strategic decisions and formulate business strategy

- Plan long, medium and short-run operations

- Determine capital structure and fund that structure

- Design reward strategies for executives and shareholders

- Inform operational decisions

- Control operations and ensure the efficient use of resources

- Measure and report financial and non-financial performances to management and other stakeholders

- Safeguard tangible and intangible assets

- Implement corporate governance procedures, risk management and internal controls'.

(CIMA Official Terminology)

7.1.1 Future uncertainty

It is worth emphasising the **uncertainty** in much strategic planning.

(a) Strategic plans may cover a **long period** into the future.

(b) Many strategic plans involve big changes and **new ventures**, such as capacity expansion decisions or decisions to develop into new product areas and new markets.

Inevitably, management accounting information for strategic planning will be based on incomplete data and will use **forecasts** and **estimates.**

(a) It follows that strategic management accounting information is unlikely to give clear guidelines for management decisions and should incorporate some **risk and uncertainty analysis** (eg sensitivity analysis).

(b) For longer term plans, DCF techniques ought to be used in financial evaluation.

(c) The management accountant will be involved in the following.

- Project evaluation
- Managing cash and operational matters
- Reviewing the outcome of the project (post implementation review)

7.1.2 External and competitor orientation

Much management accounting information has been devised for internal consumption.

However, it is important to balance this with a consideration of external factors.

- Strategic management involves **environmental considerations**
- A strategy is pursued in relation to **competitors**

7.2 The challenge for management accountants

The challenge lies in providing more relevant information for decision making. Traditional management accounting systems may not always provide this.

(a) **Historical costs** are not necessarily the best guide to decision-making. One of the criticisms of management accounting in a strategic context is that management accounting information is biased towards the **past rather than the future.**

(b) **Strategic issues** are not easily detected by management accounting systems.

(c) **Financial models** of some sophistication are needed to enable management accountants to provide useful information.

In other words, to support strategic decisions, management accounting itself needs to become more strategic.

7.3 What is strategic management accounting?   9/10

KEY TERM

STRATEGIC MANAGEMENT ACCOUNTING is a 'form of management accounting in which emphasis is placed on information which relates to factors external to the entity, as well as non-financial information and internally generated information'.   *(CIMA Official Terminology)*

Ward suggests that the role of the strategic management accountant can be analysed as follows.

(a)   **Financial analysis** indicates the **current position** of a business and its financial performance in comparison with competitors, as well as breaking it down into product and customer profitability analyses. (These are discussed in later chapters.)

(b)   **Financial planning** quantifies the goals and objectives of the business, normally in a budget.

(c)   **Financial control**. Financial information is an essential part of the **feedback** mechanism comparing planned with actual performance.

We can also appreciate something of the context of strategic management accounting by re-considering what strategy is:

'Strategy is the direction and scope of an organisation over the long term which achieves advantage in a changing environment, through its configuration of resources and competences with the aim of fulfilling stakeholder expectations.' (*Johnson, Scholes & Whittington*).

The references to the **environment** and to **stakeholders** are important here, because they highlight that strategy has an **external focus** as well as an internal one.

7.3.1 External orientation

The important fact which distinguishes strategic management accounting from other management accounting activities is its **external orientation**, towards customers and competitors, suppliers and perhaps other stakeholders. For example, whereas a traditional management accountant would report on an organisation's own revenues, the strategic management would report on market share or trends in market size and growth.

(a)   **Competitive advantage is relative**. Understanding competitors is therefore of prime importance. For example, knowledge of competitors' costs, as well as a firm's own costs, could help inform strategic choices: a firm would be unwise to pursue a cost leadership strategy without first analysing its costs in relation to the cost structures of other firms in the industry.

(b)   **Customers** determine if a firm has competitive advantage.

7.3.2 Future orientation

Another criticism of traditional management accounts is that they are **backward-looking**. Decision-making is a forward and outward looking process.

Strategic management accountants will use **relevant costs** and revenues (ie **incremental** costs and revenues and **opportunity** costs) for decision-making.

KEY TERM

RELEVANT COSTS AND REVENUES are 'costs and revenues appropriate to a specific management decision. These are represented by future cash flows whose magnitude will vary depending upon the outcome of the management decision made.   *(CIMA Official Terminology)*

7.3.3 Goal congruence

Business strategy involves the activities of many different functions, including marketing, production and human resource management. The strategic management accounting system will require the **inputs of many areas of the business**.

(a)   Strategic management accounting translates the consequences of different strategies into a **common accounting language for comparison**.

(b)   It **relates business operations to financial performance**, and therefore helps ensure that business activities are focused on shareholders' needs for profit.

It **helps to ensure goal congruence**, again by translating business activities into the common language of finance.

KEY TERM

GOAL CONGRUENCE. 'In a control system, the state which leads individuals or groups to take actions which are in their self-interest and also in the best interest of the entity. Goal incongruence exists when the interests of individuals or of groups associated with an entity are not in harmony.'

(CIMA Official Terminology)

7.4 What information could strategic management accounting provide?

Bearing in mind the need for **goal congruence**, **external orientation** and **future orientation**, some **examples** of strategic management accounting are provided below.

(a)   **Competitors' costs**. What are they? How do they compare with ours? Can we beat them? Are competitors vulnerable because of their cost structure?

(b)   **Financial effect of competitor response**.

(c)   **Product profitability**. A firm should want to know what profits or losses are being made by each of its products, and why.

(d)   **Customer profitability**. Some customers or groups of customers are worth more than others.

(e)   **Pricing decisions**. Accounting information can help to analyse how profits and cash flows will vary according to price and prospective demand.

(f)   The **value of market share**. A firm ought to be aware of what it is worth to increase the market share of one of its products.

(g)   **Capacity expansion**. Should the firm expand its capacity, and if so by how much?

(h)   **Brand valuation**. What are the costs and benefits of investing in building brands?

(i)   **Shareholder wealth**. Future profitability determines the value of a business.

(j)   **Cash-flow**. A loss-making company can survive if it has adequate cash resources, but a profitable company cannot survive unless it has sufficient liquidity.

(k)   Effect of **acquisitions** and **mergers**.

(l)   Decisions to **enter or leave a business area**.

(m)   Introduction of **new technology**.

Exam skills

Most strategic decisions are unique, so the information needed to support them is likely to be specifically tailored to the decision in hand. This is also true for your exam. Make sure any strategic decisions you recommend are supported by the detail given in the scenario.

7.5 Success factors for a strategic management accounting system (SMAS)

Strategic management accounting has to bridge a gap between financial reporting on the one hand and the uncertainties of the future on the other. We can now go on to identify the success factors of a strategic management accounting system (as outlined by *Ward*). It should:

• Aid strategic decisions
• Close the communication gap between accountants and managers

 BPP
LEARNING MEDIA

- Identify the type of decision
- Offer appropriate financial performance indicators
- Distinguish between economic and managerial performance
- Provide relevant information
- Separate committed from discretionary costs
- Distinguish discretionary from engineered costs
- Use standard costs strategically
- Allow for changes over time

These are now discussed in more detail.

7.5.1 Aid strategic decisions

As part of a strategic management system, the SMAS will provide one-off information to support and evaluate particular strategic decisions and information for strategic management, in order to monitor strategies and the firm's overall competitive position. Changes in the external environment and competitor responses should be easily incorporated into the system.

7.5.2 Close the communication gap

The SMAS converts financial data into information for strategic decision-making. Financial data is off-putting to many people. Consequently, the preparer of such information should make sure that it is tailored.

- Ask the recipient how he or she would like the **format** of the report
- Provide only the **relevant** supporting financial data
- Identify the **key assumptions** on which the information is prepared

7.5.3 Identify the types of decision

Ward states that, despite the one-off nature of many strategic decisions, it is possible to identify the following types of financial decision.

(a)   **Changing the balance of resource allocation** between different business areas, for example by increasing spending in one area.

(b)   **Entering a new business area** (eg new product development, new markets). Some account will have to be taken of the timescale in which the strategy is expected to consume resources, as benefits may be some time in coming.

(c)   **Exit decisions** which come in two forms.

   (i)   **Closing down** part of the business and selling off the assets
   (ii)   Selling the business as a **going concern**

To support such decisions, the SMAS should:

- Incorporate **future cash flows** rather than historic costs
- Include only those items which will be **changed** by the particular decision

7.5.4 Offer suitable financial performance indicators

Two general points can be made.

(a)   **Financial data is not enough.** Customers drive a business, and competitors can ruin it, so performance measures which ignore key variables of customer satisfaction or competitor activity ignore critical strategic issues.

(b)   **The financial information must suit the competitive strategies**. A report complaining about the expense of an advertising campaign ignores the fact that failing to advertise could lead to loss of market share.

7.5.5 Distinguish economic versus managerial performance

A business's **overall economic performance** results from both controllable factors and uncontrollable factors.

(a)   **Risk**. Shareholders may be happy with the risk, if it is balanced by suitable return, but a manager may be unhappy if his or her career is at risk from pursuing a strategy whose success is outside his or her control.

(b)   **Performance**. Judging a manager's contribution on the basis of the overall economic performance of the business may not reflect his or her contribution at all. Managers should therefore be judged on their contribution in areas over which they have control.

7.5.6 Provide relevant information

Relevant financial information should be provided, which presents strategic decisions from the organisation's viewpoint. Specific, tailored reports should support individual decisions and activities, perhaps with **profitability analyses** for each market segment.

7.5.7 Separate committed from discretionary costs

Ignore sunk costs. This has a number of ramifications for the making of business strategies.

- A cost may be **committed** even though it has not actually been incurred.
- **Discretionary costs** are those over which the decision-maker still has choice.

7.5.8 Distinguish between discretionary and engineered costs

Engineered costs are those which derive from a relatively predictable relationship between input materials and output units of production.

7.5.9 Use standard costs strategically

Standard costs consist of a physical usage element (eg volume of materials) and a price element. The split between the **price** and **usage** elements is indicative.

- The extent to which the firm is **vulnerable** to suppliers raising prices
- The possible impact of **trade-offs** between, say, labour and materials

Trade-offs. If the relationships between the input material and output quantities are known, or variable, then standard costing can show the financial effects of different mixes.

(a)   For example, if there is a trade off between labour and raw materials, changes in the relative costs of these factors can indicate a suitable mix: more expensive labour would result in less of a valued raw material being used.

(b)   If the price of a raw material escalates suddenly, the standard costing system can be amended with the new price, and a new mix analysis calculated which takes it into account.

Absorbing indirect/fixed overheads into products can lead to poor pricing decisions, in the short term. If a factory is working at 60% capacity utilisation, this could lead to higher indirect costs being absorbed per unit. This information, if wrongly interpreted, could be used to suggest a price rise, rather than a reduction to encourage more sales and hence an increased utilisation of capacity.

Section summary

The management accountant can play a valuable role in the process of planning and developing strategy; for example, by providing information which is relevant for strategic decision making, such as product profitability and the value of market share.

8 Directors' strategic roles and responsibilities

Introduction

There is an ethical dimension to many aspects of business strategy, including mission and objectives, organisations' dealings with their stakeholders, relationships with governments and society, and evaluating different strategic options.

However, one of most important examples of ethics can be found in the role of directors, who act as agents to run an organisation on behalf of its owners – often the shareholders.

The fundamentals of ethics, corporate governance and corporate social responsibility are covered in paper E2.

However, the Examiners for E3 assume that you are familiar with this material and can apply it as necessary to a case study scenario. If you are not comfortable you could incorporate basic ethical or CSR issues into an answer make sure you revise this material before you sit the exam.

In most businesses, a few strategic decisions can make the difference between superior long-term performance and ordinary results, and these decisions frequently affect the whole organisation and its stakeholders. Consequently there is a lot of responsibility attached to these decisions, making it appropriate that they are taken by very senior management – usually the directors of a business.

In this section, we will consider directors' roles and responsibilities to an organisation.

8.1 Corporate governance

KEY TERM

CORPORATE GOVERNANCE is 'the system by which organisations are directed and controlled' (Cadbury Report).

However, it is important to distinguish between the purpose and the objectives of corporate governance.

The main **purpose** of corporate governance is to monitor the parties within an organisation who control and use the organisation's resources on behalf its owners.

The main **objective** of corporate governance is to contribute to improved accountability and performance in creating long-term value for the owners (long-term shareholder value).

Although governance is mostly discussed in relation to large quoted companies, it is an issue for all corporate bodies, whether they are commercial or not for profit (NFP).

There are a number of key elements in corporate governance:

(a)   The management and **reduction of risk** is a fundamental issue in all definitions of good governance; whether explicitly stated or merely implied.

(b)   The notion that overall **performance is enhanced by good supervision and management** within set best practice guidelines underpins most definitions.

(c)   Good governance provides a **framework** for an organisation to pursue its strategy in an **ethical and effective** way from the perspective of **all stakeholder groups** affected, and offers safeguards against misuse of resources, physical or intellectual.

(d)   Good governance is not just about externally established codes, it also requires a willingness to **apply the spirit** as well as the letter of the law.

(e)   **Accountability** is generally a major theme in all governance frameworks.

Good corporate governance involves managing risk and internal control, being **accountable to shareholders** and other stakeholders, and conducting business in an ethical and effective way.

Directors' accountability to 'other stakeholders' beyond 'shareholders' not only highlights the importance of stakeholder management but also highlights the link between stakeholder management, ethics and corporate social responsibility which we will look at in Chapter 2 of this text.

In addition, the idea of accountability also highlights the importance of performance and performance management which are key aspects of the E3 syllabus. A company's performance has to be measured to assess how well it (and its directors and managers) are performing against the strategic objectives which have been set.

We look at performance measurement and performance management in more detail in Chapters 13 and 14 in this Text.

8.1.1 Key aspects of governance

The UK Corporate Governance Code (2010) identifies five key areas of governance:

(a)   **Leadership** – Every company should have an effective Board which is responsible for the long-term success of the company. The Board should include non-executive directors, and there should be a clear **division of responsibility** between the Chairman (responsible for running the Board) and the CEO (responsible for running the company).

(b)   **Effectiveness** – The Board and its committees should have an appropriate balance of skills, experience, independence and knowledge.

(c)   **Accountability** – The Board should present a balanced and understandable assessment of the company's current position and its future prospects.

The Board should conduct a review of the effectiveness of the risk management and internal controls within the company at least once a year.

(d)   **Remuneration** – There should be a formal and transparent procedure for developing a company's policy on executive remuneration, and no director should be involved in deciding his or her own remuneration.

(e)   **Relationship with shareholders** – The Board collectively has responsibility for ensuring that a satisfactory dialogue takes place with shareholders.

However, while corporate governance plays a beneficial role in risk management and control within organisations it could still have some less favourable implications in relation to business strategy:

(a)   Governance increases **shareholders' power** and prioritises shareholders' interests, potentially at the expense of other stakeholder groups.

(b)   The increased scrutiny to which results are exposed (particularly in listed companies) may encourage a focus on short-termism and **short term results** rather than long term plans.

(c)   The increased emphasis on risk management and risk reduction may make directors feel that they should accept lower risk (and lower return) projects in favour of ones which might generate higher returns (but which might also carry higher risk).

8.2 Role of the board of directors

Scope of role

The *King report* provides a good summary of the role of the **board of directors**.

> 'To define the purpose of the company and the values by which the company will perform its daily existence and to identify the stakeholders relevant to the business of the company. The board must then develop a strategy combining all three factors and ensure management implements that strategy.'

This highlights that the board is responsible for **taking strategic decisions** and major policy decisions, and also ensuring that these decisions are properly implemented by an organisation.

If the board is to act effectively, its role must be defined carefully. The *Cadbury report* suggests that the board should have a formal schedule of matters specifically reserved to it for decision. Some would be decisions such as **mergers and takeovers** that are fundamental to the business and hence should not be taken just by executive managers.

Other decisions would include **acquisitions and disposals of assets of the company** or its subsidiaries that are material to the company and **investments, capital projects, bank borrowing** facilities, **loans** and their repayment, foreign currency transactions, all above a certain size (to be determined by the board).

Other tasks the board of directors should perform include:

*   Monitoring the chief executive officer
*   Monitoring risks and control systems
*   Monitoring the human capital aspects of the company in regard to succession, morale, training, remuneration and so on
*   Ensuring that there is effective communication of its strategic plans, both internally and externally

Whether an organisation has a prescriptive or emergent approach to the strategy approach, the board of directors still has the key role in controlling its strategy. Although emergent strategies may emerge from the business rather than being imposed by senior management, the directors still have to ensure that the strategy is delivering value and wealth to the business, and the business is not simply being allowed to drift.

Changing the scope of the role

Directors have traditionally had quite clear ideas about what their responsibilities are in the strategic development process, and what managers' responsibilities are.

These can be summarised in as follows:

The Board of Directors' traditional role in strategy development

	Formulate	Approve	Implement	Monitor
Board		X		X
Management	X		X	

However, recently directors have been expressing a desire to have a greater input into company's growth plans.

Directors increase shareholder value by challenging the CEO to grow revenues, by asking questions about the current position, and by challenging the strategic plan. However, directors often have experience and capabilities which could be useful in formulating business strategy.

In this case, organisations can benefit if the Board is involved not only in approving and monitoring their business strategies, but also in offering concrete advice to the management team about strategic formulation.

Equally, where directors have experience of strategic implementation, they can also use this to assist the management team.

Contemporary current directors are often highly qualified business professionals, and so they can use their experience to help grow revenues and profits by increasing their role in strategy formulation.

8.3 Attributes of directors

In order to carry out effective scrutiny, directors need to have **relevant expertise** in industry, company, functional area and governance. The board as whole needs to contain a **mix of expertise** and a **balance** between **executive management** and independent non-executive directors. The *King report* stresses the importance also of having a good **demographic balance.**

New and existing directors should also have **appropriate training** to develop the knowledge and skills required.

8.4 Responsibilities of directors

The directors of a commercial enterprise are **collectively responsible** for the conduct of its affairs. There is a **scalar chain of authority and accountability** that runs hierarchically up and down the organisation. Junior managers are accountable to more senior ones and so on up the chain until the board of directors is reached. The question then arises: to whom are the directors accountable for the activities of the company as a whole?

As a matter of principle we can say that in any type of organisation there should be some external entity on whose behalf the managers at the strategic apex act and to whom they are accountable. In the case of an incorporated business in which ownership is separated from control, the answer is that the directors are ultimately accountable to the **shareholders** collectively, according to the internal rules of the company.

8.4.1 Fiduciary responsibility and due diligence

The essence of external accountability is that **organisations are not autonomous**: that is to say, they do not exist to serve their own purposes or those of their senior managers.

They exist to serve some external purpose and their managers have a duty to run them in a way that serves that purpose, whether it be to relieve distress (a charity), to keep the peace and manage the economy (a government), to promote the interests of its members (a trade union) or to make a profit (a business).

Managers have a **fiduciary responsibility** (or duty of faithful service) in this respect and their behaviour must always reflect it.

In addition to the requirement to **act in good faith**, directors are also expected not to be negligent or reckless and to bring a reasonable degree of competence to the discharge of their duties. There is thus a requirement to act with **due diligence**, a phrase you may be more familiar with in connection with business acquisitions; there, the phrase describes just one aspect of the directors' duty of care.

Due diligence - The care a reasonable person should take before entering into an agreement or a transaction with another party.

Fiduciary responsibility – Directors must try to act in a way which is most likely to promote the success of the company for the benefit of the shareholders. This needs to consider a number of statutory factors, including the long-term consequence of decisions, the firm's reputation and the interests of other stakeholders, such as employees and the community.

In the UK, the Companies Act (2006) identifies that directors have a duty to:

- Promote the success of the company

- Exercise reasonable care, skill and diligence

- Avoid conflicts of interest or of duties

This duty to 'promote the success of the company' could have important implications in the context of business strategy:

- Directors need to consider the consequences of any strategic decisions for both the long term and the short term

- Directors need to consider how different stakeholder groups can affect the company's success; for example, the company's relationships with its employees, suppliers, customers, the local community and the environment. Once again, this highlights the importance of **stakeholder management** as a key element of business strategy.

8.4.2 The objectives of commercial organisations

We implied above that the objective of a commercial organisation is to make a profit. It is possible to argue that **wider objectives** should be acknowledged and that the interests of people other than the owners should be served. This is the *stakeholder view* and is discussed later in this Study Text. Nevertheless, whatever an organisation's objectives may be, it is the duty of its managers to seek to attain them. Many senior figures in the world of business have given the impression that the organisations they run exist to serve their own personal purposes. This is not the case and managers at all levels must be aware of this.

8.4.3 Personal motivation and corruption

We must emphasise that managers need not be actually corrupt in order to fail in their fiduciary duty. The CEO who sets in motion a takeover bid that will enhance his prestige; the head of department who 'empire builds'; and the IT manager who buys an unnecessarily sophisticated system are all failing in their fiduciary duty even though they receive no material benefit themselves.

CASE STUDY

This case study is adapted from an article on the BBC news website (February 2009):

The former bosses of the two biggest casualties of the banking crisis in the UK have apologised 'profoundly and unreservedly' for their banks' failure.

Former Royal Bank of Scotland (RBS) chief executive Sir Fred Goodwin told MPs on the Treasury Committee that he 'could not be more sorry' for what happened. He also admitted that the bonus culture in banks had contributed to the crisis and needed to be reviewed.

But he added if bankers felt they were not paid enough, they would leave.

Andy Hornby, former CEO of Halifax Bank of Scotland (HBOS), also conceded that the culture of cash bonuses also needed looking at. 'The bonus system has proved to be wrong. Substantial cash bonuses do not reward the right kind of behaviour' he said.

However, when he was asked whether the bonus culture encouraged excessive risk taking and had exacerbated he banking crisis, Sir Fred Goodwin argued that traders were trading within set limits, and were simply doing 'what they were authorised to do.'

However, a rather different picture is emerging from HBOS. It has emerged that a senior HBOS employee was sacked for warning four years ago that the bank's risky sales culture could 'lead to disaster.' Paul Moore – who was head of group regulatory risk – was dismissed for pointing out that the bank was ignoring checks and balances. He argued that 'anyone whose eyes were not blinded by money, power and pride' would have realised that problems were building up for HBOS and other banks.

Mr Moore also insisted that the current banking crisis could have been avoided if there were adequate systems to hold bank chiefs to account. The real problem, and the cause of this crisis, was that people were too afraid to speak up, and the balance of power was weighted far too much in favour of the executive.

However, bonuses and poor internal controls were not the only cause of the business's problems.

Sir Fred Goodwin oversaw a number of acquisitions that made RBS one of the world's biggest banks. But his takeover of Dutch rival ABN Amro late in 2007 is now seen as ill-timed and a deal too far, in the light of RBS's inability to survive the credit crunch without a massive injection of Government funds.

Sir Fred admitted that the deal to buy ABN was 'a big mistake. We bought it at the top of the market, and anything we paid was an error. We are sorry we bought ABN Amro' he added.

Section summary

The board of directors should be responsible for taking the policy and strategic decisions in an organisation, and they should ensure the good corporate governance is maintained within the organisation.

Chapter Roundup

- ✓ Organisations need strategies to establish their direction and scope in the long term, and to determine the resources and competences needed to achieve the desired course of action.

- ✓ The **rational model** describes a highly structured approach to strategic planning. An organisation identifies its objectives, analyses its current position, develops its strategic options and then selects a strategy to implement.

- ✓ There is a basic distinction to be made between **prescriptive** and **emergent** theories of strategy. The emergent process does not identify final strategic objectives in advance, and so is more adaptable than a prescriptive approach. It also recognises the important role people play in actually designing and delivering strategies, and the importance of learning and innovation as outputs from strategy.

- ✓ Rather than looking at strategy as being either prescriptive or emergent, we could look at it in terms of design, experience or ideas, using the notion of the **three strategic lenses**. The design lens shows strategy as a rational, top-down process operating under careful controls. This contrasts with the experience lenses which presents strategy as an extension of what has worked in the past. The ideas lens suggests that strategy is formed by diversity of ideas, leading to innovation.

- ✓ *Stacey* argues that organisations operate in the chaotic region between **stability** and **instability**. This makes it difficult to predict the future with any certainty, but also highlights the importance of the strategic manager in guiding organisations through **states of flux**.

- ✓ In essence, approaches to strategy can either be **position-based** or **resource-based**. The resource-based approach to strategy starts from a consideration of strengths and weaknesses and highlights the importance of developing core competences as a basis of competitive advantage.

- ✓ The management accountant can play a valuable role in the process of planning and developing strategy; for example, by providing information which is relevant for strategic decision-making, such as product profitability and the value of market share.

- ✓ The Board of Directors should be responsible for taking the major policy and strategic decisions in an organisation, and they should ensure that good corporate governance is maintained within the organisation.

Further reading:

Although this Study Text is designed to provide you with comprehensive coverage of the material you need for your E3 exam, if you wish to do some further reading around areas of business strategy, we recommend the following texts:

Johnston, G., Scholes, K. & Whittington, R. (2011) – Exploring Corporate Strategy, (9th ed), Harlow, FT/Prentice Hall

Lynch, R. (2011) – Strategic Management, (6th ed), Harlow, FT/Prentice Hall

Quick Quiz

1   What is a strategy?

2   AZ Co is an electronics company based in a European country, and it uses a rational model approach to strategic planning. AZ is currently looking to expand aboard into other European countries. The European electronics market is known to be dynamic, and to contain a number of fast-moving, innovative companies.

Which of the following statements about AZ Co is/are true?

(i)   Its approach to strategic planning will allow it to adapt quickly to deal with unexpected changes in the market

(ii)   Its approach to strategic planning will allow AZ to develop a picture of the opportunities and threats the European market presents before it decides to enter the market.

A   Neither of them
B   (i) only
C   (ii) only
D   Both (i) and (ii)

3   Which one of the following statements about emergent strategy is NOT true?

A   Final objectives are unclear at the outset of the strategy process
B   Elements of the strategy are developed as the strategy proceeds
C   Emergent strategies are deliberately imposed on an organisation by senior management
D   Emergent strategies usually take longer to develop than planned strategies

4   What is the basic principle of resource-based strategy?

5   What are the three stages of strategic planning in the rational model?

Answers to Quick Quiz

1   A strategy is a course of action, including the specification of resources required, to achieve a specific objective.

2   C   (ii) only.

Part of the strategic analysis stage of the rational model is an environmental analysis – identifying the opportunities and threats in an environment. However, one of the perceived problems of the rational model approach to strategy is that its rigidity prevents companies from responding quickly to unforeseen opportunities or threats, or other changes.

3   C   Emergent strategies are developed out of patterns of behaviour throughout an organisation, rather than being imposed in advance by senior management.

4   Competitive advantage can only be sustained by the possession of distinctive resources or competences

5   Strategic analysis (position), strategic choice, and strategic implementation (action).

Now try this question from the Exam Question Bank	Number	Level	Marks	Time
	Q1	Introductory	n/a	30 mins

STAKEHOLDERS AND CORPORATE OBJECTIVES

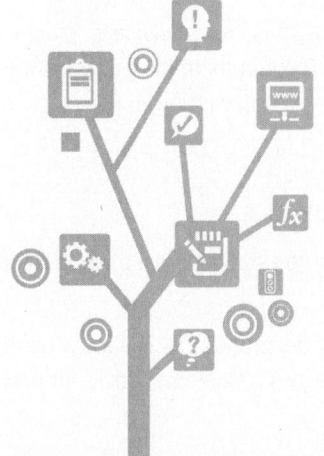 In this chapter we consider the **objectives and goals** of an organisation. A **mission** (Section 1) describes what the organisation is for and how it relates to the wider society. Many organisations, especially public sector ones, have to juggle a number of conflicting objectives, and so developing a mission may be difficult. Businesses (Section 2) generally pursue some kind of **financial return**, although a number of measures can be used. **Secondary objectives** support this return. Trade-offs have to be made between goals. **Short-term versus long-term perspectives** also affect business performance (Section 3).

Various groups of stakeholders (Section 4) have their own expectations of the organisation. Conflicts of expectations between the various stakeholder groups often arise.

The ethical stance taken by an organisation (Section 5) can affect the strategy it develops.

The theme of **social responsibility and sustainability** (Section 6) is the question of how far a business is accountable to the wider community for the effects of its operations, and the fact that resources are finite and need to be replaced.

The chapter closes with a look at the specific issues relating to the **not-for-profit** and **public sector** objectives.

topic list	learning outcomes	syllabus references	ability required
1 Mission, goals and strategy	C1(a)	C1(i)	Evaluate
2 Business goals and objectives	C1(a)	C1(i)	Evaluate
3 The short term and long term	C1(a)	C1(i)	Evaluate
4 Stakeholder management	A1(b), A1(d)	A1(i), A1(iii)	Recommend
5 Business ethics	A1(c)	A1(ii)	Discuss
6 Corporate social responsibility and sustainability	A1(c)	A1(ii)	Discuss
7 Not-for-profit organisations	A1(b)	A1(iii)	Recommend
8 The public sector	A1(b)	A1(iii)	Recommend

1 Mission, goals and strategy   11/10

Introduction

Strategies are developed in order to achieve desired outcomes. These are inherent in the organisation's mission or defining purpose. Whether stated or not, the **mission** of a business always includes return to investors. Mission guides strategic decisions and provides values and a sense of direction.

The *Ashridge College* model of mission **links business strategy to culture and ethics** by including four separate elements in an expanded definition of **mission**.

(a)   **Purpose**. Why does the company exist? Who does it exist for?

     (i)   To create wealth for shareholders, who take priority over all other stakeholders?

     (ii)   To satisfy the needs of all stakeholders, including employees, for example?

     (iii)   To reach some higher goal such as the advancement of society?

(b)   **Values** are the beliefs and moral principles that underlie the organisation's culture.

(c)   **Strategy** provides the commercial logic for the company (the **nature** of the organisation's business), and so addresses the following questions: 'What is our business? Or, what should it be?' What are our elements of sustainable competitive advantage?

     When answering these questions, the mission should look at them from the **customer's perspective**. So, for example, a company which produces study materials for professional exams, might say 'We are in the business of producing high quality books that help our readers pass their exams.' The competitive advantage will come from the quality of the books and the extent to which they help their readers pass their exams.

(d)   **Policies and standards of behaviour** provide guidance on how the organisation's business should be conducted. For example, a service industry that wishes to be the best in its market must aim for standards of service, in all its operations, which are at least as good as those found in its competitors.

1.1 The importance of mission for corporate strategy

There are several reasons why a business should give serious consideration to establishing a clear concept of its corporate mission.

(a)   Values are acknowledged as integral elements of consumers' buying decisions; this is shown by the attention paid to them in advertising, brand building and market research. Customers ask not only 'What do you sell?' but 'What do you stand for?'

(b)   Studies into organisational behaviour show that people are motivated by many things other than money: employees are likely to be both more productive and more satisfied with their work when they feel that what they are doing has significance beyond the mere pursuit of a living.

(c)   Some writers believe there is an empirical relationship between strong corporate values and profitability.

1.2 Mission statements   9/10, 3/11, 9/11, 5/12

KEY TERMS

A MISSION STATEMENT is a published statement, apparently of the entity's fundamental objective(s). This may or may not summarise the true mission of the entity.   *(CIMA Official Terminology)*

A MISSION is an entity's 'fundamental objectives... expressed in general terms'

(CIMA Official Terminology)

In essence, a mission statement describes an organisation's basic purpose and what it is trying to achieve. There is no standard format, but the four elements in the Ashridge model of mission offer a good

basis for writing a mission statement. Mission statements are likely to have some of the following characteristics:

(a)   Stating the purpose of the organisation

(b)   Stating the business areas in which the organisation intends to operate

(c)   Providing a general statement of the organisation's culture

(d)   Acting as a guide to develop the direction of the an entity's strategy and its goals/objectives

The authors of the Ashridge model also make another important point. Mission statements contain only **statements** of purpose and strategy, but in order for an organisation to develop a 'sense of mission' that 'mission' must be exhibited in the performance standards and values of the organisation.

Lynch (in *Strategic Management*) has provided the following criteria by which to judge the effectiveness of a corporate mission statement:

(a)   Is it specific enough to impact upon individuals' behaviour throughout the business?

(b)   Does it reflect the distinctive advantage of the organisation and recognise its strengths and weaknesses?

(c)   Is it realistic and attainable?

(d)   Is it flexible to the demands of a changing environment?

CASE STUDY

The following are the mission statements for some well known companies:

Coca-Cola   –   'To refresh the world... To inspire moments of optimism and happiness... To create value and make a difference.'

Google   –   'To organize the world's information and make it universally accessible and useful.'

Starbucks   –   'Our mission: to inspire and nurture the human spirit - one person, one cup and one neighbourhood at a time'

eBay   –   'To provide a global trading platform where practically anyone can trade practically anything.'

Microsoft   –   'To help people and businesses throughout the world realise their potential.'

Although a number of successful companies have mission statements, critics raise the following criticisms of mission statements:

(a)   They are often **public relations** exercises rather than an accurate portrayal of the organisation's actual values.

(b)   They can often be full of **generalisations** which are impossible to tie down to specific strategic implications, and practical objectives.

(c)   They may be ignored by the people responsible for formulating or implementing strategy.

(d)   They become obsolete, as they fail to evolve over time to reflect changes in the organisation, or in its markets or the external environment.

However, there are no fixed rules about how long an organisation should keep the same mission statement. Therefore a company's mission statement could be periodically reviewed to ensure it still accurately reflects the company's position and its environment.

1.3 Mission and planning

The mission statement can play an important role in the strategic planning process.

(a)   **Inspires and informs planning.** Plans should further the organisation's goals and be consistent with its values. In this way, the mission statement provides a focus for consistent strategic planning decisions.

(b)   **Screening**. Mission acts as a yardstick by which plans are judged.

(c)   Mission also affects the **implementation** of a planned strategy in terms of the ways in which an organisation carries out its business, and through the culture of the organisation. A mission statement can help to develop a corporate culture in an organisation by communicating the organisation's core values. A mission statement can also often help to establish an ethics framework.

CASE STUDY

The Co-operative Group in the UK, which includes the Co-operative foodstores, has explicit social objectives. In some cases it will retain stores which, although they are too small to be as profitable as a large supermarket, fulfil an important social role in the communities which host them. The Co-operative is run by its members rather than by shareholders, so instead of having to chase profits for its shareholders it can steer its business in a more socially responsible direction.

Section summary

Mission guides strategic decisions and provides value and direction. Mission statements are formal documents that state an organisation's mission. They can play an important role in the strategic planning process, but have also been criticised for being over-generalised, ignored in practice, static/obsolete, and little more than PR.

2   Business goals and objectives   11/10

Introduction

Goals and **objectives** derive from mission and support it. For a business, a primary corporate objective will be the return offered to shareholders, however this is measured. There may be other primary objectives and there will certainly be supporting objectives for costs, innovation, markets, products and so on.

2.1 Goals, objectives and targets

An understanding of an organisation's mission is invaluable for setting and controlling the overall **functioning and progress** of the organisation.

However, mission statements themselves are open-ended and are not stated in quantifiable terms, such as profits or revenues. Equally, they are not time bound.

Therefore mission statements can only be seen as a general indicator of an organisation's strategy. In order to start implementing the strategy and managing performance, an organisation needs to develop some more specific and measurable objectives and targets.

Most people's work is defined in terms of specific and immediate **things to be achieved.** If these things are related in some way to the wider purpose of the organisation, this will help the organisation to function more effectively than if these tasks are not aligned to the organisation's overall purpose.

Loosely speaking, these 'things to be achieved' are the goals, objectives and targets of the various departments, functions, and individuals that make up the organisation. In effective organisations **goal congruence** will be achieved, such that these disparate goals, objectives and targets will be **consistent** with one another and will **operate together** to support progress with the mission.

However, whilst mission statements are high-level, open-ended statements about a firm's purpose or strategy, **strategic objectives** translate the mission into more **specific milestones and targets** for the business strategy to follow and achieve.

2.1.1 A hierarchy of objectives

A simple model of the relationship between the various goals, objectives and targets is a **pyramid** analogous to the traditional organisational hierarchy. At the top is the **overall mission**; this is supported by a **small number of wide ranging goals**, which may correspond to overall departmental or functional responsibilities. Each of these goals is supported in turn by **more detailed, subordinate goals** that correspond, perhaps, to the responsibilities of the senior managers in the function concerned. This pattern is continued downwards until we reach the work targets of individual members of the organisation.

As we work our way down this pyramid of goals we will find that they will typically become **more detailed** and will relate to **shorter timeframes**. So, the mission might be very general and specify no time scale at all, but an individual worker is likely to have very specific things to achieve every day, or even every few minutes.

Note that this description is very basic and that the structure of objectives in a modern organisation may be much more complex than this, with the pursuit of some goals involving input from several functions. Also, some goals may be defined in very general terms, so as not to stifle innovation, co-operation and informal ways of doing things.

An important feature of any structure of goals is that there should be **goal congruence**; that is to say, goals that are related to one another should be **mutually supportive**. This is because goals and objectives drive actions, so if goals aren't congruent then the actions of one area of the a business will end up conflicting with those of another area of the business.

Goals can be related in several ways:

* **Hierarchically**, as in the pyramid structure outlined above

* **Functionally**, as when colleagues collaborate on a project

* **Logistically**, as when resources must be shared or used in sequence

* In **wider organisational senses**, as when senior executives make decisions about their operational priorities

A good example of the last category is the tension between long- and short-term priorities in such matters as the need to contain costs while at the same time increasing productivity by investing in improved plant.

KEY TERMS

The words *goal*, *objective* and *target* are used somewhat imprecisely and, to some extent, interchangeably. The suggestions we make below about the usage of these words are only tentative and you should read as widely as you can in order to make your own mind up about how to employ them.

A GOAL is often a longer term overall aspiration: *Mintzberg* defines **goals** as 'the intentions behind decisions or actions, the states of mind that drive individuals or collectives of individuals called organisations to do what they do.' Goals may be difficult to quantify and it may not be very helpful to attempt to do so. An example of a goal might be to raise productivity in a manufacturing department.

OBJECTIVES are often quite specific and well-defined, though they can also embody comprehensive purposes.

TARGETS are generally expressed in concrete numerical terms and are therefore easily used to measure progress and performance.

2.1.2 Management by objectives   3/12

The contrast between objectives and mission statements can be highlighted by the fact that objectives should be 'SMART'.

Specific   **M**easurable   **A**chievable   **R**elevant   **T**ime-related

Relevant is sometimes replaced with **realistic**; but 'realistic' and 'achievable' could be seen as meaning similar things. An objective is relevant if it is appropriate to an organisation's mission.

There are other variants: *achievable* may be replaced with *attainable*, which has an almost identical meaning. Achievable is also sometimes replaced with '*Agreed*'; denoting that objectives should be agreed with those responsible for achieving them. However, note that whichever version you prefer, a SMART objective corresponds very closely with our description of the way the word *target* is commonly used.

(a) **S**pecific: An objective must be a clear statement, and must be easy to understand. Whereas mission statements tend to be vague, objectives must be specific.

(b) **M**easurable: Again, in contrast to mission statements, objectives must be measurable so that performance against the objectives can be assessed. Measuring performance against objectives is a key element of control in organisations.

(c) **A**chievable: If the objectives set are not achievable, people will not bother trying to achieve them, so there is little point setting them.

(d) **R**elevant: An objective is relevant if it is appropriate to an organisation's mission, and will help it fulfil that mission. (This reiterates the link between an organisation's mission and its objectives.)

(e) **T**ime-related: Whereas mission statements tend to be open-ended, an organisation needs to define a specific time period in which objectives should be achieved. Again, this is very important for enabling management to judge whether or not the objective has been achieved. For example, if an organisation has an objective 'To increase sales revenue by 5%' how will managers know the time period over which this sales increase is expected? However, if the objective is 'To increase sales revenue by 5% per year' the time frame is clearly identified.

Functions of objectives

(a) **Planning**: objectives define what the plan is about.

(b) **Responsibility**: objectives define the responsibilities of managers and departments.

(c) **Integration**: objectives should support one another and be consistent; this integrates the efforts of different departments.

(d) **Motivation**: the first step in motivation is knowing what is to be done. Objectives must be created for all areas of performance.

(e) **Evaluation**: performance is assessed against objectives and control exercised.

2.2 Primary and secondary objectives

Some objectives are more important than others. In the hierarchy of objectives, there is a **primary corporate objective** and other **secondary objectives** which should combine to ensure the achievement of the overall corporate objective.

For example, if a company sets itself an objective of growth in profits, as its primary aim, it will then have to develop strategies by which this primary objective can be achieved. An objective must then be set for each individual strategy. Secondary objectives might then be concerned with sales growth, continual technological innovation, customer service, product quality, efficient resource management or reducing the company's reliance on debt capital.

Corporate objectives should relate to the business as a whole and can be both **financial** and **non-financial**:

• Profitability	• Customer satisfaction
• Market share	• The quality of the firm's products
• Growth	• Human resources
• Cash flow	• New product development
• Asset base	• Social responsibility

Equally, when setting corporate objectives, it is important that an organisation considers the needs of all of its **stakeholders**, to try to ensure that these are met wherever possible.

CASE STUDY

British Airways

In its 2008/9 Annual Report and Accounts, British Airways summarised its strategy and objectives:

'*In an incredibly tough trading environment, we have to focus hard on pulling ourselves through the immediate crisis [of the global recession and the decline in passenger numbers], while preparing the business for better economic times. This year we have mapped out a long-term vision for our business. It is to be the world's leading global premium airline*.'

The focus on 'premium' is important here, because it shows how British Airways (BA) is looking to differentiate itself from the budget airlines such as EasyJet. As if to reinforce this point, BA goes on to identify Five Key Goals, which it believes are the key steps in needs to take to achieve its vision of being the world's leading premium airline:

1.   *Be the airline of choice for long-haul premium customers* – so that people will want to fly with BA whenever they can. It aims to achieve this, for example, by investing in customer lounges and restyling the First class cabins.

2.   *Deliver an outstanding service for customers at every touch point* – by training colleagues on the ground and in the air so that they provide world-class hospitality and customer service. BA is also looking to improve service by making it easy for customers to check-in from their mobile phone or PDA, and by upgrading the in-flight entertainment system.

3.   *Grow presence in key global cities* – to provide the best global connectivity for customers.

4.   *Build on its leading position in London* – ensuring Heathrow remains a world-class hub is vital to give BA a strong London base to service the largest international long-haul markets. BA will work with BAA to improve baggage and terminal facilities at Heathrow.

5.   *Meet customers' needs and improve margins through new revenue streams* – by building profitable ancillary services that offer value to customers and re-enforce BA's brand. For example, BA is looking to boost revenue from third-party engineering and in-flight sales, as well as using its website (ba.com) to offer hotel and car hire options packaged with flights.

2.3 Time horizons: long-term objectives and short-term objectives

Objectives may be long-term and short-term. A company that is suffering from a recession in its core industries and making losses in the short term might continue to have a long-term primary objective of achieving a growth in profits, but in the short term its primary objective might be survival.

We return to this topic later in the chapter.

2.4 Financial objectives

For commercial businesses in the UK, the primary objective is concerned with the **return to shareholders**.

(a)   A satisfactory return for a company must be sufficient to **reward shareholders adequately** in the long run for the risks they take. The reward will take the form of **profits**, which can lead to **dividends** or to **increases in the market value** of the shares.

(b)   The size of return which is adequate for ordinary shareholders will vary according to the risk involved.

There are different ways of expressing a financial objective in quantitative terms. Financial objectives would include the following.

- Profitability
- Return on investment (ROI) or return on capital employed (ROCE)
- Share price, earnings per share, dividends
- Growth

We will look in more detail at how organisations measure their performance later in this text.

Growth

There are some difficulties in accepting growth as an overall objective.

(a)   **Growth of what?** In the long run, some elements must be expected to grow faster than others because of the dynamics of the business environment.

(b)   In the long run, growth might lead to **diseconomies of scale** so that inefficiencies will occur.

Smaller companies will usually have a greater potential for significant rates of growth, especially in new industries, and growth will be a prime objective. Larger companies grow to achieve a size which will enable them to compete with other multinationals in world markets.

2.5 Multiple objectives

A firm might identify several financial objectives.

- Scope for growth and enhanced **corporate wealth**
- Maintaining a policy of paying attractive but not over-generous **dividends**
- Maintaining an acceptable **gearing ratio**

2.6 Subsidiary or secondary objectives

Whatever primary objective or objectives are set, **subsidiary objectives** will then be developed beneath them.

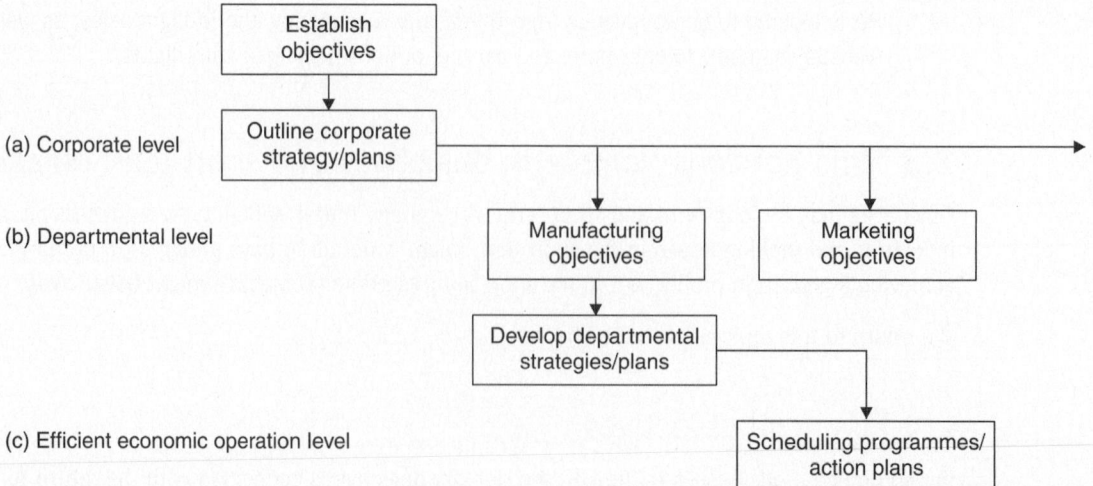

The overall objectives of the organisation will indicate different requirements for different functions.

In this respect it is important to appreciate the structure of goals or objectives in an organisation:

Strategic (corporate) **objectives**:   set the overall long-term objectives for the business as a whole

Tactical objectives: the 'middle tier' of objectives; designed to plan and control individual functions within the organisation. Tactical objectives are then implemented by setting operational objectives

Operational objectives: day-to-day performance targets to ensure that the organisation's operations are carried out efficiency or effectively.

2.6.1 Unit objectives

Unit objectives relate either to strategic business units or functions of the business.

(a)   Private sector objectives:

(i)   Increasing the number of customers by 10%
(ii)   Reducing the number of rejects by 50%
(iii)   Producing monthly reports more quickly, within five working days of the end of each month

(b)   Public sector objectives:

(i)   Responding more quickly to emergency calls
(ii)   Reducing the length of time a patient has to wait for an operation

2.6.2 Goals for markets and marketing

Goals for **markets** will involve the following type of decisions.

(a)   **Market leadership.** Whether the organisation wants to be the market leader, or number two in the market, what rate of growth it desires and so on

(b)   **Coverage.** Whether the product range needs to be expanded

(c)   **Positioning.** Whether there should be an objective to shift position in the market – eg from producing low-cost for the mass market to higher-cost specialist products

(d)   **Expansion.** Whether there should be an objective of broadening the product range or extending the organisation's markets

2.6.3 Goals for products and services

Labour productivity objectives are often quantified as targets to reduce unit costs **and increase output per employee** by a certain percentage each year.

Capital productivity is measured less often, but it can denote how efficiently a firm is using its equipment.

Quality objectives might be measured in low rejects (eg through quality targets set under 'Six Sigma' methodologies). In some environments, targets may be set for service delivery, such as speed in answering the telephone, customer satisfaction and service quality.

Goals for products include **technology**.

2.7 Ranking objectives and trade-offs

Where there are multiple objectives a problem of ranking can arise.

(a)   **There is never enough time or resources** to achieve all of the desired objectives.

(b)   **There are degrees of accomplishment.** For example, if there is an objective to achieve a 10% annual growth in earnings per share, an achievement of 9% could be described as a near-success. When it comes to ranking objectives, a target ROI of, say, 25% might be given greater priority than an EPS growth of 10%, but a lower priority than an EPS growth of, say, 15%.

When there are several key objectives, some might be achieved only at the expense of others. For example, attempts to achieve a good cash flow or good product quality, or to improve market share, might call for some sacrifice of short term profits.

For example, there might be a choice between the following two options.

Option A   15% sales growth, 10% profit growth, a $2 million negative cash flow and reduced product quality and customer satisfaction.

Option B   8% sales growth, 5% profit growth, a $500,000 surplus cash flow, and maintenance of high product quality/customer satisfaction.

If the firm chose option B in preference to option A, it would be trading off sales growth and profit growth for better cash flow, product quality and customer satisfaction. It may feel that the long-term effect of reduced quality would negate the benefits under Option A.

One of the tasks of strategic management is to ensure **goal congruence**. Some objectives may not be in line with each other, and different **stakeholders** have different sets of priorities.

2.7.1 Dealing with conflict between different types of goals

(a)   **Rational evaluation** according to financial criteria.

(b)   **Bargaining**. Managers with different goals will compete and will form alliances with other managers to achieve their goals.

(c)   **Satisficing**. Organisations do not aim to maximise performance in one area if this leads to poor performance elsewhere. Rather they will accept satisfactory, as opposed to excellent, performance in a number of areas.

(d)   **Sequential attention**. Goals are dealt with one by one in a sequence.

(e)   **Priority setting**. Certain goals get priority over others. This is determined by senior managers, but there are quite complicated systems to link goals and strategies according to certain criteria.

(f)   **Exercise of power**.

2.8 Critical success factors   5/10

The **critical success factor** approach is an alternative to the pyramid structure of objectives. It aims to identify a small number of performance areas in which satisfactory results will result in successful competitive performance overall.

KEY TERM

CRITICAL SUCCESS FACTORS (CSFs) are 'Elements of the organisational activity which are central to its future success. Critical success factors may change over time, and may include items such as product quality, employee attitudes, manufacturing flexibility and brand awareness'. *(CIMA Official Terminology)*

Johnson, Scholes and Whittington describe a six stage process for using CSFs.

(a)   **Identify the CSFs** for the process under review. (Try to restrict the number of CSFs to six or less).

(b)   **Identify the underlying competences** required to gain a competitive advantage in each of the CSFs.

(c)   Ensure the list of competences is sufficient to generate competitive advantage.

(d)   **Develop performance standards** – key performance indicators (KPIs).

(e)   Ensure these standards cannot be matched by competitors. (If they can be matched by competitors they will not form the basis of competitive advantage.)

(f)   **Monitor competitors** and assess the impact on the CSFs of any response competitors may make.

2.8.1 Mission, CSFs and KPIs

Earlier, we introduced the idea of a hierarchy in which an organisation's goals help supports its mission. We could suggest a parallel here in which the CSFs and KPIs are crucial for enabling an organisation to achieve its mission.

Vision and mission	The organisation's vision is a **statement of its aspirations** or what it wants to be in the future. The organisation's mission expresses its **fundamental objectives**; what it wants to achieve.
CSFs	The CSFs are the **building blocks** which will enable an organisation to implement its mission and thereby achieve future success.
KPIs	KPIs are the **measures** which indicate whether or not the CSFs are being achieved.
	For example, if a CSF has been identified as 'We need new products to satisfy market needs' possible KPIs to measure how well this is being achieved could be: 'Number of new products introduced in a period' or 'Proportion of revenue generated from new products.'

Exam skills

It is important to appreciate the difference between CSFs and KPIs.

CSFs represent 'what' must be done to enable the organisation to be successful. KPIs are the 'measures' of whether or not the CSFs are being achieved.

We will look at CSFs and KPIs again in the context of performance management in Chapter 14, later in this Study Text.

Section summary

Goals and **objectives** derive from and support the mission. The relationship can be modelled as a pyramid with the mission at the top. Where there are lots of objectives, problems of ranking and trade-offs can occur. Critical success factors can be used as an alternative to the pyramid structure.

3 The short term and the long term

Introduction

Objectives are set for varying time horizons. There is a trade-off between long-term and short-term objectives when they are in conflict, or its resources are scarce. For example, capital expenditure projects may be postponed or abandoned in order to protect short-term cash flow and profits.

KEY TERM

SHORT TERMISM is 'bias towards paying particular attention to short-term performance with a corresponding relative disregard to the long run'.   (CIMA *Official Terminology*)

BPP
LEARNING MEDIA

3.1 Long-term and short-term objectives

Objectives may be long-term or short-term.

(a)   For example, a company's primary objective might be to increase its earnings per share from 30c to 50c in the next five years. Strategies for achieving the objective might be selected to include the following.

     (i)   Increasing profitability in the next twelve months by cutting expenditure.

     (ii)   Increasing export sales over the next three years.

     (iii)   Developing a successful new product for the domestic market within five years.

(b)   Secondary objectives might then be re-assessed to include the following.

     (i)   The objective of improving manpower productivity by 10% within twelve months.

     (ii)   Improving customer service in export markets with the objective of doubling the number of overseas sales outlets in selected countries within the next three years.

     (iii)   Investing more in product-market research and development, with the objective of bringing at least three new products to the market within five years.

Targets cannot be set without an awareness of what is realistic. Quantified targets for achieving the primary objective, and targets for secondary objectives, must therefore emerge from a realistic 'position audit'.

3.2 Trade-offs between short-term and long-term objectives

Just as there may have to be a trade-off between different objectives, so too might there be a need to make trade-offs between short-term objectives and long-term objectives. This is referred to as **S/L trade-off**.

Decisions which involve the **sacrifice of longer-term objectives** include the following.

(a)   Postponing or abandoning capital expenditure projects, which would eventually contribute to growth and profits, in order to protect short term cash flow and profits.

(b)   Cutting R&D expenditure to save operating costs, and so reducing the prospects for future product development. Ultimately, cost leadership as a whole is a short term strategy.

(c)   Reducing quality control, to save operating costs (but also adversely affecting reputation and goodwill).

(d)   Reducing the level of customer service, to save operating costs (but sacrificing goodwill).

(e)   Cutting training costs or recruitment (so the company might be faced with skills shortages).

Section summary

Objectives may be short-term or long-term and there may be a **trade off** between the two. This occurs when they are in conflict or resources are scarce.

4   Stakeholder Management   9/10, 3/11, 5/11, 9/11

Introduction

Organisations have a variety of stakeholders, each with very different interests and requirements. This can lead to stakeholder conflict.

Stakeholder mapping is discussed in Paper E2 and is a very useful way of identifying the key stakeholders who have an interest in an organisation's activities, and the power to influence them. (A brief summary of Mendelow's matrix for stakeholder mapping is provided in the introductory chapter at the start of this Study Text.)

KEY TERM

STAKEHOLDERS are 'Those persons and organisations that have an interest in the strategy of the organisation. Stakeholders normally include shareholders, customers, staff and the local community.'

(CIMA Official terminology)

Given that, by definition, stakeholders have an interest in an organisation (and its mission and strategy) then it is very important that the organisation bears the interests of its stakeholders in mind when it is developing its mission and objectives.

4.1 Stakeholder interests

Organisations have a variety of stakeholders, each group of which is likely to have its own interests:

Internal stakeholder	Interests to defend	Response risk
Managers and employees	• Jobs/careers • Money • Promotion • Benefits • Satisfaction	• Pursuit of 'systems goals' rather than shareholder interests • Industrial action • Negative power to impede implementation • Refusal to relocate • Resignation
Connected stakeholder	**Interests to defend**	**Response risk**
Shareholders (corporate strategy)	• Increase in shareholder wealth, measured by profitability, P/E ratios, market capitalisation, dividends and yield • Risk	• Sell shares (eg to predator) or boot out management
Bankers (cash flows)	• Security of loan • Adherence to loan agreements	• Denial of credit • Higher interest charges • Receivership
Suppliers (purchase strategy)	• Profitable sales • Payment for goods • Long-term relationship	• Refusal of credit • Court action • End relationship/reduce supplies

Customers (product market strategy)	• Goods as promised • Future benefits	• Buy elsewhere • Damage reputation (eg bad publicity) • Legal action
External stakeholder	**Interests to defend**	**Response risk**
Government and regulatory agencies	• Jobs, training, tax • Investment and infrastructure • Aggregate demand • National competitiveness; protect emerging industries	• Tax increases • Regulation • Legal action • Tariffs
Interest/pressure groups (*)	• Pollution • Rights • Other	• Publicity • Direct action • Sabotage • Pressure on government
Industry associations and trade unions	• Member rights	• Legal action • Direct action
Non-Governmental organisations (**)	• Human rights	• Legal action

Notes:

*: *Braithwaite and Drahos* refer to the idea of '**mass publics**' – large groups of citizens who express a common concern about an issue.

: Braithwaite and Drahos also refer to the idea of **civil society. Civil society includes, amongst others, non-governmental organisation (NGOs), charities, trades unions, social and religious groups, environmental groups, professional associations, academic institutions, consumer groups, sports and social clubs, and the media.

When considering stakeholder groups which could have an interest in a strategy, organisations should consider these groups from 'civil society' as well as the potentially more obvious internal and connected stakeholders.

When considering stakeholders, organisations need to be aware of two important differences in stakeholder focus:

Economic or social focus   Some stakeholders' interests are primarily economic (for example, shareholders are interested in profitability, employees about salaries) while other stakeholders will care more about social issues (such as social responsibility, or environmental protection).

Local or national focus   Often, the interests of local stakeholder groups may be different from national (or international groups). Think, for example, of the debate about whether to build a third runway at Heathrow airport. Local residents are concerned about increased noise, pollution and traffic, but at a national level politicians have highlighted the economic benefits of expansion.

4.2 Stakeholder conflicts

Conflict is likely between stakeholder groups due to the divergence of their interests. This is further complicated when individuals are members of more than one stakeholder group and when members of

the same stakeholder group do not share the same principal interest. Both cases are illustrated by considering a workforce, some of whose members are also shareholders and some of whom are not.

Exam skills

Different stakeholder groups are likely to have a range of responses to possible business strategies. If you are asked to evaluate a strategy, you should always think what impact it will have on the key stakeholders.

However, you should also consider the different types of responsibility an organisation has to its stakeholders. For example:

Economic – to generate an acceptable rate of return to shareholders

Legal – to comply with relevant rules and regulations

Socially responsible – to be a good corporate citizen, and to make a positive contribution to the local community.

Question 2.1	Stakeholder influences

Learning outcome A1(d)

Ticket and Budget International is a large multinational firm of accountants. The firm provides audit services, tax services, and consultancy services for its many clients. The firm has a strong Technical Department which designs standardised audit procedures. The firm has just employed a marketing manager. The marketing manager regards an audit as a 'product', part of the entire marketing mix including price (audit fees), place (usually on the client's premises) and promotion (advertising in professional journals). The marketing manager is held in high regard by the firm's senior partner. The marketing director and the senior partner have unveiled a new strategic plan, drawn up in conditions of secrecy, which involves a tie-up with an advertising agency. The firm will be a 'one-stop shop' for business services and advice to management on any subject. Each client, or 'customer' will have a dedicated team of auditors, consultants and advertising executives. Obviously, a member of staff will be a member of a number of different teams.

The firm has recently settled a number of expensive law suits for negligence (which it has, of course, 'contested vigorously') out of court, without admitting liability. The Technical Department is conducting a thorough review of the firm's audit procedures.

In the light of what we have covered in this section, what do you think will be the organisational and stakeholder influences on the proposed strategy?

So, different stakeholders will have their own views as to strategy. As some stakeholders have **negative power**, in other words power to impede or disrupt the decision, their likely response might be considered.

4.3 Pressure groups

The members of **pressure groups** come together to promote an issue or cause.

Stakeholders may be unable to exercise any power over an organisation, whether as consumers, employees or members of the public at large. In these circumstances, individuals may seek to influence an organisation by joining a **pressure group**.

Pressure groups arise for two reasons.

- Political representatives fail to air important concerns
- Different groups in society have different interests

Pressure groups have an interest in matters of public policy, but do not aspire to control the machinery of government. There are many thousands of groups ranging from major umbrella groups to small purely local groups, often established for a specific purpose.

(a) **Cause** groups (or **promotional** groups) promote a distinct cause or issue (eg Greenpeace, or Friends of the Earth).

(b) **Interest groups** (or **defensive** or **sectional** groups) defend the wider interests of groups in society such as workers (unions), business firms (eg the CBI in the UK) or consumers (eg the AA or the RAC defending the interests of motorists in the UK).

Some of these groups have other activities than trying to influence government and might regard political activity as only one of their many roles. Some of the major charities, such as Oxfam, do good work and also try to influence government policy. A group can have one of two sorts of relationship with government.

(a) **Insider groups** are regularly consulted by government as a matter of routine in areas of policy. In fact, some insider groups *expect* to be consulted. Note that insider groups do not necessarily support the government of the day. The British Medical Association, for example, although not always supporting government policy on the NHS, is still regularly consulted.

(b) **Outsider groups** do not have a direct link to government. Some of their activities are to **promote interest** in their cause outside government (eg in the media) so that the issue is raised in the public arena and to **gain credibility** in the eyes of the public and recognition of their importance by the government, so that their pronouncements are taken seriously.

The role of pressure groups is controversial.

(a) Some argue that the existence of a pressure group means that **power** is **diffused widely**, and that they are an informal check on ever-increasing power of the state. They also help protect minorities.

(b) Others argue that some pressure groups (eg business interests) are far **more influential** than others (eg some supporters of rail transport believe that 'the road lobby' has undue influence on UK transport policy) and that this is anti-democratic.

Pressure groups may either encourage or try to discourage a policy.

This might be safeguarding the environment ('Friends of the Earth'), trying to ensure freedom of speech and human rights ('Amnesty International') or trying to ban fox hunting ('League Against Cruel Sports').

4.4 Interest groups

The main pressure groups reflecting economic interests are as follows.

(a) **Businesses**: Employers' organisations. These can be supplemented by smaller more specified trade associations in particular industries, which gang together to promote common interests (eg newspapers to oppose tax on the press).

(b) **Professional associations** are groups of people who do the same type of job or use similar skills such as accountants and doctors. Professional associations are generally involved in setting standards of skill and enforcing adherence to good practice (for example, through disciplinary schemes) on the part of members who do the same type of job or use similar skills.

(c) **Trade unions** are similar to professional associations, in that they represent people who work.

(d) **Consumers' associations** represent people as consumers, in other words, campaigning for the interests of consumers on issues such as product pricing, safety, quality and information. Consumer associations have campaigned for labelling on food, for example.

4.5 Management of stakeholders

The firm can make strategic gains from managing stakeholder relationships. Studies have revealed the following correlations:

(a)   A correlation between **employee** and **customer loyalty** (eg reduced staff turnover in service firms generally results in more repeat business).

(b)   **Continuity** and **stability** in relationships with employees, customers and suppliers is important in enabling organisations to respond to certain types of change, necessary for business as a sustained activity.

Responsibilities towards customers are mainly those of providing a product or service of a quality that customers expect, and of dealing honestly and fairly with customers.

Responsibilities towards suppliers are expressed mainly in terms of trading relationships.

(a)   The organisation's size could give it considerable power as a buyer. One ethical guideline might be that the organisation should not use its power unscrupulously. 'Fair trade' organisations illustrate the principle of large buyers giving a fair deal to their (much smaller) supplier.

(b)   Suppliers might rely on getting prompt payment in accordance with the terms of trade negotiated with its customers.

(c)   All information obtained from suppliers and potential suppliers should be kept confidential.

Successful stakeholder management presents the organisation with the opportunity of creating positive, productive and long lasting relationships. However, if the situation is mis-managed, the organisation may damage these relationships creating threats such as resource withdrawal or reputational damage.

Such opportunities and threats should be analysed in terms of:

(a)   **Impact.** How seriously will the performance of the company be affected by the interests/actions of the stakeholders?

(b)   **Direction.** Is the primary effect moving from the company to the stakeholder (such as pollution to the local community) or from the stakeholder to the company (such as …)

(c)   **Time scale.** When will the company be affected by the demands/actions of the stakeholders?

(d)   **Ability to resolve.** Does the company have the capability and resources to deal with the stakeholder demands?

Macmillian and Jones suggest that management should consider the following decisions when determining their approach to stakeholder management.

(a)   Do they deal directly or indirectly with stakeholders?
(b)   Do they take and offensive or defensive approach?
(c)   Do they accommodate, negotiate, manipulate or resist stakeholder claims?
(d)   Do they take a single course of action, or a combination of the approaches above?

4.5.1 Resolving conflicting objectives

Additionally, *Cyert and March* suggest that management should consider the following four ways of resolving conflicting objectives between different stakeholder groups:

(a)   **Satisficing** – Using negotiations between key stakeholder groups to reach a **compromise** which is acceptable to all of them.

(b)   **Sequential attention.** Instead of considering the needs of all stakeholders simultaneously, management should focus on the needs of different stakeholder groups in turn, and with the understanding that once a group has had their needs addressed they will then have to 'wait their turn' while the needs of other stakeholder groups are addressed.

(c) **Side payments.** If a stakeholder group's primary objectives cannot be met, management should ensure that the group is compensated in some other way; either through a policy concession, or - literally - a payment. For example, if local residents have argued against a new factory being built (due to concerns about the impact the factory will have on their neighbourhood) the factory company could look to appease the local community by offering to fund local projects (eg schools, sports clubs etc.)

(d) **Exercise of power**. If it appears that there is no other way of resolving conflicting views, a senior figure could force through a decision by virtue of the power they possess.

Exam skills

If you are faced with a stakeholder question in the exam, you must ensure you apply your knowledge specifically to the context given in the question. You will not earn marks by simply repeating everything you know about stakeholder management. Too often students assume that a question about stakeholder management automatically means 'Draw Mendelow's matrix, and then explain it.'

However, this is not the case! Even if you are asked to analyse stakeholders into the various categories of the matrix, the most important part of your answer is likely to be explaining *why* you believe each group has the level of power or interest in the issue at hand which you have ascribed to it. Simply explaining the model (or drawing it) will earn you very few, if any, marks.

4.6 Measuring stakeholder satisfaction

Measuring the satisfaction of stakeholder interests is likely to be difficult, since many of their expectations relate to **qualitative** rather than **quantitative** matters. It is, for example, difficult to measure good corporate citizenship. On the other hand, some of the more important stakeholder groups do have fairly specific interests, the satisfaction of which should be fairly amenable to measurement. Here are some examples of possible measures.

Stakeholder group	Measure
Employees	Staff turnover; pay and benefits relative to market rate; job vacancies
Government	Pollution measures; promptness of filing annual returns; accident rate; energy efficiency
Distributors	Share of joint promotions paid for; rate of stock-outs

4.7 Corporate political activity

How an organisation responds to external pressures and the external environment is one of the key aspects of strategic management. PEST analysis highlights how these external factors can be summarised.

The 'P' is PEST analysis (political) also suggests that governments can play a key **role in influencing an organisation's strategy** or business activities.

Governments, by definition, have a degree of **legitimate power** in a country and so can establish and enforce the **institutional environment** in which firms operate. In this respect, governments are a potential resource or threat to every firm and industry in society.

For example, government initiatives can create changes in industry cost structure by providing direct subsidies, imposing minimum wage laws, introducing tax policies, or introducing quality standards for industrial products. In this respect, governments can play a key role in shaping business strategy.

However, there is a danger that we might think that firms are simply passive players in this political environment and have to accept the institutional environment which their national government creates. This is not the case though.

Mainstream business theory considers business organisations pursuing economic goals, and in this context political factors are viewed as a constraint for a firm's activities. However, **political factors can also be considered as resources for a firm**. Although laws and regulations do affect a firm's competitive environment, firms can also try to influence political decision-making.

In this context, corporate political activity can be seen part of an organisation's strategy to generate and sustain profits. Moreover, the relationship between business and government should be seen as 'two-way' rather than just government imposing legislation and regulation on businesses.

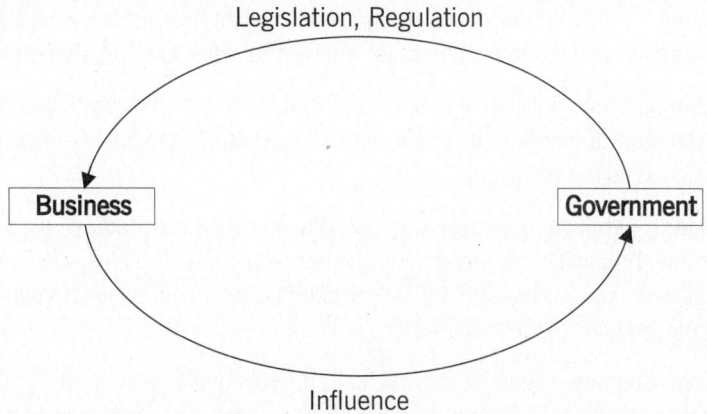

CORPORATE POLITICAL ACTIVITY can be seen as 'every deliberate attempt of a firm to influence government political decision-making'   (*Getz*)

KEY TERM

Keim & *Baysinger* offer an alternative definition which indicates more clearly why corporate political activity is relevant to business strategy. For them, corporate political activity is 'managerial decisions that represent an integrated set of activities within a firm, intended to produce public policy outcomes favourable to the firm's economic survival and continued success.'

This second definition highlights the role corporate political activity can play in securing competitive advantage over competitors. This definition also alludes to the way that corporate political activity – as a way of promoting or maintaining the competitiveness of the firm – can play an **integral part of corporate competitive strategy**.

In this respect, for a business strategy to be effective, its components must be integrated and tailored to the firms' market and non-market environments, as well as to its competencies.

4.7.1 The non-market environment

Political behaviour, in general, relates to the acquisition and use of power in relation to other entities. However, note that business political behaviour take place in the **political** (or **non-market) environment** of a firm, as opposed to the **economic** (or **market) environment** of a firm. It is important that firms recognise that **competitive advantage** can be built (or lost) in the non-market environment as well as in the market environment. For example, a firm's ability to work with regulators, or its ability to foresee relevant government actions, could contribute to its competitive advantage.

In the political environment, a firm interacts with a set of actors, such as governments (including politicians and officials), interest groups, non-government organisations and the public. However, whereas the economic environment consists of the supply and demand of goods and services, the political environment provides the supply and demand of public policies.

Also whereas the activities in the economic environment are typically voluntary (a consumer chooses whether or not to buy a good or service), in the political environment they may be either **voluntary** (for

example, if a firm cooperates with government officials) or **involuntary** (for example, when government regulates an activity).

4.7.2 Types of corporate political activity

Since the 1980s, in developed countries, firms have increasingly established public affairs offices and employed specialists in public relations in order to monitor and manage their political environment.

Alongside this, firms have used different types of political activity in order to influence public policy decision-making.

Such activities include:

Lobbying – senior represents of an organisation, or else a professional lobbyist employed by the organisation, contact political decision-makers in order to try to shape their views and their policies.

Election funding – businesses make contributions either directly to candidates or else to political parties, in an attempt to increase the chances of a favourable candidate being elected, and then to influence subsequent legislative voting.

Petitions – petitions to political decision-makers are a conventional corporate response to increased government regulation or foreign competition. Typically, firms use petitions to inform policy-makers or emergent or realised threats to their competitiveness, with a view to getting the policy-makers to take action to sustain competitiveness.

Coalition building – coalition is a tactic to improve collective power. Coalitions may be temporary (for example, a coalition may form to respond to a specific piece of legislation) or may be more permanent (for example a trade association). Coalition building typically involves collective action – for example, sending a petition to a government.

4.7.3 Levels of corporate political activity

Corporate political activity varies according to the context in which it takes place:

*   Institutional level
*   Industry level
*   Firm level

Institutional level – This is the level which affects all the firms operating in a national economy. So, for example, it includes all the laws and statutes of a country. At this level, the institutional environment can affect national competitive advantage. (Note the link here to the ideas in Porter's diamond).

Industry level – We can illustrate the distinction between industry and firm level by suggesting that the benefits from corporate political activity may be either **collective** or **selective**.

Corporate political strategies may be considered collective in that the results of political activities may benefit more than one individual firm: for example, introducing trade barriers, quotas, subsidies, or product quality standards which may act as barriers to entry to potential new entrants into an industry as a whole.

Firms can also use corporate political activity to try to get extra funding or loans. For example, the car industry has been very badly affected by the recession in 2009 and car plants in the UK have argued they need government help to ensure they can survive the recession. The UK government has set aside over £2 billion in support for the car industry, mostly in the form of loan guarantees, as well as direct aid to car makers.

In the 2009 budget in the UK, the Chancellor of the Exchequer announced that motorists trading in an old car (more than 10 years old) and buying a brand new car would get a £2,000 discount off their new car for a limited period. (The scrappage scheme only ran between 2009-2010).

This measure could be seen as a stimulus to the car industry, but also a response to the pressure the car industry had been putting on the Chancellor.

Firm level – Selective benefits, by contrast, accrue only to those who participate in the activity. Selective benefits could be gained, for example, by having access to decision-makers which competitors do not have.

In this respect, the pattern of political behaviour is likely to vary between large and small firms. In general, large firms are more politically active than small firms, because they have the resources required for potentially costly political manoeuvring. Moreover, large firms are likely to have more political bargaining power to influence political decision-making more than small firms.

However, the different levels at which corporate political activity can take place also has important implications, especially for large, diversified firms containing various business divisions which may experience different (and conflicting) political goals. In this case, each of the divisions will face different political and regulatory concerns.

4.7.4 Corporate political activity and ethics

We have noted that the corporate political activity involves organisations trying to influence politicians. However, if you need to advise about any such activity in your E3 exam, remember that any actions you suggest should meet with the standards of ethics required by the CIMA Code of Ethics for Professional Accountants.

For example, it is not appropriate for organisations to offer bribes to politicians in order to secure publicly-funded business.

Exam skills

We cannot overstate how important it is that any actions you suggest comply with CIMA's Code of Ethics. If you suggest unethical political responses in any part of your answer, you will score very poorly for that part of your answer, even if you make a number of other valid points.

Section summary

Organisations have many **stakeholders**. Conflict between stakeholder groups is likely due to the wide range of specific interests and requirements held by each group. Firms can make strategic gains by managing stakeholder relationships to create positive, productive and long-lasting relationships.

5 Business ethics   5/10, 9/10, 11/11

Introduction

Modern society is very concerned to define for itself what is and what is not 'acceptable'. This has forced businesses to become more aware of their activities and take measures to demonstrate that they are ethical organisations.

KEY TERM

BUSINESS ETHICS can be defined as the standards of behaviour in the conduct of business.

5.1 Fundamental ethical principles

CIMA has developed a 'Code of Ethics' for CIMA members (including students) which dictates that a professional accountant shall comply with five fundamental principles (Section 100.5 of the Code):

(a) **Integrity:** acting honestly, straightforwardly and truthfully in all professional and business relationships.

The principle of integrity implies that professional accountants should not be associated with any information which they believe contains a materially false or misleading statement, or which is misleading by omissions.

(b) **Objectivity:** not allowing bias, conflict of interest, or the undue influence of others to override professional or business judgments.

(c) **Professional Competence and Due Care:** maintaining professional knowledge and skill at the level required to ensure that a client or employer receives competent professional services, based on current applicable technical and professional standards.

This principle highlights that professional accountants must keep themselves up to date with current business or professional developments, hence the need for continuing professional development.

This principle also implies that staff working under the authority of a professional accountant must receive appropriate training and supervision.

(d) **Confidentiality:** respecting the confidentially of information acquired through professional and business relationships, and not disclosing any such information to third parties without proper and specific authority, unless there is a legal or professional duty to do so.

Confidentiality also requires an accountant not to use any information acquired through professional or business relationships for their own personal advantage or for the advantage of any third parties.

(e) **Professional Behaviour:** complying with relevant laws and regulations in order to avoid any action that would discredit the profession.

5.1.1 Threats to the fundamental ethical principles

CIMA's Code of Ethics identifies five categories of threat which could compromise the accountant's ability to comply with one or more of the fundamental ethical principles:

(a) **Self interest threat:** the threat that a financial or other interest (eg concern about job security) will inappropriately influence the professional accountant's judgement or behaviour. In other words, this relates to the threat of a conflict of interest.

(b) **Self review threat:** the threat that a professional accountant will not appropriately evaluate the results of a previous judgement made by themselves, or by another individual within their organisation, but will rely on that judgement as part of a service they are currently providing.

(c) **Advocacy threat:** occurs if a professional accountant is promoting a client or employer's position or opinion to the extent that the accountant's subsequent objectivity is compromised.

(d) **Familiarity threat:** If the accountant develops too close a relationship with a client or employer (for example, through length of service) the accountant could become too sympathetic to the interests of the client or employer such that their professional judgement becomes compromised.

(e) **Intimidation threat:** when an accountant is deterred from acting objectively by actual or perceived threats, including attempts to exercise undue influence over the accountant.

5.1.2 Safeguards

Safeguards are actions of other measures designed to eliminate threats or reduce them to an acceptable level.

There are two broad categories of safeguard:

(a)   **Safeguards created by the profession, legislation or regulation**. These include:

- Education, training and experience requirements for entry into the profession

- Requirements for continuing professional development

- Corporate governance regulation

- Professional standards

- Professional monitoring and disciplinary procedures

- External review by a legally empowered third party (eg an auditor) of the reports, returns and information produced by a professional accountant

(b)   **Safeguards in the work environment.** These include complaint systems within employing organisations which enable colleagues, employers and members of the public to draw attention to unprofessional or unethical behaviour. For example, employing organisations often have whistle-blowing or grievance procedures to help protect employees against threats.

Similarly, a professional accountant has an explicit duty to report breaches of ethical requirements.

CIMA's Code of Ethics adopts a 'threats and safeguards' approach to resolving ethical issues. This means that if an accountant perceives one or more of the fundamental ethical principles to be under threat (and the threat is significant), the accountant should take action to remove or mitigate the threat.

5.1.3 Resolving ethical conflicts

If one or more of the five fundamental principles is threatened, then the accountant faces an **ethical dilemma**. For example, such a situation would arise if an accountant is asked to act contrary to the law or professional standards, or to issue a report which materially misrepresents the facts in a situation. The Code of Ethics stresses that a professional accountant must actively respond to such a situation, and must not simply remain silent.

Similarly, the Code identifies that a professional accountant may be required to **resolve a conflict** in relation to compliance with the fundamental ethical principles. For example, the accountant may face a conflict between responsibility to their employer, and their obligations to the Code's fundamental principles.

The Code recommends the following as an approach for resolving ethical conflicts:

(a)   Establish the relevant facts

(b)   Establish the ethical issues involved

(c)   Identify the fundamental ethical principles related to the matter in question

(d)   Follow established internal procedures

(e)   Investigate alternative courses of action, and consider the consequences of each possible course of action.

Once they have considered the relevant factors, the professional accountant should then determine the appropriate course of action, weighing the consequences of each possible course of action.

If the matter remains unresolved, the accountant may wish to **consult with other appropriate people** within their firm or employing organisation for help in resolving it. For example, the accountant could discuss the matter with their line manager, and then, if necessary, also raise it with the people charged with governance of the organisation, such as the Directors or the audit committee.

If a significant issue cannot be resolved, the accountant should then consider obtaining **professional advice** from the relevant professional body (such as CIMA, via the ethics helpline) or from **legal advisors**.

The accountant can generally obtain guidance on ethical issues without breaching the fundamental principle of confidentiality if a matter is discussed with a relevant professional body on an anonymous basis.

Ultimately, if the accountant remains unable to resolve the matter creating the conflict, the accountant may need to reconsider their position in their organisation. In the worst case scenario, they may have to **resign from their current role** or their current employment.

Exam skills

The examiner has indicated that CIMA's Code of Ethics is an explicit part of the E3 syllabus, and students should be prepared for questions that deal either with the general principles of the Code, or that require a more detailed knowledge and application of the Code, in order to analyse how a scenario fits with the Code or what actions might be required in a given scenario.

For example, a requirement in the September 2010 exam asked candidates to explain the threats a management accountant faced in a scenario, and then to a recommend safeguards which could eliminate or reduce those threats.

WEBLINK – CIMA Code of Ethics: www.cimaglobal.com/Professional-ethics/Ethics/

5.2 Ethics in organisations

Organisations are coming under increasing pressure to adopt an ethical approach towards

- **Stakeholders** (employees, customers, competitors, suppliers and society as a whole)
- **Environmental issues** (such as pollution and recycling)
- **The disadvantaged**
- Dealings with **unethical companies or countries**

This pressure may come from

- **Government**
- UK and European **legislation**
- **Treaty obligations** (such as the Kyoto protocol)
- **Consumers**
- **Employers**
- **Pressure groups**

To be effective, a code of ethics will have to be incorporated into the entire culture of the organisation. Its ethical views can therefore directly impact on the mission statement and strategy adopted by the organisation.

You will cover governance and ethical issues in more detail in the 'Risk and Internal Control' section of Paper P3 – Performance Strategy.

5.3 Ethics and strategy

As well as presenting possible threats to a management accountant, ethics and ethical issues can also have a role in strategy more generally.

For example, strong ethical policies - that go beyond simply upholding the law - can add value to a brand. Conversely, failing to act ethically can cause social, economic and environmental damage, and in doing so can undermine an organisation's long-term reputation and prospects.

In this respect, a social and environmentally ethical approach can assist an organisation's ability to thrive in the long run. In this respect, ethical behaviour can help contribute to **sustainable competitive advantage**.

The collapse of Enron (as a result of a massive fraud) clearly showed how unethical behaviour led to a failure to create a sustainable business model. It is also possible to argue that some other corporate failures - such as Lehman Brothers, Bear Stearns or Northern Rock - came about as a result of the organisations focussing too much on trying to pursue high short-term gains, and in doing so jeopardising their longer-term survival.

These examples highlight the importance of organisations not only understanding the **risks** they are taking in their business, but also focussing on long-term sustainability as well as short term profitability.

Such considerations can be directly relevant in the context of strategic options. For example, how might a consideration of ethical behaviour affect an investment decision? In simple terms, if a project generates a positive net present value (NPV) it is likely to be accepted. If, however, the project involves exploiting cheap labour (or even child labour) it should not be accepted by an organisation; either on ethical grounds, or because of the potential risk to its reputation (and therefore future sales) if its labour practices become more widely known.

Consequently, it is important that ethics are embedded in an organisation's business model, organisational strategy and decision-making processes. Moreover, ethical issues are particularly important when considered alongside aspects of sustainability, which we are going to look at in more detail shortly.

Section summary

Organisations are coming under increasing pressure to adopt an ethical approach to stakeholders, the environment, the disadvantaged, and their dealings with unethical companies or countries. To be effective, a code of ethics must be incorporated into the entire culture of the organisation.

6 Corporate social responsibility and sustainability

3/11, 5/11, 9/11, 3/12, 5/12

Introduction

Some argue that a business has a **social responsibility** for the cost of its activities, while others argue that businesses already contribute enough to society via the taxes on their profits.

The **sustainability** of business activity is becoming a major concern as business moves into the 21st century. This considers both environmental and social pressures. The '**triple bottom line**' refers to a whole new way of measuring business performance using not only economic prosperity, but environmental quality and social equality.

6.1 Corporate social responsibility

If it is accepted that businesses do not bear the total **social cost** of their activities, it could be suggested that **corporate social responsibility** might be a way of recognising this.

KEY TERMS

SOCIAL COST. 'Tangible and intangible costs and losses sustained by third parties or the general public as a result of economic activity, for example pollution by industrial effluent'.

SOCIAL RESPONSIBILITY ACCOUNTING. 'Identification, measurement and reporting of the social costs and benefits resulting from economic activities.'   *(CIMA Official Terminology)*

Businesses, particularly large ones, are subject to increasing expectations that they will exercise **social responsibility**. This is an ill-defined concept, but appears to focus on the provision of specific benefits to society in general, such as charitable donations, the creation or preservation of employment, and spending on environmental improvement or maintenance. A great deal of the pressure is created by the activity of minority action groups and is aimed at businesses because they are perceived to possess extensive resources. The momentum of such arguments is now so great that the notion of social responsibility has become almost inextricably confused with the matter of ethics. It is important to remember the distinction.

Social responsibility and ethical behaviour are not the same thing although they are related. Business ethics is concerned with the standards of behaviour in the conduct of business. **Corporate social responsibility (CSR)** is an organisation's obligation to **maximise positive stakeholder benefits** while **minimising the negative effects of its actions**.

Johnson, Scholes & Whittington point out that 'Corporate social responsibility is concerned with the ways in which an organisation exceeds its minimum obligations to stakeholders specified through regulation.'

Importantly, CSR includes **economic** and **legal issues**, as well as **ethical ones**: reflecting the whole range of stakeholders who have an interest in an organisation. In this respect, CSR requires an organisation to go beyond simply adhering to minimum ethical standards. Ethics concerns issues such as justice, fairness and honesty, which are fundamental, unchanging values that have implications for business.

CSR is more closely associated with contemporary business issues, and concerns organisations giving something back to society, and being good citizens. Therefore, in contrast to ethics, CSR is socially mediated and likely to be specific to the time and culture in which it is considered. For example, CSR could include:

- Staff development via training and education
- Equal opportunities statements
- Written anti-discrimination policies
- Commitment to reporting on CSR
- Policies for restricting the use of child labour by suppliers
- Policies on fair trade
- Commitment to the protection of the local community

We can suggest that companies achieve society's expectation that they are good corporate citizens through their **philanthropic responsibilities**. These might include: making charitable donations; supporting local schools, arts or sports projects; or even building educational or leisure facilities in the local communities where they operate.

However, an important point to note about philanthropic responsibilities is that, while local communities may hope that companies contribute to their well-being, it does not make the companies unethical if they do not. Philanthropic responsibilities may be desired by society, but companies are not obliged to make such contributions, and they should not be considered unethical just because they do not make them.

A business managed with the sole objective of maximising shareholder wealth can be run in just as ethical a fashion as one in which far wider stakeholder responsibility is assumed. On the other hand, however, there is no doubt that many large businesses have behaved irresponsibly in the past and some continue to do so.

6.1.1 Corporate social responsibility stances

Different organisations take very different stances on social responsibility, and their different stances will be reflected in how they manage such responsibilities.

Johnson, Scholes & Whittington identify four corporate social responsibility stances, which reflect a progressively more inclusive list of stakeholder interests:

- Laissez-faire
- Enlightened self-interest (Long-term shareholder interest)
- Multiple stakeholder obligations
- Shaper of society

Laissez-faire stance: Organisations which adopt a laissez-faire stance take the view that an organisation's only responsibilities are the **short-term interests of shareholders**, and to make a profit, pay taxes and provide jobs.

Organisations adopting this view believe that it is government's role to prescribe, through legislation and regulation, the constraints which are placed on businesses in their pursuit of economic efficiency. Laissez-faire organisations will meet these minimum obligations but no more.

Enlightened self-interest (long-term shareholder interest)

The rationale behind the 'enlightened self-interest' stance is that there can be a long-term benefit to shareholders from well-managed relationships with other stakeholders. Therefore, the justification for social action is that it makes good business sense.

There are two reasons why an organisation might take a wider view of ethical responsibilities when considering the longer-term interest of shareholders:

(a)   The organisation's **corporate image** may be enhanced by an assumption of wider responsibilities. The cost of undertaking such responsibilities may be justified as essentially promotional expenditure.

(b)   The responsible exercise of corporate power may prevent a build-up of social and political **pressure for legal regulation**. Freedom of action may be preserved and the burden of regulation lightened by acceptance of ethical responsibilities.

For example, in 2012 in the UK, following a downturn in its profits, the supermarket giant Tesco has sought to reinvent its business to persuade people that it isn't simply a money-making machine, but also has 'a softer side'. To this end, the chief executive Philip Clarke said that 'We will do more to ensure that Tesco is valued and trusted in local communities all around the world for doing the right thing' - although critics were quick to point out that this is the same company which has been squeezing farmers and other suppliers for years to extract the best price they can for its customers.

Multiple stakeholder obligations

Organisations adopting this stance accept the **legitimacy of the expectations of stakeholders other than shareholders** and build those expectations into the organisation's stated purposes. Such organisations recognise that without appropriate relationships with groups such as suppliers, employers and customers, they would not be able to function.

However, organisations adopting a 'multiple stakeholder obligations' stance also argue that performance should not be measured simply through the financial bottom line. They argue that the key to long-term survival is dependent on social and environmental performance as well as economic (financial) performance, and therefore it is important to take account of the views of stakeholders with interests relating to social and environmental matters.

Shaper of society

Shapers of society regard financial considerations as being of secondary importance to changing society or social norms. For such organisations, ensuring that society benefits from their actions is more important than financial and other stakeholder interests.

6.1.2 Against corporate social responsibility

Milton Friedman argued against corporate social responsibility along the following lines.

(a) Businesses do not have responsibilities, only people have responsibilities. Managers in charge of corporations are responsible to the owners of the business, by whom they are employed.

(b) These employers may have charity as their aim, but 'generally [their aim] will be to make as much money as possible while conforming to the basic rules of the society, both those embodied in law and those embodied in ethical custom.'

(c) If the statement that a manager has social responsibilities is to have any meaning, 'it must mean that he is to act in some way that is not in the interest of his employers.'

(d) If managers do this they are, generally speaking, spending the owners' money for purposes other than those they have authorised; sometimes it is the money of customers or suppliers that is spent and, on occasion, the money of employees. By doing this, the manager is, in effect, both raising taxes and deciding how they should be spent, which are functions of government, not of business. There are two objections to this.

    (i) Managers have not been democratically elected (or selected in any other way) to exercise government power.

    (ii) Managers are not experts in government policy and cannot foresee the detailed effect of such social responsibility spending.

Friedman argues that the social responsibility model is politically collectivist in nature and deplores the possibility that collectivism should be extended any further than absolutely necessary in a free society.

A second argument against the assumption of corporate social responsibility is that the **maximisation of wealth is the best way that society can benefit from a business's activities**.

(a) Maximising wealth has the effect of increasing the tax revenues available to the state to disburse on socially desirable objectives.

(b) Maximising shareholder value has a 'trickle down' effect on other disadvantaged members of society.

(c) Many company shares are owned by pension funds, whose ultimate beneficiaries may not be the wealthy anyway.

6.1.3 Arguments in favour of CSR

Despite Friedman's arguments against it, there are a number of reasons why corporate social responsibility can be strategically beneficial for businesses:

Customer expectations – There is an increasing expectation from consumers and other stakeholders that businesses will act in a more socially responsible manner. For example, from the food they eat, to the coffee they drink and the clothes they wear, consumers are becoming more aware of the origins of the everyday things they buy, and they want to buy products that are responsibly sourced.

Given that one of the key success factors for a business is the ability to offer customers what they want, then offering products and services which are deemed to be socially responsible could help boost sales.

In this respect, CSR could provide opportunities to enter new markets or develop new products; for example, in the way that Toyota developed the 'Prius' hybrid car.

Brand name – Being seen as socially responsible can help enhance a business's reputation and therefore its brand. Customers may prefer to deal with a business they feel is socially responsible rather than with one which is not. Therefore, CSR could actually be a source of differentiation for a business.

Lower environmental costs – If firms improve the efficiency of their energy usage, for example, then as well as making lower emissions they will also have lower cost bases. If firms can achieve a lower cost base through the efficient use of resources, this could help them create (or improve) their competitive advantage.

More generally, firms could also find it is less costly to regulate their own activities voluntarily than ignoring socially responsibility in the short term and then having to comply with statutory regulations (in the form of taxes or fines, for example) which may be imposed on them later.

Trading opportunities – If firms are perceived as not being socially responsible, they may find it harder to attract trading partners, or support from nations and local communities where they might want to invest.

Access to staff - Similarly, the way firms are perceived to treat their staff may affect their ability to attract staff. For example, firms that are perceived to offer good working conditions are likely to be able to attract a higher calibre of staff than firms which are perceived to offer unfavourable working conditions. In turn, a firm which is able to attract (and retain) high quality staff may be able to generate competitive advantage over a firm which is less able to attract good quality staff.

Investment and funding – A firm's reputation may also affect its ability to attract finance, particularly from ethical investors. For example, obtaining a listing on the FTSE4Good (index of companies that meet globally recognised corporate responsibility standards) is likely to help a firm attract finance from ethical investors.

Sustainable business – Taken collectively, the arguments in favour of CSR suggest that a socially responsible business is likely to be able to operate for longer in society than a less responsible one. In turn, if the business can expect more years of cash flows in the future, it might be reasonable to expect the value of the company to be higher than that of one whose future is perceived to be less secure.

6.1.4 The stakeholder view

The **stakeholder view** is that many groups have a stake in what the organisation does. This is particularly important in the business context, where shareholders own the business but employees, customers and government also have particularly strong claims to having their interests considered. This is fundamentally an argument derived from **natural law theory** and is based on the notion of individual and collective **rights**.

It is suggested that modern corporations are so powerful, socially, economically and politically, that unrestrained use of their power will inevitably damage other people's rights. For example, they may blight an entire community by closing a major facility, thus enforcing long term unemployment on a large proportion of the local workforce. Similarly, they may damage people's quality of life by polluting the environment. They may use their purchasing power or market share to impose unequal contracts on suppliers and customers alike. And they may exercise undesirable influence over government through their investment decisions. Under this approach, the exercise of corporate social responsibility constrains the corporation to act at all times as a good citizen.

Another argument points out that corporations exist within society and are dependent upon it for the resources they use. Some of these resources are obtained by direct contracts with suppliers but others are not, being provided by government expenditure. Examples are such things as transport infrastructure, technical research and education for the workforce. Clearly, corporations contribute to the taxes that pay

for these things, but the relationship is rather tenuous and the tax burden can be minimised by careful management. The implication is that corporations should recognise, and pay for, the facilities that society provides by means of socially responsible policies and actions.

Henry Mintzberg (in *Power In and Around Organisations*) suggests that simply viewing organisations as vehicles for shareholder investment is inadequate.

(a) In practice, he says, organisations are rarely controlled effectively by shareholders. Most shareholders are passive investors.

(b) Large corporations can manipulate markets. Social responsibility, forced or voluntary, is a way of recognising this.

(c) Moreover, as mentioned above, businesses do receive a lot of government support. The public pays for roads, infrastructure, education and health, all of which benefit businesses. Although businesses pay tax, the public ultimately pays, perhaps through higher prices.

(d) Strategic decisions by businesses always have wider social consequences. In other words, says Mintzberg, the firm produces two kinds of outputs: **goods and services** and the **social consequences of its activities** (eg pollution).

6.1.5 The social audit

Firms sometimes carry out **social audits**. This generally involves:

- Recognising a firm's rationale for engaging in socially responsible activity
- Identifying programmes which are congruent with the mission of the company
- Setting objectives and priorities related to this programme
- Specifying the nature and range of resources required
- Evaluating company involvement in such programmes (past, present and future)

Whether or not a social audit is used depends on the degree to which social responsibility is part of the **corporate philosophy**. A cultural awareness must be achieved within an organisation in order to implement environmental policy, which requires Board and staff support.

In the USA, social audits on environmental issues have increased since the *Exxon Valdez* catastrophe in which millions of gallons of crude oil were released into Alaskan waters. The **Valdez principles** were drafted by the Coalition for Environmentally Responsible Economics to focus attention on environmental concerns and corporate responsibility.

- Eliminate pollutants and hazardous waste

- Conserve non-renewable resources

- Market environmentally safe products and services

- Prepare for accidents and restore damaged environments

- Provide protection for employees who report environmental hazards

- Companies should appoint an environmentalist to the board of directors, name an executive for environmental affairs and develop an environmental audit of global operations

There are many contrasting views about the responsibilities of the corporation.

(a) If the company creates a social problem, it must fix it (eg Exxon, or more recently BP clearing up the massive oil spill which resulted from the explosion on the Deepwater Horizon oil rig in the US Gulf of Mexico in April 2010).

(b) Companies already discharge their social responsibility, simply by increasing their profits and thereby contributing more in taxes. If a company was expected to divert more resources to solve society's problems, this would represent a double tax.

(c)   The multinational corporation has the resources to fight poverty, illiteracy, malnutrition, illness and so on. This approach disregards who actually creates the problems.

6.2 Strategies for social responsibility

Proactive strategy	A strategy which a business follows where it is prepared to take full responsibility for its actions. A company which discovers a fault in a product and recalls the product without being forced to, before any injury or damage is caused, acts in a proactive way.
Reactive strategy	This involves allowing a situation to continue unresolved until the public, government or consumer groups find out about it.
Defence strategy	This involves minimising or attempting to avoid additional obligations arising from a particular problem.
Accommodation strategy	This approach involves taking responsibility for actions, probably when one of the following happens. • Encouragement from special interest groups • Perception that a failure to act will result in government intervention

6.3 Environmental and green concerns

Business activities in general were formerly regarded as problems for the environmental movement, but the two are now increasingly complementary. There has been an increase in the use of the green approach to market products. 'Dolphin friendly' tuna and paper products from managed forests are examples.

Environmental impacts on business may be direct.

• Changes affecting costs or resource availability
• Impact on demand
• Effect on power balances between competitors in a market

They may also be **indirect**. Pressure for better environmental performance is coming from many quarters.

(a)   **Green pressure groups** have increased their membership and influence dramatically.

(b)   **Employees** are increasing pressure on the businesses in which they work for a number of reasons – partly for their own safety, partly in order to improve the public image of the company.

(c)   **Legislation** is increasing almost by the day. Growing pressure from the green or green-influenced vote has led to mainstream political parties taking these issues into their programmes, and most countries now have laws to cover land use planning, smoke emission, water pollution and the destruction of animals and natural habitats.

(d)   **Environmental risk screening** has become increasingly important. Companies in the future will become responsible for the environmental impact of their activities.

6.4 Strategic planning

Physical environmental conditions are important for strategic planning.

(a)   **Resource inputs.** Managing physical resources successfully (eg oil companies, mining companies) is a good source of profits.

(b)   **Logistics.** The physical environment presents logistical problems or opportunities to organisations. Proximity to road and rail links can be a reason for siting a warehouse in a particular area.

(c)   **Government.** The physical environment is under the control of other organisations.

(i)   Local authority town planning departments can influence where a building and necessary infrastructure can be sited.

(ii)   Governments can set regulations about some of the organisation's environmental interactions.

(d)   **Disasters.** In some countries, the physical environment can pose a major 'threat' to organisations.

Issues relating to the effect of an organisation's activities on the physical environment have come to the fore in recent years.

6.4.1 How green issues will impinge on business

Possible issues to consider are these.

- **Consumer demand** for products which appear to be environmentally friendly
- Demand for **less pollution** from industry
- Greater **regulation** by government and the EU (eg recycling targets)
- Demand that **businesses be charged** with the external cost of their activities
- Possible requirements to conduct **environmental audits**
- Opportunities to develop **products and technologies** which are environmentally friendly
- Taxes (eg landfill tax)

However, as with so many other areas of business, while some people advocate 'green claims' others are more cynical about them.

(a)   **Marketing.** Some critics argues that companies such as Body Shop have exploited environmental friendliness as a marketing tool.

(b)   **Publicity.** Perhaps companies have more to fear from the impact of bad publicity (relating to their environmental practices) than they have to benefit from positive ecological messages as such. Public relations is a vital competitive weapon.

(c)   **Lifestyles.** There may be a limit to which consumers are prepared to alter their lifestyles for the sake of ecological correctness. For example, how much more will consumers be prepared to pay to buy organic products compared to non-organic ones?

(d)   Consumers may be **imperfectly educated** about green issues. (For example, much recycled paper has simply replaced paper produced from trees from properly managed (ie sustainably developed) forests.) In short, some companies may have to 'educate' consumers as to the relative ecological impact of their products.

6.4.2 Renewable and non-renewable resources

KEY TERM

SUSTAINABILITY involves developing strategies so that the company only uses resources at a rate that allows them to be replenished such that the needs of the current generation can be met without compromising the needs of future generations. At the same time, emissions of waste are confined to levels that do not exceed the capacity of the environment to absorb them.

Sustainability means that resources consumed are **replaced** in some way: for every tree cut down another is planted. Some resources, however, are inherently non-renewable: for example, oil will eventually run out.

(a)   Metals can be recycled. Some car manufacturers are building cars with recyclable components.

(b)   An argument is that as the price of resources rise, market forces will operate to make more efficient use of them or to develop alternatives. When oil becomes too expensive, solar power will become economic.

Motor manufacturers are looking to a future without oil. Hydrogen power is one option, using **fuel cell** technology. Electric cars are another option.

John Elkington, chairman of the think-tank SustainAbility Ltd, has said that **sustainability** now embraces not only environmental and economic questions, but also social and ethical dimensions. He writes about the **triple bottom line**, which means 'business people must increasingly recognise that the challenge now is to help deliver simultaneously:

- Economic prosperity
- Environmental quality
- Social equity

However, a full consideration of sustainability in company reports is hampered by several difficulties.

- Lack of a standard methodology
- Accountants/auditors lack environmental expertise
- Difficulties in determining environmental costs
- Identification and valuation of potential liabilities is problematic

Elkington considers there to be three main forms of capital that businesses need to value.

- **Economic capital** (physical, financial and human skills and knowledge)
- **Natural capital** (replaceable and irreplaceable)
- **Social capital** (the ability of people to work together)

Environmental and social accounting is still embryonic, but *Elkington* believes that it will eventually develop our ability to see whether or not a particular company or industry is 'moving in the right direction'.

6.5 The Triple Bottom Line and Sustainability

Elkington's concept of the triple bottom line emphasises that, although firms can be capable of socially and environmentally responsibly action, many will only take such action if accounting conventions are changed to record and monitor the entire impact of business activities and not just the financial (profit) benefits. If such a change is made, firms may be able to improve their sustainability record without the need for excessive government regulation.

There are potentially a number of ways poor environmental behaviour can affect a firm: it could result in fines (for pollution or damages), increased liability to environmental taxes, loss in value of land, destruction of brand values, loss of sales, consumer boycotts, inability to secure finance, loss of insurance cover, contingent liabilities, law suits, and damage to corporate image.

Triple Bottom Line

The triple bottom line (TBL) is sometimes summarised as People, Planet, and Profit. It consists of:

- **Social justice**: fair and beneficial business practices toward labour and the community and the region in which a corporation conducts its business. A TBL company conceives a reciprocal social structure in which the well being of corporate, labour and other stakeholder interests are interdependent.

- **Environmental quality**: a TBL company endeavours to benefit the natural order as much as possible, or at the least do no harm and curtail environmental impact. In this way, the company tries to reduce its ecological footprint by, among other things, carefully managing its consumption of energy and non-renewable resources, and by reducing manufacturing waste, as well as rendering waste less toxic before disposing of it in a safe and legal manner.

- **Economic prosperity**: the economic benefit enjoyed by the host society. It is the lasting economic impact the organisation has on its economic environment. Importantly, however, this is not as narrow as the internal profit made by a company or organisation.

For many years, sustainability has been seen from an environmental perspective, but now the social side of sustainability is gaining increasing importance.

Issues such as the health and safety of workers, or paying workers a fair wage, are becoming increasingly important. For example, while Apple's iPhones and iPads are becoming 'must-have' consumer items in Western countries, a number of concerns have been raised about the working conditions of the employees in China who are making them; with allegations of excessive working hours, draconian workplace rules, and workers even being urged to sign an 'anti-suicide' pledge after a series of employee deaths in 2010.

Although health and safety measures do not necessarily add value to a company in their own, they can help to protect a company against the cost of accidents which might otherwise occur.

Moreover, if a company has poor health and safety controls this might result in, amongst other things, increased sick leave amongst staff and possible compensation claims for any work-related injuries, as well as higher insurance costs to reflect the higher perceived risks within the company.

Equally, the issue of social responsibility in relation to consumers has also been highlighted in recent years. The tobacco industry and the food and drink industry have received criticism in relation to the potential harm their products may cause to consumers.

Ultimately, if consumers cease to buy a product because they are concerned about the consequences of consuming a product, that product will not be sustainable because it will not generate any sales. For example, concerns about the high level of sugar in the 'Sunny D' orange drink forced Procter & Gamble to withdraw the drink's original formulation from the market.

CASE STUDY

In 2010, BP suffered its first annual loss for nearly 20 years, following the catastrophic explosion at the Deepwater Horizon oil rig in the Gulf of Mexico which will cost it at least £25 billion. Some analysts think the total cost to shareholders could exceed £40 billion over the next ten years (2010-2020).

2010 was one of the most damaging year's in BP's history as the devastating explosion, which killed 11 workers and triggered the biggest offshore oil spill in history, shattered the company's reputation.

In February 2011, BP chief executive Bob Dudley said he was determined to see BP "emerge from this episode as a company that is safer, stronger, more sustainable, more trusted and also more valuable…2011 will be a year of recovery and consolidation as we implement the changes we have identified to reduce operational risk and meet out commitments arising from the spill. But it will also be a year in which we have the opportunity to reset the company, adjusting the shape of our business, and focus on growing value for shareholders."

Meanwhile, however, the White House oil commission into the fatal blow-out on the drilling rig in April 2010 concluded that it was 'an avoidable disaster caused in part by a series of cost-cutting decisions made by BP and its partners.'

The commission's report argued that 'systemic management failure' at BP, Halliburton and Transocean [the other companies involved with the rig] was ultimately to blame for the blow-out, and many of the poor decisions taken on the drilling rig were made in order to save time and money.

'Whether purposeful or not, many of the decisions that BP, Halliburton, and Transocean made that increased the risk of the blow-out clearly saved those companies significant time (and money)', the report said.

Moreover, investors claimed that BP executives and directors breached their fiduciary duties to the company by ignoring safety and maintenance for years before the well exploded on 20 April 2010. The investors' lawyers argued that, despite warnings about the safety of the well, BP continued to systematically cut budgets.

The investors (who had filed a claim against BP claiming diminished share value) claimed that in addition to the tragic loss of life which resulted from the blow-out, the disaster is anticipated to cost the company billions of dollars damages, permanent reputational harm and intense government scrutiny.

The claimants argued that, despite existing concerns raised by federal safety regulators, BP had cut operational costs by 15% in 2009 alone (the year before disaster). In their opinion, 'This reduction in budgets and manpower further undermined the company's ability to operate safely, as personnel were stretched even thinner, and resources that should have been devoted to maintenance, monitoring and addressing crucial safety failures in every aspect of the company's operations were diverted.'

[*Extracted from*: BP press release, *www.bp.com*, 1 February 2011; and 'BP's Pursuit of Cost-Cutting Led to Gulf Spill, Lawyers Say,' *www.bloomberg.com*. 5 February 2011]

Conversely, some companies do realise the important of responding positively to environmental issues in order to protect and sustain their brand, and they can use sustainability issues to help maintain public trust in the brand.

For example, *Toyota* responded to environmental trends by successfully launching the *Prius* hybrid car, which supplements normal fuel usage with an electric-powered engine. The battery-powered electric engine starts the car, and operates it at low speeds. At higher speeds, the car switches automatically to a conventional engine and fuel. However, this combination saves on fuel compared to conventional cars and causes less pollution.

Equally, environmental and social responsibility can provide marketing opportunities for companies, and companies can even achieve competitive advantage by addressing and accommodating their customers' ethical concerns. For example, *Innocent* drinks has built its business on corporate social responsibility ideals.

CASE STUDY

Innocent Drinks has based its business model on 'leaving things a little bit better than we found them.' The company combines a belief in product purity with eco-humanist values. It sees its ethical stance as affecting five main areas.

- **Keeping things natural** – using 100% natural ingredients and only making food that has a positive health benefit, and which is therefore free of additives, concentrates and flavourings.

- **Sustainable ingredients** – favouring suppliers that look after their environment and their workers, as certified by independent environmental and social organisations. Innocent pay a premium for fruit with the highest ethical accreditations, such as those from the Rainforest Alliance. Employees and independent auditors check standards on the farms Innocent uses.

- **Sustainable packaging** – using recycled, or renewable, material as much as possible, using the least possible amount of material per pack, using material with a low carbon footprint, using material with a widely available sustainable waste management option.

- **Sustainable production** – working with suppliers to improve water and energy efficiency, to reduce waste produced, and to increase recycling levels. Importantly, Innocent also acknowledges that the need to reduce carbon emissions and climate change is directly relevant to its business. Its current sources of banana, mango, strawberry and pineapple all fall within areas that will be significantly affected by climate change, giving Innocent a strong commercial imperative to reduce carbon emissions.

- **Sharing profits** – donating 10% of profits each year to charity, mostly to the Innocent Foundation, funding rural development projects in countries where fruit comes from, promoting sustainability and best use of these projects in these communities.

Given that firms are more likely to embrace sustainability if it brings them a financial benefit, it is important to note that introducing better environmental management systems can create 'win – win' situations. For example, if introducing environmental management systems can allow a company to continue to produce the same amount of product by using less resources, and generating less waste, this is both economically efficient, and also beneficial from an environmental and ecological perspective. In this context, the cost savings more efficient resource usage, and waste minimisation can be substantial.

For example, by 2005, DuPont used 7% less energy than it did in 1990, despite producing 30% more goods – thereby saving $2 billion.

Sustainability and strategy   5/12

The challenge sustainability presents for decision-makers in organisations comes in incorporating longer-term (sustainability) issues alongside short-term issues. If they focus too much on short-term issues at the expense of the longer-term this undermine a company's long-term reputation and prospects.

Although the challenges facing companies will vary according to their specific circumstances the following summarises some possible issues to consider in relation to sustainability and the triple bottom line:

Environmental quality

- Resource usage (scope for using renewable rather than finite resources)

- Risks of contamination

- Levels of waste

- Carbon dioxide emissions

- Scope to use locally sourced inputs to reduce carbon footprint involved in transporting raw materials in

- Relations with authorities (especially if there are any legal requirements, such as planning permission for a new factory)

Social dimension

- Being seen as an attractive employer (which in turn can affect: ability to recruit high quality staff, retain staff and staff know-how, and employee motivation)

- Quality of working conditions

- Labour practices (labour/management relations, health and safety, training, diversity and opportunities (eg equal opportunities)

- Risk of accidents (and subsequent litigation against the company)

- Human rights (non-discrimination against minorities; use of child labour or forced labour; disciplinary practices, freedom for staff to belong to a union or other association)

- Relations with society: contribution to local community

- Integrity and image: not being involved with bribery and corruption, or anti-competitive prices (eg price fixing)

- Product responsibility: ensuring product's health and safety for customers, honesty in advertising and communications with consumers

Economic issues

- Business relations (security of business, relationship with banks and shareholders)
- Supplier and customer structure: quality of relationships with suppliers and customers
- Market position
- Brand name: risk to reputation and sales of negative publicity

Ethical consumerism – In relation to the sustainability of their sales, firms should also remember that, in most cases, consumers have a choice whether or not to buy their products. And individual consumers can make purchasing decisions based not only on personal interests but also the interests of society and the environment. For example, they may boycott companies whose products are made by sweatshops or child labour, choosing wherever possible fair trade products. Moreover, some customers are prepared to pay

more for products that are environmentally or socially responsible (fair trade; organic etc.) compared to cheaper, less responsibly sourced products.

However, if firms are going to portray themselves as ethical or socially responsible, for this to have any meaningful benefit, they must be genuinely committed to ethical principles, rather than just treating them as an 'ethical veneer.'

CASE STUDY

On its website (www.starbucks.com), the coffee house Starbucks tells us that, over the years, it has received input from a broad range of stakeholders that has helped the company create a holistic approach to sourcing its coffee responsibly. Starbucks is committed to continuously improving economic transparency, promoting responsible labour practices, reducing environmental impacts, and ensuring the long-term supply of its high-quality coffee. While it accepts there is much more to do, it believes it has already made a measurable impact in coffee-growing communities where it does business.

Starbuck's approach is grounded in 'Coffee and Farmer Equity' (C.A.F.E.) Practices, its comprehensive set of social, economic, environmental and quality guidelines. Farms and mills are evaluated with approximately 200 performance indicators by third-party verification organizations, overseen by Scientific Certification Systems

Starbucks complements purchases of C.A.F.E. Practices-verified coffee with third-party certified coffees grown and produced in ways that contribute to environmental preservation and/or sound production standards, including Fairtrade certified coffee and certified organic coffee.

However, alongside this commendable approach, critics present a somewhat less favourable impression of Starbucks.

Ethiopian coffee is widely recognized as one of the world's finest crops, and the coffee plantations in Ethiopia are hugely important for the future development of the country. Since 2005, the Ethiopian government has tried to support the country's farmers by trade-marking their coffee in the US market. The trademark campaign is intended to protect the product and to raise the price which farmers' earn for their coffee, thereby generating additional revenue for the national economy.

However, to the surprise of media commentators, the major opponent [of the trade-marking] has not been a bulk-buyer with a purely economic interest in Ethiopian coffee, but the world's largest premium coffee franchise, Starbucks.

The reason for the commentators' surprise was the apparent contradiction with Starbucks' policy of helping local farming communities. Moreover, once Starbuck's position in this matter became public knowledge, Starbuck's reputation as an ethically-minded company was damaged, and it was portrayed as a modern-day colonialist exploiting one of the world's poorest countries.

Short or long-term focus

Our discussion of triple bottom line stresses a key point about sustainability: that sustainability refers to the social, economic and environmental concerns of a business that aims to thrive in the **long term**. In this respect, it suggests that there is little point in a firm being profitable in the short term if it alienates customers, suppliers and/or staff. By doing so, the firm will weaken its chances of being profitable in the longer term.

However, this focus on the longer term can pose problems for the corporate decision-maker or the management accountant. Corporate reporting and performance measurement is often is biased towards the short-term. The fact that companies report their results on a yearly basis, and may be under pressure from shareholders and market analysts to deliver results, means they may be forced into measures which boosts profits in the short term, but which may create problems in the longer-term and in doing so may threaten sustainability.

Exam skills

In your exam, you may be asked to analyse or evaluate the appropriateness of a strategic option which an organisation is considering. When doing so, as well as looking at the short term financial implications of the proposal, it may also be necessary to consider how sustainable the proposal is.

Equally, you may be asked to evaluate how well a proposal fits with an organisation's objectives. Again, when considering objectives, you should be prepared to consider objectives relating to sustainability and social responsibility, as well as more narrowly defined financial or commercial objectives.

WEBLINK – CIMA article on sustainability and incorporating ethics into strategy: www.cimaglobal.com/Thought-leadership/Research-topics/Sustainability/incorporating-ethics-into-strategy

CIMA's research article (from 2010) concluded that having strong ethical principles can add significant value to a brand, whereas failing to have such principles can undermine a company's long-term prospects, as well as causing social, economic and environmental damage.

CIMA's research suggests that companies which demonstrate high ethical standards often find that these standards translate into bottom line benefits.

However, CIMA's report also highlighted that companies need good quality **management information** about social, environmental and ethical performance if they are going to monitor the environmental and social impacts of their operations.

Equally, the report warned that company reporting on sustainability needs to provide hard evidence of the actions companies are taking to address the negative effects of their operations. In this respect, it is not sufficient for companies simply to pay lip service to the 'green agenda'.

WEBLINK – CIMA article on corporate sustainability practices: www.cimaglobal.com/en-gb/Thought-leadership/Research-topics/Sustainability/ Evolution-of-corporate-sustainability-practices/

In a second report (also from 2010), produced in conjunction with the Chartered Accountants of Canada (CICA) and the American Institute of CPAs, CIMA examined the key characteristics of business sustainability and the level of the finance function's involvement in corporate sustainability initiatives.

The report identified that ten elements are integral to embedding sustainability within organisations, and noted that finance and accounting functions can play an important role in a number of them.

Strategy and oversight

- Board and senior management commitment
- Understanding and analysing the key sustainability drivers for the organisation
- Integrating the key sustainability drivers into the organisation's strategy

Execution and alignment

- Ensuring that sustainability is the responsibility of everyone in the organisation (and not just of a specific department)
- Breaking down sustainability targets and objectives for the organisation as a whole into targets and objectives which are meaningful for individual subsidiaries, divisions and departments
- Ensuring that processes are in place to enable sustainability issues to be taken into account, clearly and consistently, in day-to-day decision-making
- Extensive and effective sustainability training

Performance and reporting

- Including sustainability targets and objectives in performance appraisal
- Champions to promote sustainability and celebrate success
- Monitoring and reporting sustainability performance

One of the key messages here is that sustainability is becoming an increasingly integral part of business strategy, and therefore companies need to consider sustainability issues when developing and implementing strategic plans.

6.6 Environmental Management Accounting (EMA)

In the context of sustainability, it is also important to consider the concept of Environmental Management Accounting (EMA).

The UN Expert Working Group on EMA (2001) defined the concept as:

> 'the identification, collection, analysis and use of the two following metrics: (i) physical information on the use, flows and fates of energy, water and materials (including wastes), and (ii) money metrics on environmentally-related costs, earnings and savings'

Environmental management accounting (and sustainability accounting and reporting more generally) can be seen as an important subset of accounting and reporting that records, analyses and reports environmentally and socially-induced financial impact of a company's activities.

Therefore, in the context of business strategy, it is important that management accountants look at the potential environment and social impact of a strategic option, as well as considering only the short-term, financial consequences.

However, many companies are not able to identify their environmental or social costs accurately, and therefore they are also unable to identify the potential benefits and savings from environmental and social performance.

In the context of increased demands for environmental protection and corporate social responsibility, this highlights the need for effective managerial accounting systems which consider a company's environmental and social impacts.

Section summary

Corporate social responsibility is an organisation's obligation to maximise shareholder benefits whilst minimising the negative effects of its actions. It is not the same as ethical behaviour although the two are related. Social audits are sometimes carried out by firms that have social responsibility built into their corporate philosophy.

The issues of environmental and social sustainability are becoming increasingly important in strategic decision making.

7　Not-for-profit organisations

Introduction

Not-for-profit organisations have their own objectives, generally concerned with **efficient use of resources** in the light of specified targets.

7.1 Voluntary and not-for-profit sectors

Although most people would know one if they saw it, there is a surprising problem in clearly defining what counts as a **not-for-profit (NFP) organisation**. Local authority services, for example, would not be setting objectives in order to arrive at a profit for shareholders, but nowadays they are being increasingly required to apply the same disciplines and processes as companies which are oriented towards straightforward profit goals.

KEY TERM

Bois proposes that a NOT-FOR-PROFIT ORGANISATION be defined as: ' ... an organisation whose attainment of its prime goal is not assessed by economic measures. However, in pursuit of that goal it may undertake profit-making activities.'

This may involve a number of different kinds of organisation with, for example, differing legal status – charities, trade unions, and government departments providing services such as education, health, leisure or public utilities such as water or road maintenance.

Business strategy issues are just as relevant to a not-for-profit organisation as they are to a business operating with a profit motive. The tasks of setting objectives, developing strategies and controls for their implementation can all help in improving the performance of charities and NFP organisations. Whilst the basic principles are appropriate for this sector, differences in how they can be applied should not be forgotten.

7.2 Objectives

Objectives will not be based on profit achievement but rather on achieving a **particular response** from various target markets. This has implications for reporting of results. The organisation will need to be open and honest in showing how it has managed its budget and allocated funds raised. **Efficiency and effectiveness** are particularly important in the use of donated funds, but there is a danger that resource efficiency becomes more important than the service effectiveness.

Here are some possible objectives for a NFP organisation.

(a)　Surplus maximisation (equivalent to profit maximisation)
(b)　Revenue maximisation (as for a commercial business)
(c)　Usage maximisation (as in leisure centre swimming pool usage)
(d)　Usage targeting (matching the capacity available, as in a hospital service)
(e)　Full/partial cost recovery (minimising subsidy)
(f)　Budget maximisation (maximising what is offered)
(g)　Producer satisfaction maximisation (satisfying the wants of staff and volunteers)
(h)　Client satisfaction maximisation (the police generating the support of the public)

There are a number of different **audiences** which NFP organisations may serve.

(a)　A **target public** is a group of individuals who have an interest or concern about the charity.
(b)　Those benefiting from the organisation's activities are known as the **client public**.
(c)　Relationships are also vital with **donors and volunteers** from the general public.
(d)　There may also be a need to lobby **local and national government** and businesses for support.

The objective setting process must **balance** the interests and concerns of these audiences, which may result in a range of objectives, rather than a single overriding one. In order to allow for this balance to be

achieved, NFPs may allow wide **participation** in the objective setting process, or, indeed, may have it enforced upon them by, for example, legal requirements for consultation with interested parties, or constitutional provision for a range of constituencies to be heard.

NFP objective-setting has other complications:

(a)   Providers of funds have potentially greater influence than members or beneficiaries and may have different objectives.

(b)   There is no overall profit motive. There is often a conflict between delivering a profit or achieving social responsibilities.

(c)   Priorities may change rapidly as circumstances change, as for instance when a natural disaster occurs or a government changes.

(d)   All the factors above make it easier for powerful insiders to pursue their personal objectives for power or recognition.

Charities and NFP organisations often deal more with **services and ideas** than products.

(a)   **Appearance** needs to be business-like rather than appearing extravagant.

(b)   **Process** is increasingly important, for example, the use of direct debit to pay for council tax, reduces administration costs leaving more budget for community services.

(c)   **People** need to offer good service and be caring in their dealings with their clients.

(d)   **Distribution channels** are often shorter with fewer intermediaries than in the profit making sector. Wholesalers and distributors available to business organisations do not exist in most non-business contexts.

(e)   **Promotion is usually dominated by personal selling**. Advertising is often limited to public service announcements due to limited budgets. Direct marketing is growing due to the ease of developing databases. Sponsorship, competitions and special events are also widely used.

(f)   **Pricing** is probably the most different element in this sector. Financial price is often not a relevant concept. Rather, opportunity cost, where an individual is persuaded of the value of donating time or funds, is more relevant.

Controlling activities is complicated by the difficulty of judging whether **non-quantitative objectives** have been met. For example assessing whether the charity has improved the situation of client publics is difficult to research. Statistics related to product mix, financial resources, size of budgets, number of employees, number of volunteers, number of customers serviced and number and location of facilities, are all useful for this task.

Section summary

Not-for-profit organisations do not have profit as their primary motive, but are increasingly required to apply the same disciplines and processes as a profit orientated company. Business strategy is equally relevant to these organisations to help them improve performance, however the differing objectives set by such organisations mean that the concepts will be differently applied.

8   The public sector

Introduction

In the public sector, resources (not sales) are the limiting factor. The rationing of health care typifies the problems faced.

In a business, the level of sales often indicates the level of activity (number of goods produced). Effectively, sales are a limiting factor, and once the level of activity has been determined, resources are obtained to satisfy this demand.

While sales of services can be used in some public sector organisations as the starting point of the budgeting process, this cannot be the case when the services are not sold but are provided to meet social needs. Instead **resources are the limiting factor**, since demand is potentially limitless. Many of the concerns about rationing health care suggest precisely this problem.

8.1 'Care in the Community'

The Audit Commission in the UK published some guidelines for budgeting, in situations where levels of service provision must be matched to available resources. An example is a guideline for budgeting for local authority support for community care. Rather than look after the elderly, disabled or mentally ill in institutions, care is delivered at the patient's home. How do authorities deal with the delivery of services to dependent elderly people?

A basic problem with this sort of budget in the public sector is to find the starting point.

(a)   Planners can **budget for a set level of service provision**. The budget is based upon the number of home helps currently available and the number of day care centres to be run.

(b)   Planners can identify the **needs of service recipients**. These can be classified and ranked to establish various levels of possible demand for the service.

Relevant factors need to be identified.

- The **needs** of the local dependent elderly population
- The various **alternative policies** by which these needs can be met
- The **resources actually available**
- The amount of those resources which are already **committed**

Identifying the needs means that the level of service can be tailored more accurately to the requirements of the clients.

8.2 Responsibility accounting in health care

An example of the problems in introducing management accounting techniques to achieve the objectives of public sector stakeholders is offered by the extension since the 1970s of **responsibility accounting** to the UK National Health Service (NHS). Responsibility accounting aims to devolve budget and expenditure control to decision-makers, such as doctors.

The NHS internal market is now in place with purchasers arranging contracts with hospitals. Trust hospitals now work autonomously.

In the NHS, the introduction of management accounting techniques based on private sector practice is problematic for the following reasons.

(a)   Although NHS self-governing hospital trusts are financially autonomous, they are not profit-making businesses. The purpose of the internal market is to **allocate resources efficiently**, not to make a profit.

(b)   Many doctors resent managerial and financial involvement in medical decisions. NHS managers may seek the cheapest option rather than what the doctor considers most effective.

(c)   The level of paperwork involved in implementing the system causes a lot of resentment.

(d)   The budgetary system is often conducted on an annual basis. Strategic planning, as we have seen, should be a long-term process.

(e)   There is political interference – after all, the NHS survives on tax-payers' money and NHS funding decisions are a matter of public policy.

What is undeniably true is that there is an increased emphasis on **performance**. Schools and hospitals publicise **league tables** on certain key criteria.

(a)   Critics argue these ignore the real differences in the schools' environments (eg a school's exam success might depend on the quality of its pupils and the relative social deprivation of its catchment area).

(b)   Supporters argue that league tables give clients of services a better choice and concentrate managers' minds on improving performance.

Section summary

In a private sector commercial business, sales are the limiting factor. In most public sector organisations, services are provided to meet social needs rather than sold. This means demand is potentially limitless, and so the limiting factor is resources. Public sector business strategies must therefore look to make the best use of the resources available to them.

Chapter Roundup

✓   Mission guides strategic decisions and provides value and direction. Mission statements are formal documents that state an organisation's mission. They can play an important role in the strategic planning process, but have also been criticised as being over-generalised, ignored in practice, static/obsolete and little more than PR.

✓   **Goals** and **objectives** derive from and support the mission. The relationship can be modelled as a pyramid with the mission at the top. Where there are lots of objectives, problems of ranking and trade-off can occur. Critical success factors can be used as an alternative to the pyramid structure.

✓   Objectives may be short-term or long-term and there may be a **trade-off** between the two. This occurs when they are in conflict or resources are scarce.

✓   Organisations have many **stakeholders.** Conflict between stakeholder groups is likely, due to the wide range of specific interests held by each group. Firms can make strategic gains from managing stakeholder relationships to create positive, productive and long-lasting relationships.

✓   Organisations are coming under increasing pressure to adapt an ethical approach to stakeholders, the environment, the disadvantaged, and their dealings with unethical companies or countries. To be effective, a code of ethics must be incorporated into the entire culture of the organisation.

✓   Corporate social responsibility is an organisation's obligation to maximise shareholder wealth whilst minimising the negative effects of its actions. It is not the same as ethical behaviour although the two are related. Social audits are sometimes carried out by firms that have social responsibility built into their corporate philosophy.

✓   The issues of environmental and social sustainability are becoming increasingly important in strategic decision making.

✓   Not-for-profit organisations do not have profit as their primary motive, but are increasingly required to apply the same disciplines and processes as a profit orientated company. Business strategy is equally relevant to these organisations to help improve their performance, however the different objectives set by such organisations mean that the concepts will be differently applied.

✓   In a private sector commercial business, sales are the limiting factor. In most public sector organisations, services are provided to meet social needs rather than sold. This means demand is potentially limitless, and so the limiting factor is resources. Public sector business strategies must therefore look to make the best use of the resources available to them.

Further reading

Although this Text is designed to provide you with comprehensive coverage of the material you need for your E3 exam, if you wish to do some further reading around the areas of business strategy covered in this chapter, we recommend the following texts:

Johnston, G., Scholes, K. & Whittington, R. (2011) – Exploring Corporate Strategy, (9th ed), Harlow, FT/Prentice Hall

Lynch, R. (2011) – Strategic Management (6th ed), Harlow, FT/Prentice Hall

Quick Quiz

1   What are the four elements in the Ashridge College definition of 'mission'?

P ....

S ....

P ....

V ....

2   Mission statements have a standard format.

☐ True

☐ False

3   Distinguish between critical success factors, key tasks and priorities

4   Fill in the gaps: 'Most organisations set themselves quantified (1) .... in order to enact the corporate (2) .... Many objectives are:

(3)   S ....

(4)   M ....

(5)   A ....

(6)   R ....

(7)   T ....

5   What is corporate social responsibility?

6   As part of a restructuring exercise, AB Co will have to make some of its staff redundant. How should AB Co's staff be classified in terms of their levels of power and interest in relation to this decision?

A   Low power; low interest

B   Low power; high interest

C   High power; low interest

D   High power; high interest

7   How do questions of sustainability tie in with the long/short term debate?

8   You have been working with the Finance Director preparing a presentation for your company's shareholders. You have noticed that the FD's presentation makes the company's performance look significantly more favourable than it actually is, because the FD has excluded the results from a poorly performing division from the presentation.

When you mentioned this omission to the FD, he replied that he was already aware of it, and he had deliberately chosen to exclude the division's results.

Which fundamental ethical principle is being threatened here?

Answers to Quick Quiz

1   Purpose

      Strategy

      Policies and standards of behaviour

      Values

2   False. Although the four elements of the Ashridge model are a good basis, there is no standard format for a mission statement.

3   Critical success factors (CSFs) 'are those factors on which the strategy is fundamentally dependent for its success', and at which an organisation must excel to outperform its competitors.

      Key tasks are what must be done to ensure each critical success factor is achieved.

      Priorities indicate the order in which tasks are achieved.

4   (1) objectives (2) mission (3) specific (4) measurable (5) attainable (6) results-orientated (or realistic) (7) time bounded

5   Corporate social responsibility is an organisation's obligation to maximise positive stakeholder benefits while minimising the negative effects of its actions.

6   B   The staff will have a high level of interest in the decision (because it directly affects them) but it is likely that they will only have a low level of power to be able to influence it; not least because they don't appear to be able to prevent the redundancies from occurring.

7   Issues of sustainability challenge an organisation to look at the longer-term consequences of its actions rather than just the short term financial impact. Some decisions that are taken from an ecological sustainability standpoint may have an impact on short term performance (such as the decision to invest in a new recycling process) but the longer term consequences should also be considered in the investment decision.

8   Integrity.

      The FD appears to be deliberately presenting incomplete information in order to make the company's performance look better than it is (which is misleading to the shareholders).

Answer to Questions

2.1   Stakeholder influences

Accountants have divided loyalties – to their firm, and to their profession.

The Technical Department will almost certainly resist such a change, as the proposals devalue audit to being one of many business services to management. An audit is undertaken for the benefit of shareholders, not the company management. The Technical Department (the firm's technostructure) is also powerful as enforcement of the standards it will suggest should reduce professional negligence costs. The technostructure will thus exert a powerful influence over the strategy and business practices. External influences include professional associations which have a technostructural influence on the profession as a whole. The marketing manager may also be misled as to the degree to which customers want a 'one-stop shop' for accounting and advertising services. Perhaps he is overestimating the power of this factor in the external coalition.

Now try this question from the Exam Question Bank	Number	Level	Marks	Time
	Q2	Examination	25	45 mins

STRATEGY DEVELOPMENT AND STRATEGIC OPTIONS

Part B

STRATEGIC DECISION MAKING

 An organisation needs to use the information it gathers about its strategic position to inform its strategic options (Sections 1 and 2)

Gap analysis (Section 3) allows an organisation to compare its expected performance against its objectives. However, the effectiveness of gap analysis depends on an organisation's ability to forecast its performance in the future (Section 4).

Often information about the environment is uncertain, and can be incomplete or even ambiguous. This makes strategic decision making a complicated process.

You also need to remember that environmental changes, in any given situations, can have an impact on corporate appraisal, particularly in relation to the opportunities and threats facing an organisation.

A number of the topics covered in this chapter (for example, scenario planning and foresight) are ways organisations try to include some of the uncertainty they face in their strategic planning (Sections 5 and 6).

Despite this uncertainty, gathering strategic intelligence (Section 8) remains a very important part of strategic planning.

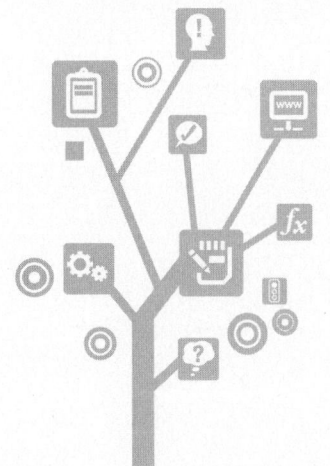

3

topic list	learning outcomes	syllabus references	ability required
1 Relating the organisation to its environment	A 1 (a); C 1 (a)	C 1 (ii)	Evaluate
2 Environmental information and analysis	A 1 (a); C 1 (a)	C 1 (ii)	Evaluate
3 Gap analysis	C 1 (a); C 2 (d)	C 1 (ii)	Evaluate
4 Forecasting	C 1 (a); C 2 (d)	C 1 (vi), C 2 (ii)	Evaluate
5 Scenario planning	C 1 (a); C 2 (d)	C 1 (v),(vi), C 2 (ii)	Evaluate
6 Foresight	C 1 (a); C 2 (d)	C 1 (vi), C 2 (ii)	Evaluate
7 Game theory	C 1 (a) ; C 2 (d)	C 1 (vii)	Evaluate
8 Strategic intelligence	C 1 (a)	–	Evaluate

1　Relating the organisation to its environment　　　5/11

Introduction

An important part of developing a strategy is analysing an organisation's position in relation to its external environment.

Organisations exist within an environment which strongly influences what they do and whether they survive and develop. Strategic planners must take account of potential environmental impacts in order to produce plans that are realistic and achievable. Where international or even global operations are undertaken, it is important to understand that there may be important differences between the environments present in the various regions and countries involved.

The environment of an organisation is everything outside its boundaries. It may be segmented according to the diagram below.

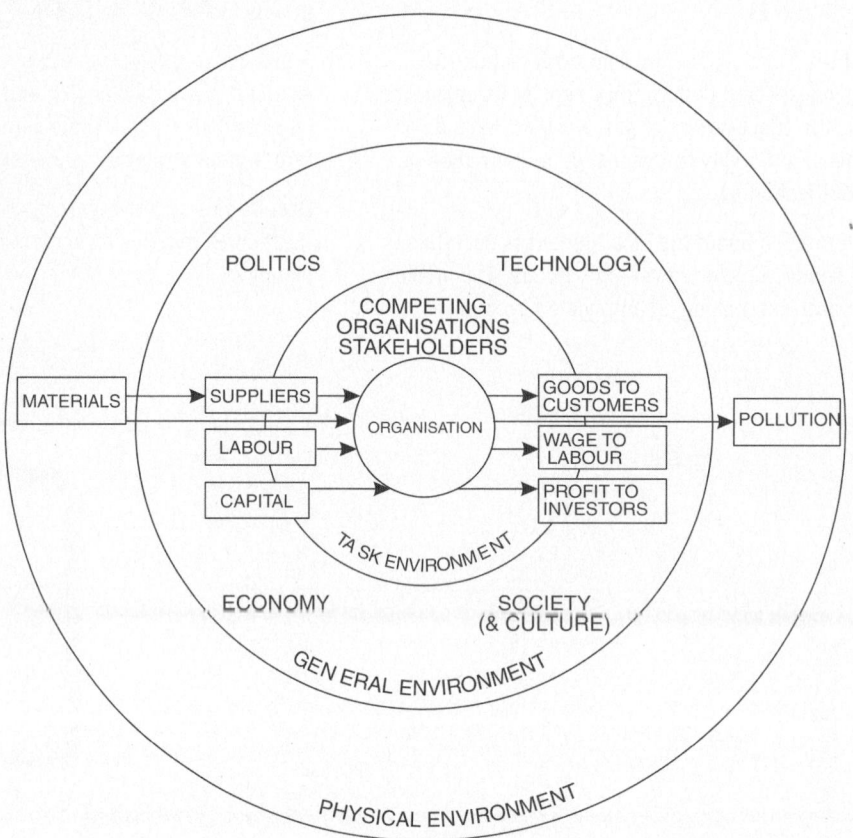

KEY TERMS

The GENERAL ENVIRONMENT covers all the political/legal, economic, social/cultural and technological (**PEST**) influences in the countries an organisation operates in.

The TASK ENVIRONMENT relates to factors of particular relevance to a firm, such as its competitors, customers and suppliers of resources.

The PEST model is covered in the syllabus for E2, and is therefore considered to be assumed knowledge for E3. A brief summary of the PEST model is provided in the Introductory chapter at the start of this Study Text, but you should refer to the E2 Study Text for more details about the way PEST factors can affect strategic business decisions.

The PEST model is often used in environmental analysis, although PEST is sometimes expanded to PESTEL. Increasing public concern for the natural environment and issues around sustainability in recent years have led to the inclusion of a second 'E' in the mnemonic, to stand for environment. Legal matters can also be considered separately from the political heading – this is the 'L' in PESTEL.

Understanding the environment is an important part of the strategic planning process. Identifying opportunities and threats is part of the corporate appraisal (**SWOT analysis**) which firms adopting a rational strategy process will prepare before generating their strategic options.

 SWOT analysis is another model we revisited briefly in the Introductory chapter because it is deemed to be assumed knowledge brought forward from E2.

SWOT analysis is an important management tool because it not only helps an organisation establish its current strategic position but also encourages the organisation to start thinking about the strategic choices it faces – for example, what opportunities might be available which would help the organisation build on its strengths or address its weaknesses.

1.1 Environmental fit

One approach to strategy is to seek **environmental fit**, relating a company to its environment.

Any strategy is made in conditions of **partial ignorance**. The environment is a major cause of such 'ignorance'.

(a)   It contains **opportunities and threats** which may influence the organisation's activities and may even threaten its existence.

(b)   The environment is sometimes so **varied** that many organisations will find it difficult to discern its effects on them. (Note the link here back to the ideas of 'chaos' and 'complexity' which we discussed in Chapter 1).

(c)   Firms can conduct **audits** to identify which of the many different sorts of environmental factors have had a significant influence. (Note: When we are talking about environmental fit and environment factors, we are referring to the business environment in which an organisation operates – in effect, all the PEST factors. We are not simply talking about the physical or 'green' environment (and, for example, issues about sustainability and pollution).

(d)   Environmental conditions change. Consequently it is important that organisations have an on-going process of **environmental scanning** to look for emerging opportunities and threats in the environment. In this respect, environmental analysis will be a key part of an emergent approach to strategy.

1.2 Complexity and dynamism

Johnson, Scholes and Whittington (in *Exploring Corporate Strategy*) contrast the concepts of **environmental complexity** (how many influences there are and the inter-relationships between them) and **environmental dynamism** (the rate of change).

Together, complexity and dynamism create **uncertainty**.

 Section summary

Analysing an organisation's position in relation to its external environment is an important part of strategy development. Strategists need to recognise potential impact the complexity and uncertainty in the environment could have on strategic decisions.

2 Environmental information and analysis

Introduction

An organisation's response to its environment is influenced by environmental complexity and its dynamism. The value of forecasts varies according to these factors.

KEY TERM

UNCERTAINTY is 'The inability to predict the outcome from an activity due to a lack of information about the required input/output relationships or about the environment within which the activity takes place.'

(CIMA Official terminology)

2.1 Environmental analysis and uncertainty

One way of identifying the environmental factors which have a significant influences on an organisation's development, or its performance in the past, is by conducting an **audit of environmental influences**.

Strategic decisions are made in partial ignorance, as we have seen, because the environment is **uncertain**. As we mentioned earlier, uncertainty arises from the **complexity and dynamism** of the environment.

(a)   **Complexity** arises from:

(i)   The **variety of influences** faced by the organisation. The more open an organisation is, the greater the variety of influences. The greater the number of markets the organisation operates in, the greater the number of influences to which it is subject.

(ii)   The amount of **knowledge** necessary. All businesses need to have knowledge of the tax system, for example, but only pharmaceuticals businesses need to know about mandatory testing procedures for new drugs.

(iii) The **interconnectedness** of environmental influences. Importing and exporting companies are sensitive to exchange rates, which themselves are sensitive to interest rates. Interest rates then influence a company's borrowing costs.

(b)   **Dynamism**. Stable environments are unchanging. Dynamic environments are in a state of change. The computer market is a dynamic market because of the rate of technological change, for example. Shortening product life cycles are a feature of dynamic environments, but as product life cycles become shorter, it becomes harder for businesses not only to predict future sales accurately but also to recoup investments in major research and development projects.

Question 3.1	Contrasting environment

Learning outcome A1(a)

Analyse the environments of the two situations below according to the criteria given above.

(a)   A new product has just been introduced to a market segment. It is proving popular. As it is based on a unique technology, barriers to entry are high. The product will not be sold outside this market segment.

(b)   A group of scientists has recently been guaranteed, by an EU research sponsoring body, funds for the next ten years to investigate new technologies in the construction industry, such as 'smart materials' (which respond automatically to weather and light conditions). This is a multi-disciplinary project with possible benefits for the construction industry. A number of building firms have also guaranteed funds.

The implication is that the type of business strategy adopted, and indeed the approach to making business strategy, will depend on the type of environment the firm inhabits.

2.2 Impact of uncertainty

If an organisation is operating in a highly uncertain environment, this will affect its strategy.

- **The planning horizon will be shortened** because the uncertainty will mean that management will not dare plan too far ahead.

- **Strategies may be more conservative** because management are unlikely to risk anything new. However, the counter argument to this is that management may want to try something new, because the uncertainty could mean that the existing strategies will no longer work.

- **Emergent strategies may be encouraged**, instead of planned strategies. Advocates of emergent strategies argue they are more appropriate to periods of uncertainty because of their adaptability to changing circumstances.

- **Increased information requirements**. Management will require more regular information to allow them to monitor and assess the changing conditions. Uncertainty will make forecasting harder, so management will need more information to gauge their strategic position.

- **Firms may follow multiple strategies**. Firms may respond to risk and uncertainty by trying to develop a number of alternative options. For example, in the current climate of uncertainty surrounding oil reserves and production, oil firms may try to develop multiple sources of oil around the world, to avoid being dependent on a particular region or a particular extraction technology.

 It is worth considering the links between the ideas of uncertainty and developing multiple strategy options and the techniques of real options and investment appraisal covered in the Financial Strategy paper F3. The Real option behaviours we will look at in section 2.3 below are modelled on the behaviours of investors in derivative markets.

2.3 Real options

Options theory can be applied to strategic decisions. There are three common types of 'real option' which are relevant to strategic projects: the option to make follow-on investments, the option to abandon a project, the option to wait.

- The **option to make follow-on investments**

   Traditional net present value (NPV) analysis means that an organisation will invest in a project if it makes a positive return on the initial investment for that project. However, there may be occasions when that initial project does not make a positive return by itself but it opens up other potential projects which the organisation can then take advantage of.

   If these subsequent projects make a positive return, and the organisation can only invest in them by undertaking the initial project, then the organisation should invest in the initial project – although conventional NPV analysis suggest it shouldn't. In this respect, NPV is not a sufficient basis for making the investment decision, and to make an informed choice managers have to consider the value of keeping their options open.

 Example: follow-on investments as options

Cornseed Publishing is a publisher of study guides in a sector of the professional training market. Over the last ten years, it has built up a share of approximately 30% of its target market. The directors of the company are now considering a project which would involve producing its study guides as electronic downloads, to be called *Online Guides*. The new *Online Guides* would not simply duplicate the material in the study guides as they would involve some interactive features. However it is thought that in the future, the *Online Guides* might be developed into a more innovative fully interactive format – provisionally called *Online Tutor* – which provides students with online tutorials and seminars, and allows

them to ask questions to an online tutor. The *Online Tutor* product offering would take much more time and would require greater software know-how than is currently available.

The initial *Online Guides* project would involve employing additional staff to develop the material required for the new format. Cornseed think that their competitors are also considering similar projects.

However, one of the directors has questioned whether the project is worthwhile. It has been calculated, using the NPV method, that the *Online Guides* project as proposed has a negative net present value of $50,000. The director has challenged why Cornseed should invest in a project with a negative NPV. He argues *Online guides* which are not fully interactive are not likely to be a success. Just because our competitors are putting money into them doesn't mean we should make the same mistake.'

However, another director has pointed out that if the initial *Online Guide* project does not go ahead, Cornseed may be missing out on the opportunity to develop *Online Tutor.* This second director argues that developing the *Online Guides* will provide Cornseed with the expertise and competences which will help it pursue the follow-on option (*Online Tutor*).

The *Online Tutor* is expected to be very profitable.

Cornseed should consider the value of the follow-on investment in *Online Tutor* when evaluating the *Online Guide* project.

- The **option to abandon a project**

  Many strategic projects involve a significant capital investment up front. If the subsequent revenue streams from the project are highly uncertain, the option to abandon the project if things go wrong would be very valuable to an organisation.

  This may be particularly important for projects involving new products where their acceptance by the market in uncertain.

- The **option to wait** before making an investment

  An organisation may opt to 'wait and see' before making a decision in the expectation of gaining more relevant information which will help inform its decision. This is not simply an excuse for doing nothing. Rather, a firm's decision making could be improved by waiting and taking advantage of new information which becomes available.

  In this case, managers need to balance the potential benefits of waiting and taking advantage of the new information, with the cost of potential cash inflows foregone.

  For example, an option to wait may be particularly valuable for a mining company, which can delay the decision to start mining a deposit until the market price of the commodity is favourable.

Real options could also be used in the following situations:

Input mix options: For example, a utility company may have the option to build a new coal-fired power station or one that burns either coal or gas. The dual fuel station costs more to build. Simply applying a discounted cash flow (DCF) analysis might suggest that the coal-fired station is preferable since it can be constructed more cheaply. However, the dual plan provides more flexibility, and gives management the ability to select which fuel to use as the relative prices of coal and gas vary. Therefore the value of this operating option should be taken into account in the initial decision.

Output mix options: Whereas the previous example looks at flexibility in the inputs to a process, this one looks at flexibility in product outputs. These options are particularly valuable in industries where goods are bought in small batches, or demand is very volatile. For example, a clothing manufacturer's ability to stop producing one line of garments that has become unfashionable to quickly being producing a popular new style of garment. Although a production facility which allows this flexibility may be more expensive than a simpler facility, the flexibility may be a valuable benefit.

2.3.1 Other issues to consider

Level of uncertainty   If there is a very high degree of uncertainty surrounding a project, the more valuable the option will be, but equally the higher the cost of the option.

Duration of the option   The length of the option will affect its value to a business. A longer option will be more valuable than a shorter one, because it provides more opportunity for evaluating different outcomes.

Interest rates   The value of an 'option to wait' will be higher when interest rates are high, because the firm benefits more from delaying its initial investment expenditure.

2.4 Forecasts

Forecasting attempts to reduce the uncertainty managers face by predicting future events and quantifying their impact. In **simple/static conditions the past is a relatively good guide** to the future.

In **dynamic/complex conditions**, this is not the case though.

- **Future developments:** the past is not a reliable guide.

- Techniques such as **scenario building** are useful as they can propose a number of possible futures.

- **Complex environments** require techniques to reduce the effects of complexity on organisational structure and decision-making.

Some firms aim to deal with planning in complex environments by techniques such as scenario building.

One way organisations can use forecasting is in analysing the **planning gap**.

Section summary

The inherent uncertainty in the environment means that strategic decisions are often made in partial ignorance. This uncertainty may also encourage organisations to adopt emergent strategies rather than prescriptive strategies.

3 Gap analysis

Introduction

Gap analysis quantifies the size of the gap between the objective for the planning period and the forecast based on the extrapolation of the current situation, and current prospects.

Once they have analysed an organisation's current position, strategic planners need to think about the extent to which new strategies are needed to enable the organisation to achieve its objectives. One technique whereby this can be done is **gap analysis**.

KEY TERM

GAP ANALYSIS is 'a comparison between an entity's ultimate objective (most commonly expressed in terms of profit or ROCE) and the expected performance of projects both planned and underway. Differences are classified in a way which aids the understanding of performance, and which facilitates improvement.'

(CIMA *Official Terminology*)

KEY POINT

The **planning gap** is **not** the gap between the current position of the organisation and the desired future position. Rather, it is the gap between the position forecast from continuing with current activities, and the desired future position.

Gap analysis is based on two questions.

(a) What are the organisation's targets for achievement over the planning period?

(b) What would the organisation be expected to achieve if it 'did nothing' – ie did not develop any new strategies, but simply carried on in the current way with the same products and selling to the same markets?

This difference is the gap. **New strategies will then have to be developed which will close this gap**, in order for an organisation to be able to achieve its targets over the planning period.

'Gap analysis' is a generic term and can be used to refer to more than one basis for analysis.

- CIMA *Official Terminology* describes an analysis of existing and potential sales.

- The term is more commonly used in connection with plans for eliminating a future gap in overall performance.

We examine these two versions below, before mentioning some other possible uses of the gap analysis idea.

3.1 A forecast or projection based on existing performance: F_0 forecasts

This is a **forecast** of the company's future results assuming that it **does nothing**. For example, if the company sells ten products in eight markets, produces them on a certain quantity and type of machinery in one factory, has a gearing structure of 30% and so on, a forecast will be prepared, covering the corporate planning period, on the assumption that none of these items are changed.

Argenti identified four stages in the preparation of such a forecast.

(a) **Review** past results and analyse.

    (i) revenues into units of sale and price
    (ii) costs into variable, fixed, and semi-variable

(b) A **projection** into the future for each major item of revenue and cost should be made up to the end of the planning period.

(c) **Consider any other factors** which might significantly affect the projections. Examples are as follows.

    (i) Internal factors such as machine breakdown, strikes and so on
    (ii) External PEST factors, such as new technology or changes in the law

(d) The forecast is then finalised. The forecast allows the company no new products or markets and no other new strategies: but the purpose of the forecast and gap analysis is to determine the size of the task facing the company if it wishes to achieve its target profits.

3.1.1 Errors in the forecast

A forecast cannot be expected to guarantee **accuracy** and there must inevitably be some **latitude for error**.

(a) By estimating **likely variations**. For example, 'in 201X the forecast profit is $5 million with possible variations of plus or minus $2 million'.

(b) By providing a **probability distribution** for profits. For example, 'in 201X there is a 20% chance that profits will exceed $7 million, a 50% chance that they will exceed $5 million and an 80% chance that they will exceed $2½ million. Minimum profits in 201X will be $2 million.'

3.2 Analysing an existing gap in sales

The diagram below is adapted from the CIMA *Official Terminology*.

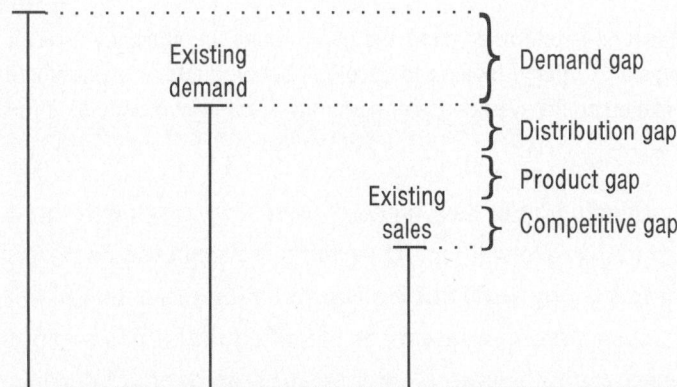

The **demand gap** is the difference between total market potential and current demand from users.

The **distribution gap**, **product gap** and **competitive gap** together make up the difference between current demand and actual sales achieved.

(a)   The **distribution gap** arises from lack of access to or utilisation of distribution channels.

(b)   The **product gap** arises from product failure or deliberate product decisions.

(c)   The **competitive gap** arises from failures of pricing or promotion.

This analysis is based on the 4Ps of the **marketing mix**. The marketing mix illustrates how an organisation needs to align **product, price, place** and **promotion** in order to market a product successfully.

3.3 The profit gap

The **profit gap** is the difference between the target profits and the profits on the forecast.

(a)   First of all the firm can estimate the effects on the gap of any projects or strategies in the pipeline. Some of the gap might be filled by a new project.

(b)   Then, if a gap remains, new strategies have to be considered to close the gap.

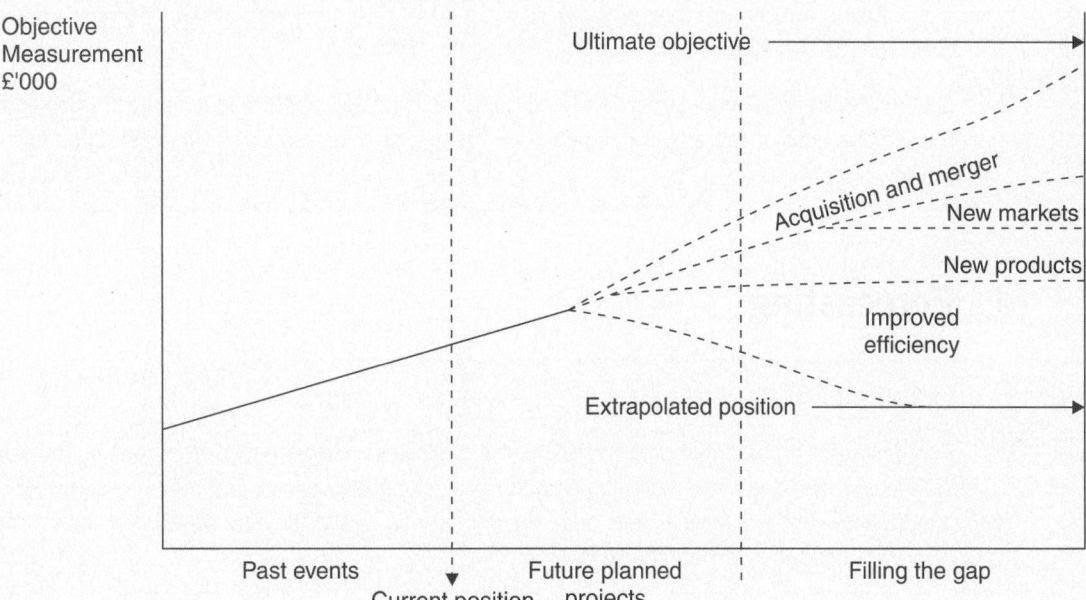

3.3.1 Filling the gap

An organisation has two broad types of strategy it can use to try to fill the gap:

(a)   **Improved efficiency**. Here an organisation seeks to boost profits by reducing costs or increasing output with the same level of inputs as a result of increased efficiency (an **efficiency drive**).

(b)   **Growth**. If an organisation is unable to close the gap through an efficiency drive, it will then have to consider an expansion strategy: looking to develop new products or expanding into new markets, or both. The organisation could even consider acquiring another company as a means of achieving the growth required.

The idea of using new products and/or new markets as sources of growth forms the basis of Ansoff's product-market matrix. We will look at Ansoff's matrix in the context of strategic choices (in Chapter 6 of this Study Text) but it is worth noting the potential link between gap analysis and the matrix. Once an organisation has identified that it has a gap, it then needs to develop potential strategies to fill the gap. Market penetration, product development, market development, and diversification are all potential strategies it could consider depending on its current strategic position and the environment in which it is operating.

Although gap analysis can be a very useful strategic tool, there could also be some problems with it.

(a)   The financial propositions may be susceptible to **inflation** – there is no easy way of dealing with this problem.

(b)   More serious, however, is risk: remember that in many cases a higher return can equate to a higher risk. In seeking to develop strategies to give a higher return, the firm may, unwittingly, be raising its **risk profile**.

(c)   In addition, gap analysis tends to give an impression that there are no restrictions on an organisation's ability to implement strategies designed to fill the gap. However, in reality this may not be the case. For example, there could be a number of different powerful stakeholder groups, with differing objectives, which could mean that the organisation has to adopt some kind of compromise, rather than simply selecting a strategy purely on the basis of its ability fill the gap.

Section summary

Gap analysis allows an organisation to compare its expected performance against its objectives. However, the effectiveness of gap analysis depends on the organisation's ability to forecast its performance in the future.

4   Forecasting

Introduction

Forecasting is an essential part of the process of strategic management. Methods include the use of statistical techniques based on extrapolation; modelling; and expert jury opinion. Sometimes individual judgement is used. The weakness of all these methods is that they are based on the assumption that the future will tend to resemble the past.

Some definitions can usefully be outlined at this stage.

A FORECAST is 'a prediction of future events and their quantification for planning purposes'.

A PROJECTION is 'expected future trend pattern obtained by extrapolation. It is principally concerned with quantitative factors, whereas a forecast includes judgements.' (CIMA *Official Terminology*)

KEY TERMS

EXTRAPOLATION is the technique of determining a projection by statistical means.

Forecasts and financial analysis are covered in more detail in the syllabus for F3 – Financial Strategy

As you know, a variety of techniques can be used in connection with forecasting, including DCF, expected values and sensitivity analysis. Different techniques are appropriate accordingly to the **degree of uncertainty** perceived in the relevant forecast.

(a) We are used to employing a **NPV** approach when the amount and timing of future cash flows are assumed to be known with something **approaching certainty**.

(b) Projects that are **repeated several times** lend themselves to the use of **expected values** and **decision trees**.

(c) **Modelling** and **sensitivity analysis** are appropriate when there is **less confidence** about the range and distribution of potential outcomes: such techniques are employed in conjunction with decision rules that reflect the degree of risk aversion of the decision makers.

(d) It is important to remember that **certainty cannot be attained in any forecast**. Major, rapid changes, such as the collapse of the dot com bubble and the oil shocks of the 1970s simply are not knowable in advance. This is perhaps the realm where **scenario planning** makes its greatest contribution.

It is also important to appreciate the implications that forecast error or uncertainty could have on decision making.

Managers can develop a reasonably reliable forecast of the future when the business environment is stable and predictable, but it is much harder to forecast successfully when the business environment is unstable or unpredictable. For example, how can a manager accurately forecast sales if there is uncertainty about whether new entrants will join the market or not? (The potential entrant may decide not to join, in which case the market will stay the same; or the new firm may decide to join. And if the entrant joins the market, will it do so in its own right – thereby creating an additional extra player in the market – or will it do so by acquiring an existing player?)

While gap analysis and rational planning approaches may be appropriate to a stable and predictable environment, they cope less well with an uncertain environment. Businesses will need to use alternative approaches to cope with uncertainty, for example scenario planning (which we will consider later in this chapter).

4.1 Statistical projections

Statistical forecasts take past data and endeavour to direct it to the future, by **assuming** that **patterns or relationships which held in the past will continue to do so**. Many statistical techniques aim to reduce the uncertainty managers face. In **simple/static conditions the past is a relatively good guide** to the future.

Statistical forecasting techniques for static conditions

(a) **Time series analysis**. Data for a number of months/years is obtained and analysed. The aim of time series analysis is to identify:

(i) Seasonal and other cyclical fluctuations
(ii) Long term underlying trends

For example, the UK's monthly unemployment statistics show a **headline figure** and the **underlying trend**.

(b) **Regression analysis** is a quantitative technique to check any underlying correlations between two variables (eg sales of ice cream and the weather). Remember that the relationship between two variables may **only hold between certain values**. (You would expect ice cream consumption to rise as the temperature becomes hotter, but there is a maximum number of ice creams an individual can consume in a day, no matter how hot it is.)

(c) **Econometrics** is the study of economic variables and their interrelationships, using computer models. Short-term or medium-term econometric models might be used for forecasting.

    (i) **Leading indicators** are indicators which change **before** market demand changes. For example, a sudden increase in the birth rate would be an indicator of future demand for children's clothes. Similarly, a fall in retail sales would be an indicator to manufacturers that demand from retailers for their products will soon fall.

    (ii) The firm needs the ability to **predict the span of time between a change in the indicator and a change in market demand**. Change in an indicator is especially useful for demand forecasting when they reach their highest or lowest points (when an increase turns into a decline or *vice versa*).

(d) **Adaptive forecasts** change in response to **recent** data.

4.1.1 Problems with statistical projections

(a) Past relationships do not necessarily hold for the future.

(b) Data can be misinterpreted, and **relationships assumed where none exist**. For example, sales of ice cream rise in the summer, and sales of umbrellas fall – the link is the weather, not any correlation between them.

(c) Forecasts do not account for special events (eg wars), the likely response of competitors and so on.

(d) The variation and depth of business cycles fluctuate.

(e) In practice statistical forecasters **underestimate uncertainty**

(f) Projections can reflect bias as outlined below:

Bias in forecasts and projections

A business forecast can become biased in two different ways:

(a) By inputting inappropriate assumptions:

    (i) having too narrow a focus so that it doesn't foresee the occurrences of future events and their relevant to the forecast

    (ii) by consistently under- or over-estimating the impact of future events

    (iii) relying too heavily on selected past events to build forecasts rather than looking at all past events

    (iv) over- or under-estimating an activity's revenue earning potential, or its associated costs

(b) Through deliberate actions within the process

    (i) the tendency to interpret information so that it supports a given belief

    (ii) having to manipulate figures so that they achieve a particular outcome (eg a manager increasing the forecast for their department to prevent subsequent budget allocations being cut)

    (iii) compensation adjustments – for example, under-forecasting in the second half of a forecast period to compensate for over-forecasting in the first half.

4.2 Judgemental forecasts

Judgemental forecasts are used principally for the long term, covering several decades. However, because of the limitations of short-term forecasting they are used for the short term too. Effectively, they are based on **hunches or educated guesses**. Sometimes, these prove surprisingly accurate. At other times they are wide of the mark.

(a)   **Individual forecasting**. A company might forecast sales on the basis of the judgement of one or more executives.

       (i)   **Advantages** are that it is cheap and suitable if demand is stable or relatively simple.

       (ii)   The **disadvantage** is that it is swayed most heavily by **most recent** experience rather than trend.

(b)   **Genius forecasting**

      An individual with expert judgement might be asked for advice. This might be the case with the fashion industry; although demand might be hard to quantify, an ability to understand the mind of the customer will be very useful.

(c)   In practice, forecasts might be prepared by an interested individual who has read the papers, say, and has promoted an item for management attention.

4.3 Consensus forecasts

4.3.1 Jury forecasts

A panel of experts and/or executives prepare their own forecasts and a consensus forecast emerges from this.

(a)   **Advantages**: expert opinions are sought and obtained.

(b)   **Disadvantages**. The jury might **dilute** the best. The **group dynamics** will interfere with the decision. Each expert might differ and, in a face-to-face situation, the more forceful or confident would win the argument.

4.3.2 Think tank

A group of experts are encouraged, in a relatively unstructured atmosphere, to speculate about future development in particular areas, and to identify possible courses of action.

(a)   **Advantages**: Provide a useful way of generating ideas and assessing their feasibility. The group nature of the activity allows views to be shaped and encourages a consensus view.

      The independence of group members, and the unstructured nature of the group, without a prescribed leader, enables free discussion and argument to take place.

(b)   **Disadvantages**. There can be a danger that think tanks (as groups of experts) may think their remit goes beyond simply forecasting and they may start planning, as sometimes happens with large organisations, including governments. However, it is important to remember that think tank proposals do not necessarily represent company, or government, policy.

4.3.3 Delphi method

This was developed to overcome problems relying on **known** experts or personalities in the jury.

(a)   Participants remain **anonymous**, known only to the organiser.

(b)   Participants respond to a **questionnaire** containing tightly-defined questions. The Delphi technique **retains anonymity**. The results are collated and statistically analysed, and are returned by the organiser to each expert. The experts respond again, having seen the opinions of the other experts.

(c)   The Delphi technique is **time consuming**.

(d).   In practice, it seems to be the case that experts are **universally optimistic**.

4.3.4 Brainstorming

A group of people from across an organisation generate ideas without any initial evaluation or criticism of those ideas. Only after the list of ideas is complete is each idea evaluated.

(a)   The lack of any initial evaluation means that everybody's ideas are heard and listed. Brainstorming differs from many other forecasting methods because it invites ideas from across all levels of an organisation; it doesn't simply rely on expects' opinions.

(b)   The initial ideas can then provoke other follow up ideas. The evaluation stage which follows the initial idea generation allows ideas to be developed and modified.

4.4 Statistical versus judgemental and consensus forecasts

David Mercer identifies the relative advantages and disadvantages of each method.

Use of forecasts	Statistical	Judgement
Changes in established patterns	Past data is no guide	Can be predicted but could be ignored
Using available data	Not all past data is used	Personal biases and preferences obscure data
Objectivity	Based on specific criteria for selection	Personal propensity to optimism/pessimism
Uncertainty	Underestimated	Underestimated, with a tendency to over-optimism
Cost	Inexpensive	Expensive

It is important to recognise that judgemental forecasting is **speculative**. However, speculation may be necessary to identify changing patterns in data, or weak signals reflecting or foreshadowing social changes.

4.5 Market forecasts and sales forecasts

Market forecasts and sales forecasts complement each other. The market forecast should be carried out first of all and should cover a longer period of time.

KEY TERM

MARKET FORECAST. This is a forecast for the market as a whole. It is mainly involved in the assessment of environmental factors, outside the organisation's control, which will affect the demand for its products/services.

(a)   Components of a market forecast.

    (i)   The **economic review** (national economy, government policy, covering forecasts on investment, population, gross national product, and so on).

    (ii)   **Specific market research** (to obtain data about specific markets and forecasts concerning total market demand).

    (iii)   Evaluation of **total market demand** for the firm's and similar products (for example, profitability and market potential).

(b)   **Sales forecasts** are estimates of sales (in volume, value and profit terms) of a product in a future period at a given marketing mix.

4.5.1 Research into potential sales

KEY TERM

SALES POTENTIAL is an estimate of the part of the market that is within the possible reach of a product.

Factors governing sales potential

- The price of the product
- The amount of money spent on sales promotion
- How essential the product is to consumers
- Whether it is a durable commodity whose purchase is postponable
- The overall size of the possible market
- Competition (or potential competition) in the market

Whether sales potential is worth exploiting will depend on the cost which must be incurred to realise the potential.

4.6 Example

Market research has led a company to the opinion that the sales potential of product X is as follows.

	Sales value	Contribution earned before selling costs deducted	Cost of selling
either	$100,000	$40,000	$10,000
or	$100,000	$44,000	$15,000

In this example, it would not be worth spending an extra $5,000 on selling in order to realise an extra sales potential of $10,000, because the net effect would be a loss of $(5,000 – 4,000) = $1,000.

Section summary

A forecast is a prediction of future events and their quantification for planning purposes. Be aware, however, that forecasts are susceptible to uncertainty and bias.

5 Scenario planning   9/10

Introduction

Most organisations are faced with great environmental complexity. Scenario planning is a technique to help enable them to allow for different possibilities, and be aware of the range of plausible alternatives.

According to *Johnson, Scholes and Whittington* scenario planning involves:

- Building plausible views about how the business environment of an organisation might develop in the future…

- …based on sets of key drivers for change about which there is a high level of uncertainty.

As with other areas of strategic management, we have to distinguish between the decision making process and the content of the decision itself. For example, it is quite possible that a decision to launch a new product could have been taken as a result of any number of strategic decision processes, for example by rational planning, visionary decision-making or incrementalism.

KEY TERM

A SCENARIO is 'an internally consistent view of what the future might turn out to be'.

In addition to their usefulness in providing some guidance in strategic planning, scenarios are also valuable in that preparing and updating them forces the managers at the strategic apex to **look carefully**

at the business environment and to monitor developments within it. This can be particularly important (and useful) in the context of rapidly changing environments.

5.1 Macro scenarios

Macro scenarios use macro-economic or political factors, creating alternative views of the future environment (eg global economic growth, political changes, interest rates). Macro scenarios were developed because the activities of oil and resource companies (which are global and at one time were heavily influenced by political factors) needed techniques to deal with uncertainties.

5.1.1 Steps in scenario planning

There is no one single way to construct a scenario. However, the ten steps which *Schoemaker* describes are a good illustration of how a scenario could be created.

 **Define the scope.** The scope should be defined with reference to time frame involved, products considered and markets considered.

 **Identify the major stakeholders** that drive change or affect the industry (within the scope of the scenario identified in step 1).

 **Identify the basic trends** that affect the industry and the business environment.

 **Identify the key areas of uncertainty** and their drivers. Uncertainties in scenario planning should be viewed as future possibilities. They could be based upon the political/legal, economic, social/cultural and technological (PEST) factors identified through environmental analysis, and also an organisation's own competencies and capabilities.

 **Construct initial scenarios** based on the key areas of uncertainties. The scenarios should be created by shaping the key areas of uncertainty (step 4) into coherent themes.

 **Check for consistency** and plausibility. In other words, re-examine the scenarios to assess whether they make sense. For scenario planning to be useful, the scenarios presented must be able to happen, and in the timescale identified by the scope of the scenario.

 **Develop learning scenarios.** At this stage, the initial frameworks identified in step 5 should be expanded into full descriptions of the scenario as if it were actually occurring.

At this point, **senior management should become involved** in the process, and should start considering the implications of each scenario in terms of the potential impacts they could have on their business.

 **Identify research needs:** understand what additional information is required to fill in any gaps in the scenario, and obtain that information to improve the coverage given by the scenario.

 **Develop quantitative models.** This stage builds on step 7, to put together business models to forecast the effects of different scenarios on an organisation's activities and future profitability/cash flow.

 **Use scenarios to formulate competitive strategy.** The value of scenario planning process is that it assists an organisation's decision-making in times of uncertainty. The process should have exposed the key areas of uncertainty which face an organisation, and in this final stage, management should develop strategic courses of action which they can apply to each of the scenarios to deal with the uncertainties they may face.

5.1.2 Using scenarios

As well as identifying the ten steps which could be followed to create a scenario, *Schoemaker* also described a four step approach for using scenarios. This approach could be useful for an organisation looking at its strategic options.

- Develop scenarios through examining the external environment and identifying key trends and uncertainties

- Conduct industry analysis and develop strategies for each scenario, to enable the organisation to fit with those scenarios

- Compare the organisation's present competences and capabilities with the future needs identified in the alternative scenarios, and strengthen the organisation's key competences and capabilities to withstand or benefit from each of the scenarios

- As the future unfolds, and key uncertainties in the environment begin to resolve themselves, adopt the appropriate strategic option.

5.2 Industry scenarios

Porter believes that the most appropriate use for scenario analysis is if it is restricted to an industry. An **industry scenario** is an internally consistent view of an **industry's** future structure. Different competitive strategies may be appropriate to different scenarios.

The **entire range**, not the most **likely** 'future', is used to design a competitive strategy. The process is as follows.

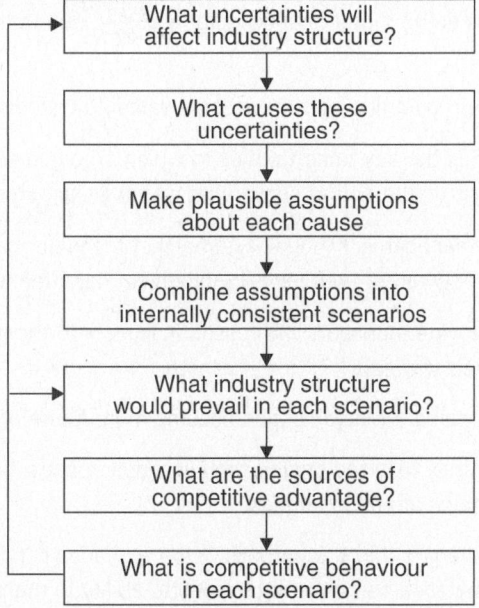

5.2.1 Using scenarios to formulate competitive strategy

(a) A strategy built in response to only **one scenario is risky**, whereas one supposed to cope with them **all might be expensive**.

(b) Choosing scenarios as a basis for decisions about competitive strategy.

Approach	Comment
Assume the most probable	This choice puts too much faith in the scenario process and guesswork. A less probable scenario may be one whose failure to occur would have the worst consequences for the firm.
Hope for the best	A firm designs a strategy based on the scenario most attractive to the firm: wishful thinking.
Hedge	The firm chooses the strategy that produces satisfactory results under all scenarios. Hedging, however, is not optimal. The low risk is paid for by a low reward.
Flexibility	A firm taking this approach plays a 'wait and see' game. It is safer, but sacrifices first-mover advantages.
Influence	A firm will try and influence the future, for example by influencing demand for related products in order that its favoured scenario will be realised in events as they unfold, or even by attempting to influence government and regulatory bodies.

5.3 Evaluating scenario planning

It is unusual for scenario planning to create an accurate prediction of what actually happens. Also, managers are often criticised for identifying trends and uncertainties from their own cultural perspectives rather than adopting a more 'universalist' perspective.

These limitations mean it could be tempting to dismiss scenario planning as a worthless exercise. Moreover, critics argue that it is unacceptably costly, due to the resources and time required to develop the scenarios.

However, scenario planning does have some valuable benefits:

- It **identifies the key uncertainties** to which an organisation is exposed, allowing it to plan for how to deal with them and to know what warning signs to look for as time goes on.

- It forces management to look externally at the wider business environment (and potential change triggers in it) rather then focusing purely on the internal operations of an organisation.

- It may provide managers with useful insights into the future of their industry which can then help shape their strategy.

  – It helps the organisation become more future orientated.

  – It may help the organisation expect surprises, because it has already started to try to anticipate uncertainties.

  We could argue that the purpose of the scenarios is not forecasting but **competence building,** with the competence being the organisation's ability to manage the future strategically.

  Developing the scenarios can also encourage communication between different managers and departments in an organisation, and this improved communication could, by itself, be beneficial to the organisation.

Note, although we have mainly described scenario planning in terms of medium to long timescales, it could also be useful in the shorter run. Encouraging managers to consider responses to the question of 'What if such and such happens' are still an important part of strategic management because they increase the organisation's ability to respond flexibly to circumstances. For example, short term scenario planning could be useful for an airline company or a tour operator in response to the question 'What if there is an outbreak of pandemic influenza, such as Swine flu?'

CASE STUDY

Leading through uncertainty

In December 2008, The McKinsey Quarterly published an online article called 'Leading through uncertainty'.

This article argued that the economic downturn in 2008 requires executives to find new ways of operating that are suited to the uncertain business environment. 'They need greater flexibility to create strategic and tactical options they can use defensively or offensively as conditions change. They need a sharper awareness of their own and their competitors' positions.

The article argues that instead of focusing on quarterly performance companies need to take a more flexible approach to planning, and should develop several coherent, multipronged strategic action plans.

These plans shouldn't just be academic exercises. Executives must be ready to pursue them as the future unfolds. Which acquisitions could be attractive, and on what terms? How much capital or management capabilities would be required? What new products would best fit different scenarios? If one or more major competitors falter, how will the company react? In which markets can it gain market share? If one or more major suppliers falter, how will the company react?

As the problems in the global credit markets create volatility and destroy current business models, organisations need to understand how their revenues, costs, profits, and cash flows will fare under different scenarios, and what the risks that they face are. This information will help executives plan for the future. Is the firm prepared for the bankruptcy of major customers? Could it halve capital spending quickly if necessary?

The value of asking these questions is that it should help organisations be better prepared and to recognise as early as possible which scenario is developing. Such knowledge is critical in a crisis, when lead times disappear quickly, and organisations can only seize the initiative if they act before everyone else understands the probable outcome.

Business intelligence is also vital, because it promotes faster, more effective decision making. Organisations can often gain insights into the potential moves of competitors by analysing news reports about their activities, reviewing stock market analysts report. They can also gather information by talking to customers and suppliers. All of this information is important. In difficult economic conditions it can make the difference between missing opportunities to buy distressed assets and leaping in to catch them. And it can also make the difference between rushing in to buy what appeared a bargain but was actually a business which should have been avoided at all costs.

Adapted from *'Leading through uncertainty'* by Lowell Bryan and Diana Farrell, December 2008
www.mckinseyquarterly.com/Strategy/

5.4 Scenario planning and the rational model?

The rational model, and prescriptive approaches to strategy, assumes there is a degree of predictability and control in the strategy process.

In other words, **a forecast** is a prediction of relevant environmental trends, and a plan is the organisation's way to **control** its own behaviour in the future.

But scenario planning takes a rather different approach to strategic planning. It suggests there is an inherent ambiguity and uncertainty in future. Such an approach suggests that successful strategy can only be developed by acknowledging this uncertainty.

Importantly, this approach also suggests that planning for the future should not be treated as a one-off activity, but should be an on-going learning proposition.

By looking at a number of **alternative** futures, scenario planning **does not pretend to predict** one of them – it is of more benefit to **management learning processes** to take a variety of perspectives into account.

This is one of the key benefits of scenario planning. By identifying a range of possible scenarios and outcomes, scenario planning can help management respond to real situations when they arise. In this way, however, scenario planning fits more comfortably with an emergent, flexible approach to strategy then the more prescriptive, rational model.

Scenario planning also encourages managers to challenge their assumptions and the ways the think about their organisations.

Exam skills

We have mentioned the impact of environmental uncertainty on strategy a number of times in this chapter.

This highlights one of the limitations of the rational model and the prescriptive approach to strategic planning: this approach assumes a degree of order and predictability is often not present in the real world.

In the exam, if you have to consider the effectiveness of an organisation's strategy, try to establish whether the organisation has a prescriptive or emergent approach to strategy. Then consider, is this suitable to the environment in which it is operating?

Section summary

Scenario planning is one of the techniques an organisation can use to help it cope with uncertainty. Scenario planning helps identify the key uncertainties to which an organisation is exposed, and can therefore help the organisation plan how to deal with some of those uncertainties.

6 Foresight

Introduction

Whereas scenario planning allows an organisation to identify the uncertainties to which it could be exposed, foresight is a process of identifying possible ways in which the future could develop.

Scenario planning, jury forecasts and the Delphi method are all ways management can attempt to get **insights into the future**, and therefore prepare itself to deal with the opportunities and threats the future holds for it.

The business environment is said to be changing at a faster pace than ever before. A number of factors - including technological change, changing lifestyles and consumer tastes, the rise of international competitors from developing countries, and regulatory upheavals - are presenting challenges to the competitive advantage of the existing dominant companies in an industry.

These changes present a challenge to business managers, in that successful management no longer simply involves reviewing current results, but also requires **visioning** the opportunities and threats that may lie ahead, to develop an organisation's strategic vision. Competitive advantage no longer simply comes from the way an organisation manages its tangible resources, but from the way it reinvents its business model before circumstances force it to do so.

In this context, senior managers must develop 'vision' and **'foresight.'** Foresight can be described as the art and science of anticipating the future. However, unlike forecasting, foresight does not attempt to predict the future, but rather to identify a range of possible outcomes based on an understanding and analysis of current trends.

Foresight can be particularly useful in relation to research and development, and in identifying new technologies which could have major long-term benefits for society in the future.

In this respect, we can identify five key aspects of the foresight process (which John Irvine and Ben Martin have called the 'five Cs'):

- **Communication**: bringing together disparate groups of people, and providing a structure in which they can communicate

- **Concentration** on the **longer term**

- **Co-ordination**: enabling different groups to align their future research and development activities

- **Consensus**: about the future directions and research priorities for an organisation

- **Commitment**. Getting those people who are responsible for translating the results of the foresight to be committed to turning them into research advances, technological developments and innovations for the benefit of society.

KEY POINT

Do not confuse 'foresight' with 'forecasting'. The two are very different concepts.

Futurists argue that the future is continuous with the present, so by analysing the present we can learn a lot about what might happen in the future.

A foresight project can be divided into four stages:

- **Monitoring** – identifying relevant current trends

- **Analysis** – understanding the drivers of change

- **Projection** – anticipating the future

- **Transformation** – drawing implications for the business based on the projected futures (in terms of new product or new business development, and in terms of strategic management).

An organisation can use of number of techniques to improve its foresight. These include:

- **Scenario planning** - We have already discussed scenario planning as a way of generating a range of possible futures derived from the current environment and the uncertainties contained within it.

- **Delphi technique** – where a number of experts are asked to independently and anonymously give their opinions and insights on a particular trend and how it may develop. These initial results are summarised and the summary is returned to the experts, who are then asked to respond again once they have seen the responses of the group. The process is repeated until a consensus is achieved.

- **Cross-impact analysis** - A basic limitation of many forecasting methods (including the Delphi technique) is that they produce only isolated forecasts. In other words, events and trends are projected one by one, without explicit reference to their possible influence on each other. However, most events and developments are connected to each other in some way, and so the interdependencies between them need to be considered to develop more consistent and accurate foresight. Cross-impact analysis addresses these interdependencies.

  Cross-impact analysis involves recording events on a matrix, and at each matrix intersection questioning what impact the event in the row occurring would have on the likelihood of the event in the column occurring. In this way, cross-impact analysis provides a more systematic way of examining a range of possible future events and outcomes.

- **Morphological analysis** – All the attributes of a product or strategy are listed as column headings in a table and then as many variations of each attribute as possible are listed in each column. In effect, a matrix of components is created. One entry from each column is then chosen to create a new mixture of components. This new mixture could represent a new product or strategy.

Morphological analysis can be used to identify a range of opportunities for an organisation which would not otherwise be obvious. Also, if an organisation carried out a morphological analysis on its competitors it may be able to identify new products or strategies that they are considering.

- **Visioning** – Visioning requires an organisation's management to develop an image of a possible or desirable future state. This image may initially be quite vague, but then needs to be developed into a more definite goal, accompanied by a strategic plan for how to achieve that goal. However, for visioning to be useful for an organisation, the image or goal articulated has to be a realistic and achievable alternative to the current state, and one which is preferable to the current state.

- **Opportunity mapping** - An opportunity map is a qualitative and experience-based analysis aimed at identifying gaps in the current user experience of an organisation's product portfolio. Opportunity maps allow an organisation to discover the desired qualities of its products, which may in turn prompt it to change its priorities and strategies in order to provide those desired qualities.

- **Trend extrapolation** - This is a projection technique based on the assumption that certain social, economic or technological trends or patterns identified in the past will manifest themselves in the future and that one can forecast future trends by observing how certain patterns have changed in the past and projecting or extrapolating those changes into the future.

- **Role-playing** – This is another technique where alternative options are generated by a group, but unlike the Delphi technique it does not use experts. A group of people are given a description of a hypothetical future situation, and told to act as they think they would if that situation was actually happening. Analysing their actions can give useful insights into what might happen if that hypothetical situation actually occurs.

However, one of the disadvantages of foresight is that it **relies on the future being shaped by actions that can be imagined now**. It cannot take account of sudden one-off events which could dramatically change the business environment. For example, a person at the start of the 20th century may not have been able to foresee that by the end of that century the world would be shaped by (among other things) television, computers, aeroplanes, the rise and the decline of communism, and atomic energy and weapons. Nevertheless, foresight can help organisations plan for the uncertainties which they will inevitably face in the future.

Section summary

Foresight is a process of identifying a range of possible outcomes which could develop, based on an understanding and analysis of current trends.

7 Game theory

Introduction

Scenario planning and foresight both highlight the inherent uncertainty in trying to predict the future.

One particular aspect of this uncertainty comes from how competitors will react to any new strategy an organisation introduces.

KEY TERM

GAME THEORY is the study of the ways in which the strategic interactions among rational players produce *strategic outcomes* which were not intended by any of the players.

7.1 Game theory approach to strategy

Game-based approaches to strategy treat **strategy as an interaction** between an organisation and its competitors. To this end, an organisation cannot simply develop its strategy by analysing its current

position in the environment, and looking at its internal resources. Instead it also needs to look at its competitors, identify their strengths and weaknesses and examine how their responses to a strategy could affect the effectiveness of that strategy. Anticipating competitors' moves is a crucial part of strategic thinking: gauging competitors' likely reactions to a strategy greatly improves an organisation's ability to choose a strategy that will be successful.

We can illustrate this with a simple example.

Example: soft drinks market

Firms A and B are the two market-leaders in the soft drinks market, and between them they hold virtually 100% of the market share. Firm A is considering launching a major advertising campaign, because its marketing director believes this will not only increase its own sales and profit, but will also reduce those of its rival (B).

However, the marketing director has not considered B's response. B has become aware of A's campaign, and is now considering launching a campaign of its own to restore its market share.

At the moment, both A and B make profits of $250m per year. A is thinking of spending $25m on its campaign, because it wants a major campaign to generate a significant increase in revenue. The anticipated increase of revenue from the campaign is $75m.

Because A and B essentially share the market, A's revenue increase is expected to come from customers who switch to it from B. Therefore, alongside A's revenue increase of $75m, B will suffer a revenue reduction of $75m.

Consequently, at the end of A's initial campaign, and in the short term, B will have suffered a reduction in profit of $75m, while A will have enjoyed an increase in profit of $50m ($75m revenue less $25m marketing cost). This is a **'win – lose'** situation, because A has 'won' while B has 'lost'.

However, B then runs a rival campaign, also costing $25m, and which also generates $75m additional revenue following the logic from before, this is now a **'lose – win'** situation because A has 'lost' and B has 'won'.

Let us look at the impact these campaigns have on A and B's profits, and the overall profits earned by the soft drink industry.

Option	A's profit	B's profit	Industry profit
Currently (no advertising)	$250m	$250m	$500m
A advertises	$300m	$175m	$475m
B then launches counter advert	$225m	$225m	$450m

Interestingly, after the advertising campaigns **both firms are worse off** than they were before, and the industry profit has reduced by the cumulative cost of the advertising campaigns. So overall the advertising campaign, created a **'lose – lose'** situation.

The figures show that although one firm can gain in the short run from a competitive strategy, in the long run both firms are likely to be better off by working together and not advertising, rather than competing with each other.

One of the assumptions of game theory is that the firms do not have any collusive agreements and do not know what the other is going to do. So A and B must select their strategies based solely on the outcome which they think is best for them regardless of the decision made by their rival.

Under these circumstances, both firms will choose to advertise, because their own campaign increases their own profit by $50m. However, collectively this course of action causes them both to lose $25m each.

In this way, game theory illustrates the key problem of **interdependent decision-making** which organisations face. Organisations need to consider the possible responses of their competitors when making strategic decisions or introducing new strategies.

Moreover, game theory also suggests that it may benefit firms to **co-operate** and **negotiate** with others in the search for optimal solutions rather than simply working alone and **competing** with all the other players in a market place. In order to create a **'win – win'** scenario, firms are likely to have to compromise and co-operate rather than always seeking to compete with each other.

In this context of networks and co-operation being preferable to constant competition, game theory can help explain the reasoning behind **strategic alliances**. Game theory also supports the cartel arrangement which the OPEC nations have established to control the production and price of oil.

CASE STUDY

GlaxoSmithKline's strategy for the developing world

GlaxoSmithKline (GSK), the world's second biggest pharmaceutical company is to radically shift its attitude to providing cheap drugs to millions of people in the developing world.

In a major change of strategy, Andrew Witty, the new head of GSK has announced he will slash prices on all medicines in the poorest countries, give back profits to be spent on hospitals and clinics and – most ground-breaking of all – share knowledge about potential drugs that are currently protected by patents.

Witty says he believes drug companies have an obligation to help the poor get treatment, and he has challenged other pharmaceutical giants to follow his lead.

Pressure on the industry has been growing over the past decade as drug companies have been repeatedly criticised for failing to drop their prices for HIV drugs while millions died in Africa and Asia. Campaigners have criticised the drug companies for defending the patents, which allow them to maintain high prices.

Campaigners have also been critical of the way drug companies have attempted to crush competition from generic manufacturers, who undercut them dramatically in countries where patents do not apply.

However, the moves which Witty has announced go a long way to addressing these concerns, and mark a significant change to the way GSK does business in the developing world.

He said that GSK will:

- Cut its prices for all drugs in the 50 least developed countries to no more than 25% of the levels in the UK and US – and less if possible and make drugs more affordable in middle-income countries such as Brazil and India

- Put any chemicals or processes over which it has intellectual property rights that are relevant to finding drugs for neglected diseases into a "patent pool", so they can be explored by other researchers

- Reinvest 20% of any profits it makes in the least developed countries in hospitals, clinics and staff

The extent of these changes is likely to stun not only critics of drug companies but also other pharmaceutical companies, who risk being left exposed.

Witty accepts that his stance may not win him friends in other drug companies, but he is inviting them to join him in an attempt to make a significant difference to the health of people in poor countries.

Witty explained that the changes reflect his desire that GSK finds solutions for developing and developed countries alike. However, he is aware that the move may raise concerns among GSK's shareholders.

"I think the shareholders understand [the need to help the developing countries as well as the richer, developed countries] and it's my job to make sure I can explain it. I think we can. I think it's absolutely the kind of thing large global companies need to be demonstrating, that they've got a more balanced view of the world than short-term returns."

The move on intellectual property, until now regarded as the sacred cow of the pharmaceutical industry, will be seen as the most radical of his proposals. "I think it's the first time anybody's really come out and said we're prepared to start talking to people about pooling our patents to try to facilitate innovation in areas where, so far, there hasn't been much progress" he said.

However, a key question now is how the other major pharmaceutical companies will respond.

(Based on an article by Sarah Boseley in guardian.co.uk, 13 February 2009. *Drug giant GlaxoSmithKline pledges cheap medicine for world's poor.*)

The value of game theory is that it highlights that both competition and co-operation can exist in an industry. An important part of an organisation's strategy is how it interacts with the other players in an industry in this respect.

Although both scenario planning and foresight aim to assist an organisation in designing their future strategies, their effectiveness will depend in part on the organisation's current strategic intelligence.

Specifically, game theory highlights the importance of **competitor analysis**, and of having an insight into competitors' strategies.

Three key purposes of competitor analysis are:

- To gain an insight into competitors' strategies and to forecast competitors' future strategies and decisions

- To predict competitors' likely reactions to a firm's own strategic decisions

- To determine how competitors' behaviour can be influenced to make it more favourable for the firm.

The second of these, in particular, has a significant overlap with the ideas of game theory.

However, critics of game theory argue that its value to strategic management is limited because it focuses on only a small fraction of the strategy process. For example, it does not provide any insight into the development of the competitive resources or capabilities of an organisation. Equally, it does not provide any useful guidance as to how to actually **implement** whatever co-operative strategies may have been negotiated.

Section summary

Game theory illustrates that an organisation cannot develop its strategy without considering the possible reactions of its competitors. Competitor reaction may mean that the outcomes of a strategy are very different to what was initially intended.

8 Strategic intelligence

Introduction

An organisation should plan to obtain **strategic intelligence** as a basis for future strategies. Internal and external databases should be maintained and the data they contain assessed and applied.

If a key task of strategic management is to ensure environmental fit, managers need a willingness and an ability to understand the environment and to anticipate future trends.

- A separate strategic planning department collects data on trends
- The marketing department identifies customer needs
- The R&D department identifies new technology
- The production department suggests process innovation

Arguably, as strategy is about the whole organisation, there are dangers in restricting the gathering of strategic information to functional departments. The whole firm needs to be aware of **strategic intelligence**.

In the Introductory chapter at the start of this text, we revised PEST analysis and Porter's five forces model. These are very useful models for environmental analysis, which in turn could help an organisation improve its knowledge of its business environment.

8.1 Creating strategic intelligence

KEY TERM

STRATEGIC INTELLIGENCE, according to *Donald Marchand*, is defined as 'what a company needs to know about its business environment to enable it to anticipate change and design appropriate strategies that will create business value for customers and be profitable in new markets and new industries in the future'.

A model of the process of creating strategic intelligence is outlined below.

Sensing	Identify appropriate external indicators of change
↓	↓
Collecting	Gather information in ways that ensure it is relevant and meaningful
↓	↓
Organising	Structure the information in the right format
↓	↓
Processing	Analyse information for implications
↓	↓
Communicating	Package and simplify information for users
↓	↓
Using	Apply strategic intelligence

Key dimensions of strategic intelligence

Information culture	What is the role of information in the organisation? Is it only distributed on a 'need to know basis' or do people have to give specific reasons for secrecy?
Future orientation	Is the focus on specific decisions and trade-offs, or a general attitude of enquiry?
The structure of information flows	Is communication vertical, up and down the hierarchy, or lateral?
Processing strategic intelligence	Are 'professional' strategists delegated to this task or is it everybody's concern?
Scope	Is strategic intelligence dealt with by senior management only, or is intelligence built throughout the organisation?
Time horizon	Short-termist or orientated towards the long term?
The role of IT	Some firms are developing sophisticated knowledge management systems to capture the information?
Organisational 'memory'	In other words, do managers keep in mind the lessons of past successes or failures?

There are many **sources** of strategic intelligence.

(a) **Internal sources** or sources relatively close to the company.

    (i) The **sales force** deals with customers, and so is in a position to obtain customer and competitor information.

(ii)   Many companies conduct **market research**. Although generally this deals with specific issues, it can indicate general environmental concerns (eg consumers' worries).

(iii)   The **management information system** may generate information about the environment, although its main focus is internal.

(b)   **External sources** of environmental data are various.

(i)   **Media**. Newspapers, periodicals and television offer environmental information.

(ii)   Sometimes, more detailed country information is needed than that supplied by the press. **Export consultants** might specialise in dealing with particular countries, and so can be a valuable source of information. The **Economist Intelligence Unit** offers reports into particular countries.

(iii) Academic or **trade journals** might give information about a wide variety of relevant issues to a particular industry.

(iv)   **Trade associations** also offer industry information.

(v)   The government can be a source of statistical data relating to money supply, the trade balance and so forth, which is often summarised in newspapers. In the UK, the Department for Business, Innovation and Skills also publishes **Overseas Trade**, concentrating on export opportunities for UK firms. Official statistical sources also include government censuses, and demographic and expenditure surveys.

(vi)   Sources of technological environmental information can include the national patents office (because patents for new products are registered with the patent office).

(vii) Stockbrokers produce investment reports for the clients which involve analysis into particular industries.

(viii) Specialist consultancy firms (eg CACI census data) provide information.

(ix)   The **Internet** (for example, 'current awareness services' where subscribers can register particular key words related to their industry with media vendors and then receive automatic emails of articles and announcements that include those key words as tags). However, the websites of rival firms may also give an insight into their mission, objectives, strategy and financial performance.

(x)   **Annual reports** of competitors, suppliers or firms in a potential target market can also provide useful information.

8.2 Database information

A **management information system** or **database** should provide managers with a useful flow of relevant information which is easy to use and easy to access. Information is an important corporate resource. Managed and used effectively, it can provide considerable competitive advantage and so it is a worthwhile investment. Large scale databases are created and stored on **computer systems,** using **database application packages** such as **Microsoft Access**.

Knowledge management (KM) is becoming an increasingly important issue in contemporary business. We will look in more detail at KM and related topics, such as data warehousing and data mining, later in this Study Text.

It is now possible to access large volumes of generally available information through databases held by public bodies and businesses.

(a)   Some **newspapers** offer free or paid-for access on the web to both current and archived editions, with search facilities looking for information on particular companies or issues.

(b)   Public databases are also available for inspection. **Dun and Bradstreet** provide general business information. **AC Nielsen** operate on-line information regarding products and market share.

(c) Developments in information technology allow businesses to have access to the databases of **external organisations**. Reuters, for example, provides an on-line information system about money market interest rates and foreign exchange rates to firms involved in money market and foreign exchange dealings, and to the treasury departments of a large number of companies. The growing adoption of technology at **point of sale** provides a potentially invaluable source of data to both retailer and manufacturer.

Legislation and regulation exists to protect consumers from misuse of **personal details** held on computer, unsolicited mail and invasion of privacy.

For example, in the UK, the Data Protection Act (1998) regulates how personal information should be used, and means that companies can only access personal data in relation to the use for which it was originally registered.

8.2.1 Environmental data

Nine areas of environmental data that ought to be included in a database for strategic planners could be as follows.

(a) **Competitive data.** This would include information derived from an application of Porter's Five Forces analysis

(b) **Economic data**. Details of past growth and predictions of future growth in GDP and disposable income, the pattern of interest rates, predictions of the rate of inflation, unemployment levels and tax rates, developments in international trade and so on

(c) **Political data**. The influence that the government is having on the industry

(d) **Legal data**. The likely implications of recent legislation, legislation likely to be introduced in the future and its implications

(e) **Social data**. Changing habits, attitudes, cultures and educational standards of the population as a whole, and customers in particular

(f) **Technological data**. Technological changes that have occurred or will occur, and the implications that these will have for the organisation

(g) **Geographical data**. Data about individual regions or countries, each of them potentially segments of the market with their own unique characteristics

(h) **Energy suppliers' data**. Energy sources, availability and price of sources of supply generally

(i) **Data about stakeholders in the business**. Employees, management and shareholders, the influence of each group, and what each group wants from the organisation

In other words data which covers the key elements of the general and market environment should be included in a database for strategic and marketing planners.

As well as obtaining data from its own internal database system an organisation can obtain it from an **external database** operated by another organisation.

8.2.2 A word of caution

Most external databases are on-line databases, which are very large computer files of information, supplied by **database providers** and managed by **host** companies whose business revenue is generated through charges made to **users**.

Information sources have to be used with caution. The Internet, in particular, has made data more available: but this data is often unchecked and unmediated. For example, *Wikipedia* can often be a source of useful information, but the fact that it can be edited by any of its readers means that the reliability of the data on it cannot always be guaranteed.

8.3 Market research

One of the key aspects of the research a firm should undertake about its environment before considering a strategic action is market research.

Market research will help establish:

(a)   The size of a potential market (and the potential revenues which could be earned from it)

(b)   Potential bases of segmentation in the market (for example, by age, income or cultural differences; or by frequency and type of purchase, such as frequent vs infrequent purchasers, or industrial vs personal customers)

(c)   Who the main competitors are, and what products or services they are offering

8.3.1 Customer behaviour

In relation to customer needs and expectations, it is also important to understand why buyers purchase particular goods or services.

Such an understanding could be useful for two different reasons:

(a)   It could help an organisation to identify the **critical success factors** (CSFs) required to satisfy those customers successfully, which in turn should help an organisation establish whether it has the core competences required to meet those CSFs (for example, to be able to produce goods more cheaply than competitors, or produce goods which are smaller, more lightweight, more reliable, more energy-efficient etc.)

(b)   It could help an organisation design its advertising messages so that they highlight those aspects of the product or service which are most important to the customer's buying decision. For example, when choosing which washing powder to buy, some people will choose according to which removes stains best; others may choose according to which leaves their white clothes 'whitest'; while others may choose according to the price of the powder.

This very short example is also interesting because it raises the idea that within a single product class (washing powder) a manufacturer could offer several different products or brands, each aimed at a different specific benefit which customers value.

 When analysing why customers buy goods and services, it is important to distinguish between individual consumers and industrial buyers. We will look at the characteristics of industrial buying decisions later in this Study Text in the context of marketing strategy.

 ## Section summary

An organisation needs strategic intelligence about its environment to allow it to anticipate changes and to design strategies that will allow it to respond effectively to those changes.

Chapter Roundup

✓   Analysing an organisation's position in relation to its external environment is an important part of strategy development. Strategists need to recognise potential impact the complexity and uncertainty in the environment could have on strategic decisions.

✓   The inherent uncertainty in the environment means that strategic decisions are often made in partial ignorance. This uncertainty may also encourage organisations to adopt emergent strategies rather than prescriptive strategies.

✓   Gap analysis allows an organisation to compare its expected performance against its objectives. However, the effectiveness of gap analysis depends on the organisation's ability to forecast its performance in the future.

✓   A forecast is a prediction of future events and their quantification for planning purposes. Be aware, however, that forecasts are susceptible to uncertainty and bias.

✓   Scenario planning is one of the techniques an organisation can use to help it cope with uncertainty. Scenario planning helps identify the key uncertainties to which an organisation is exposed, and can therefore help the organisation plan how to deal with some of those uncertainties.

✓   Foresight is a process of identifying a range of possible outcomes which could develop, based on an understanding and analysis of current trends.

✓   Game theory illustrates that an organisation cannot develop its strategy without considering the possible reactions of its competitors. Competitor reaction may mean that the outcomes of a strategy are very different to what was initially intended.

✓   An organisation needs strategic intelligence about its environment to allow it to anticipate change and design strategies that will allow it to respond effectively to those changes.

Quick Quiz

1   The planning gap is the gap between the current position of the organisation and the forecast desired position.

☐   True

☐   False

2   What is the difference between a forecast and a projection?

3   What is foresight?

4   What are the 10 steps in scenario planning (according to *Schoemaker*)?

5   List three common types of real options could be relevant to strategic projects.

6   An organisation follows a strategy which it thinks will be beneficial to it, but because of the response of its competitors the strategy turns out to be detrimental to both the organisation and the industry as a whole.

Which one of the following does this demonstrate best:

A: Emergent strategy

B: Game theory

C: Gap analysis

D: Delphi technique

Answers to Quick Quiz

1   False. It is the gap between the forecast position from continuing with current activities, compared to the desired future position.

2   A forecast is 'a prediction of future events and their quantification for planning purposes'. (CIMA)

A projection is 'an expected future trend pattern obtained by extrapolation. It is principally concerned with quantitative factors, whereas a forecast includes judgements'. (CIMA)

3   Foresight is the art and science of anticipating the future. It is a process of identifying a range of possible outcomes which could develop, based on an understanding and analysis of current trends.

4   Step 1   Define the scope

Step 2   Identify the major stakeholders

Step 3   Identify basic trends

Step 4   Identify key areas of uncertainty

Step 5   Construct initial scenarios

Step 6   Check for consistency and plausibility

Step 7   Develop learning scenarios

Step 8   Identify research needs

Step 9   Develop quantitative models

Step 10   Use scenarios to formulate competitive strategy

5   Option to make follow-on investments

Option to abandon a project

Option to wait

6   B   Game theory.

Game theory illustrates the way that strategic interactions between competitors produce outcomes that were not intended by any of the players.

Answer to Questions

3.1 Contrasting environment

(a)   The environment is simple, as the product is only being sold in one market. The environment is dynamic, as the product is still at the introduction stage and demand might be predicted to increase dramatically

(b)   The environment is complex, but stable. The knowledge required is uncertain, but funds are guaranteed for ten years.

Now try this question from the Exam Question Bank	Number	Level	Marks	Time
	Q3	Intermediate	20	36 mins

RESOURCE AUDIT

 In earlier chapters we reviewed both the general and competitive environments. In this chapter we examine some of the key aspects of the organisation's current **position** and its resources.

A **resource audit** (Sections 1 and 2) identifies any gaps in resources and limiting factors on organisational activity.

Value chain analysis (Section 3) identifies how the business adds value to the resources it obtains, and how it deploys these resources to satisfy customers. Supply chain management (Section 4) extends this idea to demonstrate the possible gains available through developing strong relationships with all parties who add value to the finished product/service.

We then review the organisation's current outputs, its **product portfolio**, in Section 5. A review of its current portfolio may encourage an organisation to develop new products (Section 6).

An organisation's resources and competences are difficult to assess in isolation, so some form of comparison is needed. **Benchmarking** (Section 7) is now common, and involves comparing an organisation's processes with those of best practice, such as those employed by an exemplar organisation, which may be an organisation in a different industry. Such an exercise will highlight areas where improvements can be made, notably in the value chain.

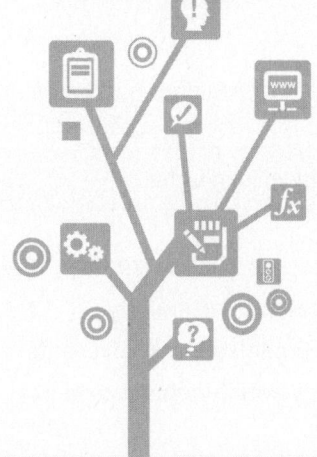

4

topic list	learning outcomes	syllabus references	ability required
1 The position audit	C2(a)	C2(i)	Evaluate
2 Resources and limiting factors	C2(a)	C2(i)	Evaluate
3 Converting resources: the value chain	C2(c)	C2(iv)	Produce
4 The supply chain	A1(e)	A1(v)	Recommend
5 Outputs: the product portfolio	C2(b)	C2(iii)	Recommend
6 New products and innovation	–	C2(iii)	–
7 Benchmarking	C2(a)	C2(i)	Evaluate

1   The position audit

Introduction

To develop a strategic plan, an organisation's management must be aware of the current position of the organisation.

KEY TERM

POSITION AUDIT is 'part of the planning process which examines the current state of the entity in respect of:

- Resources of tangible and intangible assets and finance
- Products, brands and markets
- Operating systems such as production and distribution
- Internal organisation
- Current results
- Returns to stockholders'.   (CIMA *Official Terminology*)

The rest of this chapter is concerned with how this vital task may be successfully carried out.

Section summary

It is necessary to develop an understanding of an organisation's current position before a strategic plan can be developed.

2   Resources and limiting factors

Introduction

Firms do not have unlimited resources, so have to do the best they can from limiting factors.

In Chapter 1, we highlighted the contrast between a position-based approach to strategy and a resource-based approach. The ideas we will look at in this chapter are particularly important in relation to the resource-based approach, in which an organisation analyses its own internal resources and competences and then adopts a strategy which helps it exploit those resources and competences.

A resource audit is an internal review. The **Ms model** categorises the limiting factors as follows.

Resource	Example
Machinery	Age, condition, and utilisation rate of assets. Technologically up-to-date? Cost. Quality of outputs?
Make-up	Culture and structure of organisation. Other intangibles such as: Patents. Goodwill. Brands.
Management	Skills, experience and vision of senior management. Loyalty. Career progression. Structure.
Management information	Ability to generate and disseminate ideas accurately and on a timely basis. Innovation. Information systems. Availability of information to support strategic decision-making

Resource	Example
Markets	Markets (and market segments) the organisation operates in. Position of the organisation and its products/services in those markets.
Materials	Relationships with suppliers. Quality and reliability of inputs. Waste. New materials. Cost. Availability. Future provision.
Men and women	Human resources: Number of staff. Skills. Wage costs (as a proportion of total costs). Efficiency. Labour turnover. Staff morale. Industrial relations.
Methods	How are activities carried out? Capital-intensive or labour-intensive, outsourcing, JIT.
Money	What is the organisation's cash position? Credit and turnover periods. Cash surpluses/ deficits. Short term and long term finance. Gearing levels. Investment plans.

Resources are of no value unless they are organised into systems. A resource audit considers how well resources have been utilised and the efficiency and effectiveness of the organisation's systems. This includes the quality and timeliness of information available to managers.

2.1 Limiting factors

Every organisation operates under resource **constraints**.

KEY TERM

A LIMITING FACTOR or **key factor** is 'anything which limits the activity of an entity. An entity seeks to optimise the benefit it obtains from the limiting factor.

Examples are a shortage of supply of a resource or a restriction on sales demand at a particular price'.

(CIMA *Official Terminology*)

Examples of limiting factors are:

- A shortage of production capacity
- A limited number of key personnel, such as salespeople with technical knowledge
- A restricted distribution network
- Too few managers with knowledge about finance, or overseas markets
- Inadequate research design resources to develop new products or services
- A poor system of strategic intelligence
- Lack of money
- A lack of adequately trained staff

Once the limiting factor has been identified, the planners should:

- In the short term, make best use of the resources available.
- Try to reduce the limitation in the long term.

2.2 Resource use

Resource use is both the **efficiency** with which resources are used, and the **effectiveness** of their use in achieving the planning objectives of the business. Resources can be a source of competitive advantage when used efficiently and effectively.

KEY TERMS

EFFICIENCY is 'how well the resources have been utilised irrespective of the purpose for which they have been employed'.

EFFECTIVENESS is 'whether the resources have been deployed in the best possible way'.

Section summary

Limiting factors are anything which limit the activity of an entity. Resources should be used as effectively and efficiently as possible in order to make the best use of them. Firms should aim to reduce the limitation in the long-run.

3 Converting resources: the value chain   5/10

Introduction

The **value chain** models all the activities of a business and the linkages between them. It shows how value is created, how costs are caused and how competitive advantage can be gained.

The **value chain**, developed by *Michael Porter*, offers a bird's eye view of the firm and what it does. Competitive advantage, says Porter, arises out of the way in which firms organise and perform **activities**. Businesses are made up of value-creating activities. It is important to consider the structure of an organisation in terms of these activities.

KEY TERMS

The VALUE CHAIN is the 'sequence of business activities by which, in the perspective of the **end-user**, value is added to the products or services produced by an entity'.   (*CIMA Official Terminology*)

ACTIVITIES are the means by which a firm creates value in its products. (They are sometimes referred to as **value activities**.)

Activities incur costs, and, in combination with other activities, provide a product or service which earns revenue.

3.1 Example of the value chain

A **restaurant's** activities are buying, cooking and serving food. The customer is prepared to **pay more than the cost of** the resources (food, wages etc). The ultimate value created is the amount customers are willing to pay above the cost of carrying out value activities. A firm is profitable if the value to customers exceeds the cost of activities.

(a) Customers **purchase value**, which they measure by comparing a firm's products and services with those of competitors.

(b) The business **creates value** by carrying out its activities either more efficiently than other businesses, or combining them in such a way as to provide a unique product or service.

Question 4.1   Creating value

Learning outcome C 2 (iv)

Outline different ways in which the restaurant can 'create' value.

Porter (in *Competitive Advantage*) grouped the various activities of an organisation into a value chain:

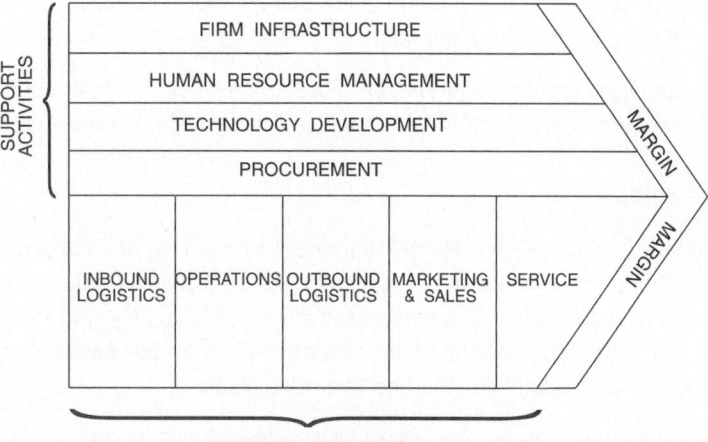

The **margin** is the excess the customer is prepared to **pay** over the **cost** to the firm of obtaining resource inputs and providing value activities. And in this respect the chain highlights the underlying business logic that a firm's activities should be designed to **create a margin** by producing outputs which have a greater sale price (or value to customers) than the cost of the inputs.

3.2 Activities

Primary activities are directly related to production, sales, marketing, delivery and service.

	Comment
Inbound logistics	Receiving, handling, storing and distributing inputs to the production system (warehousing, transport, inventory control etc).
Operations	Convert resource inputs (people and materials) into a final product. Testing and packaging of the product.
Outbound logistics	Storing the product and distributing it to customers
Marketing and sales	Informing customers about the product, persuading and enabling them to buy it (advertising, promotion, selling etc.)
After sales service	Installing, repairing and upgrading products, providing spare parts, providing training and so on.

Support activities provide purchased inputs, human resources, technology and infrastructural functions to **support the primary activities**.

Activity	Comment
Procurement	Acquire the resource inputs to the primary activities (eg purchase of materials, subcomponents equipment).
Technology development	Product design, improving processes and/or resource utilisation.
Human resource management	Recruiting, training, developing and rewarding people.
Firm infrastructure	Planning, finance, quality control: Porter believes these are crucially important to an organisation's strategic capability in all primary activities.

Linkages connect the activities of the value chain.

(a)   **Activities in the value chain affect one another**. For example, more costly product design or better quality production might reduce the need for after-sales service.

(b)   **Linkages require co-ordination**. For example, Just In Time requires smooth functioning of operations, outbound logistics and service activities such as installation.

Exam skills

The value chain provides a rational framework for carrying out analysis so is potentially useful in exam questions. At this level you may not earn marks simply by reproducing the value chain, so you should expect to have to apply it to a scenario situation. Alternatively, you may need to apply the model in the context of further applications such as benchmarking, or business process improvements. You may also need to consider how IS/IT can affect the value chain.

However, the syllabus requires you to be able to 'produce an organisation's value chain' so you do need to be able to draw the diagram if a question asks you to.

The value chain helps managers identify the activities which create value for a firm's customers. In doing so it can also help managers identify the key processes and areas in which a firm has to perform successful to secure a competitive advantage.

These key areas are the firm's critical success factors (CSFs). Therefore, it is important to note the potential link between this area of the syllabus and CSFs, targets and key performance indicators as elements of performance management (which we will look at in Chapter 14 of this Study Text.)

3.3 Value system

Activities that add value do not stop at the organisation's **boundaries**. For example, when a restaurant serves a meal, the quality of the meat and vegetable ingredients is determined by the farmer who supplies them. The farmer has added value. The farmer's ability is as important to the customer's ultimate satisfaction as the skills of the chef. A firm's value chain is connected to what Porter calls a **value system**.

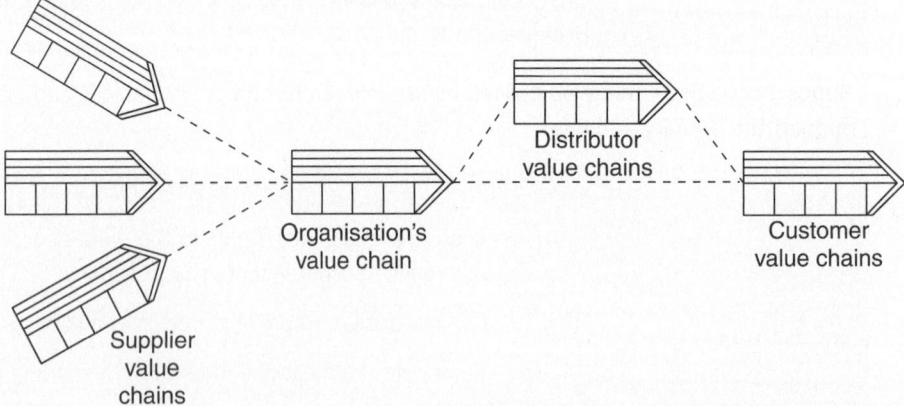

It may be possible to capture the benefit of some of the value generated both upstream and downstream in the value system. An obvious way to do this is by **vertical integration** through the acquisition of supplies and customers.

It is possible for large and powerful companies to exercise less formal power over suppliers and customers by using their **bargaining power** to achieve favourable purchase and selling prices.

A more subtle advantage is gained by fostering good relationships that can promote **innovation** and the **creation of knowledge**. Businesses are increasingly looking to work together in **partnerships** with other member of their value system.

3.4 Using the value chain

A firm can secure competitive advantage by:

- Inventing new or better ways to do activities
- Combining activities in new or better ways
- Managing linkages in its own value chain to increase efficiency and reduce cost
- Managing the linkages in the value system. This links to the ideas of **supply chain management**.

The **value system** offers the potential to improve efficiency and reduce cost through negotiation, bargaining, collaboration and vertical integration. Vertical integration offers the chance to increase profitability by **migrating** to the part of the value system that has the most potential for adding value.

Note also that Information Technology (IT) can transform the value chain, and a number of current improvements in value chain activities have been IT driven. (We will look at the strategic significance of IT, including its impact on the value chain, in Chapter 9 of this Study Text.)

Question 4.2	Value chain and value system

Learning outcome C 2 (iv)

Sana Sounds is a small record company. Representatives from Sana Sounds scour music clubs for new bands to promote. Once a band has signed a contract (with Sana Sounds) it makes a recording. The recording process is subcontracted to one of a number of recording studio firms which Sana Sounds uses regularly. (At the moment Sana Sounds is not large enough to invest in its own equipment and studios.) Sana Sounds also subcontracts the production of CDs to a number of manufacturing companies. Sana Sounds then distributes the disks to selected stores, and engages in any promotional activities required.

What would you say were the activities in Sana Sounds' current value chain?

Also, stop and think how the development of MP3 technology might permit Sana Sounds to re-engineer its value chain.

The value chain is an important analytical tool because it helps management to:

- See the business as a whole

- Identify potential sources of competitive advantage

- Suggest strategies

- Analyse competitors

- Implement activities such as benchmarking, outsourcing, business process re-engineering, performance measurement and activity based costing and management

3.5 The value chain and management accounting

There is a clear link between the concept of value activities that cut across departments and the principles of activity based costing.

A summary of the failure of traditional costing systems, and a contrast based on the value chain, is outlined in the table below.

	Traditional costing system	Value chain cost analysis: an alternative
Focus	Manufacturing operations	Customers Value perceptions
Cost objects	Products Functions Expense heads	Value-creating activities Product attributes
Organisational focus	Cost and responsibility centres	Strategic business units (SBUs) Value-creating activities
Linkages	1 Largely ignored 2 Cost allocations and transfer prices used to reflect interdependencies	Recognised and maximised
Cost drivers	Simple volume measures	Strategic decisions
Accuracy	Manufacturing operations	Low precision Indicative answers

Example

The practical application of value chain cost analysis can be seen with the following illustration which relates each element to the example of a supermarket's operations.

	Value chain cost analysis	Practical example
Focus	Customers	The supermarket is heavily focused on customers as the key source of value. Specific customers are targeted through marketing campaigns and 'customer delight' is sought. Competition forces retailers to invest more in customer service, systems and price.
Cost objects	Value-creating activities and profit attributes	Activities which promote customer loyalty and bigger spend are investigated and developed. For example, giving a 10% discount to new mothers could increase sales and profit margin above the cost of the discount. Self-scanning technology increases sales in stores.
Linkages	Recognised and maximised	Supplier and customer relationships are nurtured. Suppliers are ranked for their ability to meet the supermarket's demand and customers are constantly reminded via in-store promotions of the supermarket's commitment to giving them value.
Cost drivers	Strategic decisions	These are prompted either by competitor activity (eg price cuts) or new business initiatives such as investment in new technology or development of overseas markets. Target rates of return are required, often also measured in terms of the required sales uplift and related margin to justify an activity.
Accuracy	Indicative answers	Details of sales and margin by product are collected and individual customer spends are analysed. Customer surveys, and level of customer complaints may highlight weak areas of the business.

In this context, we should also acknowledge how the value chain could be useful when developing key performance indicators (KPIs). KPIs should monitor how well a business is performing against its critical success factors (CSFs), and these CSFs, in turn, should be linked to the key processes that deliver the organisation's strategy. So, the value chain should highlight the activities whose performance should be measured in the KPIs.

3.5.1 How the value chain drives costs

What might influence the costs of the value chain?

(a) **Structural cost drivers** are major strategic choices made by the firm which determine its underlying cost base.

(i) **Scale** of operations, capacity etc, giving rise to economies or diseconomies of scale
(ii) **Scope**: to what extent is the firm vertically integrated?
(iii) **Experience**: has the firm climbed the learning curve?
(iv) **Technology** used in the value chain
(v) **Complexity** and breadth of product range

(b) **Management** influences how well a firm manages the value chain operationally.

(i) Capacity utilisation
(ii) Product and process design
(iii) Learning opportunities offered by continuous improvement programmes
(iv) How well external linkages (eg liaison with suppliers) are exploited

Firms might create a more **outward-looking focus** in their costing systems as follows

(a) Most products are a collection of benefits, which is why customers buy them. The provision of customer benefits is the real cost driver of the business. It should be possible to work backwards from these benefits to the underlying costs.

$$\begin{array}{l}\text{Input} \xrightarrow{} \textit{Activities} \xleftarrow{} \begin{array}{l}\xleftarrow{}\text{Cost driver A}\xleftarrow{} \\ \xleftarrow{}\text{Cost driver B}\xleftarrow{} \\ \xleftarrow{}\text{Cost driver C}\xleftarrow{}\end{array}\begin{array}{l}\text{A} \\ \text{B} \\ \text{C}\end{array}\begin{array}{l}\text{Customer} \\ \text{benefit} \\ \text{sought}\end{array}\end{array}$$

(b) For different products, it should be possible to identify the customer's perception of the value of the benefit and the cost of providing it.

For the accountant, problems with this approach are:

- A lack of precision in the data
- The subjectivity in deciding what customers value as a benefit

3.6 Limitations of the value chain

(a) It was originally designed for use in a manufacturing context, so can be difficult to apply to **service businesses**.

(b) The value system is difficult to apply to **network organisations**.

(c) Making the best use of the value chain idea is dependent on adopting at least some part of **activity based costing** to establish the costs of value activities. This can be time consuming and expensive.

(d) The costs of the analysis may exceed the potential benefits.

(e) The value chain takes little account of the increasing role of IT in business. In response to this criticism Porter and Millar revisited the model and stressed the importance of using technology to increase linkages.

3.7 Alternative approaches

Stabell and Fjeldstad address the first two limitations listed above by proposing **new lists of primary activities** that relate better to service and network organisations respectively.

In their model, *Stabell and Fjeldstad* refer to the idea of a **value shop** rather than value chain.

3.7.1 The value shop and service organisations

The value shop model is based on the idea that an organisation needs to use its resources to address customers' issues or to solve their problems, so it can perhaps be seen most clearly in relation to a professional practice such as a firm of accountants or lawyers, or in medical services. **Expertise is the principal asset**, and is built by experience.

Primary activities include:

- **Problem-finding and acquisition**: Recording, reviewing and formulating the problem to be solved, and choosing an overall approach to solving the problem. Marketing effort could be required here as well as professional expertise.
- **Problem solving**: more extensive professional expertise must be deployed to identify and evaluate potential solutions to the issue at hand.
- **Choice between solutions**: A preferred solution is chosen (in consultation with the client) from the alternative solutions which have been identified.
- **Solution implementation.** This activity involves communicating, organising and implementing the chosen solution.
- **Control and feedback**: Measuring and evaluating the extent to which the solution has solved the initial problem, to ensure the effectiveness of the solution

The **secondary activities** in the value shop are the same as those in *Porter*'s value chain.

An organisation which can be viewed as a value shop will:

- Use a variety of skills, expertise, disciplines and specialties
- Be able to cope with unique situations
- Perform repetitive and cyclical activities. (Whereas *Porter*'s value chain is essentially linear, the primary activities in the value shop are arranged as a circle to reflect the process of identifying, evaluating (and possibly rejecting) different solutions before reaching a conclusion.)
- Co-ordinate across different activities
- Rely on reputation-based referrals

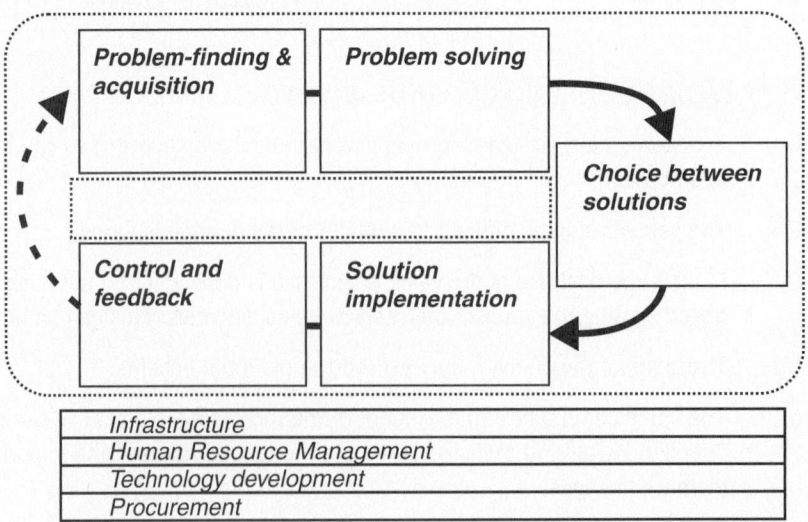

The value shop (after *Stabell and Fjeldstad*)

3.7.2 Network organisations

The emphasis here is on the wider network of unrelated stakeholders, not the network approach to internal structure.

Primary activities include:

* **Network promotion and contract management:** this combines marketing with administration
* **Service provisioning:** day to day liaison, communication and decision making
* **Infrastructure operation:** physical and intangible resources must be maintained and exploited; this is perhaps clearest in the context of IT systems

Section summary

The value chain shows how value is created and how competitive advantage can be gained. Value adding activities do not stop at the organisation's boundaries, and a firm's value chain is connected to others in a value system.

4 The supply chain

Linked to the value chain is the concept of supply chain management. By establishing **closer links** with companies in the supply chain, firms can obtain best value for money and reduce inventory holdings. The adversarial, arms length relationship with a supplier is replaced by one which is characterised by closer co-operation.

Supply chain linkage is demonstrated in the following model.

4.1 Supply chain model

The supply chain is the network of organisations involved in the different processes and activities necessary to transform raw materials into finished goods and services in order to produce value for the ultimate customer.

There are three main themes to supply chains and supply chain management:

* **Responsiveness:** The combination of shortening product life cycles and increasing customer expectations mean firms must be able to supply their customers quickly. Increased integration – for example, electronic data interchanges (EDI) – can be very useful here; allowing orders to be transmitted quickly and accurately.

* **Reliability:** Deliveries through the supply chain must be reliable, in terms of timeliness, quality and quantity. Reliability will be greatly assisted by **transparency** in the supply chain: so that upstream firms can see orders coming from customers and deliveries coming from downstream suppliers.

* **Relationships:** The need for responsiveness and reliability means that the members of the supply chain need to develop a mutual understanding and trust of each other. In this respect, the supply chain needs to be seen as a network based on collaboration and common interest, instead of the traditional dichotomy of the buyer/seller relationship.

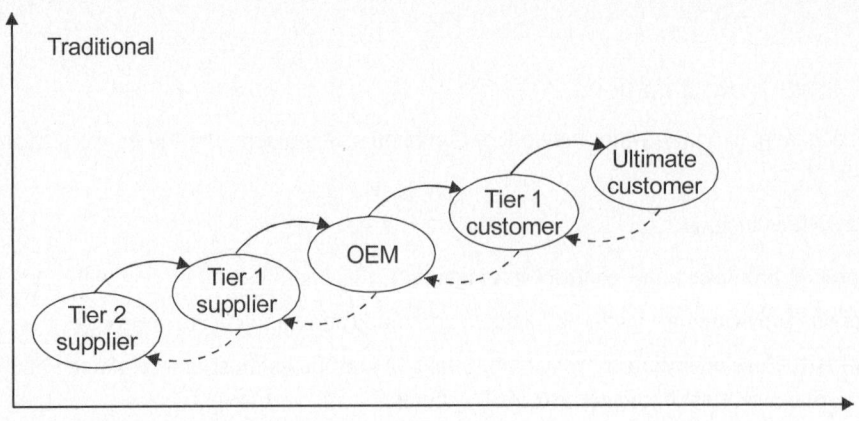

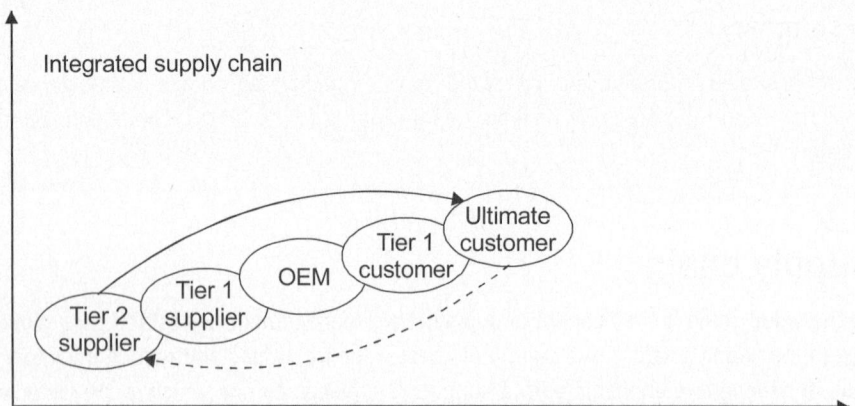

Historically, businesses in the supply chain operated relatively independently of one another to create value for an ultimate customer. Independence was maintained by buffers of material, capacity and lead-times. This is represented in the 'Traditional' model shown above.

Market and competitive demands are now **compressing lead times** and businesses are reducing inventories and excess capacity. Linkages between businesses in the supply chain must therefore become tighter. This is shown in the 'Integrated supply chain' model.

Monczka (who developed this supply chain model) further claims that in the future **whole supply chains** will compete, not just individual firms. This will continue to have a great impact upon distribution methods.

The traditional model of a supply chain is as a 'push' system, in which manufacturers create products and then supply them to customers who are, effectively, passive receivers at the end of the supply chain.

However, many companies are now moving to a more customer-driven 'pull' model. In a 'pull' model, customers are able to give direction to suppliers about the specifications of the products they want. For example, customers buying Dell PCs are able to customise their machines when they place their order, and their PCs are then made according to that order.

Just-in-time (JIT) systems are also an illustration of 'pull' systems, and we look at JIT systems in more detail in Chapter 10 of this Study Text.

4.2 Supply chain management

KEY TERM

SUPPLY CHAIN MANAGEMENT means optimising the activities of companies working together to produce goods and services, to be responsive to customers demands and reliable in the delivery of them.

Supply chain management (SCM) is a means by which the firm aims to manage the chain from input resources to the consumer. It involves the following:

(a)   Reduction in the number of suppliers

(b)   Reduction in customers served, in some cases, to focus on customers of high potential value

(c)   Price and inventory co-ordination. Firms co-ordinate their price and inventory policies to avoid problems and bottlenecks caused by short-term surges in demand, such as promotions

(d)   Linked computer systems – electronic data interchange saves on paperwork and warehousing expense. The internet and XML allow businesses to have a more automated procurement policy (e-procurement). Technology now also enables firms to track the status of purchases from order to dispatch and delivery.

(e)   Early supplier involvement in product development and component design

(f)   Logistics design. Hewlett-Packard restructured its distribution system by enabling certain product components to be added at the distribution warehouse rather than at the central factory, for example user-manuals which are specific to the market (ie user manuals in French would be added at the French distribution centre)

(g)   Joint problem solving

(h)   Supplier representative on site

KEY POINT

The aim is to co-ordinate the whole chain, from raw material suppliers to end customers. The chain should be considered as a **network** rather than a **pipeline** – a network of vendors support a network of customers, with third parties such as transport firms helping to link the companies.

CASE STUDY

Comet

A turbulent economic climate often prompts companies to impose tougher supplier terms. An extreme attempt at this was made by Kesa, the owners of Comet, in January 2009 in a bid to improve the cash position of the struggling electrical retail chain.

New terms were imposed on Comet's suppliers insisting they pay fees in exchange for having their products displayed on the shop floor. The terms require manufacturers to pay a listing fee for each item stocked, as well as a 2% discount on invoices and an additional 0.5 % fee for sales and stocks data. This translates to £5,504 for a small item such as an iron up to a staggering £15,431 for white goods such as washing machines.

Many suppliers refused the new terms.

Service Level Agreements

Given the importance of companies collaborating and working together within the supply chain, it is also important for companies to be able to measure and manage the performance of key partners within the supply chain (for example, to control the number of late or incomplete deliveries).

A key issue will be whether upstream suppliers are delivering the agreed quantity and quality of goods or services on time. However, in order to measure whether the suppliers are meeting such requirements, the requirements first have to be established.

This highlights the importance of establishing service level agreements between organisations and their suppliers.

A service level agreement should include:

- An explanation of the service the supplier has agreed to provide (and details of any information the company has agreed to provide the supplier).

- The benchmarks being used to measure performance, details of how they are measured/calculated, and the implications for failing to meet them.

- Procedures for dealing with any complaints arising from the actual level of performance provided, and details of expected response times for responding to any queries or complaints raised.

- Procedures for cancelling the contract between the parties.

Once a service level agreement is in place, both parties have a structure against which to measure their performance in the relationship, and to assess whether a satisfactory level of performance is being achieved.

4.2.1 Lean supply chain

The objective of developing a lean supply chain is to completely remove waste from the process in order to achieve a competitive advantage.

Advantages	Counter arguments
Reduced cost	Focuses on reducing cost rather than improving quality. Too much cost reduction may actually worsen quality.
Improved quality (and lower costs of re-working and quality problems)	
Reduced inventories	There may be insufficient slack in the system to deal with fluctuations in damage.
Shorter lead times	Lean supply chain consists of a series of preferred supplier relationships. These may be akin to monopolies, so good for firms involved but not for the consumer, because the market operates most efficiently under perfect competition.

CASE STUDY

Li & Fung which began life as a Hong Kong-based export trading company but has now evolved into a multi-national trading, retailing and distribution group, takes the following approach to its manufacturing supply chain.

'Say we get an order from a European retailer to produce 10,000 garments. It's not a simple matter of our Korean office sourcing Korean products or our Indonesian office sourcing Indonesian products. For the customer we might decide to buy yarn from a Korean producer but have it woven and dyed in Taiwan. So we pick the yarn and ship it to Taiwan. The Japanese have the best zippers and buttons, but they manufacture them mostly in China. Okay, so we go to *YKK*, a big Japanese zipper manufacturer and we order the right zippers from their Chinese plants. Then we determine that, because of quotas and labour conditions, the best place to make the garments is Thailand. So we ship everything there. And because the customer needs quick delivery, we may divide the order across five factories in Thailand. Effectively, we are customising the value chain to best meet the customer's needs.

'Five weeks after we have received the order, 10,000 garments arrive on the shelves in Europe, all looking like they came from one factory with colours, for example, perfectly matched. Just think about the logistics and the co-ordination.

'This is a new type of value added, a truly global product that has never been seen before. The label may say "Made in Thailand", but it's not a Thai product. We dissect the manufacturing process and look for the best solution to each step. We're not asking which country can do the best job overall. Instead, we're pulling apart the value chain and optimising each step – and we're doing it globally... . The classic

supply-chain manager in retailing is *Marks & Spencer*. They don't own any factories, but they have a huge team that goes into the factories and works with the management.'

CASE STUDY

In turn, Li & Fung itself has evolved from being a sourcing agent to becoming a global supply chain manager by being an innovator in the development of supply chain management.

Through its practice and research in this area, Li & Fung has derived the following *seven principles* which constitute the pillars of its supply chain management methodology:

(a)   Be customer-centric and market demand driven

(b)   Focus on one's own core competency and outsource non-core activities, in order to develop a positioning in the supply chain

(c)   Develop a close, risk- and profit-sharing relationship with business partners

(d)   Design, implement, evaluate and continuously improve the work flow, physical flow, information flow and cash flow in the supply chain

(e)   Adopt information technology to optimise the operation of the supply chain

(f)   Shorten production lead time and delivery cycles

(g)   Lower costs in sourcing, warehousing and transportation

4.3 The importance of context

Managing the supply chain **varies from company to company**. A company such as Unilever will provide the same margarine to both Tesco and Sainsbury. The way in which the product is delivered, transactions are processed and other parts of the relationship are managed will be different since both supermarket chains have their own ways of operating. The focus will need to be on customer interaction, account management, after sales service and order processing.

A supplier that 'knows' what his customers want does not have to guess or wait until the customer places an order. It will be able to better plan its own delivery systems. The **Internet** has allowed customers and suppliers to acquire more up to date information about forecast needs and delivery schedules than ever before.

The greatest changes in supply chain management have taken place in the implementation of **software applications**. Managers today have a wider choice of systems with quick implementation times – important in a competitive market where a new supply chain system is required. Supply chains at local, regional and global level are often managed simultaneously, via a standardised infrastructure that nevertheless allows for local adaptation where this is important.

As well as tactical issues, what might be the underlying strategic concerns?

(a)   Close partnerships are needed with suppliers whose components are essential for the business unit.

(b)   A firm should choose suppliers with a distinctive competence similar to its own. A firm selling 'cheap and cheerful' goods will want suppliers who are able to supply 'cheap and cheerful' subcomponents.

Problems with the **partnership approach** to supply chain management are these.

- Each partner needs to remain competitive in the long term.
- There is a possible **loss of flexibility.**
- The **relative bargaining power** may make partnership unnecessary.
- Arguments about sharing profits may arise.

4.4 Choosing suppliers

Although there are a few occasions when an organisation has no choice about which supplier to buy goods and services from, in most cases there is a degree of choice. An organisation's choice of supplier should take account of factors such as the following:

- The **price** the supplier is charging (relative to other potential suppliers).
- Whether the supplier can deliver the required **quality** of product or service.
- Whether the supplier has the capacity to deliver the required **quantity** of product, and whether the supplier has sufficient space capacity to increase the quantity if necessary, or deal with special orders at short notice.
- How **quickly** the supplier will be able to deliver orders.
- How **reliable** the supplier is at fulfilling orders; on time, in the correct quantity, and to the desired standard of quality.
- Levels of **customer service** and how the supplier handles returns or other problems. (If the organisation is buying a complex product (for example, some software) it should also consider what level of technical support is available if required.)
- Where the supplier is **located**. For multi-national companies, there is also a question of whether different suppliers will be needed in different parts of the world.
- The **number of suppliers** the organisation wants to use. Using a small number of suppliers may allow the organisation to benefit from bulk purchase discounts, but could increase the suppliers' bargaining power in relation to the company.
- The credit period and **credit terms** offered.
- Whether the supplier is **financially secure**.
- The **relative size** of the supplier to the company (which will affect the strength of the bargaining power between the organisation and the supplier). However, while using a small supplier may give the organisation more bargaining power over the supplier, it may mean that the supplier is less easily able to fulfil large orders, or it could be less financially secure.

4.5 E-procurement

The procurement process covers all the activities needed to obtain goods or services from a supplier. However, as with many other areas of business, developments in IT have enabled elements of the procurement process to be automated.

E-procurement is the purchase of supplies and services through the internet and other information and networking systems, such as Electronic Data Interchange (EDI). It is typically operated through a secure website, possibly using a paperless system based around a purchasing card.

Traditionally, e-procurement has been seen as a simple process, from identifying a requirement to purchase something, to placing an electronic purchase order with a supplier, and then paying for the order through an electronic bank payment system such as BACS.

Today the transactional process is considered to be only part of the e-procurement function as a whole. It includes purchasing, transportation, goods receipt and warehousing before the goods are used. A properly implemented system can connect companies and their business processes directly with suppliers, while managing all interactions between them. This includes management of correspondence, bids, questions and answers, previous pricing, and multiple emails sent to multiple participants.

It focuses on the complete purchasing mix, or the 'five rights of purchasing', which are that goods and services must be delivered:

- At the right **time**
- At the right **price**
- In the right **quantity**
- From the right **vendor**
- At the right **quality**

4.5.1 Methods

Typically, e-procurement websites allow authorised and registered users to log in using a password. The supplying organisation will set up its website so that it recognises the purchaser once they have logged in and presents a list of items that the purchaser regularly buys. This saves searching for the items required and also avoids the need to key in the purchaser's name, address and delivery details. Depending on the approach, buyers or sellers may specify prices or invite bids. Transactions can then be initiated and completed. Once the purchases are made, the purchasing organisation will periodically be billed by the supplier. Ongoing purchases may qualify customers for volume discounts or special offers.

A very limited form of electronic procurement is a **purchasing card**, which is a paperless purchase and payment system aimed at the end-user who can order and pay for goods directly with a small number of suppliers. Buyers identify themselves by their card number when placing an order; the supplier checks the purchase card number and, if correct, authorises it with the bank. The bank pays the supplier in 2 to 5 days, and the supplier ships the goods.

4.5.2 Benefits of e-procurement

Cost reduction	Might include process efficiencies, reduction in the actual cost of goods and services, and reduced purchasing agent overheads.
Reduced inventory levels	Because orders are cheaper to place and process, organisations can afford to place orders more frequently, and can therefore hold lower levels of inventory.
Control	The ability to control parts inventories more effectively. E-procurement also provides greater financial transparency and accountability over the procurement process.
Wider choice of supplier	In theory, resources can be sourced from suppliers anywhere in the world, perhaps at much lower prices than could be obtained if an organisation only considered local suppliers.
	In this respect, one of the key stages in e-procurement is **e-sourcing**: using electronic methods to find new suppliers and establish contacts with them.
Quicker ordering	A second key stage of e-procurement is **e-purchasing,** which covers product selection and ordering. E-purchasing allows organisations to select standard items from electronic catalogues and then automatically send electronic purchase orders to the supplier via an extranet.
Intangible benefits	Staff are able to concentrate on their prime function and there is financial transparency and accountability.
Benefits to suppliers	Reduction in ordering and processing costs, reduced paperwork, improved cash flow and reduced cost of credit control.

4.5.3 Risks of e-procurement

(a) **Control.** If anyone can order goods from anywhere, there is a risk that unauthorised purchases will be made. There is also an increased likelihood that purchases will be made from suppliers who cannot deliver the required quality (or cannot deliver at all!)

(b) **Organisational risk.** In moving to an e-procurement tool, an adopting company will make a substantial investment in the software, but for any number of reasons the implementation may never be successful. Users may not adapt to it well. Suppliers may reject the technology or new

process. Technical issues may stall the implementation. Also, managing the internal processes around the changeover is challenging.

(c)   **Data security.** Putting a company's spending online means dealing with the security issues that come with any internet-related deployment. This brings up questions like: Who has access to our data? Where is it stored? How is it protected? What happens if we change providers? Do we get our data back? Do they sell spending data to our competitors?

(d)   **Management loses spending control.** There is a perceived risk that moving to e-procurement will put spending decisions in the wrong hands internally and management will lose decision-making control over who spends how much on what.

(e)   **Supply chain problems.** Moving to e-sourcing speeds up the sourcing process dramatically, but the increased efficiency and speed can also destabilise the rest of a supply chain if it is not able to step up its performance to meet the increased speed in the purchasing link of the chain.

Section summary

By establishing closer links with companies in the supply chain, firms can obtain best value for money and reduce inventory holdings. Supply chain management is a means by which firms aim to manage the chain from input resources through to the final customer.

5 Outputs: the product portfolio

Introduction

Many firms make a number of different products or services. Each product or service has its own financial, marketing and risk characteristics. The combination of products or services influences the attractiveness and profitability of the firm.

5.1 The product life cycle

The **product life cycle** concept holds that products have a life cycle, and that a product demonstrates different characteristics of profit and investment at each stage in its life cycle. The life cycle concept is a model, not a prediction. (Not all products pass through each stage of the life cycle.) It enables a firm to examine its portfolio of goods and services as a whole.

The profitability and sales of a product can be expected to change over time. The **product life cycle** is an attempt to recognise distinct stages in a product's sales history. Marketing managers distinguish between different aspects of the product.

(a)   **Product class:** this is a broad category of product, such as cars, washing machines, newspapers' also referred to as the **generic product**.

(b)   **Product form:** within a product class products take different forms, for example five-door hatchback cars or two-seater sports cars.

(c)   **Brand:** the particular type of the product form (eg *Ford Focus*).

The product life cycle applies in differing degrees to each of the three cases. A product-class (eg cars) may have a long maturity stage, and a particular make or brand (eg Rolls Royce) *might* have an erratic life cycle or not. Product forms tend to conform to the classic life cycle pattern however.

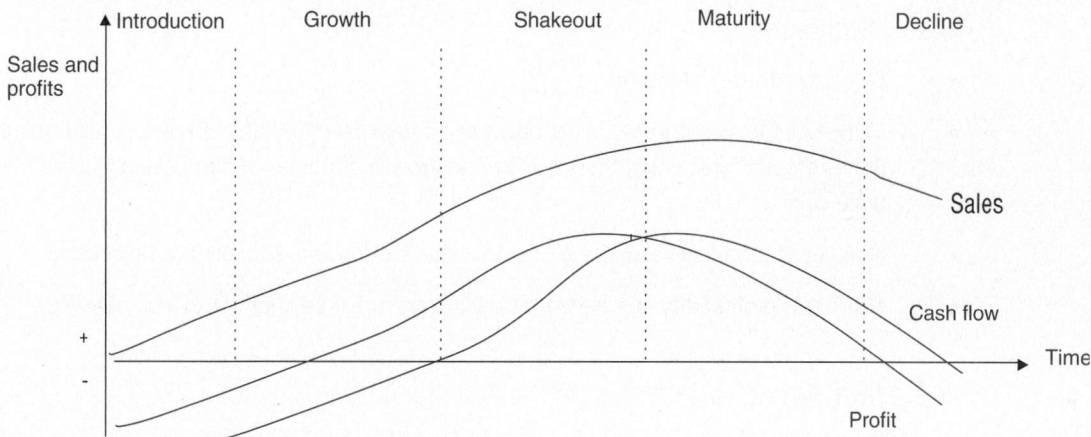

5.1.1 Introduction

- A new product takes time to be accepted. There is a slow growth in sales. Unit costs are high due to low output and costly promotions. High marketing costs in order to get product recognised by customers.

- There may be early teething troubles with production technology

- Limited product range

- The product for the time being is a loss-maker, and has negative cash flows

- The product is high risk because it is new and has not yet been accepted by the market

- The product has few, if any, competitors (because they are not willing to take similar risks)

- The product is only likely to be purchased by 'innovators'

Pricing strategy will be influenced by price elasticity of demand. If demand is likely to be inelastic, **price skimming** is appropriate. If demand is expected to be elastic, and/or gaining market share is an important objective, **penetration pricing** is likely to be appropriate.

5.1.2 Growth

- If the new product gains market acceptance, sales will eventually rise more sharply and the product will start to make profits

- Capital investments are needed to fulfil levels of demand, meaning cash flows remain lower than profit. However, cash flows increase as sales increase and the market becomes profitable.

- Competitors are attracted with similar products, but as sales and production rise, unit costs fall (eg due to economies of scale)

- Sales for the market as a whole increase

- Need to add additional features to differentiate from competitors as buyers become more sophisticated. Product complexity is likely to rise. Alternatively, a firm may choose to lower price and compete on price grounds.

- Continued marketing expenditure required to differentiate the firm's product from competitors' offerings. New market segments may be developed.

- Growth sustained by attracting new types of customers

5.1.3 Shakeout

- Sales growth rate slows down.

- Market becomes saturated, as supply begins to exceed demand. Excess supply (resulting from producers not forecasting the slowdown in growth of demand) can possibly be addressed through price cuts.

- Number of producers reduces either as a result of business failures or takeovers.

- Maximum profitability is reached, but will start to fall as supply exceeds demand.

5.1.4 Maturity

- The market is no longer growing. Purchases are now based on repeat or replacement purchases, rather than new customers.

- High levels of competition, because in order to increase sales a firm needs to capture market share from competitors.

- This is probably the longest period of a successful product's life as customers buy to replace existing products when they reach the end of their useful lives. (Most products on the market at any time will be at the mature stage of their life cycle.)

- Profits remain good, and levels of investment are low, meaning cash flow is also positive.

- Price becomes more sensitive. Prices likely to start to decline, as firms compete with one another to try to increase their share of a fixed-size market.

- Equally, companies need defensive strategies to protect their current positions from competitors.

- Firms try to capitalise on existing brand name by launching spin-off products under the same name. By now, buyers are sophisticated and fully understand the product.

- Environmental analysis is important. Companies need to detect or anticipate changes in the market so that they can be ready to undertake modifications in product-market strategies to lengthen the life cycle.

- The number of firms in industry reduces again, due to consolidation in the industry in an attempt to restore profitability.

5.1.5 Decline

Eventually, the product is superseded by **technically superior substitutes**. Sales begin to decline and there is over-capacity of production in the industry. Prices fall in order to try to attract business. Severe competition occurs, **profits fall** and some **producers leave the market**. The remaining producers try to prolong the product life by modifying it and searching for new (niche) market segments. Investment is kept to a minimum. Although some producers are reluctant to leave the market if they haven't found alternative industries to move into, many inevitably do because of falling profits.

CASE STUDY

Television

Over time, the design and specification of television sets has changed. Black and white screens have been superseded by colour; cathode ray tubes have been superseded by flat screen and plasma screens, and manufacturers have developed home cinema systems.

However, the switch to online distribution methods of video content is also now having significant implications for the television set industry, and there are already indications that viewer habits are changing.

Online TV, mobile phone TV and free TV catch up services offered by the major channels give viewers much greater choice and flexibility, allowing them to watch programmes at their own convenience. Figures now indicate that TV audience figures are dropping, whilst internet access is on the rise.

Suggestions have even been made that television sets will become a thing of the past in the UK when the analogue signal is turned off and viewers watch a digital service only.

To prevent decline, the TV industry has to adapt to cope with the changes, perhaps through internet enabled televisions, or sets that connect directly with PCs as part of a complete home media system.

5.1.6 The relevance of the product life cycle to strategic planning

In reviewing outputs, planners should assess products in three ways in order to determine an appropriate strategy.

(a)   The **stage of its life cycle** that any product has reached. For example, in the growth stage, a firm's strategy might focus on trying to differentiate its product from competitors', and it might have to incur high marketing costs to achieve this. However, for a mature product, the focus will be on controlling costs.

(b)   The **product's remaining life**, ie how much longer it will contribute to profits.

(c)   How **urgent is the need to innovate**, to develop new and improved products?

A product's stage in its life cycle can also affect the suitability of different performance measures. Traditional performance measures (such as ROCE or ROI) are most applicable for the mature phase, but are less useful in the introduction or growth phases when the focus is on investing for future success.

 Firms should also consider the range of products (or services) they offer, and what stages they are at in their life cycles. For example, mature products (which generate positive cash flows) could help fund the development of new products. This idea of creating a portfolio of products is expanded further in the BCG matrix which we look at later in this chapter.

5.1.7 Difficulties of the product life cycle concept

(a)   **Recognition**. How can managers recognise where a product is in its life cycle?

(b)   **Not always true**. Some products have no maturity phase, and go straight from growth to decline. Some never decline if marketed competitively.

(c)   **Descriptive not predictive**. Managers cannot use the lifecycle to predict future sales, because the model describes general trends, rather than having any value for detailed predictions.

(d)   **Changeable**. Strategic decisions can change or extend a product's life cycle.

(e)   **Competition varies** in different industries. The financial markets are an example of markets where there is a tendency for competitors to copy the leader very quickly, so that competition has built up well *ahead* of demand.

(f)   **Focus on the product**. Sometimes a customer group or market is a better unit of strategic analysis than a single product. A product may be at different stages of its life cycle in different **markets**.

(g)   **Lack of clarity** about 'the product'. For example, for a car manufacturer, is its 'product' a car in general terms, a type of car (eg petrol vs diesel car) or a specific brand or model of car?

(h)   **Single product only**. The model only looks at a single product at a time. It does not consider the connections between that product and other products in a company's product portfolio. For example, are some products which are mature necessary in order to attract customers who will then buy products which are in their growth stage?

5.1.8 The industry life cycle concept

In the same way we can identify a product life cycle, it may also be possible to discern an **industry life cycle**, which will have wider implications for the nature of competition and competitive advantage.

An industry is a group of firms producing the same product or products that are close substitutes for one another. So, the stages of the industry life cycle do not relate just to products, but to aspects such as the number of competitors in the industry, the number of customers, and the level of profits which firms can sustain.

This cycle reflects changes in demand and the spread of technical knowledge among producers. Innovation creates the new industry, and this is normally product innovation. Later, innovation shifts to processes in order to maintain margins. The overall progress of the industry lifecycle is illustrated below.

	Introduction	Growth	Maturity/shakeout	Decline
Products	Basic, no standards established	Better, more sophisticated, differentiated	Superior, standardised	Varied quality but fairly undifferentiated
Competitors	None to few	Many entrants Little concentration in industry	Competition increases, weaker players leave	Few remain. Competition may be on price
Buyers	Early adopters, prosperous, curious must be induced	More customers attracted and aware	Mass market, brand switching common	Enthusiasts, traditionalists, sophisticates
Profits	Negative – high first mover advantage	Increasing as sales increase rapidly	High, but beginning to decline	Falling, as sales and prices have fallen
Objectives & Strategy	Build product awareness Dominate market, build quality	Try to maximise market share React to competitors with marketing spend	Maximise profit while defending market share Cost reductions sought	Control costs Possibly harvest or divest

Notice the last row in the table: objectives and strategy. This is important because it highlights that the most suitable strategy for a firm to adopt is likely to depend on the stage of the industry in its life cycle.

5.2 Portfolio planning

Portfolio analysis examines the current status of the organisation's products and their markets. Portfolio analysis is the first stage of **portfolio planning**, which aims to create a balance among the organisation's market offerings in order to maximise competitive advantage.

Four **major strategies** can be pursued with respect to products, market segments and, indeed, SBUs.

(a) **Build**. A build strategy forgoes short term earnings and profits in order to increase market share. This could be either done through organic growth, or through external growth (acquisition; strategic alliances etc.)

(b) **Hold**. A hold strategy seeks to maintain the current position, defending it from the threat of would-be 'attackers' as necessary.

(c) **Harvest**. A harvesting strategy seeks short-term earning and profits at the expense of long-term development.

(d)   **Divest**. Disposal of a poorly performing business unit or product. Divestment stems the flow of cash to a poorly performing area of the business and releases resources for use elsewhere.

5.2.1 The Boston classification (BCG matrix)   3/11, 11/11

The **Boston classification** (BCG matrix) classifies products or business units in terms of their capacity for growth within the market and the market's capacity for growth as a whole. A firm should have a balanced **portfolio of products or business units**. The GE Business Screen and the Shell matrix are similar tools.

The Boston Consulting Group **(BCG) matrix** assesses a company's products in terms of potential cash generation and cash expenditure requirements. Products or SBUs are categorised in terms of **market growth rate** and a firm's **relative market share**.

KEY TERM

RELATIVE MARKET SHARE: 'One entity's sales of a product or service in a specified market compared to the total sales earned by the largest entity offering that product or service.'

(a)   The rate of **market growth** depends on market conditions, and new markets often grow explosively while mature ones grow hardly at all. As a guide, 10% is often used as a dividing line between high and low growth. High market growth rate can indicate good opportunities for profitable operations. However, intense competition in a high growth market can erode profit, while a slowly growing market with high barriers to entry can be very profitable.

(b)   **Relative market share** is assessed as a ratio: it is a firm's market share compared with the market share of the **largest competitor**. A relative market share greater than one indicates that the product or SBU is the market leader, and this is used as the dividing line between high and low relative market share. Therefore, only market leaders (with a relative market share greater than 1) should be said to have a high relative market share.

The BCG matrix uses market share to estimate costs associated with given products. This is used as there is a connection between lower costs and higher market share. However, **correlation does not necessarily prove causation**: just because a firm is large doesn't necessarily mean its costs are lower than a smaller firm's would be.

(c)   Note that there is an unspoken assumption that the **market** itself is easily defined. This may not be the case and it is likely that much thought will have to be given to this problem, even if only to decide whether the analysis should be in terms of brand, generic product or product form.

(d)   Be aware also that the **matrix ignores potential links between products**. However, it is important to consider such links: for example, if a firm stops producing one product will it have a knock on effect on say other products?

	Relative market share	
	High	*Low*
High	Stars	Question marks/ Problem children
Low	Cash cows	Dogs

Market growth (label on left, rows: High, Low)

The product portfolio should be balanced, with cash cows providing finance for stars and question marks; and a minimum of dogs.

(a)   **Stars**. In the short term, these require capital expenditure in excess of the cash they generate, in order to maintain their market position, and to defend their position against competitors' attack strategies, but they promise high returns in the future. Strategy: **build**.

(b)   In due course, stars will become **cash cows**. Cash cows need very little capital expenditure (because opportunities for growth are low) and generate high levels of cash income. However apparently mature products can be invigorated, possibly by competitors, who could come to dominate the market. Cash

cows can be used to finance the stars or question marks which are in their development stage. Strategies: **hold,** or **harvest** if weak.

(c)   **Question marks**. Do the products justify considerable capital expenditure in the hope of increasing their market share, or will they be squeezed out of the expanding market by rival products? Question marks have the potential to become stars if they are successfully developed. However, if their development is not successful, they may end up consuming a lot of investment and management time but ending up as 'problem adults' rather than stars as had been intended. Strategies: **build, harvest or divest**.

(d)   **Dogs**. They may be ex-cash cows that have fallen on hard times. Although they will show only a modest net cash outflow, or even a modest net cash inflow, they are cash traps which tie up funds and provide a poor return on investment. However, they may have a useful role, either to complete a product range or to keep competitors out. There are also many smaller niche businesses in market that are difficult to consolidate that would count as dogs but which are quite successful. Strategy: **divest** or **hold**.

Although developed for use with a *product* portfolio, the BCG matrix is also used in diversified conglomerates to assess the strategic position of subsidiary **SBUs**. This is an important point to note: the BCG matrix can be applied either to a **product portfolio** or a **business portfolio**.

The BCG matrix offers management a simple and convenient way of looking at a diverse range of businesses and products, within a single overall portfolio. In doing so, it encourages management to look at the portfolio as a whole rather than simply assessing the needs and performance of each unit independently. For example, the portfolio would allow a group of companies to consider the cash flow requirements of the group as a whole rather than focusing on individual units in isolation.

Also, the matrix should help management with long-term strategic planning: for example, by highlighting the need for new question marks or stars to be developed, to eventually replace the current crop of cash cows. In this respect, the matrix may also highlight the need for a firm to consider acquisitions if its portfolio is currently unbalanced, and only offers limited opportunities for growth and development.

However, critics argue the axes are too simplistic.

- A high market share is assumed to indicate competitive strength but this is not necessarily true.

- A strong brand may yield competitive strength despite a relatively low market share.

- High market growth is deemed to indicate an attractive industry. But fast growing industries are likely to require significant investment, so they may not be attractive to a firm with limited available capital.

- The requirement that firms have a high relative market share is justified by the ability of large producers to benefit from scale economies and experience effects, and thereby to assist in surviving price pressure in late life cycle markets. However, following a *differentiation* strategy or a *niche* strategy allows a firm to prosper even with a small relative share.

- The approach sees the Board as working on behalf of shareholders as a super-investor seeking to balance the demands of cash returns now with future growth to make the firm's equity attractive. This overlooks other synergies from combining businesses together in the same portfolio, such as cross-selling, supply and demand integration, knowledge spreading etc.

Question 4.3	Juicy drinks

Learning outcome C 2 (iii)

The marketing manager of Juicy Drinks Co has invited you in for a chat. Juicy Drinks Co provides fruit juices to a number of supermarket chains, which sell them under their own label.

'We've got a large number of products, of course. Our freshly squeezed orange juice is doing fine – it sells in huge quantities. Although margins are low, we have sufficient economies of scale to do very nicely in

this market. We've got advanced production and bottling equipment and long-term contracts with some major growers. No problems there. We also sell freshly squeezed pomegranate juice: customers loved it in the tests, but producing the stuff at the right price is a major hassle: all the seeds get in the way. We hope it will be a winner, once we get the production right and start converting customers to it. After all the market for exotic fruit juices generally is expanding fast.'

What sort of products, according to the Boston classification, are described here?

5.2.2 The General Electric Business Screen

The approach of the GE Business Screen (GEBS) is similar to that of the BCG matrix. The GEBS includes a broader range of company and market factors. This matrix **classifies products (or businesses)** according to **industry attractiveness** and **company strengths**. The approach aims to consider a variety of factors which contribute to both these variables.

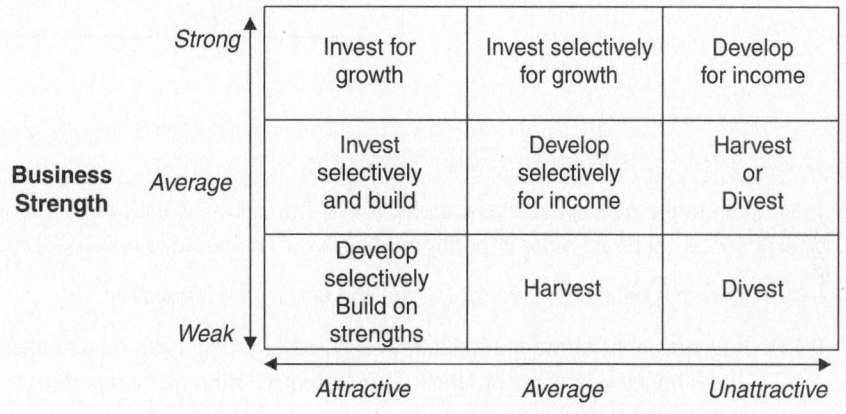

The broader approach of the GE matrix attempts to match competences within the company to conditions within the market place. Difficulties associated with measurement and classification mean that again the results must be interpreted with care.

5.2.3 The Shell directional policy matrix

There have been several other matrices designed as guides to strategy. The **Shell directional policy matrix** is similar to the GEBS in that its classifications depend upon **managerial judgement** rather than simple **numerical scores**, as in the BCG matrix. Its axes are **competitive capability** and **prospects for sector profitability**. Clearly, these measures are very similar to those used in the GEBS.

Prospects for sector profitability

		Unattractive	Average	Attractive
	Weak	Disinvest	Phased withdrawal	Double or quit
Enterprise's competitive capabilities	Average	Phased withdrawal	Custodial Growth	Try harder
	Strong	Cash generation	Growth Leader	Leader

5.2.4 Problems with portfolio planning

In addition to the questionable assumptions that the market is easy to define and that low cost is a result of experience, there are other important criticisms of the portfolio matrix approach.

(a)   Its recommendations are over-simplistic and ignore **innovation**.

(b)   It ignores links between products. A successful product can be damaged if a less successful one is discontinued or starved of funds. **Completeness of range** is important to both consumers and distributors.

(c)   It considers the position of the market leader but **ignores other rivals** that may be growing more effectively.

Also, it is difficult to put into practice as it gives no guidance on:

(a)   How the market position of the products should be **improved** – ie how much extra or less market share to go for.

(b)   What the **mix** of question marks, stars and cash cows ought to be.

(c)   How a policy of developing question marks into stars and stars into cash cows can be implemented in **practice**.

5.3 Direct product profitability

Management accountants may be asked to review the profitability of a product or product line. This can be done using direct product profitability analysis.

5.3.1 Direct product profitability (DPP)

Direct product profitability is a technique to analyse the profit on each individual product line, to arrive at relative profitabilities of different products.

KEY TERM

DIRECT PRODUCT PROFITABILITY is a measure 'used primarily within the retail sector, (and) involves the attribution of both the purchase price and other indirect costs (for example distribution, warehousing and retailing) to each product line. Thus a net profit, as opposed to a gross profit, can be identified for each product. The cost attribution process utilises a variety of measures (for example warehousing space and transport time) to reflect the resource consumption of individual products.'   (CIMA *Official Terminology*)

DPP arose from the need for manufacturers to encourage retailers to place new products onto their shelves. Supermarkets analyse the direct profitability of every branded and non-branded product they sell. This helps them decide on what ranges to present in store and provides a focus for individual marketing initiatives. The profitability of entire commodity groups is presented after taking account of factors in addition to cost, such as supplier discounts and wastage levels.

DPP is calculated by determining the sales revenue from a product (less any discounts or refunds given) and then deducting the costs incurred by stocking that product. These costs will be:

*   The purchase price charged by the supplier (less any discounts)
*   The costs of ordering the product
*   The costs of storing the product
*   Transport costs incurred in getting the product to its point of sale
*   Wastage and obsolescence

It is useful to analyse how DPP can be used in practice. We can take the limiting factor to be shelf space in this example.

	Product		
	X	Y	Z
Selling price	£1.50	£1.25	£1.30
Purchase cost	£1.00	£0.80	£1.00
Gross profit	£0.50	£0.45	£0.30
Gross profit % of sales price	33%	36%	23%
Shelf space per unit	15 cm^2	9 cm^2	12 cm^2
Gross profit per cm^2	3.3p	5p	2.5p

This would imply that Y was the most profitable for the retailer: however this ignores stock turnover. In other words, if sales volumes of Y are higher than for X or Z, the product makes a higher profit in total. Let us add sales volumes into the calculation and estimate as to how much shelf space the product takes up.

	Product		
	X	Y	Z
Gross profit per product	£0.50	£0.45	£0.30
Total shelf space	750 cm^2	600 cm^2	1,200 cm^2
Weekly sales volume	30	20	60
Gross profit per cm^2 per week	$\frac{50p \times 30}{750} = 2p$	$\frac{45p \times 20}{600} = 1.5p$	$\frac{30p \times 60}{1,200} = 1.5p$

This analysis, based on sales volume suggests that for the retailer X is the better bet. Why might this be so?

(a)   **Inventory turnover**. The manufacturer of X might offer to replenish the shelves twice a week, thereby halving the amount of space needed to support the same sales volume. This increases the profit per unit of scarce resource.

(b)   **Product size**, as indicated, is a reason why the unit profit might differ. This is why packaging decisions can, from the retailer's viewpoint, affect a product's attractiveness.

This example demonstrates the importance of obtaining sufficient information before a meaningful analysis can be carried out. Simple information on cm^2 occupied per unit was insufficient. Sales volumes, total shelf space required and probably in some cases additional direct costs (such as handling, administration) all need to be taken into account.

DPP can also be useful in a **marketing context**. There are two broad approaches to marketing: one is that products are the source of an organisation's profits, the other is that customers are the source of profits. (We will look at marketing in more detail in a later chapter of this Study Text.)

DPP can be useful in the first of these approaches to marketing, because it suggests that the way to commercial success is to make (and sell) more of the products which generate the highest product profitability.

However, DPP analysis might also lead companies to try alternative ways of increasing product profitability: for example, by reducing the costs of stocking the product by reducing the size of product packaging.

Alternatively, manufacturers may also directly reduce retailers' costs in selling their product by offering point of sale support. For example, a frozen food manufacturer may provide a retailer with a refrigerator unit in which to store their products in the shop. This will increase the DPP of that supplier's products compared to rival products for which the supermarket may have to provide its own refrigeration units and so may influence which supplier the supermarket buys its products from.

Problems with DPP:

(a) Brand expenditure can be spread over a number of different products, making accurate allocation difficult.

(b) DPP focuses internally on product characteristics, but in doing so ignores the needs of the customers.

(c) **Cross-subsidisation** is a feature of many product strategies. An example is provided by computer games.

    (i) The hardware (eg the games console) may be priced relatively cheaply:

        – To deter competitors (raising entry barriers)
        – To encourage customers to buy

    (ii) The software, or games which are run, will be priced relatively expensively, to recoup some of the cost. Also, barriers to entry will exist as the manufacturer will own patents, have exclusive distribution deals etc, and there will be a switching cost, of course.

However, DPP overlooks these interrelations between products.

Section summary

The **product life cycle** shows that, generally, products pass through five stages: introduction, growth, shakeout, maturity, and decline. Portfolio planning aims to create a balance among the firm's products in order to maximise competitive advantage. Matrices such the Boston Classification (BCG matrix), the GE business screen, or the Shell matrix can assist firms in achieving a balanced portfolio of products.

6 New products and innovation

Introduction

Innovation can be a major source of competitive advantage but brings a burden of cost and uncertainty. To avoid waste, there should be a programme of assessment for major product development.

6.1 Innovation

This section looks at how an organisation can develop its capacity for new products. This idea is developed further in Chapter 6 where we look at how product development can be used as a strategy for growth.

6.1.1 Innovation and competitive advantage

For many organisations, product innovation and being the **first mover** may be a major source of competitive advantage.

(a) A reputation for innovation will attract **early adopters**, though it depends in part on promotional effort.

(b) Customers may find they are locked in to innovative suppliers by unacceptable **costs of switching** to competitors.

(c) The **learning** (or experience) **curve** effect may bring cost advantages.

(d) The first mover may be able to **define the industry standard**.

(e) A **price skimming** strategy can bring early profits that will be denied to later entrants.

(f) Legal protection, such as patents, for intellectual property may bring important revenue advantages. This is particularly important in the pharmaceutical industry.

However, the first mover also has particular problems:

- Gaining regulatory approval where required
- Uncertain demand
- High levels of R&D costs
- Lower cost imitators
- Costs of introduction such as training sales staff and educating customers

PIMS (Profit Impact of Market Strategy) data indicate that there is a **negative correlation** between **profitability** and a high level of expenditure on **R&D**, perhaps because of the costs associated with these problems.

6.1.2 Technology and the value chain

Porter points out in Competitive Advantage that 'every value activity uses some technology to combine purchased inputs and human resources to produce some output.' He discusses the varied role of information technology and emphasises the importance of administrative or office technology. The significance of this for strategy lies in the area of core competences. Just as R&D is as much concerned with processes as with products, so improvement in the linkages of the value chain will enhance competitive advantage.

6.2 New product strategies

The development of new products might be considered an important aspect of a firm's competitive and marketing strategies.

(a) New and innovative products can lower **entry barriers** to existing industries and markets, if new technology is involved.

(b) The interests of the company are best met with a balanced product portfolio. Managers must plan when to introduce new products, how best to extend the life of mature ones and when to abandon those in decline.

A strategic issue managers must consider is their approach to new product development.

(a) Features of a **Leader strategy**:

- An innovative strategy is taken to gain competitive advantage
- Heavy **R&D** emphasis
- Shortened likely length of product life cycles
- Reduced potential profitability due to high **R&D costs**

(b)   Features of a **Follower strategy**:

- Lower costs

- Less emphasis on **R&D**

- Sacrifices early rewards of innovation but avoids its risks

- May have to license certain technologies from a leader

- Can be a **more profitable strategy** especially when the follower can learn from the leader's mistakes

A matrix of new product strategies and new market strategies can be set out as follows.

Product

	No technological change	*Improved technology*	*New technology*
Market unchanged	–	*Reformulation* A new balance between price/quality has to be formulated	*Replacement* The new technology replaces the old
Market strengthened (ie new demand from same customers)	*Remerchandising* The product is sold in a new way – eg by re-packaging	*Improved product* Sales growth to existing customers sought on the strength of product improvements	*Product line extension* The new product is added to the existing product line to increase total demand
New market	*New use* By finding a new use for the existing product, new customers are found	*Market extension* New customers sought on the strength of product improvements	*Diversification*

6.3 Research and development

Research may be **pure, applied** or **development**. It may be intended to improve **products** or **processes**. New product development should be controlled by requiring strategic approval at key points of development.

R&D should support the organisation's strategy and be closely co-ordinated with marketing.

6.4 Product and process research

There are two categories of R&D.

KEY TERMS

PRODUCT RESEARCH is based on creating new products and developing existing ones.

PROCESS RESEARCH is based on improving the way, or efficiency with which, those products or services are made or delivered.

Product research – new product development

The product development process must be carefully controlled. New products are a major source of competitive advantage but are expensive to bring to market. A screening process is necessary to ensure

that resources are concentrated on projects with a high probability of success and not wasted on those that have poor prospects.

Idea generation and **strategy formulation** are also important features of new product development.

(a) To be effective, **idea generation** requires a system to promote, and reward creativity and innovative ideas. Cooper suggests a four point plan.

    (i)   Nominate one manager to be the **focal point for ideas**.

    (ii)   That manager establishes where ideas may **arise**.

    (iii)   Those sources are **encouraged**.

    (iv)   The ideas they produce are **captured**.

(b) **Strategy formulation**. A business should have a detailed new product strategy, specifying goals, priorities, funding and methods. This is a top management responsibility.

Product research is not confined to dealing with new products. It has an important role in connection with **existing products**.

(a) **Value engineering** may be used to continue the development of existing products so that they use cheaper components or processes without compromising the perceived value of the market offer.

(b) As products near the end of their **life cycle**, it may be possible to develop them for launch in a different market, or simply to extend their lives.

(c) Where products are replaced by new versions it may be advantageous to ensure new products are **backwards compatible** with the installed base. This is an important consideration in software engineering, for example.

6.5 Process research

Process research looks at how the goods/services are produced. Process research has these aspects.

(a) **Processes** are crucial in service industries (eg fast food), where processes are part of the services sold.

(b) **Productivity**. Efficient processes save money and time.

(c) **Planning**. If you know how long certain stages in a project are likely to take, you can plan the most efficient sequence.

(d) **Quality management** for enhanced quality.

Advances in process research are much harder to imitate than product developments. Competitors can purchase and **reverse engineer** new products. With good physical security in place, they will find it much harder to imitate new processes.

The strategic role of R&D. R&D should support the organisation's chosen strategy. For example, if a strategy of **differentiation** has been adopted, it would be inappropriate to research ways of minimising costs. If the company has a competence in R&D, this may form the basis for a strategy of product innovation. Conversely, where product lifecycles are short, as in consumer electronics, product development is fundamental to strategy.

Customer needs, as identified by marketers, should be a vital input to new product developments.

The R&D department might identify possible changes to product specifications so that a variety of marketing mixes can be tried out and screened.

6.6 Problems with R&D

(a) **Organisational**. Problems of authority relationships and integration arise with the management of R&D. The function will have to liaise closely with marketing and with production, as well as with senior management responsible for corporate planning: its role is both strategic and technical.

(b)   **Financial**. R&D is by nature not easily planned in advance, and financial performance targets are not easily set. Budgeting for long-term, complex development projects with uncertain returns can be a nightmare for management accountants.

(c)   **Evaluation and control**. Pure research or even applied research may not have an obvious pay off in the short term. Evaluation could be based on successful application of new ideas, such as patents obtained and the commercial viability of new products.

(d)   **Staff problems**. Research staff are usually highly qualified and profession-orientated, with consequences for the style of supervision and level of remuneration offered to them.

(e)   **Cultural problems**. Encouraging innovation means trial and error, flexibility, tolerance of mistakes in the interests of experimentation, high incentives etc. If this is merely a subculture in an essentially bureaucratic organisation, it will not only be difficult to sustain, but will become a source of immense 'political' conflict. The R&D department may have an 'academic' or university atmosphere, as opposed to a commercial one.

6.6.1 Drivers for innovation

Market pull: Marketers suggest that the best way to competitive advantage is to find out what the market wants and give it to them.

Technology push: Unfortunately, market pull innovation tends merely to produce better versions of products that already exist. A more fruitful approach may be 'product orientation'. The world is full of products that no-one asked for, including post-it notes and mobile phones that are also cameras. This approach we might call **technology push**.

Collaboration: Perhaps the best approach would be a combination of the two, where technologists try to solve customers' problems and marketers try to find applications for new and emerging technologies. Many new developments are the result of **collaboration between suppliers and customers**.

CASE STUDY

Procter & Gamble – Open innovation

Historically, companies have looked for their own staff to provide them with their sources of innovation and new products. However, why should a company restrict the generation of new ideas to its own staff only? There are many external sources – for example, scientists, engineers, universities and other companies – who could all have the know-how and technical expertise to contribute to new product development.

As with many mature organisations, in 2000 Procter & Gamble's R&D productivity was flat, while innovation costs were increasing faster than sales growth. Therefore, the CEO at the time, challenged the company to stop spending more and more on R&D for diminishing returns, and reinvent Procter & Gamble's innovation business model. Put simply, the company's existing 'invent-it-yourself' approach was not capable of sustaining sales growth.

This prompted Procter & Gamble (P & G) to recognise the potential of the pools of expertise and ideas, and the opportunities for innovation which existed outside the company, and it sought to make use of them through its Connect+Develop programme.

The CEO set the business a target of acquiring 50% of its innovations from *outside* the company.

P & G practises 'open innovation,' which is a means of accessing externally developed intellectual property and at the same time allowing its own internally developed assets and know-how to be used by others. So, for P & G innovation has become a two-way process.

Through Connect+Develop, P & G actively seeks to collaborate with external partners to generate and develop new products ideas. P & G employs about 7,500 researchers, but the logic was that for every P & G researcher there were another 200 scientists or engineers elsewhere in the world who were just as good. This meant that there were a further 1.5 million scientists out there who did not work for P & G. The logic of the Connect+Develop programme was that P&G's R&D programme should use ideas from the full 1,507,500.

By identifying promising ideas from this pool throughout the world, P&G could then apply its R&D, manufacturing, marketing and purchasing capabilities to them to create better and cheaper products, faster than it could otherwise have done.

This attempt to 'un-source' ideas appears to be working. By 2006, more than 35% of P & G's new products had elements that originate from outside the company, and 45% of the initiatives in their product development portfolio had key elements that were discovered externally. At the same time, R&D productivity within P&G had increased by nearly 60%.

Section summary

Innovation can lead to competitive advantage, but it is very expensive and results are not guaranteed. Research may be pure, applied or development and may be intended to improve products or processes.

7 Benchmarking   3/12

Benchmarking enables a firm to meet industry standards by copying others, but it is perhaps less valuable as a source of innovation.

KEY TERM

BENCHMARKING is the 'establishment, through data gathering, of targets and comparators, through whose use relative levels of performance (and particularly areas of underperformance) can be identified. By the adoption of identified best practices it is hoped that performance will improve.

(CIMA Official Terminology)

Benchmarking provides management with a means of identifying how well areas of an organisation are performing, with a view to improving the performance of those areas which are currently underperforming.

In this respect, benchmarking could be an important performance management tool. Managing performance is an important underlying theme in strategy implementation, and we will look at aspects of performance management in more detail in Chapter 14 of this Study Text.

7.1 Types of benchmarking

(a)   **Internal benchmarking**. This involves comparing one operating unit or function with similar ones within the same organisation. This is easier to do than comparing performance with that of external organisations, but it is unlikely to lead to innovative or best-practice solutions.

(b)   **Competitive benchmarking**: in which performance information is gathered about direct competitors. From a strategic perspective, the value of competitor benchmarking is that if an organisation can match a competitor's performance in an area which was previously a core competence for the competitor, that area is no longer a source of competitive advantage for the competitor.

      However, at a practical level, the biggest problem with competitor benchmarking could be in obtaining information about the competitor. In particular, a competitor is unlikely to disclose information about a process or area of performance which it knows relates to an area of competitive advantage for it.

(c)   **Functional benchmarking**. This involves comparing the performance of internal functions with that of the best external practitioners, regardless of their industry. (This type of benchmarking is also known as operational benchmarking or generic benchmarking).

(d)   **Process (or activity) benchmarking**. This involves comparing work processes to similar processes in other organisations which are not competitors but which have innovative or best practice processes (for example, comparing the processes for serving customers in banks and supermarkets).

Through process benchmarking, an organisation can try to find new, innovative ways to create competitive advantage, as well as solving threshold problems. And, because the comparator is not a competitor, there is likely to be less resistance to sharing information than would be case in relation to competitive benchmarking.

Benchmarking can be divided into eight stages.

Obtain management support

Senior management commitment to the benchmarking process is only genuinely available when senior managers have a full appreciation of the objectives of the project, its benefits and its costs. Senior management are can change their minds when it becomes apparent that they did not anticipate the actual levels of cost or inconvenience a project may bring. For the project to be a success it is essential that senior management endorse it.

Determine the areas to be benchmarked and set objectives

Determine areas to benchmark by identifying the critical business processes or those which are the main drivers of revenues and costs.

Set objectives. Note that here, the objectives will not be in the form of aspirations for improvement to specific processes and practices, but more in the nature of stating the extent and depth of the enquiry.

Understand processes and identify key performance measures

Understand processes. Before any key performance measures can be set, the benchmarking team will need to understand the processes which drive them. This will require discussion with **key stakeholders** plus observation and documentation of the way work is carried out.

Identify key performance measures. Once the team understand the processes, then they can identify key performance measures for the processes (for example, the length of time between receiving a customer order and despatching the goods ordered).

Choose organisations to benchmark against

This can either be done **internally** (comparing one division against another) or through **external** competitive benchmarking (comparing performance with rival companies). Firms often want to compare their performance against the **'best in class'** external performer. However, they have to be realistic about whether that 'best in class' performer will be willing to share performance information with them.

Measure performance

Measure own and others' performance. Negotiation should take place to establish who does the measurement. Ideally, a joint team made up of people from both the organisations being benchmarked should do it, but there may be issues of confidentiality or convenience that mean each organisation does its own measuring.

Compare performance and discuss results

Raw data must be carefully analysed if appropriate conclusions are to be drawn.

Discuss results with management and staff. The **stakeholders** concerned are likely both to have useful comments and also to be anxious about the possibility of adverse reflection upon them. It is important to remember that the purpose of benchmarking is not to apportion blame for poor performance, but to act as an opportunity to improve performance.

Improvement programmes

Design and implement improvement programmes. It may be possible to import complete systems or it may be appropriate to combine various elements of best practice. Sometimes, improvements require extensive **reorganisation** and **restructuring**, and may sometimes also involve **outsourcing**.

In many cases, there is likely to be a requirement for **training**. Improvements in administrative systems often call for investment in new equipment, particularly in IT systems.

Monitor improvements

The continuing effectiveness of improvements must be monitored. At the same time, it must be understood that **improvement is a continuous process rather than a one-off change** and so further adjustments (and follow-up benchmarking exercises) may be beneficial.

Johnson, Scholes and Whittington set out questions that should be asked when carrying out a benchmarking exercise as part of a wider strategic review.

- **Why** are these products or services provided at all?
- Why are they provided **in that particular way**?
- What are the examples of **best practice** elsewhere?
- How should activities be **reshaped** in the light of these comparisons?

They see three levels of benchmarking.

Level of benchmarking	Through	Examples of measures
Resources	Resource audit	Quantity of resources • revenue/employee • capital intensity
		Quality of resources • Qualifications of employees • Age of machinery • Uniqueness (eg patents)
Competences in separate activities	Analysing activities	Sales calls per salesperson Output per employee Materials wastage
Competences in linked activities	Analysing overall performances	Market share Profitability Productivity

When selecting an appropriate **benchmark basis**, companies should ask themselves the following questions.

(a) Is it possible and easy to obtain reliable competitor information?

(b) Is there any wide discrepancy between different internal divisions?

(c) Can similar processes be identified in non-competing environments and are these non competing companies willing to co-operate?

(d) Is best practice operating in a similar environmental setting?

(e) What is our timescale?

(f) Do the chosen companies have similar objectives and strategies?

7.2 Advantages of benchmarking

Benchmarking has the following advantages.

(a) **Position audit**. Benchmarking can assess a firm's existing position, and provide a basis for establishing standards of performance.

(b) The comparisons are **carried out by the managers** who have to live with any changes implemented as a result of the exercise.

(c) Benchmarking **focuses** on improvement and sets targets which are challenging but achievable.

(d) The sharing of information can be a **spur to innovation**.

(e) The result should be **improved performance**, particularly in cost control and delivering value.

(f) Benchmarking can provide an organisation with an early warning if its performance begins to slip compared to the organisations against which it is being benchmarked.

7.3 Dangers of benchmarking

Many companies have gained significant benefits from benchmarking but there may be dangers.

(a) It concentrates on **doing things right** rather than **doing the right thing**: the difference between **efficiency** and **effectiveness**. A process can be efficient but its output may not be useful. Other measures (such as amending the value chain) may be a better way of securing competitive advantage.

(b) The benchmark may be **yesterday's solution to tomorrow's problem**. For example, a cross-channel ferry company might benchmark its activities (eg speed of turnround at Dover and Calais, cleanliness on ship) against another ferry company, whereas the real competitor is the Channel Tunnel.

(c) It is a **catching-up exercise rather than the development of anything distinctive**. After the benchmarking exercise, the competitor might improve performance in a different way.

(d) It depends on **accurate** information about comparator companies.

(e) It is **not cost-free** and can divert **management attention**. The benchmark measures have to be collated, turned into a report and then discussed. This takes time and effort, but at the end of it management may just feel they are being overloaded with information.

(f) It can become a hindrance and even a threat: **sharing information** with other companies can be a burden and a security risk.

(g) It may reduce managerial motivation, if the performance of the managers' areas is compared unfavourably to rival organisations. For benchmarking to be useful, the ultimate outcome of the benchmarking exercise should not be the measures themselves but improvements in the underlying processes which drive performance.

Section summary

Benchmarking enables a firm to identify relative levels of performance and best practice. Performance levels can then be improved by implementing the best practice identified by the benchmarking process.

Chapter Roundup

✓   It is necessary to develop an understanding of an organisation's current position before a strategic plan can be developed.

✓   Limiting factors are anything which limit the activity of an entity. Resources should be used as effectively and efficiently as possible in order to make the best use of them. Firms should aim to reduce the limitation in the long-run.

✓   The value chain shows how value is created and how competitive advantage can be gained. Value adding activities do not stop at the organisation's boundaries, and a firm's value chain is connected to others in a value system.

✓   By establishing closer links with companies in the supply chain, firms can obtain best value for money and reduce inventory holdings. Supply chain management is a means by which firms aim to manage the chain from input resources through to the final customer.

✓   The **product life cycle** shows that, generally, products pass through five stages: introduction, growth, shake out, maturity, and decline. Portfolio planning aims to create a balance among the firm's products in order to maximise competitive advantage. Matrices such as the Boston classification (BCG matrix), the GE business screen, or the Shell matrix can assist firms in achieving a balanced portfolio of products.

✓   Innovation can lead to competitive advantage, but it is very expensive and results are not guaranteed. Research may be pure, applied or development and may be intended to improve products or processes.

✓   Benchmarking enables a firm to identify relative levels of performance and best practice. Performance levels can then be improved by implementing the best practice identified by the benchmarking process.

Quick Quiz

1   What are the 9 'Ms' categorised in the Ms model?

2   What is a limiting or key factor? Give an example.

3   Which of these describes 'efficiency', and which 'effectiveness'?

       (a)   Whether the resources have been deployed in the best possible way.

       (b)   How well the resources have been utilised irrespective of the purpose for which they have been employed.

4   Is logistics a primary or secondary activity in the value chain?

5   In Porter's value chain model, who is value ultimately created for?

6   What are the stages of the product life cycle?

7   Complete the BCG matrix below

Market ....

		High	Low
	High	....	....
Market	**Low**	....	....

Answers to Quick Quiz

1   Machinery; Make-up; Management; Management Information; Markets, Materials; Men and women; Methods; Money

2   A limiting factor or key factor is 'a factor which at any time or over a period may limit the activity of an entity, often one where there is shortage or difficulty of supply.' An example would be a shortage of production capacity.

3   (a)   effectiveness
     (b)   efficiency

4   Primary

5   The end-user consumer. The value chain expresses the way value is added to the products or services produced by an entity from the perspective of the end-user consumer (not from the perspective of the organisation.)

6   Introduction, growth, shakeout, maturity, decline.

7

| | | *Relative market share* | |
		High	*Low*
Market growth	*High*	Stars	Question marks
	Low	Cash cows	Dogs

Answers to Questions

4.1 Creating value

Here are some ideas for organising the activities of buying, cooking and serving food in a way that customers will value.

(a) It can become more efficient, by automating production, as in fast food chains.

(b) The chef can develop commercial relationships with growers, so he or she can obtain the best quality fresh produce.

(c) The chef can specialise in a particular type of cuisine (eg Nepalese, Korean).

(d) The restaurant can be sumptuously decorated for those customers who value 'atmosphere' and a sense of occasion, in addition to good food.

(e) The restaurant can serve a particular type of customer (eg celebrities).

4.2 Value chain and value system

Sana Sounds is involved in the record industry from start to finish. Although recording and CD manufacture are contracted out to external suppliers, this makes no difference to the fact that these activities are part of Sana Sounds' own value chain. Sana Sounds earns its money by managing the whole set of activities. If the company grows then perhaps it will acquire its own recording studios.

Note the subsidiary point (in the 'Stop and think…') that changes in technology are offering new opportunities in the way music is distributed. Consumers can now download tracks from the internet rather than having to buy physical discs.

4.3 Juicy drinks

(a) Orange juice is a cash cow
(b) Pomegranate juice is a question mark, which the company wants to turn into a star.

Now try this question from the Exam Question Bank	**Number**	**Level**	**Marks**	**Time**
	Q4	Intermediate	n/a	45 mins

GENERIC STRATEGIES

After looking at the context in which strategic planning decisions are made, and the internal and external factors which affect strategic decisions, we will now look at the range of strategic options which organisations can choose from.

There are three key aspects to these options:

- How to compete
- Direction of growth
- Method of growth

In this chapter we will look at the first of these three options, and consider the competitive strategies by which a firm can compete. Michael Porter identified two underlying generic strategies: cost leadership, or differentiation.

In Chapter 6 we will then look at the different directions and methods of growth a firm can choose from.

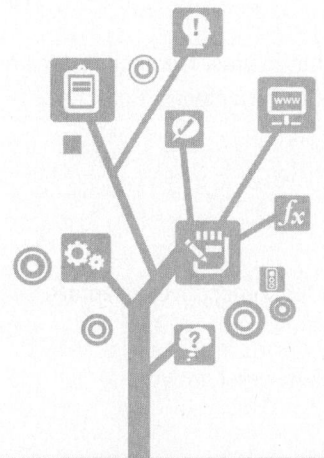

topic list	learning outcomes	syllabus references	ability required
1 Factors affecting strategic options	C 1 (b)	C 1 (iii)	Evaluate
2 Generic competitive strategies	C 1 (b)	C 1 (iv)	Evaluate
3 Using the value chain in competitive strategy	C 1 (b)	C 1 (iv)	Evaluate
4 Pricing and competition	C 1 (b)	C 1 (iv)	Evaluate

1 Factors affecting strategic options

Introduction

Once an organisation has identified the opportunities and threats in its external environment and its internal strengths and weaknesses, it must make choices about what **strategies** to pursue in order to achieve its targets and objectives.

1.1 Core businesses

A business should have a **common thread** running through all of its activities, which gives them a purpose or logic.

(a) The aim of some businesses is to pursue **diversified activities**. The common thread in such businesses will usually be to earn a high return on investments, largely through acquisitions and disposals.

(b) Many organisations, however, identify themselves with **certain products or markets**, to which most of their activities are devoted. These are the organisation's **core businesses**.

In seeking to define their core businesses, firms should not confuse the **market** with the **industry**.

(a) **The market** is defined by consumer needs and reflects consumer demands.

(b) **The industry** is defined by related firm capabilities and industries are based on supply technologies. Washing machines and refrigerators are products of the same industry, despite their wholly different purposes.

If a company recognises that it is in a declining business, or in one where future growth will be restricted, it should seek to expand in other areas or to exploit the remaining competitive advantages it has.

1.2 Strategic choices

It is possible to analyse strategic choice into three categories.

(a) Competitive strategies are the strategies an organisation will pursue for competitive advantage. They determine **how you compete**.

(b) Product-market strategies determine **where you compete** and the direction of growth.

(c) Institutional strategies determine the **method of growth**.

Exam skills

It is very important that you appreciate these three categories of strategic choice. Many of the exam questions you will face in E3 will require you to analyse or evelute one or more aspects of a strategic choice. If you are asked to advise an organisation about a proposed strategic choice, then you should be prepared to consider its implications for these three aspects of the organisation's strategy.

1.2.1 Horizontal boundaries

A firm's **horizontal boundaries** define the variety of products and services that it produces. The optimum horizontal boundary for a firm depends on **economies of scale**. In some industries, such as pharmaceuticals, company size is influenced by a preference for mergers ('bigger is better') and corporate giants emerge, such as *Du Pont*. A few large firms account for the vast proportion of industry sales.

Economies of scale occur when large scale processes, such as production and distribution, have cost advantages over smaller scale processes. Economies of scale affect both the size of firms and the structure of markets, and so consideration of them, and therefore where organisational boundaries should be, is vital in any business strategy decision about possible merger or expansion.

1.2.2 Vertical boundaries

The **vertical boundaries** of a firm define which activities the firm performs itself and which it purchases from independent firms. A number of firms now **outsource** activities which they feel are not part of their core competencies.

The concept of vertical boundaries is allied to the concepts of the **value chain and value networks. For example, a value chain might** with the acquisition of raw materials and culminate in distribution and sale of the finished goods. In this case, a firm needs to decide how much of the value creation process it wants control internally and how much of the value passes outside the firm.

We will look at horizontal and vertical integration again later in Chapter 6 in the context of **related diversification** as a product-market strategy.

1.2.3 Products and strategy

The right strategy depends on the type of product or service that the firm is producing.

(a) **Search products**. These are products whose attributes the consumer can discern, evaluate and compare fairly easily, eg size and colour.

(b) **Experience products**. These are products whose attributes cannot be discerned until the consumer has had experience of using the product – eg taste in the case of food.

(c) **Credence products**. These are products whose important attributes cannot be evaluated by the consumer either because the product's attributes might vary the next time (eg quality of service in a restaurant) or because the product's attributes cannot easily be evaluated (eg pet food).

Products may be categorised as follows.

(a) **Breakthrough products** offer either a radical performance advantage over competition, drastically lower price, or ideally, may offer both.

(b) **Improved products** are not radically different to their competition but are obviously superior in terms of better performance at a competitive price.

(c) **Competitive products** show no obvious advantage over others, but derive their appeal from a particular compromise of cost and performance.

1.3 Strategic marketing issues

A **standard** product might satisfy the needs of all customers in the market. On the other hand, **variations** in a product's design might appeal more strongly to some prospective customers than others.

Customers differ in various respects – according to age, sex, income, geographical area, buying attitudes, buying habits etc. Each of these differences can be used to **segment** a market.

By creating a new market segment or entering a growing market segment a company can hope to achieve the following.

(a) **Increase sales and profits**, by meeting customer needs in a number of different ways
(b) Extend the **life cycle** of the product
(c) Capture some of the overall **market share** from competitors
(d) Survive in the face of competition

Section summary

A firm has to make strategic choices about **how** to compete, **where** to compete (products, markets), and **how to grow** (organically or externally).

2 Generic competitive strategies

Introduction

Porter suggests there are three generic strategies: **cost leadership**, **differentiation** and **focus**. These ideas have subsequently been extended into the idea of the **strategy clock**.

In any market where there are competitors, strategic and marketing decisions will often be taken in response to what a competitor has done.

Competitive advantage is anything which gives one organisation an edge over its rivals. Porter argues that a firm should adopt a competitive strategy which is intended to achieve some form of competitive advantage for the firm. A firm that possesses a **competitive advantage** will be able to make profit exceeding its cost of capital: in terms of economic theory, this is '**excess profit**' or '**economic rent**'. The existence of excess profit tends to be temporary because of the effect of the **five competitive forces**. When a company can continue to earn excess profit despite the effects of competition, it possesses a **sustainable competitive advantage**.

KEY TERM

COMPETITIVE STRATEGY means 'taking offensive or defensive actions to create a dependable position in an industry, to cope successfully with ... competitive forces and thereby yield a superior return on investment for the firm. Firms have discovered many different approaches to this end, and the best strategy for a given firm is ultimately a unique construction reflecting its particular circumstances'. *(Porter)*

Porter's five forces model is discussed in the E2 syllabus and is assumed knowledge for E3, although we have included a brief recap of the model in the Introductory chapter at the start of this Study Text. Make sure you could apply the five forces model to help answer a question in your exams.

2.1 The choice of competitive strategy   11/10, 5/11, 3/12

Porter believes there are three **generic strategies** for competitive advantage. To be successful, Porter argues, a company must follow only one of the strategies. If they try to combine more than one they risk losing their competitive advantage and becoming '**stuck in the middle.**'

KEY TERMS

COST LEADERSHIP means being the lowest cost producer in the industry as a whole.

DIFFERENTIATION is the exploitation of a product or service which the **industry as a whole** believes to be unique.

Focus involves a restriction of activities to only part of the market (a segment) through:

- Providing goods and/or services at lower cost to that segment (**cost-focus**)
- Providing a differentiated product or service to that segment (**differentiation-focus**)

Cost leadership and differentiation are industry-wide strategies. Focus involves segmentation but involves pursuing, within the segment only, a strategy of cost leadership or differentiation.

2.1.1 Cost leadership

A cost leadership strategy seeks to achieve the position of lowest-cost producer in the **industry as a whole**.

By producing at the **lowest cost**, the manufacturer can could either charge the same price as its competitors knowing that this would enable it to generate a greater profit per unit than them, or it could decide to charge a lower price than them. This could be particularly beneficial if the goods or services which the organisation sells are price sensitive.

How to achieve overall cost leadership

- Set up production facilities to obtain **economies of scale**

- Use the **latest technology** such as CAD/CAM and computerised stock and logistics control to reduce costs and/or enhance productivity

- Exploit the **learning curve effect**

- Concentrate on **improving productivity**

- **Minimise overhead costs**

- **Get favourable access to sources of supply** and buy in bulk wherever possible (to obtain discounts for bulk purchases)

- **Relocate to cheaper areas** (possibly in a different country)

- Use **IT** to record and analyse costs

The airline industry provides some good examples of where companies have deliberately pursued cost leadership strategies: for example, *South West Airlines* in the US, and *EasyJet* or *Ryanair* in Europe.

Value chain analysis, which we looked at in the previous chapter, could be very useful when considering which generic strategy to pursue. If a company wishes to pursue a cost leadership strategy, it will need to ensure that its costs are as low as possible across all the different activities in its value chain.

Exam skills

Remember that Porter identified the importance of *cost* leadership (not price leadership) as one of the generic strategies. Although companies which are pursuing a cost leadership strategy might then choose to compete on price, the focus of Porter's model is on how companies can *produce* goods or services at a lower cost than their rivals, rather than selling price *per se*.

2.1.2 Differentiation

A differentiation strategy assumes that competitive advantage can be gained through **particular characteristics** of a firm's products or processes. Differentiation is often used to justify a firm charging a higher price for its products than its rivals do. This can allow the firm to earn higher margins than its rivals.

Products may be categorised as:

(a)   **Breakthrough products** offer a radical performance advantage over competition, perhaps at a drastically lower price (eg float glass, developed by Pilkington).

(b)   **Improved products** are not radically different from their competition but are obviously superior in terms of better performance at a competitive price (eg microchips).

(c) **Competitive products** derive their appeal from a particular compromise of cost and performance. For example, cars are not all sold at rock-bottom prices, nor do they all provide immaculate comfort and performance. They compete with each other by trying to offer a more attractive compromise than rival models.

How to differentiate

- **Build up a brand image** (for example, as Levi's has done in relation to jeans)
- **Give the product special features** to make it stand out
- **Exploit other activities of the value chain** such as marketing and sales or service
- Use **IT** to create new **services** or **product features**

CASE STUDY

Bang & Olufsen

The audio and television equipment manufacturer, Bang & Olufsen, has used a differentiation strategy, based on style, to distinguish its products from those of its competitors.

Bang & Olufsen has built an international reputation for quality, and has developed a very loyal customer base. Its sleek, tastefully discreet designs and high standards of production have earned it elite status in the market. For decades, these factors have formed the basis of Bang & Olufsen's advertising and marketing strategy, and the company has recognised that 'style' needs to be displayed distinctively in retail outlets.

This has led to the creation of 'concept shops' where subtle images are projected onto walls, and products are displayed in free-standing areas constructed from translucent walls.

The company's view is that one cannot sell Bang & Olufsen equipment when it is sandwiched amongst a densely-packed range of electrical goods or domestic appliances. By contrast, the concept shop gives the right look and feel to make the most of the products.

Bang & Olufsen has focused on the importance of style and aesthetics rather than technology or low prices in buying decisions. It sells products on the basis of ambience as much as sound.

However, one of the key challenges Bang & Olufsen faces is to keep its brand (and strategy) relevant in a world where customers' audio-visual habits (eg listening to music via downloads and portable devices) are changing. At the same time, Bang & Olufsen also needs to maintain its style distinction in the face of high-end equipment being produced, for example, by Samsung and Sony.

(Based on a case study in Jobber 'Principles and Practices of Marketing')

Advantages and disadvantages of industry-wide strategies

Competitive force	Advantages		Disadvantages	
	Cost leadership	Differentiation	Cost leadership	Differentiation
New entrants	Economies of scale raise entry barriers	Brand loyalty and perceived uniqueness are entry barriers		
Substitutes	Firm is not as vulnerable to the threat of substitutes as its less cost-effective competitors	Customer loyalty is a weapon against substitutes		
Customers	Customers cannot drive down prices further than the next most efficient competitor	Customers have no comparable alternative Brand loyalty should lower price sensitivity and prevent price wars		Customers may no longer need the differentiating factor. Sooner or later, customers become price sensitive
Suppliers	Flexibility to deal with cost increases	Higher margins can offset vulnerability to supplier price rises	Increase in input costs can reduce price advantages	
Industry rivalry	Firm remains profitable when rivals collapse due to excessive price competition	Unique features reduce direct competition	Technological change will require capital investment, or make production cheaper for competitors. Competitors learn via imitation. Cost concerns ignore product design or marketing issues	Imitation narrows differentiation

2.1.3 Focus (or niche) strategy

In a focus strategy, a firm concentrates its attention on one or more particular segments or niches of the market, and does not try to serve the entire market with a single product. For example, a firm could look to establish a nice based on: location, market segment and consumer type, product quality or product features.

Information technology (IT) can be useful in establishing the exact determining characteristics of the chosen niche, using existing customer records.

(a)   A **cost-focus strategy:** aim to be a cost leader for a particular segment. This type of strategy is often found in the printing, clothes manufacture and car repair industries.

(b)   A **differentiation-focus strategy:** pursue differentiation for a chosen segment. Luxury goods suppliers are the prime exponents of such a strategy. *Ben and Jerry's* ice cream is a good example of a product offering based on differentiation-focus.

CASE STUDY

Tyrell's

The crisp manufacturer, Tyrell's, has successfully implemented a focus differentiation strategy, by seizing an opportunity to produce better-quality potato chips than those traditionally found in the supermarkets. Tyrrell's has targeted its chips at a market segment that would be prepared to pay a higher price for good quality produce. A major feature of its strategy is to sell mainly through small retailers at the upper end of the grocery and catering markets – thereby avoiding direct competition with the market leader (Walkers crisps).

Tyrell's differentiates itself by cooking its potato chips by hand using the finest home-grown potatoes. All the chips are produced on the farm where the potatoes have been grown, so Tyrell's are in total control of the process 'from seed to chip'. (The company was set up by a potato farmer, who saw crisp production as a way to add extra value to his basic product, potatoes.)

- **Branding**. Tyrrell's marketing taps into the public's enthusiasm for 'authenticity' and 'provenance'. Its crisp packets tell the story of Tyrrell's. Pictures of employees growing potatoes on the Herefordshire farm and then cooking them illustrate the journey from 'seed to chip'.

- **Quality**. Tyrrell's chips are made from traditional varieties of potato and 'hand-fried' in small batches.

- **Distribution**. Tyrrell's sells directly to 80 per cent of its retail stockists. Students from a local agricultural college were employed to trawl through directories and identify fine-food shops to target with samples. After winning their business, Tyrrell's develops the relationship though personal contact.

- **Diffusion strategy**. Selling to the most exclusive shops creates a showcase for Tyrrell's to target consumers who are not sensitive to price, allowing it to grow profitably.

- **New product development**. The Tyrrell's product family consists of sixteen potato chip varieties, including exciting seasonal editions, a 'Best of British' range, and several locally inspired seasonings such as Ludlow Sausage & Wholegrain Mustard, and Worcester Sauce & Sundried Tomatoes. However, in addition to potato chips, they also now produce Root Vegetable Chips: 'Beetroot, Parsnip and Carrot Chips cooked to perfection'.

- **Exporting**. This has created a further sales channel through fine-food stores. Yet it has also forced greater dependency on distributors, introducing an unwelcome layer between itself and its customers.

Porter suggests that a focus strategy can achieve competitive advantage when '**broad-scope**' businesses fall into one of two errors.

(a)   **Underperformance** occurs when a product does not fully meet the needs of a segment and offers the opportunity for a **differentiation focus** player.

(b)   **Overperformance** gives a segment more than it really wants and provides an opportunity for a **cost focus** player.

Advantages of a focus strategy

- A niche is more secure and a firm can insulate itself from competition.
- The firm does not spread itself too thinly and can specialise in one particular area of expertise.
- Because the segment is relatively small, this reduces the investment in marketing operations required, compared to a strategy which involves competing across the whole market.

Drawbacks of a focus strategy

- The firm sacrifices economies of scale which could be gained by serving a wider market.
- The segment may not be sufficiently large to enable sufficient returns to be earned in the long run to satisfy investors.
- Competitors can move into the segment, with increased resources (eg the Japanese moved into the US luxury car market, to compete with Mercedes and BMW).
- The segment's needs may eventually become less distinct from the main market

In effect, in order to be successful, a niche must be large enough in terms of potential buyers, and must have sufficient growth potential to generate returns for a firm, yet it must remain of negligible interest to major competitors so that they don't enter it.

2.2 Which strategy?

Although there is a risk with any of the generic strategies, Porter argues that a firm must pursue one of them. A **stuck-in-the-middle** strategy is almost certain to make only low profits. 'This firm lacks the market share, capital investment and resolve to play the low-cost game, the industry-wide differentiation necessary to obviate the need for a low-cost position, or the focus to create differentiation or a low-cost position in a more limited sphere.'

CASE STUDY

Woolworths – Stuck in the middle

A company in the UK that suffered fatally from 'stuck-in-the-middle syndrome' was *Woolworths*.

Historically, Woolworths offered a diverse range of children's clothing, homewares, toys and games, music and entertainment, and confectionery. However, it found itself trying to compete against specialist retailers (such as *Game* for video games, and *HMV* for DVDs and CDs*)* and at the same time being squeezed by cheaper operators such as the supermarkets and Poundland (which offers a range of snack foods, healthcare products, and home- and kitchen-wares, all priced at £1).

In January 2009, Woolworths went into administration with the loss of approximately 27,000 jobs.

Exam skills

If you are asked to consider which generic strategy an organisation should pursue, or whether a particular strategy might be appropriate for it, it is vital to consider how well that strategy would 'fit' with the organisation's existing resources and culture. For example, if an organisation looks to provide high quality services, a cost leadership strategy is unlikely to be suitable for it, because some of its competitors who provide lower quality services are likely to have lower cost bases.

Question 5.1   Hermes

Learning outcomes C 1 (iv)

The managing director of Hermes Telecommunications plc is interested in corporate strategy. Hermes has invested a great deal of money in establishing a network which competes with that of Telecom UK, a recently privatised utility. Initially Hermes concentrated its efforts on business customers in the South East of England, especially the City of London, where it offered a lower cost service to that supplied by Telecom UK. Recently, Hermes has approached the residential market (ie domestic telephone users) offering a lower cost service on long-distance calls. Technological developments have resulted in the possibility of a cheap mobile telecommunication network, using microwave radio links. The franchise for this service has been awarded to Gerbil phone, which is installing transmitters in town centres and stations etc.

What issues of competitive strategy have been raised in the above scenario, particularly in relation to Hermes Telecommunications plc?

2.3 Using the generic strategies

Porter's three generic strategies can help managers in their strategic planning in a number of different ways.

(i) **Encourage them to analyse competitors' positions**. For example, firms which are competing as cost leaders will need to analyse rivals' cost structures and value chains to identify if there are any areas where cost savings can be made. By contrast, firms which want to pursue differentiation strategies should undertake market research information to get an understanding of brand perceptions in the market.

(ii) **Choose a competitive strategy**. This is the key point behind Porter's model: to be successful a firm needs to follow one of the generic strategies.

(iii) **Analyse the risks of their present strategy.** Porter identifies that each generic strategy has some inherent risks. For example:

Differentiation

– The brand loyalty underpinning differentiation may fail if the cost differential between the price difference with cost leading products becomes too great.

– Buyers may value the differentiating factor less, and so may become more willing to buy generic products instead of differentiated products.

Cost leadership

– Technological change could mean that existing low-cost technology becomes superseded by newer, cheaper technology.

– Inflation or exchange rates may destroy cost advantages.

Focus

– The distinctions between segments narrows so that individual segments are no longer clearly identifiable

– Segment collapses and leaves the firm with no other source of earnings

The value of Porter's model is in reminding managers they need to focus on these threats and risks, and develop strategies to deal with them and to maintain their competitive advantage.

2.4 Limitations of Porter's model

In practice, it is rarely simple to draw hard and fast distinctions between the generic strategies as there are conceptual problems underlying them.

(a) **Problems with cost leadership**

(i) **Internal focus.** Cost refers to internal measures, rather than the market demand. It can be used to gain market share: but it is the **market share that is important,** not cost leadership as such. Economies of scale are an effective way to achieve low costs, but they depend on high volumes. In turn, high volumes may depend on low prices, which, in turn, require low costs. There is a circular argument here.

(ii) **Only one firm.** If cost leadership applies cross the whole industry, only one firm will pursue this strategy successfully. However, more than one firm might **aspire** to cost leadership, especially in dynamic markets where new technologies are frequently introduced. Firms competing across the industry as a whole might have different competence or advantages that confer cost leadership in different segments.

(iii) **Higher margins can be used for differentiation.** Having low **costs** does not mean you have to charge lower prices or compete on **price**. A cost leader can choose to 'invest higher margins in R&D or marketing'. Being a cost leader arguably gives producers more freedom to choose other competitive strategies.

There is often confusion about what cost leadership actually means. In particular, cost leadership is often assumed to also mean low price. However, '**cost leadership**' and '**low price**' **are not necessarily the same thing**.

(b)   **Problems with differentiation**. Porter assumes that a differentiated product will always be sold at a higher price.

(i)   However, a **differentiated product** may be sold at the same price as competing products in order to **increase market share.**

(ii)   **Choice of competitor.** Differentiation from whom? Who are the competitors? Do they serve other market segments? Do they compete on the same basis?

(iii)   **Source of differentiation**. This includes **all** aspects of the firm's offer, not only the product. For example, restaurants try to distinguish themselves from their competitors through their ambience and the quality of their service as well as by serving high quality food.

Focus probably has fewer conceptual difficulties, as it ties in very neatly with ideas of market segmentation. In practice most companies pursue this strategy to some extent, by designing products/ services to meet the needs of particular target markets.

'Stuck-in-the-middle' is therefore what many companies actually pursue quite successfully. Any number of strategies can be pursued, with different approaches to **price** and the **perceived added value** (ie the differentiation factor) in the eyes of the customer.

In this way, Porter's model no longer reflects the full range of competitive strategies an organisation can choose from.

CASE STUDY

Tesco

Tesco has established itself as the largest retailer in the UK, and is the third largest retailer in the world (by revenue) behind Wal-mart and Carrefour.

One of Tesco's guiding principles is if you want to be a supermarket superpower you have to 'be everywhere', and so it actively seeks out new locations in pursuit of the best sites.

But being everywhere isn't enough. The second key idea which Tesco follows is that to be a supermarket superpower you have to sell to everyone.

One analyst remarked "They've pulled off a trick that I'm not aware of any other retailer achieving; that is to appeal to all segments of the market."

The analysts comment highlights that Tesco offers three distinct ranges of own-brand products, from Value to Finest, priced to attract all types of shoppers to its stores.

Tesco's 'Value' ranges appeal to customers who are looking for a low price option, while the 'Finest' range appeals to more upmarket customers who are prepared to spend more.

One commentator wrote "Whether you're a prince or a pauper you can go into Tesco and find something you want."

2.5 The strategy clock

The idea that firms can successfully pursue a number of strategies based on price and perceived added value has led to a re-assessment of Porter's original arguments. Moreover, the emphasis on **price** and **added value** recognises the importance of the customer – in a competitive situation, rational customers will seek **value for money** in their purchases, and value for money is provided through the combination of **price** and **perceived product/service benefits**.

To this end, it is worth considering the strategy clock (developed by *Bowman*) as a successor to Porter's generic strategies. The **strategy clock identifies eight different strategies** a firm can take in terms of price and adding value.

The eight strategies on the clock represent different approaches to creating value for the customer, with the logic being that each customer will buy from the provider whose offering most closely matches their own view of the proper relationship between price and perceived benefits.

Each position on the clock has its own **critical success factor**, since each strategy is defined in market terms. Positions 1 and 2 will attract customers who are price conscious above all, with position 2 giving a little more emphasis to serviceability. These are typical approaches in commodity markets. By contrast, strategies 4 and 5 are relevant to consumers who require a customised product; for example, professional service firms have often used these strategies as a basis for competition.

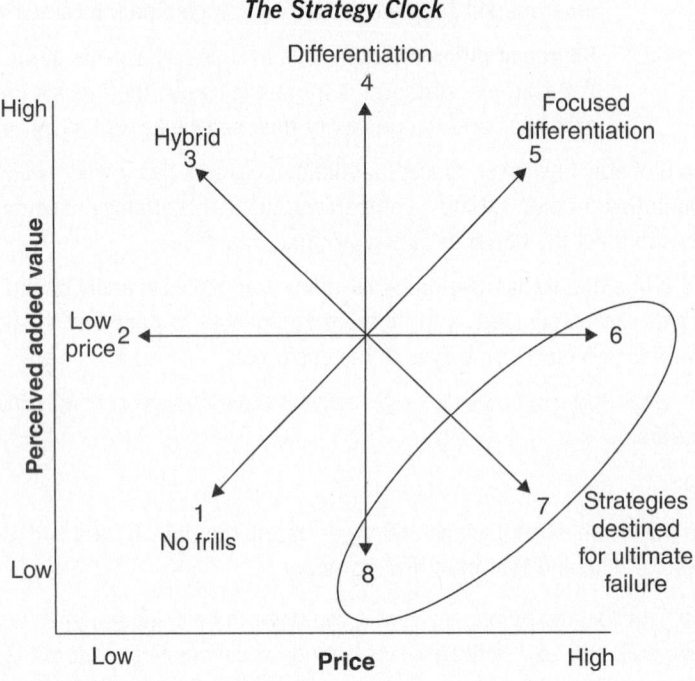

Figure 5.1: Bowman's Strategy clock

2.5.1 No Frills

A **no frills strategy** combines a low price with low perceived product /service benefits.

A no frills strategy is appropriate for commodity-like products or for markets where customers are strongly price-conscious. It is also suitable where customers' switching costs are low and where there is little opportunity for competition on product features.

A no frills strategy may be used for **market entry**, to **gain experience** and **build volume**. If the market leaders are competing on other bases, a no frills strategy may give new entrants a viable way of establishing themselves in the market before moving on to other strategies.

This was done by Japanese car manufacturers in the 1960s, and has also more recently been seen in the airline industry, where companies such as *EasyJet* and *Ryanair* have successfully adopted a no-frills approach.

2.5.2 Low Price

A firm pursuing a **low price** strategy aims to **offer better value than its competitors**. It seeks to do this by offering the same perceived product or service benefits as its competitors, but at a lower price.

However, a potential drawback with such a strategy is that it **could lead to a price war**, if competitors lower their prices as well. A price war would reduce profit margins for all players in the market, and also lead to **lack of reinvestment** because the lower margins will reduce the amount of resources available.

Porter's generic strategy of **cost leadership** is appropriate to a firm adopting this strategy. However, low cost in itself is not the basis for a sustainable competitive advantage. The challenge which firms face is how to reduce their costs to a level that competitors cannot match. If a firm can establish unique cost competences, then a low price strategy could afford it a sustainable competitive advantage.

Differentiation strategies

Strategies 3, 4 and 5 on the strategy clock are differentiation strategies. Each one represents a different trade-off between market share (with its cost advantages) and margin (with its direct impact on profit). Differentiation can be created in three ways.

– Product features
– Marketing, including powerful brand promotion
– Core competences

2.5.3 Hybrid strategy

A firm pursuing a hybrid strategy seeks both **differentiation** and a **lower price** than its competitors. The firm's cost base must be low enough to permit reduced prices and yet still retain high enough margins to be able to reinvest. Reinvestment is necessary to maintain differentiation.

Nonetheless it could be argued that a firm which has a differentiated product should not need to have a lower price than its competitors, because differentiation should enable it to achieve prices that are equal to its competitors. Following this logic, we might question whether a hybrid strategy can be a successful competitive strategy or whether it will be a sub-optimal compromise between differentiation and low price.

If a hybrid strategy is merely a compromise strategy, then it is very likely it will be sub-optimal and therefore unsuccessful. However, there are circumstances where a hybrid strategy may be more advantageous than differentiation alone:

• If it allows a firm to achieve much greater sales volumes than competitors, and therefore also better margins as a result of economies of scale which give it low-cost base.

• If differentiation rests on core competences, and costs can be reduced elsewhere. For example, *Ikea* builds differentiation on the basis of its product range and design logistics, store operations and marketing, but can save costs because customers are prepared to transport and build their products themselves.

• If a low price approach is suited to a particular market segment

• Where it is used as a market entry strategy

2.5.4 Broad differentiation

A broad differentiation strategy seeks to provide products or services that offer benefits which customers value and which are different from competitors' offerings.

The basic differentiation strategy comes in two variants:

• Offering better products or services than competitors at a higher price (**price premium**) than them to enhance margins

• Offering better products or services at the same price as competitors (**competitive price**) in order to build **market share.**

If a firm wants to pursue a differentiation strategy it will need detailed and accurate **market intelligence** about **strategic customers,** and the **key competitors.** The **strategic customers** and their preferences and values must be clearly identified, as must the firm's competitors and their likely responses to its strategy.

The chosen basis for differentiation, which will probably need to be developed over time, should be inherently **difficult to imitate** so that it gives the firm a basis for a sustainable competitive advantage. One way a firm can create sustainable advantage is by creating **strategic lock-in** (establishing its product or service as the industry standards, like Microsoft Windows has done for computer operating systems).

A differentiation strategy can, however, still be **vulnerable to price based competition**. There may be occasions when differentiation is not sufficient to affect customers' purchasing decisions in the face of lower prices. For example, in the recession which has affected Western economies in 2008-9, a number of customers have changed their shopping patterns from branded goods to own-label goods in an effort to curtail their spending. (Interestingly, this example also illustrates why a hybrid strategy can be so effective: allowing firms to offer superior products at lower prices than competitors).

CASE STUDY

Discount retailers

At the start of 2009 some of Britain's leading consumer businesses – from retailer Asda to pub chain J D Wetherspoon – announced that they were marking the beginning of the year with more price cuts.

This had become a familiar story. The economic downturn in developed countries across the world in 2008-9 has meant that consumers were being more careful about how they spent their cash. This carefulness affected a number of retail companies who saw their margins suffer as customer numbers fell away.

However, while established retailers were suffering, discounters became much more popular, as cost-conscious shoppers started snapping-up cut price goods.

The growth of grocery discounters in Europe is not a new phenomenon though. They have been steadily increasing market share since the early 1960s when the Albrecht family founded Aldi in Germany.

Now chains such as Aldi, Lidl and Netto operate throughout Europe, with discounters accounting for just below 18% of grocery spending across the continent (2008). In Germany, where consumers are even more cost-conscious than in many other nations, discounter chains accounted for 43% of total food spend in 2007.

However, the growth of discount chains has mirrored the economic downturn. From Dollar General in the US, to Uniqlo, the Japanese clothing chain, the conditions were near perfect for those promoting thrift.

In the UK, discounters such as Aldi and Lidl, which had previously been kept at bay by supermarket chains Tesco and Asda, began enjoying an unprecedented growth spurt. And the supermarkets are taking note. Tesco, the UK's biggest retail chain, launched an aggressive price-cutting strategy – marketing itself as 'Britain's biggest discounter' – in an attempt to stem the flow of customers leaving it for cheaper rivals.

The supermarket industry research body, IDG, says that the discounters' growth is likely to be sustained throughout a recession. 'The historic perspective provides insight into key growth periods for discounters; namely times of economic uncertainty.'

Discounters had a strong year in 2002 when the introduction of the Euro prompted consumers, in search of greater reassurance over prices, to turn to discount stores. And the IDG believes that the coming years will offer another growth spurt for the sector. Discounters are expected to increase their market share from 18% in 2008 to 20% by 2012, as they move more firmly into the mainstream of people's lives.

Adapted from: 'Cost-cutters move into mainstream', *Financial Times*, January 2, 2009

2.5.5 Focused differentiation

A firm pursuing a strategy of **focused differentiation** seeks a high price premium in return for a high degree of differentiation in a well-defined and probably quite restricted market segment (niche). Focused differentiation strategies are often used for premium products which are heavily branded.

However, focused differentiation raises some important issues:

(a)   A firm may have to choose between focused differentiation and broad differentiation (position 4 on the clock). A firm looking at international growth is likely to have to choose between building competitive advantage at a global level and with a global product (broad), or tailoring its products/services to specific markets (focus).

(b)   It is difficult to pursue focused differentiation for only part of an organisation: the less focussed part, even if it is to some extent differentiated, can damage the brand values of the focussed part.

(c)   In the public sector, stakeholders expecting universal provision will object to a focus on particular segments. For example, a dentist's surgery may feel it could generate increased revenue by focusing on cosmetic dentistry rather than traditional dental care. However, this would exclude patients who want traditional work on their teeth (such as fillings).

(d)   Focus is a common start-up strategy: expansion may prompt or require a gradual move to a less focused differentiation. Moving from focused to broad differentiation may require a lowering or price, and therefore also cost, while still maintaining the differentiating features of a product or service.

(e)   Focus is aimed at a specific segment, but that segment or its requirements may not remain constant. For example, if a non-focused product is improved enough to become acceptable to this segment, the advantage of focus will be eroded. Alternatively, competitors may make even more focused offerings to sub-segments, again eroding the focuser's original advantage.

2.5.6 Failure strategies

Combinations 6, 7 and 8 on the strategy clock are likely to result in failure. A failure strategy is one which does not provide customers will perceived value for money – either with respect to product features, or price, or both.

Increased price/standard value

The logic here is to increase margins by increasing price while keeping costs (and by inference, value) constant. However, unless the firm pursuing this strategy is a monopoly or is somehow protected by legislation or high barriers to entry, it is likely that such a strategy would cause it to lose market share, as customers switch to a competitors product which offers the same value for a lower price.

One possible example of Position 6 on the strategy clock is the way oil producing countries increased the price of crude oil in 2007/2008, by restricting supply in the face of excess demand. However, although there are significant barriers to entry, we can still see the potential problems with this strategy in terms of sustaining a competitive advantage because it has prompted people (and countries) to look at ways of reducing energy and fuel consumption, as well as stepping up their drive to discover alternative sources of energy.

Increased price/low value

Position 7 on the clock is even more likely to result in failure than option 6. A strategy which sees a firm increasing its price while lowering the value it offers its customers would be expected to result in that firm losing all its customers to its competitors. Position 7 on the clock is only likely to be feasible in a monopoly situation.

Low value/standard price

Again, the logic here is to increase margins, effectively by cutting costs (reducing value) but keeping price the same. However, this strategy is again likely to lead to a loss of market share as customers become aware of the reduction in value, and switch their purchases to competitors whose products or services cost the same but offer greater value.

2.6 Overall limitations of the generic strategy approach

Problems in defining the 'industry' - Porter's model depends on clear notions of what the **industry** and **firm** in question are, in order to establish how competitive advantage derives from a firm's position in its industry. However, identifying the industry and the firm may not be clear, since many companies are part of larger organisations, and many 'industries' have boundaries that are hard to define. For example, what industry is a car manufacturer in? Cars, automotive (cars, lorries, buses), manufacturing, transportation?

Defining the strategic unit - As well as having difficulties in defining the industry, we can also have difficulties in determining whether strategies should be pursued at **SBU** or **corporate level**, and in relation to exactly which category of products. For example, *Proctor and Gamble* have a huge range of products and brands; are they to follow the same strategy with all of them? Similarly, the *Volkswagen-Audi Group* own the Seat, Audi, Bentley and Skoda car marques.

Porter's theory states that if a firm has more than one competitive strategy this will dilute its competitive advantage. But does this mean that the Volkswagen-Audi's strategy for Skoda needs to be the same as for Bentley? Clearly not, and this is a major problem with Porter's theory.

It is impractical to suggest that a whole group should follow a single competitive strategy and so it seems more appropriate to suggest that the model should be applied at business unit level. Yet if the theory is only applied at individual SBU level, then it could lead managers to overlook sources of competitive advantages which emerge from being part of a larger group – for example, economies of scale in procurement.

Another criticism which is sometimes made of Porter's model is that it doesn't look at how firms might use their competitive advantages and distinctive competences to **expand into new industries**, perhaps as the result of creative innovation. Porter only looks at how a firm might use its resources to develop strategy in its existing line of business. However, we could argue that this criticism isn't really valid. Although Porter doesn't talk about expansion into new industries, his model does not preclude it, and his arguments about following a competitive strategy would still ultimately need to be applied in the new industry.

Section summary

Porter's **generic strategies** suggest that a firm generates competitive advantages by either being a **cost leader**, or by **differentiating itself** from its competitors. Porter's ideas have subsequently been expanded to create the concept of the **strategy clock**.

3 Using the value chain in competitive strategy   5/10

Introduction

The generic strategies model illustrates that firms have a choice of whether to compete as cost leaders of quality leaders (differentiators). Once they make this choice, they can use the **value chain** to help design a competitive strategy.

The value chain can be used to design a competitive strategy, by deploying the various activities strategically. The examples below are based on two supermarket chains, one concentrating on low prices, the other differentiated on quality and service. See if you can tell which is which.

(a)

	INBOUND LOGISTICS	OPERATIONS	OUTBOUND LOGISTICS	MARKETING & SALES	SERVICE
Firm infrastructure	Minimum corporate HQ				
Human resource management		De-skilled store- ops	Dismissal for checkout error		
Technology development	Computerised warehousing		Checkouts simple		
Procurement	Branded goods only – big discounts	Low cost sites			Use of concessions
	Bulk warehousing	1,000 lines only		Low price promotion	Nil
		Price points		Local focus	
		Basic store design			

(b)

	INBOUND LOGISTICS	OPERATIONS	OUTBOUND LOGISTICS	MARKETING & SALES	SERVICE
Firm infrastructure	Central control of operations and credit control				
Human resource management	Recruitment of mature staff	Client care training	Flexible staff to help with packing		
Technology development		Recipe research	Electronic point of sale	Consumer research & tests	Itemised bills
Procurement	Own label products	Prime retail positions		Adverts in quality magazines & poster sites	
	Dedicated refrigerated transport	In store food halls	Collect by car service	No price discounts on food past sell-by dates	No quibble refunds
		Modern store design			
		Open front refrigerators			
		Tight control of sell-by dates			

The two supermarkets represented are based on the following.

(a)   The value chain in (a) is the 'discount' supermarket (perhaps similar to *Lidl or Aldi* in the UK) which sells on price, pursuing a cost leadership strategy. This can be seen in the limited product range and its low-cost sites.

(b)   The value chain in (b) is for the supermarket which seeks to differentiate on quality and service (for example, *Waitrose* in the UK). Hence the 'no quibble' refunds, the use of prime retail sites, and customer care training.

You can probably think of other innovations, such as loyalty cards and Internet shopping, which supermarkets have introduced to try to improve the quality and service they provide their customers.

Section summary

A firm needs to ensure that its **value chain** is appropriate to the strategy it is pursuing.

4 Pricing and competition

Introduction

Pricing strategy is an important component, both as part of the marketing mix and as a company's competitive weapon.

KEY TERMS

PRICING . 'Determination of a selling price for the product or service produced. A number of methodologies may be used.

COMPETITIVE PRICING. Setting a price by reference to the prices of competitive products.

COST PLUS PRICING. Determination of price by adding a mark-up, which may incorporate a desired return on investment, to a measure of the cost of the product/service.

MARKET-BASED PRICING. Setting a price based on the value of the product in the perception of the customer. Also known as perceived value pricing.

PENETRATION PRICING. Setting a low selling price in order to gain market share.

PREDATORY PRICING. Setting a low selling price in order to damage competitors. May involve dumping, ie selling a product in a foreign market at below cost, or below the domestic market price (subject to, for example, adjustments for taxation differences, transportation costs, specification differences).

PRICE SKIMMING. Setting a high price in order to maximise short-term profitability, often on the introduction of a novel product.

RANGE PRICING. The pricing of individual products such that their prices fit logically within a range of connected products offered by one supplier, and differentiated by a factor such as weight of pack or number of product attributes offered.

SELECTIVE PRICING. Setting different prices for the same product or service in different markets. Can be broken down as follows:

- **Category pricing**. Cosmetically modifying a product such that the variations allow it to sell in a number of price categories, as where a range of 'brands' are based on a common product.

- **Customer group pricing**. Modifying the price of a product or service so that different groups of consumers pay different prices.

- **Peak pricing**. Setting a price which varies according to level of demand.

- **Service level pricing**. Setting a price based on the particular level of service chosen from a range.

- **Time material pricing.** A form of cost plus pricing in which price is determined by reference to the cost of the labour and material inputs to the product/service.'

(CIMA Official Terminology)

4.1 Price

All profit-seeking organisations and many non-profit organisations face the task of **setting a price** on their products or services. Price can go by many names: fares, tuitions, rent, assessments and so on.

Price can be defined as a measure of the **value exchanged by the buyer for the value offered by the seller**. It might be expected, therefore, that the price would reflect the costs to the seller of producing the product and the benefit to the buyer of consuming it.

Unlike the other marketing mix elements, pricing decisions affect profits through their impact on **revenues** rather than costs. It also has an important role as a **competitive tool** to differentiate a product and an organisation and thereby exploit market opportunities.

Although pricing can be thought of as fulfilling a number of roles, in overall terms a price aims to produce the desired level of sales in order to meet the objectives of the business strategy.

Two broad categories of objectives may be specified for pricing decisions.

(a)   **Maximising profits** is concerned with maximising the returns on assets or investments. This may be realised even with a comparatively small market share depending on the patterns of cost and demand.

(b)   **Maintaining or increasing market share** involves increasing or maintaining the customer base which may require a different, more competitive approach to pricing, while the company with the largest market share may not necessarily earn the best profits.

4.2 Pricing and the customer

4.2.1 Price sensitivity

Price sensitivity will vary amongst purchasers. Those that can pass on the cost of purchases will be the least sensitive and will therefore respond more to other elements of perceived value.

(a)   The family on holiday is likely to be very price sensitive when choosing an overnight stay.

(b)   In industrial marketing the purchasing manager is likely to be more price sensitive than the engineer who will use the new equipment that is being sourced.

4.2.2 Price perception and quality connotations

Price perception is an important factor in the ways customers react to prices. For example, customers may react to a price increase by buying more. This could be for a variety of reasons.

(a)   They expect further price increases to follow (they are 'stocking up')

(b)   Many customers appear to judge quality by price

      (i)   They assume the quality has increased, if there is a price rise

      (ii)   The brand takes on a 'snob appeal' because of the high price (eg the advertising slogan used by Stella Artois – "reassuringly expensive")

4.2.3 Intermediaries' objectives

If an organisation distributes products or services to the market through independent **intermediaries**, the objectives of these intermediaries complicate the pricing decision. Such intermediaries are likely to deal with a range of suppliers and their aims concern their own profits rather than those of suppliers.

4.2.4 Multiple products and loss leaders

Most organisations sell a range of products. The management of the pricing function is likely to focus on the profit from the whole range rather than the profit on each single product. Take, for example, the use of **loss leaders**: a very low price for one product is intended to make consumers buy additional products in the range which carry higher profit margins.

4.2.5 Ethics

Ethical considerations are a further factor, for example whether or not to exploit short-term shortages through higher prices. The outcry surrounding the series of petrol price rises following the outbreak of the first Gulf Crisis in 1990 was a good example of public sensitivity to pricing decisions.

An alternative aspect of ethics and social responsibility in pricing is ensuring that all suppliers are paid a fair price for what they produce. '**Fair Trade**' products illustrate this. And although they may be slightly more expensive than some rival products, the 'fair trade' aspect may be an important factor in leading consumers to buy them in preference to some cheaper alternatives.

4.3 New product pricing: market penetration and market skimming

There are three elements in the pricing decision for a new product.

- Getting the product **accepted**
- Maintaining a **market share** in the face of competition
- Making a **profit** from the product

4.3.1 Penetration

Market penetration pricing is a policy of low prices when the product is first launched in order to gain sufficient penetration into the market. It is therefore a policy of sacrificing short-term profits in the interests of long-term profits.

(a)   The firm wishes to **discourage rivals** from entering the market.

(b)   The firm wishes to **shorten the initial period of the product's life cycle**, in order to enter the growth and maturity stages as quickly as possible. (This would happen if there is high elasticity of demand for the product.)

4.3.2 Skimming

Market skimming. The aim of market skimming is to gain high unit profits very early on in the product's life.

(a)   The firm charges high prices when a product is first launched.

(b)   The firm spends heavily on advertising and sales promotion to win customers.

(c)   As the product moves into the later stages of its life cycle (growth, maturity and decline) progressively lower prices will be charged. The profitable 'cream' is thus 'skimmed' off in progressive stages until sales can only be sustained at lower prices.

(d)   The firm may lower its prices in order to attract more price-elastic segments of the market; however, these price reductions will be gradual. Alternatively, the entry of competitors into the market may make price reductions inevitable.

Introductory offers and temporary **discounts** may be used to attract an initial customer interest.

4.4 Other pricing decisions

Promotional prices are short-term price reductions or price offers which are intended to attract an increase in sales volume. (The increase is usually short-term for the duration of the offer, which does not appear to create any substantial new customer loyalty). Loss leaders and 'money off' coupons are a form of promotional pricing.

A temporary **price cut** may be preferable to a permanent reduction because it can be ended without unduly offending customers and can be reinstated later to give a repeated boost to sales.

4.5 Pricing and the management accountant

The decision about pricing is one which involves both the accountant and the marketing manager.

Short-term pricing. Marketing management should have the responsibility for estimating the price-demand inter-relationship for their organisation's products. The accountant should become involved in short-term pricing decisions because of cost.

(a)   The sales-revenue maximising price for a product and the profit-maximising price might not be the same.

(b)   Simple CVP analysis can be used to estimate the breakeven point of sales, and the sales volume needed to achieve a target profit figure.

(c)   Many organisations use a **cost-plus** approach to pricing. Accounting figures are needed for cost in order to establish a floor for making a cost-plus pricing decision.

By analysing **product profitability**, the accountant also provides information for pricing control, because profit statements indicate whether prices have been high enough, given the sales demand, to provide a satisfactory return.

4.6 Price and competition

In classical economic theory, price is the major determinant of demand and brings together supply and demand to form an equilibrium market price. However, economic theory can only determine the optimal price structure under the two extreme market conditions.

(a)   **Perfect competition**: many buyers and many sellers all dealing in an identical product. Neither producer nor user has any market power and both must accept the prevailing market price.

(b)   **Monopoly:** one seller who dominates many buyers. The monopolist can use his market power to set a profit maximising price.

However, in practice most of British industry can be described as an **oligopoly:** where relatively few competitive companies dominate the market.

4.6.1 Price leadership

Given that price competition can have disastrous consequences in conditions of oligopoly, it is not unusual to find that large corporations emerge as price leaders.

A price leader will have the dominant influence on price levels for a class of products. Price increases or decreases by the price leader provide a direction to market price patterns.

However, a danger with price leadership is that it might appear to limit the impact of competition. If firms actively collude to keep prices to a certain level, and to divide the 'spoils' between them, they are forming a cartel. Cartels are illegal under UK and European competition law.

Generally speaking, therefore, price cuts to increase market share will be matched by competitors in some way. If a rival firm cuts its prices in the expectation of increasing its market share, a firm has the following options.

(a)   **Maintain its existing prices**. This would be done if the expectation is that only a small market share would be lost, so that it is more profitable to keep prices at their existing level. Eventually, the rival firm may drop out of the market or be forced to raise its prices.

(b)   **Maintain prices but respond with a non-price counter-attack**. This is a more positive response, because the firm will be securing or justifying its current prices with a product change, advertising, or better back-up services, etc.

(c)   **Reduce prices**. This should protect the firm's market share so that the main beneficiary from the price reduction will be the consumer.

(d)   **Raise prices and respond with a non-price counter-attack**. A price increase would be based on a campaign to emphasise the quality difference between the rival products.

Predatory pricing is the use of price to drive a competitor out of business. It is a grey area, as competing on price is legitimate and economically efficient.

The intensely competitive supermarket sector in the UK and US provides a prime example of periodic price cutting activity that can lead, in extreme cases, to all-out price 'wars' between the largest competitors. **Price competition** like this will undermine the value of the market that is being competed for. (Note the link here between price competition and game theory which we looked at earlier.)

When faced with price competition, firms might ask themselves the following questions.

- What is the minimum potential **sales loss** that justifies meeting a **lower competitive price**?
- What is the minimum potential **sales gain** that justifies **not following** a competitive price **increase**?
- What is the minimum potential **sales loss** that justifies **not following** a competitive price **decrease**?

4.7 Competitive pricing actions

Different competitive pricing actions can say a lot about a company's strategy and send signals to the market.

(a)   **Reducing price below that of competitors** in order to win a contract gives certain messages.

   (i)   The company is desperate for sales volume
   (ii)   It believes it is the lowest cost supplier
   (iii)   The target customer is strategically important

(b)   **Reducing price by the same amount as a competitor,** in order to win back business, demonstrates to that competitor that contracts cannot be won or lost on price considerations alone.

(c)   **Substantial price reductions** and public announcements of new manufacturing facilities show the market that despite price reductions, sales are set to expand and revenues will not decrease in the long term.

(d)   A **quick negotiation of lower prices** without alerting the competition indicates a belief that a gain can be made through the short term winning of a customer.

 Section summary

A firm needs to ensure that its **pricing strategy** supports its overall strategy. Price is a key element of the **marketing mix**.

Chapter Roundup

✓ A firm has to make strategic choices about **how** to compete, **where** to compete (products, markets) and **how to grow** (organically or externally).

✓ Porter's **generic strategies** suggest that a firm generates competitive advantages by either being a **cost leader**, or by **differentiating itself** from its competitors. Porter's ideas have subsequently been expanded to create the concept of the **strategy clock**.

✓ A firm needs to ensure that its **value chain** is appropriate to the strategy it is pursuing.

✓ A firm also needs to ensure that its **pricing strategy** supports its overall strategy. Price is a key element of the **marketing mix**.

Quick Quiz

1   What are the three categories of strategic choice?

....

....

....

2   **Fill in the blanks**.

In the context of Porter's three generic strategies:

(1) .... and (2) .... are industry wide strategies

(3) .... involves segmentation

3   According to Bowman's Strategy Clock, a hybrid strategy is one in which a firm:

(a)   Combines low price with low perceived product or service benefits
(b)   Pursues a low price strategy but offers better value than its competitors
(c)   Pursues a strategy which seeks both differentiation and a lower price than its competitors
(d)   Enhances margins by offering better products or services at a higher price than its competitors

4   What are two overall limitations of Porter's generic strategy approach?

5   The car manufacturer, Morgan, makes all its cars by hand and only serves a very small part of the market – car enthusiasts who like cars with a traditional design but performance resembling that of a sports car. Because the cars are hand made, they are expensive to buy.

What kind of generic strategy is Morgan pursuing?

BPP
LEARNING MEDIA

Answers to Quick Quiz

1   How you compete
     Where you compete
     Method of growth

2   (1)   cost leadership
     (2)   differentiation
     (3)   focus

3   C   A firm pursuing a hybrid strategy seeks both differentiation and a lower price than its competitors.

          Option A describes a 'no frills' strategy: B describes a low price strategy; and Option D is a differentiation strategy.

4   •   Problems in defining the 'industry'.
     •   Problems in deciding whether strategies should be pursued at corporate level or SBU level.

5   Differentiation – focus. Morgan make luxury cars for a narrowly defined sector of the market.

Answer to Questions

5.1 Hermes

(a)   Arguably, Hermes initially pursued a cost-focus strategy, by targeting the business segment.

(b)   It seems to be moving into a cost leadership strategy over the whole market although its competitive offer, in terms of lower costs for local calls, is incomplete.

(c)   The barriers to entry to the market have been lowered by the new technology. Gerbil phone might pick up a significant amount of business.

Now try this question from the Exam Question Bank	Number	Level	Marks	Time
	Q5	Examination	10	18 mins

DIRECTIONS AND METHODS OF GROWTH

As well as deciding how to compete, a firm also has to choose its preferred direction of growth and method of growth.

Direction of growth. Product/market strategy refers to the mix of product and markets (new or existing) and what the firm should do.

Method of growth – Does the organisation look to grow organically or externally? External growth can be through an acquisition or merger, or through a strategic alliance of some kind?

Each method of growth has its own particular advantages and disadvantages, relating to a whole variety of factors, including risk, resources and corporate culture.

Given the increasingly global nature of business, **international expansion** is an important topic within any discussion of growth.

However, as well as growth and acquisition, business also need to know when to dispose of underperforming assets, or rationalise divisions whose costs are too high.

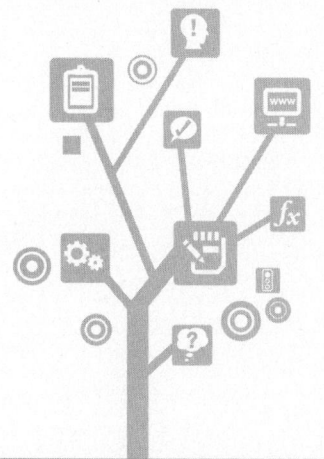

topic list	learning outcomes	syllabus references	ability required
1 Product-market strategy: direction of growth	C 1 (b)	C 1 (iv)	Evaluate
2 Methods of growth	C 1 (b)	C 1 (viii)	Evaluate
3 Organic growth and in-house innovation	C 1 (b)	C 1 (viii)	Evaluate
4 Mergers and acquisitions	C 1 (b)	C 1 (viii)	Evaluate
5 Joint ventures and strategic alliances	C 1 (b)	C 1 (viii)	Evaluate
6 Divestment and rationalisation	C 1 (b)	C 1 (viii)	Evaluate
7 Public and not-for-profit sectors	C 1 (b)	C 1 (iv)	Evaluate

1 Product-market strategy: direction of growth   5/10, 9/11

Introduction

Product-market strategy looks at the mix of products and markets a firm can use to try to increase its sales.

Ansoff demonstrates the choices available in the form of a matrix with four options.

- **Market penetration**: current products, current markets
- **Market development**: current products, new markets
- **Product development**: new products, current markets
- **Diversification**: new products, new markets

All of these can secure growth. **Diversification** is often perceived to be most **risky**. Although it can be justified by 'synergies' (common assets, expertise etc which can be applied in a number of different business areas), these are often more apparent than real.

KEY TERM

PRODUCT MARKET MIX is a short hand term for the **products/services** a firm sells (or a service which a public sector organisation provides) and the **markets** it sells them to.

1.1 Product-market mix: Ansoff's growth vector matrix

Ansoff drew up a **growth vector matrix**, describing how a combination of a firm's activities in current and new markets, with existing and new products, can lead to **growth**. Ansoff's original model was a 4 cell matrix based on product and market.

Ansoff's matrix

	PRODUCT	
	Present	*New*
MARKET *Present*	Market penetration	Product development
New	Market development	Diversification • related • unrelated

Lynch has produced an enhanced model that he calls the **market options matrix.** This adds the external options shown in this second diagram.

Lynch – Market options matrix

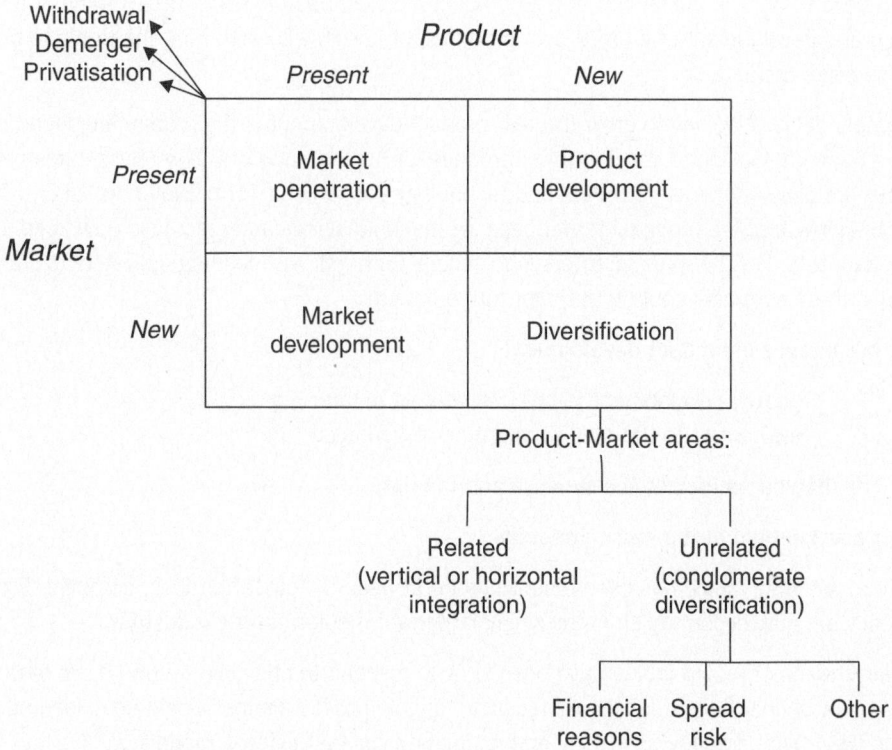

Exam alert

If an exam question refers to Ansoff's growth vector of Ansoff's product-market matrix, you should use Ansoff's original model as the framework for you answer, not Lynch's enhanced version.

1.1.1 Current products and current markets: market penetration

The firm seeks to:

- Maintain or increase its share of current markets with current products, eg through competitive pricing, advertising, sales promotions, quality discounts (designed to increase purchases by existing customers)

- Secure dominance of growth markets

- Restructure a mature market by driving out competitors

- Acquire a rival in the same market

- Increase usage by existing customers (eg airmiles, loyalty cards)

1.1.2 Current products and new markets: market development

- **New geographical areas** and export markets

- **New demographic segments** (eg different age groups)

- **New distribution channels** to attract new customers (eg different age groups, industrial or domestic customers). Accompanied by advertising in different media, and in different ways, to reflect the new customer segments being targeted.

- **Differential pricing policies** to attract different types of customer and create **new market segments**

1.1.3 New products and current markets: product development

Product development is the launch of new products to existing markets, either through the internal research and development of a firm's own products, or possibly by acquiring the rights to produce someone else's product.

An example of firms looking to grow through product development is the mobile telephone manufacturers who are currently looking to develop and introduce fourth generation (4G) wireless infrastructure. 4G networks are based on wireless broadband technology called Long Term Evolution (LTE). LTE is expected to fuel the growth of the mobile internet because it should significantly increase download speeds on mobile handsets. For the manufacturers who secure contracts with leading operators to supply 4G networks, these contracts could a basis for future growth.

(a) **Advantages of product development**

    (i)   Product development forces competitors to innovate

    (ii)   Newcomers to the market might be discouraged

(b)   The **drawbacks** include the expense and the risk.

CASE STUDY

Product development in the music industry

Over time, recorded music has been distributed on LP records, cassette tapes, compact discs, but digital downloads are now becoming an increasingly important medium in the industry.

However, the major record labels have been slow to respond to changes in how music fans want to access music online. Record labels are facing an ongoing battle against illegal downloading, but it is possible they might actually benefit by embracing new digital business models.

Although digital distribution and piracy have troubled record companies over the last few years, the digital sector has emerged as one of the few still growing in the recorded music industry. Online music piracy could be seen as a response to the record labels' slow response to consumers' demands for how they want to listen to music.

However, record labels are now beginning to understand that the industry is changing. Although they were initially scared of the digital revolution, they now realise the only way for them to survive is to get onboard.

And getting industry members to work together to develop with licensed music services has actually benefited them.

Tom Findlay from Groove Armada pointed out "Now people have decided that they want to consume music in different ways, all the subscription services seem to be doing well, and I think the labels have got leaner and cleverer."

One way music retailers have mounted a defence to online piracy is by offering in-store kiosks where customers can download music direct to their MP3 players.

However, the future of the industry may well involve exploiting the web. Web retailers such as iTunes allow users to browse huge back catalogues, but they expect the user to actually pay for each track they listen to. Other services include subscription-based website Napster that allows paying members to consume as much music as they want.

Another approach is ad-supported downloads, such as We7, where consumers can downloads songs for free, but each track is preceded by an advertisement.

However, the record industry is not alone in trying to exploit the net, as artists themselves are taking a more active role in using the download to dominate pop charts.

Tom Findlay pointed out that artists have to work a lot harder now to earn a living.

"The bottom line is the revenue from the actual recording royalties have really gone down massively and that is something you got to live with. What you are seeing now is that the artists really have to go out and have to really perform," he said.

These developments may lead to a revival in the number of live performance, but they are also leading to artists developing their own marketing ventures.

For example, Groove Armada launched its own marketing venture by releasing an EP in conjunction with a drinks brand. Fans were able to receive the first track of the EP for free, but to get the rest of the EP, they had to share that track with a certain amount of users. The more songs they shared, the more they got for free.

However, as a note of caution, Tom Findlay admitted that this is quite a dynamic time in the music industry. "I think it is in a massive state of flux and nobody knows where it is going to go," he said

Source: Adapted from bbc news 'Click' online article, 13 February 2009.
http://news.bbc.co.uk/go/pr/fr/-/1/hi/programmes/click_online/7889289.stm

1.1.4 New products: new markets (diversification)

Diversification occurs when a company decides to make **new products for new markets**. It should have a clear idea about what it expects to gain from diversification.

(a)   **Growth.** New products and new markets should be selected which offer prospects for growth which the existing product-market mix does not.

(b)   **Investing surplus** funds not required for other expansion needs. (The funds could be returned to shareholders.)

CASE STUDY

HMV

The music and entertainment chain, HMV, was hoping to turn around a decline in its sales with a move into fashion when it launched an "entertainment-inspired" clothing range in 2010.

Like-for-like sales at HMV had fallen by 12.4% while total sales had declined by 8.5% in the 16 weeks to April 24, 2010. As sales of compact discs (CDs) have gone into decline, HMV has had to seek out new sources of revenue, and to try to transform itself away from being seen simply as a CD retailer.

The move into fashion consisted initially of a range of clothing, with iconic rock and film imagery aimed at the 18-30 year-old male market.

In conjunction with its CD business, HMV already sold T-shirts featuring bands such as the Rolling Stones. However, the new range will go beyond traditional band merchandise, and the chief executive said it will represent "pure fashion in its own right."

While many of HMV's designs will be "closely linked" to music and film, the group is also moving into non-branded goods including a range of "festival chic" clothing, with checked woven shirts and scarves. HMV will also launch a range of accessories, such as trilby hats and sunglasses inspired by Michael Jackson, and is in talks with jean manufacturers. It also intends to sign up music artists to design clothing lines.

HMV will be competing with high-street fashion retailers such as Topshop and River Island, which already offer a limited range of music and film-inspired clothes. However, HMV's Chief Executive feels his company will be offering something different: "While you can buy some of these products elsewhere there is nothing on the high street quite like this. What we are doing is totally unique," he said.

The clothing range is part of a wider strategy aimed at moving the company away from traditional lines such as CDs and DVDs. HMV has also acquired Mama Group, the live music venue, and improved its technology range.

[*Based on*: HMV hopes to cut a dash with new fashion range as sales fall, *Times Online*, April 29, 2010]

1.2 Related diversification

KEY TERM

RELATED DIVERSIFICATION is 'development beyond the present product market, but still within the broad confines of the industry ... [it] ... therefore builds on the assets or activities which the firm has developed' (*Johnson, Scholes & Whittington*). It takes the form of vertical or horizontal integration.

Horizontal integration is development into activities which are competitive with or directly **complementary** to a company's present activities; for example, a newspaper company moving into magazine production. The firm's advantage lies in using its technical and technological competences. This form of integration is also called **concentric diversification**.

Vertical integration occurs when a company becomes its own:

(a) **Supplier** of raw materials, components or services (**backward vertical integration**). For example, backward integration would occur where a milk producer acquires its own dairy farms rather than buying raw milk from independent farmers.

(b) **Distributor** or sales agent (**forward vertical integration**), for example: where a manufacturer of synthetic yarn begins to produce shirts from the yarn instead of selling it to other shirt manufacturers.

Advantages of vertical integration

- A **secure supply of components** or **materials,** thus lower supplier bargaining power
- **Stronger relationships** with the 'final consumer' of the product (thereby reducing the bargaining power of consumers)
- Win a share of the **higher profits** at all stages of the **value chain**
- Avoiding costs of **intermediate transactions** (eg packaging of component parts required if bought in from an external supplier)
- Pursue a **differentiation strategy** more effectively (because more of the product is under the firm's control)
- Raise **barriers to entry**
- Improvements in **quality** and **innovation**

Disadvantages of vertical integration

(a) **Overconcentration.** A firm places 'more eggs in the same end-market basket' (*Ansoff*). Such a policy is fairly inflexible, more sensitive to instabilities and increases the firm's dependence on a particular aspect of economic demand. For example, the flexibility to change suppliers is reduced if a firm is using an 'in-house' supplier.

(b) The firm **fails to benefit from any economies of scale or technical advances** in the industry into which it has diversified. This is why, in the publishing industry, most printing is subcontracted to specialist printing firms, who can work machinery to capacity by doing work for many firms.

(c) **Fixed costs**. Vertical integration increases the proportion of a firm's costs which are fixed. If a firm buys in inputs from an external supplier, the costs of those inputs are variable costs. If the input is produced internally, the firm has to bear all the fixed costs of production. The increase in fixed costs as a proportion of total costs increases the firm's **operating gearing** and the business risk associated with this.

(d) **Inefficiency**. The internal relationship between buyer and seller can lead to inefficiencies, as the seller no longer faces the same level of competition as it would in an open market transaction. As a result, production costs could start to rise, and this cost inefficiency, in turn, could be passed through to the group's final product. This will mean that the price of the final product will either have to be higher than that of competitors' products, or – if the price is held the same as competitors' prices – the group will earn lower margins on its product that competitors do on theirs.

1.3 Unrelated diversification

KEY TERM

UNRELATED OR CONGLOMERATE DIVERSIFICATION 'is development beyond the present industry into products/ markets which, at face value, may bear no close relation to the present product/market'.

Conglomerate diversification is now very unfashionable. However, it has been a key strategy for companies in Asia, particularly South Korea, where the diversified conglomerates known as *chaebol* have been very popular.

CASE STUDY

Hutchinson Whampao

Hutchinson Whampoa Limited is among the largest companies listed on the main board of the Hong Kong Stock Exchange. Flagship companies within the Hutchinson group include: Hutchinson Port Holdings, Hutchinson Whampoa Properties, A S Watson (health, beauty and lifestyle retailer) Cheung Kong Infrastructure, and Hutchinson Telecom.

The group has businesses spanning the globe, but its diverse array of holdings includes five different core businesses:

- Ports and related services
- Property and hotels
- Retail (in particular, health and beauty)
- Energy and infrastructure
- Telecommunications – including mobile phones and networks under the '3' brand.

1.3.1 Advantages of conglomerate diversification

- Risk-spreading by entering new products into new markets
- An improvement of the overall profitability and flexibility of the firm through synergy
- Escape from the present business
- Better access to capital markets
- Organisational learning by buying in expertise
- Use surplus cash
- Exploit under-utilised resources
- Obtain cash, or other financial advantages (such as accumulated tax losses)
- Use a company's image and reputation in one market to develop into another

1.3.2 Disadvantages of conglomerate diversification

- The dilution of shareholders' earnings

- Lack of a common identity and purpose in a conglomerate organisation

- Failure in one of the businesses will drag down the rest

- Lack of management experience may reduce management's ability to run the new business properly

- Increased risk: the business is either entering a new market or producing a new product. Because they are new, they carry an increased risk that the venture may not be successful – for example, have the needs of the customer been correctly identified? Will the organisation's culture be appropriate to the new market?

1.4 Trade-offs

Conglomerate diversification can lead to a wide rage of organisational characteristics. Generally there will be trade-offs to be made between elements such as those listed below.

- Economies of scale (increasing the utilisation of dedicated assts)

- Economies of scope (increasing the utilisation of general assets)
- Overhead cost structure and level
- Responsiveness to changing customer needs and wants
- Exploitation of resources and competences
- Organisational learning
- Competition reaction
- Management attention and capacity

1.5 Diversification and synergy

Synergy is the 2 + 2 = 5 effect, where a firm looks for **combined results** that reflect a better rate of return than would be achieved by the same resources used independently as separate operations. Synergy is used to justify diversification. Much of the benefit of synergy is derived from **economies of scale and scope**.

1.5.1 Obtaining synergy

(a) **Marketing synergy:** use of common marketing facilities such as distribution channels, sales staff and administration, and warehousing.

(b) **Operating synergy:** arises from the better use of operational facilities and personnel, bulk purchasing, a greater spread of fixed costs whereby the firm's competence can be transferred to making new products. For example, although there is very little in common between sausages and ice cream, both depend on a competence of refrigeration.

(c) **Investment synergy:** the joint use of plant, common raw material inputs, transfer of research and development from one product to another – ie from the wider use of a common investment in fixed assets, working capital or research.

(d) **Management synergy:** the advantage to be gained where management skills concerning current operations are easily transferred to new operations because of the similarity of problems in the two industries.

Question 6.1   Road transport

Learning outcomes C 1 (iv)

A large organisation in road transport operates nationwide in general haulage. This field has become very competitive and with the recent down-turn in trade, has become only marginally profitable. It has been suggested that the strategic structure of the company should be widened to include other aspects of physical distribution so that the maximum synergy would be obtained from that type of diversification.

Suggest two activities which might fit into the suggested new strategic structure, explaining each one briefly. Explain how each of these activities could be incorporated into the existing structure. State the advantages and disadvantages of such diversification.

1.6 Withdrawal

It might be the right decision to cease producing a product and/or to pull out of a market completely. This is a hard decision for managers to take if they have invested time and money or if the decision involves redundancies.

Exit barriers make this difficult.

- Cost barriers include redundancy costs and the difficulty of selling assets

- Managers might fail to grasp opportunity costing
- Political barriers include government attitudes
- Marketing considerations may delay withdrawal
- Managers hate to admit failure
- People might wrongly assume that carrying on is a low risk strategy

Reasons for exit

- The company's business may be in buying and selling firms
- Resource limitations mean that less profitable businesses have to be abandoned
- A company may be forced to quit, because of insolvency
- Change of competitive strategy
- Decline in attractiveness of the market
- Funds can earn more elsewhere

1.7 Guidelines for a product-market strategy

Johnson, Scholes & Whittington suggested the following principles and guidelines for product-market planning.

(a)   **The potential for improvement and growth**. It is one thing to eliminate unprofitable products but will there be sufficient growth potential among the products that remain in the product range?

(b)   **Cash generation**. New products require some initial capital expenditure. Retained profits are by far the most significant source of new funds for companies. A company investing in the medium to long term which does not have enough current income from existing products, will go into liquidation, in spite of its future prospects.

 Exam skills

In this context it would be useful to look at an organisation's product portfolio matrix (BCG matrix) as part of the preparation of a product-market strategy. Has the organisation got a balanced portfolio, with enough cash cows to fund present growth, and stars and question marks to sustain future growth?

(c)   **The timing decision for killing off existing products**. There are some situations where existing products should be kept going for a while longer, to provide or maintain a necessary platform for launching new models.

(d)   **The long-term rationale of a product or market development**.

(e)   **Diversification by acquisition**. It might pay to buy product ranges or brands in a takeover deal. If the product-market strategy includes a policy of diversification, then the products or services which the expanding company should seek to acquire should provide definite benefits.

1.7.1 Closing the profit gap and product-market strategy

The aim of product-market strategies is to **close the profit gap** that is found by gap analysis. A mixture of strategies may be needed to fill the gap between the current profit forecast (F_0 in the following diagram) and the target profit.

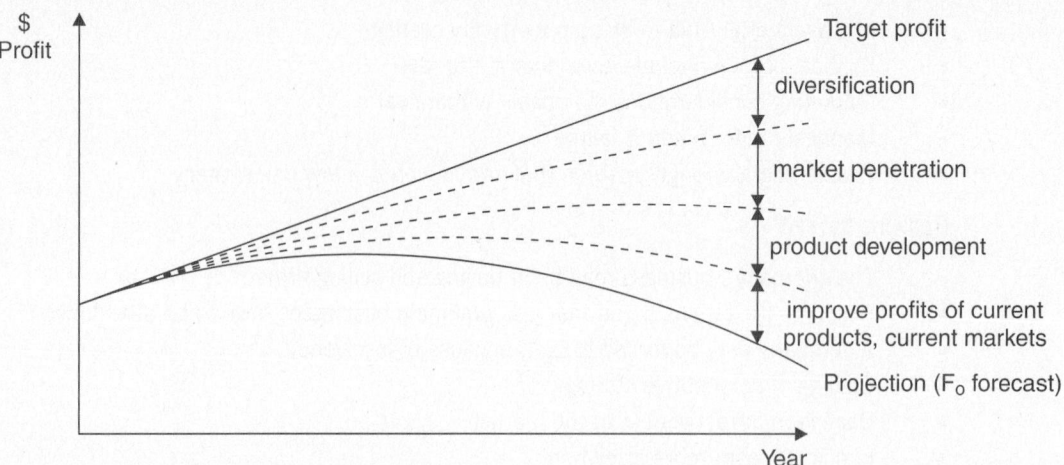

It is worth remembering that **divestment** is also a product-market option to close the profit gap, if the business being divested is making losses.

A related question in what do you do with spare capacity – go for market penetration, or go into new markets. Many companies begin exporting into new overseas markets to use surplus capacity.

The strategies in the Ansoff matrix are not mutually exclusive. A firm can quite legitimately pursue a penetration strategy in some of its markets, while aiming to enter new markets.

However, remember that the strategies in the *Ansoff* matrix have different levels of **risk** attached to them. Diversification involves a much greater degree of risk than market penetration does.

1.7.2 Levels of risk   5/12

If a firm is looking to implement product-market growth strategies it needs to be aware of the potential risks it will be facing.

Market risk

- If a firm enters a new market, it will face competition from the existing firms in the market who will want to protect their market share.

- The new entrant needs to understand the culture of the market and the needs of the customers if it is to be able to compete successfully.

- The new entrant needs to persuade customers to buy from it in preference to the existing firms.

Product risk

- If a firm is developing a new product, or a new production process, production costs may be increased to lack of experience.

- There may be problems with quality and reliability to begin with, and these could severely damage the firm's reputation and its prospects in the market.

- Because the firm is making a new product, it may have to develop new supply-chain relations, and the absence of an existing supply chain infrastructure could adversely affect cost and quality.

Managerial risk

- The management team may not be able to run the new business effectively, especially if it is in a significantly different business area to its existing business.

- There is a related risk here that if management devote too much time to the new business at the expense of the existing business, the performance of the existing business will suffer.

Financial risk

- The cash flows from a new business are likely to be volatile.

- The business may need to raise additional funds to support a new investment, but there is a risk the new venture will not be successful meaning that the new assets may have to be written off.

- The need for funds to support the business may reduce the level of dividend paid to shareholders. The firm will need to reassure shareholders about the respective levels of risk and return, so that they support the new projects.

- Equally the company will need to try to reassure the markets that the projects will be successful, because uncertainty tends to lead to a fall in a company's share price.

1.8 Brand switching and competitive rivalry

A company may introduce measures to counteract **brand switching** by customers (and consequent loss of market share). One example is provided by the loyalty card schemes used by supermarkets to encourage repeat (and increased) spending by customers who may otherwise defect to the opposition.

Section summary

Ansoff's growth vector matrix identifies the four product-market strategies firms can use to try to increase sales: **market penetration; market development; product development; and diversification**. The degree of risk involved varies between strategies, with diversification being the most risky.

---

2 Methods of growth   11/10

Introduction

So far we have considered the basis on which firms might look to develop (for example, as cost leaders or differentiators) and the product / market strategies they might adopt in order to do so.

However, we now need to look at **how firms grow**. Do they develop internally, or do they look for external growth, through mergers and acquisitions or strategic alliances?

Once a firm has made its choice about which strategies it wants to pursue, it needs to choose an appropriate **mechanism** to deliver that strategy.

- Develop the business from scratch
- Acquire or merge with an already existing business
- Co-operate in some way with another firm

The main issues involved in choosing a method of growth are these.

- **Resources.** Does a firm have enough resources and competences to go it alone, or does it have plenty of **resources** to invest?

- Two different businesses might have **complementary skills**

- **Speed**. Does a firm need to **move fast**?

- A firm might wish to **retain control** of a product or process

- **Cultural fit.** Combining businesses involves integrating **people and organisation culture**

- **Risk**. A firm may either increase or reduce the level of risk to which it is subject. External growth often involves more risk than organic (internal) growth.

The type of relationships between two or more firms can display differing degrees of intensity.

- **Formal integration**: acquisition and merger
- **Formalised ownership/relationship**, such as a joint venture
- **Contractual relationships**, such as franchising

2.1 Expansion method

Lynch summarised possible expansion methods in an expansion method matrix that analysed them on two axes: **internal-external** development, and **home country-international** location.

(a)   Internal development in the home country is simply organic growth

(b)   Internal development internationally

(i)	Exporting	(iv)	Multi national operation
(ii)	Overseas office	(v)	Global operation
(iii)	Overseas manufacture		

(c)   External development in the home country or internationally

(i)	Merger	(iii)	Joint venture or alliance
(ii)	Acquisition	(iv)	Franchising or licensing

Company

	Inside	Outside
Home country	Organic growth	Merger Acquisitions Joint venture Alliance Franchise Licence
International	Exporting Overseas office Overseas manufacture Multi-national operation Global operation	Merger Acquisitions Joint venture Alliance Franchise Licence Contract manufacturing

Location

Lynch – Expansion method matrix

Section summary

A firm can either choose to grow internally or else it can link with another firm.

3   Organic growth and in-house innovation

Introduction

Organic growth is a popular method of growth for many organisations. It is achieved through the development of an organisation's own internal resources, rather than combining with any other firms.

KEY TERM

ORGANIC GROWTH. Expansion of a firm's size, profits, activities achieved without taking over other firms.

Why might a firm pursue organic growth?

- The **process of developing** a new product gives the firm the best understanding of the market and the product

- It might be the only sensible way to pursue **genuine technological innovations**

- There is **no suitable target for acquisition**

- The firm has **sufficient current resources** to comfortably plan, finance and deliver the growth itself

- The same **style of management** and **corporate culture** can be maintained

- There are no issues with trying to integrate the firm's **operating systems** with those of another firm

- May be less onerous on cash flow than an acquisition. Investment on internal growth can be funded in stages, but to make an acquisition a firm is likely to have to commit a large amount of funds in one go.

- **Hidden or unforeseen losses** are less likely with organic growth. There are also no issues with having to **value a potential acquisition**.

If we assume that existing products have a finite life, a strategy of organic growth must include plans for **innovation**.

- It provides the organisation with a **distinctive competence**, and with the ability to maintain such a competence

- It maintains the organisation's **competitive advantage** and market share

There are two key triggers for innovation:

Market pull – new market opportunities may generate growth opportunities for firms

Technology push – technological change provides new opportunities. Often technological change can migrate from one industry to another. If firms monitor technological changes in other industries they can sometimes identify opportunities for their own.

CASE STUDY

Organic growth by innovation is not always the guarantee of success. *The Economist* reported a research study into successful innovations.

(a) Pioneers often fail to conjure up a mass market. The first video recorder was developed in 1956 by *Ampex* – they sold for $50,000. The firm made no attempt to expand the market. *Sony*, *JVC* and *Matsushita* spent 20 years turning it into a mass market product.

(b) Another reason is financial strength. *Coca-Cola's Fruitopia* brand (subsequently *Minute* Maid) was positioned against firms such as *Snapple* which had pioneered the market in non-cola 'alternative beverages'.

Innovative companies are not necessarily the most successful. Success is based upon other factors such as distribution capability, technical expertise and marketing skills. The anti-ulcer drug *Zantac* from *Glaxo* was an imitative product, but it overtook *Tagamet* from *SmithKline* due to Glaxo's commercial skills in exploiting it.

Potential disadvantages of organic growth

- **Time**. It will take longer for a firm to grow organically, than by acquiring another firm. This may be a problem in an industry which is changing rapidly, and where an acquisition could allow the firm to 'buy in' new skills and knowledge.

- If the firm is looking to break into new markets, it may lack the **access** to key suppliers or customers which established players have.

- The firm has to bear all the **risk** of any new product development or market entry strategies. By contrast if, for example, the firm entered into a joint venture, this risk would be shared with the venture partner.

Capacity issues: critical mass and economies of scale

For some firms, organic growth must result in a target **critical mass** being achieved, in order to achieve economies of scale. In an industry where fixed costs are high, and variable costs relatively small, significant reductions in unit costs can be achieved by producing on a larger scale.

For example, suppose that in the widget-manufacturing industry, the following costs are applicable.

Factory capacity (output in units pa)	Fixed costs $	Unit variable costs $
10,000	400,000	5.00
50,000	800,000	4.80
200,000	1,600,000	4.60

Unit costs of producing at maximum capacity in each size of factory would be as follows.

Capacity Units	Unit costs Fixed $	Unit costs Variable $	Total $	
10,000	40.0	5.0	45.00	Effect of
50,000	16.0	4.8	20.80	economies of
200,000	8.0	4.6	12.60	scale

If an organisation plans to achieve a certain capacity of output, it will not minimise its costs unless actual production volumes reach the capacity level. In the table above, the factory with 200,000 units capacity can achieve unit costs of $12.60 when operating at full capacity; but if actual production were only 50%, say, unit fixed costs would double to $16, and unit costs would be $20.60 (very nearly as high as in a factory with a 50,000 units capacity operating at full capacity).

3.1 International expansion

International expansion is a big undertaking and firms must know their reasons for it, and be sure that they have the resources to manage it, both strategically and operationally. The decision about which overseas market to enter should be based upon assessment of **market attractiveness**, **competitive advantage**, and **risk**.

Some key decisions for international expansion

Firms must deal with three major issues.

- Whether to market abroad at all
- Which markets to enter
- The mode(s) of entry

3.1.1 Why expand overseas?

Firms may be **pushed** into international expansion by domestic adversity, or **pulled** into it by attractive opportunities abroad. More specifically, some of the reasons firms expand overseas are the following. They can be classified as either **internal** or **external** factors.

(a) **Chance.** Firms may enter a particular country or countries by chance. A company executive may recognise an opportunity while on a foreign trip or the firm may receive chance orders or requests for information from potential foreign customers.

(b) **Life cycle.** Home sales may be in the mature or decline stages of the product life cycle. International expansion may allow sales growth since products are often in different stages of the product life cycle in different countries. For example, if a product is at the mature stage of its life cycle in a firm's home market, it could be beneficial to expand into an emerging market where the product may be at the introductory or growth stages of the life cycle.

(c)   **Competition.** Intense competition in an overcrowded domestic market sometimes induces firms to seek markets overseas where rivalry is less keen.

(d)   **Reduce dependence.** Many companies wish to diversify away from an over-dependence on a single domestic market. Increased geographic diversification can help to **spread risk**.

(e)   **Economies of scale.** Technological factors may be such that a large volume is needed either to cover the high costs of plant, equipment, R&D and personnel or to exploit a large potential for economies of scale and experience. For these reasons firms in the aviation, ethical drugs, computer and automobile industries are often obliged to enter multiple countries.

(f)   **Variable quality.** International expansion can facilitate the disposal of discontinued products and seconds since these can be sold abroad without spoiling the home market. Conversely, many companies, such as most UK pottery manufacturers, reserve their first quality outputs for sale in lucrative high income countries like the USA, selling only seconds in the home country.

(g)   **Cheaper sources of raw materials.** Access to cheaper raw materials, or cheaper labour, could be a source of competitive advantage for an organisation, particularly if it is pursuing a cost leadership strategy.

(h)   **Finance.** Many firms are attracted by favourable opportunities such as the following.

   (i)   The development of lucrative emerging markets (such as China and India)
   (ii)   Depreciation in their domestic currency values
   (iii)   Corporate tax benefits offered by particular countries
   (iv)   Lowering of import barriers abroad

(i)   **Familial.** Many countries and companies trade because of family or cultural connections overseas. For example, the Kenyan horticultural industry exports to the UK.

3.1.2 Involvement overseas

(a)   **Reasons supporting involvement overseas**

   (i)   **Profit margins** may be higher abroad.

   (ii)   Increase in **sales volume** from foreign sales may allow large reductions in unit costs.

   (iii)   The **product life cycle** may be extended if the product is at an earlier stage in the life cycle in other countries.

   (iv)   **Seasonal fluctuations** may be levelled out (peak periods in some countries coinciding with troughs in others).

   (v)   It offers an opportunity of **disposing of excess production** in times of low domestic demand.

   (vi)   International activities **spread the risk** which exists in any single market (eg political and economic changes).

   (vii)   **Obsolescent products** can be sold off overseas without damage to the domestic market.

   (viii) The firm's prestige may be enhanced by portraying a **global image**.

(b)   **Reasons for avoiding involvement**

   (i)   Profits may be unduly affected by factors outside the firm's **control** (eg due to fluctuation of exchange rates and foreign government actions).

   (ii)   The **adaptations** to the product (or other marketing mix elements) needed for success overseas will diminish the effects of economies of scale.

   (iii)   Extending the product life cycle is not always **cost effective**. It may be better to develop new products for the domestic market.

   (iv)   The **opportunity costs** of investing abroad may be better utilised at home.

(v)   In the case of marginal cost pricing, **anti-dumping duties** are more quickly imposed now than in the past.

Before getting involved in overseas expansion, the company must consider both strategic and tactical issues.

(a)   **Strategic issues**

     (i)   Does the strategic decision fit with the company's overall mission and objectives? Or will 'going international' cause a mis-match between objectives on the one hand and strategic and tactical decisions on the other?

     (ii)   Will the operation make a positive contribution to shareholders' wealth?

     (iii)   Does the organisation have (or can it raise) the resources necessary to exploit effectively the opportunities overseas?

(b)   **Tactical issues**

     (i)   How can the company get to understand customers' needs and preferences in foreign markets? Are the company's products appropriate to the target market?

     (ii)   The company's performance will reflect the local economic environment, as well as management's control of the business. So the company needs to understand the economic stability and prospects of the target country before investing in it.

     (iii)   Cultural issues. Does the company know how to conduct business abroad, and deal effectively with foreign nationals? For example, will there be language problems? Are there any local customs to be aware of?

     (iv)   Are there foreign regulations and associated hidden costs?

     (v)   Does the company have the necessary management skills and experience?

     (vi)   Have the foreign workers got the skills to do the work required? Will they be familiar with any technology used in production processes?

Before moving to a foreign country, an organisation should also consider whether there are any **corporate social responsibility** (CSR) implications of such an expansion. For example, if local labour laws allow workers to be employed for low wages and in poor working conditions, does the organisation take advantage of this, or does it treat it its workers better than it has to? Similarly, if pollution laws are not very strict, does the organisation comply with the minimum requirements or does it build more environmentally friendly facilities than it has to?

In both cases, the socially responsible course of action may not be the one which maximises profits. But the organisation needs to consider its reputation as a whole, and its CSR position as a whole. If it is seen to be exploiting workers in one country, this could damage its brand more widely.

3.1.3 Preliminary considerations

In making a decision as to which market(s) to enter the firm must start by establishing its objectives. Here are some examples.

(a)   What proportion of total sales will be overseas?

(b)   What are the longer term objectives?

(c)   Will it enter one, a few, or many markets? In most cases it is better to start by selling in countries with which there is some familiarity and then expand into other countries gradually as experience is gained. Reasons to enter fewer countries at first include the following.

     (i)   Market entry and market control costs are high
     (ii)   Product and market communications modification costs are high
     (iii)   There is a large market and potential growth in the initial countries chosen
     (iv)   Dominant competitors can establish high barriers to entry

(d)   What types of country should it enter (in terms of environmental factors, economic development, language used, cultural similarities and so on)? Three major criteria should be as follows.

(i)   Market attractiveness
(ii)   Competitive advantage
(iii)   Risk

The matrix below can be used to bring together these three major criteria and assist managers in their decisions.

Evaluating which markets to enter

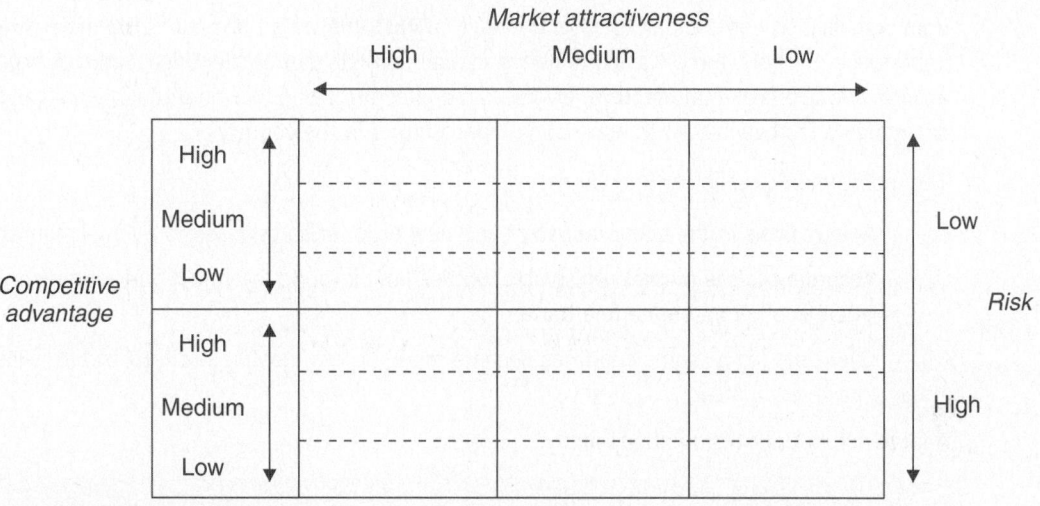

Source: Kotler

(a)   **Market attractiveness**. This concerns such indicators as GNP/head and forecast demand, and market accessibility.

(b)   **Competitive advantage**. This is principally dependent on prior experience in similar markets, language and cultural understanding.

(c)   **Risk**. This involves an analysis of political stability, the possibility of government intervention and similar external influences.

The best markets to enter are those located at the top left of the diagram. The worst are those in the bottom right corner. Obtaining the information needed to reach this decision requires detailed and often costly international marketing research and analysis. Making these decisions is not easy, and a fairly elaborate screening process will be instituted.

In international business there are several categories of risk.

(a)   **Political risk** relates to factors as diverse as wars, nationalisation, arguments between governments etc.

(b)   **Business risk.** This arises from the possibility that the business idea itself might be flawed. As with political risk, it is not unique to international marketing, but firms might be exposed to more sources of risk arising from failures to understand the market.

(c)   **Currency risk.** This arises out of the volatility of foreign exchange rates. Given that there is a possibility for speculation and that capital flows are free, such risks are increasing.

(d)   **Profit repatriation risk.** Government actions may make it hard to repatriate profits.

If a firm is considering investing in new production facilities in a foreign country, the choice of which country to invest in is a key strategic decision. Porter's 'diamond' is a useful model for analysing the factors which make a country attractive as a place to invest.

Porter's diamond is covered in the syllabus for E2. However, a brief reminder of the model is included in the Introduction section at the start of this Study Text.

3.1.4 Involvement in international markets

If an organisation has decided to enter a foreign market, the way it does so is of crucial strategic importance. Broadly, three ways of entering foreign markets can be identified: **indirect exports**, **direct exports** and **overseas manufacture**. Overseas manufacture can either be through wholly owned production or through a joint venture with an existing manufacturer in the country.

The most suitable mode of entry varies:

(a)   **Among firms in the same industry** (eg a new exporter as opposed to a long-established exporter)

(b)   **According to the market** (eg some countries limit imports to protect domestic manufacturers whereas others promote free trade)

(c)   **Over time** (eg as some countries become more, or less, hostile to direct inward investment by foreign companies).

A large number of considerations apply.

Consideration	Comment
The firm's marketing objectives	These relate to volume, time scale and coverage of market segments. Thus setting up an overseas production facility would be inappropriate if sales are expected to be low in volume.
The firm's size	A small firm is less likely than a large one to possess sufficient resources to set up and run a production facility overseas.
Mode availability	Some countries only allow a restricted level of imports, but will welcome a firm if it builds manufacturing facilities which provide jobs and limit the outflow of foreign exchange.
Mode quality	All modes may be possible in theory, but some are of questionable quality or practicality. The lack of suitably qualified distributors or agents would preclude the export, direct or indirect, of high technology goods needing installation, maintenance and servicing by personnel with specialist technical skills.
Human resources requirements	When a firm is unable to recruit suitable staff either at home or overseas, indirect exporting or the use of agents based overseas may be the only realistic option.
Market feedback information	In some cases a firm can receive feedback information about the market and its marketing effort from its sales staff or distribution channels. In these circumstances direct export or joint ventures may be preferred to indirect export.
Learning curve requirements	Firms which intend a heavy future involvement in an overseas market might need to gain the experience that close involvement in an overseas market can bring. This argues against the use of indirect exporting as the mode of entry.
Risks	Firms might prefer the indirect export mode as assets are safer from expropriation.
Control needs	Production overseas by a wholly owned subsidiary gives a firm absolute control while indirect exporting offers only limited control over the marketing mix to the exporter.

3.1.5 Exporting

Goods are made at home but sold abroad. It is the easiest, cheapest and most commonly used route into a new foreign market.

Advantages of exporting

(a)   Exporters can **concentrate production** in a single location, giving **economies of scale** and **consistency of product quality**.

(b)   Firms lacking experience can try international marketing on a **small scale**.

(c)   Firms can **test** their international marketing plans and strategies before risking investment in overseas operations.

(d)   Exporting **minimises operating costs**, administrative overheads and personnel requirements.

Disadvantages of exporting

(a)   **Distance**. The firm remains a long way from its customers. This could make it harder to develop relationships with the customer, or to find out information about the customer (for example, their credit status)

(b)   **Working capital.** The firm's working capital cycle could be extended due to the time taken to ship produce to the customer

(c)   Potential **foreign exchange risk**

Indirect exports

Indirect exporting is where a firm's goods are sold abroad by other organisations who can offer greater market knowledge.

(a)   **Export houses** are firms which facilitate exporting on behalf of the producer. Usually the producer has little control over the market and the marketing effort.

(b)   **Specialist export management firms** perform the same functions as an in-house export department but are normally remunerated by way of commission.

(c)   **UK buying offices of foreign stores and governments**.

(d)   **Complementary exporting** ('piggy back exporting') occurs when one producing organisation (the carrier) uses its own established international marketing channels to market (either as distributor, or agent or merchant) the products of another producer (the rider) as well as its own.

Direct exports

Direct exporting occurs where the producing organisation itself performs the export tasks rather than using an intermediary. Sales are made directly to customers overseas who may be the wholesalers, retailers or final users.

(a)   **Sales to final user**. Typical customers include industrial users, governments or mail order customers.

(b)   Strictly speaking an **overseas export agent** or distributor is an overseas firm hired to effect a sales contract between the principal (ie the exporter) and a customer. Agents do not take title to goods; they earn a commission (or profit).

(c)   **Company branch offices abroad**. A firm can establish its own office in a foreign market for the purpose of marketing and distribution as this gives greater control.

3.1.6 Foreign (overseas) production

A firm can either choose to manufacture in a foreign country because it wants to **sell to that country**, or it may choose to relocate its production to a foreign country but **continue to sell in its 'home' market**.

The firm can either undertake the overseas production itself or it can use an overseas manufacturer.

Benefits of foreign manufacture

(a)   A **better understanding of customers** in the overseas market.

(b)   **Economies of scale** in large markets.

(c)   **Production costs are lower** in some countries than at home (for example, labour costs or costs of raw materials may be cheaper).

(d)   **Lower storage and transportation costs**, because the distance between production and market is reduced.

(e)   **Overcomes the effects of tariff and non-tariff barriers**. For example, governments might relax trading restrictions if the foreign investment is going to create jobs in their country.

(f)   Manufacture in the overseas market **may help win orders from the public sector**.

(g)   Removes foreign exchange risk if goods are sold in the same country as they are produced in.

If a firm wants to move its manufacturing operations to a foreign country, it can either establish its own plant in the country (foreign direct investment), or it can look to negotiate production contracts with existing producers in that country.

We have identified that one of the reasons a firm may move production overseas is to take advantage of lower production costs. However, it is possible that a firm can benefit from lower costs by relocating within its existing country.

For example, there may be regional development incentives available for relocating to less affluent areas.

So a firm need not necessarily relocate overseas to benefit from lower costs.

Wholly owned overseas production

Production capacity can be built from scratch, or, alternatively, an existing firm can be acquired.

(a)   **Acquisition** has all the benefits and drawbacks of acquiring a domestic company.

(b)   **Creating new capacity** can be beneficial if there are no likely candidates for takeover, or if acquisition is prohibited by the government.

Advantages

(a)   The firm does **not have to share its profits** with partners of any kind.
(b)   The firm does **not have to share or delegate decision-making**.
(c)   There are **none of the communication problems** that arise in joint ventures.
(d)   The firm is able to operate completely **integrated** international systems.
(e)   The firm gains a more **varied experience** from overseas production.

Disadvantages

(a)   **Significant initial investment** needed. The investment needed prevents some firms from setting up operations overseas.

(b)   Suitable **managers** may be **difficult to recruit** at home or abroad.

(c)   Some overseas **governments discourage**, and sometimes prohibit, **100% ownership** of an enterprise by a foreign company.

(d)   This mode of entry **forgoes the benefits of an overseas partner's market knowledge**, distribution system and other local expertise.

You should also note that if a firm is considering foreign direct investment it needs to conduct an investment appraisal on the project. Foreign Investment appraisals are covered in the syllabus for paper F3 'Financial Strategy'.

Contract manufacture

As an alternative to setting up a wholly owned production facility in a foreign country, a firm could set up a production contract with an existing manufacturer in that country. (This is sometimes known as a **turnkey operation**)

That way, the firm can take advantage of the cheaper production costs in the foreign country without incurring the capital expenditure involved in setting up its own factory. And when the firm needs goods to be produced it can exercise its contract (ie turn its key) and get the foreign plant to produce the goods it needs.

Contract manufacture is suited to **countries** where the **small size of the market** discourages investment in plant and to firms whose main **strengths are in marketing** rather than production.

Advantages of contract manufacture

(a)   No need to invest in plant overseas
(b)   Lower risk of asset expropriation (because assets owned by the contractor)
(c)   Lower transport costs and lower production costs (from overseas production)

Disadvantages of contract manufacture

(a)   Suitable overseas producers cannot always be easily identified
(b)   The need to train the contractor's personnel
(c)   The contractor may eventually become a competitor
(d)   Quality control problems in manufacturing may arise

Outsourcing and Off-shoring

Although outsourcing or off-shoring are not primarily growth strategies they are business strategies which could relate in an organisation relocating some of its activities. A number of companies in developed countries have outsourced some of their operations to foreign countries where they can be performed more cheaply.

KEY TERM

OUTSOURCING is the contracting out of specified operations or services to an external provider.

By removing some of an organisation's work, outsourcing allows an organisation to devote more time to the activities which it continues to perform in house. Generally speaking, outsourcing is appropriate for peripheral activities, meaning an organisation has more time to concentrate on its core activities and competences.

A further advantage of outsourcing is that external suppliers may capture economies of scale and experience effects. This allows them to provide the function being outsourced at a lower cost than if the organisation had retained it in house.

Getting the best out of outsourcing depends on **successful relationship management** rather than through the use of formal control systems.

Outsourcing of non-core activities is widely acknowledged as having the potential to achieve important cost savings.

Advantages

(a) Can save on costs by making use of a specialist provider's **economies of scale**

(b) Can **increase effectiveness** where the supplier deploys higher levels of expertise (eg in software development)

(c) Allows the organisation to focus on its own **core activities** / competencies

(d) Can deliver benefits and change more quickly than business process reorganisation in-house

(e) Service level agreements mean that the company knows the level of service they can expect

(f) **Cost control**. The creation of a 'customer/contractor' relationship introduces a focus on cost control which is sometimes lost when functions are performed internally.

Disadvantages

(a) There may be problems finding a single supplier who can manage complex processes in full. If more than one supplier has to be used for a single process then the economies of scale are likely to be reduced.

(b) Firms may be **unwilling to outsource whole processes** due to the significance of those processes or the confidentiality of certain aspects of them. (This could be a particular problem if the contractor company is also working for competitors.) Again, if processes are fragmented in this way, the economies of scale may be reduced.

(c) Outsourcing can lead to **loss of control** particularly in relation to **quality issues**. This occurs when agreed service levels are not met. The firm which is outsourcing activities now has to develop competences in relationship management (with the outsourced suppliers) in place of its competences in the processes it has outsourced.

(d) Firms may be tied to **inflexible, long term contracts.**

(e) If there are specialist skills involved in the work, it may be difficult to switch to a new supplier if there are problems, or at the end of a contract period. This gives the external contractor significant bargaining power.

(f) Firms may be unwilling to give up an area of threshold competence that may be difficult to reacquire. If they lose the competence, they will become dependent on suppliers; again, giving the supplier significant bargaining power.

The outsourcing decision needs to be treated with care. The advantages it delivers will largely be seen in the short-term, but there could be longer-term disadvantages in relation to loss of control, quality or knowledge. Therefore both the short-term and longer-term implications need to be considered before an organisation chooses to outsource.

Joint ventures

Some governments discourage or even prohibit foreign firms setting up independent operations, so joint ventures are the only option. That said, a joint venture with an indigenous firm provides local knowledge, quickly.

3.1.7 Summary of entry strategies

The different entry strategies a firm could use for entering a foreign market can be summarised diagrammatically as below:

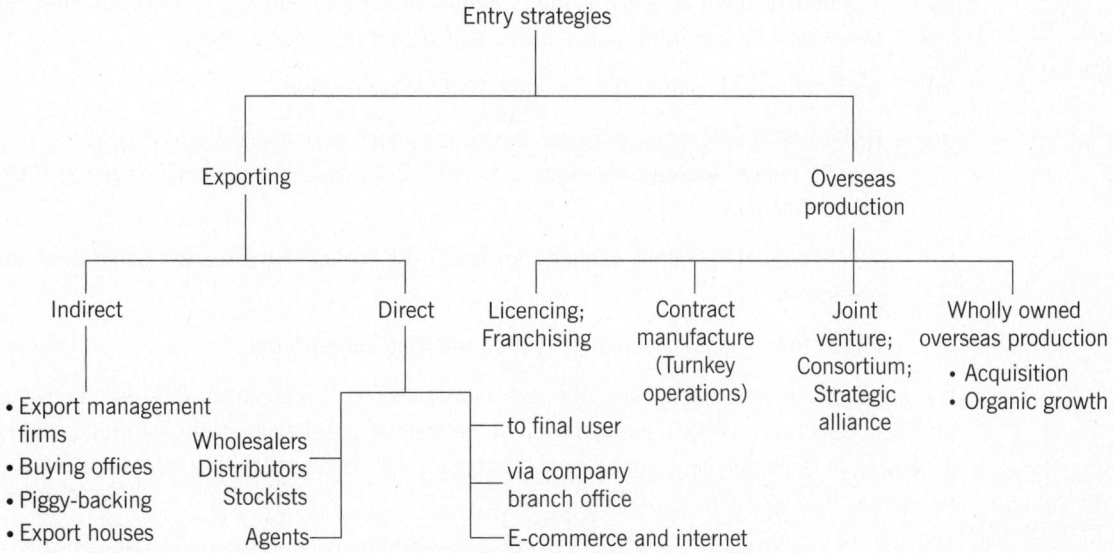

3.2 Multinational and global companies

In our analysis of exporting and foreign direct investment, we have implied a business model in which there is a 'home' market and one single foreign market. However, this oversimplifies the reality of international business.

Instead of just dealing between two countries, many organisations are now **transnational** (or **multinational**). Transnational corporations (TNC) are able to co-ordinate and control operations in a variety of countries, even if they do not have full ownership of all of those operations.

The geographical range of their operations provides a number of opportunities for TNCs:

(a)   They can co-ordinate **various stages** of the **production chain** between different countries.

(b)   They can take advantage of differences in geographical distribution in factors of production (eg raw materials, skilled labour, access to capital) and government policies (eg taxes, subsidies).

(c)   They have geographical flexibility; they can switch resources and operations at an international and global scale.

However, although TNCs have operations in a number of countries, they still have a 'home' base, and the culture of the company is like to reflect this home.

But the continuing process of globalisation may mean that in time we see the emergence of **truly global organisations**. Their activities will transcend national boundaries; and the company will have a single 'corporate culture' across all its operations, wherever they are located. Similarly, the company will develop standard products and procedures across all its operations, and management will treat all their business units the same – wherever they are located.

Global firms also raise capital from a number of different sources, and may be listed on several different stock markets.

However, we shouldn't think that globalisation will remove cultural and political boundaries between countries. It won't – there will remain significant differences between countries.

Moreover, in practice, there are a number of aspects which challenge the notion of the global firm:

(a)   **Workforce.** Most multinationals, other than those based in small nations, have less than half of their employees abroad.

(b)   **Ownership and control of multinationals remain restricted.** Few so-called global companies are currently quoted on more than two stock markets, but more and more are seeking a listing in a number of financial markets.

(c)   **Top management is rarely as multinational in composition** as the firm's activities. (A foreigner is rarely seen on the Tokyo-based board of a Japanese multinational.)

(d)   National residence and status is important for **tax reasons**.

(e)   **R&D.** The bulk of a typical multinational's research and development is generally done in the home country, where strategic decisions are made. But this is changing, especially as R&D is sometimes subcontracted.

(f)   Where **capital is limited**, 'global' companies stick to the home market rather than developing overseas ones.

(g)   Profits from a global company must be **remitted somewhere.**

It is important to acknowledge that the internationalisation of a business does not remove cultural and political boundaries. While there has been an increasing internationalisation of production through the expansion of multinational companies and foreign direct investment, the extent to which the economy can be seen as truly global is still debatable.

However, it is possible that the growth of the internet and e-commerce may change this in future.

Section summary

Organic growth allows a firm to expand by developing its own resources rather than by combining with any other firms. A firm growing organically can **expand internationally**, but managing an international operation will require different resources and competences than managing an operation in a single country. Decisions about **which countries to enter**, and **how to enter them**, are key strategic decisions.

4   Mergers and acquisitions

Introduction

So far, we have looked at the issues surrounding a firm growing by itself. However, a firm can also grow by combining with other firms, through merger or acquisition. A **merger** is the integration of two or more businesses. An **acquisition** is where one business purchases another.

Many companies consider growth through acquisitions or mergers.

KEY TERMS

A MERGER is the joining of two separate companies to form a single company.

An ACQUISITION is the purchase of a controlling interest in another company

It is important for a company to understand its reasons for acquisition and that these reasons are valid in terms of its strategic plan. The classic reasons for acquisition as a part of strategy are as follows:

Reason	Effect on operations
Marketing advantages	New (or extended) product range Market presence Rationalise distribution and advertising Eliminate competition Combine adjoining markets
Production advantages	Economies of scale: synergies Acquire technology and skills Greater production capacity Safeguard future supplies Bulk purchase opportunities
Finance and management	Management team improve running of the business Cash resources Gain assets, including intellectual property Tax advantages (eg losses bought) Asset stripping Turn round opportunities
Risk-spreading	Diversification
Retain independence	
Overcome barriers to entry	
Outplay rivals	

Acquisitions provide a means of entering a market, or building up a market share, more quickly and/or at a lower cost than would be incurred if the company tried to develop its own resources. Corporate planners must however consider the level of **risk** involved. Acquiring companies in overseas markets is more risky, for a number of reasons, such as differences in culture and/or language, and differences in the way the foreign company is used to being managed.

The acquirer should attempt an evaluation of the following.

- The prospects of technological change in the industry
- The size and strength of competitors
- The reaction of competitors to an acquisition
- The likelihood of government intervention and legislation
- The state of the industry and its long-term prospects
- The amount of synergy obtainable from the merger or acquisition
- The cultural fit between predator and target

Exam skills

Whatever the reason for the merger or acquisition, it is unlikely to be successful unless it offers the company opportunities that cannot be found within the company itself and unless the new subsidiary fits closely into the strategic plan outlined for future growth.

If you asked to assess the appropriateness of an acquisition, you should also consider whether the company being acquired will gain any competitive advantage from the acquisition.

4.1 Better off tests

Michael Porter suggests that one of the key issues behind acquisitions should be in realising synergies between the existing company and the new acquisition.

To this end, he suggests that potential acquisitions should be assessed against three tests:

(a) **Better off test** – Will the company being acquired be better off after the acquisition? Will it gain competitive advantage from being in the group?

(b) **Attractiveness test** – Is the target industry structurally attractive? (Porter originally developed his tests in relation to diversification, and so was looking at companies making acquisitions in unrelated industries. However, the point about 'attractiveness' could be applied more generally to look at target companies, countries.)

(c) **Cost of entry** – The cost of the acquisition (or the cost of entering a new market) must not capitalise all future profits from that acquisition (or market). In other words, will the future cash flows from the acquisition be greater than the amounts paid to acquire it?

Porter also identified another key point in relation to successful acquisitions, which could be called the **parenting test**. Has the company making the acquisition got the necessary skills as a corporate parent to get the best value out of the company being acquired? For example, have they got any **experience of previous acquisitions**?

4.2 The mechanics of acquiring companies

You will look at the financial issues involved in evaluating options for mergers and acquisition in Paper F3 – Financial Strategy.

As a management accountant you may be required to assess the value of an acquisition. A number of methods are available.

(a) **Price/earnings ratio:** the markets expectations of future earnings. If it is high, it indicates expectations of high growth in earnings per share and/or low risk.

(b) **Accounting rate of return**, whereby the company will be valued by estimated future profits over return on capital.

(c) **Value of net assets** (including brands).

(d) **Dividend yield**.

(e) **Discounted cash flows**, if cash flows are generated by the acquisition. A suitable discount rate (eg the acquirer's cost of capital) should be applied.

(f) **Market prices.** Shareholders may prefer to hang on for a better bid.

4.2.1 Takeovers or mergers financed by a share exchange arrangement

Many acquisitions are paid for by **issuing new shares** in the acquiring company, which are then used to buy the shares of the company to be taken over in a 'share exchange' arrangement. An enlarged company might then have the financial 'muscle' and borrowing power to invest further so as to gain access to markets closed to either company previously because they could not individually afford the investment.

4.2.2 Acquisitions and earnings per share

Growth in EPS will only occur after an acquisition in certain circumstances.

(a) When the company that is acquired is bought on a lower P/E ratio or

(b) When the company that is acquired is bought on a higher P/E ratio, but there is profit growth to offset this.

4.2.3 Debt finance

Another feature of takeover activities in the USA especially, but also in the UK, has been the **debt-financed takeover**. This is a takeover bid where most or all of the purchase finance is provided by a syndicate of banks for the acquisition. The acquiring company will become very highly geared and will normally sell off parts of the target company.

A **leveraged buy-out** (LBO) is a form of debt-financed takeover where the target company is bought up by a team of managers in the company.

4.3 Acquisitions and organic growth compared   11/10

Advantages of acquisition

Acquisitions are probably only desirable if organic growth alone cannot achieve the targets for growth that a company has set for itself.

(a)   Acquisitions can be made to enter new product or geographical areas, or to expand in existing markets, much more **quickly**

(b)   **Can avoid barriers to entry**. If there are significant barriers to entry into a market (or if there is already intense competitive rivalry) then it might not be possible for a new entrant to join the market in its own right. However, acquiring an existing player in the market would enable a group to join that market.

(c)   Acquisitions can be made **without cash**, if share exchange transactions are acceptable to the company

(d)   When an acquisition is made to diversify into new product areas, the company will be **buying technical expertise, goodwill and customer contracts**

Disadvantages (or risks) of acquisitions

(a)   **Cost**. They might be too expensive, and will involve high initial capital costs to acquire shareholdings in the target company. If the acquisition is resisted by the directors and shareholders of the target company this may force the offer price to be increased further.

(b)   There could also be **valuation issues** here. The management of the target company are likely to know more about its true value than the acquiring company, and so it could be difficult to arrive at a fair price for the sale.

(c)   **Customers** of the target company might consider going to other suppliers for their goods.

(d)   **Incompatibility**. In general, the problems of assimilating new products, customers, suppliers, markets, employees and different systems of operating might create 'indigestion' and management overload in the acquiring company. One of the main reasons why acquisitions and mergers fail is because of the **lack of 'fit'** between the two companies.

(e)   **Post-acquisition costs**. Even if the acquisition goes ahead, there will be significant costs involved in integrating the acquired company's systems (production systems, IT systems etc) with those of the parent company.

(f)   **Lack of information**. Commentators have suggested that the 'acquisitions' market for companies is rarely efficient. This means that companies making an acquisition do not have perfect information about the company they are acquiring. This could mean that the price they pay for the acquisition is too high, and/or the future value the company brings to the group is lower than they had anticipated.

(g)   **Cultural differences**. There may be clashes if the culture and management style of the acquired company is different to the acquiring one. There is potential for human relations problems to arise *after* the acquisition.

(h)   **Rationalisation costs**. As the parent organisation looks to benefit from synergies after an acquisition, they often streamline the workforce, leading to redundancy costs, but possibly also damaging morale amongst the workforce.

It is worth considering the **stakeholders** in the acquisition process:

(a)   Some acquisitions are driven by the personal goals of the acquiring company's **managers**. For example, some managers may want to make the acquisition and increase the size of the firm as a means of increasing their own status and power. Alternatively, other managers may view an acquisition as a means of preventing their own company being taken over, thereby making their job safer.

(b)   **Corporate financiers and banks** also have a stake in the acquisitions process as they can charge fees for advice.

Takeovers often benefit the shareholders of the acquired company more than the acquirer. According to the Economist Intelligence Unit, there is a consensus that fewer than half all acquisitions are successful. One of the reasons for failure is that firms rarely **take into account non-financial factors**.

(a)   All acquirers conduct financial audits of target companies but many do not conduct anything approaching a **management audit**.

(b)   Some major problems of implementation relate to **human resources and personnel issues** such as morale, performance assessment and **culture**. If key managers or personnel leave, the business will suffer.

Another common problem following a merger or acquisition is that the **post-acquisition phase is not properly managed**, so the two component companies are never properly integrated. In this way, the potential benefits of the deal cannot be fully realised.

Section summary

Mergers and acquisitions allow firms to grow by combining with others. A merger or acquisition can provide quicker growth than organic growth, but strategic planners must consider the levels of risk involved.

5 Joint ventures and strategic alliances

Introduction

There are other types of arrangement whereby businesses pool resources

*   **Joint ventures**, consortia and other alliances

*   **Franchising**, where the franchiser provides expertise, a brand name etc, and the franchisee offers some of the capital.

Short of mergers and takeovers, there are other ways by which companies can co-operate.

Consortia: organisations co-operate on specific business prospects. Airbus is an example, a consortium including British Aerospace, Daimler, Aerospatiale and Casa.

Joint ventures: two or more organisations set up a **new, separate organisation** in which they each hold an equity stake. This is very common in entering normally closed markets.

CASE STUDY

Joint Venture

In May 2010, the US glass packaging manufacturer Owens-Illinois Inc. announced that it is teaming up with a Thai company to buy four plants in China and Southeast Asia that make beverage and food containers.

The joint venture of Owens-Illinois and Thailand's Berli Jucker Public Co. signed a deal to buy Fraser & Neave Holdings' Malaya Glass plants in Sichuan Province, China; Saraburi Province, Thailand; Johor Bahru, Malaysia and Ho Chi Minh City, Vietnam.

BPP
LEARNING MEDIA

The plants make containers for the beer, non-alcoholic beverage and food markets, and employ about 1,900 people.

The joint venture is buying the plants for $221.7 million, according to a news release. Owens-Illinois will pay $132.4 million of the total.

The plants in Malaysia and Vietnam will be operated by a joint venture owned 50 percent by Owens-Illinois and 50 percent by Berli Jucker. The acquired interest in the Chinese plant will be managed as part of Owens-Illinois' existing China operations. Berli Jucker will assume majority ownership of the Thai operation.

Owens-Illinois Chairman and CEO Al Strucken said the deal fits his company's objective of seeking "a leadership position in China and Southeast Asia."

He said the plant in Sichuan expands its presence in China, while the joint venture gives it a competitive position in the growing markets in Vietnam and Malaysia.

5.1 Joint ventures

KEY TERM

A JOINT VENTURE is a 'contractual arrangement whereby two or more parties undertake an economic activity which is subject to joint control'.
(CIMA Official Terminology)

Advantages of joint ventures

Like any acquisition, joint ventures provide a way of building scale quickly. Joint ventures are especially attractive to **smaller or risk-averse firms,** or where very expensive new technologies are being researched and developed because they allow **risks and capital commitment to be shared between the venture partners**. This could be particularly useful for expensive technology and research projects.

Other advantages are these:

- Joint ventures permit coverage of a **larger number of countries** since each one requires less investment.

- A joint venture can reduce the risk of **government intervention.**

- Joint ventures can provide close **control** over operations.

- A joint venture with an indigenous firm provides **local knowledge,** and can also allow firms a **route into markets** they might otherwise struggle to enter.

- A joint venture can also be a **learning exercise,** as each party gains **access to the other's competences.**

- A joint venture is often an alternative to seeking to buy or build a wholly owned manufacturing operation abroad.

Disadvantages of joint ventures

The major disadvantage of joint ventures is that there can be major **conflicts of interest**. Disagreements may arise over profit shares, amounts invested, the management of the joint venture, and the marketing strategy.

Other disadvantages are:

- The **profits** from the venture **have to be shared among the venture partners,** reducing the amount earned by each partner

- The joint venture may **not be fully supported by its parent companies** because none of them feel they really own it

- Partners can **gain confidential information** about each other which could subsequently be used competitively by one partner against the other

One partner may ultimately take over the joint venture.

5.2 Strategic alliances

Unlike a joint venture where two or more partners set up a new, separate entity, alliances occur where firms work together to enhance their competitive advantages, but do not create a new legal entity. For example, the '*One World*' alliance brings together 10 of the world's biggest airlines, including American Airlines, British Airways, Cathay Pacific and Qantas. The alliance allows them to offer an integrated service, including code-sharing, and the common use of passenger terminals.

Firms may enter **strategic alliances** with others for a variety of reasons.

(a)   They **share development costs** of a particular technology, and **share the risks** associated with developing them. Alliances can also be used more to share risks more generally.

(b)   The regulatory environment prohibits take-overs (eg most major airlines are in strategic alliances because in most countries – including the US – there are limits to the level of control an 'outsider' can have over an airline). In this respect, an alliance could be a way of overcoming a barrier to entry into a market.

(c)   Alliances can facilitate entry into new markets on a global or regional basis. For example, BP's alliance with the Russian oil producer TNK gave BP access to Russian oil fields. In return, TNK benefited from BP's extensive resources and oil exploration skills.

(d)   **Complementary markets, technology,** or **competences**. By working together, alliance partners may be able to exploit synergies between their different businesses.

(e)   Smaller firms can often work together in an alliance to act as **more effective competition to a dominant player** in the market then they could if they all acted independently.

(f)   **Knowledge**. An important potential benefit from alliances is the opportunity to get access to the knowledge and expertise of the partners involved.

Strategic alliances only go so far, as there may be disputes over control of strategic assets leading to a breakdown of trust and co-operation among the partners.

If a firm enters an alliance as a means of learning from, or gaining knowledge about, an alliance partner this could also ultimately cause a problem. If the partners do not want others to learn from them, or if they feel there is an unfair exchange between the alliance partners this could signal the end of the alliance. In a well-structured alliance, the risk, rewards and resource commitments are fairly apportioned among the alliance partners.

Nevertheless, it is worth noting that a number of **alliances end in takeover**, possibly after one of the organisations has gained knowledge from their partners. Firms entering an alliance need to be aware of this risk.

An additional issue which alliances face is that because the partners remain separate entities they may fail to achieve the level of integration (synergies) needed to deliver any significant competitive advantage or economies of scale.

5.2.1 Choosing alliance partners

Hooley et al suggest the following factors should be considered in choosing alliance partners.

Drivers	What benefits are offered by collaboration? What are the objectives of the alliance?
Partners	Which partners should be chosen? What competencies and capabilities will the partners bring to the alliance? In a well-structured alliance, the partners will be selected such that the strengths of one partner complement the weaknesses of another partner.
Facilitators	Does the external environment favour a partnership?
Components	Activities and processes in the network.
Effectiveness	Does the previous history of alliances generate good results? Is the alliance just a temporary blip? For example, in the airline industry, there are many strategic alliances, but these arise in part because there are legal barriers to cross-border ownership.
Market-orientation	Alliance partners are harder to control and may not have the same commitment to the end-user.

In addition, when considering an alliance it is also important that the alliance's targets/objectives, methods and resource commitments are clearly understood by all the alliance partners, and that the prospective partners are prepared to co-operate fully with the alliance. If they are not, the alliance could be doomed to failure from the outset.

Limitations of alliances

(a)   **Core competence**. Each organisation should be able to focus on its core competence. Alliances do not enable it to create new competences.

(b)   Because alliance partners remain separate entities, many **fail to achieve the integration or commitment** needed to gain any significant competitive advantage.

(c)   **Strategic priorities.** If a key aspect of strategic delivery is handed over to a partner, the firm loses flexibility. A core competence may not be enough to provide a comprehensive customer benefit.

5.2.2 IS based alliances

The cost of major IS based methods of working, combined with their inherent communications capability have made alliances based on IS a natural development. There are four common types.

(a)   **Single industry partnerships**: for example, the 'Oneworld' alliance in the airline industry allows passengers to cross-book across all the member airlines' networks and it also introduced interline e-ticketing across all the member airlines' networks.

(b)   **Multi-industry joint marketing partnerships**: some industries are so closely linked with others that it makes sense to establish IS linking their offerings. A well-known example is holiday bookings, where a flight reservation over the Internet is likely to lead to a seamless offer of hotel reservations and car hire.

(c) **Supply chain partnerships**: as discussed in Chapter 4, greater and closer co-operation along the supply chain has led to the need for better and faster information flows. Electronic data interchange between customers and suppliers is one aspect of this improvement, perhaps seen most clearly in the car industry, where the big-name manufacturers effectively control the flow of inputs from their suppliers.

(d) **IT supplier partnerships**: a slightly different kind of partnership is not uncommon in the IT industry itself, where physical products have their own major software content. The development of these products requires close co-operation between the hardware and software companies concerned.

5.3 Other arrangements

5.3.1 Licensing agreement

A **licensing agreement** is a commercial contract whereby the licenser gives something of value to the licensee in exchange for certain performances and payments.

(a) The licenser may provide any of the following.

    (i) Rights to produce a patented product or use a patented production process

    (ii) Manufacturing know-how (unpatented)

    (iii) Technical advice and assistance

    (iv) Marketing advice and assistance

    (v) Rights to use a trademark, brand etc

(b) The licenser receives a royalty.

(c) Production is higher with no investment.

(d) The licensee might eventually become a competitor.

(e) The supply of essential materials, components, plant.

5.3.2 Agency agreement   5/10

Instead of opening its own sales distribution channel, a firm may grant agency agreements so that agents market and sell its products.

The agent receives a set of sample products, sales literature (eg brochures) and product training.

In return for selling the product, the agent receives a commission based on the number of sales they generate. Although the agent generates the sale, the firm still supplies the customer, so they can tell how many sales each agent has generated.

While agency agreements can be useful where customers like to compare between products (eg for financial services products) or where sales are enhanced by social networks (eg cosmetics, like *Avon* ladies), they can have some disadvantages:

There is a danger that an agent could mis-sell a product simply to gain a commission; the mis-selling could damage the underlying brand though.

*   The firm doesn't establish any relationships with its customers, so it misses out on customer feedback or the opportunity for relationship marketing

*   There is a risk that agents could desert the firm, taking their customers with them

5.3.3 Subcontracting

Subcontracting is also a type of alliance. Co-operative arrangements also feature in supply chain management.

5.3.4 Franchising   5/12

Franchising is a method of expanding the business on less capital than would otherwise be possible. The franchisee pays a capital lump sum to enter the franchise and also bears some of the running costs of its outlet.

Franchisers include McDonalds, Holiday Inn, Kall-Kwik Printing, KFC, and the Body Shop.

The franchiser offers the franchisee:

- Use of the franchise name, and any goodwill associated with it
- Use of its business systems and support services (including central marketing support)
- Its product/service to sell, and relevant instructions for selling the product/service
- Management and staff training programmes

In return:

- The franchisee pays the franchisers for being granted these rights.

- The franchisee has responsibility for the day-to-day running, and for the ultimate profitability, of – his own franchise.

- The franchisee supplies capital, personal involvement (staff, and human resources management) and local market knowledge. As well as reducing costs for the franchiser, this can also allow barriers to entry to be overcome effectively.

5.3.5 Benefits of Franchising

(a)   **Reduces capital requirements.** Firms often franchise because they cannot readily raise the capital required to set up company-owned stores. John Y. Brown, former president of Kentucky Fried Chicken, maintained that it would have cost KFC $450 million to establish its first 2,700 stores, and this was a sum that was not available to the corporation in the early stages of its life.

(b)   **Reduces managerial resources.** A firm may be able to raise the capital required for growth, but it may lack the managerial resources required to set up a network of company-owned stores. Recruiting and training managers and staff account for a significant percentage of the cost of growth of a firm.

        Under a franchise agreement, the franchisees supply the staff required for the day-to-day running of the operation.

(c)   **Improves return on promotional expenditure through speed of growth.** A retail firm's brand and brand image are crucial to the success of its stores. Companies often develop their brand through extensive advertising and promotion, but this only translates into sales if they have a number of stores that customers can visit after seeing their advertisements.

        To reap the benefits of its national or regional advertising efforts, the company needs to attain the minimum efficient scale, in terms of number of stores, as quickly as possible.

        Because franchising provides quicker access to capital and managerial resources, a firm can **expand more quickly through franchising than through opening company-owned stores.** Faster expansion through franchising, in turn, should allow companies to achieve a favourable return from their promotional campaigns.

(d)   **Benefits of specialisation**. Because the franchisee and the franchiser both contribute different resources to the franchise, franchising provides an effective way of reducing costs: each party concentrates on their core areas, and increases their efficiency in those areas.

        In general, franchisers are more cost efficient than franchisees in performing functions that decrease in cost with a substantial level of output. By contrast, franchisees are more efficient in performing functions which are more efficient at a smaller scale. For example, in the fast-food business, product development and national promotion are more efficiently handled on a large

scale (by the franchisor), whereas the production of food itself is handled better on a relatively smaller scale (by the franchisee).

(e)   **Low head office costs.** The franchiser only needs a small number of head office staff because there is a considerable delegation of operational responsibility to the franchisees. For example, in the fast-food business, the franchisees provide the staff who work in the restaurants, and so the franchisees incur the HR and payroll costs associated with that.

(f)   **Reduced supervision costs**. Company-owned retail stores are run by employee managers who may often perform poorly if they are not supervised. A company, therefore, has to supervise its store managers, and this will result in central overhead costs. However, under a franchise arrangement, because franchisees have invested capital in their own stores, and because their earnings come from the profits of those stores, they are motivated to work hard to maximise the success of the stores. Consequently the franchiser will have much lower supervision costs.

(g)   **Risk Management**. When opening new stores, a corporation does not know with certainty the business potential and the chances of success of different locations. Under a franchising arrangement, the franchiser can judge the profitability potential of different sites without incurring a significant business risk. If a particular store fails, the franchisee bears the brunt of the failure.

However, franchising also helps franchisees reduce their risks. Franchised stores typically open more quickly, and become profitable more quickly, than independent company-owned stores. The franchisee benefits from the franchisors managerial experience and from the established brand name. In effect, when a franchisee enters a lease agreement with the franchisor, it is leasing managerial know-how and brand recognition, as well as the physical store it is operating.

5.3.6 Disadvantages of franchising (for the franchiser)

(a)   The **search for competent candidates** is both costly and time consuming where the franchiser requires many outlets (eg *McDonald's* in the UK).

(b)   **Reduced profits**, because part of the profit has to be paid to franchisee

(c)   Danger that poor franchisee performance can **harm the brand**. The franchiser has to monitor its franchisees to ensure they are all offering a consistent product or service (for example, that all *McDonald's* outlets prepare their meals to the same recipe, sell them for the same price, and serve them in restaurants that are clean and follow the correct branding guidelines)

(d)   Danger that franchises can gain **confidential information** about the franchiser and subsequently set up as competitor.

Section summary

Joint ventures and **strategic alliances** are ways firms can combine resources. This can allow them growth opportunities which would not have been available to them acting in isolation. **Franchising** can be a useful method of expanding a business with limited capital.

6 Divestment and rationalisation

Introduction

So far we have looked at growth and acquisition strategies. However, history has shown that not all growth strategies prove successful. In particular, companies which have pursued diversification strategies have subsequently decided to refocus on their core competences rather than trying to have a wider range of interests. In such situations, groups need to divest the business units which no longer fit into their corporate portfolio.

Most strategies are designed to promote growth, but management should consider what rate of growth they want, whether they want to see any growth at all, or whether there should be a contraction of their business.

KEY TERM

DIVESTMENT is 'disposal of part of its activities by an entity'.   (CIMA *Official Terminology*)

Reasons for divestment are these.

(a)   To **rationalise** a business as a result of a strategic appraisal, perhaps as a result of portfolio analysis. For example, if a group has a business unit (SBU) which is a dog in a BCG and is unlikely to generating positive net cashflow for the group, the corporate parent may try to find a buyer for that SBU.

(b)   **Satisfy investors**: diversified conglomerates are unfashionable. Modern investment thinking is that investors prefer to provide their own portfolio diversification. So firms may divest business units which are not core to their business, and make their groups into a more coherent investment for investors.

(c)   **Focus on core competences**. If a group is too widely diversified it is likely to include some operations that could be more effectively bought in than retained in house. The group should focus on those areas that it can do better than any outside sides: its core competences.

(d)   **Improve control**. Similarly, if a group is too diverse, it can be difficult for management to control, and to appraise the performance of individual divisions.

(e)   To **allow market valuation to reflect growth and income prospects**. Where a low growth, steady income operation exists alongside a potentially high growth new venture, the joint P/E is likely to be too high for the cash cow and too low for the star. The danger is that the two businesses are not split so that their share prices correctly reflect their value, a predator will take over the whole operation at a discounted price. The predator will then split the business in two, allowing each part to settle at its own level, in effect doing what the business had failed to do itself.

(f)   To sell off **subsidiary companies** at a profit, perhaps as an **exit route** after managing a turnaround. If the subsidiary was struggling it could have been acquired at a low price. If the group then **turned it around** so that it became profitable, the group could then sell it at a profit. In this way, the subsidiary could be seen as an investment by the group, and the divestment allows the group to realise its investment.

(g)   To **raise funds** to invest elsewhere or to reduce debt. This may be particularly important if a group is suffering cash flow shortages and needs to raise cash.

CASE STUDY

Divestment

In January 2010, the US confectionery, food and beverage company Kraft acquired the UK confectionery business, Cadbury, in a deal costing £11.5bn ($18.9bn).

Kraft (whose group companies include Oscar Meyer, Philadelphia, Jacobs, Maxwell House and Nabisco) said the deal would create a 'global confectionery leader.'

However, by contrast, in 2008 Cadbury had been involved in divestment activity – selling the drinks businesses which it had previously held in its portfolio.

In December 2008, it sold its Australian drinks arm, Schweppes Beverages, to Japan's biggest brewer, Asahi.

That sale completed Cadbury's exit from the drinks market, following the demerger of Dr Pepper Snapple Group early that year (May 2008).

Talking about the Schweppes sale, Cadbury Chief Executive, Todd Stitzer, said: "The successful sale of Schweppes Australia will complete Cadbury's divestment of its beverage operations. As a result, Cadbury will focus solely on growing its chocolate, gum and candy portfolio in line with our strategy announced in June 2007."

Market analysts also looked favourably on the sale. One commented, "Strategically and financially, we think that this is an excellent deal for Cadbury. Their exit from soft drinks is now complete and they can focus exclusively on confectionery. They are exiting a 'so-so' asset for a price well ahead of our expectations."

Methods of divestment

Methods of divestment are these.

- **Sold as a going concern** to another business (in return for cash and/or shares). This option allows the business to continue, and so should allow staff to keep their jobs. It should also provide continuity for customers.

- **Assets are liquidated**: the business is closed and its assets are sold. This is likely to create job losses. While this option may be necessary if no buyer can be found, it can create negative publicity. For example, it the business being closed is part of a group, it may raise questions about the group as a whole.

- **Demerger**

- **Management buyout** (MBO)

- **Management buy in** (MBI)

6.1 Demergers

One term that describes divestment is **demerger**. This is sometimes referred to as **unbundling**. The main feature of a demerger is that one corporate entity becomes two or more separate entities. The newly-separated businesses might have the same shareholders, but they will usually have different people on their board of directors. In other words the supposed synergies are negative (a '2 + 2 = 3' effect, rather than a '2 + 2 = 5' effect).

Exam alert

A question in E3's predecessor paper (P6) featured a Group with three divisions whose estimated market capitalisations – if they had been operating separately – were $400m, $260m and $690m. This meant the total 'value' of the component businesses was $1,350m. However, the Group overall was only valued at $1,000m suggesting that the Group had 'destroyed' $350m of value. In such situation, a demerger would be a sensible strategic option.

6.2 Management buyout (MBO)

KEY TERM

A MANAGEMENT BUY-OUT is 'purchase of a business from its existing owners by members of the management team, generally in association with a financing institution. Where a large proportion of the new finance required to purchase the business is raised by external borrowing, the buy-out is described as leveraged'.

(CIMA Official Terminology)

Typically, a better price can be obtained by selling a business as a unit, and there might well be many other firms interested in buying. In recent years there have been a large number of **management buyouts**, whereby the subsidiary is sold off to its managers.

This option may appear attractive to managers because it gives them the chance to **control their own business**, with the absence of any head office constraints.

Moreover, it removes any concerns about **redundancy or imposed changes** if the business is sold to a new owner.

Finally, the management team should know the **business's potential**, and if they think it is profitable they should be well-positioned to maximise that profitability.

However, the MBO option may also be attractive for the divesting company because they can present the MBO as being an opportunity for the business to **develop its own talent**.

The managers put in some of their own capital, but obtain the rest from venture capital organisations and hope to make a bigger success of the business than the company which is selling it off.

CASE STUDY

Green & Black's

When Craig Sams sold his organic chocolate company Green & Black's to Cadbury for £20m in 2005, he was anxious to emphasise that his ultra-ethical brand (the holder of Britain's first Fairtrade designation) was in good hands.

Following Cadbury's takeover by Kraft in 2010, it seems that Green & Black's is less than keen to remain in a group headed by one of the globe's most ruthlessly efficient conglomerates. Green & Black's management are reportedly trying to engineer a buy-out from Kraft's empire, with Mr Sams seemingly keen to take back the brand.

Green & Black's (which has an annual turnover of about £40m) claims it is struggling to maintain its "entrepreneurial spirit" under Kraft (which has an annual turnover of £25 bn). Reports suggest that the company was keen to return to being a separate company, with its managers incentivised by linking performance to compensation.

There are suggestions that the chocolate maker approached Kraft at the end of 2010 with an initial proposal to spin off the company via a management buy-out, but this approach seems to have been rejected by Kraft.

However, Green and Black's position highlight the potentially uneasy relationship between brands which start out as small-scale, highly ethical products and are eventually swallowed by multi-national suitors.

There was already a degree of discontent within Green & Black's at being part of the Cadbury group, but the arrival of Kraft seems to have exacerbated these. Annual growth which had been close to 70% in 2005, has fallen sharply and some staff within Green & Black's have been bemoaning the amount of time devoted to projects that seldom came off.

6.2.1 Strategic factors in a buyout decision

Particularly important questions are as follows.

(a)   Can the buyout team **raise the finance** to pay for the buyout? Buyouts are well-favoured by venture capital organisations, which regard them as less risky than new start-up businesses.

(b)   Can the bought-out operation generate enough **profits** to pay for the costs of the acquisition?

6.3 Management buy ins (MBI)

An MBI is similar to an MBO, but the new management team comes from outside the existing business, rather than being the current management team.

6.4 Cost Rationalisation

Divestments occur when a group wants to sell off part of its business. However, firms may also want to reduce their costs and overheads, without actually selling off any parts of the business.

This is particularly relevant in periods of economic downturn, when firms have to deal with tighter margins or falling sales.

Firms are likely to review all their spending more closely, and many will look to make job cuts to reduce their wage bills.

However, as a cautionary note, firms should try to take a balanced approach between short-term cost cutting and longer-term robustness. If firms cut back too much in the short term (for example, by not investing in their staff or in maintaining their infrastructure) this could weaken their competitive position in the longer term.

Many organisations who lay people off in recessionary times struggle to meet renewed business demand when the economy picks up. Moreover, those employers who treat their staff well during hard times will benefit from having a committed workforce which will serve them well in the longer term. By contrast, simply making workers redundant can have serious negative impacts on morale and performance.

6.5 Relocation Strategies

In Section 3 above, we looked at some of the ways firms may relocate internationally as part of a growth strategy.

However, firms may also look to relocate within the same country, and this can often be as a means of saving costs. For example, in the UK a number of government and quasi-government bodies have relocated from London to Manchester because office costs and wages are much lower there.

Nonetheless, relocation strategies within a single country are not necessarily driven solely by the need to save costs.

There are a number of factors an organisation should consider when thinking about relocating:

- The savings that could be achieved through reduced accommodation costs (land, buildings, refurbishment, rent, rates etc) and staff costs

- Improved recruitment / retention of staff (if moving to an area of higher unemployment)

- Enhanced productivity (for example, if reduced accommodation costs allow new machinery and equipment to be purchased)

- Increase in operational efficiency (for example, by moving into purpose-built premises)

- Improved quality of service

- Improved working environment / quality of life

- Creation of a new corporate image, brand or new look

However, it is important that the relocation strategy reflects the business' needs, and the views of stakeholders, including staff and customers.

In some cases, a firm may need to relocate because it is expanding and needs to recruit additional staff. In this case, the choice of location will be influenced by 'positive' factors such as the availability of labour (with suitable qualifications), quality of life, amenities, and transport links.

Nevertheless, economic factors still need to be considered alongside these non-economic ones – with accommodation costs, and salary expectations still being important factors in the location decision.

It will also be important to consider the transitional costs which may be involved in the relocation. These will include:

- Transfer of staff (relocation allowances)
- Redundancies (for staff who do not wish to relocate)
- Recruitment and training costs (for replacement staff in the new location)
- Productivity losses (over the period of the move and as new staff get established)
- Plant and equipment, fixtures and fittings for the new premises
- Telecommunications and IT infrastructure of the new premises
- Costs of parallel running (if new offices are run alongside existing offices during the period of the move)

Section summary

Although strategic planning often focuses on growth and expansion, management need to be aware they can sometimes benefit from **disposing** (divesting) of part of their activities. This can often be true for diversified groups who need to refocus on their core activities.

Organisations can also make savings by relocating activities to new locations.

7 The public and not-for-profit sectors

Introduction

Public sector and **not-for-profit organisations** will find some commercial strategic management techniques useful, particularly in the fields of marketing and innovation.

7.1 The public sector

Just as business organisations' objectives are set according to the priorities of their stakeholders, with owners having priority and managers great influence, so public sector organisations' objectives are set in theory for the benefit of the public in general and the defined client groups in particular. Nonetheless, public sector organisations still need strategic management – in theory – to ensure that appropriate value chains, processes and resources are in place to allow them to achieve their objectives. In practice, however, public sector organisations' objectives often become subjected to politicians' and civil servants' own personal and professional priorities.

Political forces, in particular, can introduce **rapid policy changes**, while budgetary stringency or *largesse* can lead to the imposition of sudden spending cuts or the equally sudden availability of funds for which there are no planned applications. In the second case, actually spending the money can be more important than what it is spent on, so that an **underspend** need not be reported.

These considerations make much business strategy theory irrelevant to this sector. However, *Montanari and Bracker* proposed a matrix for the analysis of services provided by public sector bodies. This might be applied at the level of local or national government, or an executive agency with a portfolio of services. The axes are an assessment of service efficiency and public attractiveness: naturally, political support for a service or organisation depends to a great degree on the extent to which the public need and appreciate it.

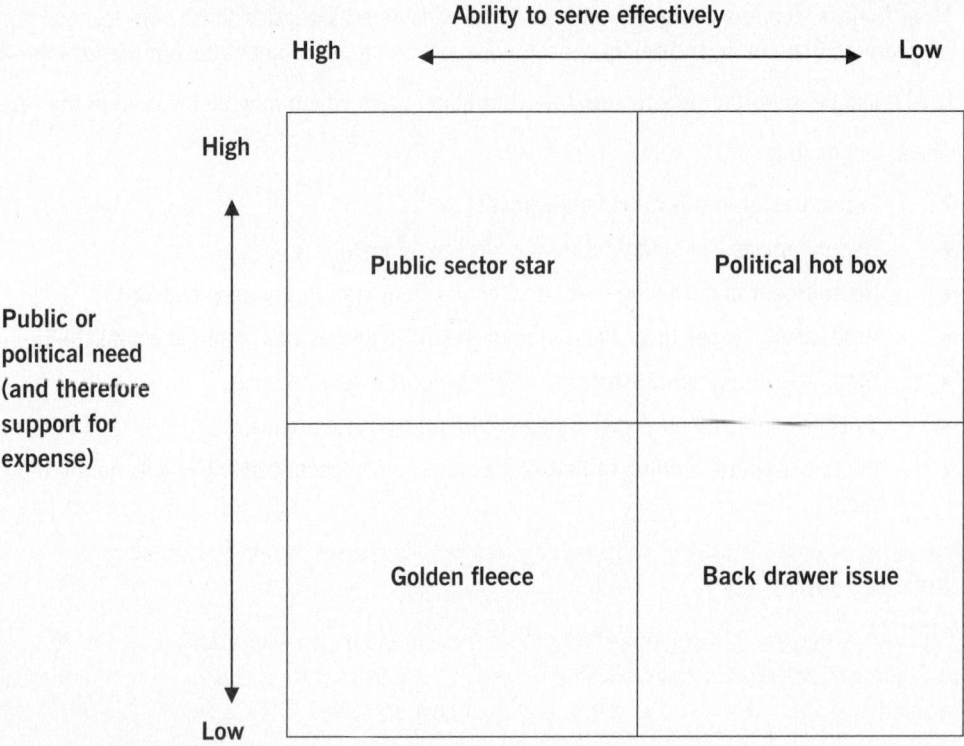

(a)   A **public sector star** is something that the system is doing well and should not change. They are essential to the viability of the system.

(b)   **Political hot boxes** are services that the public want, or which are mandated, but for which there are not adequate resources or competences.

(c)   **Golden fleeces** are services that are done well but for which there is low demand. They may therefore be perceived to be undesirable uses for limited resources. They are potential targets for cost cutting.

(d)   **Back drawer issues** are unappreciated and have low priority for funding. They are obvious candidates for cuts, but if managers perceive them as essential, they should attempt to increase support for them and move them into the **political hot box** category.

A similar concept, the Maslin Multidimensional matrix has been proposed. This is also a two axis, four cell structure, with one axis dedicated to **client group needs** and wants and the other for any dimension that users might see as useful. This dimension might be, for example, the level of concern of the local community, of national government, the level of finance available, the level of staff expertise, or the level of activities currently undertaken.

The four cells are then defined by high and low levels of needs or wants and the extremes of the chosen second dimension.

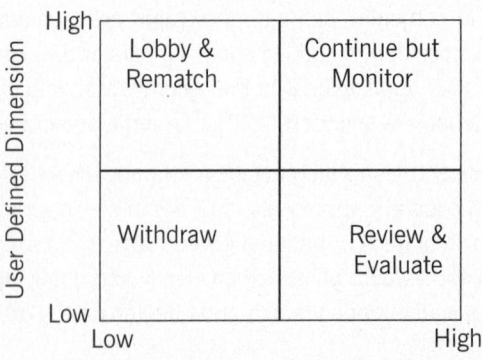

Public servants are under an obligation to deliver certain services in an effective and economical fashion. This implies that certain problems and choices are likely to appear repeatedly.

(a)   Plans must be made for the **delivery of services**. This may involve consideration of which **core competences** to maintain and develop, which services to carry on providing in-house and which to outsource.

(b)   Choices must also be made about procurement policy and the selection of suppliers to provide services required.

(c)   Budgets must be managed to provide mandated services. Choices must be made about **investment in physical and human resources** of all kinds.

(c)   Some **marketing** activity will be required, certainly in the form of **communication** with politicians, departmental staff, client groups and the wider public; and possibly in the form of **market research**, particularly in relation to the design and effectiveness of services.

(d)   Just as in business, there will be a requirement for continuing **innovation** in products and methods in the search for increased effectiveness and economy to deliver (for example) new services, or to find new ways of delivering services. These new ways of delivering services might include **public-private partnerships**, in which a public sector authority and one or more private sector companies combine to deliver a project. This will require the development of knowledge, assets and competences.

A public sector organisation's strategy will have three major elements.

*   Marketing
*   Service delivery
*   Resource utilisation

As we have seen, co-operation between business organisations is now commonplace, both across and along the supply chain. Similar **cross-boundary links** are required in the public sector, both to meet client needs and to ensure that difficult problems do not disappear into the gaps between agencies.

7.2 Not-for-profit organisations

Even more than public sector organisations, charities need to operate both **economically** and **effectively**: they have an obligation both to those who depend on them and to those who finance them to do so. The techniques of business strategy are more applicable to charities than to the public sector, however, because their income is derived from **providing satisfaction to the donating public**, albeit in the form of providing a worthy cause to support. In addition, many charities do, in fact, operate mainstream businesses as a source of funds. They must therefore be particularly alive to **changing public concerns** when setting their objectives and be prepared to market their purpose as though it were a consumer product. Charities are, effectively, in competition with one another for donations.

The strategic management of charities is complicated by the element of **voluntary work** that exists within them. This is likely to be driven, at least in part, by very high ideals and may produce **ideological pressure** concerning the courses of action undertaken. Volunteers are likely to have their own ideas about how the organisation should be run, which is likely to constrain management ideas about control and reporting.

A major strategic concern will be to market the organisation's priorities and methods to its **internal stakeholders** as well as to the external donors who may be perceived to be its 'customers'. Both groups must be satisfied that the organisation is making proper use of the resources entrusted to it.

Strategic concern for charities

Haberberg and Rieple recognise three strategic concerns for charities.

*   Organise and manage **internal structure** and systems so as to achieve the mission
*   Develop and manage **fundraising** to provide consistent and predictable levels of income
*   Demonstrate good **governance**

Section summary

Although **public sector** and **not-for-profit organisations** have different objectives to commercial organisations, they still need to develop strategies to deliver their objectives economically and effectively.

Chapter Roundup

✓ Ansoff's growth vector matrix identifies the four product-market strategies firms can use to try to increase sales: **market penetration; market development; product development; and diversification**. The degree of risk involved varies between strategies, with diversification being the most risky.

✓ A firm can either choose to grow internally or else it can link with another firm.

✓ **Organic growth** allows a firm to expand by developing its own resources rather than by combining with any other firms. A firm growing organically can **expand internationally**, but managing an international operation will require different resources and competences than managing an operation in a single country. Decisions about **which countries to enter**, and **how to enter them**, are key strategic decisions.

✓ **Mergers and acquisitions** allow firms to grow by combining with others. A merger or acquisition can provide quicker growth than organic growth, but strategic planners must consider the levels of risk involved.

✓ **Joint ventures** and **strategic alliances** are ways firms can combine resources. This can allow them growth opportunities which would not have been available to them acting in isolation. **Franchising** can be a useful method of expanding a business with limited capital.

✓ Although strategic planning often focuses on growth and expansion, management need to be aware they can sometimes benefit from **disposing** (divesting) of part of their activities. This can often be true for diversified groups who need to refocus on their core activities.

✓ Organisations can also make saving by relocating activities to new locations.

✓ Although **public sector** and **not-for-profit organisations** have different objectives than commercial organisations, they still need to develop strategies to deliver their objectives economically and effectively.

Quick Quiz

1 Fill in the Ansoff matrix

Product

		Present	New
Market	Present	....	....
	New	....	....

2 Why is innovation important in an organic growth strategy?

3 Distinguish a merger from an acquisition.

4   **Fill in the blanks** in the statement below, using the words in the box.

(1) .... provide a means of entering a (2) .... or building up (3) .... more (4) .... than would be the case if the company tried to develop its own (5) .... Corporate planners must however consider the level of (6) .... involved.

- risk
- market share
- quickly
- resources
- market
- acquisitions

5   Define a joint venture. What is the chief disadvantage of joint ventures?

6   What are the methods of divestment?

Answers to Quick Quiz

1

		Product	
		Present	New
Market	Present	Market penetration; (for growth) or consolidation (to maintain position) or withdrawal	Product development
	New	Market development	Diversification

2   Innovation provides the organisation with a distinctive competence, and with the ability to maintain such a competence. Also it maintains the organisation's competitive advantage and market share

3   A merger is the joining of two separate companies to form a single company.
An acquisition is the purchase of a controlling interest in another company.

4   (1) Acquisitions (2) market (3) market share (4) quickly (5) resources (6) risk

5   A joint venture is an arrangement where two firms (or more) join forces for manufacturing, financial and marketing purposes and each has a share in both the equity and the management of the business. The major disadvantage of joint ventures is that there can be conflicts of interest.

6   Sale as a going concern
Sale of assets
Demerger
Management buyout / buy in

Answer to Questions

6.1 Road transport

The first step in a suggested solution is to think of how a company operating nationwide in general road haulage might diversify, whilst benefitting from synergies between its new business and its existing business. Perhaps you thought of the following.

(a)   To move from nationwide to international haulage, the company might be able to use its existing contacts with customers to develop an international trade. Existing administration and depot facilities in the UK could be used. Drivers should be available who are willing to work abroad, and the scope for making reasonable profits should exist. However, international road haulage might involve the company in the purchase of new vehicles (eg road haulage in Europe often involves the carriage of containerised products on large purpose-built vehicles). Since international haulage takes longer, vehicles will be tied up in jobs for several days, and a substantial investment might be required to develop the business. In addition, in the event of breakdowns, a network of overseas garage service arrangements will have to be created. It might take some time before business builds up sufficiently to become profitable.

(b)   Moving from general haulage to 'speciality' types of haulage, perhaps haulage of large items of plant and machinery, or computer equipment. The same broad considerations apply to speciality types of haulage. Existing depot facilities could be used and existing customer contacts might be developed. However, expertise in specialist work will have to be 'brought in' as well as developed within the company and special vehicles might need to be bought. Business might take some time to build up and if the initial investment is high, there could be substantial early losses.

Now try these questions from the Exam Question Bank	Number	Level	Marks	Time
	Q6	Examination	15	27 mins
	Q7	Examination	25	45 mins

EVALUATING STRATEGIC OPTIONS

 This chapter describes how management accountants can apply decision techniques to strategic issues such as investment appraisal, risk and operational gearing, and uncertainty.

The basic theory and mathematics of techniques such as discounting and breakeven analysis should already be familiar to you. The aim of this chapter is to illustrate the way these methods can be used to support *strategic* decision making. Such decision-making is complicated by such factors as incompleteness of information and the need to apply more than one set of ideas to a problem in order to analyse it fully. Management accountants operating at a strategic level must, for example, appreciate the constraints applied by the marketing function and be prepared to incorporate them into their analyses.

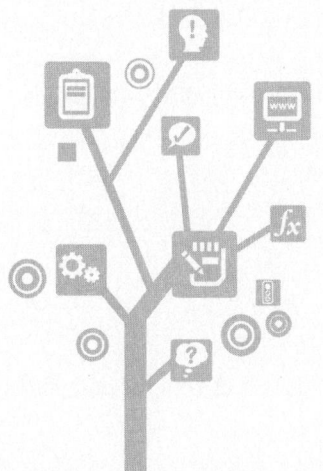

topic list	learning outcomes	syllabus references	ability required
1 Evaluating strategic options	C1 (b), C2(d)	C1 (iii), C2 (v)	Evaluate
2 Strategic management accounting, DCF and investment appraisal	C2 (d)	C2 (v)	Discuss
3 Risk and cost behaviour	C2 (d)	C2 (v)	Discuss
4 Decision techniques	C2 (d)	C2 (v)	Discuss

1 Evaluating strategic options   3/11

Introduction

Strategic choices are evaluated according to their suitability (to the organisation and its current situation), their feasibility (eg in terms of usefulness or competences) and their acceptability (eg to relevant stakeholder groups).

Once an organisation has identified its current strategic position, and the different potential strategic options available to it, it then has to choose which of these options it wants to pursue.

According to the rational model, individual strategies have to be evaluated against a number of criteria before a strategy or a mix of strategies is chosen. *Johnson, Scholes and Whittington* narrow these criteria down to three: **suitability**, **acceptability** and **feasibility**.

Exam skills

If you are asked to *evaluate a strategy* you should consider its suitability, acceptability and feasibility – relating these specifically back to the context given in the question scenario.

Suitability differs from feasibility and acceptability in that little can be done with an unsuitable strategy. However, it may be possible to adjust the factors that suggest a strategy is not acceptable or not feasible. Therefore **suitability should be assessed first**.

1.1 Suitability

Suitability relates to the **strategic logic** of the strategy. The strategy must fit the company's operational circumstances.

- **Exploit** company strengths and distinctive **competences**?
- Rectify company **weaknesses**?
- **Neutralise** or deflect environmental **threats**?
- Help the firm to seize **opportunities**?
- **Satisfy the goals** of the organisation? (And, at a more general level, does it fit with the company's mission and objectives?)
- **Fill the gap** identified by gap analysis?
- Generate/maintain **competitive advantage**?
- Involve an acceptable level of **risk**?
- Suit the **politics** and corporate **culture**?

An organisation should also consider two overall important strategic issues when assessing the suitability of an option:

- Does it **fit with any existing strategies** which the company is already employing, and which it wants to continue to employ?
- How well will the option actually address the company's strategic issues and **priorities**?

A number of the models which we have looked at in the preceding chapters in this Text could be useful for assessing the suitability of a strategy:

Porter's generic strategies – For example if an organisation is currently employing a cost leadership strategy and the basis of a proposed strategy is differentiation, this might not be suitable.

Value chain – Similar issues could be identified in relation to the activities in the organisation's value chain: will the activities required for the proposed strategy 'fit' with the nature of the activities in the organisation's current value chain?

BCG matrix – How will any new products or business units fit with the existing ones in an organisation's portfolio? Will they improve the balance of the portfolio?

Ansoff's matrix – Is the choice of product-market strategy suitable? For example, in order for a market development strategy to be suitable there have to be unsaturated markets available which the organisation could move into. And, at the same time, the organisation's product or service has to be more attractive to customers than any existing competitor offerings so that the customers in the new market will want to switch to the organisation's product. Furthermore, the organisation needs sufficient spare production capacity and distribution channels to be able to satisfy demand in the new market.

1.2 Acceptability (to stakeholders)

The acceptability of a strategy relates to people's expectations of it. It is here that stakeholder analysis can be brought in.

(a)   **Financial considerations**. Strategies will be evaluated by considering how far they contribute to meeting the dominant objective of increasing **shareholder wealth**.

   (i)   Return on investment
   (ii)   Profits
   (iii)   Growth
   (iv)   EPS
   (v)   Cash flow
   (vi)   Price/Earnings
   (vii)   Market capitalisation

(b)   **Customers**. Will the strategy give customers something they want? How will customers react to the strategy? Customers may object to a strategy if it means reducing service or raising price, but on the other hand they may have no choice but to accept the changes.

(c)   **Management** have to implement the strategy via their staff.

(d)   **Staff** have to be committed to the strategy for it to be successful. If staff are unhappy with the strategy they could leave.

(e)   **Suppliers** have to be willing and able to meet the input requirements of the strategy.

(f)   **Banks** are interested in the implications for cash resources, debt levels etc.

(g)   **Government**. A strategy involving a takeover may be prohibited under monopolies and mergers legislation. Similarly, the environmental impact may cause key stakeholders to withhold consent.

(h)   **The public**. The environmental impact may cause key local stakeholders to protest. Will there be any pressure groups who oppose the strategy?

(i)   **Risk**. Different shareholders have different attitudes to risk. A strategy which changed the risk/return profile, for whatever reason, may not be acceptable.

1.3 Feasibility

Feasibility asks whether the strategy can in fact be implemented.

- Is there enough **money**?
- Is there the **ability** to deliver the goods/services specified in the strategy?
- Can we deal with the likely **responses that competitors** will make?
- Do we have access to **technology, materials and resources**?
- Do we have enough **time** to implement the strategy?

The 'Ms' model (which we considered in connection with the resource audit) could be useful for assessing feasibility. Does the organisation have the resources it needs to implement the strategy successfully?

Strategies which do not make use of the existing competences, and which therefore call for new competences to be acquired, might not be feasible.

- Gaining competences via organic growth takes time
- Acquiring new competences can be costly

We look at budgets and financial resources in the next section.

1.4 Sustainability

Some organisations may feel it is appropriate to consider the longer term prospects for a strategy under a separate heading of sustainability. This indicates that a firm should aim to adopt strategies which will deliver a long-term competitive advantage.

Section summary

Strategies should be assessed to ensure they are **suitable**, **acceptable** and **feasible**. Suitability should be assessed first as little can be done with an unsuitable strategy, whereas it may be possible to adjust the factors to make a strategy more acceptable or feasible.

2   Strategic management accounting, DCF and investment appraisal

Introduction

Decisions about investment can be illuminated by the use of relevant costs and discounting.

The principles of relevant costs for decision-making and the techniques of DCF should be familiar to you already. Remember that a cost that is relevant to one decision may not be relevant to another one. This is particularly true of opportunity costs.

Investment decisions are covered in more detail in Paper F3 – Financial Strategy.

Exam skills

For strategic management accounting, you must be able to apply these principles and techniques to situations where the data is either subject to uncertainty in the estimates, or else is incomplete. State your

assumptions clearly. In the context of strategic management accounting, as a general guideline, the following is suggested as an approach.

(a)   Recognise why the accounting information is needed – what are we trying to do?

(b)   Assess whether the data is incomplete. If so, make any suitable assumptions that might be necessary.

(c)   Recognise whether any estimated data is uncertain, and of dubious reliability. If possible, assess how variations in the estimates would affect your financial analysis and recommendation style.

2.1 Example: strategic management accounting and DCF analysis

Booters plc is a company which specialises in purchasing and re-selling land with development potential. The following data is available.

Market value of agricultural land	£20,000 per acre
Market value of land that can be developed	£200,000 per acre
Maintenance cost of land, per acre	£2,500 pa
Booters plc's cost of capital	19%

Agricultural land that is held by Booters plc can be let to farmers on short term leases for £300 per acre per annum, but maintenance costs would be payable by Booters.

The company has now received invitations to bid for two properties.

Property 1. 1.5 acres of land near a planned major road. Some of the land is about to be made subject to a compulsory purchase order, for sale to the local authority for £25,000. The remaining land (0.8 of an acre) can be re-sold to a property developer for £190,000, but not until about five years' time.

Property 2. A country estate of 160 acres, of which 15 acres might be released for residential housing development at any time in the next four years. Development of the remaining 145 acres will not be allowed.

This land will be put up for auction, unless Booters plc agrees now to pay a price of £1,400,000 beforehand. If the land goes up for auction, it is believed that a local businessman might offer £1,600,000, but the reserve price will be only £900,000.

Required: In the case of each property, what should Booters bid for the property, if anything?

Discussion

In this example, the data is incomplete. Some of the missing items would be readily available in a real-life situation, but other data would be unobtainable, except as guesswork.

Property 1. Most of the data we need for a simple financial analysis exists, but the data does not state whether the land is agricultural land or not, and so whether it can be let out to a farmer.

Otherwise, we have a straightforward DCF analysis.

	Year	Value/Cost £	Discount factor 19%	Present value £
Sale value of land, subject to compulsory purchase order	0	25,000	1.000	25,000
Sale value of remaining land	5	190,000	0.419	79,610
Maintenance cost of land, assumed to be £2,500 × 0.8 pa	1-5	(2,000)	3.058	(6,116)
Maximum purchase price				98,494

If the land sold under the compulsory purchase order takes time to sell, say one year, the value of the land would be lower, with the £25,000 sale value having to be discounted by a factor of 0.840 and a maintenance cost of land to be included (0.7 acres × £2,500, as a year 1 cost).

A maximum price of £98,000 might be indicated.

Property 2. Here the data is incomplete and uncertain.

(a)   How likely is it that the 15 acres will be released for housing development?

(b)   When is it most likely to be released?

(c)   Is it agricultural land, and so could it be leased out to tenant farmers?

(d)   Would the unwanted 145 acres be saleable at agricultural land prices, and if so, when would Booters plc know which land it did not want? Have the 15 acres for re-development been specifically identified?

(e)   If the land goes for auction, would a bid above the reserve price be likely?

It is only by recognising what data is missing or uncertain that we can begin to carry out a sensible financial analysis.

Here the following assumptions are made.

(a)   The land is agricultural land.

(b)   The 15 acres for redevelopment have not been identified specifically. The remaining 145 acres cannot be re-sold until the planning permission has been obtained on the other 15 acres.

(c)   The 145 acres could then be resold at agricultural land prices.

Two further assumptions call for business judgement.

(a)   The 15 acres will be released for residential housing. There is a risk, of course, that it won't be.
(b)   The land will not be released for four more years. It could, of course, be sooner.

Now we can carry out a DCF analysis.

	Year	Value/cost £	Discount factor 19%	Present value £
Sales value of 15 acres (15 × £200,000)	4	3,000,000	0.499	1,497,000
Sales value of 145 acres (145 × £20,000)	4	2,900,000	0.499	1,447,100
Sub-letting of 160 acres at £300 per acre	1-4	48,000	2.639	126,672
Maintenance cost of 160 acres at £2,500 pa	1-4	(400,000)	2.639	(1,055,600)
Maximum value of the land				2,015,172

Since Booters plc has been offered the chance to buy the property prior to auction for £1,400,000, the key questions are as follows.

(a)   Is buying the land too much of a risk? If the land is not released for development, the 15 acres would be sold for only £300,000, and the PV of this would be only around £150,000. The maximum value of the land would now be about £1,350,000 less, at approximately £671,000.

(b)   If the risk is considered to be worth accepting, should a price of £1,400,000 be accepted, or is it worth trying to get the land for something near the reserve price of £900,000 and running the risk of having to outbid a rival, by offering as much as £1,600,000 or even more?

Exam alert

There is no clear answer to either question, but a decision has to be taken. This is what strategic management is about! Now try this exercise:

Question 7.1   Domestic gas

Learning outcomes C 1 (iii)

A public company responsible for the supply of domestic gas has received several requests from prospective customers in the Matsfold area to be connected to the gas supply system. Matsfold, an area consisting of about 8,000 residential dwellings, does not currently have any connection to the gas mains, and the company is now trying to reach a decision whether or not to provide gas supplies to the area.

(a)   New customers are each charged £300 for being connected to the system and having a meter installed.

(b)   Charges per quarter are:

   (i)   standing charge of £15, plus

   (ii)   a charge for gas consumed, at the rate of £500 per 1,000 metered units. The average domestic consumption is about 120 metered units per month.

(c)   Supplies of gas cost the company £0.08 per metered unit. Wastage of 20% must be allowed for.

(d)   A postal market research survey of the Matsfold area elicited a 50% response, and 90% of the respondents indicated their wish to be connected to a gas supply.

(e)   The company's cost of capital is 17%.

Required

What is the maximum capital project cost that the company should be willing to incur to persuade it to provide gas supplies to the Matsfold area?

2.2 Target returns for new capital investments: the cost of capital

You will look at evaluating investment projects and the cost of capital in more detail in Paper F3 – Financial Strategy.

KEY TERM

COST OF CAPITAL. 'Minimum acceptable return on an investment, generally computed as a discount rate for use in investment appraisal exercises. The computation of the optimal cost of capital can be complex, and many ways of determining this opportunity cost have been suggested.'   (CIMA *Official Terminology*)

Setting target returns for new capital investments could help ensure that future returns are sufficient to allow a company to achieve its overall target return.

In practice, things are not so simple.

(a)   The return on new capital investments is only one aspect of making an adequate return. For most companies, it is the **return on existing products** that is the major influence on profitability and return.

(b)   The actual return on capital is measured **retrospectively**, as ROI, profits, earnings per share or dividends plus capital growth. A DCF return, in contrast, is measured by future cash flows.

Many groups of companies have a corporate treasury function within the holding company, which controls the use of the group's internally-generated funds by means of a central 'banking system.' The holding company will 'loan' capital to subsidiary operating units and charge out the funds at the corporate cost of capital. The target DCF rate of return selected by an organisation might be based on the following:

(a)   The **weighted average cost of capital** (WACC of the organisation).

(b)   The **marginal cost of capital** – ie the cost of the extra capital required to finance a specific project.

(c)   The **opportunity cost** of the capital required to finance the project.

(d)   A cost of capital that is adjusted to allow for the **risk element** in the particular capital investment.

(e)   A return based on the **capital asset pricing model**.

2.3 Strategic value analysis

Ultimately, investment decisions are supposed to increase **shareholder value** (a measure of shareholders' wealth as reflected in the share price).

Strategic value analysis is an approach which measures the potential financial benefit or loss to shareholders from pursuing strategic options.

(a)   **Shareholder value analysis** suggests the following '**value drivers**' generate a company's future cash flows.

- Sales growth rate (percentage)
- Operating profit margin
- Cash tax rate
- Incremental fixed capital investment
- Incremental working capital investment
- Planning period
- Cost of capital

> The resulting free cash flows over the planning period can be discounted at the cost of capital to get an estimated shareholder value from pursuing an option

(b)   **Economic value added** is a similar approach, structured in a different way.

The model above can be used as a decision making tool. For example, moving into a new market might be associated with **sales growth**, but cash flows will be under pressure from incremental **fixed and working capital investment**.

2.4 Strategic problems in investment appraisal

Strategic decisions cannot be reduced entirely to computation. Qualitative factors must also be considered.

KEY TERM

STRATEGIC INVESTMENT APPRAISAL. 'Method of investment appraisal which allows the inclusion of both financial and non-financial factors. Project benefits are appraised in terms of their contribution to the strategies of the organisation either by their financial contribution, for non-financial benefits, by the use of index numbers or other means. (CIMA *Official Terminology*)

It is not always easy, or even possible, to quantify some of the strategic issues which affect an investment decision, for example **trends in the industry** as a whole.

2.4.1 External orientation

As a firm's strategy is linked very much with its position in the market place, any investment appraisal of a project must take the broader strategic issues into account.

Two questions can be posed of a strategic investment therefore, in addition to financial evaluation.

(a)   Does a project generate value to **customers**, so that the cash generated will provide a return?

(b)   Will these cash flows be **sustained** in the light of the competitive environment?

Exam alert

Strategic investment decisions must be assessed with regard to their:

- Immediate financial viability
- Effect on competitive advantage in the light of environmental uncertainties

2.4.2 Procedure for strategic investment appraisal

The following ten steps for approaching strategic projects have been suggested.

1	Determine the investment project to be analysed.
2	Determine the strategic objectives for the project.
3	Determine alternative ways of achieving the same strategic objectives.
4	Analyse a small number of alternatives.
5	Try to determine what will happen if nothing is done (but this does not mean that you assume that competitors will do nothing).
6	Determine key internal and external assumptions.
7	Collect data on areas of greatest uncertainty.
8	Carry out sensitivity analysis tests.
9	Redefine the project on the basis of 8.
10	Expose key assumptions and debate them.

2.4.3 Investment decisions

There are a number of different types of spending which can be conceived as **strategic investment issues** even though not all of them are recorded as such in financial statements.

- Investing in brands and marketing
- Investing in corporate image
- R&D to create knowledge for future exploitation
- Information technology
- Acquisitions

2.4.4 Marketing expenditure

There is some justification for treating certain types of **marketing expenditure** as investment. Levels of marketing expenditure are often significant, and any marketing strategy will have to be evaluated accordingly. However, according to *Keith Ward*, 'levels of marketing expenditure…are often subjected to far less rigorous financial evaluations than smaller financial commitments on more tangible assets.'

Marketing expenditure can be evaluated using a variety of methods.

- Cash flow modelling with **NPV**
- Use of **non-financial measures** to benchmark spend
- **Modelling competitor responses**

We will look at strategic marketing in greater detail in Chapter 8.

Section summary

Relevant costs for decision making and discounting analysis can provide information which can help make decisions about investments. It is important to take non-financial information, along with the financial information, into consideration when making strategic decisions.

3 Risk and cost behaviour

Introduction

Among the problems associated with strategic decision making is the lack of certainty associated with the forecasting techniques used. Whether or not probabilities can be assigned to outcomes, techniques exist for minimising the impact of this uncertainty, including CVP analysis.

Strategies deal with future events: the future cannot be predicted.

We can make a distinction between risk and uncertainty, but often the terms are used interchangeably.

(a)   **Risk** is sometimes used to describe situations where outcomes are not known, but their probabilities can be estimated.

(b)   **Uncertainty** is present when the outcome cannot be predicted or assigned probabilities.

Note: You will look at the strategic and operational risks an organisation faces in much more detail in Paper P3 – Performance Strategy.

The material we are looking at here does not attempt to replicate the material from P3, but it is a brief illustration of the way organisations need to take account of a wide range of potential risks when evaluating their strategic options.

3.1 Types of risk   5/12

KEY TERM

RISK is taken to mean both general unquantifiable uncertainty (eg political risk) and volatility, often measured by standard deviation.

Risk	Comment
Physical risk	Earthquakes, fire, flooding, and equipment breakdown. In the long-term, climatic changes: global warming, drought (relevant to agriculture and water firms).
Economic risk	Assumptions about the economic environment might turn out to be wrong. Not even the government forecasts are perfect.
Financial risk	This term has a specific technical meaning: the risk to shareholders caused by debt finance. The risk exists because the debt finance might prevent capital growth or the payment of dividends, particularly when trading is difficult. The converse is that when businesses buoyant, interest payments are easily covered and shareholders receive the benefit of the remaining profits.
Business risk	Lowering of entry barriers (eg new technology); changes in customer/supplier industries leading to changed relative power; changes to the firms internal structure (eg its culture or technical systems); management misunderstanding of core competences; volatile cash flows; uncertain returns; changed investor perceptions increasing the required rate of return.
Political risk	Nationalisation, sanction, civil war, political instability, can all have an impact on the business.
Exchange risk	This is the risk that changes in exchange rates affect the value of a transaction in a currency, or how it is reported.
Competitor risk	The risks to cash flows arising from the actions of competitors: for example if a competitor introduces a new product, or reduces the price of their existing products.

CASE STUDY

Risk

The eruption of a volcano in Iceland in April 2010 turned into a major headache for businesses across Europe and around the world, as a spreading cloud of ash closed a number of European airports.

Airlines were forced to ground their places, and alongside the disruption to passenger travel there was also disruption to the transportation of food supplies and other essential goods.

Airline shares suffered on stock markets, and the Geneva-based International Air Transport Association estimated that the disruption cost the airline industry some $200 million a day in revenues.

Eurocontrol, the European air traffic agency, said approximately 16,000 flights were cancelled on the day after the volcano erupted, more than half the 28,000 that usually operate. The flight ban was imposed because of concerns about pilot visibility and jet engine failure from the ash.

The Chief Executive of Ryanair, the leading low-cost airline in Europe, said "This spreading cloud of volcanic ash is an unprecedented event in Ryanair's 26 year history, and we are continuing to work around the clock to minimise its effects on our schedules."

As well as the airlines themselves, other businesses were affected by the inability to get freight in and out of countries. The main problems related to goods that are perishable (for example, fresh fruit and vegetables, fish and flowers). The pharmaceutical industry is also particularly reliant on air freight because of the high value and low weight of their products.

3.2 Who suffers risk?

Risk and return are related. An investor will want a higher return to compensate for the increased risk of a project.

For example, investors in a company in a low-risk business might be satisfied with a return of, say, 15%, whereas in a comparable high-risk business the required return might be a minimum of 25%.

There may be a **minimum return** that shareholders will accept, allowing for the risk of the investment.

Different stakeholders in a company or a decision have different attitudes to risk.

(a)   **Shareholders** are able to **diversify their portfolios**, so they can have shares in a number of firms, some offering high return for high risk, others offering a low return for a low risk.

(b)   Key decision makers are **managers**, and their perceptions of risk are likely to be quite different.

3.3 The management accountant and risk

3.3.1 Targets for risk

If the primary financial target can be converted into a target rate of return for individual capital projects, how can risk be expressed in practical terms for decision-makers?

(a)   A **premium** for risk can be added to the target DCF rate of return.

(b)   To protect cash flows, it might be made a condition of all new capital projects that the project should **pay back** within a certain period of time, say three to four years.

When assessing future cash flows and net present values of projects it may also be useful to consider the value of leaving different options open. This is the essence of real options theory, which we discussed in Chapter 3.

3.3.2 Risk appraisal in strategy evaluation

One of the problems arising when evaluating alternative strategies is the reliability of the data used.

(a) Business planners use operational research techniques to measure levels of uncertainty.

(b) Basic **probability theory** can be used to express the likelihood of a forecast result occurring. This would evaluate the data given by informing the decision-maker that there is, for example, a 50% probability that an acceptable result will be achieved, a 25% chance that the worst result will occur and a 25% chance that the best possible result will occur. This evaluation of risk might help the executive to decide between alternative strategies, each with its own risk profile.

When evaluating a strategy, management should consider the following.

(a) Whether an individual strategy involves **an unacceptable amount** of risk. If it does, it should be eliminated from further consideration in the planning process.

(b) However, the risk of an individual strategy should also be considered in the context of the **overall portfolio** of investment strategies adopted by the company.

3.3.3 Risk and cost behaviour: operational gearing

CVP analysis (breakeven analysis) can be useful in strategic planning to assess the share of the market needed to break even or to achieve a target return with a particular strategy. For example, if a company is planning to make a new product for a particular market, and estimates of capital investment costs and fixed and variable running costs were fairly reliable, the company could assess the following for a number of different sales prices.

(a) How many sales would be needed to break even each year, and so what market share would be needed.

(b) How many sales would be needed over a given period (of say, three years) assuming a gradual increase in annual sales, in order to break even in DCF terms (ie achieve an NPV = 0). The required market share per year for each year of the project could then be assessed.

KEY TERM

COST-VOLUME-PROFIT ANALYSIS (CVP) . 'Study of the effects on future profit of changes in fixed cost, variable cost, sales price, quantity and mix.' *(CIMA Official Terminology)*

A related risk is the **cost structure** of the business.

(a) A **high level of fixed costs** means that large losses are made if sales are less than breakeven, but that once breakeven is achieved, larger profits follow.

(b) A **high proportion of variable product costs** means that the total costs are always sensitive to actual production volumes. Losses are lower, but so are profits.

In other words, the business's **operational gearing** (the ratio of fixed to variable costs) is an important indicator of risk. Where there is a high proportion of fixed costs, a strategy might be more risky, although it promises a higher return. A high proportion of genuinely variable costs can mean more flexibility.

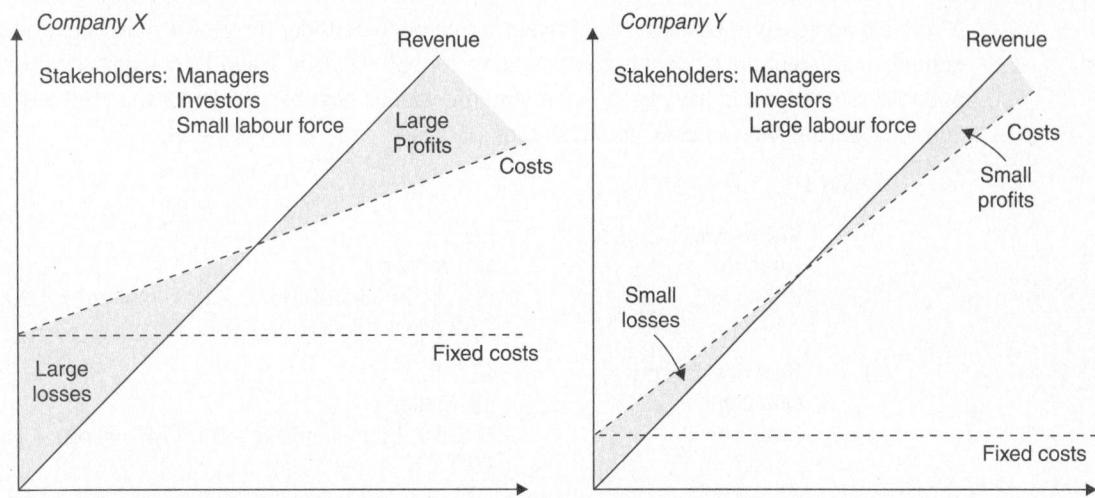

The two graphs have the same breakeven point, but X is much more sensitive to lower sales. It is more volatile. X promises higher profits, but risks higher losses than Y.

With any strategy there is a **stakeholder response risk**, an environmental factor which can intrude on the management accountant's cost behaviour diagrams. Bankers, employees and the government are all interested in a business. If a business pursues a particular strategy, this might antagonise the government of the country in which it is operating.

3.3.4 Probabilities and risk

Higher risks tend to be associated with higher returns. This is the principle underlying the Capital Asset Pricing Model, and we have already seen that the target DCF rate of return for capital expenditure projects may be varied according to the project's risk.

Some risks can be measured by probabilities.

(a)   An average expected profit or NPV can be measured as an expected value (EV) of the different probabilities.

(b)   Risk can be quantified as a standard deviation of expected profit or NPV.

You will look at the Capital Asset Pricing Model in Paper F3 – Financial Strategy.

3.4 Example: uncertainty about sales demand, costs and profits

A company is trying to make a strategic decision about whether to introduce a new production process. The process would reduce unit variable costs of production significantly but would increase fixed costs of production substantially. Forecast sales demand is uncertain, for a range of different selling prices. Non-production costs are also uncertain. The key information in the question could be reduced to the following.

(a)   **Option 1**. Keeping existing system

(i)   Sales price could be anywhere in the range £9 – £10.5 per unit
(ii)   Sales quantity could be anywhere in the range 8.5 million to 11 million units
(iii)   Profits in £ would be (PQ)0.8 – 0.2Q – 100,000 where

P = price
Q = quantity sold

(b)   **Option 2**. Introduce new production system

(i)   Sales price had to be £9 per unit or less
(ii)   Sales quantity could be anywhere above 11 million units at the chosen price
(iii)   Profit would be (PQ)0.8 – 0.15Q – 400,000

A suitable approach to tackling this problem would be to consider the profits that would be earned at a number of different price/quantity combinations, for both Options 1 and 2. A 'worst possible' and 'best possible' estimate could have been made, and the various possible outcomes analysed and discussed. Some figures are shown below, for illustration purposes.

(a)   **Option 1**

       (i)   Worse possible price   £9
                Quantity   8.5 million
                Profit   = $(9 \times 8.5$ million$)0.8 - 0.2$ (8.5 million) $- 100{,}000$
                        =   £59.4m

       (ii)   Best possible price   £10.5
                Quantity   11 million
                Profit   = $(10.5 \times 11$ million$)0.8 - 0.2$ (11 million) $- 100{,}000$
                        =   £90.1m

(b)   **Option 2**

       Best possible price   £9
       Worst possible volume   11 million units
       Profit   = $(9 \times 11$ million$)0.8 - 0.15$ (11 million) $- £400{,}000$
                    =   £77.15m

These could be used in a number of ways.

(a)   If the probabilities of different outcomes were known they could be plotted on a decision tree.

(b)   The outcomes might be used in a decision matrix, if they could be related to different sets of circumstances.

(c)   An assessment of risk might be carried out.

Section summary

Strategies deal with future events, and the future cannot be predicted. Techniques such as CVP analysis can be used to reduce this risk of uncertainty.

4   Decision techniques

Introduction

Decision-making processes can be supported by rational techniques, including decision trees, cost/benefit analysis, ranking and scoring, scenario building, decision matrices and sensitivity analysis.

This section describes a number of techniques to enable a systematic approach to be taken to certain strategic decisions.

4.1 Decision trees

KEY TERM

DECISION TREE. 'Pictorial method of showing a sequence of interrelated decisions and their expected outcomes. Decision trees can incorporate both the probabilities of, and values of, expected outcomes, and are used in decision making.'   (CIMA *Official Terminology*)

Decision trees are a useful tool for helping managers choose between different courses of action. The tree structure allows them to lay out options and investigate the possible outcomes of choosing these options.

There are **two stages in preparing a decision tree**.

(a)   **Drawing the tree itself**, to show all the choices and outcomes

(b)   **Putting in the numbers**: the probabilities, outcome values and expected values (EVs). (Expected value is calculated as **probability** × **outcome**.) For example, if you have a 1% chance of winning £100, the expected value of the winning is £1.

The role of decision trees in strategic planning is to assess which choices are **mutually exclusive**, and to try and give them some quantitative value. As such, they are useful in:

*   Clarifying strategic decisions when they are complex
*   Using risk (in probability terms) as an **input** to quantifying the decision options
*   Ranking the relative costs and benefits of the options

4.2 Cost/benefit analysis

Cost/benefit analysis is a strategy evaluation technique often used in the public sector, where many of the costs and benefits of a project are intangible.

KEY TERM

COST/BENEFIT ANALYSIS involves a comparison between the cost of the resources used, plus any other costs imposed by an activity (eg pollution, environmental damage) and the value of the financial and non-financial benefits derived.

In many public sector decisions, a cost/benefit analysis is conducted on the following basis.

(a)   The project and its overall objectives are defined.

(b)   The benefits, including social benefits, are analysed in detail. It is not always easy to put a value on social costs.

(c)   The net benefits for the project are estimated, if possible. A road might reduce journey times, and so save money.

It can help businesses negotiate with public sector officials. For example, most large building projects have to get planning permission from the local authority. Local government officials will sometimes insist on certain social benefits to be included in a project.

4.3 Ranking and scoring

Ranking and scoring methods are less precise than decision trees. Some goals may be hard to quantify, and strategic decisions generally take more matters into account than can be dealt with by uncertain estimates of probability.

This is best illustrated by means of a simple example. The objectives are weighted in relative importance (so that minimising competitive threats is the most important).

	Objectives				
Strategic option	Growth in profit by over 10%	Reduce dependence on suppliers	Minimise competitive threats	Score	Rank
Do nothing	X	X	X	–	
Cut costs by subcontracting	✓	X	X	4	3rd
Expand product range	✓	X	✓	9	1st
Offer discounts to customers for fixed term contract	X	X	✓	5	2nd
Objective weighting	4	3	5		

In the example, expanding the product range would be chosen as the firm believes this will enhance profits and minimise competitive threats. Note that this is a deliberately simple example. In many cases, the strategies may not be mutually exclusive.

4.4 Scenarios

Scenario building is the process of identifying alternative futures. A strategy can be evaluated in terms of the various models of the future a company has.

 Scenario planning and forecasting were discussed in more detail in Chapter 3 of this Text.

4.5 Decision matrices

A **decision matrix** is a way of comparing outcomes with a variety of circumstances. Outcomes can be selected on a number of bases, and the decision matrix clarifies the choice.

When a decision has to be made, there will be a range of possible actions. Each action will have certain consequences, or **payoffs**. The payoff from any given action will depend on the circumstances (for example, high demand or low demand).

For a decision with these elements, a **payoff table** can be prepared. This is simply a table with rows for circumstances and columns for actions (or vice versa) and the payoffs in the cells of the table. Here is an example.

Payoff table for decision on level of advertising expenditure: payoffs in $'000 of profit after advertising expenditure

		Actions: expenditure		
		High	*Medium*	*Low*
Circumstances	I	+50	+30	+15
of the economy	II	+20	+25	+5
	III	−15	−10	−5

Having worked out the consequences of different actions under different circumstances, we need to select a criterion for making our decision. Two basic decision rules cater for optimists and pessimists respectively.

(a)   **Hope for the best**: the maximax rule can be applied in two equivalent ways:

(i)   Maximise the maximum profit

(ii)   Minimise the minimum costs or losses

Using this rule, we would decide on high expenditure as this offers the best of the favourable outcomes. Note that in this case, we are looking at economy condition 1, since this offers the highest profit: minimising cost or loss does not apply.

(b)   **Expect the worst**: the minimax rule also has two equivalent versions:

(i)   Maximise the minimum profit

(ii)   Minimise the maximum costs or losses

Using this rule we examine economy condition 3 since this cause the greatest losses. Here we would choose low expenditure.

To consider only one payoff of each action may be thought unrealistic. The Hurwicz criterion seeks to remedy this by taking a **weighted average** of the best and worst payoffs of each action:

Weighted payoff = $\alpha \times$ worst payoff $\times (1 - \alpha) \times$ best payoff

α is a number between 0 and 1, sometimes called the **pessimism-optimism index**. The value chosen reflects one's attitude to the risk of poor payoffs and the chance of good payoffs. The action with the highest weighted payoff is selected.

Another possible approach is to consider the extent to which we might come to regret an action we had chosen. This is the **minimax regret** rule.

Regret for any combination of action and circumstances	=	Payoff for best action in those circumstances	–	Payoff of the action actually taken in those circumstances

To apply this rule it is necessary to calculate the regret for each cell for each course of action.

Another technique which organisations could use to help consider the possible outcomes from a course of action is game theory, which we discussed in Chapter 3 of this Text.

4.6 Sensitivity analysis

KEY TERM

SENSITIVITY ANALYSIS 'Modelling and risk assessment procedure in which changes are made to significant variables in order to determine the effect of these changes on the planned outcome. Particular attention is thereafter paid to variables identified as being of special significance.'   (CIMA *Official Terminology*)

Sensitivity analysis involves asking 'what if?' questions. By changing the value of different variables in a decision model, a number of **different outcomes** will be produced. For example, wage increases can be altered to 10% from 5%; demand for a product can be reduced from 100,000 to 80,000, the introduction of new processing equipment can be deferred by six months, on the revised assumption that there will be delays, and so on.

A particularly powerful decision-related technique is to establish the percentage change in each assumption that would lead to a different decision. This can give a good indication of overall risk and also show which variables need the closest monitoring.

4.7 Complications of strategic decisions

Remember that strategic decisions often involve a long time scale, and are based on data which may be unreliable. (For example, projected sales forecasts for a new product may be little more than educated guesses).

The level of uncertainty involved means that strategic investment appraisal and analysis cannot ensure that an organisation makes the 'correct' investment decision. However, just as the rational model provides a framework for strategic planning overall, strategic investment analysis can give organisations a framework in which to make logical investment decisions.

Section summary

Rational techniques such as decision trees, cost/benefit analysis, ranking and scoring, scenario building, decision matrices and sensitivity analysis are useful to support the decision making process.

Chapter Roundup

✓ Strategies should be assessed to ensure they are **suitable**, **acceptable** and **feasible**. Suitability should be assessed first as little can be done with an unsuitable strategy, whereas it may be possible to adjust the other factors to make a strategy more acceptable or feasible.

✓ Relevant costs for decision making and discounting analysis can provide information that can help make decisions about investments. It is important to take non-financial factors, along with the financial information, into consideration when making strategic decisions.

✓ Strategies deal with future events, and the future cannot be predicted. Techniques such as CVP analysis can be used to reduce this risk of uncertainty.

✓ Rational techniques such as decision trees, cost/benefit analysis, ranking and scoring, scenario building, decision matrices and sensitivity analysis are useful to support the decision making process.

Quick Quiz

1   What are the three criteria organisations should use for evaluating individual strategies?

2   What is strategic value analysis?

3   List the steps for analysing strategic investment projects.

4   Identify some types of risk.

5   Explain the relationship between risk and operational gearing.

6   Define cost/benefit analysis.

7   How is 'expected value' calculated when preparing a decision tree?

8   What is being described here? 'Study of the effect on future profit of changes in fixed cost, variable cost, sales price, quantity and mix'.

Answers to Quick Quiz

1   Suitability, acceptability and feasibility

2   Strategic value analysis is an approach which measures the potential financial benefit or loss to shareholders from pursuing strategic options.

3   (i)   Determine the investment project to be analysed.

     (ii)   Determine the strategic objectives for the project.

     (iii)   Determine alternative ways of achieving the same strategic objectives.

     (iv)   Analyse a small number of alternatives.

     (v)   Try and determine what will happen if nothing is done (but this does not mean that you assume that competitors will do nothing).

     (vi)   Determine key internal and external assumptions.

     (vii)   Collect data on areas of greatest uncertainty.

     (viii)   Carry out sensitivity analysis tests.

(ix)   Redefine the project on the basis of (viii).

(x)   Expose key assumptions and debate them.

4   • Physical
     • Economic
     • Financial
     • Business
     ` Stakeholder response risk

5   The business's operational gearing (the ratio of fixed to variable costs) is an important indicator of risk. Where there is a high proportion of fixed costs, a strategy might be more risky, although it promises a higher return. A high proportion of genuinely variable costs can mean more flexibility.

6   Cost/benefit analysis involves a comparison between the cost of the resources used, plus any other costs imposed by an activity (eg pollution, environmental damage) and the value of the financial and non-financial benefits derived.

7   Probability × outcome

8   Cost – volume profit analysis (CVP); also known as breakeven analysis

Answers to Questions

7.1 Domestic gas

(a)   The main area of uncertainty here is the number of customers who would actually wish to be connected to the gas supply.

(b)   To start with, it is assumed that gas supplies can be provided fairly quickly (ie in year 0), but this assumption can be changed quite easily later on.

(c)   Other assumptions

      (i)   The company might seek a payback on its investment within a specific time horizon – say ten or 15 years. However, cash flows in perpetuity will be used here to assess the project financially.

      (ii)   A cost of capital of 17% pa is equal to a cost of 4% per quarter. This quarterly cost will be used to evaluate the PV of future revenues.

      (iii) A PV of net benefit per customer will be calculated, before an assessment is made of the maximum acceptable project cost.

(d)   Workings, per customer

	£
Quarterly standing charge	15.0
Quarterly revenue for gas consumed	
(120 units × 3 months × £500 ÷ 1,000)	180.0
Cost of gas, including wastage	
(120 units × 100/80 × 3 months × £0.08)	(36.0)
Net income per quarter	159.0

(e)   Financial evaluation, per customer

	Year	Discount factor per qtr 4%	Cash flow £	Present value £
Connection charge	0	1.0	300	300
Quarterly net income	In perpetuity	1/0.04 = 25.0	159	3,975
NPV of all future net income, per customer				4,275

(f)   Financial evaluation for the area

(i)   The key issue is how many customers will actually want connecting to the gas supply, and how long will it take to connect them?

(ii) The postal survey, taking an optimistic viewpoint, might suggest demand from 90% of 8,000 dwellings – 7,200 dwellings.

(iii) A more realistic estimate might be just 50% of this, or even less. The company's experience with similar projects in the past could provide data to help in reaching a realistic estimate about this. Without further information about the likely margin of error in the data from the postal survey, its reliability is hard to assess. After all, it is one thing to reply to a survey saying that you would like to be connected to the gas supply, but faced with a connection charge of £300, you might easily change your mind!

(g)   The estimate of demand is crucial.

Possible demand (customers)		Maximum acceptable project cost £
3,000	(× £4,275)	12,825,000
5,000		21,375,000
7,000		29,925,000

As you can see, the potential variation in the figures is enormous. What would your judgement be, and how would you advise the company's senior management?

Now try this question from the Exam Question Bank

Number	Level	Marks	Time
Q8	Examination	25	45 mins

STRATEGIC MARKETING

Marketing plays a key part in a business' strategy, and can help a business fulfil its mission and maximise long-term owner value.

Products and customers are two key aspects of marketing, because both are sources of revenue for an organisation.

The product views of marketing looks at issues such as direct product profitability and branding.

Customers' demands will dictate decisions for investment in new products, development of existing ones and setting-up of new outlets. They will also affect the standards adopted for quality control, and the extent to which they can be enticed away by competitors'

products will affect the planned advertising spend.

In this chapter we have included an overview of some key marketing issues, considering both the importance of attracting new customers and also retaining existing (profitable) customers.

We have also highlighted the increasing importance of information in strategic marketing, and the role of databases, data warehouses and data mining in enabling organisations to store data about their customers (section 5).

We finish the chapter by looking at the way the internet has allowed organisations to develop new marketing activities (e-marketing; section 6).

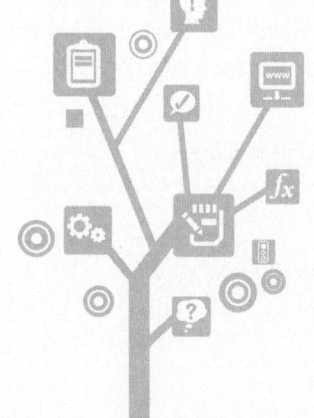

topic list	learning outcomes	syllabus references	ability required
1 Marketing	A1(e)	A1(iv)	Recommend
2 Marketing: products, customers and segmentation	A1(e)	A1(iii), (iv)	Recommend
3 Customer relationship marketing and loyalty	A1(e)	A1(iv)	Recommend
4 Reviewing the customer portfolio	A1(e)	A1(iv)	Recommend
5 Databases and marketing	A2(b)	A2(ii)	Evaluate
6 E-Marketing	A1(e)	A1(iv)	Recommend

1 Marketing

Introduction

Marketing as a concept of the way business should be done must be distinguished from marketing as a business function. Operational marketing is the best developed form of the latter.

1.1 The nature of marketing

'Strategic management' and 'marketing' share a number of ideas and models but they are not the same thing. 'Marketing' contributes to strategic management and is ultimately subordinate to it.

What is marketing?

> **Marketing** is the management process responsible for identifying, anticipating and satisfying customer requirements profitably.   *(Chartered Institute of Marketing)*

While useful in its way, the CIM definition is not the only one we might consider; in fact there are many. Here is what *Dibb, Simkin, Pride and Ferrel* have to say:

> 'Marketing consists of individual and organisational activities that facilitate and expedite satisfying exchange relationships in a dynamic environment through the creation, distribution, promotion and pricing of goods, services and ideas.'

This is a more detailed definition and has the advantage of being very specific about the activities it includes under the umbrella term 'marketing'.

Finally, let us consider what *Philip Kotler* says

> 'The marketing concept holds that the key to achieving organisational goals lies in determining the needs and wants of target markets and delivering the desired satisfactions more efficiently and effectively than the competition.'

Kotler's statement is very important because it identifies four key concepts in marketing:

(a)   Identifying **target markets**.
(b)   Determining the **needs and wants** of those markets.
(c)   Delivering a **product offering** which meets the needs and wants of those markets.
(d)   Meeting the needs of the market **profitability**.

1.2 Models of marketing

The material below is taken from the introduction to the syllabus for the Chartered Institute of Marketing (CIM) qualification. It therefore represents an authoritative view of just what marketing is.

'The type, or model, of marketing practised in any organisation depends on a number of factors, not least of which are the activities to be performed according to the nature of the business and the organisation's dominant orientation. Marketing activities in organisations can be grouped broadly into four roles.

(a)   **Sales support**: the emphasis in this role is essentially reactive: marketing supports the direct sales force. It may include activities such as telesales or telemarketing, responding to inquiries, co-ordinating diaries, customer database management, organising exhibitions or other sales promotions, and administering agents. These activities usually come under a sales and marketing director or manager.

(b)   **Marketing communications**: the emphasis in this role is more proactive: marketing promotes the organisation and its product or service at a tactical level. It typically includes activities such as providing brochures and catalogues to support the sales force.

(c) **Operational marketing**: the emphasis in this role is for marketing to support the organisation with a co-ordinated range of marketing activities including marketing research; brand management; product development and management; corporate and marketing communications; and customer relationship management. Given this breadth of activities, planning is also a function usually performed in this role but at an operational or functional level.

(d) **Strategic marketing**: the emphasis in this role is for marketing to contribute to the creation of competitive strategy. As such, it is practised in customer-focused and larger organisations. In a large or diversified organisation, it may also be responsible for the coordination of marketing departments or activities in separate business units.

Operational marketing activities.

- Research and analysis
- Contributing to strategy and marketing planning
- Managing brands
- Implementing marketing programmes
- Measuring effectiveness
- Managing marketing teams

The operational marketing role, where it exists, will be performed by a marketing function in a business.'

So, what is the relationship between marketing and strategic management? The two are closely linked since there can be no corporate plan which does not involve products/services and customers.

Corporate strategic plans guide the overall development of an organisation. Marketing planning is subordinate to corporate planning but makes a significant contribution to it and is concerned with many of the same issues. The marketing department is probably the most important source of information for the development of corporate strategy. The corporate audit of product/market strengths and weaknesses, and much of its external environmental analysis is directly informed by the **marketing audit**.

Specific marketing strategies will be determined within the overall corporate strategy. To be effective, these plans will be interdependent with those for other functions of the organisation.

(a) The **strategic** component of marketing planning focuses on the direction which an organisation will take in relation to a specific market, or set of markets, in order to achieve a specified set of objectives.

(b) Marketing planning also requires an **operational** component that defines tasks and activities to be undertaken in order to achieve the desired strategy. The **marketing plan** is concerned uniquely with **products** and **markets**.

Marketing management aims to ensure the company is pursuing effective policies to promote its products, markets and distribution channels. This involves exercising strategic control of marketing, and the means to apply strategic control is known as the **marketing audit**. Not only is the marketing audit an important aspect of **marketing control**, it can be used to provide much information and analysis for the **corporate planning process**.

1.3 Marketing audit

KEY TERM

In his text, *Principles and Practice of Marketing*, *Jobber* defines a MARKETING AUDIT as 'a systematic examination of a business's marketing environment, objectives, strategies, and activities, with a view to identifying key strategic issues, problem areas and opportunities'.

The marketing audit provides the basis upon which a plan of action to improve marketing performance can be built. It also provides answers to the following questions in relation to a firm's marketing strategy:

- Where are we now?
- How did we get here?
- Where are we heading?

Jobber points out that the answers to these questions depend on an analysis of the **internal** and **external** environment of a business, invoking models such as PESTEL and SWOT.

(In effect, the marketing audit is the marketing equivalent of the corporate **strategic analysis** which is carried out in the strategic analysis stage of the rational model.)

The **internal marketing audit** focuses on those areas which are under the control of marketing management, whereas the **external marketing audit** looks at those forces over which marketing has no control (eg GDP growth).

The results of the marketing audit are a key determinant of the future direction of the business, and may even give rise to a redefined missions statement for the business as a whole.

Jobber identifies five aspects of a marketing audit:

(a) **Market analysis.** This looks at:

   – Market size, market growth and trends

   – Customer analysis and buyer

   – Competitor analysis – competitors' objectives and strategies; market shares and profitabilities; competitors' strengths and weaknesses; barriers to entry

   – Analysis of different distribution channels and their relative strengths and weaknesses

   – Supplier analysis – trends in the supply chain; power of suppliers; strengths and weaknesses of key suppliers

(b) **Strategic issues analysis.** This involves considering the suitability of the organisation's marketing objectives in relation to the market place and any changes in the market. Points to consider are likely to include: market segmentation; basis of competitive advantage; core competences; positioning; and product portfolio.

(c) **Review of marketing mix effectiveness:** looking at product, price, promotion and distribution

(d) **Marketing structure** – including marketing **organisation** (does the organisation of the marketing department fit with the strategy and the market); marketing **training**; and intra- and inter-departmental **communication** (for example, how well does the marketing department communicate with production departments).

(e) **Marketing systems.** Three different types of system are considered:

   – Marketing information systems: What information is provided? Is it sufficient?

   – Marketing planning systems

   – Marketing control systems: Can the systems provide an evaluation of marketing campaigns (accurately and on a timely basis)? Do the systems evaluate the key variables affecting company performance?

1.4 Marketing and the management accountant

The role of the management account in marketing is to provide the company with the information it requires in order to be able to market itself successfully. However, in order to do this, the accountant must first understand the nature of the information he or she will be asked to provide, and whether it is product led or customer led.

Products or Customers?

The aim of most commercial organisations is to maximise the wealth of their shareholders via the twin aims of increasing revenues and minimising costs. In order that an organisation can analyse its revenues (and thereby work out how to increase them) it is important that the management accountant can produce information on **where revenues come from**.

However, there is a debate over whether these revenues ultimately come from products or customers:

The **product view** follows the idea that the products a company sells are the source of its earnings and so the more products a company sells, the greater its revenues will be.

The **customer view** believes that customers are the source of revenue and as such customer relationships and loyalty are the drivers of success.

The distinction between these two views of marketing – and which one a firm decides to follow – can have important implications for how the firm decides its strategy.

1.5 The Product view

Direct product profitability analysis (DPP)

If an organisation adopts the product view and decides that products are its source of revenue, then issues such as its **product portfolio** and the **product lifecycle** (which we discussed earlier in this Study Text) will be crucial considerations in developing its strategy.

It will also be important that an organisation can accurately assess the profitability of its products in order to maximise the returns it can make.

In this respect, direct product profitability can also play a key part in helping an organisation develop its strategy.

We introduced the idea of direct product profitability in Chapter 4 earlier in this Study Text.

DPP was originally introduced developed by consumer goods' manufacturers to help them assess the profits that retailers generated by stocking their products. The manufacturers could then use that information when negotiating terms and conditions with the retailers.

However, today DPP is primarily used by retailers in order to determine which products to put on their shelves. For example, supermarkets can analyse the relative profitability of every branded and non-branded product they sell, and thus maximise the contribution to profit being generated by the limited retailing space they have available.

1.6 Brand strategies   5/12

If organisations are adopting a product view of marketing, then brands and brand strategy are also likely to be an important aspect of their marketing approach. For example, should the organisation brand its products or not; and if it does, what should its branding strategy be?

1.6.1 Why brand?

According to *Kotler* a **brand** is 'a name, term, sign, symbol or design or combination of them, intended to identify the goods or services of one seller or group of sellers and to differentiate them from those of competitors'.

Another way of considering this issue is the concept of **brand equity**. Brand equity is the asset that the marketer builds to ensure continuity of satisfaction for the customer and profit for the supplier. The 'asset' consists of consumer attitudes, distribution channels and other relationships.

The reasons for branding are as follows.

(a)   It is a form of **product differentiation** that can make it possible to change premium prices. (Think, for example, of designer clothes labels. The kudos attached to the brand means that the clothes can be sold for significantly higher prices than non-branded equivalents.)

(b)   The more a product is similar to competing goods, the more branding is necessary to create a separate **product identity**.

(c)　It leads to a more ready **acceptance** of a manufacturer's goods by wholesalers/retailers. The power of the retailer is reduced and it is easier for the manufacturer to enter new markets.

(d)　It facilitates **self-selection** of goods in self-service stores and also makes it easier for a manufacturer to obtain the optimum **display space** in shops and stores.

(e)　It reduces the importance of **price differentials** between goods.

(f)　**Brand loyalty** in customers gives a manufacturer more control over marketing strategy and his choice of channels of distribution.

(g)　Strong brands form **barriers to entry**.

(h)　Brands can have much **longer lifecycles** than products, especially when the technology is developing rapidly.

(i)　A strong brand name may allow a firm to **enter unfamiliar markets** or **introduce new products** or marketplaces more quickly and with less risk than a firm without a strong brand would be able to.

(i)　Where products form a range and are marketing as such it is difficult to analyse revenues and marketing costs by product, service the availability of each product can influence sales of the others. Analysis of costs and revenues is simplified by the use of brands.

1.6.2 Branding strategies

Kotler has identified the following five strategies a company can use once it has established its brand(s):

(a)　**Line extension** – an existing name is applied to new variants of existing products, for example Coca-cola launching Diet coke.

(b)　**Brand extensions** – using an existing brand to launch a product in a new category, for example chocolate bars such Mars or Galaxy and Mars / Galaxy ice creams.

(c)　**Multi-branding** – launching several brands in the same category, for example Kellogg's offers a breakfast cereals with their own brands – for example, All-bran, Cornflakes, Cocopops, Rice Krispies.

(d)　**New Brands** – new products are launched under their own brand, for example Coke attempting to sell bottled water under the 'Dasani' brand.

(e)　**Co-branding** – two brands are combined in an offer, for example Sony Playstations were offered in a package with Tomb Raider game.

The decision as to whether a brand name should be given to a range of products or whether products should be branded individually depends on quality factors.

(a)　If the brand name is associated with quality, all goods in the range must be of that standard.

(b)　If a company produces different quality (and price) goods for different market segments, it would be unwise to give the same brand name to the higher and the lower quality goods because this could deter buyers in the high quality/price market segment.

Section summary

Marketing plays an important role in strategic management since an organisation cannot have a strategic plan which does not involve products/services and customers. The marketing audit is an important aspect of marketing control, but can also provide information and analysis for the corporate planning process.

Another important factor in shaping an organisation's marketing strategy will be whether it views revenue as coming ultimately from products or customers.

2 Marketing: products, customers and segmentation

Introduction

The strategy of a business is often orientated towards its customers. Marketing seeks to identify customers and their needs, and to encourage them to buy. Segments are groups of customers with similar needs that can be **targeted** with a distinctly **positioned** marketing **mix**.

2.1 Products and customers

KEY TERM

A **PRODUCT** (goods or services) is anything that satisfies a need or want. It is not a 'thing' with 'features' but a package of benefits. For example a compact disc and hifi system provide recorded music, and other benefits. From most customers' point of view, the electronics inside are not important as long as they are reliable and deliver a certain quality of sound.

The immediate task of a marketing manager with respect to the **products** of the organisation may be any of the following.

- To create demand (where none exists)
- To develop a latent demand
- To revitalise a sagging demand
- To attempt to smooth out (synchronise) uneven demand
- To sustain a buoyant demand (maintenance marketing)
- To reduce excess demand

Many products might satisfy the same customer need. On what basis might a customer choose?

(a)   **Customer value** is the customer's estimate of how far a product or service goes towards satisfying his or her need(s).

(b)   Every product has a cost, so the customer must trade-off between expenditure and value.

(c)   According to *Kotler* customers must feel they get a better deal from buying an item than by the alternatives.

Companies must make a distinction between the **customer** and the **consumer**.

(a)   The **customer** is the person or organisation buying the product or service. For example, a cat's owner will buy food for the cat.

(b)   The **consumer** is the person who uses the product or receives the benefit of the service. In the case of cat food, the cat is the consumer, not the purchaser.

Marketing has a role in the organisation's **value chain**. The end result of a value chain is a product or service which has both a price in line with **customer perceptions of value** and a cost that allows the producer to make a **margin or profit**.

2.2 The importance of developing a market orientation in strategic planning

An organisation commits itself to supplying what customers need. As needs change, so must the goods or services produced. **Marketing orientation enables a firm to adapt to the environment**.

(a)   By applying the marketing concept to product design the company might hope to make more attractive products, hence to achieve sustained sales growth and make higher profits.

(b)   Profits do not only come from individual transactions with customers, but also from the customer's propensity to deal with the firm rather than its competitors.

Strategic planning involves making decisions about the choice of **product-market strategies** – developing new products and new markets that will fill the '**profit gap**'. A marketing orientation should help planners to identify more successfully what products or markets would earn good profits for the organisation.

Having decided on a competitive strategy a firm must then decide on the following.

- Which target markets should be developed.
- How the firm should offer its product or service in comparison with competitors.
- How to establish a **marketing system** and organisation for the firm.
- How to develop a **marketing plan** and then implement and control it.

2.3 Buyer behaviour

The decision to make a purchase can be very simple, very complex or somewhere between the two.

Nonetheless, it is important that organisations try to understand **why** buyers purchase their goods or services.

It might be tempting to think that consumers make purchasing decisions wholly on the basis of the value-for-money they obtain from buying a particular product or service. However, consumer behaviour is also shaped by a range of different needs and requirements, which Maslow identified as a 'hierarchy of needs':

- Physiological needs
- Safety needs
- Social needs
- Status/ego needs
- Self-fulfilment needs

The type of need which a product or service addresses could in turn help shape the strategy which a firm uses for marketing and selling that product or service. For example, the purchasing decisions involved in buying a luxury sports car (fulfilling a status/ego need) are likely to be very different to those involved in buying everyday groceries such as bread and milk (to meet physiological needs). Equally, the marketing and sales strategies a sports car company uses to sell sports cars are likely to be very different to the approach a supermarket takes in relation to selling bread and milk.

It is also important to remember that buyers do not always proceed rationally. In this respect, the distinction between individual consumers and industrial buyers can be significant, because the purchasing decisions and motivations of industrial buyers tend to be more logical than those of individual consumers.

In marketing, a market is defined in terms of its **buyers** or **potential buyers**.

- **Consumer markets** (eg for soap powder, washing machines, TV sets, clothes)
- **Industrial markets** (eg for machine tools, construction equipment)
- **Government markets** (eg for armaments, and, in the UK, medical equipment)
- **Reseller markets**
- **Export markets**

2.3.1 Consumer goods

Consumer goods are ready to be used by the consumer without the need for any further commercial processing. Consumer goods are further classified according to the method by which they are purchased.

	Features	Examples
Convenience goods	Purchased regularly in small amounts of low unit value. Has close substitutes. Everyday purchases and likely to be produced by several manufacturers. Promoting a unique image for the product, for example by **branding**, is important.	Toothpaste Bread Coffee Chocolate
Shopping goods	Goods for which customers are more discriminating. Usually have a higher unit value and are bought less frequently, usually from a specialist outlet with a wide range on offer.	Cars Furniture Hi-fi equipment Household appliances, such as washing machines and cookers
Speciality goods	The manufacturer, either by product design or advertising, has become associated in the public mind with a particular product. The customer will ask for it by name and seek out a dealer who sells it.	Rolls Royce cars Wedgwood pottery

2.3.2 Industrial or business-to-business markets

In industrial markets, the customer is another firm. The industrial market, more than the consumer market, is influenced by the general state of the economy and the government's economic policy.

Derived demand. The demand for industrial goods and services is derived from the demand for the product or service to which they contribute. For example, the demand for aluminium is in part derived from the demand for cans, which might itself be derived from demand for beer or soft drinks.

Industrial buyers are more **rationally motivated** than consumers in deciding which goods to buy. Sales policy decisions by a supplier are therefore more important than sales promotion activities in an industrial market. Special attention should be given in selling to quality, price, credit, delivery dates, after-sales service, etc. The size of order which can be supplied may also be an important factor; whether or not the supplier has the capacity to meet the buyer's demands.

These rational motivations make it difficult for an untried newcomer to break into an industrial goods market.

2.3.3 Organisational buying behaviour

The organisational buying behaviour process has some similarities with consumer buyer behaviour, but is supposedly more rational.

- How are needs recognised in a company?
- What is the type of buying situation?
- How is a supplier selected?
- How will performance be reviewed after purchase?

2.3.4 Factors in the motivation mix of business or government buyers

Business or government buyers are motivated as follows:

(a) **Quality** and reliability.

(b) **Price**. Where profit margins in the final market are under pressure, the buyer of industrial goods will probably make price the main purchasing motivation (particularly if the buyer's own competitive strategy is focused on cost minimisation and cost leadership).

(c) **Budgetary control** may encourage the buying department to look further afield for potential suppliers to obtain a better price or quality of goods.

(d) **Fear of breakdown**. Where a customer has a highly organised and costly production system, he will want to avoid a breakdown in the system due to a faulty machine or running out of inventory.

(c) **Credit**. The importance of credit could vary with the financial size of the buyer.

(f) **Delivery**. Generally, buyers want delivery without delay; even for orders which can sometimes be on a much larger scale than those made by individual consumers.

(g) **Purchasing procedures**. The availability of written quotations, legal contracts, or service level agreements could be important for business buyers. Again, the buyers are also likely to be interested in the credit terms (and/or bulk discounts) available.

2.4 Market segmentation

Both consumer and industrial markets can usefully be segmented, and several bases exist for the process. The aim is to identify a coherent segment that is both valid and attractive.

Much marketing planning is based on the concepts of **segmentation and product positioning.** Segmentation identifies target markets in which the firm can take a position. A market is not a mass, homogeneous group of customers, each wanting an identical product. Market segmentation recognises that every market consists of potential buyers with different needs, and different buying behaviour. It is relevant to a **focus strategy**.

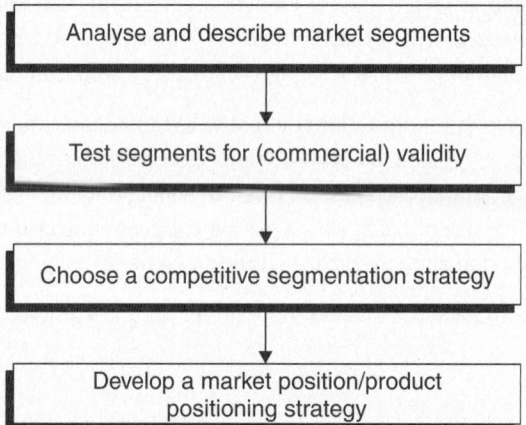

Analyse and describe market segments

↓

Test segments for (commercial) validity

↓

Choose a competitive segmentation strategy

↓

Develop a market position/product positioning strategy

KEY TERM

MARKET SEGMENTATION is 'the subdividing of a market into distinct and increasingly homogeneous subgroups of customers, where any subgroup can conceivably be selected as a target market to be met with a distinct marketing mix'. *(Kotler)*

There are two important elements in this definition of market segmentation.

(a) Although the total market consists of widely different groups of consumers, each group consists of people (or organisations) with **common needs and preferences**, who perhaps react to 'market stimuli' in much the same way.

(b) Each market segment can become a **target market for a firm**, and would require a unique marketing mix if the firm is to exploit it successfully.

Reasons for segmenting markets

Reason	Comment
Better satisfaction of customer needs	One solution will not satisfy all customers
Growth in profits	Some customers will pay more for certain benefits
Revenue growth	More customers may be attracted by what is on offer, in preference to competing products
Customer retention	By targeting customers, a number of different products can be offered to them
Targeted communications	Segmentation enables clear communications as people in the target audience share common needs
Innovation	By identifying unmet needs, companies can innovate to satisfy them
Segment share	Segmentation enables a firm to implement a focus strategy successfully

2.5 Identifying segments

An important initial marketing task is the **identification of segments** within the market. Segmentation applies more obviously to the consumer market, but it can also be applied to an **industrial market**. An important basis for segmentation is the nature of the customer's business.

(a)   One basis will not be appropriate in every market, and sometimes two or more bases might be valid at the same time.

(b)   One basis or 'segmentation variable' might be 'superior' to another in a hierarchy of variables. These are **primary and secondary segmentation variables.**

CASE STUDY

An airport cafe conducted a segmentation exercise of its customers. It identified a number of possible segments.

- Business travellers
- Airport employees
- Groups
- Single tourists

However, further analysis revealed that running through each of these categories was the same fault line.

- Those 'in a hurry'
- Those with time to spare

For marketing purposes, this latter segmentation exercise was more useful, and the firm was able to develop an 'express menu' for those in a hurry.

Customers could be classified into customer segments using a variety of other **segmentation** bases such as:

(a)   Geography – location of the customers

(b)   Socio-economic group, or social class

(c)   Stage in the family life cycle

(d)   Level of education

(e)   Personal wealth

(f)   Lifestyle

(g)   Behaviour – based on their attitudes to and use of the product, and the benefits they expect to receive

CASE STUDY

Market segmentation

Tourism NT (the Northern Territories tourism board in Australia) uses market segmentation to identify similar characteristics in visitors and to establish what types of visitors represent the most attractive market. Characteristics include demographic and sociological variables such as attitudes, values and interest.

Tourism NT distinguishes visitors according to whether they come from within Australia or whether they are international. However, Tourism NT has found that a key market segment is what is refers to as 'Experiential travellers'.

Experiential travellers seek a holiday experience with meaning and purpose. They want an authentic holiday that is not just 'sight-seeing'.

Experiential travellers want a holiday that fulfils the particular reason for which they have travelled. This is often a holiday based around the Territory's natural and cultural strengths; and one which will provide the traveller with a sense of personal enrichment. Experiential travellers also tend to be environmentally and socially conscious and seek out ecologically sustainable experiences.

For an experiential traveller, the experience of the holiday itself matters more than the actual destination. Experiential travellers are willing to travel great distances and pay substantial amounts towards an experience. Consequently, they often yield higher profits for tourism operators, than many other market segments. However, in keeping with this experiential travellers also expect superior quality and value-for-money.

Tourism NT uses this knowledge about a key market segment to:

    –   Inform the style and tone of marketing communications
    –   Locate and place communications in appropriate media channels
    –   Inform destination development needs and
    –   Guide product development

2.6 Segmentation of the industrial market

Industrial markets can be segmented with many of the bases used in consumer markets such as geography, usage rate and benefits sought. Additional, more traditional bases include customer type, product/technology, customer size and purchasing procedures.

(a)   **Geographic location**. Some industries and related industries are clustered in particular areas. Firms selling services to the banking sector might be interested in the City of London.

(b)   **Type of business** (eg service, manufacturing)

       (i)   **Nature of the customers' business**. Accountants or lawyers, for example, might choose to specialise in serving customers in a particular type of business. An accountant may choose to specialise in the accounts of retail businesses, and a firm of solicitors may specialise in conveyancing work for property development companies.

       (ii)   **Components manufacturers specialise in the industries of the firms to which they supply components.**

(c)   **Use of the product.** In the UK, many new cars are sold to businesses, as company cars. Although this practice is changing with the viability of a 'cash alternative' to a company car, the varying levels of specification are developed with the business buyer in mind (eg junior salesperson gets a Ford Fiesta, Regional Manager gets a Ford Mondeo).

(d)   **Type of organisation.** Organisations in an industry as a whole may have certain needs in common. Employment agencies offering business services to publishers, say, must offer their clients personnel with experience in particular desk top publishing packages. Suitable temporary staff offered to legal firms can be more effective if used to legal jargon. Each different type of firm can be offered a tailored product or service.

(e)   **Size of organisation**. Large organisations may have elaborate purchasing procedures, and may do many things in-house. Small organisations may be more likely to subcontract certain specialist services.

2.7 Segment validity

A market segment will only **be valid if it is worth designing and developing a unique** marketing mix for that specific segment. The following questions are commonly asked to decide whether or not the segment can be used for developing marketing plans.

Criteria	Comment
Can the segment be measured?	A market segment might be easy to define but hard to measure. For example, if 'people with a conservative outlook to life' is a segment, how would this be measured?
Is the segment big enough?	There has to be a large enough potential market to be profitable.
Can the segment be reached?	There has to be a way of getting to the potential customers via the organisation's promotion and distribution channels.
Do segments respond differently?	If two or more segments respond in the same way to a marketing mix, the segments are effectively the same. There is no point in distinguishing them from each other.
Can the segment be reached profitably?	Do the identified customer needs cost less to satisfy than the revenue they earn?

2.8 Segment attractiveness

A segment might be valid and potentially profitable, but is it potentially **attractive?**

(a)   A segment which has **high barriers to entry** might cost more to enter but will be less **vulnerable to competitors.**

(b)   For firms involved in **relationship marketing**, the segment should be one in which a **viable relationship** between the firm and the customer can be established.

The most attractive segments are those whose needs can be met by building on the company's strengths and where forecasts for **demand**, **sales profitability** and **growth** are favourable.

Target markets

Because of limited resources, competition and large markets, organisations are not usually able to sell with equal efficiency and success to the entire market, that is to every market segment. It is necessary to select **target markets.** The marketing management of a company may choose one of the following policy options.

KEY TERMS

UNDIFFERENTIATED MARKETING: produce a single product and hope to get as many customers as possible to buy it; that is, ignore segmentation entirely.

CONCENTRATED MARKETING: the company attempts to produce the ideal product for a single segment of the market (eg Rolls Royce cars for the wealthy).

DIFFERENTIATED MARKETING the company attempts to introduce several product versions, each aimed at a different market segment. For example, manufacturers of soap powder make a number of different brands, marketed to different segments.

It is important to assess company strengths when evaluating attractiveness and targeting a market. This can help determine the appropriate strategy, because once the attractiveness of each identified segment has been assessed it can be considered along with relative strengths to determine the potential advantages the organisation would have. In this way preferred segments can be targeted.

Market segment attractiveness

		Unattractive	Average	Attractive
Current and potential company strengths in serving the segment	Weak	Strongly avoid	Avoid	Possibilities
	Average	Avoid	Possibilities	Secondary targets
	Strong	Possibilities	Secondary targets	Prime targets

The major **disadvantage of differentiated marketing** is the additional costs of marketing and production (more product design and development costs, the loss of economies of scale in production and storage, additional promotion costs and administrative costs etc). When the **costs of further differentiation of the market exceed the benefits** from further segmentation and **target marketing**, a firm is **over-differentiated**.

The major **disadvantage of concentrated marketing** is the business risk of relying on a single segment of a single market. On the other hand, specialisation in a particular market segment can give a firm a profitable, although perhaps temporary, competitive edge over rival firms.

The choice between undifferentiated, differentiated or concentrated marketing as a marketing strategy will depend on the following factors.

(a)   The extent to which the product and/or market is **homogeneous**. **Mass marketing** may be 'sufficient' if the market is largely homogeneous (for example, for safety matches).

(b)   The **company's resources** must not be over extended by differentiated marketing. Small firms may succeed better by concentrating on one segment only.

(c)   The product must be sufficiently **advanced in its life cycle** to have attracted a substantial total market; otherwise segmentation and target marketing is unlikely to be profitable, because each segment would be too small in size.

Remember, the ideal mix for a convenience good (requiring a heavy emphasis on distribution and sales promotion) will be different from that for an industrial good (where price, design, quality and after-sales service are more important).

Section summary

Segments are groups of customers with similar needs that can be targeted with a distinct marketing mix. Both consumer and industrial markets can be segmented, and the aim is to identify coherent segments that are both valid and attractive.

3 Customer relationship marketing and loyalty

Introduction

Customer relationship marketing means using marketing resources to retain, rather than simply attract, customers. It focuses on establishing **loyalty** among the existing customers.

We mentioned earlier in this chapter that organisations can adopt either a product view or a customer view of marketing. We are now going to look at customer-based aspects of marketing, in particular customer relationship management and customer profitability analysis.

Customer relationship marketing

In his text, *Principles and Practice of Marketing*, *David Jobber* notes that many companies find that 80% of their sales come from 20% of their customers. This highlights how important it is for companies to retain their existing high-volume and highly profitable customers, as well as those with strong potential to become high-volume, high profit customers in the future.

This emphasis on **customer retention** has led to an increasing focus on customer relationship management. Sales and marketing staff should no longer be looking solely to make a one-off sales, but to create a long term relationship, which is mutually beneficial for the company and the customer.

This is the logic behind relationship marketing and customer relationship management.

Relationship marketing is the use of marketing resources to maintain and exploit a firm's **existing customers**, rather than using marketing resources solely to attract new customers.

Firms can implement their relationship marketing strategy through effective **customer relationship management.**

KEY TERM

CUSTOMER RELATIONSHIP MANAGEMENT is the establishment, development, maintenance and optimisation of long-term, mutually valuable, relationships between consumers and organisations.

What Customer Relationship Management involves	Company benefits realised as a result
• Organisations must become 'customer centric'	• Improved customer retention
• Organisations must be prepared to adapt so that they take customer needs into account and then deliver them	• Improved cross-selling
• Market research must be used to assess customer needs and satisfaction	• Improved profitability (per customer and in general)

3.1 The need for customer relationship management (CRM)

There are several reasons why CRM is an important consideration:

- Customers are inherently more willing to switch suppliers and less likely to be loyal to a specific company or brand than they have been in the past. (The internet has also had an impact on

customer loyalty. For example, price comparison websites may reduce customer loyalty if customers see that an alternative supplier offers a product or service more cheaply than their current provider. However, by developing a relationship with its customers, an organisation will move away from competition based on price alone.)

- It is cheaper to focus on retaining existing customers than to have to attract new ones. Attracting new customers is expensive due to low initial prices or promotion expenses for instance

- In mature markets, existing customers provide the most likely source of future earnings

- Strategy to widen the range of products available would make no sense if existing customers could not be retained.

Dave Chaffey outlines three phases of CRM (particularly in relation to e-business and e-commerce management)

- Customer **acquisition**
- Customer **retention**
- Customer **extension**

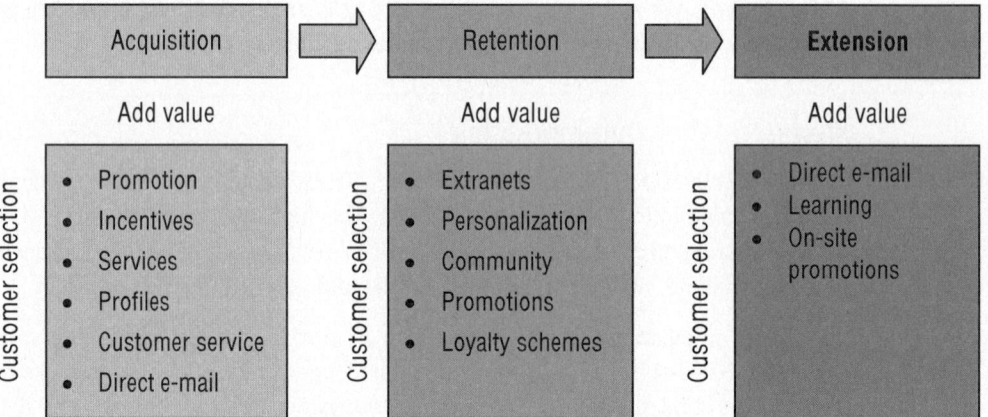

Chaffey's three phases of customer relationship management

Customer acquisition is the process of attracting customers for their first purchases.

Customer retention ensures that customers return and buy for a second time. The organisation keeps them as customers. This is most likely to be the purchase of a similar product or service, or the next level of product or service.

Customer extension introduces products and services to loyal customers that may not wholly relate to their original purchases. These are additional, supplementary purchases.

In recent times emphasis has increased on building and **maintaining good long-term relationships** with customers. This is because such relationships are more profitable than constantly searching for new customers.

3.1.1 Customer retention in service businesses

An important element in a service business' ability to retain customers will be its ability to continue to meet the needs of its customers.

However, in order to able to do this, the business will need to research the needs of their customers, so that they can then measure how well they are performing in relation to their customers' needs. These needs are likely to vary according to the nature of the business: for example, reliability is important in a bank; comfort is more likely to be important in a hotel.

One framework which business can use for assessing the quality of service they provide their customers is the **SERVQUAL methodology** (developed by Zeithanl, Parasurman & Berry). This covers five dimensions of service quality, and customer feedback is sought in relation to the five dimensions:

(a)   **Tangibles**: for example, appearance of facilities; is equipment up-to-date equipment; are staff well dressed?

(b)   **Reliability**: for example, are bookings processed accurately; if services are promised by a certain time, are they delivered by that time?

(c)   **Responsiveness**: Do staff react to queries promptly, and courteously?

(d)   **Assurance**: Do staff inspire confidence: if customers have problems, are staff sympathetic and reassuring?

(e).   **Empathy**: Are customers are treated as individuals; do staff have the customers' best interests at heart?

The SERVQUAL methodology then allows businesses to improve their performance by gauging the gap between how well they think they are performing and customers' expectations of how well they should be performing. Staff and managers may believe they are delivering a good quality service; customers may not agree though.

3.2 Differences between transactional and relationship marketing

Transactional	Relationship
Importance of single sale	Importance of customer relations
Importance of product features	Importance of customer benefits
Short time scale	Longer time scale
Less emphasis on service	High customer service
Quality is concern of production	Quality is concern of all
Competitive commitment	High customer commitment
Persuasive communication	Regular communication

Marketing, Principles and Practice: Adcock, Bradfield, Halborg and Ross

3.3 Relationship marketing strategies

A number of strategies can be implemented in relation to customer relationship marketing and to develop loyalty towards an organisation.

Strategy	CRM implications	Examples
Develop appropriate staff incentive schemes	Encourages staff to work harder to retain existing customers	Reward staff based on customer satisfaction and feedback, rather than number of new customers attracted
Provide consistent standards	Customers more likely to return if they receive consistently good service Familiarity with good staff encourages loyalty	Implement measures to reduce staff turnover
Obtain senior management buy-in	If senior management prioritise staff retention, staff will too	Build customer retention into the organisational strategy Develop a customer focused approach at all levels
Monitor customer relationships and act appropriately	By understanding the behaviour of customers, improvements to secure their loyalty can be made	Establish regular contact with customers Assess customer satisfaction and loyalty Determine reasons for loss of a customer Address reasons to prevent future loss of custom
Obtain detailed customer information	Allows the firm to: • Identify customer needs • Develop improved ways of meeting those needs • Specifically target customers and bring relevant new products or services to their attention	Customer loyalty/reward cards can provide invaluable information about the buying habits and patterns of customers
Develop specific loyalty focused strategies	Directly encourages the customer to return	Introduce loyalty cards Appoint dedicated account managers for key customers
Implement procedures to monitor and influence all aspects of the customer relationship	Provides the customers with a good experience of the company encouraging them to be loyal Monitors the success of the relationship allowing weak areas to be identified and improved	Total quality management (TQM)
Implement systems that can support Customer Relationship Management	Provides high level of information to the firm, allowing better understanding of the relationship. This in turns helps understand how it can be improved.	Analytical customer databases Automated sales management systems Systems to track customer spending and profitability

3.4 Wider relationship marketing

Adrian Payne and his colleagues at the Cranfield School of Management have suggested that relationship management extends beyond the customer. They developed the **Six Markets model** which recommends building relationships in six markets as shown in the following table.

Market	Who they are	CRM implications
Customer Markets	Customers are the final buyers of the product or service	Superior customer value can only be delivered if appropriate relationships exist in each of the markets.
Referral Markets	People/institutions that introduce new customers, for instance banks, agencies or existing customers	Build strong relationships in this market to ensure new customers are introduced.
Supplier Markets	All suppliers to the company	By working closer with suppliers the firm can better meet the needs of the final consumer.
Recruitment Markets	Potential staff, as well as key stakeholders in the recruitment market such as agencies and careers advisors.	Good staff are crucial to provide good service to customers. To attract good staff the firm must • Develop an appealing corporate image • Build relationships with the key stakeholders in this market
Influence Markets	Any person, group or company that can influence customer purchases, such as analysts, pressure groups, brokers or consumer groups	The firm needs a good Personal Relations (PR) department to ensure the firm is presented favourably in this market.
Internal Markets	Everyone internal to the organisation. Each department is a customer and a supplier to other departments.	Develop strategies that • Ingrain a client service mentality • Discourage departmental rivalry • Encourage each department to view its work in relation to serving the customers

Section summary

Customer relationship marketing focuses on establishing loyalty in the existing customer base. Payne suggested that relationship marketing extends beyond the customer and developed the six market model to demonstrate where relationships should be built.

4 Reviewing the customer portfolio

Introduction

The **customer base** is an asset to be invested in, as future benefits will come from existing customers, but not all customers are as important as others. It will help you in evaluating the customer portfolio if you consider the customer base as an asset worth investing in.

CASE STUDY

(a) In September 2009, the online jewellery retailer Bidz.com acquired the intellectual property and trademark registration of Whitehall Jewelers (also incorporating Lundstrom Jewelers, Mark Bros. Jewelers, and White Star Private Label). However, as well as acquiring a well-known brand (Whitehall Jewelers) with its associated history and goodwill, Bidz.com also acquired the customer mailing list with over 800,000 names and addresses.

BPP
LEARNING MEDIA

(b)   Supermarket loyalty cards reward customers with bonus points, saving them money, or allowing them to redeem points for products according to how much they spend.

(c)   Many banks lose money on student accounts, in the hope that they will earn it back later in the customer's life cycle.

A **marketing audit** involves a review of an organisation's products and markets, the marketing environment, and its marketing system and operations. The profitability of each product and each market should be assessed, and the costs of different marketing activities established.

Information obtained about markets

(a)   **Size of the customer base**. Does the organisation sell to a large number of small customers or a small number of big customers?

(b)   **Size of individual orders**. The organisation might sell its products in many small orders, or it might have large individual orders. Delivery costs can be compared with order sizes.

(c)   **Sales revenue and profitability.** The performance of individual products can be compared, perhaps as follows:

Product group	Sales revenue		Contribution to profits	
	£'000	% of total	£'000	% of total
B	7,500	35.7	2,500	55.6
E	2,000	9.5	1,200	26.7
C	4,500	21.4	450	10.0
A	5,000	23.8	250	5.6
D	2,000	9.5	100	2.2
	21,000	100.0	4,500	100.0

An imbalance between sales and profits over various product ranges can be potentially dangerous. In the figures above, product group A accounts for 23.8% of turnover but only 5.6% of total contribution, and product group D accounts for 9.5% of turnover but only 2.2% of total contribution.

(d)   **Segments.** An analysis of sales and profitability into export markets and domestic markets.

(e)   **Market share.** Estimated share of the market obtained by each product group.

(f)   **Growth.** Sales growth and contribution growth over the previous four years or so, for each product group.

(g)   Whether the **demand** for certain products is **growing, stable or likely to decline.**

(h)   Whether **demand is price sensitive** or not.

(i)   Whether there is a growing tendency for the market to become **fragmented**, with more specialist and 'custom-made' products.

Information about current marketing activities

- Comparative pricing
- Advertising effectiveness
- Effectiveness of distribution network
- Attitudes to the product, in comparison with competitors

4.1 Customers

Key customer analysis investigates six main areas of customers, in order to identify which customers offer most profit.

Many firms – especially in business-to-business markets – sell to a relatively small number of customers. **Not all customers are as important as others.** The checklist below can help identify the most important.

Strategic importance evaluation guide	High	Medium	Low	N/A
1 Fit between customer's needs and our capabilities, at present and potentially.				
2 Ability to serve customer compared with our major competitors, at present and potentially.				
3 'Health' of customer's industry, current and forecast.				
4 'Health' of the customer, current and forecast.				
5 Customer's growth prospects, current and forecast.				
6 What can we learn from this customer?				
7 Can the customer help us attract others?				
8 Relative *significance:* how important is the customer compared *with other* customers?				
9 What is the *profitability* of serving the customer?				

4.2 Customer analysis

Key customer analysis considers six main areas of customer analysis. A firm might wish to identify which customers offer most profit. Small businesses are especially prone to overtrading.

Area	Detail
Key customer identity	• Name of each key customer • Location • Status in market • Products they make and sell • Size of firm (capital employed, turnover, number of employees)
Customer history	• First purchase date. • Who makes the buying decision in the customer's organisation? • What is the average order size, by product? • What is the regularity/ periodicity of the order, by product? • What is the trend in size of orders? • What is the motive in purchasing? • What does the customer know about the firm's and competitors' products? • On what basis does the customer reorder? • How is the useful life of the product judged? • Were there any lost or cancelled orders? For what reason?
Relationship of customer to product	• What does the customer use the product for? • Do the products form part of the customer's own service/product?
Relationship of customer to potential market	• What is the size of the customer in relation to the total end-market? • Is the customer likely to expand, or not? Diversify? Integrate?
Customer attitudes and behaviour	• What interpersonal factors exist which could affect sales by the firm and by competitors? • Does the customer also buy competitors' products? • To what extent may purchases be postponed?

Area	Detail
The financial performance of the customer	How successful is the customer?

4.3 Customer profitability analysis (customer account profitability)
11/10

Customer profitability analysis is an analysis of the total sales revenue generated from a customer or customer group, less all the costs that are incurred in servicing that customer group.

KEY TERM

CUSTOMER PROFITABILITY ANALYSIS (CPA). 'Analysis of the revenue streams and service costs associated with specific customers or customer groups.'
(CIMA *Official Terminology*)

The total costs of servicing customers can vary depending on how customers are serviced.

(a) **Volume discounts**. A customer who places one large order is given a discount, presumably because it benefits the supplier to do so (eg savings on administrative overhead in processing the orders – as identified by an ABC system).

(b) **Different rates** charged by power companies to domestic as opposed to business users. This in part reflects the administrative overhead of dealing with individual customers. In practice, many domestic consumers benefit from cross-subsidy.

Customer profitability is the 'total sales revenue generated from a customer or customer group, less all the costs that are incurred in servicing that customer or customer group.'

It is possible to analyse customer profitability over a single period but more useful to look at a longer time scale. Such a multi period approach fits in with the idea of **relationship marketing** discussed earlier in this chapter, with its emphasis on customer retention for the longer term.

Question 8.1	Profitable customers

Learning outcomes A1(iv)

Seth Ltd supplies shoes to Narayan Ltd and Kipling Ltd. Each pair of shoes has a list price of £50 each; as Kipling buys in bulk, Kipling receives a 10% trade discount for every order over 100 shoes. it costs £1,000 to deliver each order. In the year so far, Kipling has made five orders of 100 shoes each. Narayan Ltd receives a 15% discount irrespective of order size, because Narayan Ltd collects the shoes, thereby saving Seth Ltd any distribution costs. The cost of administering each order is £50. Narayan makes ten orders in the year, totalling 420 pairs of shoes. Which relationship is the most profitable for Seth?

Customer profitability analysis (CPA) focuses on profits generated by customers, and suggests that **profit does not automatically increase with sales revenue**. CPA can benefit a company in the following ways.

• It allows a company to **identify and retain the most profitable customers**

• It enables a company to **focus resources** on the most profitable areas

• It identifies unexpected **differences in profitability** between customers

• It enables a company to **stop supplying to unprofitable customers**, or to **work out a way of increasing the profitability of those customers**; for example, imposing a minimum order size, or varying delivery charges depending on the size of an order

• An appreciation of the costs of servicing clients assists in **negotiations** with customers

• It helps quantify the **financial impact** of proposed changes

- It helps highlight the **cost** of obtaining **new** customers and the **benefit** of retaining existing customers

- It helps to highlight whether **product** development or **market** development is to be preferred

4.3.1 Limitations of CPA

However, there are also some limitations of CPA.

- Practical **calculations can be very difficult** – in particular assigning indirect costs to different activities or customers. If costs are wrongly apportioned then customer profitability will be distorted.

- CPA tends to be used on single products, but in practice **customers may buy a range of products**. Although a customer may not be profitable on the single product being assessed, they may be across the range of products they buy. CPA could overlook this leading to **flawed decision-making**.

- CPA may also lead to flawed decision-making if it only looks at **current revenues and costs**, and **overlooks the lifecycle value** of the customer. Although a customer may not currently be very profitable, their profitability may increase as they move through their lifecycle. For example, university students may not be very profitable customers for banks during their student days, but if they become business executives in the future they could then become very profitable.

4.4 Identifying profitable customers/segments

To analyse customer profitability successfully, it may be necessary to structure **accounting information systems** to take account of the many factors by which customers can be analysed.

An important area in marketing strategy is **retaining** customers, so as to generate new business from them. But how do you identify which customers, or customer groups generate the most profit?

- First divide the customer base into segments (for example, by purchase value, by frequency of purchases, by geographic region, by method of ordering (in store, by phone, or online), by number of different products bought, or by payment method)

- Then calculate the annual revenues earned (net of direct production costs) from each of the segments.

- Finally, calculate the annual costs of serving each of the segments (for example, delivery costs, promotional costs, cost of processing orders, sales returns or warranty costs, and any special costs due to last minute orders. This will involve the adoption of Activity Based Costing techniques).

- By comparing revenues with costs it is possible to identify which segments are the most profitable.

Remember, this consideration must be brought into the design of management information and administration systems. The firm's existing customer groupings, as reported in management accounts, may reflect administrative measures rather than their strategic value.

Question 8.2	Choosing data

Learning outcomes A1(iv)

Busqueros Ltd has 1,000 business customers spread fairly evenly over the UK. The sales force is organised into ten regions, each with 100 customers to be serviced. There are sales force offices at the heart of each region. Information is collected on a regional basis. The marketing director has recently carried out an analysis of the major customers by sales revenue. There are five significant customers, who between them account for 20% of the sales revenue of the firm. They do not get special treatment. What does this say about customer profitability analysis in Busqueros Ltd?

4.4.1 Accounting systems

To analyse customer profitability successfully it may be necessary to structure accounting information systems to take account of the many factors by which customers can be analysed. A **relational database**, whereby information can be structured in many different ways, offers a useful approach.

How do you apportion costs to customer segments? Assume you have a customer base of 15,000 people. You have just spent £20,000 on an advertising campaign and 5,000 new customers have been found. How do you allocate the cost of the campaign? You do not know whether each new customer was attracted by the campaign, or by word-of-mouth.

Different customer costs can arise out of the following.

* Order size
* Sales mix
* Order processing
* Transport costs (eg if JIT requires frequent deliveries)
* Management time
* Cash flow problems (eg increased overdraft interest) caused by slow payers
* Order complexity (eg if the order has to be sent out in several stages)
* Inventory holding costs can relate to specify customers
* The customer's negotiating strength

4.4.2 Product attributes

The nature of the product (its **attributes**) may be a mix of the varying requirements of different customers. Hence some customers will be offered greater value than they need at a price they are unwilling to pay. The sales volume to this market segment and resulting profit will be less than it might be with a simpler product. This must be set against the potential extra cost and complication of offering a special product.

4.4.3 Example

Here is a possible layout for a **customer profitability analysis.**

		£'000
Gross sales		1,072
Less discounts		(45)
Net sales		1,027
Production		
Less production costs		(510)
		517
Marketing		
Less specific marketing costs:		
sales calls		(10)
in-store promotions		(5)
customer bonuses		(5)
Less share of other marketing costs:		
sales force management		(10)
customer service		(10)
		477
Distribution		
Less specific distribution costs:		
Transportation		(5)
Packaging		(17)
Refusals		(2)
outstanding debts		(30)
		423

[Cont'd]

BPP LEARNING MEDIA

Less shares of distribution costs:
order processing   (4)
inventory holding   (24)
Warehousing   (20)
collecting debts   (10)
Customer Contribution   365

Such a report can highlight the differences between the cost of servicing different individuals or firms which can then be applied as follows.

(a) **Directing effort to cutting customer specific costs**. Installing an electronic data interchange system (EDI) can save the costs of paperwork and data input.

(b) **Identifying those customers who are expensive to service**, thereby suggesting action to increase profitability.

(c) **Using CPA as part of a comparison with competitors' costs**. A firm which services a customer more cheaply than a competitor can use this cost advantage to offer extra benefits to the customer.

(d) Indicating cases where **profitability might be endangered**, for example by servicing customers for whom the firm's core competence is not especially relevant.

CPA might provide answers to the following questions. (Obviously a firm doing work for one major customer will find it easier to answer these questions than one which works for many customers.)

- What **profit/contribution** is the organisation making on sales to the customer, after discounts and selling and delivery costs?

- What would be the **financial consequences** of losing the customer?

- Is the customer buying in order sizes that are **unprofitable** to supply?

- What is the level of **inventory** required specifically to supply these customers?

- Are there any other **specific costs** involved in supplying this customer, eg technical and test facilities, R&D facilities, special design staff?

- What is the ratio of net contribution per customer to total investment?

4.5 Customer lifecycle value

Customer lifecycle value (CLV) is the present value of the future cash flows attributed to the lifecycle of an organisation's relationship with a customer.

In theory, CLV shows how much each customer is worth to an organisation; and therefore shows that organisation how much they should be prepared to spend on acquiring and retaining that customer. For example, it is not worth an organisation offering promotions and incentives whose value is greater than the customer's lifecycle value to that organisation.

The concept of the **customer lifecycle** is less developed than the product and industry lifecycle models, however it could still usefully be used in conjunction with customer account profitability by considering the following:

(a) **Promotional expense** relating to a single customer is likely to be heavily **front-loaded**: it is much cheaper to retain a customer than to attract one.

(b) It is likely that **sales** to a customer will start at a low level and increase to a higher level as the customer gains confidence, though this is not certain and will vary from industry to industry.

(c) A customer who purchases a basic or commodity product initially may move on to **more differentiated products** later.

(d) In consumer markets, career progression is likely to provide the individual with steadily increasing amounts of disposable income, while the **family lifecycle** will indicate the ranging nature of likely purchases as time passes.

In practice, firms have to make some assumptions in order to calculate CLV. Two key assumptions are:

(a) **Churn rate**: The percentage of customers that end their relationship with the organisation in any given period. Organisations tend to assume that churn rate remains constant, but if, for example, churn rate turns out to be lower than this assumed level, CLV should be higher than anticipated.

(b) **Retention cost**. The amount of time and money the company has to spent in order to retain an existing customer, for example through customer service, or special offers and other promotional incentives.

In addition, any attempt to estimate lifecycle costs and revenues should also consider existing and potential environmental impacts, including, in particular, the likely actions of competitors and the potential for product and process innovation.

However, these external factors increase the degree of uncertainty in any customer value calculations over the longer term. For example, what is the probability of retaining customers in the future if competitors introduce new products? Or what is the probability that customers will buy additional products in the future if the company develops new products?

Section summary

Key customer analysis investigates six main customer characteristics in order to identify which customers offer most profit.

Customer profitability analysis is an analysis of total sales revenue generated from a customer or customer group, less all the costs incurred in servicing that customer or group.

5 Databases and marketing

Introduction

Information and knowledge about customers can help organisations manage their marketing campaigns more effectively. **Database marketing** illustrates how organisations can use databases to assist with the direct marketing of products.

However, a consequence of the increasing importance of data is that businesses are having to hold and manage ever-increasing amounts of data (about sales, revenues, customers, competitors etc). Two techniques designed to utilise the ever-increasing amounts of data held by organisations are **data warehousing** and **data mining**.

KEY TERM

DATABASE MARKETING is the analysis and use of customer databases to aid in the direct marketing of products.

Obviously, an organisation must be careful that is does not distribute spam (unsolicited or unwanted emails) via the internet.

However, database marketing can offer significant benefits to a business.

- **Identify the best customers**. By using RFM analysis (**R**ecency of the latest purchase, **F**requency of purchases, and **M**onetary value of purchases) a business can determine which customers are the most profitable to market to.

- **Tailor messages based on customer usage**. E-mails can be targeted based on the type and frequency of purchases indicated by the customer's purchase profile.

- **Cross-sell related and complementary products**. The customer purchase database can be used to identify opportunities to suggest additional products to the customer while they are making a purchase.

- **Develop new customers**. Collect lists of potential customers to incorporate into the database.

Databases and new customers

An organisation's customer database and potential customer database represents a major source of trade. The company can use it to generate repeat business, or to stimulate new business.

When advertising, companies don't always target new customers, but also the existing ones they already have listed in their databases. **Keeping contact with existing customers** is a good way to generate repeat business, but also to be able to promote new products to the right people – the people who would be most interested in buying them.

Obtaining **names of potential new customers** is now quite easy, because there are companies who specialise in selling the information of individuals who wish to be contacted by relevant businesses.

However, there is a cost involved in this method, which is why it is also important for organisations to keep records of all the potential customers they come into contact with so that they can build up their own database.

Ultimately, the **aim of marketing databases is to generate revenues**, so the more information organisations can hold about customers and potential customers the better. The more the organisation knows about potential customers the better chance it should have of targeting the right people in a marketing campaign.

In an effort to **target potential customers more effectively**, organisations can use database marketing to build models of their target demographic group. These models then allow them to focus their advertising budgets on these target groups, in the hope that this will result in an improved return on investment (ROI) on their advertising spend.

Information gathering is therefore an important process, and organisations need to attract potential customers who are willing to divulge information about themselves. Offering prizes or and promotional campaigns through newsletters or 'ezines' can help achieve this.

If **records and stored and organised effectively**, an organisation should be able to implement new marketing strategies and (targeted) campaigns more quickly and easily. For example, by grouping individuals together according to shared characteristics (age, income, gender etc) organisations can generate targeted mailing lists of potential customer who share a set of desired characteristics.

Moreover, having a comprehensive database can also **help with forecasting**. Future trends for sales and marketing can be modelled based on the results of previous projects. By studying the past purchases of consumers, analytical software allows data analysts to predict broad trends in purchasing habits which can give an insight into customers' future purchasing behaviour.

However, it is important that organisations keep their database **up to date, and well-organised**. Having outdated or invalid entries could cause confusion and waste time. For example, there is no point in trying to contact business customers who have gone out of business.

There is also an **ethical/legal dimension** to consider when managing databases. Often unsolicited calls do not generate any business and can be annoying for the recipient. But more importantly companies need to ensure their databases comply with the law. In the UK, data must be kept up to date, be relevant, and must only be used for the purpose the customer intended or can reasonably expect it to be used for.

5.1 Data warehousing

KEY TERM

A DATA WAREHOUSE consists of a database, containing data from various operational systems, and reporting and query tools.

Data warehouse – A data warehouse is a large-scale data collection and storage area, containing data from various operational systems, plus **reporting** and **query tools** which allow the data to be analysed. The key feature of a data warehouse is that it provides a single point for **storing a coherent set of information** which can then be used across an organisation for **management analysis** and decision making.

The data warehouse is not an operational system, so the data in it remains static until it is next updated. For example, if a supermarket introduces a customer credit card, the history of customers' transactions on their cards could be stored in a data warehouse, so that management could analyse spending patterns.

However, although the reporting and query tools within the warehouse should facilitate management reporting and analysis, data warehouses are primarily used for **storing** data rather than analysing data.

A data warehouse contains data from a range of **internal** (eg sales order processing system, nominal ledger) and **external sources**. One reason for including individual transaction data in a data warehouse is that if necessary the user can drill-down to access transaction level detail. Data is increasingly obtained from newer channels such as customer care systems, outside agencies or websites.

Maintenance of a data warehouse is an iterative process that continually refines its content. Data is copied to the data warehouse as often as required – usually either daily, weekly or monthly. The process of making any required changes to the format of data and copying it to the warehouse is usually automated.

The result should be a coherent set of information available to be used across the organisation for management analysis and decision making. The reporting and query tools available within the warehouse should facilitate management reporting and analysis.

The reporting and query tools should be flexible enough to allow multidimensional data analysis, also known as **on-line analytical processing** (OLAP). Each aspect of information (eg product, region, price, budgeted sales, actual sales, time period etc) represents a different dimension. OLAP enables data to be viewed from each dimension, allowing each aspect to be viewed and in relation to the other aspects.

5.1.1 Features of data warehouses

A data warehouse is subject-oriented, integrated, time-variant, and non-volatile.

(a) **Subject-oriented**

A data warehouse is focussed on data groups not application boundaries. Whereas the operational world is designed around applications and functions such as sales and purchases, a data warehouse world is organised around major **subjects** such as customers, supplier, product and activity.

(b) **Integrated**

Data within the data warehouse must be consistent in format and codes used – this is referred to as **integrated** in the context of data warehouses.

For example, one operational application feeding the warehouse may represent **sex** as an 'M' and an 'F' while another represents **sex** as '1' and '0'.

While it does not matter how **sex** is represented in the data warehouse (let us say that 'M' and 'F' is chosen), it **must** arrive in the data warehouse in a **consistent integrated** state. The data import routine should cleanse any inconsistencies.

(c)   **Time-variant**

Data is organised by time and stored in time-slices.

Data warehouse data may cover **a long time horizon**, perhaps from five to ten years. Data warehouse data tends to deal with **trends** rather than single points in time. As a result, each data element in the data warehouse environment must carry with it the time for which it applies.

(d)   **Non-volatile**

Data **cannot be changed** within the warehouse. Only load and retrieval operations are made.

Organisations may build a single central data warehouse to serve the entire organisation or may create a series of smaller **data marts**. A data mart holds a selection of the organisation's data for a specific purpose.

A data mart can be constructed more quickly and cheaply than a data warehouse. However, if too many individual data marts are built, organisations may find it is more efficient to have a single data warehouse serving all areas.

The components of a data warehouse are shown in the following diagram.

Components of a data warehouse

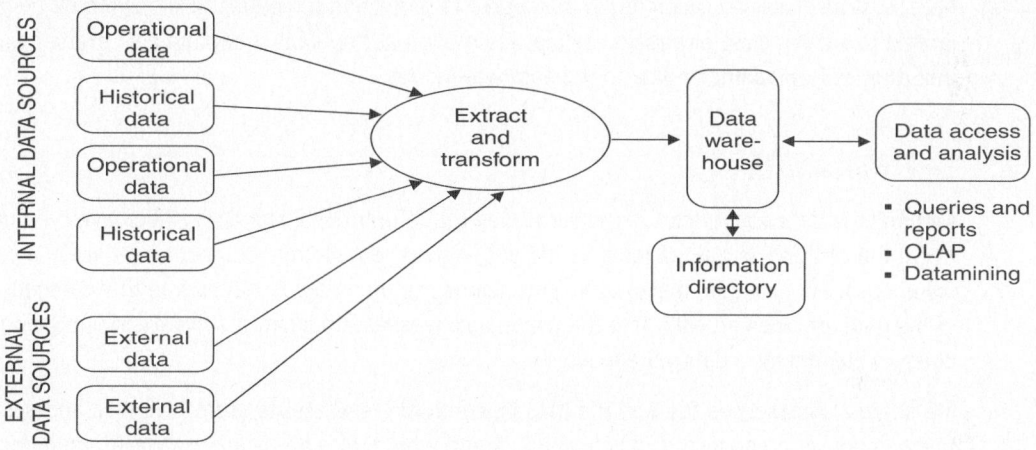

5.1.2 Advantages of data warehouses

Advantages of setting up a data warehouse system include the following.

(a)   **Supports strategic decision making**: The warehouse provides a single source of authoritative data which can be analysed using data making techniques to support strategic decision making.

(b)   Decision makers can access data without affecting the use of operational systems.

(c)   **Data quality**. Having a single source of data available will reduce the risk of inconsistent data being used by different people during the decision making process.

(d)   Having a wide range of data available to be queried easily encourages the taking of a wide perspective on organisational activities.

(e)   **Speed**. Data warehousing can enable faster responses to business queries, not only by storing data in an easily accessible central repository, but also by using OLAP technologies.

(f)   Data warehouses have proved successful in some businesses for:

   (i)   Quantifying the effect of marketing initiatives.
   (ii)   Improving knowledge of customers.
   (iii)   Identifying and understanding an enterprise's most profitable revenues streams.

In this way, data warehouses (and data mining) allow organisations to use the data they hold to help improve their competitiveness, and could help them gain a competitive advantage over their rivals.

5.1.3 Limitations of data warehouses

Some organisations have found they have invested considerable resources implementing a data warehouse for little return. To benefit from the information a data warehouse can provide, organisations need to be flexible and prepared to act on what they find. If a warehouse system is implemented simply to follow current practice it will be of little value.

Other limitations exist, particularly if a data warehouse is intended to be used as an operational system rather than as an analytical tool. For example:

(a) The data held may be outdated.

(b) An efficient regular routine must be established to transfer data into the warehouse.

(c) A warehouse may be implemented and then, as it is not required on a day-to-day basis, be ignored.

There is also an issue of **security**. The management aim of making data available widely and in an easily understood form can be at variance with the need to maintain confidentiality of, for example, payroll data.

This conflict can be managed by **encrypting** data at the point of capture and **restricting access** by a system of authorisations entitling different users to different levels of access. For this to work, the data held must be classified according to the degree of protection it requires: users can then be given access limited to a given class or classes of data. Encryption at the point of capture also exerts control over the **unauthorised uploading** of data to the data warehouse.

5.2 Metadata

Metadata is data about data. In the same way that a nutritional standards label gives you information about the contents of a tin of food, so metadata gives you information about the data in a data warehouse. For example, metadata might include the time data is loaded into the warehouse, the source of the data, or when an entry into the warehouse was last updated. A software information model can create metadata for a data warehouse.

Metadata also describes the way the data is structured, and assists users in finding and accessing data in the warehouse. It can also help users understand what that data means. However, metadata also plays an important role in ensuring the quality of data held in a warehouse. Metadata specifies what is supposed to be in the data warehouse, and documents what is actually there. Good metadata allows data to be loaded into a database more quickly, and equally allows users to fulfil subsequent information requests more quickly.

CASE STUDY

Data warehouses

The New York Central Mutual Fire Insurance Company (NYCM) sells home and auto insurance through a network of more than 1,000 independent agents.

Historically NYCM had no formal data warehouse and used legacy databases to create reports for its agents. However, this meant it became increasingly difficult to keep up with NYCM's data-related needs as they became more complex. The vice president (VP) of information and technology commented that the company 'essentially had a static reporting environment'.

NYCM was reluctant to spend vast amounts of money on a data warehouse, but hoped it could find a warehouse robust enough to handle its growing data needs at an affordable price.

Although the VP and his IT team were hesitant about the potentially high cost of deploying a comprehensive data warehouse, they realised the value the warehouse could offer the business. The VP noted that "Based on where we stand in the marketplace and where we need to be, we need to take a serious look at what our data can tell us about our business. We need to delve deeper into what our experience has been."

NYCM began working with business intelligence provider Kalido, and decided to implement a data warehouse deployment early in 2006. The implementation process has been time consuming as Kalido had to cleanse NYCM's customer and financial data, and then integrate it into the warehouse.

However, the VP hopes that, by using the reporting tools on the front end, NYCM insurance agents will be able to auto-generate reports and access data which will allow them to identify new and better ways to serve the company's 500,000-plus customers.

For example, the VP hopes that in upstate New York - an area prone to weather-related emergencies during the long winters – staff and agents will be able to examine historical trends via the Kalido data warehouse to better prepare customers before a catastrophe happens. He also said Kalido's ad hoc query capabilities should help agents resolve insurance claims faster.

5.3 Data mining

While a data warehouse is effectively a large database which collates information from a wide variety of sources, data mining is concerned with the discovery of meaningful relationships in the underlying data.

KEY TERM

DATA MINING software looks for hidden patterns and relationships in large pools of data.

Data mining is primarily concerned with **analysing data**. It uses statistical analysis tools to look for **hidden patterns and relationships** (such as trends and correlations) in large pools of data. The value of data mining lies in its ability to highlight previously unknown relationships.

In this respect, data mining can give organisations a **better insight into customer behaviours**, and can lead to **increased sales through predicting future behaviour**.

For example, a number of supermarkets now have customer loyalty cards (for example, *Tesco's Clubcard*). When a customer pays for their shopping using a loyalty card, the supermarket can also create a record of the items the customer has bought. The purchasing behaviour of customers can be used to create a profile of what kind of people the cardholders are.

Data mining techniques could be applied to customers' purchasing information to identify patterns in the items which were purchased together, or what types of item were omitted from shopping baskets, and how the make-up of customers' baskets varied by different types of customer. The supermarket could then target its promotions to take advantage of these purchasing patterns.

In this way, by identifying patterns and relationships, data mining can **guide decision-making**.

True data mining software discovers **previously unknown relationships**. The hidden patterns and relationships the software identifies can be used to guide decision making and to **predict future behaviour**, as with the Wal-Mart beer and nappies example given earlier.

Data mining uses statistical analysis tools as well as neural networks, fuzzy logic and other **intelligent techniques**.

The types of relationships or patterns that data mining may uncover may be classified as follows.

Relationship/ Discovery	Comment
Classification or cluster	These terms refer to the identification of patterns within the database between a range of data items. For example, data mining may find that unmarried males aged between 20 and 30, who have an income above $75,000 are more likely to purchase a high performance sports car than people from other demographic groups. This group could then be targeted when marketing material is produced/distributed.
Association	One event can be linked or correlated to another event – such as in Wal-Mart example.
Forecasting	Trends are identified within the data that can be extrapolated into the future.

Section summary

Data warehouses and data mining are important techniques for using the data held by an organisation.

A **data warehouse** consists of a database, containing data from various operational systems, and reporting and query tools, and is used to collate a coherent set of information which can be used in decision making. **Data mining** involves discovering new patterns and relationships in the underlying data.

6 E-marketing

Introduction

E-marketing is the application of IS and internet techniques to achieve marketing objectives. Most marketing activities can be enhanced by the use of such techniques, including branding, customer service and sales.

6.1 E-marketing – scope and media

KEY TERM

E-MARKETING is described by *Chaffey* in *E-business and E-commerce Management* as 'the application of the Internet and related digital technologies to achieve marketing objectives'.

Marketing objectives include identifying, anticipating and satisfying customer requirements profitably.

- **Identifying** – using the Internet to find out customers' needs and wants

- **Anticipating** – the demand for digital services

- **Satisfying** – achieving customer satisfaction raises issues over whether the site is easy to use, whether it performs adequately and how are the physical products dispatched.

Essentially, e-marketing means using digital technologies to help sell goods or services. The basics of marketing remain the same – creating a strategy to deliver the right messages to the right people. What has changed is the number of options available. These include pay per click advertising, banner ads, e-mail marketing and affiliate marketing, interactive advertising, search engine marketing (including search engine optimisation) and blog marketing.

Though businesses will continue to make use of traditional marketing methods, such as press and television advertising, direct mail and PR, e-marketing adds a whole new element to the marketing mix and is a valuable complement. It gives businesses of any size access to the mass market at an affordable price and, unlike TV or print advertising, it allows truly **personalised marketing**.

6.1.1 Key marketing functions the Internet can perform

(a) **Creating company and product awareness** – communicating essential information about the company and its brands. Such information may have a financial orientation to help attract potential investors, or it may focus on the unique features and benefits of its product lines.

(b) **Branding** – is a marketing communications activity. The intent is to have the public perceive a brand in a positive manner. With the amount of advertising being devoted to the Internet increasing each year, the frequency of visits to a site will also increase. Consequently, a company's web site will play a more prominent role in building its brand image. Online communications should therefore be similar in appearance and style to communications in the traditional media so as to present a consistent brand image.

(c)   **Offering incentives** – many sites offer discounts for purchasing online. Electronic coupons, bonus offers, and contests are now quite common. Such offers are intended to stimulate immediate purchase before a visitor leaves a web site, and also to encourage repeat visits.

(d)   **Lead generation** – the Internet is an interactive medium. Visitors to a site leave useful information behind when they fill in boxes requesting more information (eg, name, address, telephone number, and e-mail address). A site may also ask for demographic information that can be added to the company's database. This information is retained for future mailings about similar offers, or they can be turned over to a sales force for follow-up if it is a business-to-business marketing situation.

(e)   **Customer service** – in any form of marketing, customer service is important. Satisfied customers hold positive attitudes about a company and are therefore more likely to return to buy more goods. Right now, customer service is perceived as a weak link in Internet marketing. Customers are concerned about who they should call for technical assistance or what process to follow should goods need to be returned.

Some customer service tactics commonly used include frequently asked questions (FAQs) and return e-mail systems. It is apparent that organisations will have to spend more time and money developing effective customer service systems.

(f)   **E-mail databases** – organisations retain visitor information in a database. E-mailing useful and relevant information to prospects and customers helps build stronger relationships. An organisation must be careful that it does not distribute spam (unsolicited/unwanted e-mail) on the Internet.

(g)   **Online transaction** – organisations are capable of selling online if the web site is user friendly. Sites that are difficult to navigate create frustration in visitors. Presently, the business-to-business market is booming with business transactions. Organisations in the supply chain are linking together to achieve efficiencies in the buying-selling process.

 Earlier in the chapter we discussed the concept of customer relationship, and its three elements of customer acquisition, retention and extension.

The internet and on-line techniques can play an important role in these, perhaps most extensively in relation to customer acquisition.

The internet offers a number of methods for **acquiring customers**:

Search engines – Search engines (such as Google) mean that when users search for relevant key words or phrases links to the company's website will appear in their search results. In turn, **search engine optimisation** can be used as a technique for improving the company's position in the search engine listings.

Pay per click (or cost per click) advertising – Companies can pay other websites to display a banner on their website, with the hope that potential customers will click on the banner which then links through to the company's own website.

Affiliate marketing – A company rewards affiliates for each visitor or customer who comes to the company's website through the affiliate's own marketing efforts. Amazon is probably the best known example of an affiliate network; with an extensive range of sites directing customers to Amazon to buy books or music tracks that the affiliates have mentioned on their web pages.

Business blogs – Companies can use blogs to showcase the knowledge and expertise of their employees, and thereby hopefully attract new customers.

Comparison sites – Comparison sites (such as *moneysupermarket.com*) allow potential customers to compare the price and features of different products, and if a product compares favourably to competitor products this should encourage potential customers to buy it.

Viral marketing – Social networks are used to increase brand awareness, for example through video clips or images being passed from one user to another.

Retention

The internet can also be useful for helping to **retain customers,** for example through the use of **personalised reminder emails**, possibly with discount codes or other incentives, to customers who have not purchased anything recently.

Online communities – the creation of online communities and forums could also help retain customers' interest in a product or service. However, these forums can also have an additional benefit from companies. By reading customers' feedback and comments, businesses can improve their understanding of customer needs, and can take steps to improve their products or services to address any issues which are currently attracting criticism on the forums.

Extension

Recommendations – Probably the best known examples of customer extension are the 'recommendations' which customers are given on Amazon. Amazon's data modeling software allows them to monitor products which customers often buy together. Therefore, when existing customers log back in to Amazon they are given recommendations of other products they might like to buy, based on their previous purchases.

However, recommendations are not only made when customers log on, they also occur at the point a customer makes a purchase. For example, if a customer purchases a television, they might then be asked at the checkout if they also want to buy a television stand to go with their televisions.

6.1.2 Specific benefits of e-marketing

(a)   **Global reach** – a website can reach anyone in the world who has Internet access. This allows you to find new markets and compete globally for only a small investment.

(b)   **Lower cost** – a properly planned and effectively targeted e-marketing campaign can reach the right customers at a much lower cost than traditional marketing methods.

(c)   **The ability to track and measure results** – marketing by email or banner advertising makes it easier to establish how effective your campaign has been. You can obtain detailed information about customers' responses to your advertising.

(d)   **24-hour marketing** – with a website your customers can find out about your products even if your office is closed.

(e)   **Personalisation** – if your customer database is linked to your website, then whenever someone visits the site, you can greet them with targeted offers. The more they buy from you, the more you can refine your customer profile and market effectively to them.

(f)   **One-to-one marketing** – e-marketing lets you reach people who want to know about your products and services instantly. For example, many people take their mobile phone or *Blackberry* hand-held devices with them wherever they go. Combine this with the personalised aspect of e-marketing, and you can create very powerful, targeted campaigns.

(g)   **More interesting campaigns** – e-marketing lets you create interactive campaigns using music, graphics and videos. You could send your customers a game or a quiz – whatever you think will interest them.

(h)   **Better conversion rate** – if you have a website, then your customers are only ever a few clicks away from completing a purchase. Unlike other media which require people to get up and make a phone call, post a letter or go to a shop, e-marketing is seamless.

Together, all of these aspects of e-marketing have the potential to add up to more sales.

As a component of e-commerce, it can include information management; public relations; customer service and sales.

6.2 Developing an effective e-marketing plan

Planning for e-marketing does not mean starting from scratch. Any online e-communication must be **consistent with the overall marketing goals** and **current marketing efforts** of the organisation.

The key strategic decisions for e-marketing are common with strategic decisions for traditional marketing. They involve selecting target customer groups and specifying how to deliver value to these groups. Segmentation, targeting, differentiation and positioning all contribute to effective digital marketing.

The **SOSTAC® planning framework** developed by *Paul Smith* provides a structured and effective approach to marketing strategy. It can be used by managers in the private, public and non-profit sectors.

S = Situation Analysis	Where are we now? What is the external environment in which we are operating? What are our own strengths and weaknesses?
O = Objectives	Where do we want to get to? What is our goal?
S = Strategies	How do we get there? What do we need to do to be successful?
T = Tactics	What are the individual steps we need to take to achieve our objective?
A = Actions	What are the things we need to do? What is our 'to-do' list? Who will do what?
C = Control	What will we measure to know we are succeeding? How will we know when we have arrived?

The planning framework is expanded in the diagram below to show the techniques/actions that make up each stage:

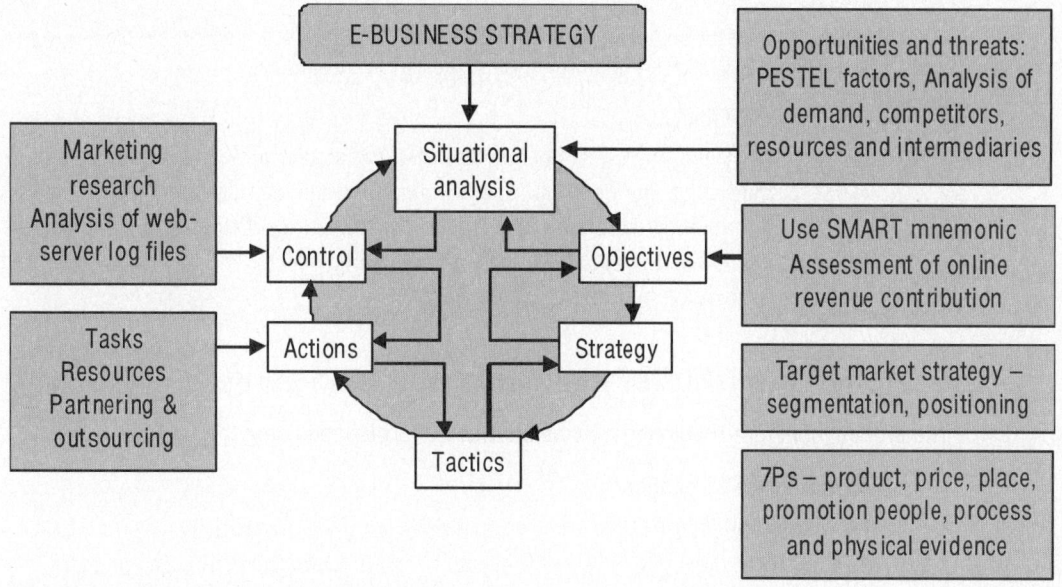

SOSTAC® Framework for e-marketing planning

In developing an effective e-marketing plan, the media of e-marketing used at certain stages will include the following.

Competitor analysis	Scanning competitor Internet sites.
	Competitor benchmarking to compare e-commerce services within a market.
	Competitive intelligence systems give a structured approach to monitoring and disseminating information on competitor activities
Intermediary analysis	Identify and compare intermediaries for a marketplace
	Search portals and look for new approaches for traffic building
	Research whether competitors are using disintermediation or reintermediation
Internal marketing audit	Focus on e-market measurement:

Channel promotion › Channel behaviour › Channel satisfaction › Channel outcomes › Channel profitability

Acquisition costs Referrers	Who? How?	Opinions? Attitudes? Brand impact?	Leads? Sales?	ROI? Profitability?

	Applying web analytics tools to measure the contribution of leads, sales and brand involvement currently delivered by online communications such as search engine marketing, online advertising and E-mail marketing in conjunction with the web site
	Create online CRM capabilities to understand customers' characteristics, needs and behaviours and to deliver targeted, personalised value
Objective setting	Online revenue contribution
Strategy	Identify target market by assessing size, segments, needs and competitive action
	Online value proposition (OVP)
Tactics	Use Internet to vary the extended product
	Look at new channel structures
	Research people replacements: autoresponders, e-mail notification, call-back facility, FAQs, on-site search engines and virtual assistants
	Branding
	Managing the continuous online marketing communications such as search engine marketing, partnerships, sponsorships and affiliate arrangements and campaign-based e-marketing communications such as Online advertising, E-mail marketing and microsites to encourage usage of the online service and to support customer acquisition and retention campaigns

6.3 Characteristics of the media of e-marketing

The employment of e-marketing may be analysed and planned using the six Is.

- Independence of location
- Industry structure
- Integration
- Interactivity
- Individualisation
- Intelligence

The six Is of marketing developed at Cranfield by *McDonald and Wilson* in 1999, summarise the ways in which the Internet can add customer value and hence improve the organisation's marketing effectiveness.

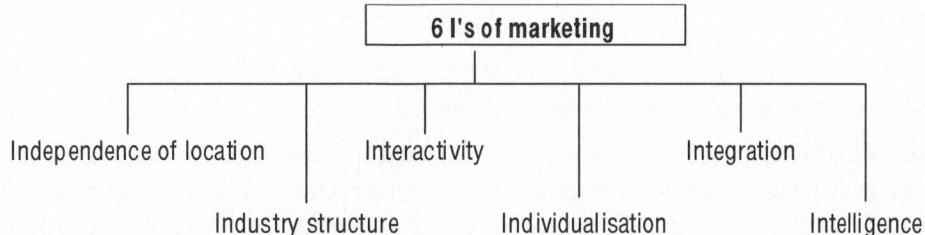

By considering and questioning each of these aspects of the new media, marketing managers can develop plans to accommodate the characteristics of the new media.

Independence of location	Do you exploit any opportunities to deliver information-based products and services electronically?
	Electronic media gives the possibility of communicating globally – giving opportunities of selling into markets that may not have been previously accessible.
Industry structure	Industry restructuring includes the following:
	Redesigning business processes
	Redrawing the market map in form of new market segments or increasing the marketing boundaries
	Adopting IT enabled services (ITeS).
Integration	Do you have detailed knowledge of individual customers, influencers or consumers?
	Do you share this knowledge across all customer-facing parts of the business?
	Advertising products/services on the Web is easy. It is more difficult, but absolutely crucial, to gather vital customer information, obtain customer feedback, use existing knowledge about the customer and exploit the Web's interactive nature to add value through product configuration, online pricing and so on.
Interactivity	Do you use interactive media to allow your customers to communicate with you?
	Do you listen to what they say and respond appropriately in a continuing dialogue?
	Traditional media are mainly 'push' media –the marketing message is broadcast from company to customer – with limited interaction. On the Internet it is usually a customer who seeks information on a web – it is a 'pull' mechanism.
	The growing use of carefully targeted direct mail as a means of communicating with individual customers has led some to call this 'the age of addressability'
Individualisation	Do you use your customer knowledge to tailor products and services to the needs of particular individuals or segments?
	Do you tailor all your communications to the characteristics of the recipients?
	Communications can be tailored to the individual unlike traditional media where the same message is broadcast to everyone
Intelligence	Do you inform your marketing strategy with intelligence gleaned from your operational systems at the customer interface eg, through analysis of customer needs, segmentation, prioritising segments according to customer lifetime value etc?
	The Internet can be used as a low cost method of collecting marketing information about customer perceptions of products and services. The web site also records information every time a user clicks on a link. Log file analysers will identify the type of promotions or products customers are responding to and how patterns vary over time

Example

The best-known example of electronic commerce – book-selling, exemplifies how the Internet can be used for an interactive dialogue with a known customer.

Web sites such as *Amazon.com* exploit the web's interactive nature to allow the customer to search for books on particular topics, track the status of an order placed earlier, and ask for recommendations of books similar to their favourites, read reviews placed by other customers, and so on. The web site builds knowledge of the customer which allows it, for example, to notify them by e-mail if a new book appears on a topic of particular interest.

6.4 E-marketing and the 7Ps

More specific concepts for the development of e-marketing may be based on the seven Ps of the service marketing mix.

- The augmented **product** can be extended through web information and interactivity.
- **Pricing** can be made transparent; dynamic pricing may be used.
- The global reach of the Internet has great implications for **place**, with the creation of new marketplaces and channel structures.
- **Promotion** can be previously targeted *via* customer databases.
- **People** can be replaced by software to a varying extent.
- **Processes** may be automated.
- **Physical evidence** consists of the customer's experience of using the organisation's e-marketing tools in general and of its website in particular

Marketing on the Internet brings many new opportunities not readily available or affordable using conventional marketing methods.

The marketing mix is the combination of marketing activities that an organisation engages in so as to best meet the needs of its targeted market. Because of changes in the market and the behaviour of the customers, future marketing should focus more on delivering value to the customer and become better at placing the customer – and not the product – in the centre. In some texts, the 4 Ps have been renamed the 4 Cs.

- Product becomes **customer value**
- Place becomes **customer convenience**
- Promotion becomes **customer communication**
- Price becomes **customer cost**

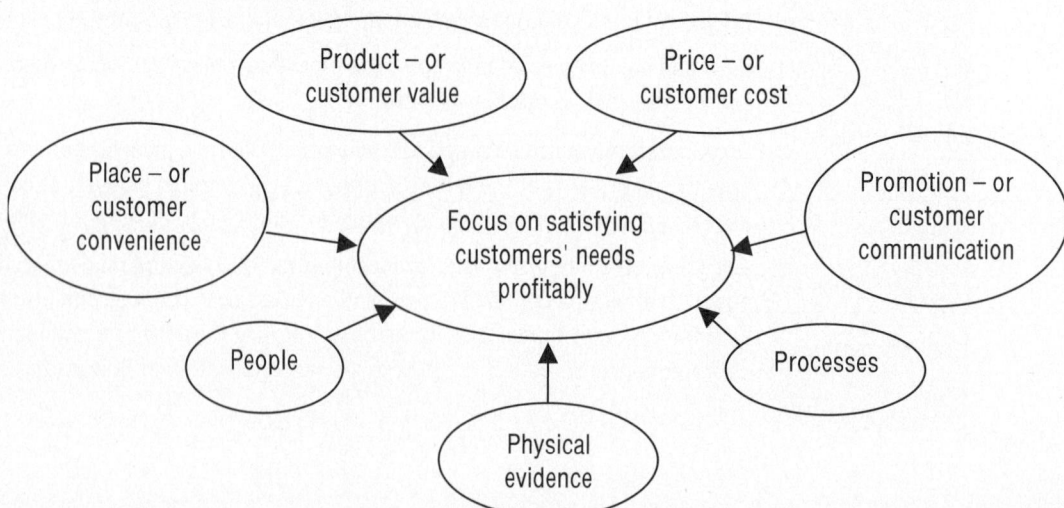

We will now show how the internet and e-commerce provides the opportunities for the marketer to vary the seven elements of the marketing mix.

Exam skills

We have mentioned above how the traditional 4Ps of the marketing mix have been extended to 7Ps for the service marketing mix. If you are faced with a question about marketing issues for a service company, make sure you think about the characteristics of services which distinguish them from products: they are **intangible** so customers cannot physically see the features of the item they are buying; they cannot be stored for later use, because the customer is an essential part of the transaction. This customer involvement means there is a very large degree of **variability** in the customers' experiences of service transactions.

6.4.1 Product (or customer value)

This is the element of the marketing mix that involves researching customers' needs and developing appropriate products. *Philip Kotler,* in *Principles of Marketing,* devised a very interesting concept of benefit building with a product. He suggested that a product should be viewed in three levels.

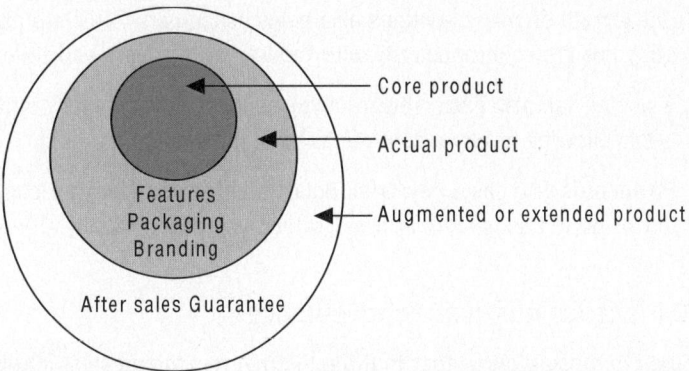

Core product – what is the core benefit the product offers? Customers who purchase a camera are buying more then just a camera they are purchasing memories.

Actual product – all cameras capture memories. The strategy at this level involves organisations **branding**, **adding features** and benefits to ensure that their product offers a differential advantage from their competitors.

Augmented or **extended product**: What additional non-tangible benefits can you offer? Competition at this level is based around after sales service, warranties, delivery and so on.

What does buying products online offer over one to one sales?

(a)   The ability to deliver interactivity and more detailed information through the Internet is the key to enhancing the augmented or extended product offering online.

(b)   The buyer knows immediately about product features, the facts, not a sales person's interpretations.

(c)   The buying process is customised for returning visitors, making repeat purchases easier. Organisations can also offer immediately ancillary products along with the main purchase. *EasyJet* for example, can readily bundle its flights, hotels and car hire through suitable design of its web site

(d)   The product can also be customised to consumers needs eg *www.nike.com* offer customised trainers to users online. Users can design and see their trainers online before they order

6.4.2 Price (or customer cost)

The Internet has made **pricing very competitive**. Many costs such as store cost and staff cost have disappeared for completely online stores, placing price pressures on traditional retailers.

(a) The Internet increases customer knowledge through **increased price transparency** since it becomes much quicker to shop around and compare quoted prices by visiting supplier web sites. Even more significant is the use of price comparison sites by consumers. Sites such as *Kelkoo.com (or Kelkoo.co.uk* in the UK) give a single location that empowers the consumer to quickly find out the best price from a range of suppliers for a range of products from books and CDs to white goods. Such easy access to information helps to maintain prices within the online world.

(b) **Dynamic pricing** gives the ability to test prices or to offer differential pricing for different segments or in response to variations in demand. For some product areas such as ticketing it may be possible to dynamically alter prices in line with demand. *Tickets.com* adjusts concert ticket prices according to demand and have been able to achieve 45% more revenue per event as a result.

(c) Different types of pricing may be possible on the Internet, particularly for digital, downloadable products. Software and music has traditionally been sold for a continuous right to use. The Internet offers new options such as payment per use; rental at a fixed cost per month or a lease arrangement. Bundling options may also be more possible.

(d) The growth of online auctions also helps consumers to dictate price. The online auction company *eBay* has grown in popularity with thousands of buyers and seller bidding daily.

(e) E-pricing can also easily reward loyal customers. Technology allows repeat visitors to be tracked, easily allowing loyalty incentives to be targeted towards them.

(f) Payment is also easy; *PayPal* or online credit cards allow for easy payments. However the downside to this is Internet fraud, which is growing rapidly around the world.

6.4.3 Place (or customer convenience)

Allen and Fjermestad argue that that the Internet has the greatest implications for **place** in the marketing mix since it has a global reach.

E-Business Models

Types of marketplaces	Set up by	Main aim
Controlled by sellers	Single vendor seeking many buyers	To retain value and power in any transaction
Controlled by buyers	One or more buyers	To shift value and power in marketplace onto the buyer's side Buyer intermediaries can also be there to act as agents
Neutral marketplaces	Third party intermediaries to match many buyers to many sellers	To match buyers to sellers at an auction Commission based

Choosing a marketplace depends on four factors:

- Are there transactions or benefits to be realised?
- Is the electronic market for the product developing quickly?
- Does company have substantial market share or buying power?
- Would a neutral intermediary be beneficial?

Types of e-commerce marketplace

- B2C and B2B (can be combined or separate eg, *Dell*)
- C2C (*eBay*)
- Cuctions, (*eBay)*
- Consumer reviews (*Bizrate*)
- Customer bids (*priceline*)

The emergence of new **channel structures** – disintermediation, reintermediation and countermediation – (which we will consider in connection with e-commerce in Chapter 9) also affect the 'place' where online transactions take place.

Navigation – there are three aspects of navigation that are key to achieving competitive advantage online.

(a) **Reach** – this is the potential audience of the e-commerce site. Reach can be increased by moving from a single site to representation with a large number of different intermediaries.

(b) **Richness** – this is the depth or detail of information which is both collected about the customer and provided to the customer. This is related to the product element of the mix.

(c) **Affiliation** – this refers to whose interest the selling organisation represents – consumers or suppliers. This particularly applies to retailers. It suggests that customers will favour retailers who provide them with the richest information on comparing competitive products.

Localisation – providing a local site, usually a language-specific version, is referred to as localisation. A site may need to support customers from a range of countries; they may have different product needs, language differences and cultural differences.

6.4.4 Promotion (or customer communication)

Marketing communications are used to inform customers and other stakeholders about an organisation and its products.

(a) There are new ways of applying each of the elements of the **communications mix** (advertising, sales promotions, PR and direct marketing), using new media such as the web and e-mail. Most organisations today have some form of webpage used in most if not all advertisements. Placing banner advertisements on other web pages is a common form of e-promotion. Web public relations (WPR) is another approach to promoting online. Newsworthy stories based on product or service launches can be placed on the company's webpage, or WPR articles sent to review sites for consumers to read.

(b) The Internet can be used at different stages of the **buying process**. For instance, the main role of the web is often in providing further information rather completing the sale. Think of a new car purchase. Many consumers will now review models online, but most still buy in the real world.

(c) Promotional tools may be used to assist in different stages of **customer relationship management** from customer acquisition to retention. In a web context this includes gaining initial visitors to the site and gaining repeat visits using eg, direct e-mail reminders of site proposition and new offers.

(d) The Internet can be integrated into **campaigns**. For example, we are currently seeing many direct response print and TV ad campaigns where the web is used to manage entry into a prize draw and to profile the entrant for future communications.

These general technological trends have an impact across the promotional mix.

Promotion activity	Impact/opportunity	Examples of supporting technology
Advertising	Reach more customers worldwide	Websites and ads
	Target audiences more specifically	Specialist TV channels
	Increase response via interactivity	Direct Response TV, SMS text messaging
Sales promotion	Target segment/individual interests and preferences	Customer databases, EPOS data
	Facilitate/motivate response	Online entry/coupons
	Online discounts (lower admin costs)	Online transaction
Direct marketing	Personalised, one-to-one messages	Database
	Permission-based database/contacts to enhance response rate	E-mail, website, SMS requests for info
	Speed and interactivity of response	E-mail + website links
	Direct response/transaction	E-commerce sites
PR and publicity	Speed of information dissemination and response to crisis/issues	E-mail media releases and online information
Marketing/sales support	Publicising sponsorships	Website
	Publicising exhibition attendance	Website/e-mail clients
	Up-to-date information for sales force & call centre staff	Access to product/inventory and customer database
Internal marketing	Staff access to information relevant to their jobs	Intranet newsletters, bulletins, policy info
	Co-ordination/identification of dispersed offices and off-site staff	E-mail, tele– and video-conferencing
Network marketing	Supplier/client access to information relevant to business relationship	Extranet: access to selected information

6.4.5 People

The **people** element of the marketing mix is the way an organisations' staff interact with customers and other stakeholders during sales and pre and post sales. *Smith and Chaffey* suggest that online, part of the consideration for the people element of the mix is the consideration of the tactics by which people can be replaced or automated.

(a)   **Autoresponders** automatically generate a response when a company e-mails an organisation, or submits an online form.

(b)   **E-mail notification** may be automatically generated by a company's systems to update customers on the progress of their orders. Such notifications might show, for example, three stages: order received; item now in stock; order dispatched.

(c)   **Call-back facility** requires that customers fill in their phone number on a form and specify a convenient time to be contacted. Dialling from a representative in the call centre occurs automatically at the appointed time and the company pays

(d)   **Frequently Asked Questions (FAQ)** can pre-empt enquires. The art lies in compiling and categorising the questions so customers can easily find both the question and a helpful answer

(e)   **On site search engines** help customers find what they are looking for quickly. Site maps are a related feature

(f)   **Virtual assistants** come in varying degrees of sophistication and usually help to guide the customer through a maze of choices.

6.4.6 Process

The **process** element of the marketing mix is the internal methods and procedures companies use to achieve all marketing functions such as new product development, promotion, sales and customer service. The restructuring of the organisation and channel structures described for product, price, place and promotion all require new **processes**.

6.4.7 Physical evidence

The physical evidence element of the marketing mix is the tangible expression of a product and how it is purchased and used. In an online context, physical evidence is **customers' experience of the company through the web site** and associated support. It includes issues such as ease of use, navigation, availability and performance. Responsiveness to e-mail enquiries is a key aspect of performance. The process must be right to enable an acceptable response within the notified service standards such as 24 hours.

Benefits of e-marketing
It promotes **transparent pricing** – because potential customers can readily compare prices not only from suppliers within any given country, but also from suppliers across the world.
It facilitates **personalised attention** – even if such attention is actually administered through impersonal, yet highly sophisticated IT systems and customer database manipulation.
It provides sophisticated **market segmentation** opportunities. Approaching such segments may be one of the few ways in which e-commerce entrepreneurs can create **competitive advantage**.
The web can either be a **separate** or a **complementary** channel.
A new phenomenon is emerging called **dynamic pricing**. Companies can rapidly change their prices to reflect the current state of demand and supply.

These new trends are creating **pressure** for companies. The main threat facing companies is that **prices will be driven down by consumers' ability to shop around**.

6.5 Comparison of traditional and on-line branding

IT and the Internet have particular implications for branding.

*   The domain name is a vital element of the brand

*   Brand values are communicated within seconds *via* the experience of using the brand website

*   Online brands may be created in four ways

    –   Migrate the traditional brand
    –   Extend the traditional brand
    –   Partner with an existing digital brand
    –   Create a new digital brand

KEY TERM

A BRAND is a name, symbol, term, mark or design that enables customers to identify and distinguish the products of one supplier from those offered by competitors.

A brand is a tool which is used by an organisation to differentiate itself from competitors. For example, what is the value of a pair of *Nike* trainers without the brand or the logo?

The value of brands in today's environment is phenomenal. Brands have the power of instant sales; they convey a message of confidence, quality and reliability to their target market, which is particularly important in e-commerce where there are often concerns over privacy and security.

Aspects of a well-formed brand in traditional delivery channels
Brand name awareness – achieved through marketing communications to promote the brand identity and the other qualities of the brand
Perceived quality – awareness counts for nothing if the consumer has had a bad experience of a product or associated customer service
Positive brand associations – include imagery, the situation in which a product is used, its personality and symbols
Brand loyalty – the commitment of a segment to a brand

These customer touch-points combine to build a good brand presence. However, screen-based delivery adds a new level of complexity to the problem. For the first time customers are interacting in machine-mediated experiences as opposed to human-mediated. How can a machine be made to express a company's positive brand attributes, like respect and reliability, the same way a person does?

There are essential elements common to both traditional media and new screen-based systems. A successful brand, online or off, represents an entire customer experience. In a bricks-and-mortar environment this includes such matters as: how the customer is welcomed into the store; how products are packaged and presented and how staff and customers interact.

These elements can be translated to the online shopping experience to include the e-tailer's home or welcome page web site design and page navigation and online support.

6.5.1 Visual identity

An effective visual identity is important online, as is a memorable **domain name**. The one big difference in branding on the internet from branding in conventional marketing is introduced by domain names. For example, the domain name *www.coca-cola.com* is fast becoming the brand first seen by the consumer rather than the distinctive red and white label on the can. Unfortunately, there are a limited number of names available, and each name has been given to the first applicant. The World Intellectual Property Organisation has now taken up this issue, at least in terms of the worst exploitative excesses. Even so there may be many legitimate claimants for a .com name who operate in very different sectors, and the new extensions (such as *.biz* and *.TV*) do not totally resolve the problem. Every supplier still wants *.com* since this is where the customers look first.

Despite these similarities, online branding differs in important ways from traditional branding and must be approached differently. A company's entire character, identity, products, and services, can be communicated in seconds on the web and customers make judgments just as fast.

6.5.2 Online brand options

Migrate traditional brand online – this can make sense if the brand is well known and has a strong reputation eg, *Marks & Spencer*, *Orange* and *Disney*. However, there is a risk of jeopardising the brand's good name if the new venture is not successful.

Extend traditional brand – a variant. For example, *Aspirin*'s land-based brand positioning statement used to be 'Aspirin – provides instant pain relief'. However, management felt this didn't work as a meaningful web statement, because you can't get instant pain relief on the web. So it was changed to 'Aspirin – your self help brand', and the web site offered 'meaningful health oriented intelligence and self help'.

Partner with existing digital brand – co-branding occurs when two businesses put their brand name on the same product as a joint initiative. This practice is quite common on the Internet and has proved to be a good way to build brand recognition and make the product or service more resistant to copying by

private label manufacturers. A successful example of co-branding is the *Senseo* coffeemaker, which carries both the *Philips* and the *Douwe Egberts* brands.

Create a new digital brand – because a good name is extremely important, some factors to consider when selecting a new brand name are that it should suggest something about the product (eg *Betfair*), be short and memorable, be easy to spell, translate well into other languages and have an available domain name.

Section summary

E-marketing means using IS and internet technologies to achieve marketing objectives and enhance marketing activities.

The employment of e-marketing may be analysed and planned using the 6 Is:

- Independence of location
- Industry structure
- Integration
- Interactivity
- Individualism
- Intelligence analysed

More specific concepts for the development of e-marketing may be based on the 7 Ps:

- Product
- Pricing
- Place
- Promotion
- People
- Processes
- Physical evidence

Chapter Roundup

✓   Marketing plays an important role in strategic management since an organisation cannot have a strategic plan which does not involve products/services and customers. The marketing audit is an important aspect of marketing control, but can also provide information and analysis for the corporate planning process.

✓   Another important factor in shaping an organisation's marketing strategy will be whether it views revenues as coming ultimately from products or customers.

✓   Segments are groups of customers with similar needs that can be **targeted** with a distinct **marketing mix**. Both consumer and industrial markets can be segmented, and the aim is to identify coherent segments that are both valid and attractive.

✓   **Customer relationship marketing** focuses on establishing **loyalty** in the existing customer base. Payne suggested that relationship marketing extends beyond the customer and developed the six market model to demonstrate where relationships should be built.

✓   **Key customer analysis** investigates six main areas of customer characteristics, in order to identify which customers offer most profit.

✓   **Customer profitability analysis** is an analysis of the total sales revenue generated from a customer or customer group, less all the costs that are incurred in servicing that customer or group.

✓   Data warehouses and data mining are important techniques for using the data held by an organisation.

✓   A **data warehouse** consists of a database, containing data from various operational systems, and reporting and query tools, and is used to collate a coherent set of information which can be used in decision making. **Data mining** involves discovering new patterns and relationships in the underlying data

✓   **E-Marketing** means using IS and internet technologies to achieve marketing objectives and enhance marketing activities

✓   The employment of e-marketing may be analysed and planned using the six Is.

- Independence of location
- Industry structure
- Integration
- Interactivity
- Individualism
- Intelligence analysed.

✓   More specific concepts for the development of e-marketing may be based on the 7 Ps.

- Product
- Pricing
- Place
- Promotion
- People
- Processes
- Physical evidence

Quick Quiz

1   Give an example showing why there should be a correlation between employee and customer loyalty.

2   Which of the statements below describes differentiated marketing?

    (a)   The company attempts to produce the ideal product for a single segment of the market (eg Rolls Royce cars for the wealthy).

    (b)   This policy is to produce a single product and hope to get as many customers as possible to buy it, ignoring segmentation entirely.

    (c)   The company attempts to introduce several product versions, each aimed at a different market segment. For example, manufacturers of soap powder make a number of different brands, marketed to different segments.

3   How can different costs arise with different customers? Give five examples.

4   What are the three categories of consumer goods?

5   Data warehousing involves discovering new patterns and relationships in underlying data.

    True or false?

6   What are the six 'I's of e-marketing?

7   What are the four ways an online brand be created?

Answers to Quick Quiz

1   Reduced staff turnover in service firms can result in more repeat business because of improved service quality due to more knowledgeable staff.

2   (c)

3   Five from:

- Order size
- Sales mix
- Order processing
- Transport costs (eg if JIT requires frequent deliveries)
- Management time
- Cash flow problems (eg increased overdraft interest) caused by slow payers
- Order complexity (eg if the order has to be sent out in several stages)
- Inventory holding costs can relate to specify customers
- The customer's negotiating strength

4   Convenience, shopping and speciality

5   False. Data mining involves discovering new patterns and relationships in underlying data

6   Independence of location, industry structure, interactivity, individualisation, integration and intelligence

7
- Migrate the traditional brand
- Extend the traditional brand
- Partner with an existing digital brand
- Create a new digital brand

Answers to Questions

8.1 Profitable customers

You can see below that the profit earned by Seth in servicing Narayan is greater, despite the increased discount.

	Kipling	Narayan
Number of shoes	500	420
	£	£
Revenue (after discount)	22,500	17,850
Transport	(5,000)	–
Administration	(250)	(500)
Net profit	17,250	17,350

8.2 Choosing data

The information reflects sales force administration and convenience. However, it might obscure an analysis of customer profitability, in which case presenting information by customer size might be more important than geography.

Now try this question from the Exam Question Bank	Number	Level	Marks	Time
	Q9	Examination	25	45 mins

INFORMATION SYSTEMS AND STRATEGY

 In this chapter we examine some aspects of information management that have strategic significance.

Organisations need to use information about both the external environment and internal performance to help determine strategy (Section 3). Information is also important for allowing management to maintain strategic control over an organisation (Section 4).

The increasing amounts of data and information which organisations have to manage mean that it is important data is organised efficiently and can be accessed easily (Sections 5-6).

Information and information systems also play an increasingly more dynamic role in contemporary organisations, and the internet has had a major impact on the structure of many organisations and how they do business. One significant aspect of this is the way the internet has opened up new business models through e-commerce activities (Section 7).

The internet also allows new marketing opportunities and ways of interacting with potential customers through the application of Web 2.0 technologies (Section 8).

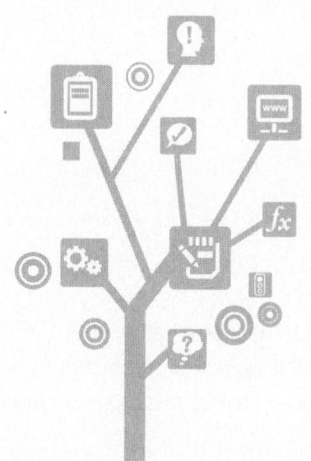

9

topic list	learning outcomes	syllabus references	ability required
1 Strategic information systems	A2(b)	A2(ii)	Evaluate
2 Information strategy	A2(b), D1(d)	A2(i), D1(viii), D1(ix)	Evaluate
3 Information sources and management	A2(b)	A2(ii)	Evaluate
4 Information for planning and control	A2(b)	A2(ii)	Evaluate
5 Knowledge management	A2(b), D1(d)	A2(ii)	Evaluate
6 Databases and models	A2(b)	A2(ii)	Evaluate
7 E-commerce	A2(a)	A2(iii)	Evaluate
8 Web 2.0 technologies and business strategy	A2(a)	A2(iii)	Evaluate
9 The IT department	A2(b)	–	Evaluate

1   Strategic information systems

Introduction

Strategic information is used to **plan** the **objectives** of the organisation, and to **assess** whether the objectives are being met in practice. Therefore it is important that organisations have an information systems strategy so that it can meet its information requirements.

Organisations often have to consider three different strategies in relation to information: information systems (IS) strategy, information technology (IT) strategy and information management (IM) strategy. We will look at these in more detail throughout this chapter, but it is important you are aware of the different aspects of information strategy overall as you are reading through the chapter.

1.1 Strategic information

Strategic planning, management control and operational control may be seen as a hierarchy of planning and control decisions. (This is sometimes called the Anthony hierarchy, after the writer *Robert Anthony*.)

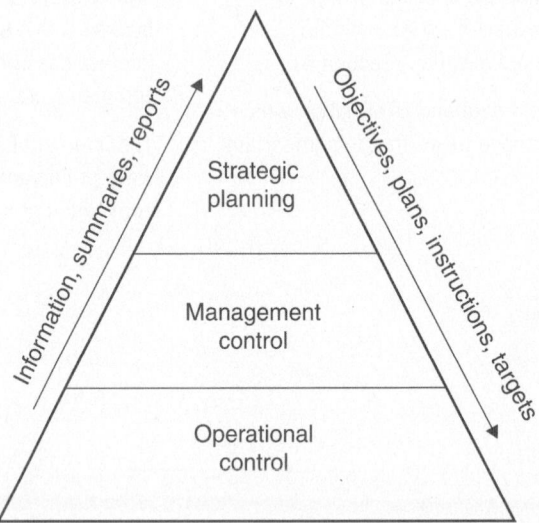

Strategic information is used to **plan** the **objectives** of the organisation, and to **assess** whether the objectives are being met in practice. Such information includes overall profitability, the profitability of different segments of the business, future market prospects, the availability and cost of raising new funds, total cash needs, total manning levels and capital equipment needs.

Strategic information is:

*   Derived from both **internal and external** sources
*   **Summarised** at a high level
*   Relevant to the **long term**
*   Concerned with the **whole organisation**
*   Both **quantitative** (numerical) and **qualitative** (descriptive, based on qualities)
*   **Uncertain**, as the future cannot be accurately predicted

KEY TERMS

DATA is the raw material for data processing. Data consists of numbers, letters and symbols and relates to facts, events, and transactions.

INFORMATION is data that has been processed in such a way as to be meaningful to the person who receives it.

INFORMATION SYSTEMS AND STRATEGY

In this chapter we examine some aspects of information management that have strategic significance.

Organisations need to use information about both the external environment and internal performance to help determine strategy (Section 3). Information is also important for allowing management to maintain strategic control over an organisation (Section 4).

The increasing amounts of data and information which organisations have to manage mean that it is important data is organised efficiently and can be accessed easily (Sections 5-6).

Information and information systems also play an increasingly more dynamic role in contemporary organisations, and the internet has had a major impact on the structure of many organisations and how they do business. One significant aspect of this is the way the internet has opened up new business models through e-commerce activities (Section 7).

The internet also allows new marketing opportunities and ways of interacting with potential customers through the application of Web 2.0 technologies (Section 8).

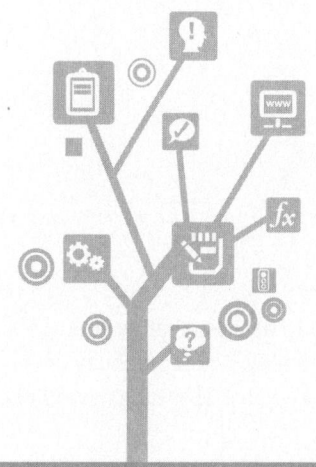

9

topic list	learning outcomes	syllabus references	ability required
1 Strategic information systems	A2(b)	A2(ii)	Evaluate
2 Information strategy	A2(b), D1(d)	A2(i), D1(viii), D1(ix)	Evaluate
3 Information sources and management	A2(b)	A2(ii)	Evaluate
4 Information for planning and control	A2(b)	A2(ii)	Evaluate
5 Knowledge management	A2(b), D1(d)	A2(ii)	Evaluate
6 Databases and models	A2(b)	A2(ii)	Evaluate
7 E-commerce	A2(a)	A2(iii)	Evaluate
8 Web 2.0 technologies and business strategy	A2(a)	A2(iii)	Evaluate
9 The IT department	A2(b)	–	Evaluate

1   Strategic information systems

Introduction

Strategic information is used to **plan** the **objectives** of the organisation, and to **assess** whether the objectives are being met in practice. Therefore it is important that organisations have an information systems strategy so that it can meet its information requirements.

Organisations often have to consider three different strategies in relation to information: information systems (IS) strategy, information technology (IT) strategy and information management (IM) strategy. We will look at these in more detail throughout this chapter, but it is important you are aware of the different aspects of information strategy overall as you are reading through the chapter.

1.1 Strategic information

Strategic planning, management control and operational control may be seen as a hierarchy of planning and control decisions. (This is sometimes called the Anthony hierarchy, after the writer *Robert Anthony*.)

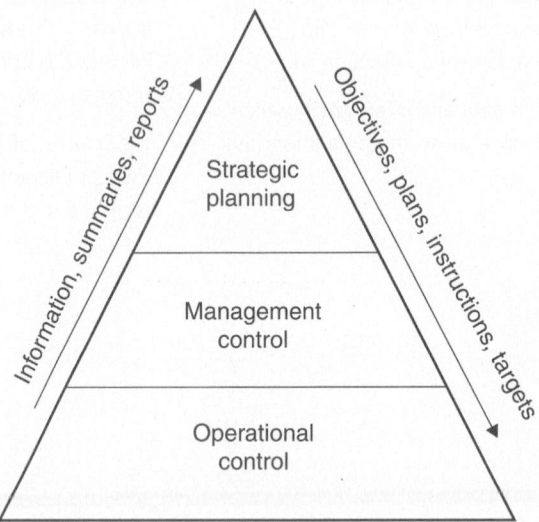

Strategic information is used to **plan** the **objectives** of the organisation, and to **assess** whether the objectives are being met in practice. Such information includes overall profitability, the profitability of different segments of the business, future market prospects, the availability and cost of raising new funds, total cash needs, total manning levels and capital equipment needs.

Strategic information is:

- Derived from both **internal and external** sources
- **Summarised** at a high level
- Relevant to the **long term**
- Concerned with the **whole organisation**
- Both **quantitative** (numerical) and **qualitative** (descriptive, based on qualities)
- **Uncertain**, as the future cannot be accurately predicted

KEY TERMS

DATA is the raw material for data processing. Data consists of numbers, letters and symbols and relates to facts, events, and transactions.

INFORMATION is data that has been processed in such a way as to be meaningful to the person who receives it.

1.2 Strategic information systems

Strategic IT systems include Executive Information Systems **(EIS)**, Management Information Systems **(MIS)** and Decision Support Systems **(DSS)**. **Value added networks** facilitate the strategic use of information in order to add value.

1.2.1 Executive Information Systems (EIS)

KEY TERM

An EXECUTIVE INFORMATION SYSTEM (EIS) pools data from internal and external sources and makes information available to senior managers in an easy-to-use form. EIS help senior managers make strategic, unstructured decisions.

An EIS should provide senior managers with easy access to key **internal and external** information. The system summarises and tracks strategically critical information, possibly drawn from internal MIS and DSS, but also including data from external sources eg competitors, legislation, external databases such as Reuters.

An EIS is likely to have the following **features**.

- Flexibility
- Quick response time
- Sophisticated data analysis and modelling tools

A model of a typical EIS is shown below.

An Executive Information System (EIS)

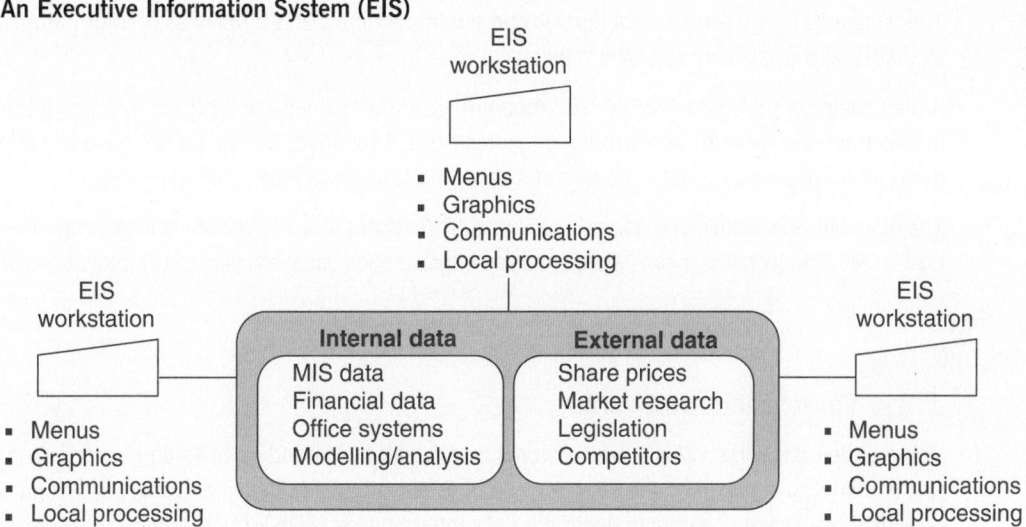

1.2.2 Management Information Systems (MIS)

KEY TERM

MANAGEMENT INFORMATION SYSTEMS (MIS) convert data from mainly internal sources into information (eg summary reports, exception reports). This information enables managers to make timely and effective decisions for planning, directing and controlling the activities for which they are responsible.

An MIS provides regular reports and (usually) on-line access to the organisation's current and historical performance.

MIS usually transform data from underlying transaction processing systems into summarised files that are used as the basis for management reports.

MIS have the following characteristics:

- Support **structured** decisions at operational and management control levels
- Designed to report on **existing** operations
- Have little analytical capability
- Relatively **inflexible**
- Have an **internal** focus

1.2.3 Decision support systems (DSS)

KEY TERM

DECISION SUPPORT SYSTEMS (DSS) combine data and analytical models or data analysis tools to support semi-structured and unstructured decision making.

DSS are used by management to assist in making decisions on issues which are subject to high levels of uncertainty about the problem, the various **responses** which management could undertake or the likely **impact** of those actions.

Decision support systems are intended to provide a wide range of alternative information gathering and analytical tools with a major emphasis upon **flexibility** and **user-friendliness**.

DSS have more analytical power than other systems enabling them to analyse and condense large volumes of data into a form that helps managers make decisions. The objective is to allow the manager to consider a number of **alternatives** and evaluate them under a variety of potential conditions.

CASE STUDY

Executives at small and medium sized companies are making critical business decisions every day based on the information available to them.

This information can come from a variety of sources: opinions from peers and colleagues; a personal sense of intuition or business judgment; or data derived internally or externally to the organisation. This is worrying, however, given the lack of confidence in the data available to decision makers.

A 2007 report conducted by the Economist Intelligence Unit (EIU) found that nine out of ten corporate executives admit to making important decisions on the basis of inadequate information.

This suggests that there are problems in the quality, amount and timeliness of information which is available as the basis for decision making.

It also suggests that today's small and medium sized companies are destined to make a number of uninformed decisions on an alarmingly regular basis. Executives simply do not have the relevant information required to make the best decision in a timely manner.

Therefore business solutions software – such as *SAP Business One* – is becoming increasingly valuable for businesses. The technology can help companies improve operational efficiency, customer service and innovation.

1.2.4 Value added networks

Value added networks (VANs) are networks that facilitate the adding of value to products and (particularly) to services by the strategic use of information. Typically, VANs will link separate organisations together through electronic data interchanges (EDIs), contributing to the development of **business networks**.

Also, they are often business ventures in their own right, with companies subscribing to the services available. Good examples are the SABRE, Amadeus and Galileo airline flight booking system. A simpler example is the electronic data interchange systems between manufacturers and their suppliers that facilitate the operation of just-in-time (JIT) logistics.

VANs give mutual competitive advantage to all their subscribers, but only so long as some competitors are left outside of the system. As soon as membership of the VAN (or a competing VAN) becomes a standard feature of the industry, the original competitive advantage is lost. Competitive advantage based on VAN membership can then only exist if there is more than one VAN and each VAN in the industry offers a different degree of benefit in terms of cost reduction or differentiation.

Section summary

Strategic information is used to **plan** the **objectives** of the organisation, and to **assess** whether the objectives are being met in practice. Strategic information (such as EIS and MIS) help managers make strategic decisions.

2 Information strategy

Introduction

Information strategy can be divided into **information systems strategy**, **information technology strategy** and **information management strategy**. The strategic significance of information requires that information itself be managed strategically so that the systems, the technology and the information itself support the overall strategic policy.

As with so many other aspects of business strategy, the terminology used in the world of information strategy is not clearly defined. Terms such as 'information management' are used in slightly different ways by different groups of professionals. In this section we will provide you with information that will help you to gain a fuller understanding of the ways in which various terms are used and some of the range of meanings and connotations they possess.

2.1 Information and information systems

To begin with, let us consider the difference between **information** itself and the **means by which it is collected, processed, moved around and stored**. Information is intangible and in its most basic form exists in people's minds. However, there is a limit to the amount of information any one person can remember and make effective use of; as a result, **physical records** of information have been with us for thousands of years.

So, right from the beginning, we have a **distinction between information itself and the means by which it is handled**. Inscribed clay tablets that survive from ancient civilizations are an example of information technology; we can hold them in our hands, but the information they store is lost to us unless we can decipher the symbols used by the person who inscribed them.

Today we have a huge array of means in which we can store and manipulate information; many of these are electronic, but paper records are still fundamental to many aspects of information handling. We would not necessarily think of a hand-written memo as an example of information technology, such is its simplicity, but, in principle, it is.

Generally, today, information technology means **computers**: electronically-based processing and storage systems and all the **peripherals**, **communication links** and **software** that go with them. The extreme complexity of these systems leads to the creation of large amounts of information relating specifically to their design, maintenance and operation, but this information is not their purpose: it is part of the technology itself.

The **information technology systems** we use in business exist to help us to make use of **information that is external to the overall system itself**, information that we need to carry on our business operations.

The immense potential of computer-based systems provides an increasingly wide range of ways in which we can exploit information in business. We need to decide how we are going to use the information we have, how we are going to obtain more information and how we are going to exploit the information technology that we use to handle it. The decisions we make about these problems constitute our **information strategy**.

2.2 Information strategy   11/10, 3/11

KEY TERMS

The INFORMATION SYSTEMS (IS) STRATEGY is the long-term plan for systems to exploit information in order to support business strategies or create new strategic options.

The INFORMATION TECHNOLOGY (IT) STRATEGY is concerned with selecting, operating and managing the technological element of the IS strategy.

The INFORMATION MANAGEMENT (IM) STRATEGY deals with the roles of the people involved in the use of IT assets, the relationships between them and design of the management processes needed to exploit IT.

STRATEGIC INFORMATION SYSTEMS are systems at any level of an organisation that change goals, processes, products, services or environmental relationships with the aim of gaining competitive advantage.

Earl's analysis of information strategy into three elements (IS, IT and IM) is useful. The first distinction he made was between the strategies for **information systems** and **information technology.**

2.2.1 Levels of Information strategy

Information systems (IS) strategy

An information systems (IS) strategy is concerned with specifying the systems (in the widest meaning of the word) that will best **enable the use of information to support the overall business strategy** and to deliver tangible benefits to the business (for example, through increased productivity, or enhanced profits). In this context, a 'system' will include all the **activities, procedures, records** and **people** involved in a particular aspect of the organisation's work, as well as the **technology** used.

The information systems strategy is focussed on **business requirements**, the demands they make for information of all kinds and the nature of the benefits that information systems are expected to provide.

This strategy is very much **demand-led** and **business-driven**: each SBU in a large organisation is likely to have its own information systems strategy.

Information technology strategy (IT)

The information technology strategy, by contrast is technology-focussed and looks at the resources, technical solutions and systems architecture required to enable an organisation to implement its information systems (IS) strategy.

IT strategies are likely to look at the **hardware and software** used by the organisation to produce and process information. They may also include aspects of data capture and data storage, as well as the transmission and presentation of information.

Information management strategy (IM)

Earl subsequently also highlighted the need for an information management strategy. The emphasis here is on management: managing the role and structure of IT activities within an organisation, and managing the relationships between IT specialists and the users of information. In this respect, a key feature of IM strategy is its focus on **roles and relationships.**

IM strategy also plays an important part in ensuring that information can be accessed by all the people who need it, but, at the same time, access to information is restricted to those people who need to access to it.

We might sum up the three levels of information strategy in very simple terms by saying that: IS strategy defines **what** is to be achieved; IT strategy determines **how** hardware, software and telecommunications can achieve it; and the IM strategy describes **who** controls and uses the technology provided.

This model of information strategy has the advantage of being **internally consistent** and quite **simple** to understand. Unfortunately, the picture is spoiled by a different use of the term information management.

You may come across a rather narrow use of this term to mean 'the approach taken to storing and accessing data'. Since this is really just an aspect of the information technology strategy as defined above, we do not recommend the use of the term in this way.

Exam skills

Although you are not expected to have a detailed knowledge of IT systems, IS and IT are core elements of modern businesses, and they are likely to become increasingly important to business strategies.

The E3 examiner has noted that students often display a poor knowledge of IS and IT.

So, make sure you do not overlook this area of the syllabus. Very often an organisation's ability to deliver a strategy may depend having sufficient IT capabilities to do so. Equally, an organisation's IT capabilities may be instrumental in shaping its strategy. For example, does it have sufficient competences to support an e-commerce strategy?

Also remember that an organisation needs to be able to collect data and turn it into useful information, for example either for management information or marketing information.

2.3 The need for a strategic approach

Earl says that information systems and information strategy are too important to leave in the hands of technology professionals alone. He suggests the following characteristics of IT/IS strategy support this view:

- Involves **high costs**

- Is **critical to the success** of many organisations

- Is now used as part of the commercial strategy in the battle for **competitive advantage**

- Impacts on **customer service**

- Potentially affects **all levels of management and staff** in an organisation

- May **lead to structural changes** within an organisation which require HR planning

- Affects the way **management information** is created and presented

- **Requires effective management** to obtain the maximum benefit

- Involves many **stakeholders** inside and outside the organisation, therefore stakeholder analysis is required

2.3.1 IS/IT is a high cost activity

Many organisations invest large amounts of money in IS, but not always wisely. The unmanaged proliferation of IT is likely to lead to expensive mistakes. Two key benefits of IT, the ability to **share** information and the **avoidance of duplication**, are likely to be lost. All IT expenditure should therefore require approval to ensure that it enhances rather than detracts from the overall information strategy. There is also the possibility that the failure of a very large IT investment might have strategic negative impact on the organisation concerned, possibly even leading to business failure.

2.3.2 IS/IT is critical to the success of many organisations   09/10

When developing an IS/IT strategy a firm should assess **how important IT is** in the provision of products and services. The role that IT fills in an organisation will vary depending on the type of organisations. IS/IT could be:

- A **support** activity
- A **key** operational activity
- **Potentially** very important
- A **strategic** activity (without IT the firm could not function at all; eg Amazon, eBay)
- A source of **competitive advantage**

CASE STUDY

Increasing infrastructure capacity and speed – Betfair

The online gambling company, Betfair, is the world's largest internet betting exchange.

In 2009, the technology supporting Betfair's IT systems was heavily under pressure after the Grand National race meeting (in April) because of a high volume of new customers, so a transformation programme dubbed 'Performance 2010' was introduced. In this project, the firm sought to replace "virtually every piece of kit" such as network, hardware and software.

As part of the project, Betfair replaced legacy Sun SPARC database systems running Oracle, with horizontal, scalable Linux boxes also running Oracle. With the new set-up, capacity was improved by more than 50% and running costs decreased by 20%.

Betfair's Chief Technology Officer (CTO) acknowledged that companies would usually take 18-20 months to do something like that, but their IT team was given just nine months to do it, because the new systems had to be ready in time for the major horse racing Festival at Cheltenham in March 2010.

Reflecting on the project, Befair's CTO noted that 'Some competitors had problems during the horse racing season, but [our upgrade] went through smoothly and we are now ready for the [2010 football] World Cup. That was a huge changeover though and a bit frightening, as it is the infrastructure the company is sitting on. The team did an amazing job and I am particularly proud of this project.'

Exam skills

When considering IS/IT in a strategic context it could be useful to consider how they contribute to an organisation's current strategic position. One way of doing this could be through a SWOT analysis.

For example:

Strength: A business might have a sophisticated customer database which allows it send out targeted marketing messages to customers. Or a retailer might have an inventory management system which automatically re-orders stock lines according to sales being recorded on the shop tills, thereby allowing it to minimise the levels of inventory it needs to hold.

Weakness: A business' ordering system (either online or manual) is unreliable, and so customers cannot be confident that the goods they order will be delivered correctly or within an acceptable time scale.

Opportunity: If a business does not currently have a web site which allows customers to purchase items online, the opportunity to develop such a website could provide a significant boost to its sales.

Threat: Conversely, if a competitor has recently upgraded their IT systems with the result that they can now offer a greater range of services to their customers and provide them with improved levels of service, this could pose a threat to an organisation, because customers may switch to using the competitor instead.

2.3.3 Information and competitive advantage

It is now recognised that information can be used as a source of competitive advantage. Many organisations have recognised the importance of information and developed an **information strategy**, covering both IS and IT.

Information systems should be tied in some way to **business objectives**.

(a)   The **corporate strategy** is used to plan functional **business plans** which provide guidelines for information-based activities.

(b)   On a year-by-year basis, the **annual plan** would try to tie in business plans with information systems projects for particular applications, perhaps through the functioning of a steering committee.

2.3.4 IT can impact significantly on the business context

IT is an **enabling** technology, and can produce dramatic changes in individual businesses and whole industries. For example, the deregulation of the airline industry encouraged the growth of computerised seat-reservation systems. IT can be both a **cause** of major changes in doing business and a **response** to them.

2.3.5 IT affects all levels of management

IT has become a routine feature of office life, **a facility for everyone to use**. IT is no longer used solely by specialist staff.

2.3.6 IT and its effect on management information

The use of IT has permitted the design of a range of information systems. Executive Information Systems (EIS), Management Information Systems (MIS), Decision Support Systems (DSS), Knowledge Work Systems (KWS) and Office Automation Systems (OAS) can be used to improve the quality of management information.

IT has also had an effect on **production processes**. For example, Computer Integrated Manufacturing (CIM) changed the methods and cost profiles of many manufacturing processes. The techniques used to **measure and record costs** have also adapted to the use of IT.

2.3.7 IT and stakeholders

Parties interested in an organisation's use of IT are as follows.

(a)   **Other business users** – for example to facilitate Electronic Data Interchange (EDI).

(b)   **Consumers** – for example as reassurance that product quality is high, consumers may also be interested if information is provided via the Internet.

(c)   **Employees** – as IT affects work practices.

(d)   **Governments** – eg telecommunications regulation, regulation of electronic commerce.

(e)   **IT manufacturers** looking for new markets and product development. User-groups may be able to influence software producers.

2.3.8 Other aspects

In addition to these arguments we might also identify the reasons below.

(a)   IS are by their nature open to external influences, particularly improvements and updates. A strategic view should be taken in order to obtain optimum benefit from these influences and prevent the proliferation of incompatible developments.

(b)   Environmental dynamism means that the need for information is constantly recreated in new ways.

(c)   Information is fundamental to strategic planning and so it should be managed strategically.

2.3.9 Advantages of a strategic approach

(a)   Competitive advantage is more easily attained.

(b)   There is **congruence** between the goal structure of the IS strategy and the overall corporate strategy.

(c)   Technical developments can be monitored and assessed with a view to introduction at a suitable time, rather than being ignored or introduced before they are properly developed.

(d)   Expenditure can be controlled strategically.

Note at this point we could also question whether IS/IT strategy is best developed through a formal plan or whether a more emergent strategy could sometimes be more appropriate. In other words, it is important to think about the process of how information strategy is developed, just as it is important to think about the process of how business strategy is developed.

Question 9.1	Babbage and Newman

Learning outcome A2(b)

Babbage and Newman plc is a company with an established base of IT applications. The finance department has a fully computerised accounting system. The marketing department has developed a primitive customer modelling package. The production department 'does not need IT'.

The Finance Director is in charge of IT at Babbage and Newman. He proposes in the annual corporate budget a 10% increase in IT expenditure based on last year, for the relevant departments. This will enable system upgrades.

Comment briefly on the information strategy at Babbage and Newman.

2.4 How IT is changing corporate strategy

It should be obvious that information systems and information technology should **support** corporate strategy, but there are also a number of ways IS/IT can **influence** corporate strategy.

In 1985, the Harvard Business Review published an article by *Michael Porter* and *Victor Millar* aimed at general managers facing the changes resulting from the rapid and extensive development of information technology. Although it is was written a number of years ago, the article still has great relevance to the **strategic employment of information** systems and the use of information technology. It dealt with three main interlinked topics.

- The ways in which IT had become **strategically significant**
- How the **nature of competition** had changed
- **How to compete** in the new, IT influenced environment

2.4.1 The strategic significance of IT

IT transforms the **value chain**. The value chain model (which *Michael Porter* devised) illustrates the way that businesses **add value** for the customers, through nine different activities: five primary, and four support.

We have looked at the value chain in Chapter 4 of this text.

Think also of the way the value chain links to Porter's generic strategies of cost leadership or differentiation (covered in Chapter 5).

Porter and Millar's article remarks that each of the value chain activities has both **physical** and **information** aspects and points out that, while until quite recently, technical advances were concentrated in the physical aspects, **current improvements tend to be IT driven**.

Simple improvements are made by faster and more accurate processing of existing forms of data; more dramatic ones by creating new flows of previously unavailable information. This has a particular effect on the linkages between the various activities and extends the company's **competitive scope**, which is the range of activities it can efficiently undertake.

Porter and Millar provide a diagram of the value chain in which they give examples of the ways in which IT was influencing the various activities at the time the article was written (1985). Although the technologies themselves have developed since then, the ideas in the model are still very relevant.

Support activities	Firm infrastructure	Enterprise Resource Planning Intranets Extranets				
	Human resource management	Automated personnel scheduling				
	Technology development	Computer aided design Electronic market research				
	Procurement	Online procurement of parts (e-procurement)				
		Automated warehouse Electronic data interchange (EDI)	Flexible manufacturing	Automated order processing Vehicle tracking	Electronic marketing CRM EPOS Remote terminals for salespersons	Remote servicing of equipment Computer scheduling and routing of repair trucks
		Inbound logistics	Operations	Outbound logistics	Marketing and sales	Service
	Primary activities					**Margin**

IT transforms the **product**. It is possible to view products as having physical and informational content, with the mix varying from product to product. **Diesel fuel**, for example, is an almost **entirely physical** product, though it is necessary to be aware that it will not work with petrol-engined vehicles. This Study Text, on the other hand, consists almost entirely of information, though, obviously, it has a physical aspect. An intermediate case would be an aircraft, which has a very obvious physical existence, but which cannot be used without a great deal of information on servicing, handling characteristics and the operation of its systems.

Porter and Millar make the point that there is an unmistakeable trend towards **supplying increasing amounts of information with products** as, for instance, in the case of freight and courier services that provide on-line tracking of consignments.

Exam skills

As well as thinking specifically how IT can affect the value chain, you should also be prepared to think how IT and e-business have affected business more generally.

For example:

The use of computer aided design can lead to the faster production of new products and designs. Organisations could either use this speed as a basis for making designs cheaper (cost leadership) or, for example, in the clothing and fashion industry, as a means of getting the latest fashions to market more quickly than their rivals (differentiation).

Websites and email have changed the nature of communications between organisations and customers.

The internet has also changed the nature of the supply chain and channel structure; for example, by allowing customers to book flights and hotel rooms for their holidays directly from the airline company and the hotel online, rather than having to use travel agents. (This is an example of disintermediation which we will discuss in more detail later in the chapter).

2.4.2 How IT changes the nature of competition

IT changes the **structure of industry** through its effect on the **five competitive forces**.

Porter's five forces model is covered in the syllabus for E2, however there is a brief summary of it in the Introductory chapter at the front of this text. The model looks at the competitive forces which affect the level of profit which can be sustained in an industry.

The relevance of it here is to consider how IT can change the nature of these five forces and therefore change the level of profits which can be sustained - for better or for worse.

Competitive rivalry – Developments in IT have been fundamental in the growth of online companies, which has meant that there is now increased competition, in many industries, between online and offline companies.

Threat of new entrants – IT could help create barriers to entry. For example, it could increase economies of scale through computer-controlled production methods, thereby meaning that potential new entrants would have to have similar technology to be able to compete effectively. Equally, improved levels of service based on expensive IT systems could also act as a potential barrier to new entrants.

Conversely, IT could also break down barriers to entry. For example, the development of telephone banking and online banking means that banks can be established without the need for an extensive network of high street branches (which would otherwise require large amounts of capital to establish).

Bargaining power of customers – One of the ways of reducing the bargaining power of customers is through 'locking them in' to a particular product or brand. A number of supermarkets and retailers have adopted this idea in their 'loyalty card' programmes. However, loyalty card programmes (such as Tesco's Clubcard) are also linked to data warehouses which then provide the retailer with information for targeted marketing campaigns. If supermarkets have detailed information about individual customers' spending habits and patterns, they can then send personalised marketing messages to customers with offers relating to products which they have bought previously or may be likely to buy in the future.

Threat of substitutes – In some cases, IS/IT can itself be the substitute product; for example in the way that videoconferencing could be seen as a substitute for business travel, or possibly in the way that e-books could be seen as a substitute for traditional printed copies of books.

Conversely, however, computer-aided design and manufacturing systems could be used to introduce new and reconfigured versions of existing products more rapidly to help fend off the threat from substitutes.

IT and competitive strategy

IT **enhances competitive advantage** in two principal ways:

* by **reducing costs**
* by making it easier to **differentiate products**.

Perhaps the most obvious examples of IT-driven cost reductions have occurred in the automation of much clerical work that has apparent since the introduction of mainframe computers in the middle of the twentieth century.

However, although IT can be used to reduce costs, it is perhaps debatable whether this generates a long-term competitive advantage. For example, businesses increasingly use virtual conferencing as a means of cutting costs and imposing operational efficiency due to the ease with which data can be shared. However, if all the firms in an industry start using virtual conferencing, will this actually generate any competitive advantage for any individual firms in that industry?

Differentiation. One way an organisation might seek to differentiate itself from its competitors is by meeting customers' needs and requirements more closely than their competitors. The greeting card company 'Moonpig.com' has adopted such an approach by allowing customers to design their own cards online.

IT could also enhance competitive advantage by forming the basis of complete **new businesses**. It makes new businesses technically feasible; it creates derived demand for new products; and it creates new businesses inside old ones. The impact of *Apple's iPod* gives examples of all three effects. The device itself is based on the MP3 file format; a large **iPod ecosystem** of accessories has been created; and the product itself represents a departure from Apple's previous hardware and software strategies.

2.4.3 Competing in the information age

Porter and Millar propose a five step process to take advantage of new information-based opportunities.

 **Assess information intensity**. A high level of information content in either products or processes indicates that IT can play a strategic role.

 **Determine the role of IT in industry structure**. IT may have the potential to radically change the way in which the industry operates, including changing the basis of competition and moving its boundaries.

 **Identify and rank the ways in which IT might create competitive advantage**. Possible value chain-based applications include opportunities for reducing cost or enhancing differentiation and establishing new links between activities. There may also be opportunities to enter new market segments and to introduce new products.

 **Investigate how IT might spawn new businesses**. These might be based on the exploitation of new categories of information and the sale of information-processing capacity.

 **Develop a plan to exploit IT**. Effectively, this is the creation of a comprehensive strategy and has implications for most parts of the organisation.

An important role of the information technology and finance functions is to help ensure the agreed strategy is proceeding according to plan. The table below outlines the rationale behind this view.

	Traditional view	Strategic implications
Cost	The finance and information technology functions can be relatively expensive	Shared services and outsourcing could be used to capture cost savings
IT	IT has traditionally been transaction based	IT/IS should be integrated with business strategy
Value	The finance and IT functions do not add value	Redesign the functions
Strategy	Accountants and IT managers are seen as scorekeepers and administrators rather than as a business partner during the strategic planning process	Change from cost-orientated to market-orientated ie development of more effective strategic planning systems

2.4.4 The importance of managing technology

The success of an organisation's use of technology depends largely on how technology is selected, implemented and **managed**. For example, **information systems** may **fail to deliver the benefits expected** for any of the following reasons.

(a)   They are used to tackle the **wrong problem** (ie the use of IT has not been thought through in the context of the wider organisation).

(b)   Senior management are not interested.

(c)   Users are ignored in design and development.

(d)   No attention is given to behavioural factors in design and operation.

If an organisation develops and follows a realistic information strategy and information systems plan for information systems and technology then there is less chance that these problems will arise.

Organisations have typically gone through a process of evolution in the development and management of their IS strategy. *Nolan* identified six stages based on the level of expenditure involved.

Initiation: computers are introduced, usually by financial staff, in order to make cost savings.

Contagion: computers are introduced into other areas in an uncontrolled fashion, with varying degrees of success.

Control: Senior managers, concerned about expenditure, create a central IT staff and concentrate control in its hands.

Integration: a need for innovative joint development by users and specialists is accepted and controls are loosened.

Data administration: the value of information is recognised and drives development; databases are set up.

Maturity: a strategic view is taken and IS strategy is incorporated into overall organisational strategy.

Obviously, factors other than the progression outlined in this model will affect expenditure, including the rapid fall in the cost of IT and the development of completely new technologies, such as video conferencing. The value of Nolan's model is the guidance it gives on how the **management of IT resources** might reasonably proceed and evolve.

Organisations typically go through a process of evolution in their IT strategy, moving from **simple automation of processes** such as bookkeeping to fully-fledged **information-based business strategy**. Along the way they may pass through stages of expansion, centralised control of IT and wider dispersion of IT development. Different management techniques tend to be used as the process continues.

Exam skills

You should look out for question scenarios in which the management of IS and IT strategies appears to be deficient, and be prepared to offer sensible advice. The aim of IS and IT strategies should be to achieve strategic objectives while controlling costs: this will require the input of user needs and practical experience to be combined with the IT specialist's knowledge of the available technology and how to make the best use of it.

However, note that it is important to distinguish between IS strategy (the business's requirements from the systems) and IT strategy (focusing on the hardware and software necessary to deliver the business requirements).

2.5 Developing IT strategy

Just as business strategy should be subject to continuing review and development, it would be inappropriate to consider an information strategy as a fixed and immutable. Developments both within the organisation and in the environment will inevitably require that the **information strategy be developed and subject to change**. Obvious potential influences include technical developments in hardware and software and changes in the business strategy itself. A simple guide to the continuing development of an information strategy might include the features outlined below.

(a)   There should be **constant reference to the overall business strategy**. This will shape the demand for information and thence the IS, IT and IM strategies. There may be companies in which the overall strategy is driven by the appearance of new technology, but it is important to be aware that, generally, this will not be the case and it will be **inappropriate to seek to adopt new technology for its own sake**.

(b)   **Compatibility of technologies** should be carefully considered.

(c)   Similarly, the **wider implications** of proposed developments must be thoroughly considered. Each part of the organisation should be able to make appropriate inputs into plans for change.

(d)   Where significant change is envisaged, it must be **properly planned**, possibly using a methodology such as Structured Systems Analysis and Design Methodology (SSADM). Hardware and software choices must be made; decisions must be taken about the extent to which work should be outsourced, if at all, and costs and benefits should be considered.

A successfully developed strategy will contribute to the success of the organisation. Its success may also be judged by the extent to which it performs three specific functions:

(a)   Prediction and definition of major areas of strategic choice

(b)   Indication of the degree of common ground between business and information managers on such matters as strategic assumptions, objectives and policies

(c)   Timely identification of the information resources required to implement the business strategy

2.5.1 Information needs

The identification of organisational **information needs** and the information systems framework to satisfy them is at the heart of a strategy for information systems and information technology.

The IS and IT strategies should complement the overall strategy for the organisation. It follows therefore that the IS/IT strategy should be considered whenever the organisation prepares other long-term strategies such as marketing or production.

2.5.2 Earl's three leg analysis

The writer *Earl* observed that, in practice, there are three ways in which IS strategies develop. He identified these as the three 'legs' of IS strategy development:

- Business led (top down emphasis, focuses on business plans and goals)
- Infrastructure led (bottom up emphasis, focuses on current systems)
- Mixed (inside out emphasis, focuses on IT/IS opportunities)

A diagrammatic representation of the three legs follows.

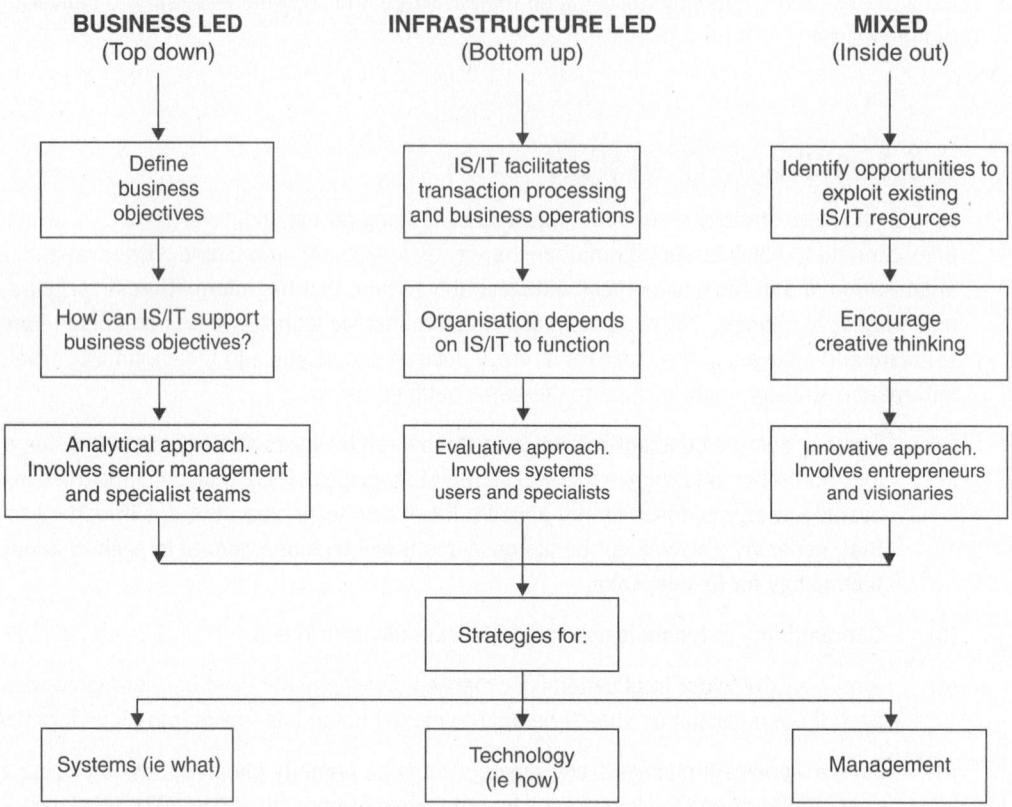

Earl's three leg analysis is explained in the following table.

Leg or approach	Comment
Business led (top down)	The **overall objectives** of an organisation are identified and then IS/IT systems are implemented to enable these objectives to be met. This approach relies on the ability to break down the organisation and its objectives to a series of business objectives and processes and to be able to identify the information needs of these. This is an analytical approach. The people usually involved are senior management and specialist teams.
Infrastructure led (bottom up)	Computer based **transaction systems** are critical to business operations. The organisation focuses on systems that facilitate transactions and other basic operations. This is an evaluative approach. The people usually involved are system users and specialists.
Mixed (inside out)	The organisation encourages ideas that will **exploit existing IT and IS resources**. Innovations may come from entrepreneurial managers or individuals outside the formal planning process. This is an innovative/creative approach. The people involved are entrepreneurs and/or visionaries.

We will now look at a number of other methodologies and frameworks that may be used as part of the information systems strategy development process.

2.5.3 Enterprise analysis

KEY TERM

ENTERPRISE ANALYSIS involves examining the entire organisation in terms of structure, processes, functions and data elements to identify the key elements and attributes of organisational data and information.

Enterprise analysis is sometimes referred to as **business systems planning**. This approach involves the following steps.

STEP 1   Ask a large sample of managers about:

- How they use information
- Where they get information
- What their objectives are
- What their data requirements are
- How they make decisions
- The influence of the environment

STEP 2   Aggregate the findings from *Step 1* into subunits, functions, processes and data matrices. Compile a Process/data class matrix to show:

- What data classes are required to support particular organisational processes
- Which processes are the creators and users of data

STEP 3   Use the matrix to identify areas that information systems should focus on, eg on processes that create data

Enterprise analysis approach – strength	Comment
Comprehensive	The enterprise analysis approach gives a comprehensive view of the organisation and its use of data and systems.

Enterprise analysis approach – weaknesses	Comment
Unwieldy	The enterprise analysis approach results in a mountain of data that is expensive to collect and difficult to analyse.
Focussed on existing information	Survey questions tend to focus on how systems and information are currently used, rather than on how information that is needed could be provided. The analysis has tended to result in existing systems being automated rather than looking at the wider picture.

2.5.4 Critical success factors

Critical success factors (**CSFs**) are the small number of key operational goals which are vital to the success of an organisation.

The use of CSFs can help to determine the information requirements of an organisation. CSFs are operational goals. If operational goals are achieved the organisation should be successful.

The CSF approach is sometimes referred to as the **strategic analysis** approach. The philosophy behind this approach is that managers should focus on a small number of objectives, and information systems should be focussed on providing information to enable managers to monitor these objectives. A key aspect

of the successful introduction and application of CSFs is the negotiation between the business manager and the information systems manager which identifies what information is required and how it can be obtained and delivered.

Where measures use quantitative data, performance can be measured in a number of ways.

- In **physical quantities**, for example units produced or units sold
- In **money terms**, for example profit, revenues, costs or variances
- In **ratios** and **percentages**

2.5.5 Data sources for CSFs

In general terms *Rockart* identifies four **general sources** of CSFs.

(a) The **industry** that the business is in.

(b) The **company** itself and its situation within the industry.

(c) The **environment**, for example consumer trends, the economy, and political factors of the country in which the company operates.

(d) Temporal organisational factors, which are **areas of corporate activity** which are currently **unacceptable** and represent a cause of concern, for example, high inventory levels.

More specifically, possible internal and external data sources for CSFs include the following.

(a) **The existing system**. The existing system can be used to generate reports showing **failures to meet CSFs.**

(b) **Customer service department**. This department will maintain details of **complaints** received, **refunds** handled, **customer enquiries** etc. These should be reviewed to ensure all failure types have been identified.

(c) **Customers**. A survey of customers, provided that it is properly designed and introduced, would reveal (or confirm) those areas where **satisfaction** is high or low.

(d) **Competitors**. Competitors' operations, pricing structures and publicity should be closely monitored.

(e) **Accounting system**. The **profitability** of various aspects of the operation is probably a key factor in any review of CSFs.

(f) **Consultants**. A specialist consultancy might be able to perform a detailed review of the system in order to identify ways of satisfying CSFs.

2.5.6 CSF approach: strengths and weaknesses

CSF approach – strengths	Comment
Takes into account environmental changes	The CSF approach requires managers to examine the environment and consider how it influences their information requirements.
Focuses on information	The approach doesn't just aim to establish organisational objectives. It also looks at the information and information systems required to establish and monitor progress towards these objectives.
Facilitates top management participation in system development	The clear link between information requirements and individual and organisational objectives encourages top management involvement in system (DSS, ESS) design.

CSF approach – weaknesses	Comment
Aggregation of individual CSFs	Wide-ranging individual CSFs need to be aggregated into a clear organisational plan. This process relies heavily on judgement. Managers who feel their input has been neglected may be alienated.
Bias towards top management	When gathering information to establish CSFs it is usually top management who are interviewed. These managers may lack knowledge of operational activities.
CSFs change often	The business environment, managers and information systems technology are subject to constant change. CSFs and systems must be updated to account for change.

2.6 Information audit

KEY TERM

An INFORMATION AUDIT aims to establish the information needs of users **and** how these needs could be met.

The audit has three stages.

Information needs assessment

This stage involves **gathering information**, usually through interviews and questionnaires.

Information users are asked what information they require, why they require it, when they require it and the preferred format.

People should be encouraged to think laterally about what information would help them do their job, rather than simply listing the information they currently receive.

To encourage wide-ranging thought, users should be asked to state the information they would like in an 'ideal world'. Unrealistic and uneconomic needs can be rejected (tactfully) at a later stage.

Information analysis

This stage **examines the information** provided by the existing information system. Both the quantity and the quality of the information are analysed. For example, the timing of information may reduce the quality of otherwise excellent information as it is provided too late to influence decision-making. Slightly less accurate information, provided earlier, may be more desirable.

Gap analysis

This stage **compares** the information needs identified in stage 1 with the information identified as being provided in stage 2. Gaps between what is required and what is currently provided are identified.

'Information gaps' are analysed to evaluate the costs and benefits of closing the gap.

An information system **resource analysis** involves a review of **all** information systems and information technology used within an organisation. The review includes all aspects of hardware, software, communications devices, network topologies, systems development methodologies, maintenance procedures, contingency plans and IS/IT personnel. The review looks at all of these aspects in the context of the organisation's overall strategy and the IS/IT strategy.

Resource analysis is sometimes called **Current Situation Analysis (CSA)**. The analysis establishes the current status of IS/IT within the organisation. The CSA has similar problems to that of a cost-benefit analysis in that it relies on the **subjective judgements** of information users. A group of people using the same system for the same purpose may come up with different ratings for system efficiency and user-friendliness.

Two techniques that could be useful when conducting a CSA are **Earl's grid** and the **applications portfolio**.

2.6.1 Earl's grid

Earl suggests a grid to analyse an organisation's current use of information systems. Current systems are plotted on the following grid.

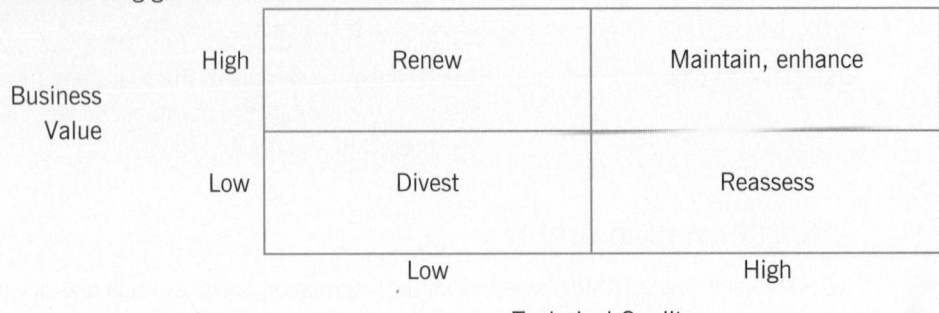

(a) A system of poor quality and little value should be **disposed of** (divest).

(b) A system of high business value and low technical quality should be **renewed (**invested in). An important system of low quality carries a high business risk.

(c) A system of high quality but low business value should be **reassessed**. Is the system meeting an information need? Why is it under-utilised?

(d) High quality systems with a high business value should be **maintained** to preserve the high quality, and if possible **enhanced** in the quest for competitive advantage.

Establishing where to place systems on the grid is the difficult part. Consultation with system users and those for formulating and implementing information system strategy would be undertaken to form an opinion of each system. Again, judgements are subjective.

2.6.2 The strategic grid

The importance of IS/IT to an organisation was studied by *McFarlan and McKenney* in 1983.

They devised a matrix designed to show the level of dependence on IS/IT within an organisation. The grid classifies four levels of dependence.

Strategic importance of **planned** information systems	High	Turnaround	Strategic
	Low	Support	Factory
		Low	High

Strategic importance of **current** information systems

(a) Organisations in the **strategic** quadrant currently depend on IS/IT for competitive advantage, and expect to continue to do so.

(b) Organisations in the **turnaround** quadrant do not currently view IS/IT as having strategic importance, but expect IS/IT will be strategically important in the future.

(c) Organisations in the **support** quadrant see no strategic value in IS/IT.

(d)   Organisations in the **factory** quadrant sees IS/IT as strategically significant at the moment, but predict this will not be the case in the future.

2.6.3 Applications portfolio

The strategic grid is interesting, but of limited use for detailed planning. *Peppard* developed it into the **applications portfolio**. This is used to analyse the strategic impact of **individual applications** within an organisation. It therefore is intended to offer more detailed analysis.

		Low	High
Strategic importance of individual applications in the predicted **future** competitive environment	**High**	High potential	Strategic
	Low	Support	Key operational

Strategic importance of individual applications
in the **current** competitive environment

(a)   **Support applications** are not critical to business success, but are designed to improve the productivity and efficiency of the internal activities of an organisation. Examples include an accounting system, or a payroll package.

(b)   **Key operational applications** support established core business activities. A production planning system is a good example, inventory control is another example. These are critical for a business to maintain its performance relative to its competitors.

(c)   **Strategic applications** are vital to the organisation's future success. They seek to gain competitive advantage through innovation in support of business strategies. Finance/service companies are becoming increasingly dependent on information systems and technology.

(d)   **High potential applications** are applications likely to have a significant impact in the future environment. They are often innovative. However, a business must be careful not to invest too much too quickly in these systems in case there is no market acceptance. A supermarket on-line ordering application is an example, an expert system is another example.

Section summary

Information strategy can be divided into **information systems strategy**, **information technology strategy** and **information management strategy**. The strategic significance of information requires that information itself be managed strategically so that the systems, the technology and the information support the business' overall strategic policy.

IT has the potential to **transform competition** in three ways: its effect on the **five competitive forces**, its potential for implementing **generic strategies**, and its contribution to the **emergence of completely new businesses**. However, IT strategy needs to support the overall business strategy.

3   Information sources and management

Introduction

Data and information come from sources both **inside** and **outside** an organisation. An organisation's information systems should be designed so as to obtain – or **capture** – all the relevant data and information required.

3.1 Internal information

Capturing data and information from **inside** the organisation involves designing a system for collecting or measuring data and information which sets out procedures for:

- What data and information is collected
- How frequently
- How data and information is processed, filed and communicated
- By whom
- By what methods

The accounting records

The accounting ledgers provide an excellent source of information regarding what has happened in the past. This information may be used as a basis for predicting future events.

3.2 External information

Formal collection of data from outside sources includes the following.

(a) A company's **tax specialists** will be expected to gather information about changes in tax law and how this will affect the company.

(b) Obtaining information about any new legislation on health and safety at work, or employment regulations, must be the responsibility of a particular person – for example the company's **legal expert** or **company secretary** – who must then pass on the information to other managers affected by it.

(c) Research and development (R & D) work often relies on information about other R & D work being done by another company or by government institutions. An **R & D official** might be made responsible for finding out about R & D work in the company.

(d) **Marketing managers** need to know about the opinions and buying attitudes of potential customers. To obtain this information, they might carry out market research exercises.

Informal gathering of information from the environment occurs naturally, consciously or unconsciously, as people learn what is going on in the world around them – perhaps from newspapers, television reports, meetings with business associates or the trade press.

Organisations hold external information such as invoices, letters, advertisements and so on **received from customers and suppliers**. But there are many occasions when an active search outside the organisation is necessary.

KEY TERM

The phrase ENVIRONMENTAL SCANNING is often used to describe the process of gathering external information, which is available from a wide range of sources.

Sources of external information include:

(a) The government

(b) Annual reports and press statements of competitors or other firms

(c) Advice or information bureaux

(d) Consultants

(e) Newspaper and magazine publishers

(f) Market research and other report, for example from Mintel or the Economist Intelligence Unit

(f) Libraries and information services

(g) Increasingly businesses can use each other's systems as sources of information, for instance via extranets or electronic data interchange (EDI)

(h) **Electronic sources** of information are becoming increasingly important

(i)   For some time there have been 'viewdata' services such as **Prestel** offering a very large bank of information gathered from organisations such as the Office for National Statistics, newspapers and the British Library. **Topic** offers information on the stock market. Companies like **Reuters** operate primarily in the field of provision of information.

(ii)   The **Internet** is a vast source of information. A number of journals and articles are now published on line, and many organisations now also display information about themselves on their home pages.

Exam skills

Information is only useful to an organisation if it is relevant to the organisation's situations and activities.

If you are asked to recommend sources of information for an organisation, make sure the sources you recommend are both practical and relevant to the context of the organisation style

Section summary

An information system should be designed to obtain information from **all relevant sources** – both internal and external – so that managers have the information they need to make properly informed strategic decisions.

4   Information for planning and control

Introduction

In order for it to be useful, control information must aid the decision-making process.

KEY TERM

STRATEGIC PLANNING is a process of deciding on objectives of the organisation, on changes in these objectives, on the resources used to attain these objectives and on the policies that are to govern the acquisition, use and disposition of these resources.

Strategic decision making:

- Is medium– to **long-term**
- Involves high levels of **uncertainty** and risk (the future is unpredictable)
- Involves situations that **may not recur**
- Deals with **complex** issues

KEY TERM

OPERATIONAL CONTROL ensures that specific tasks are carried out effectively and efficiently. It focuses on individual tasks, and is carried out within the strictly defined guidelines issued by strategic planning and tactical control decisions.

4.1 The decision-making process

The stages in making a decision are as follows.

   Problem recognition.

   Problem definition and structuring.

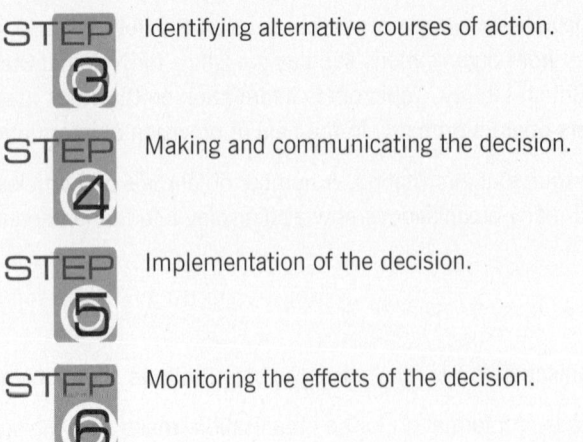

STEP 3   Identifying alternative courses of action.

STEP 4   Making and communicating the decision.

STEP 5   Implementation of the decision.

STEP 6   Monitoring the effects of the decision.

Information and decision-making

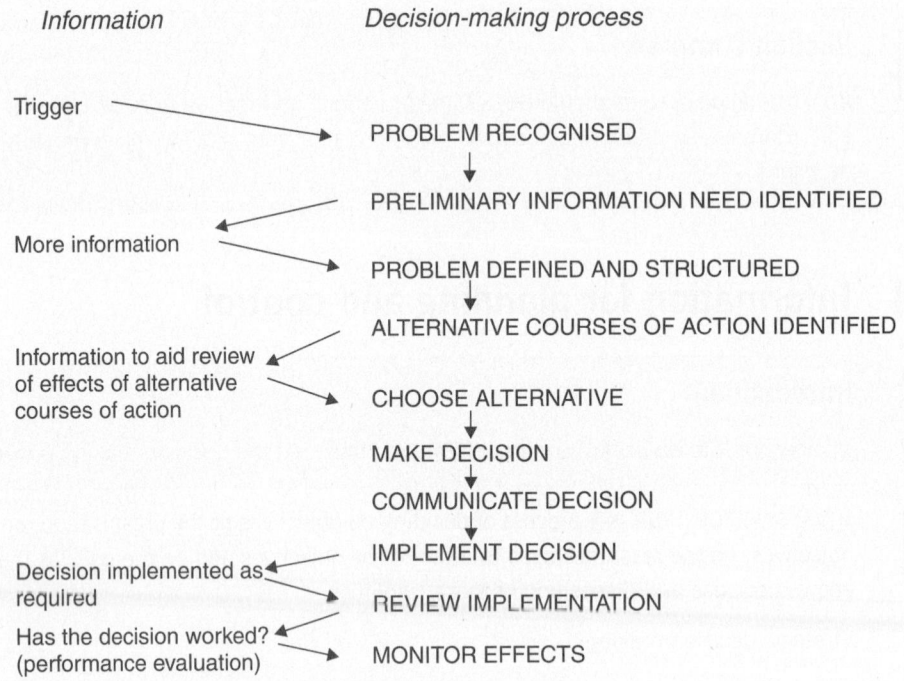

4.1.1 Problem recognition

Decisions are not made without **information**. The decision-maker needs to be informed of a problem in the first place. This is sometimes referred to as the **decision trigger**.

4.1.2 Problem definition and structuring

Normally **further information** is then required. This further information is **analysed** so that the problem can be **defined** precisely.

Consider, for example, a company with falling sales. The fall in sales would be the **trigger**. **Further information** would be needed to identify where the deficiencies were occurring. The company might discover that sales of product X in area Y are falling, and the problem can be **defined** as:

'Decline of sales of product X in area Y due to new competitor: how can the decline be reversed?'

One of the purposes of **defining** the problem is to identify the **relationships** between the **various factors** in it, especially if the problem is complex.

4.1.3 Identifying alternative courses of action

Where alternative courses of action are identified, **information** is needed about the likely effect of each, so they can be assessed.

As a simple example, if our company wishes to review the price of product X in area Y, information will be needed as to the effect of particular price levels on demand for the product. Such information can include external information such as market research (demand at a particular price) and the cost of the product, which can be provided internally.

4.1.4 Making and communicating the decision

The decision is **made** after review of the information relating to alternatives. However, the decision is useless if it is not **communicated**. So, in our example, if the **marketing director** decides to lower the price of product X and institute an intensive **advertising** campaign, nothing will happen unless the advertising department is informed, and also the **manufacturing** department, who will have to prepare new packaging showing the lower price.

4.1.5 Implementation of the decision

The decision is then **implemented**. For large-scale decisions (for example to relocate a factory 100 miles away from its current site), implementation may need substantial **planning**, detailed information and very clear communication.

4.1.6 Monitoring the effects of the decision

Once a decision has been implemented, information is needed so that its effects can be **reviewed**. For example, if a manufacturing organisation has installed new equipment in anticipation of savings in costs, then information will need to be obtained as to whether these are achieved in practice.

Exam skills

You could use this six-stage process as a means of analysing an exam question scenario and as a structure for your answer. What is the problem? What are the alternatives? How will your solution be implemented? And so on.

4.2 Risk and uncertainty in decision making

Decision making involves **making decisions now about what will happen in the future**. Obviously, decisions can turn out badly, or actual results can prove to be very different from the estimates on which the original decision was made because the necessary **information is not available** when the decision is made.

KEY TERMS

RISK involves situations or events which may or may not occur, but whose probability of occurrence can be calculated statistically and the frequency of their occurrence predicted from past records.

UNCERTAINTY involves situations or events whose outcome cannot be predicted with statistical confidence.

The management accountant, who must present relevant cost and revenue data to assist a manager who is about to make a decision, should consider two things.

(a) If the figures are **only slightly in doubt** or the amounts themselves are not material, a **best estimate** with a note that the figures are not certain may be good enough.

(b) If the amount or the **degree of uncertainty was large**, to present just one set of forecast figures would be unwise. For example, if a forecast of sales demand is 'anywhere between 1,000 and 10,000 units', it would be naive and unhelpful to prepare a **single point estimate** of sales – just one forecast figure – of, say, 5,000 units.

If the uncertainty in a situation does warrant special attention in the figures, the next problem is **how the uncertainty** in the figures should be presented.

There are various methods of bringing uncertainty and risk analysis into the evaluation of decisions. They include the following.

(a)   **Conservative estimates:** estimating outcomes in a conservative manner in order to provide a built-in safety factor.

(b)   Looking at the **worst possible** and **best possible** outcomes, as well as the most likely outcome, and reaching a decision which takes these into account.

(c)   **Sensitivity analysis:** any technique that tests decision options for their vulnerability to changes in a 'variable' such as expected sales volume.

(d)   Assessing **probabilities** and calculating, for each decision alternative, either the **expected value** of costs or benefits with, possibly, the standard deviation of the possible outcomes, or a probability distribution of the possible outcomes. **Decision trees** might be used to illustrate in a 'pictorial' or 'graphical' form the alternatives facing the decision-maker.

4.3 Perfect information

Obtaining more information first about what is likely to happen can sometimes reduce the uncertainty about the future outcome from taking a decision. We can categorise information depending upon **how reliable** it is likely to be for predicting what will happen in the future and hence for helping managers to make better decisions.

PERFECT INFORMATION is information that predicts the future with perfect accuracy.

KEY TERMS

IMPERFECT INFORMATION is information which cannot be guaranteed to be completely accurate. Almost all information is therefore imperfect – but may still be very useful.

Section summary

In order to be useful, control information must aid the decision-making process. However, information is often imperfect, because it is impossible to predict the future with perfect accuracy.

---

5   Knowledge management   3/11

Introduction

The aim of **knowledge management** is to capture, organise and make widely available all the knowledge the organisation possesses, whether in recorded form or in people's heads.

KEY TERMS

KNOWLEDGE MANAGEMENT is the systematic process of finding, selecting, organising, distilling and presenting information so as to improve comprehension of a specific areas of interest. Specific activities help focus the organisation on acquiring storing and utilising knowledge for such things as problem solving, dynamic learning, strategic planning and decision making.   *(CIMA Official Terminology)*

ORGANISATIONAL KNOWLEDGE is the collective and shared experience accumulated through systems, routines and activities of sharing across the organisation.   *(Johnson, Scholes and Whittington)*

Knowledge management is a relatively new concept in business theory. It is connected with the theory of the **learning organisation** and founded on the idea that knowledge is a major source of competitive advantage in business.

Studies have indicated that 20 to 30 percent of company resources are wasted because organisations are not aware of what knowledge they already possess. *Lew Platt,* Ex-Chief Executive of *Hewlett Packard,* has articulated this, saying 'If only HP knew what HP knows, we would be three times as profitable'.

Knowledge is thus seen as an important **resource** and may in itself constitute a **competence**: it can certainly **underpin** many competences, and knowledge management should be seen as a strategy to achieve competitive advantage, for example, through the sharing of cost reduction ideas across divisions, or through the diffusion of innovation.

In a knowledge management system, an organisation will appoint **knowledge managers** who are responsible for collecting and categorising knowledge, and encouraging other people in the organisation to use the available knowledge. The knowledge managers also monitor the use of knowledge in their organisation.

Some companies are now taking the idea of knowledge sharing one stage further and are adopting the practice of **knowledge brokering**. In knowledge brokering, companies look externally to find ways of improving internal business processes. In effect, knowledge brokering resembles benchmarking by allowing companies to find world-class solutions to problems, rather than having to invent their own solutions.

For example, a bank faced frequent complaints from customers about the length of the queues in its local branches. The bank staff responsible for reducing queuing times identified three potential sources of brokers: amusement parks, supermarkets and department stores. In each of these, it is important to keep queuing times under control. In time, the bank worked with an amusement park and a supermarket to redesign layout of the windows in its branches, and the way it deployed staff between back office and customer-facing windows at busy times.

5.1 Organisational learning

Organisational learning is particularly important in the increasing number of task environments that are both complex and dynamic. It becomes necessary for strategic managers to promote and foster a **culture that values intuition, argument from conflicting views, and experimentation**. A willingness to back ideas that are not guaranteed to succeed is another aspect of this culture: there must be freedom to make mistakes.

The aim of **knowledge management** is to exploit existing knowledge and to create new knowledge so that it may be exploited in turn. This is not easy. All organisations possess a great deal of data, but it tends to be unorganised and inaccessible. It is often locked up inside the memories of people who do not realise the value of what they know. This is what *Nonaka* calls **tacit knowledge**. Even when it is made **explicit**, (available to the organisation) by being recorded in some way, it may be difficult and time consuming to get at, as is the case with most paper archives. This is where knowledge management technology (discussed below) can be useful. Another important consideration is that tacit knowledge is inherently more **robust** (in the sense explained in the previous Section) than explicit knowledge.

From 'tacit' to 'explicit' knowledge

Nonaka and Takeuchi describe four ways in which knowledge moves within and between the tacit and explicit categories.

(a)   **Socialisation** is the informal process by which individuals share and transmit their tacit knowledge.

(b)   **Externalisation** converts tacit knowledge into explicit knowledge; this is a very difficult process to organise and control.

(c)   **Internalisation** is the learning process by which individuals acquire explicit knowledge and turn it into their own tacit knowledge.

(d)   **Combination** brings together separate elements of explicit knowledge into larger, more coherent systems; this is the arena for meetings, reports and computerised knowledge management systems.

5.2 The learning organisation

Continuing challenge to assumptions and search for improvement are typical of a **learning organisation**.

KEY TERM

A LEARNING ORGANISATION is capable of continual regeneration from the variety of knowledge, experience and skills of individuals within a culture that encourages mutual questioning and challenge around a shared purpose or vision.   *(Johnson, Scholes and Whittington)*

A learning organisation emphasises the **sharing of information and knowledge** both up and down the normal communication channels and horizontally through **social networks** and **interest groups**. It challenges notions of hierarchy and managers are facilitators rather than controllers. Such an organisation is inherently capable of change, because behaviours are adapted to reflect new knowledge. The concept has much in common with that of **logical incrementalism**. The challenge is to combine the advantages of rational planning with the resilience and adaptability provided by the learning approach.

5.3 Data, information and knowledge

There is an important conceptual hierarchy underpinning knowledge management. This distinguishes between **data, information** and **knowledge**. The distinctions are not clear-cut and, to some extent, are differences of degree rather than kind. An understanding of the terms is best approached by considering the relationships between them.

5.3.1 Data

We start with **data**. Data typically consists of individual facts, but in a business context may include more complex items such as opinions, reactions and beliefs. It is important to realise that a quantity of data, no matter how large, does not constitute **information**.

5.3.2 Information

Information is data that is **organised** in some useful way. For instance, an individual credit sale will produce a single invoice identifying the goods, the price, the customer, the date of the sale and so on. These things are data: their usefulness does not extend beyond the purpose of the invoice, which is to collect the sum due. Even if we possess a copy of every invoice raised during a financial year, we still only have data.

However, if we **process** that data we start to create information. For instance, a simple combination of analysis and arithmetic enables us to state total sales for the year, to break that down into sales for each product and to each customer, to identify major customers and so on. These are pieces of information: they are useful for the **management** of the business, rather than just inputs into its administrative systems.

5.3.3 Knowledge

Nevertheless, we still have not really produced any knowledge. Information may be said to consist of the relationships **between items of data**, as when we combine turnover with customer details to discover which accounts are currently important and which are not. We need to go beyond this in order to create knowledge.

The conceptual difference between data and information is fairly easy to grasp: it lies chiefly in the **processes** that produce the one from the other. The difference between information and knowledge is more complex and varies from setting to setting. This is not surprising, since knowledge itself is more complex than the information it derives from.

5.3.4 Differences between data, information and knowledge

A good starting point for understanding the difference is an appreciation of the importance of pattern: knowledge tends to originate in the **discovery of trends or patterns in information**. To return to our invoicing example, suppose we found that certain combinations of goods purchased were typical of certain customers. We could then build up some interesting customer profiles that would enhance our market segmentation and this in turn might influence our overall strategy, since we could identify likely prospects for cross-selling effort.

Another important aspect of the differences between data, information and knowledge is the relevance of **context**. Our sales invoice is meaningless outside its context; if you, as a marketing person, found an invoice in the office corridor, it would be little more than waste paper to you, though no doubt, the accounts people would like it back. However, if you found a list of customers in order of annual turnover, that would be rather more interesting from a marketing point of view. The information is **useful outside of its original context** of the accounts office.

This idea also applies to the difference between information and knowledge. If you were a visitor to a company and found a copy of the turnover listing, it would really only be useful to you if you were trying to sell the same sort of thing to the same customers. Its value outside its context would be small. However, if you found a marketing report that suggested, based on evidence, that customers were becoming more interested in quality and less interested in price, that would be applicable to a wide range of businesses, and possibly of strategic importance. This highlights another characteristic of knowledge: that it is a key **source of comparative advantage**.

Here is a table that summarises the progression from data to knowledge.

	Data	Information	Knowledge
Nature	Facts	Relationships between processed facts	Patterns discerned in information
Importance of context	Total	Some	Context independent
Importance to business	Mundane	Probably useful for management	May be strategically useful: Source of comparative advantage.

There is one final important point to note here and that is that the **progression** from data to knowledge is not the same in all circumstances. The scale is moveable and depends on the general complexity of the setting. Something may be **information** within its own context. Something similar may be **knowledge** in a different context. The difference will often be associated with the scale of operations. Take the example of a customer going into insolvent liquidation with $200,000 outstanding on its account. For a small supplier with an annual turnover of, say, $10 million, a bad debt of this size would be of strategic importance and might constitute a threat to its continued existence. Advance notice of the possibility would be valuable **knowledge**. However, for a company operating on a global scale, the bad debt write-off would be annoying but still only one item in a list of bad debts – **data**, in other words.

5.4 Other ideas about knowledge

Individuals acquire knowledge in a variety of ways including those listed below.

- Education and training
- Experience of work
- Observation of others
- Informal exchanges such as coaching and brain storming

Davenport and Prusak echo our earlier description of the relationship between data, information and knowledge and suggest that people **create knowledge from information by four processes**.

- **Comparison** with earlier experience
- **Consequences**: the implication of information
- **Connections**: relationships between items

- **Conversation**: discussion with others

5.5 Knowledge management (KM) systems

Recognition of the value of knowledge, and understanding of the need to organise data and make it accessible, have provoked the development of sophisticated IT systems. Such systems deal, by definition with **explicit knowledge**: that is, knowledge that is widely distributed.

Office automation systems are IT applications that improve productivity in an office. These include word processing and voice messaging systems.

Groupware is 'a collection of tools to assist collaborative work in an organisation'.

(CIMA Official Terminology)

Groupware products are designed to assist communication between members of a group, and capture information that the group is working with.

In a sales context, for instance, it would provide a facility for recording and retrieving all the information relevant to individual customers, including notes of visits, notes of telephone calls and basic data like address, credit terms and contact name. These items could be updated by anyone who had contact with a customer and would then be available to all sales people.

Groupware also provides such facilities as discussion databases and message boards, appointment scheduling, to-do lists, and jotters. Lotus Notes is a good example of a groupware product.

Workflow systems

KEY TERM

'A WORKFLOW is a series of tasks, which must be performed in order to achieve a specific result of outcome in an organisation.'   *(CIMA Official Terminology)*

For example, in order to purchase a new piece of equipment, a department may need to get some quotes from suppliers, prepare a business case, raise a purchase order (once the business case is approved) and match the purchase order to supplier invoice before approving the invoice for payment.

In a manual system, there is a chance that documents can get lost or out of order. Automated workflow systems avoid such problems by enabling documents to be moved over a network or maintained in a single database, which the appropriate users have access to at the required time. An automated workflow system can also include reminders which alert staff (or managers) when actions become due.

Intranet

An intranet is an internal network used to share information using Internet technology and protocols. The **firewall** surrounding an intranet fends off unauthorised access from outside the organisation. Each employee has a browser, used to access a server computer that holds corporate information on a wide variety of topics, and in some cases also offers access to the Internet. Applications include company newspapers, induction material, procedure and policy manuals and internal databases.

(a)   Savings accrue from the **elimination of storage**, **printing** and **distribution of documents** that can be made available to employees online.

(b)   Documents online are often **more widely used** than those that are kept filed away, especially if the document is bulky (eg manuals) and needs to be searched. This means that there are improvements in productivity and efficiency.

(c)   It is much easier to **update information in electronic form**.

Extranet

An extranet is a collaborative network which uses internet technology to join organisations, for example to link businesses with their suppliers. Extranets may be divided into **intronets** and **supranets**.

Intronet

When access to an intronet is extended to trusted external agencies, such as suppliers and customers, it becomes an **intronet**. The intronet's system content and functionality are under the control of the organisation that provides it. Intronets allow suppliers and customers to again privileged access to data held by the host. This may form the basis of a long-term relationship if the external user becomes dependent on the system's information content

Supranet

A **supranet** differs from an intronet in that it is set up in a co-operative fashion and control is not exercised by a single host. The aim is to insure the overall efficiency of the consortium of entities concerned.

Security is a major issue for extranets and may require firewalls, server management, encryption and the issue of digital certificates.

Expert system

An **expert system** is a computer program that captures **human expertise** in a limited domain of knowledge. Such software uses a knowledge base that consists of facts, concepts and the relationships between them and uses pattern-matching techniques to solve problems. For example, many financial institutions now use expert systems to process straightforward loan applications. The user enters certain key facts into the system such as the loan applicant's name and most recent addresses, their income and monthly outgoings, and details of other loans. The system will then:

(a)   Check the facts given against its **database** to see whether the applicant has a good previous credit record.

(b)   Perform **calculations** to see whether the applicant can afford to repay the loan.

(c)   Make a **judgement** as to what extent the loan applicant fits the lender's profile of a good risk (based on the lender's previous experience).

(d)   **A decision is then suggested**, based on the results of this processing.

IT systems can be used to store vast amounts of data in accessible form. A **data warehouse** receives data from operational systems, such as a sales order processing system, and stores it in its most fundamental form, without any summarisation of transactions. Analytical and query software is provided so that reports can be produced at any level of summarisation and incorporating any comparisons or relationships desired.

The value of a data warehouse is enhanced when **datamining** software is used. True datamining software **discovers previously unknown relationships** and provides insights that cannot be obtained through ordinary summary reports. These hidden patterns and relationships constitute **knowledge**, as defined above, and can be used to guide decision making and to predict future behaviour. Datamining is thus a contribution to organisational learning. (See Section 7 for more detail on data warehouses and data mining.)

The American retailer Wal-Mart discovered an unexpected relationship between the sale of nappies and beer! Wal-Mart found that both tended to sell at the same time, just after working hours, and concluded that men with small children stopped off to buy nappies on their way home, and bought beer at the same time. Logically, therefore, if the two items were put in the same shopping aisle, sales of both should increase. Wal-Mart tried this and it worked.

The following table is an amended version of our earlier table distinguishing data, information and knowledge. This one includes the relevant IT systems:

	Data	Information	Knowledge
Nature	Facts	Relationships between processed facts	Patterns discerned in information
Importance of context	Total	Some	Context independent
Importance to business	Mundane	Probably useful for management	May be strategically useful
Relevant IT systems	Office automation Data warehouse	Groupware Expert systems Report writing software Intranet	Datamining Intranet Expert systems

However, note that knowledge management is not just about IT systems. A successful knowledge management implementation must also involve people and processes; for example, changing the corporate culture to encourage knowledge sharing.

5.6 A strategy for knowledge management

An organisation that wishes to exploit its knowledge resource strategically should take a strategic approach.

A **top-down** strategy uses the **overall strategic plan** to identify the areas in which knowledge can be best exploited.

A **bottom-up** strategy is based on **research into existing key business processes** in order to determine important needs and issues.

However, in terms of actually developing and implementing a knowledge management strategy, there are five main steps to consider:

(a) **Support from senior management.** Senior management support will be needed, not only to provide the necessary **resources** and to lead the development of a knowledge-based culture, but also because if senior managers are not seen to be supporting the strategy then other staff will not do so either.

(b) **Installing the IT infrastructure**. IT hardware and software will need to be acquired to ensure that the organisation has the capabilities to **capture, store and communicate knowledge**.

(c) **Developing the databases**. Advanced databases and database management systems may need to be developed, with the details of their design and structure being tailored to the type of knowledge the organisation is looking to capture.

(d) **Develop a sharing culture**. Knowledge is widely known to represent **power**, and staff are likely to want to hoard the knowledge they have already accumulated, rather than to share it. A **culture** of **knowledge sharing** must be developed.

(e) **Capturing and using the knowledge**. Existing knowledge needs to be capture and recorded in the databases. Staff then need to be trained how to use the databases and encouraged to do so.

Importantly, however, although there is an IT element to knowledge management systems and their infrastructure, a knowledge management strategy need not be IT-driven. **IT should support rather than dominate the strategy**. The **cultural aspects** of a knowledge management strategy (particularly encouraging staff to share knowledge) are likely to be just as critical to its success as the IT elements.

5.7 The benefits of knowledge management

As well as increasing an organisation's ability to compete and add value by virtue of its **greater knowledge base**, knowledge management may also improve productivity through higher workforce **motivation**.

Also, if staff are encouraged to use knowledge this can help **improve efficiency**, and possibly lead to greater **innovation**. After all, the staff who work on a process are best placed to see whether that process could be improved, rather than management always telling them what to do.

5.7.1 Potential issues in implementing a knowledge management system

Structure and culture – The current structure and culture of an organisation may not be conducive to sharing knowledge; for example, if there is little communication between departments in an organisation, or if staff are reluctant to share knowledge for fear that it will reduce their power within the organisation. These inherent barriers will have to be overcome in order for the system to be successful.

Technological infrastructure – If an organisation does not have a suitable network which will allow information to be stored and accessed, one will have to be installed before knowledge can be shared across the organisation. There may be significant costs associated with installing such a network.

Incompatible systems and sources of information – Problems could arise if some divisions or departments record data or information in systems which are incompatible with those used by other divisions or departments. Such a situation will mean that data or information will have to be transferred into a new common format before they can be shared; but there is a risk that errors or omissions could result from the resulting conversion process.

Equally, it is possible that some information is not stored in a digital form at all, and so the organisation will have to decide how this material can be indexed and archived such that it can be accessed if it is needed in future.

Resistance to change – Staff in different areas of an organisation may already have their own preferred ways of organising data. However, this may not be compatible with the common format in which data is being held on the network. Staff may be reluctant to change their current practices, particularly if they are not given adequate training in any new systems they are required to use, and if they are not given sufficient time to adapt to them.

Section summary

There is a hierarchy between **data**, **information** and **knowledge**, and knowledge is the most useful as a source of competition advantage.

Knowledge management aims to exploit existing knowledge and create new knowledge which in turn can be exploited.

All organisations possess a great deal of data, but much of it is disorganised and inaccessible. Knowledge management technology helps structure data in a way that makes it easily accessible so that it can be used to support knowledge.

6 Databases and models

Introduction

A database is a collection of data organised to service many applications. The database provides convenient access to data for a wide variety of users and user needs.

The way in which data is held on a system affects the ease by which the data is able to be accessed and manipulated. Many modern software packages are built around a database. A database provides a comprehensive set of data for a number of different users.

KEY TERMS

A DATABASE is a collection of data organised to service many applications. The database provides convenient access to data for a wide variety of users and user needs.

A DATABASE MANAGEMENT SYSTEM (DBMS) is the software that centralises data and manages access to the database. It is a system which allows numerous applications to extract the data they need without the need for separate files.

6.1 The characteristics of a database system

(a) **Shared**. Different users are able to access the same data for their own processing applications. This removes the need for duplicating data on different files.

(b) **Controls** to preserve the **integrity** of the database. Users should not be able to alter the data on file so as to **spoil** the database records for other users. However, users must be able to make **valid** alterations to the data.

(c) **Flexibility.** The database system should provide for the **needs of different users**, who each have their own processing requirements and data access methods. The database should be capable of **evolving** to meet **future** needs.

6.2 Advantages and disadvantages

The **advantages** of a database system are as follows.

(a) Avoidance of unnecessary duplication of data

It recognises that data can be used for many purposes but only needs to be input and stored once.

(b) **Multi-purpose data**

From (a), it follows that although data is input once, it can be used for several purposes.

(c) **Data for the organisation as a whole, not just for individual departments**

The database concept encourages management to regard data as a resource that must be properly managed just as any other resource. Database systems encourage management to analyse data, relationships between data items, and how data is used in different applications.

(d) **Consistency**

Because data is only held once, it is easier to ensure that it is up-to-date and consistent across departments.

(e) **New uses for data**

Data is held independently of the programs that access the data. This allows greater flexibility in the ways that data can be used. New programs can be easily introduced to make use of existing data in a different way.

(f)   **New applications**

Developing new application programs with a database system is easier as a central pool of data is already available to be drawn upon.

(g)   **Flexibility**

Relational systems are extremely flexible, allowing information from several different sources to be combined and providing answers to ad-hoc queries.

The **disadvantages** of a database systems relate mainly to security and control.

(a)   There are potential problems of **data security** and **data privacy**. Administrative procedures for data security should supplement software controls.

(b)   Since there is only one set of data, it is essential that the data should be **accurate** and free from corruption. A back-up routine is essential.

(c)   Initial **development costs** may be high.

(d)   For hierarchical and network structures, the access paths through the data must be **specified in advance**.

(e)   Both hierarchical and network systems require intensive **programming** and are **inflexible**.

6.3 Using databases for planning

Planning will always involve an element of risk – as it deals with the **future**. Databases can at least ensure that information we have about the present and the past is available to aid planning. Organised data retrieval techniques make the data available in an effective way. In a world in which decisions must be ever more rapid, it is crucial to be able to access diverse, complex, multiple data sources and to analyse them to rapidly and correctly extract the knowledge they contain.

Databases can be used in conjunction with a variety of tools and techniques, eg Decision Support Systems, Executive Information Systems, data warehousing, and data mining.

CASE STUDY

Using models for strategic planning

Financial and business planning is one of the most important activities an organisation will undertake. Often organisations use spreadsheets as the basis for their financial planning. However, spreadsheets were never designed for planning, although they have inherited the tasks. There may often be a benefit from using dedicated software to support planning decisions, rather than relying on spreadsheets to do the job.

CASE STUDY

Continental Airlines

Forecasting is critical to the airline industry. Managers at major airlines track many indicators and statistics—fluctuations in travel demand, oil prices, and changing currency rates—to make educated business decisions. All these data have significant impact on the costs of doing business and the profitability of a company.

The environment is very dynamic, so senior management need up-to-date information and forecasts, reflecting the rapid changes in the business and economic environments.

The US airline Continental Airlines traditionally recorded key performance indicators such as load factors, fuel efficiency, and on-time rates in Excel spreadsheets. This necessitated the time-consuming manual creation of thousands of monthly reports to get business decision-makers the information they needed.

There was a huge price for such inefficiency. Because they spent so much time preparing reports and information, the financial planning and analysis team at Continental spent less than 20 percent of its time actually on analysis. This was much less than desired.

Moreover, the dependence on spreadsheets meant that much of the business logic used to prepare the numbers remained in individual employees' heads and on their desktop computers.

The head of Financial Planning and Analysis at Continental pointed out: "Excel is a great tool—I don't think anyone can do without it. But Excel is just a spreadsheet. It shouldn't be a database tool, it shouldn't be a reporting tool, and it shouldn't be a communication tool."

In 2008, although travel demand fell and oil prices skyrocketed, Continental executives saw an opportunity to change systems and processes to navigate the challenging times and emerge more efficient than ever.

They moved away from relying exclusively on Excel and implemented a suite of Hyperion EPM applications.

Within weeks of going live, Continental saw significant new efficiencies in analysing industry trends and performing strategic analysis. Additionally, Continental achieved the goal of generating an 18-month rolling forecast every month, updating executive insight and enabling better decision-making. The financial planning and analysis team increased time spent on analysis by 80 percent. Uploading data for reports on actuals was slashed from four hours to a matter of minutes. And moving critical data off of both people's laptops and network storage also represented a huge improvement in data security.

However, potentially the most important benefit was the information and insights which became available for senior management. The goal for the Financial planning team at Continental is simple: to give senior management the quickest, most complete picture of business conditions possible.

The head of Financial Planning and Analysis sums this up as follows: "Our CFO needs to be able to come in every day, sign on to his dashboard, click on the button and see, 'What's my outlook as of yesterday? What's changed since the prior day?"

In the fast-changing airline industry, having that insight could be crucial for the success of the business.

6.4 Databases and marketing

The growth of the internet and e-commerce are allowing customers to build up information about online customers in databases. E-mailing useful and relevant information to customers helps build stronger relationships with customers and may encourage them to make additional purchases.

We looked at database marketing in more detail in Chapter 8..

 Section summary

Databases provide convenient access to data for a wide variety of uses and users needs. Databases can be used in strategic planning, and play an important role in database marketing.

7   E-commerce   5/10

 Introduction

Very few businesses can afford to ignore the potential of the Internet for driving forward strategy and activity at all levels. Internet usage can range from use of email at one extreme to the almost entirely virtual business model represented by audio and video downloads at the other

E-commerce challenges traditional business models, makes global markets available to small businesses, transforms transparency of pricing, and offers new opportunities for market segmentation.

KEY TERM

E-COMMERCE is the use of electronic techniques, including the Internet, to sell products and services.

(CIMA Official Terminology)

The detail of this definition is important, because it highlights the distinction between e-commerce and e-marketing. E-commerce involves selling products and services, whereas e-marketing involves using electronic techniques for solely for communication and promotion.

7.1 The Internet, e-commerce and the challenge to traditional business models

There are several features of the Internet which make it radically different from traditional 'offline' business models.

(a) It **challenges traditional business models** – because, for example, it enables product/service suppliers to interact directly with their customers, instead of using intermediaries (like high street retail shops, travel agents, insurance brokers, and conventional banks).

(b) Although the Internet is global in its operation, its benefits are not confined to large (or global) organisations. **Small companies** can move instantly into a global market place, either on their own initiative or as part of what is known as a 'consumer portal'.

(c) It offers a **new economics of information** – because, with the Internet, much information is free. Those with Internet access can view all the world's major newspapers and periodicals without charge.

(d) It supplies an almost incredible **level of speed** of communication, giving virtually instant access to organisations, plus the capacity to complete purchasing transactions within seconds.

(e) **24 hour access**. Customers have access to a website 24 hours a day, 7 days a week. So an online 'shop' is never closed.

(f) It has created **new and cheaper networks of communication** – between organisations and their customers (either individually or collectively), between customers themselves (through mutual support groups), and between organisations and their suppliers.

(g) It stimulates the appearance of **new intermediaries** and the disappearance of some existing ones. Businesses are finding that they can cut out the middle man, with electronic banking, insurance, publishing and printing as primary examples.

CASE STUDY

A university can put its reading list on a website and students wishing to purchase any given book can click directly through to an online bookseller such as Amazon.com. The university gets a commission; the online bookseller gets increased business; the student gets a discount. Everyone benefits except the traditional bookshop.

(h) It has led to **new business partnerships** through which small enterprises can gain access to customers on a scale which would have been viewed as impossible a few years ago.

(i) Work is becoming **independent of location**. Clerical, administrative and knowledge work can be done at any location. This can reduce establishment and travelling costs, especially if people work at home, but the loss of personal interaction can affect **motivation** and **job satisfaction**.

(j) The **nature of work** is changing since increased quantities of available data and more powerful methods of accessing analysing it mean that greater attention can be paid to customising product offerings to more precisely defined target segments.

(k) It promotes **transparent pricing** – because potential customers can readily compare prices not only from suppliers within any given country, but also from suppliers across the world.

(l)   It facilitates **personalised attention** – even if such attention is actually administered through impersonal, yet highly sophisticated IT systems and customer database manipulation.

(m)   It provides sophisticated **market segmentation** opportunities. Approaching such segments may be one of the few ways in which e-commerce entrepreneurs can create **competitive advantage**.

(n)   The web can either be a **separate** channel or a **complementary** channel to an existing 'offline' business.

(o)   A new phenomenon is emerging called **dynamic pricing**. Companies can rapidly change their prices to reflect the current state of demand and supply.

These new trends are creating **pressure** for companies. The main threat facing companies is that **prices will be driven down by consumers' ability to shop around**.

A key difference between e-commerce and 'traditional' commerce can also be seen from the 'role' of the consumer in marketing activity. In traditional marketing media, such as advertising and direct mail, the marketing message is initiated by the **supplier sending out a message** to potential customers. However, there is limited interaction with the customer. In electronic media, the **customer plays a much more active role**, for example visiting a website to find out information about a product or a supplier. There is a much greater degree of **interaction** between customer and supplier.

7.2 Varieties of e-commerce

E-commerce can be divided into four main categories.

B2B (Business-to-Business) – involves companies doing business with each other, as when manufacturers sell to distributors and wholesalers sell to retailers. Pricing is based on quantity of order and is often negotiable.

B2C (Business-to-Consumer) – involves businesses selling to the general public, typically through catalogues with **shopping cart software**.

C2B (Consumer-to-Business) – a consumer posts his project with a set budget online and within hours companies review the consumer's requirements and bid on the project. The consumer reviews the bids and selects the company that will complete the project.

C2C (Consumer-to-Consumer) – an excellent example of this is found at *eBay*, where consumers sell their goods and services to other consumers. Another technology that has emerged to support C2C activities is that of the payment intermediary *PayPal*. Instead of purchasing items directly from an unknown, un-trusted seller, the buyer can instead send the money to Pay Pal, who forward it to the vendor's account.

The transaction alternatives between businesses and consumers are shown in the matrix below:

		Delivery by	
		Business	Consumer
Exchange initiated by	Business	B2B Business models eg *BusyTrade.com*	B2C Business models eg *Amazon.com*
	Consumer	C2B Business models eg *Priceline.com*	C2C Business Models eg *eBay.com*

BPP LEARNING MEDIA

7.3 Market place channel structures

Channel structures are the means by which a manufacturer or selling organisation delivers products and services to its customers. The simplest channel structure is **direct**: the business deals directly with the customer without the assistance of any **intermediaries**. The more complex the channel structure, the more intermediaries (wholesalers and/or retailers) are used in the supply chain. Intermediaries offer a wide range of services and facilities: they include agents, traders, brokers, dealers, wholesalers/distributors and providers of specialised information.

The main changes to channel structures facilitated through the Internet include **disintermediation** (direct selling), **reintermediation** (new intermediaries) and **countermediation** (the creation of a new intermediary by an established company).

7.3.1 Disintermediation

Disintermediation is the removal of intermediaries in a supply chain that formerly linked a company to its customers. Instead of going through traditional distribution channels, with intermediaries such as a distributor, wholesaler, broker or agent, companies may now deal with every customer directly via the Internet.

Examples

You can already bypass publishers to get a book printed at tiny cost through self-publishing sites such as *Lulu.com*. Gambling is being changed by online sites arranging bets directly between individuals, not through bookmakers, with *Betfair* being the market leader in this respect.

Disintermediation process

Disintermediation may be initiated by **consumers** because they are aware of **supply prices** direct from the manufacturer or wholesaler. Alternatively, it may be instigated by the author or creator of a work, such as *Steven King* selling his books directly to the public. Similarly, when *Radiohead* issued their album In Rainbows in October 2007, it was offered as a download directly from the band's official website (rather than being produced by a record company).

Disintermediation has seen the emergence of third party aggregators or buyer's clubs that link consumers with producers to obtain lower prices.

Reverse auction sites that allow consumers to specify an item they wish to purchase, allowing producers and others to bid on the item.

Traditional value chain in publishing

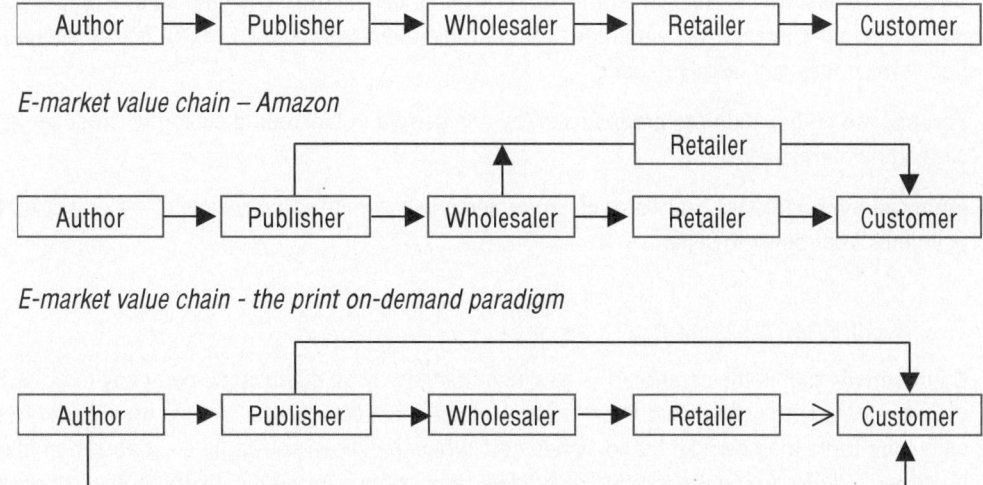

E-market value chain – Amazon

E-market value chain - the print on-demand paradigm

7.3.2 Reintermediation

Reintermediation is the establishment of new intermediary roles for traditional intermediaries that were disintermediated. In some cases, a new element of a supply chain simply replaces a single displaced element, such as Amazon.com replacing retailers. In other cases, a reintermediating entity replaces multiple supply chain elements. These new intermediaries do one of two things.

(a)   Provide customers with **new**, **important value-added services** not provided in the new direct customer-supplier relationship. An example is *Kelkoo* which is a shopping/price comparison search engine.

(b)   Provide customers with **more efficient means** of transacting business.

The ever-increasing number of 'hubs', 'portals', 'aggregators', 'clearinghouses' and 'exchanges' shows that entirely new ways of doing business are being created. Those organisations (or individuals) clever enough to recognise the opportunities provided by the Web and are reinventing themselves as 'cybermediaries' or 'infomediaries' – intermediaries offering value-added services to consumers and vendors over the Internet.

7.3.3 New types of intermediary

Search engines and directories – search engines, such as *Google* and *Alta Vista* provide search facilities based on data generated by software engines, that search the web. Directories such as *Yahoo* provide a general index of a large variety of different sites.

Search agents (Search bots) gather material from other sites. For example *Shopbot* searches across online shops.

Portals provide a gateway to the Web and may also offer **signposting**, selected **links** and other services to attract users. Examples of Web portals include *Excite, Google, MSN* and *Yahoo*. Variations on the portal as gateway are: a horizontal portal or user customised gateway (eg *my Yahoo*); a vertical portal or special interest portal eg, *CNET* – a portal for users interested in developments in IT; and an enterprise information portal, which is an organisation's home page for employees, including corporate info and selected links.

'E-tailers' or consumer shopping sites such as *Amazon*. While starting as simply a bookshop on the web it has added a variety of products and types of services. By contrast, *Tesco* is an offline retailer which is offering web-based order and delivery services.

Auction sites such as *eBay* support online auctions.

Publisher web sites are traffic generators that offer content of interest to consumers.

Virtual resellers are intermediaries that exist to sell to consumers. They are able to obtain products directly from manufacturers, who may hesitate to go directly to consumers for fear of **alienating retailers** upon which they still largely depend.

Forums, **fan clubs**, and **user groups** can play a large role in facilitating customer-producer feedback and supporting market research.

Financial intermediaries. Any form of e-commerce will require some means of making or authorising payments from buyer to seller.

7.3.4 Countermediation

Countermediation is the creation of a new intermediary by an established company in order to compete *via* e-business with established intermediaries. Examples include *B&Q* setting up *diy.com* to help people who want to do their own DIY, and *Opodo.com* which has been set up by a collaboration of nine European airlines. Countermediation also refers to possible partnerships with another independent intermediary eg, mortgage broker *Charcol*.

CASE STUDY

Airlines. The impact of the Internet is seen clearly in the transportation industry. Airlines now have a more effective way of bypassing intermediaries (ie travel agents) because they can give their customers immediate access to flight reservation systems. *EasyJet* introduced online bookings in April 1998, and within a year more than 50% of bookings were made using the website. By 2004, this figure had jumped to 98%, and now flights can only be booked over the Internet except during the three months immediately before the flight when telephone booking is also available

Travel agents. The Internet has also produced a new set of online travel agents who have lower costs because of their ability to operate without a High Street branch network. Their low-cost structure makes them a particularly good choice for selling low margin, cheap tickets for flights, package holidays, cruises and so forth.

In 2004 *British Airways* stopped paying commission to travel agents for flight bookings, intending to move to an entirely Internet-based system for bookings. In 2005 the European industry saw significant consolidation when the online travel agency *Travelocity*, bought *Lastminute.com*.

Tesco has operated on the internet since 1994 and is the UK's largest internet grocery business. In 2000 it formally launched its Tesco.com site and by 2009 annual sales had grown to £1.9 bn. In addition to its online grocery business, Tesco has also established Tesco Direct, its online marketplace for electrical appliances, home furnishings and other non-grocery products.

Financial services. The impact of the Internet is especially profound in the field of financial services. New intermediaries enable prospective customers to compare the interest rates and prices charged by different organisations for pensions, mortgages and other financial products. This means that the delivering companies are **losing control of the marketing** of their services, and there is a **downward pressure on prices**, especially for services which can legitimately be seen as mere commodities (eg house and contents insurance).

7.4 Disadvantages of e-commerce

E-commerce presents a range of **new management and organisational issues** compared to 'traditional' business.

E-commerce involves an unusual mix of people – security people, web technology people, designers, marketing people – and this can be very difficult to manage. The e-business needs supervision by expensive specialists.

In spite of phenomenal growth the market is still fuzzy and undefined. Many e-businesses have only recently reported making any **profit**, the best-known example being **Amazon.com** the Internet book-seller.

Unless the e-business is one started completely from scratch, any new technology installed will **need to link up with existing business systems**, which could potentially take years of programming. Under-estimating the time and effort involved is a common obstacle.

The international availability of a website means that the **laws of all countries** that transactions may be conducted from have to be considered. The legal issues surrounding e-commerce are complex and still developing.

7.5 The Internet in context

Commentators highlight so-called 'megatrends' which, coupled with the Internet, are changing the face of organisations:

(a) New **distribution channels**, revolutionising sales and brand management. In this respect, we can suggest that e-commerce may be increasing the **rivalry** between competitors in an industry.

(b) The continued **shift of power** towards the consumer. For example, the ability to compare prices directly between different online retailers increases the **bargaining power of customers**.

(c) **Growing competition** locally, nationally, internationally and globally. The internet removes some of the **barriers to entry** to an industry. For example, a 'shop' no longer has to incur overheads such as rent and rates because it can be set up online.

(d) An acceleration in the **pace of business**, and linked to this an increased automation of business transactions and workflows.

(e) The **transformation of companies** into 'extended enterprises' involving 'virtual teams of business, customer and supplier' working in collaborative partnerships.

(f) **Reduced importance of location**. The availability of internet connections is making the physical location where people work less important.

(g) A re-evaluation of how companies, their partners and competitors **add value** not only to themselves but in the wider environmental and social setting.

(h) Recognition of '**knowledge**' as a strategic asset.

Most observers and experts agree that a successful strategy for e-commerce cannot simply be bolted on to existing processes, systems, delivery routes and business models. Instead, management groups have, in effect, to start again, by asking themselves such **fundamental questions** as:

- What do customers want to buy from us?
- What business should we be in?
- What kind of partners might we need?
- What categories of customer do we want to attract and retain?

In turn, organisations can visualise the necessary changes at three interconnected levels.

Level 1   The simple **introduction of new technology** to connect electronically with employees, customers and suppliers (eg through an intranet, extranet or website).

Level 2   **Re-organisation** of the workforce, processes, systems and strategy – in order to make best use of the new technology.

Level 3   **Re-positioning** of the organisation to fit it into the emerging e-economy.

So far, very few companies have gone beyond levels (1) and (2). Instead, pure Internet businesses such as *Amazon.com* and *eBay* have emerged from these new rules: unburdened by physical assets, their competitive advantage lies in knowledge management and customer relationships.

CASE STUDY

Conventional thinking says that a company should pay no more to bring in a customer than the net present value of the stream of profits that the customer will subsequently generate. Yet in the e-commerce context, investors have often rewarded companies for customer acquisition without asking any questions about how quickly those customers may disappear. The evidence suggests that many 'dot.com' enterprises remain unable to achieve sustained profitability or indeed any profitability at all.

7.6 Building an 'e-commerce strategy'

A **strategy for e-commerce**, while not necessarily constituting the organisation's overall strategy, is likely to have wide implications and to involve and affect more than one function or department within the organisation. It should, therefore, be considered at the highest level of management and it should conform to the **standard criteria for strategic choice**: suitability, acceptability and feasibility.

7.6.1 Suitability

There are a few large organisations, such as Amazon, whose overall strategy is based on e-commerce. However, for most companies, e-commerce will be a **supplement to more traditional operations**, with the

website forming a supplementary medium for communication and sales. It is important that the e-commerce strategy supports the overall strategy. One way of approaching this would be to consider the **extended marketing mix** and the need for **balance**, **consistency** and **mutual support** between the elements.

A very simple example would be to consider the question of whether to confine the website to an essentially communications role, or to incorporate a fully featured on-line shopping facility. A specialist chain store dealing in, say, camping and outdoor equipment would expect to expand its market if it developed on-line shopping. On the other hand, a manufacturer of specialist luxury goods, such as the most expensive fountain pens, would probably have a policy of distributing through carefully selected retailers. It is unlikely that on-line shopping would appeal to the target market segment: they would probably enjoy the shopping experience and would want to try the products before they bought them.

7.6.2 Acceptability

The e-commerce strategy must be **acceptable to important stakeholders**. Distributors are particularly important here. Pursuing our luxury goods example we would expect that retailers chosen for their attractive premises, skilled and attentive staff and air of luxury would be unhappy to find their position usurped by a website.

7.6.3 Feasibility

Feasibility is a matter of **resources**. The fundamental resource is cash, but the availability of the **skilled labour** needed to establish and administer a website will be crucial to the e-commerce strategy. It may be appropriate to employ **specialist consultants** for these purposes.

Under this heading, we might identify the following points for consideration.

(a)   The first thing to do is to try to establish precise **objectives** for the new strategy element. It may not be possible to do this conclusively, and consideration of objectives may have to proceed alongside the processes outline below, all passing through several iterations.

(b)   An estimate and analysis of **costs** and **benefits** should be undertaken. This should cover all the possible options, such as what services are to be offered, whether a full catalogue is to be put online, whether Internet selling is envisaged, whether a search function is required and so on.

(c)   A detailed **budget** should be prepared, probably using estimates from the cost and benefit analysis. Where Internet selling is to be offered, pricing policy must be established: there is a theory that customers expect goods and services to be discounted when sold online, since they are aware that administrative costs are likely to be lower than in more traditional forms of distribution.

(d)   **Specific technical requirements**

- Web hosting software
- Server computers (more than one system to provide redundancy)

7.6.4 Launch

It may be appropriate to launch the website to a restricted number of potential customers in order to ensure that its functionality is satisfactory. This might be done on a regional basis, with promotion through appropriate press and TV channels. When a national launch is approved, it will be necessary to promote the website nationally and to ensure that the web address is included in all corporate stationery and display material.

7.6.5 e-commerce and e-marketing

Just as a marketing strategy needs to support the business strategy for a 'traditional' business model, so an organisation's marketing strategy needs to support its e-commerce strategy.

However, the interactive nature of e-commerce means that e-marketing has a number of characteristics which differentiate it from traditional marketing.

These can be summarised as **6 Is**:

*   **Independence of location** – global communications potentially allow access to markets that couldn't be reached before

*   **Industry structure** – redesigning business process; redrawing market segments

*   **Integration** – sharing customer feedback and customer requirements throughout the whole business

*   **Interactive** – customers can seek information and initiate dialogue rather than receiving marketing information

*   **Individualisation** – communications can be tailored to specific customers, rather than sending one standard message to everyone

*   **Intelligence** – information gathered about customer perceptions of products and services can be used to help shape marketing strategy.

We looked at e-marketing in more detail in the previous chapter, but it is important to be aware of the links between e-commerce and e-marketing.

Exam skills

Although an organisation can gain a number of benefits from having a website, not all websites have the same levels of functionality, or user-friendliness.

For example, is a website which simply allows customers to look at a range of products likely to have as much business benefit as one which also allows customers to make orders online?

If you are asked to advise how an organisation could benefit from having a website, or how it could benefit from improving its website, try to think of practical issues about the functionality of the website. However, also consider any issues it would need to address in making the improvements; for example, the potential security issues involved in taking online transactions.

Also, the design of the website itself could affect its effectiveness. Is it easy for users to navigate or search? Does it make it easy for users to contact the organisation (eg by email or phone)? What information does the website provide users (eg Frequently Asked Questions)? Does the website have any animations which brings its products and services to life? Do all users get the same information, or is there a 'members' section which can only be accessed via a username and password? Are viewers invited to provide an email address and then receive e-newsletters from the organisation? Can the website be viewed in different languages or is it restricted to one language?

Section summary

The **internet and e-commerce** allow organisations to challenge traditional business models, and have changed the relationship between vendors and customers. However, a business' e-commerce strategy needs to be consistent with its overall business strategy.

8   Web 2.0 technologies and business strategy

Introduction

Technologies known collectively as Web 2.0 have spread rapidly among consumers in recent years. As the popularity of Web 2.0 has grown, companies have noted the way consumers have engaged with the technologies, and have realised this could have important business implications – particularly in relation to marketing and new product development strategies.

Web 2.0 technologies can provide firms with opportunities in a range of activities – from market research, marketing, collaboration, innovation and design.

The phrase 'Web 2.0' has become synonymous with a new generation of web technologies and softwares, and, possibly more importantly, their impact on how web users interact with content, applications and each other. Web 2.0 allows people across the world to connect with each other 24 hours a day, 365 days a year.

8.1 User experience and participation

Web 2.0 allows internet users (and potential customers for businesses) to no longer simply be recipients of information, but to participate in the creation, sharing and evaluation of content. In other words, users can actively take part in 'many-to-many' communications. A crucial aspect of Web 2.0 is that it focuses on **user experience** and **participation**.

Again this is important for businesses, Web 2.0 allows firms of all sizes to engage with customers, staff and suppliers in new ways. In particular, it allows firms to have a more customer-focused approach to new product development – because customers can actually be involved in the design of the new products.

Web 2.0 has highlighted the significance of **dynamic social interactions** in the environment, rather than considering business and business transactions as a set of static business processes.

We have already identified the **importance of knowledge** to businesses, and Web 2.0 plays an important role in this 'knowledge economy' through supporting creativity, **collaboration**, **knowledge sharing**, and ultimately, innovation.

The idea of **collaboration** is also very important when considering how Web 2.0 technologies could affect business strategies. The potential impact could be huge if organisations find it becomes as efficient to do business through collaborating **outside** the organisation's structure, rather than doing business within the organisation's own structure.

In effect, collaboration is an extension of the idea of **outsourcing**, although whereas in outsourcing specific processes are outsourced **to** specific companies, in collaboration anybody can contribute to the discussion in progress. (The collaborative online encyclopaedia – Wikipedia – is probably the best known illustration of this.)

We will now look at some of the key aspects of Web 2.0.

Web-based communities

Probably the most popular aspect of Web 2.0 has been social networking sites, such as *Facebook*, which now has more than 500 million unique visitors.

Web-based communities are enhanced by:

*   **Social networking** – Social Networks (such as *Facebook* and *MySpace)* allow users to make contact with other users. As well as mass-market social networks, a number of smaller, more focused **niche social networks** have also begun to emerge. The value of these sites is that they allow users to connect with others whom they share a common interest with. For example,

LinkedIn is a network for business people looking to build business contacts, and also to advertise their skills and experience to potential employers or clients.

- **Blogs** – Blogs provide an easy way for users to publish their own content. Blogs are usually text based. Users can publish audio and visual content as podcasts, and the growth of sites such as *YouTube* illustrates how popular podcasts have become.

  The microblogging site, *Twitter*, provides a platform for people who want to publish very short blogs – of up to 140 characters each.

- **Wikis** – Wikis allow user groups to collaborate in contributing and editing content. *Wikipedia*, the collaborative online encyclopaedia is the best known example of this

- **Instant messaging** – This allows real time conversations between two or more participants using pop-up dialogue boxes (eg instant messaging is now available in *Skype*)

These web-based communities mean that web **users are now participants in the web experience** rather than simply being observers. Moreover, these communities allow people to get to know each other and to interact, regardless of their physical, geographical location.

A key aspect behind Web 2.0 is **open source software**. Open source software such as Linux (the software which Google runs on) is free to use. Because open source services are free, they can reach a far greater number of people than services which users have to pay for.

8.2 Socialisation of knowledge sharing

Web 2.0 technologies encourage the socialisation of knowledge sharing through:

- **Tagging of information** – A tag is a keyword assigned by a user to describe a piece of information (such as a file, an image, or an internet bookmark). Tagging is a key feature of many Web 2.0 applications and is commonly used on file storing and file sharing sites. Once a file has been tagged, the tag allows it to be found again when a relevant search enquiry is made.

  Tags are examples of **metadata**, which is 'data about other data'. The title, author and publication date of a book are examples of metadata about a book, and this data could help a user find the book he or she is looking for.

  Tagging also highlights an important point which businesses need to consider. The new technologies mean that the amount of information on the internet is rising constantly. However, information is no use if it can't be found. Search Engine Optimisation is therefore increasingly important for businesses – making sure web the information on the businesses website is findable and relevant.

- **Mashups** – A mashup is a web publication that combines data from more than one source into a singe web page. For example, a restaurant review website, could take the location details of all the local restaurants in an area and map them onto a single *Google* map page.

- **Feedback** on sources of information

- **Promoting collective intelligence** – Collective intelligence refers to both structured and unstructured group collaboration. It describes the way people's opinions or behaviours can be aggregated so that others can learn from their collective decision making.

  The online auction site *eBay* uses collective intelligence to let potential buyers see how efficient and trustworthy vendors are. Equally, *Amazon* and a number of online sites include product reviews allowing people who have purchased an item to comment on the item and rate its performance.

  Amazon also uses collective intelligence to make product recommendations based on purchasing patterns. When a user selects an item to buy, he or she is presented with a list of other items

purchased by people who have already bought the current selection, which may encourage a user to make follow up purchases.

User generated content (UGC): websites can now have sections of content created by their readers. One of the main ideas behind Web 2.0 technologies is that users can now generate the content of sites themselves, and the technologies allow users to create, capture and share information across the web. The video streaming website, *YouTube*, and, the image and video hosting website *Flickr*, are popular examples of content sharing sites.

Consumer generated content (CGC): websites can now contain shared feedback from consumers; for example, product reviews. This has important implications for businesses, because it means customers can communicate with other (potential) customers very easily. If a customer receives poor customer service, they can now tell everyone else about it, which could damage the business' reputation, and lead to a decline in sales.

The most widely known example of CGC is the user reviews developed by Amazon noted above. Many customers review users' product reviews when assessing prospective purchases.

In this respect, an important feature of Web 2.0 technologies is that they use **open standards** to enable connectivity between applications.

(Open standards mean that the rights normally reserved for copyright holders are provided in the public domain. Open standards are publicly available, and are developed, approved and maintained via a collaborative and consumer–driven process. Consequently users can share technologies with each other.)

Collaboration, based on shared knowledge can be assisted by:

- Virtual team management
- File sharing
- Collaborative working - both internally and with partners, suppliers and customers. This improves the ability to customise and integrate applications.

8.2.1 Enterprise 2.0

Enterprise 2.0 technology enables businesses to work across the web, regardless of location. This will increase the use of virtual teams (involving people inside and outside a business) to identify and exploit new business opportunities.

Enterprise Resource Planning software (ERP) was an important development in business technologies, allowing business systems to be integrated and automated. But a potential danger with ERP software is that it can understate the role that people still have to play in business. Even when systems are automated, people are still required to identify new opportunities for growth, or to intervene when the systems flag up problems.

In an increasingly knowledge-based society, people are critical to the development, evolution, and overall success of a business. Enterprise 2.0 recognises this and recognises that **businesses need people**, **processes** and **technology** all working together to be successful.

8.3 Evolution of web services

Although would be wrong to think of Web 2.0 as simply being a software upgrade from some kind of 'Web 1.0' it is useful to look at the evolution of Web 2.0 web functionalities and services compared to the first generation equivalents.

Web 2.0	Web 1.0 (predecessor)
Wikipedia (collaborative encyclopaedia)	Britannica Online (online version of published encyclopedia)
Content published through wikis (participative)	Content managed through content management systems (published)
Participation (many to many knowledge sharing)	Publishing (one to many knowledge dissemination)
Syndication (sharing content across sites)	Stickiness (keeping people on your site)
Cost per click advertising (revenues charged on the basis of content being actively accessed)	Page views (advertising revenues being charged on the basis of content displayed)
Web services (real connectivity between applications)	Screen scraping (accessing data being displayed by another IT application)
Tagging	Directories
Napster (peer to peer file sharing)	Mp3.com (online music store)
Flickr (photo sharing site)	Ofoto (photo repository site)
Blogging	Personal websites

8.4 Applications of Web 2.0 for business

In recent years, we have seen the emergence of a number of new online companies. Most are probably also run by young entrepreneurs for whom technology will play a key role in their business strategy:

- The business can find partners, collaborators, customers and suppliers through social networks and blogs

- It can use blogs, and social networks for publicity and to market itself, and it can encourage customers to leave feedback on its site (customer generate content)

- It can manage the development, creation and delivery of its products through virtual workspaces and wikis that support collaboration, innovation and the management of workflow. The collaborative nature of Web 2.0 enables external 3rd parties to participate in product development

- It can get market intelligence through blogs and online reference sites. It can also get feedback on how customers perceive its own products or services.

Staff - Importantly also, if the businesses want to attract and retain young, dynamic employees they will need to provide them with tools they are familiar with, and offer a work environment that fits with their lifestyle.

Marketing - Web 2.0 can also have significant implications for marketing approaches. Teenagers and young adults can be an important demographic for many businesses, and sites such as *Facebook* and *Twitter* play an important part in their lives. In this way, running campaigns through popular social networking sites can offer businesses a way of engaging with these users, allowing them to reach a demographic which has traditionally been difficult to reach. Marketers can also use pre-existing social networks as a mechanism for promoting **viral marketing** campaigns. In these, a company will generate an initial marketing message, but people then pass it along to their friends and contacts through their social networks.

However, if companies do engage in social networking or publish blogs they need to monitor how these are perceived by the online communities. **Brand management** remains very important – perhaps even more so because of the way users can publish negative feedback on poorly designed or presented content.

Conversely though, favourable customer review comments on products or services can be very useful PR material for an organisation.

Ethical and legal implications of Web 2.0

While Web 2.0 technologies could offer businesses a number of advantages, it is important that they are managed responsibly.

Security considerations – The increased use of web-based interfaces makes businesses vulnerable to malicious attacks on their internet applications. There have been a number of 'phishing' scams where hackers have tried to obtain financial information about customers and users.

Consequently, businesses need to ensure they have real-time sufficient security systems in place to detect any suspicious activities, and thereby to protect their customers.

Data protection – When handling personal data, businesses must ensure data is only used for the purpose it was provided. Data must be fairly and lawfully processed, and data requests must be relevant and not excessive. If companies hold data, they are responsible for ensuring it is accurate, and kept up-to-date. Data must not be kept for longer than is necessary, and it must be kept secure.

Copyright – Web 2.0 technologies make it much easier for staff to publish material on the internet. However, businesses need to ensure that they do not publish material if they do not have permission to do so, and if they do not credit copyright holder. This applies to videos, images, pictures and music as well as text.

Employment policies – Businesses will need to ensure their HR policies are up-to-date and deal with flexible working arrangements, e-mail use, privacy, use of social networking sites during office hours etc.

Staff also need to recognise that they are in a **position of trust**. For example, staff dealing with personal details have a duty to keep them confidential. Equally, they must not post any libellous or inappropriate content on their company's website. To this end, anonymous postings should be prohibited.

However, it appears that a number of businesses are aware of the legal and HR issues relevant to Web 2.0 technologies. In interviews with a number of business executives, *McKinsey & Company* found that 'participatory initiatives' had been stalled by legal and HR concerns. These risks differ markedly from previous technology adoptions, where the chief downsides were perceived as high costs and poor execution.

8.5 Web 2.0 and emergent strategies?

The nature of Web 2.0 technologies means that they encourage participation and a bottom-up approach.

In the context of business strategy, this is a very different approach to the prescriptive, top-down approach suggested by the rational model.

By allowing web users to provide feedback and share ideas, Web 2.0 is encouraging a model in which people outside an organisation can have an impact on that organisation's strategy.

Moreover, the internet becomes, in effect, a research tool, where companies can find out about customers' opinions about products and services. Web 2.0 allows businesses to aggregate opinions from many different individuals to guide idea generation and strategic decision making.

In this way, customer networks and social interaction have become much more important in marketing. Perhaps the most dramatic illustration of this can be seen through the virtual world of 'Second Life'.

CASE STUDY

Second Life

Second Life is the world's largest 3D virtual environment, and offers an example of how technologies are allowing companies to engage with their potential customers.

Companies can introduce new products and design ideas on the Second Life Grid and benefit from fast, cost-effective feedback, as well as planting the seeds of brand loyalty in consumers' minds.

Phillips uses the Second Life Grid to gain insights and co-design products with consumers. By presenting prototypes early on, the company can use consumer feedback to improve their design process. As a result, they are able to perfect new products before launching them in the 'real' world.

The worldwide hotel chain, Starwood, built a virtual replica of a new hotel concept. This virtual hotel functioned as a laboratory. The company observed how people moved through the space, where they gathered, and even how they used the furniture. Virtual hotel customers posted feedback on a blog, and the company used this information to modify its building plans.

However, Starwood has now left Second Life, because it discovered that avatars don't need to sleep, so ultimately it didn't make much sense to create a virtual hotel. Unlike Adidas or General Motors which sell digital versions of sportswear or cars in the online world, Starwood didn't have any goods to sell and so found itself unable to sustain avatars' interest.

Section summary

Web 2.0 technologies allow businesses new ways of interacting with customers, suppliers and staff. What distinguishes Web 2.0 technologies from previous technologies is the degree of participation they require to be effective. Web 2.0 technologies are truly interactive and rely on users to participate in the creation and sharing of ideas, rather than simply being recipients of information.

Our references to e-commerce and Web 2.0 technologies have highlighted how important technologies are to contemporary businesses. In this context, therefore, we need to acknowledge the role that IT departments play in maintaining business' IT infrastructures, but we also need to consider the issue of how the IT departments themselves are structured.

9 The IT department

Introduction

The main choice about organising the IT specialists is whether they should be centralised or decentralised. There is a tension between **control** and **relevance to local conditions**. An **information centre** is an important aspect of the IT department, providing rapid support to users together with an element of supervision.

KEY TERMS

A CENTRALISED IS/IT department involves all IS/IT staff and functions being based out at a single central location, such as head office

A DECENTRALISED IS/IT department involves IS/IT staff and functions being spread out throughout the organisation

There is no single 'best' structure for an IS/IT department – an organisation should consider its IS/IT requirements and the merits of each structure.

9.1 Centralisation

Advantages of a centralised IS/IT department:

(a) Assuming centralised processing is used, there is only one set of files so everyone uses the same data and information.

(b) It gives better security/control over data and files so it is easier to enforce standards.

(c) Head office is in a better position to know what is going on.

(d) There may be economies of scale available in purchasing computer equipment and supplies.

(e) Computer staff are in a single location, more expert staff are likely to be employed and career paths may be more clearly defined.

Disadvantages of a centralised IS/IT department:

(a) Local offices might have to wait for IS/IT services and assistance.
(b) Reliance on head office, so local offices are less self-sufficient.
(c) A system fault at head office will impact across the organisation.

Centralisation is appropriate in a coherent integrated organisation where all locations or departments are doing much the same thing and there is no equivalent for specialised systems. A chain of supermarkets would be a good example. This is sometimes called the 'star organisations' approach.

A degree of decentralisation or **partial distribution** may be appropriate where departments or sites are doing similar things but with different data: there can be commonality of systems but local processing may be appropriate. An example would be a manufacturer operating on several sites and using the same production control system at each installation: different products, manufacturing processes and inventory levels might make distributed systems appropriate.

9.2 Decentralisation

Advantages of a decentralised IS/IT department:

(a) Each office can introduce an information system specially **tailored** for its individual needs so local changes in business requirements can be taken into account.

(b) Each office is more self-sufficient.

(c) Offices are likely to have quicker access to IS/IT support/advice.

(d) A decentralised structure is more likely to facilitate accurate IS/IT cost/overhead allocations.

Disadvantages of a decentralised IS/IT department:

(a) Control may be more difficult – different and uncoordinated information systems may be introduced.

(b) Self-sufficiency may encourage a lack of co-ordination between departments.

(c) Increased risk of data duplication, with different offices holding the same data on their own separate files.

Full decentralisation may be seen in a network organisation, especially where there are incompatible legacy systems. There is unlikely to be any central IT management function; though there will probably be co-ordination by agreement. Information sharing and integration will be a priority, but may be difficult to achieve.

9.3 The information centre

KEY TERM

An INFORMATION CENTRE (IC) is a small unit of staff with a good technical awareness of computer systems, whose task is to provide a support function to computer users within the organisation.

Information centres, sometimes referred to as **support centres**, are particularly useful in organisations which use distributed systems and so are likely to have hardware, data and software scattered throughout the organisation.

9.3.1 Help

An IC usually offers a **Help Desk** to solve IT problems. Help may be via the telephone, e-mail, through a searchable knowledge base or in person. **Remote diagnostic software** may be used which enables staff in the IC to take control of a computer and sort out the problem without leaving their desk. The help desk needs sufficient staff and technical expertise to respond quickly and effectively to requests for help. IC staff should also maintain good relationships with hardware and software suppliers to ensure their maintenance staff are quickly on site when needed.

9.3.2 Problem solving

The IC will maintain a **record of problems** and identify those that occur most often. If the problem is that users do not know how to use the system, training is provided. Training applications often contain analysis software, drawing attention to trainee progress and common problems. This information enables the IC to identify and address specific training needs more closely. If the problem is with the system itself, a solution is found, either by modifying the system or by investment in new hardware or software.

9.3.3 Improvements

The IC may also be required to consider the viability of suggestions for improving the system, and to bring these improvements into effect.

9.3.4 Standards

The IC is also likely to be responsible for setting, and encouraging users to conform to, common **standards**.

(a) Hardware standards ensure that all of the equipment used in the organisation is compatible and can be put into use in different departments as needed.

(b) Software standards ensure that information generated by one department can easily be shared with and worked upon by other departments.

(c) Programming standards ensure that applications developed by individual end-users (for example complex spreadsheet macros) follow best practice and are easy to modify.

(d) Data processing standards ensure that certain conventions such as the format of file names are followed throughout the organisation. This facilitates sharing, storage and retrieval of information.

9.3.5 Security

The IC may help to preserve the security of data in various ways.

(a) It may develop utility programs and procedures to ensure that back-ups are made at regular intervals.

(b) The IC may help to preserve the company's systems from attack by computer viruses, for instance by ensuring that the latest versions of anti-virus software are available to all users, by reminding users regularly about the dangers of viruses, and by setting up and maintaining 'firewalls', which deny access to sensitive parts of the company's systems.

9.3.6 End-user applications development

An IC can help applications development by providing technical guidance to end-user developers and to encourage comprehensible and well-documented programs. Understandable programs can be maintained or modified more easily. Documentation provides a means of teaching others how the programs work. These efforts can greatly extend the usefulness and life of the programs that are developed.

9.4 Outsourcing IT/IS services

KEY TERM

OUTSOURCING is the contracting out of specified operations or services to an external vendor.

The arrangement varies according to the circumstances of both organisations.

Outsourcing arrangement			
Feature	Timeshare	Service	Facilities Management (FM)
What is it?	Access to an external processing system on a time-used basis	Focus on specific function, eg payroll	A outside agency manages the organisation's IS/IT facilities. The client retains equipment but all services provided by FM company
Management responsibility	Mostly retained	Some retained	Very little retained
Focus	Operational	A function	Strategic
Timescale	Short-term	Medium-term	Long-term
Justification	Cost savings	More efficient	Access to expertise; better service; management can focus on core business activities

Managing such arrangements involves deciding **what** will be outsourced, choosing a supplier and the supplier **relationship**.

9.4.1 How to determine what will be outsourced?

(a)   What is the system's **strategic importance**? A third party IT specialist cannot be expected to possess specific business knowledge.

(b)   Functions with only **limited interfaces** are most easily outsourced, eg payroll.

(c)   Do we know enough about the system to manage the arrangement?

(d)   Are our requirements likely to **change**?

The arrangement is incorporated in a contract sometimes referred to as the **Service Level Contract** (SLC) or **Service Level Agreement** (SLA).

Element	Comment
Service level	Minimum levels of service with penalties for example: • Response time to requests for assistance/information • System 'uptime' percentage • Deadlines for performing relevant tasks
Exit route	Arrangements for an exit route, transfer to another supplier or move back in-house.
Timescale	When does the contract expire? Is the timescale suitable for the organisation's needs or should it be renegotiated?
Software ownership	This covers software licensing, security and copyright (if new software is to be developed)?
Dependencies	If related services are outsourced, the level of service quality agreed should group these services together.
Employment issues	If the organisation's IT staff to move to the third party, employer responsibilities must be specified clearly.

9.4.2 Advantages of outsourcing arrangements

(a)   Outsourcing can remove uncertainty about **cost**, as there is often a long-term contract where services are specified in advance for a **fixed price**.

(b)   Long-term contracts (maybe up to ten years) encourage **planning** for the future.

(c)   Outsourcing can bring the benefits of **economies of scale**. For example, an IT company's research into new software may benefit several of their clients.

(d)   A specialist organisation is able to **retain skills and knowledge**. Many organisations' IT departments are too small to develop good people.

(e)   New skills and knowledge become available. A specialist company can **share** staff with **specific expertise** between several clients.

(f)   **Flexibility**. Resources may be scaled up or down depending upon demand.

9.4.3 Disadvantages of outsourcing arrangements

(a)   Information and its provision is **an inherent part of business and management**. If the information system is outsourced, the organisation will have less control over the system. If controls are subsequently relaxed, or the quality of information falls, this could damage the organisation's competitive position.

(b)   Information strategy can be used to gain **competitive advantage**. Opportunities may be missed if a third party is handling IS services.

(c)   The organisation will lose the **knowledge of key staff**, which again may weaken its competitive position.

(d)   An organisation may have highly **confidential information** and to let outsiders handle it could be seen as **risky** in commercial and/or legal terms.

(e)   The organisation is vulnerable if the outsourced company stops trading. For example, if an organisation outsources some of its software systems, and then the software provider goes bankrupt, the organisation could lose important information (such as software codes and updates).

(f)   An organisation may find itself **locked in** to an unsatisfactory contract.

Section summary

The growth of e-commerce highlights the importance of business' IT systems being well maintained. However, businesses face a number of questions about how their IT departments should be structured: in particular, whether they should be centralised or decentralised, and whether IT services should be retained in-house or outsourced.

Chapter Roundup

✓ **Strategic information** is used to **plan** the **objectives** of the organisation, and to **assess** whether the objectives are being met in practice. Strategic information systems (such as EIS and MIS) help managers make strategic decisions.

✓ Information strategy can be divided into **information systems strategy**, **information technology strategy** and **information management strategy**. The strategic significance of information requires that information itself managed strategically so that the systems, the technology and the information support the business' overall strategic policy. IT has the potential to **transform competition** in three ways: its effect on the **five competitive forces**; its potential for implementing the **generic strategies**; and its contribution to the **emergence of completely new businesses**. However, IT strategy needs to support the overall business strategy.

✓ An information system should be designed to obtain information from **all relevant sources** – both internal and external – so that managers have the information they need to make properly informed strategic decisions.

✓ In order to be useful, control information must aid the decision-making process. However, information is often imperfect because it is impossible to predict the future with perfect accuracy.

✓ There is a hierarchy between **data**, **information** and **knowledge**, and knowledge is the most useful as a source of competitive advantage.

✓ **Knowledge management** aims to exploit existing knowledge and create new knowledge which in turn can be exploited.

✓ All organisations possess a great deal of data, but much of it is disorganised and inaccessible. Knowledge management technology helps structure data in a way that makes it easily accessible so that it can be used to support knowledge.

✓ Databases provide convenient access to data for a wide variety of users and user needs. Databases can be used in strategic planning, and play an important role in database marketing.

✓ The **internet and e-commerce** allows organisations to challenge traditional business models, and have changed the relationship between vendors and customers. However, a business' e-commerce strategy needs to be consistent with its overall business strategy.

✓ **Web 2.0 technologies** allow businesses new ways of interacting with customers, suppliers and staff. What distinguishes Web 2.0 technologies from previous technologies is the degree of participation they require to be effective. Web 2.0 technologies are truly interactive and rely on users to participate in the creation and sharing of ideas, rather than simply being recipients of information.

✓ The growth of e-commerce highlights the importance of business IT systems being well maintained. However, businesses face a number of questions about how their IT departments should be structured: in particular, whether they should be centralised or decentralised, and whether IT services should be retained in-house or outsourced.

BPP
LEARNING MEDIA

Quick Quiz

1   Strategically useful information will rarely be obtained from sources internal to the organisation.

☐   True

☐   False

2   The decision making process may be said to commence with

A   Identifying courses of action
B   Problem definition
C   Problem recognition
D   None of the above

3   What are the three 'legs' of IS strategy development which Earl identified?

4   What is the difference between data and information?

5   What are the three main changes to channel structures which the Internet and e-commerce have facilitated?

6   Which one of the following is not associated with Web 2.0 technologies?

A   Wikipedia
B   Tagging
C   Screen scraping
D   Blogging

7   List three advantages of outsourcing.

Answers to Quick Quiz

1   False. Many organisations possess large amounts of strategically useful information in their internal records.

2   C. The need for a decision must first be recognised; defining the problem comes next.

3   Business led; infrastructure led; mixed.

4   Information is data that is organised in some useful way.

5   Disintermediation; Reintermediation; Countermediation.

6   C. Screen scraping involves accessing data being displayed by another IT application. This is the predecessor technology to web services which allow real connectivity between applications.

7   Any three of: removes uncertainty about cost; benefit from economies of scale; benefit from specialist knowledge: scalability of resources.

Answer to Question

9.1 Babbage & Newton

There is no strategy at all. The Finance Director regards IT as a cost. Moreover the IT 'strategy' is directed to enhancing its existing base (eg in the accounts department) rather than areas where it might prove competitively valuable (eg in marketing).

Now try this question from the Exam Question Bank	Number	Level	Marks	Time
	Q10	Examination	15	27 mins

ISSUES IN STRATEGIC MANAGEMENT

This chapter considers some discrete issues that require management attention. Each is in itself a major business management activity.

Section 1 is about project management. Major projects both have impact at the strategic level and wide-ranging effects across the organisation. Senior management attention is required if they are to remain under control.

Lean systems are covered in Section 2. Most businesses attempt to control their costs, but the best results are achieved when a comprehensive, strategic view is taken.

Section 3 examines business process re-engineering. This is an innovative response to the challenge of established methods and can bring both cost savings and efficiency improvements.

In Section 4 we look at some new ideas in the field of organisational structure. It is important that a business' structure is appropriate for, and supports, its strategy.

topic list	learning outcomes	syllabus references	ability required
1 Managing projects	D1(a)	D1(iii)	Recommend
2 Lean systems	D1(a)	D1(iv)	Recommend
3 Re-engineering and innovation	–	D1(iv)	Recommend
4 Organisation structure	C1(c)	C1(ix), D1(v)	Evaluate

1   Managing projects

Introduction

Project management is an important aspect of strategic implementation, and project management and change management are closely linked.

Knowledge brought forward

The concepts and techniques of project management, including a discussion of the PRINCE2 methodology, form part of the syllabus for Paper E2 Enterprise Management and are covered in the BPP Study Text for that paper. From here on we will assume that you are familiar with them.

If you are unsure about these matters, you should refer back to your BPP Study Text or Passcards for paper E2.

1.1 Projects and strategy

1.1.1 Linking projects with strategy

Grundy and Brown identify three links between **strategic thinking** and **project management**.

(a)   Many projects are undertaken as **consequences of the overall strategic planning process**. These projects may change the relationship between the organisation and its environment or they may be aimed at major organisational change.

(b)   Some important projects arise on a bottom-up basis. The need for action may become apparent for operational rather than strategic reasons: such projects must be given careful consideration to ensure that their overall effect is **congruent with the current strategy**.

(c)   Strategic thinking is also required at the level of the **individual project**, in order to avoid the limitations that may be imposed by a narrow view of what is to be done.

1.1.2 Project managing strategy

Project management in its widest sense is fundamental to much strategy. This is because very few organisations are able to do the same things in the same ways year after year. Continuing **environmental change** forces many organisations to include extensive processes of **adaptation** into their strategies. Business circumstances change and new conditions must be met with new responses or initiatives. Each possible new development effectively constitutes a project in the terms we have already discussed.

Grundy and Brown suggest three reasons for taking a project management view of strategic management.

(a)   **Strategic planning**. Much strategy appears to develop in an incremental or fragmented way; detailed strategic thinking may be best pursued through the medium of a **strategic project** or group of projects. Project management is a way of making *ad hoc* strategy more deliberate and therefore better-considered.

(b)   **Strategic implementation** is more complex than strategic analysis and choice; a project management approach, as outlined above, has an important role to play here, but must become capable of handling more complex, ambiguous and political issues if it is to play it effectively. When an apparent need for a project emerges, it should be screened to ensure that it supports the overall strategy.

(c)   Even at the smaller, more traditional scale of project management, **wider strategic awareness is vital** if project managers are to deliver what the organisation actually needs

Of course, not all new developments are recognised as worthy of project management. For example, the installation of a new, shared printer in an office would probably be regarded as a matter of routine, though it would no doubt have been authorised by a responsible budget holder and installed and networked by a suitable technician. There would probably have been a small amount of training associated with its use and maintenance and it might have been the subject of a health and safety risk assessment. All these processes taken together look like a project, if a very small one.

In contrast to the multitude such small events, modern organisations are likely to undergo significant change far less often, but sufficiently frequently and with developments that have sufficiently long lives for project management to be an **important aspect of strategic implementation**. Project management and **change management** are thus intimately linked.

An atmosphere of change and continuing development will be particularly evident in relation to information systems and technology, organisation structure and organisation culture.

Exam skills

Change management is an important element of project management. Successful projects inevitably lead to change, and change management is vital to successfully implement them. Therefore, for a project to be successfully managed and implemented, the project management process must contain an element of change management.

1.2 Project management

PRINCE2 defines a clear **management structure** of roles and responsibilities which can be adapted to suit both the organisation and the specific project.

PRINCE2 recognises **four layers of management responsibility.** These levels may be combined or eliminated if appropriate. A major project of strategic significance will be of interest to the organisation's **strategic apex**, which may appoint one of its members to manage the project or form a **steering committee** to set policy to support business objectives. An **executive committee** below strategic apex level may have the job of translating policies into specific projects that support them.

The top level of management for an individual project is the **project board**. This provides overall guidance and represents the business interests of the organisation. Two other constituencies are also represented.

(a)   The **senior user** represents the interests of those affected by the introduction of the new system and is accountable for the quality of the specification.

(b)   The **senior supplier/senior technical** person represents the implementers of the project. This role may be filled by an external prime contractor or a person within the organisation. For example, for an IT project this might be the senior IT person.

Clearly, Chartered Management Accountants working in senior roles may well find themselves involved in project management at one of these levels.

1.3 Business case

A fundamental aspect of PRINCE2 is that a project is **driven by its business case.** The continuing viability of the project is checked at regular intervals.

• A business case is simply a statement of what is to be achieved and the benefits of doing so.

• Occasions when the business case must be referred to should be specified at the outset to ensure focus is not lost.

• The business case may require updating as the project progresses.

• It is a strategic management role to ensure that this principle is adhered to.

1.4 Control

The project board restricts authorisation to one project stage at a time and manages by exception.

1.5 Processes

PRINCE2 Processes are approximately equivalent to stages of the **project lifecycle**, though they also relate to aspects of continuing project management activity. There are eight processes, several of which require senior management input.

- Directing a project
- Starting up a project
- Initiating a project
- Planning

- Controlling a stage
- Managing stage boundaries
- Managing product delivery
- Closing a project

Directing a project is the responsibility of the senior management team or project board. This process continues throughout the life of the project but is limited to **higher aspects of control and decision-making**.

Starting up a project is also a senior responsibility. It is a short scene-setting pre-project process concerned with fundamentals such as the project's aims and the appointment of the project board and project manager.

Controlling a stage includes a structure of reports and meetings.

(a)   A **project initiation meeting** involving senior management agrees the scope and objectives of the project and gives approval for it to start.

(b)   The completion of each project stage is marked by an **end stage assessment**, which includes reports from the project manager and the project assurance team to higher authority. The next stage does not commence until its plans have been reviewed and approved.

(c)   **Mid stage assessments** are optional and may arise if, for example, a stage runs for a particularly long time or it is necessary to start a new stage before the current one is complete.

(d)   **Highlight reports** are submitted regularly to the project board by the project manager. These reports are the main overall routine control mechanism and their frequency (often monthly) is agreed at project initiation. They are essentially progress reports and should include brief summaries of project schedule and budget status.

Closing a project is the process by which the project manager brings the project to a conclusion. It consists of checking and reporting on the extent that the project has been a success. The completion of the project is formally marked by the **project closure meeting**. This is held to ensure that all planned work has been carried out, including any approved variations to the plan, and that the work has been accepted.

1.6 Implementing a project

The objective of project management is to deliver a successful project. A project will be deemed successful if it is completed at the **specified level of quality**, **on time** and **within budget**.

Constraint	Comment
Quality	The end result should conform to the project specification. In other words, the result should achieve what the project was supposed to do.
Budget	The project should be completed without exceeding authorised expenditure.
Timescale	The progress of the project must follow the planned process, so that the 'result' is ready for use at the agreed date. As time is money, proper time management can help contain costs.

Quality, **cost** and **time** are traditionally regarded as the yardsticks against which project success is measured, although it is increasingly common to add a fourth constraint, **scope**, and even to use it to **replace quality** as a fundamental constraint and target. The **scope** of a project defines all the work that is to be done and all the deliverables that constitute project success. Under this analysis, the quality constraint is restricted to a narrower meaning and the difference between scope and quality becomes the difference between doing a job and doing it well – or badly.

The process involved in project management can be summarised in the figure below.

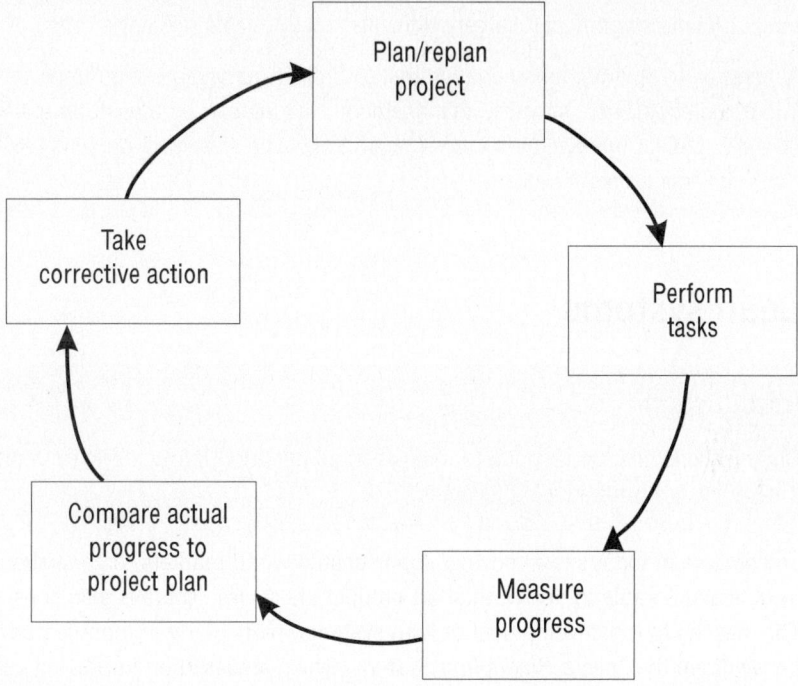

1.6.1 Management challenges presented by projects

Challenge	Comment
Teambuilding	The work is carried out by a team of people often from varied work and social backgrounds. The team must 'gel' quickly and be able to communicate effectively with each other.
Expected problems	Expected problems should be avoided by careful design and planning prior to commencement of work.
Unexpected problems	There should be mechanisms within the project to enable these problems to be resolved quickly and efficiently.
Delayed benefit	There is normally no benefit until the work is finished. The 'lead in' time to this can cause a strain on the eventual recipient who is also faced with increasing expenditure for no immediate benefit.
Specialists	Contributions made by specialists are of differing importance at each stage.
Potential for conflict	Projects often involve several parties with different interests. This may lead to conflict.

Section summary

PRINCE2 defines a clear **management structure** of roles and responsibilities within the system which can be adapted to suit both the organisation and the specific project.

A fundamental aspect of PRINCE2 is that a project is **driven by its business case**, so it will only be undertaken if it is going to add value to the organisation.

A project will be deemed successful if it is completed at the specified level of **quality**, **on time** and within **budget**. Achieving this can be very difficult: most projects present a range of significant challenges.

Adaptation to environmental change makes project management an important feature of strategic implementation. Also, strategic management thinking can be a useful input into project management. Strategic project management envisages strategy as a stream of projects intended to achieve organisational breakthroughs.

2 Lean systems

Introduction

Organisations need to respond to intensified competition, particularly from other countries, by improving their efficiency and reducing its costs.

To compete in today's fast-moving, sophisticated world markets, organisations need to be innovative, flexible and be able to deal with short product life cycles. There is also constant pressure to reduce costs. This has led to the development of **lean systems**, particularly in manufacturing. Lean manufacturing derives from the *Toyota Production System*, which focussed on improving customer value by reducing waste in the production system.

You should already be familiar with the ideas of lean production and continuous innovation which are covered in the syllabus for Paper E1. However, as with the other topics covered in E3, at this level you will be expected to analyse or evaluate the production systems being used in an organisation, rather than simply describing lean production or Just-in-time systems.

Lean production is a philosophy of production that aims to minimise the amount of resources (including time) used in all activities of an enterprise. It involves identifying and eliminating all non-value-adding activities.

The concepts behind lead production may also be applied to services and systems in the organisation. To summarise, the lean philosophy (lean) requires the organisation to focus on:

(a)   Continuous improvement
(b)   Increased productivity
(c)   Improved quality
(d)   Improved management

Lean involves the **systematic elimination of waste**. In this respect, Toyota identified seven 'wastes' to be eliminated:

(a)   **Over-production** and early production
(b)   **Waiting** – time delays, idle time, any time during which value is not added to the product
(c)   **Transportation** – multiple handling, delay in materials handling, unnecessary handling

(d)   **Inventory** – holding or purchasing unnecessary raw materials, work in process and finished goods

(e)   **Motion** – actions of people or equipment that do not add value to the product

(f)   **Over-processing** – unnecessary steps or work elements/procedures (non added value work)

(g)   **Defective units** – production of a part that is scrapped or requires rework

The aim of lean production is to eliminate waste, and to improve product flow and quality. Instead of devoting resources to planning what would be required for future manufacturing (as in a 'push' system), lean production focuses on reducing system response time so that the production system is capable of rapid change to meet market demands (a 'pull' system).

It is also important to understand the **importance of the customer** in lean thinking.

In the book 'Lean Thinking' *Womack and Jones* define five principles of Lean Thinking:

(a)   **Specifying value** – The critical starting point for lean thinking is value, and value can only be defined by the customer.

Therefore the first principle is to specify **what creates value from the customer's perspective**.

(b)   **Value stream** - Identify all the processes that are involved in the supply chain: the 'value stream.'

(c)   **Flow** – Make the value stream flow without interruptions.

(d)   **Pull** – Let the customer 'pull' value from the producer. The producer should only make what is valued (pulled) by the customer, and make it just in time to satisfy customer demand.

(e)   **Perfection** - Strive for perfection (zero defects) by constantly removing layers of waste (as identified in the seven types of waste above), and by removing delays and discontinuities in the supply chain process.

 Note the potential links between the first principle of lean thinking (creating value for the customer) and Porter's value chain, which also emphasises that value created needs to be measured from the customer's perspective.

2.1 Implementing lean systems

There are a number of specific tools that organisations can use to implement lean production systems. **Just in time** (see Section 2.2 below) is one of the core methods, but **Kaizen** (continuous improvement), **5S**, and **Six Sigma** are also techniques which could be used.

2.1.1 Kaizen

'Kaizen' focuses on making small, incremental changes to continuously improve the processes within an organisation.

Kaizen can be an effective way of reducing costs in processes (through kaizen costing.)

Under a kaizen costing approach, a target cost is applied for each function required to make a new product. These functional target costs are then added together to become the product target cost. Once the product has been in production for a year, the actual cost of the first year then becomes the starting point for cost reductions in the next year, and a similar process is applied for all subsequent years. This process of continuous improvement, encouraging constant reductions by tightening the 'standards' is known as kaizen costing.

However, another important aspect of kaizen is the role of workers in identifying improvements. Instead of viewing workers as the cause of problems, kaizen views workers as the source of solutions, and it empowers workers to find solutions to enable the continuous improvements.

2.1.2 '5S'

5S is an approach to achieving and maintaining a high-quality work environment, and it is underpinned by the idea that there is 'a place for everything, and everything goes in its place.'

The 5S concept should be used with the aim of creating a workplace with real organisation and order, which creates employees' price in their work, improves safety, and results in better quality outputs.

Sort (seiri) – eliminate unnecessary items from the work place

Set in order (seiton) – have efficient and effective storage methods

Shine (seiso) – clean the work area thoroughly

Standardise (seiketsu) – standardise work practices to achieve 'best practice'

Sustain (shitsuke) – sustain the new standards

2.1.3 Six Sigma

Six Sigma was initially envisaged as a quality management technique, but it has now developed into a system for process improvement.

Once again, though, there is a focus on the customer, and achieving levels of performance which are acceptable to the customer.

Six Sigma methodology can be used by project teams to improve processes by implementing the 5 stage 'DMAIC' pattern:

Define customer requirements for the process

Measure existing performance and compare to customer requirements. (The reference to customer requirements is important: the measurement principles in Six Sigma dictate that a business should only measure what the customer thinks is important).

Analyse existing process and assess causes for performance falling short of requirements

Improve process design and implement improvements

Control the results, and maintain new performance levels

2.2 Just-In-Time (JIT) Systems

An important element of the **lean approach** is that it focuses on a **production plan based on actual demand** (a 'pull' system), rather than production being based on a plan which it is hoped demand will follow (a 'push' system). This idea is also encapsulated in Just-in-time production systems.

JIT aims for zero inventory and perfect quality and operates by demand-pull. It consists of **JIT purchasing** and **JIT production** and results in lower investment requirements, space savings, greater customer satisfaction and increased flexibility.

The 'Toyota system' commonly known as **Just in Time** is the archetypal lean manufacturing system. It draws its inspiration from the need to **eliminate waste**.

'Traditional' responses to the problems of improving manufacturing capacity and reducing unit costs of production might be described as follows.

- Longer production runs
- Economic batch quantities
- Fewer products in the product range
- More overtime
- Reduced time on preventive maintenance, to keep production flowing

In general terms, longer production runs and large batch sizes should mean less disruption, better capacity utilisation and lower unit costs. Just-in-time systems challenge such 'traditional' views of manufacture.

KEY TERMS

JUST-IN-TIME (JIT) is a 'system whose objective is to produce or to procure products or components as they are required by a customer or for use, rather than for inventory.

JUST-IN-TIME SYSTEM is a 'pull' system, which responds to demand, in contrast to a 'push' system, in which inventories act as buffers between the different elements of the system, such as purchasing, production and sales'.

JUST-IN-TIME PRODUCTION is 'a production system which is driven by demand for finished products, whereby each component on a production line is produced only when needed for the next stage'.

JUST-IN-TIME PURCHASING is 'a purchasing system in which material purchases are contracted so that the receipt and usage of material, to the maximum extent possible, coincide'.   (CIMA *Official Terminology*)

Although described as a **technique** in the *Official Terminology*, JIT is more of a **philosophy or approach to management** since it encompasses a **commitment to continuous improvement** and the **search for excellence** in the design and operation of the production management system.

JIT has the following **essential elements**.

Element	Detail
JIT purchasing	Parts and raw materials should be purchased as near as possible to the time they are needed, using **small frequent deliveries rather than bulk orders**.
Close relationship with suppliers	In a JIT environment, the responsibility for the **quality of goods lies with the supplier**. A **long-term commitment** between supplier and customer should be established. The supplier is guaranteed a demand for his products since he is the sole supplier and he is able to plan to meet the customer's production schedules. If an organisation has confidence that suppliers will deliver material of 100% quality, on time, so that there will be no rejects, returns and hence no consequent production delays, **usage of materials can be matched with delivery of materials and inventories can be kept at near zero levels**. Suppliers are also chosen because of their close proximity to an organisation's plant.
Uniform loading	All parts of the productive process should be operated at the speed with which customers demand the final product. As output is closely matched to demand, there will be shorter production runs, smaller inventories of finished goods and reduced storage costs.
Set-up time reduction	Machinery set-ups are **non-value-added activities** (see below) which should be reduced or even eliminated.
Machine cells	Machines or workers should be **grouped by product or component** instead of by the type of work performed. The **non-value-added activity of materials movement** between operations is **minimised by** eliminating space between work stations. Products can flow from machine to machine without having to wait for the next stage of processing or returning to stores. **Lead times and work in progress are reduced**.

Element	Detail
Quality	Production management should **eliminate scrap and defective units** during production, and avoid the need for reworking of units since this stops the flow of production and leads to late deliveries to customers. Product quality and production quality are important 'drivers' in a JIT system.
Pull system (Kanban)	A Kanban, or signal, is used to ensure that products or components are only produced when needed by the next process. Nothing is produced in anticipation of need, to then remain in inventory, consuming working capital and resources.
Total productive maintenance (TPM)	Production systems must be reliable and prompt, without unforeseen delays, breakdowns or accidents. Machinery must be kept fully maintained, and so autonomous maintenance is an important aspect of production: workers are trained to take care of the equipment and machinery they work with. The aim of TPM is to achieve zero equipment breakdowns and zero product defects, thereby maximising the utilisation of production assets and plant capacity.
Employee involvement	Workers within each machine cell should be trained to operate each machine within that cell and to be able to perform routine autonomous maintenance on the cell machines (ie to be **multiskilled and flexible**).

2.2.1 Value added

JIT aims to eliminate all **non-value-added costs**. Value is only added while a product is actually being processed. Whilst it is being inspected for quality, moving from one part of the factory to another, or waiting for further processing and held in store, value is not being added. Non value-added activities (or **diversionary** activities) should be eliminated.

KEY TERM

'A VALUE-ADDED cost is incurred for an activity that cannot be eliminated without the customer's perceiving a deterioration in the performance, function, or other quality of a product. The cost of a plasma screen in a television set is value-added.

The costs of those activities that can be eliminated without the customer's perceiving deterioration in the performance, function, or other quality of a product are non-value-added. The costs of handling the materials of a television set through successive stages of an assembly line may be non-value-added. Improvements in plant layout that reduce handling costs may be achieved without affecting the performance, function, or other quality of the television set.'   *(Horngren)*

Question 10.1   Value-added activity

Learning outcomes D1(iv)

Which of the following is a value-added activity?

A   Setting up a machine so that it drills holes of a certain size
B   Repairing faulty production work
C   Painting a car, if the organisation manufactures cars
D   Storing materials

2.2.2 Problems associated with JIT

JIT, like any other system, has its faults and may not be appropriate in all situations.

(a)   It is not always easy to predict patterns of demand.

(b)   JIT makes the organisation far more vulnerable to disruptions in the supply chain.

(c)   JIT, originated by Toyota, was designed at a time when all of Toyota's manufacturing was done within a 50 km radius of its headquarters. Wide geographical spread, however, makes this difficult.

CASE STUDY

JIT and supply chains

The flight ban which affected much of Europe after the volcanic eruption in Iceland in April 2010 threatened to force worldwide car production to grind to a halt, as manufacturers were unable to source key electronic components.

The flight disruption highlighted the car industry's dependence on complex, worldwide supply chains that need multiple modes of transport to deliver goods and components just in time, to where they are needed.

Although air freight accounts for a tiny amount of world trade by weight - about 0.5 per cent for the UK - the disruption has highlighted how it plays a vital role in supplying key, high-value components to many manufacturers. In spite of its tiny volume, air freight accounts for 25 per cent of UK trade by value.

Among the carmakers, BMW and Nissan said they planned to suspend some production because of disruption to supplies. Audi said it might have to cancel shifts because of missing parts.

Although all three mainly use suppliers based near their factories and use road and sea for most deliveries, they depend on air freight for a small number of high-value electronic components. Nissan UK, for example, said it might have to halt production of its Cube, Murano SUV and Rogue crossover models because it lacked supplies of a critical sensor made in Ireland.

Although some components could be transported by sea freight (instead of air freight) this is a much slower means of transport, and so would lead to a delay in the components becoming available.

Some commentators have questioned whether this disruption will make companies re-examine their arrangements for sourcing goods. Companies have become more vulnerable to disruption since moving to just-in-time production methods, where hardly any inventory of products is held.

On the other hand, it would makes little sense to carry large quantities of excess inventory given the very slim chance of further severe disruption of this kind. Carrying excess inventory is a cost in itself.

However, there is an argument that companies should set up supply chains that reduce their reliance on a single mode of transport, and could be adapted to meet different circumstances.

As Emma Scott from the Chartered Institute of Purchasing & Supply in the UK commended "It's a case of taking a sensible approach and having a flexible approach to your supply chain."

Adapted from article 'Pressure grows on supply chains'

Financial Times, 21 April, 2010

Question 10.2 JIT

Learning outcomes D1(iv)

Batch sizes within a JIT manufacturing environment may well be smaller than those associated with traditional manufacturing systems.

What costs might be associated with this feature of JIT?

1   Increased set-up costs

2   Opportunity cost of lost production capacity as machinery and the workforce reorganise for a different product

3   Additional materials handling costs

4   Increased administrative costs

    A   None of the above
    B   1, 2, 3 and 4
    C   1 only
    D   2 and 3 only.

2.3 World class manufacturing (WCM)

World class manufacturing (WCM) aims for high quality, fast production, and the flexibility to respond to customer needs.

WCM arose in the mid-1980s to **describe the fundamental changes taking place in manufacturing companies** we have been examining. WCM is a very broad term.

KEY TERM

The *Official Terminology*'s definition of WORLD CLASS MANUFACTURING is a 'position of international manufacturing excellence, achieved by developing a culture based on factors such as continuous improvement, problem prevention, zero defect tolerance, customer-driven JIT-based production and total quality management'.

In essence, however, WCM can be taken to have four key elements.

Key element	Description
A new approach to product quality	Rather than detecting defects or poor quality in production as and when they occur, WCM sets out to **identify the root causes of poor quality, eliminate them, and achieve zero defects, that is 100% quality**, thereby incorporating the principles of **TQM**.
Just-in-time manufacturing	See section 2.2 above.
Managing people	WCM aims to utilise the skills and abilities of the work force to the full. Employees are **trained** in a variety of skills and so can **switch from one task to another**. They are also given more responsibility for production scheduling and quality. A **team approach** is encouraged, with strong trust between management and workers.
Flexible approach to customer requirements	The WCM policy is to **develop close relationships** with customers in order to know what their requirements are, supply them on time, with short delivery lead times and change the product mix quickly and develop new products or modify existing products as customer needs change.

A WCM manufacturer will have a clear **manufacturing strategy** aimed at issues such as quality and reliability, short lead times (the time from start to finish of production), flexibility and customer satisfaction. A **clear understanding** of the **value chain** is equally vital.

The value chain is made up of the following.

*   Research and development
*   Design
*   Production
*   Marketing

*   Distribution
*   Customer service
*   Customers

It **starts externally** with suppliers, links them to the internal functions of R&D, design, production, marketing, distribution and customer service, and **ends externally** with suppliers.

To improve quality, reduce costs and increase innovation, the manufacturer must ensure that the **functions within the value chain are coordinated** within the overall organisational framework.

2.4 Manufacturing location

An important aspect of cost control has been the emergence of low-wage countries as preferred centres for manufacturing. This process has encouraged '**off-shoring**', particularly of unskilled and semi-skilled work; the economies of less-developed countries are helped to grow and costs are contained. The process has been going on for many years, especially in basic, highly competitive industries, such as textiles, footwear and consumer electronics, and it has been suggested that manufacturing in high wage Western economies must inevitably decline.

CASE STUDY

The *Financial Times* reported in 2005 that the picture is more complex and indicated five strategic influences on decisions about the location of manufacturing.

(a)   **Market location and shipping costs**. It makes sense to locate production of breakable, bulky and low value items close to major markets.

(b)   **Customisation**. Where products are manufactured to specific user requirements, such as large commercial air conditioning systems, customer satisfaction is enhanced if supply chains are short and service is flexible.

(c)   **Commercial confidentiality**. It is easier to preserve a competitive edge in technology if manufacturing is concentrated in a small number of secure sites. *Toyota* keeps it most advanced technology at home in Japan.

(d)   **Automation**. Ease of automation of manufacturing processes can remove the cost advantage of off-shoring by cutting labour costs even in high-wage economies.

(e)   **Competition**. Competition is often limited in highly specialised niche markets, especially where there is a dominant proprietary technology. This can reduce pressure to reduce costs, since low price is less of a selling advantage.

Section summary

The need to be innovative, flexible and able to deal with short product life-cycles, as well as the constant pressure to reduce costs, has led to the development of **lean systems**, particularly in manufacturing.

JIT aims for zero inventory and perfect quality and operates by demand pull. It consists of **JIT purchasing** and **JIT production** and results in lower investment requirements and increased flexibility.

World Class Manufacturing (WCM) aims for high quality, fast production, and the flexibility to respond to customer needs.

3 Re-engineering and innovation

Introduction

As businesses, their market and the wider environment develop and change, it is appropriate to reconsider the way they do things from time to time. **Business process re-engineering** is a useful approach based on challenging basic assumptions about business methods and even the objectives they are designed to achieve. IT can be very useful here, but simply automating a process is not the same as re-engineering it.

In recent years the emphasis has been the **use of information technology for competitive advantage**. An earlier trend (still relevant to many situations) involved focussing attention **inwards** to consider how **business processes** could be redesigned or re-engineered to improve efficiency.

Changes made to processes may be classified as **automation**, **rationalisation** or **re-engineering**.

KEY TERMS

BUSINESS AUTOMATION is the use of computerised working methods to speed up the performance of existing tasks.

BUSINESS RATIONALISATION is the streamlining of operating procedures to eliminate obvious inefficiencies. Rationalisation usually involves automation.

Automation and rationalisation are the most common forms of organisational change. They usually offer modest returns and little risk. **Automation** usually involves assisting employees to carry out their duties more efficiently – for example introducing a computerised accounting package. **Rationalisation** involves not only the automation of a process but also efficient process design. For example, an automated banking system requires the standardisation of account number structure and standard rules for calculating daily account balances – in this situation automation encouraged a certain amount of rationalisation.

KEY TERM

BUSINESS PROCESS RE-ENGINEERING is the 'selection of areas of business activity in which repeatable and repeated sets of activities are undertaken; and the development of improved understanding of how they operate and of the scope for radical redesign with a view to creating and delivering better customer value'.

(CIMA *Official Terminology*)

Business process re-engineering involves fundamental changes in the way an organisation functions. For example, processes developed in a paper-intensive environment may be unsuitable for an environment underpinned by IT.

The main writing on the subject is *Hammer and Champy's Reengineering the Corporation* (1993), from which the following is taken.

> **Business Process Re-engineering** is the fundamental rethinking and radical redesign of business processes to achieve dramatic improvements in critical contemporary measures of performance, such as cost, quality, service and speed.

The key words here are **'fundamental'**, **'radical'**, **'dramatic'** and **'process'**.

(a)   **Fundamental** and **radical** indicate that BPR assumes nothing. It starts by asking basic questions such as 'why do we do what we do', without making assumptions or looking at what has always been done in the past.

(b)   **'Dramatic'** means that BPR should achieve 'quantum leaps in performance', not just marginal, incremental improvements.

(c)   **'Process'** is explained in the following paragraphs.

KEY TERM

A PROCESS is a collection of activities that takes one or more kinds of input and creates an output.

For **example**, order fulfilment is a process that takes an order as its input and results in the delivery of the ordered goods. The aim of BPR manufacturing is **not merely to make** the goods but to **deliver the goods that were ordered.** Any aspect of the manufacturing process that hinders this aim should be re-engineered. The first question to ask might be 'Do they need to be manufactured at all or should they be purchased from another organisation?'

A re-engineered process has certain **characteristics**.

- Often several jobs are **combined** into one
- Workers often **make decisions**
- The **steps** in the process are performed in **a logical order**
- Work is performed **where it makes most sense**
- Checks and controls may be reduced, and **quality 'built-in'**
- One manager provides a **single point of contact**
- The advantages of **centralised and decentralised** operations are combined

3.1 Principles of BPR

Hammer presents **seven principles** for BPR.

(a)   Processes should be designed to achieve a desired **customer-focused outcome** rather than focusing on existing **tasks**. (Evaluating customer satisfaction is an important aspect of BPR: how well do the current processes deliver the quality, flexibility, speed, cost or service which customers expect?)

(b)   Personnel who use the **output** from a process should **perform** the process. For example, a company could set up a database of approved suppliers; this would allow personnel who actually require supplies to order them themselves, perhaps using on-line technology, thereby eliminating the need for a separate purchasing function.

(c)   Information processing should be **included** in the work which **produces** the information. This eliminates the differentiation between information gathering and information processing.

(d)   **Geographically-dispersed** resources should be treated as if they are **centralised.** This allows the benefits of centralisation to be obtained, for example, economies of scale through central negotiation of supply contracts, without losing the benefits of decentralisation, such as flexibility and responsiveness.

(e)   Parallel activities should be **linked** rather than **integrated.** This would involve, for example, co-ordination between teams working on different aspects of a single process.

(f)   Workpeople should be **self-managing**, exercising greater autonomy over their work. The traditional distinction between workers and managers can be abolished: decision aids such as expert systems can be provided where they are required.

(g)   Information should be captured **once** at **source.** Electronic distribution of information makes this possible.

3.1.1 Is there a BPR methodology?

Davenport and *Short* prescribe a **five-step approach** to BPR.

 Develop the **business vision and process objectives**. BPR is driven by a business vision which implies specific business objectives such as cost reduction, time reduction, output quality improvement, Total Quality Management and empowerment.

 **Identify the processes** to be redesigned. Most firms use the 'high impact' approach, which focuses on the most important processes or those that conflict most with the business vision. Far fewer use the Exhaustive approach that attempts to identify all the processes within an organisation and then prioritise them in order of redesign urgency.

 Understand and **measure the existing processes** – to ensure previous mistakes are not repeated and to provide a baseline for future improvements.

 **Identify change levers**. Awareness of IT capabilities could approve useful when designing processes.

 Design and **build a prototype** of the new process. The actual design should not be viewed as the end of the BPR process – it should be viewed as a prototype, with successive alterations. The use of a prototype enables the involvement of customers.

3.2 IT and BPR

Simply computerising existing ways of doing things does not mean a process has been re-engineered. Technology may be able to add value by re-designing business processes.

IT is not the solution in itself, it is an **enabler**. BPR uses IT to allow an organisation to do things that it is not doing already. For example, teleconferencing reduces the cost of travelling to meetings – a re-engineering approach takes the view that teleconferencing allows more frequent meetings.

As *Hammer* and *Champy* put it, 'It is this disruptive power of technology, its ability to break the rules that limit how we conduct our work, that makes it critical to companies looking for competitive advantage.'

Examples of how technology has changed the way work is conducted include:

(a) **Shared databases** allow information to be accessed simultaneously from many locations.

(b) **Expert systems** may allow non-specialists to do work that previously required an expert.

(c) **Telecommunications networks** mean that businesses can simultaneously reap the rewards of centralisation and decentralisation.

(d) **Decision support tools** allow decisions to be made by a larger number of staff.

(e) **Wireless communication technology** allows staff 'in the field' to send and receive information wherever they are.

(f) **Interactive websites** allow personalised contact with many customers (or at least the appearance of personalised contact).

(g) Automatic identification and **tracking technology** allows the whereabouts of objects or people to be monitored.

(h) High performance computing allows **instant** revision of plans rather than periodic updates.

3.3 Why focus on processes?

Many businesses recognise that value is delivered **through processes,** and in this respect our focus on processes builds on Porter's ideas in the **value chain**. However, many businesses still define themselves in terms of their functional roles. To properly harness the resources within a business a clear agreement of the management and implementation of processes is needed. **Without this focus** on processes:

(a)   It is **unclear how value is achieved** or can continue to be achieved.

(b)   The **effects of change** on the operation of the business are **hard to predict**.

(c)   There is no basis to achieve **consistent** business improvement.

(d)   **Knowledge is lost** as people move around or out of the business.

(e)   Cross-functional interaction is not encouraged.

It is **difficult to align the strategy** of an organisation with the people, systems resources through which that strategy will be accomplished.

One way of portraying the relationship between organisation strategy, process, people and technology is shown below.

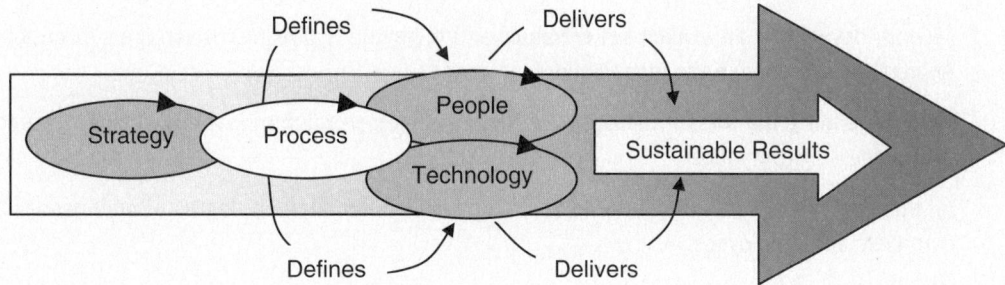

3.4 Dangers of BPR

There are concerns that BPR has become misunderstood. According to an independent study of 100 European companies, BPR has become allied in managers' minds with narrow targets such as **reductions in staff numbers** and other **cost-cutting** measures.

3.4.1 Problems with BPR

In addition to the misperception of BPR as being simply a cost-cutting exercise, several other criticisms have been made.

(a)   Successful BPR programmes result in significant **changes** that affect staff widely. Personal and management problems (as discussed in Chapters 11 and 12) will arise as a result of these changes.

   However, writings on BPR appear to overlook the impact of a BPR exercise on the staff involved. A BPR exercise may lead to new patterns of work, changing the composition of work groups and teams, as well as possible redundancies. These changes may come at a cost. This might be the direct costs associated with redundancies, or less immediately obviously, the loss of goodwill among staff, or increased stress among the workforce as a result of the reduction in staff numbers.

(b)   BPR **improves efficiency** but may ignore **effectiveness**. For example, fewer managers may lead to reduced innovation and creativity. *Hamel and Prahalad* call this process **hollowing out**.

(c)   While BPR practice generally seeks to empower workers, it assumes they will work within structures and systems imposed by others. This places strict limits on the scope for releasing their potential.

(d)   Established systems often have valuable but unrecognised features, particularly in the area of **control**. When a process is re-engineered from scratch, particularly when done with a view to cutting costs, such desirable features as segregation of duties and management supervision may be lost.

3.4.2 Beyond BPR

Champy suggests that management itself should be re-engineered. Managers are not used to thinking in systems terms, so, instead of looking at the **whole picture** (which might affect their own jobs), they tend to **seize on individual aspects** of the organisation.

It is argued that process re-engineering is really only a part of the **wider picture**. A report in the *Financial Times* on an unnamed company suggested four sets of changes as important to the transformation from a company which **satisfies** customers, to a company that **delights** them – and from a company which is **competent** to a company which is the **best** in its industry. Extracts from the report follow.

'... **first, breaking down barriers** between its different disciplinary specialists and national units by a series of procedural and structural steps, of which the re-engineering of cross-unit processes is only one;

second, developing an explicit set of values and behaviour guidelines which are subscribed to (or 'shared') by everyone in the organisation;

third, redefining the role of management in order to foster much more empowerment, responsibility and decisiveness at every level.

All this requires the creation of the **fourth factor: an unprecedented degree of openness** and trust among managers and employees'.

CASE STUDY

Workflow systems/process re-engineering

Work design, whether it is related to work in the factory or at the desk, is a process of arriving at the most **efficient** way of completing tasks and activities that minimises effort and reduces the possibility of mistakes. It is involved in increasing productivity and efficiency whilst maintaining or improving quality standards.

Today, work design is often referred to as process re-engineering and has a bad press because the perceived outcome is reduced employee numbers or downsizing. As we move increasingly to a computerised workplace the use of workflow systems is growing and changing the nature of work from one of social contact to service to the system.

A **workflow system** is a system that organises work and allocates it to particular workstations for the attention of the person operating the workstation. The system usually also incorporates a document-management facility. There are three main forms in which workflow systems operate. These are on the **casework basis**, the **flowline basis** or an **ad hoc basis**.

The **casework** basis functions by knowing the individual caseload of staff and directs existing cases to the appropriate caseworker and new cases or customers are allocated on the basis of equalising caseload.

The **flowline** approach allocates a small number of tasks to each operator and the case flows along the line from screen to screen. The **ad hoc** system works on the basis of equalising workload, regardless of who may have dealt with the case previously. The choice depends on the particular circumstances of the business and the approach taken to customer service.

Workflow management provides supervisors with information on screen about the workloads of individuals and information on their processing capabilities with statistics for average time taken to deal with a case, errors detected by the system as a percentage of cases, and so on. This information is intended to ensure that staff receive appropriate support and training, but can be and is used for bonus payments and league tables of performance.

In one organisation where workflow has been used in sales-order processing, the use of the management statistics has become quite draconian and the average period of employment of sales-order staff is three months.

The **advantages** and benefits of workflow systems come mainly from improvements in productivity and efficiency and better or speedier services to customers.

Offset against these benefits are the **disadvantages** stemming from the way that workflow systems are implemented and managed.

A list of the **benefits from the employer's point of view** would be:

- More efficient office procedures
- Providing workflow management
- Equalising of workloads
- Monitoring of operator performance
- Better security
- Ensuring work gets done when it should get done

The **dangers** lie in the segmentation or specialisation in a small number of tasks before passing the work on to the next person's screen, almost like a production line. This **de-skilling** of work increases boredom and leads to high staff turnover. It also reduces social contact to a minimum and the contact that does exist takes place via the system.

So far the casework approach, where staff deal with cases as a 'one stop shop', is the most empowering and beneficial for staff. The skills needed are high and there is a greater sense of completion and satisfaction for operators.

In the flowline approach people are demoralised at the repetitive nature of the work. Ad hoc approaches seem to fall between two stools – there is work satisfaction to a degree and no sense of continuing customer contact.

Adapted from: 'Computer talk' – Workflow systems Trevor Bentley – CIMA Articles database

3.5 Automate, informate, transformate

The **automate, informate** and **transformate** framework is very similar to BPR's **automation, rationalisation** and **re-engineering**, as is **process innovation**, which focuses on the creation of new processes to achieve business objectives.

The implementation and development of information systems can impact upon an organisation in different ways. Automation, rationalisation and re-engineering provide one framework for analysing and explaining this impact. *Zuboff* devised a similar framework, using the terms **automate**, **informate** and **transformate**. These terms are explained in the following table.

Stage/term	Comment
Automate	This involves the automation of repetitive manual tasks. Automate type changes typically take place during the initial introduction of information systems and information technology into an organisation. The new system replaces or speeds up previously manual tasks. (Corresponds to the automation stage in the **automation**, rationalisation, re-engineering framework.)

Stage/term	Comment
Informate	Some processes are redesigned to exploit the potential of information technology.
	Operating procedures are streamlined and the organisation infrastructure becomes more integrated, for example linking the order processing system with the stock control system.
	(Corresponds to the **rationalisation** stage in the automation, rationalisation, re-engineering framework.)
Transformate	Information systems and information technology are used to change the way the organisation operates and the way business is done. Systems are utilised that allow the organisation to conduct business in a way that was previously not possible.
	Transformate type changes may involve significant changes in organisation structure. This is a more risky strategy, which goes much further than rationalisation of processes. A traditional retail business moving to web-based e-commerce could be viewed as a fundamental change.
	Transformate type changes may bring competitive advantage.
	(Corresponds to the **re-engineering** stage in the automation, rationalisation, re-engineering framework.)

3.6 Process innovation

Davenport introduced the theory of Process Innovation (PI) in 1993.

KEY TERM

PROCESS INNOVATION (PI) combines the adoption of a process view of the business with the application of innovation to key processes. What is new and distinctive about this combination is its enormous potential for helping any organisation achieve major reductions in process cost or time, or major improvements in flexibility, service levels, or other business objectives.

Process innovation is similar to BPR but there are two main differences between BPR and PI.

• PI focuses to a greater extent on the **creation of new processes** so perhaps is an even more radical approach. Whereas BPR focuses on improving and redesigning **existing** processes, PI aims for a whole new way of performing each process.

• The role of IT in PI may be contrasted with its role in BPR. In BPR, IT is normally an **enabler**, allowing the organisation to achieve its desired outcome in ways that were previously impossible. In PI, IT is often the **trigger for change.** New technology creates the possibility of **completely new outcomes.**

Davenport identifies five steps of PI.

 Identify business areas or processes suitable for innovation.

 Identify the tools that can be used to innovate (change levers).

 Develop statements of purpose for the process ('process vision').

 Understand existing processes and prepare for new systems and processes.

 STEP 5   Design and prototype new processes.

Compare this procedure with that for BPR given in subsection 3.1.1.

 Exam skills

It is important to understand the differences between PI and BPR, and appreciate that while **IT** is often a **change trigger** for **PI**, it is usually an **implementation** tool for **BPR**.

 Section summary

Changes to business processes may be classed as **automation**, **rationalisation**, or **re-engineering**. Business process re-engineering involves making fundamental changes to the way an organisation functions.

Computerising existing methods is not re-engineering, but IT can add value as an **enabler**, rather than the solution.

The **automate**, **informate** and **transformate** framework is very similar to BPR's **automation**, **rationalisation** and **re-engineering**, as is **process innovation**, which focuses on the creation of new processes to achieve business objectives.

4 Organisation structure

 Introduction

You should already be reasonably familiar with basic ideas about how organisations are structured and managed. This section develops these ideas further.

4.1 The traditional organisation and the management accountant

The three essential aspects of the nature of organisations – social arrangements, agreed goals and controlled performance – make it inevitable that an organisation's strategy, its structure and the work of the management accountant are intimately entwined. The **classical approach** is being replaced by more **flexible methods** as a result of the pressure from environmental developments, including **globalisation** and **developments in IS**.

Developing and managing an **efficient organisation** is an important aspect of **strategic implementation.**

An important point to note here is that strategy is delivered *through* the organisation and so the two should support each other. *Chandler* and others have shown that **structure and strategy are closely linked**. There is a similar relationship between organisational structure and the management methods, culture and philosophy that make it work.

Drucker emphasised this point by noting that 'Structure is a means for attaining the objectives and goals or an institution.'

Management accountants and their work are embedded in an organisational setting so developments in either organisational structure or the way management accountants do their work are bound to interact with one another.

Buchanan and Huczynski suggest that there are three essential aspects that define an organisation:

(a) **Social arrangements**. People make up a major part of any organisation. Management accountants must remember that the systems, procedures and rules that they design and operate will both affect and be affected by such matters as motivation, conflict and ambition.

(b) **Collective goals**. Organisations pursue collective goals. The definition of those goals and their priorities require management accounting input such as cost estimates, project evaluation and budget preparation.

(c) **Controlled performance**. Organisations are about controlled performance. This is obviously a major theme of the management accountant's role both in strategic management and more generally within the organisation.

A large part of the management accountant's work in the field of strategy will either influence or be influenced by organisation structure. Accountants are used to working within a rational, deterministic framework of rules and procedures that trace their roots back to the classical school of management theory.

4.2 Types of organisational structure   5/10

The syllabus for Paper E2 includes discussion of different types of organisational structure, so students are assumed to already be aware of these by the time they come to study E3.

It is important that you know the different structures an organisation could take, and the characteristics of different structures, so that you could assess whether they are appropriate for an organisation or a proposed strategy being described in a question scenario in E3.

The below table summaries seven basic organisational structures:

Structure	Advantages	Disadvantages
Functional (also called **Unitary (U) organisational form**) • Departments defined by their function, ie what they do • Traditional, common sense approach used by many organisations • Centralised authority (so suited to centralised organisations)	• Based on work specialisation, therefore logical • Pooling of expertise, by grouping specialised tasks and staff together • Firm can benefit for economies of scale • Relatively simple lines of control • Senior managers close to the operation of their function • Controlled by strategic leaders/CEO • Offers career structure	• Doesn't reflect business processes by which value is created • Hard to identify where profits/losses are made on individual products • People do not have an understanding of how the whole business works • Problems in co-ordinating the work of different specialisms • Communication problems between functions • Unlikely to be entrepreneurial • Managers focus on short-term routine activities rather than longer-term strategic developments

Structure	Advantages	Disadvantages
Multi-divisional (also called **M–form**) • Business divided into autonomous regions or product businesses, each with its own revenues, expenditures and profits • Appropriate if organisation produces a number of different products or services, so relevant divisional/business splits exist • Communication between the divisions and head office is restricted • Corporate centre focuses on higher level strategic controls, aimed at ensuring divisions play their part in ensuring corporation as a whole achieves its goals • Divisions focus on managerial and operational controls	• Focuses attention of subordinate management on business performance and results • Enables contribution of various activities to be evaluated • Management by objectives is the natural control default • Corporate centre focuses on corporate strategy • Gives authority to junior managers therefore prepares them for future senior positions • Increases motivation among divisional managers	• Division is partly insulated by holding company from shareholders and capital markets, which ultimately reward performance • Different product divisions may function better as independent companies • Divisions more bureaucratic than they would be as independent companies • Can be hard to identify completely independent products/markets • Divisionalisation only possible at a high level • Conflict between divisions for resources • Divisions may think short-term and concentrate on profits rather than shareholder value • Can be difficult to evaluate relative performance of different divisions
Holding company • An extreme form of multi-divisional structure in which the divisions are separate legal entities		
Matrix • Attempts to ensure co-ordination across functional lines via **dual authority** in the organisation structure • Management control between different functions, whilst at the same time maintaining functional departmentalisation • Can be a mixture of functional, product and territorial organisation	• Offers flexibility • Improves communication • Dual authority gives the organisation multiple orientation so that functional specialists do not get wrapped up in their own concerns • Provides a structure for allocating responsibility to managers for end-results • Provides for inter-disciplinary co-operation and a mixing of skills and expertise	• Difficult to implement • Dual authority threatens a conflict between managers. Managers may also feel their authority is threatened • One individual with two or more bosses is more likely to suffer role stress at work • Can be more costly – eg project managers are additional jobs that would not be required in a more simple structure • The consensus and agreement required may slow down decision making

Structure	Advantages	Disadvantages
Transnational • Attempts to reconcile global scope and scale with local representatives • Similar to matrix, but responds specifically to globalisation challenges • National units are independent operating entities, but also provide capabilities, such as R&D, that are used by the rest of the organisation	• Shared capabilities allow national units to achieve global, or at least regional, economies of scale • Responsiveness to local conditions	• Makes great demands on managers both in their immediate responsibilities and in the complexity of their relationships with the organisation • Complexity of the organisation can lead to difficulties of control and the complications introduced by internal political activity
Team-based • Extends matrix structure by utilising cross-functional teams • Business processes used as the basis of the organisation, with each team being responsible for the processes relating to an aspect of the business		
Project-based • Similar to team-based except that projects have finite life and so, therefore, do the project teams dealing with them		

4.3 Centralisation vs decentralisation   5/10

Another important aspect of an organisation's structure is the level at which decisions are taken, and here there is a contrast between centralised organisations (in which the authority for most decisions remains with the upper levels of the organisation's hierarchy) and decentralised organisations (in which the authority to make specific decisions is delegated to people at lower levels in the organisation's hierarchy.) Consequently, decentralisation allows local managers to respond flexibly to local market conditions without constantly having to refer back to head office.

Advantages of centralisation

(a)   Decisions can be **co-ordinated** more easily, and management have better control over decisions.

(b)   **Goal congruence**. Decisions taken centrally should be based on overall objectives, whereas decentralised decisions may be influenced by short-term or local objectives of the people making the decisions.

(c)   **Standardisation**. For example, in any country McDonald's customers expect to find standard menus and pricing. If local managers were allowed to take decisions about changing menus or prices, this could undermine the business model.

(d)   **Resource allocation**. Centralised decision-making should allow resource usage to be co-ordinated effectively between different functions and divisions, based on overall corporate objectives.

(b)   Improve **lateral communication** – encouraging teams and departments to work together and share ideas.

(c)   Widen the **distribution of information** about company plans, so that people throughout the organisation can influence change and make suggestions.

(d)   Devolve and decentralise power as low down the hierarchy as possible, **delayering** where possible to reduce unnecessary layers of hierarchy.

(e)   Increase **opportunities for innovation** – allow teams more time to research and develop ideas.

4.5.3 The third wave

It is now commonplace to see the influence of advances in IS as creating a 'third wave' of economic development comparable to the development of agriculture and the industrial revolution. Whether or not a change of such magnitude is taking place, there is no doubt that there have been a number of very important IS based developments in the nature of work and the way it is organised.

(a)   **Mass customisation** of products *via* one-to-one marketing, web-based trading, the accumulation of customer information and the development of large **relationship marketing** databases.

(b)   **Disintermediation** is taking place both within organisations, as a result of delayering made possible by IS, and in the market place. Customers can deal direct with producers *via* their websites, or with a new kind of distributor typified by *Amazon*. **Network organisations** represent a mosaic of productive relationships that transcend older models based on the ownership of resources.

(c)   **Network economies** arising from the number of devices in use are becoming more important than economies of scale, which depend on the number of items produced. As the take up of any device incorporating an aspect of communications increases, so the usefulness and hence the value of an individual device grows as well.

(d)   The importance of the **service sector** and the **knowledge worker** is accelerating and the **leveraging of knowledge** itself is rising in importance as a business resource.

Hope and Hope identified 'the ten key issues of the management information wave'.

•   **Strategy** should be innovative (thinking 'outside the box'), based on core competences and organised using networks and alliances (for example, with suppliers and customers).

•   **Customer value** should be based on product leadership, operational excellence or customer knowledge.

•   **Knowledge management**: leverage human capital, market data and internal IS, to create competitive advantage.

•   **Business organisation**: base on networks rather than hierarchies.

•   **Market focus** should be on the best (most profitable) customers, not on volume of sales. (Customer Account Profitability could be a useful measure here.)

•   **Management accounting** should be relevant and empowering. It should look to manage the business (for example, processes and business drivers), not just the numbers. So rather than simply reporting costs, management accountants should also look for ways to reduce costs, for example through value chain analysis, benchmarking, or business process re-engineering.

•   **Measurement and control** measures should not constrain innovation. There needs to be a balance between control and empowerment.

•   **Shareholder value** depends on human capital, not physical assets. Human capital plays a crucial role in delivering future returns to shareholders.

•   **Productivity** is about people's ability to create value, not simply utilising non-current assets.

- **Transformation**: abandon the classical approach and Scientific Management; embrace the third wave.

Ezzamel et al suggest the following characteristics of 'new wave management'.

- Flexible supervision and employee self-discipline, rather than rules and regulation with discipline imposed by management.

- Development of people, rather than hierarchical control.

- Participative problem-solving, rather than having solutions directed by management.

- Multi-functional teams, instead of 'silos' of single-function specialists.

- Continuously evolving responsibilities and tasks, instead of narrowly defined jobs and responsibilities.

When looking at different forms of management, it may also be useful to consider *Stacey's* concepts of ordinary and extraordinary management (which we introduced in Chapter 1 of this Study Text).

Ordinary management is based on hierarchy and bureaucracy, with an emphasis on team-building and consensus. It essentially follows a rational model approach to strategy, with changes being introduced progressively and incrementally. Control is mainly exerted through 'negative feedback control': any deviations from expected results or patterns of behaviour are investigated and controlled.

Extraordinary management is much more informal. It involves a system of self-organisation, through informal creative networks and contacts, rather than formal structures. These creative networks build on 'tacit' knowledge and encourage organisational learning and innovation.

Interestingly, however, *Stacey* does not suggest that an organisation should adopt one type of management or the other. Rather, he suggests that operational matters and operational staff should be managed using ordinary management, while strategic management and organisational development may actually be better suited to an extraordinary management context.

4.6 New structural models

New approaches to the structure of organisations form an important part of the syllabus for Paper E2 and you should revise this topic from the BPP Study Text for that Paper as part of your preparation for this exam. Aspects of flexibility and the flexible firm are becoming increasingly common and so they could be examined at E3 as well as E2.

Flexibility may be important in a strategic context for a number of reasons:

(a)   **Speed of change**. Firms have to respond quickly to the need for change in turbulent and dynamic business conditions.

This may also include being able to respond quickly to new competitors who enter a market.

(b)   **Impact of technology**. New technologies lead to changes in the products produced by suppliers and demanded by consumers. Shortening product life cycles mean firms need to be able to respond to changes in product specification more quickly.

Technology has also led to changes in the **nature of the competition** firms face, with new online companies entering the market alongside established competitors.

In addition, technology has changed the ways people can work, with the growth of the internet leading to an increase in levels of **remote- or home-working**, meaning workers no longer need to be based at a firm's own offices.

(c)   **Flexibility and staffing**.

Multi-skilling: One element of flexibility is in the multi-skilling of staff; which gives firms the ability to redeploy staff in different roles as required.

Flexible remuneration: A second element of flexibility could be the flexibility of remuneration packages offered to employees. This could include not only profit-sharing and performance-related pay, but also the offer of 'cafeteria' approaches where employees are allowed to customise their own reward packages to a degree (for example, through health care, gym memberships, or buying additional leave). Such an approach allows employees to design a remuneration package which best suits their needs, and in doing so, it could also help boost employee morale and staff retention.

Flexible hours: A third element of flexibility relates to the hours which staff work: for example, the use of **flexible working hours, shift working,** or **job sharing schemes**. The increasing use of **home-working** could also be seen as an extension of the idea of greater flexibility around working hours – giving staff the flexibility to work from remote locations rather than having to come into a central office. The attraction of being able to work at home some days should be obvious for employees, but it can also be an advantage to a business: for example, by using systems like 'hot desking,' a firm can reduce the amount of office space and office furniture it needs.

Flexible numbers of staff: A fourth element of flexibility – and the one which could potentially have the greatest impact on the structure of firms – is flexibility in relation to the **numbers of staff** employed.

If a firm employs staff on a temporary contract basis, rather than on a full time basis, the number of staff it uses can be increased or decreased according to changes in demand for its services or the products those staff help to make.

This idea of using contract staff to perform non-core work was taken up by Charles Handy in his concept of the '**shamrock**' organisation.

New organisational structures include **virtual**, **network**, and **shamrock** organisations. Typically these modern approaches feature loose, delayered, organic relationships, exploitation of IS by empowered knowledge workers, and a flexible approach to mission and strategy. However, the shamrock organisation in particular, with its emphasis on **core staff** and **peripheral workers** (with activities either outsourced or performed by self-employed contract staff) is indicative of a new casualisation of labour, with implications for security and benefits at all levels.

Boundaryless organisations

Jack Welch (the long time CEO of General Electric) introduced the idea of 'The Boundaryless Organisation.'

Welch's view was that cultural, geographical and organisational boundaries which separated employees hindered efficiency, and so companies should look to make these boundaries more permeable; for example, by encouraging the exchange of information and ideas between different departments, and by developing cross-functional teams.

This idea of breaking down boundaries can also be extended to organisations' relationships with their customers and suppliers. For example, if organisations develop closer relationships with their suppliers this could help supply chain management. Equally, developing relationships with customers could help organisations gain a better understanding of what their customers want.

However, interdependency and trust are crucial in the boundaryless organisation. Staff will have to trust their co-workers, and recognise that they are all mutually accountable for the organisations successes (or mistakes).

Nonetheless, despite (or perhaps because of) the proliferation of new models of organisational structure, it is crucial that management adopt the most appropriate structure for the organisation they are running.

Although there may now be more variables to choose from, the underlying concept of aligning structure and strategy remains a key aspect of strategy implementation.

4.7 The new organisation and the management accountant

The new approaches will involve **management accountants in providing more information** to more people than previously, for decision making, for control and for reward and motivation. This may also lead to the management accountant having to deliver more detailed measures of performance.

The looser, more innovative ways of working mentioned above will be of particular significance to the management accountant. Here are some examples.

(a)   All **traditional routines** such as invoice processing will be challenged by, for instance, empowerment and network approaches.

(b)   **Cost management**. Challenging traditional routines will lead to challenging all cost areas to identify whether they add value or not. This means the accountant's role is no longer confined to **cost control**, but also extends to identifying opportunities for **cost reduction**.

(c)   **Activity based management** of costs may come to prominence within an organisation, with cross-functional responsibility centres predominating. This is likely to require a **revision of budgetary control systems**.

(d)   Functions, including some aspects of finance work, may be **outsourced** and **network structures** may be used both inside and outside the organisation: the accountant will have to provide and use control information in new ways.

(e)   **Decisions** may be made lower down the organisation, but they must still be made on sound grounds. Management accounting information will be more widely distributed, especially to **self-managing teams**, and there may be a requirement for control systems that will facilitate dispersed decision-making but prevent its abuse.

(f)   **Flexible patterns of employment** may lead to increased staff turnover with consequent loss of experience and cultural control. This may increase the need for closer rather than looser control of the work of temporary staff and teleworkers.

(g)   **Performance measurement**. Similarly, there may be a greater need for performance measurement for knowledge and contract workers. At the same time, normal cost accounting for labour will become more complicated as pay rates and the split into direct and indirect labour become more problematical.

The way labour costs are budgeted will also need to be revised, to reflect any changes in the mix between contract staff and permanent employees.

(h)   The overall system of control will depend on whether the organisation is one that depends on the knowledge and skills of its workforce, invests in and trusts them, or whether it uses flexible approaches to **exploit** them more effectively. A balance must be struck between empowerment and control.

(i)   The problem of motivating and rewarding the creative individual will be complicated by the move to **team working**.

Section summary

Three essential aspects define an organisation: social arrangements, collective goals, and controlled performance. The way organisations are structured has been affected by major environmental changes such as **globalisation** and **developments in IS**.

A number of writers on organisations and management have recommended the need for **innovation**, **flexibility**, **communication**, **empowerment**, **leveraging of knowledge** and a **network approach to organising resources** both within the organisation and outside its boundaries.

The new approaches to the structuring of organisations will involve **management accountants in providing more information** to more people than previously, for decision making, for control, and for reward and motivation.

Chapter Roundup

✓ PRINCE2 defines a clear **management structure** of roles and responsibilities within the system which can be adapted to suit both the organisation and the specific project. A fundamental aspect of PRINCE2 is that a project is **driven by its business case**, so it will only be undertaken if it is going to add value to the organisation.

✓ A project will be deemed successful if it is completed at the specified level of **quality**, **on time** and within **budget**. Achieving this can be very difficult: most projects present a range of significant challenges.

✓ Adaptation to environmental change makes project management an important feature of strategic implementation. Also, strategic management thinking can be a useful input to project management. Strategic project management envisages strategy as a stream of projects intended to achieve organisational breakthroughs.

✓ The need to be innovative, flexible and able to deal with short product life cycles, as well as the constant pressure to reduce costs, has led to the development of **lean systems**, particularly in manufacturing.

✓ **JIT** aims for zero inventory and perfect quality and operates by demand-pull. It consists of **JIT purchasing** and **JIT production** and results in lower investment requirements, space savings, greater customer satisfaction and increased flexibility.

✓ **World class manufacturing (WCM)** aims for high quality, fast production, and the flexibility to respond to customer needs.

✓ Changes to business processes may be classed as **automation**, **rationalisation**, or **re-engineering**. Business process re-engineering involves fundamental changes in the way an organisation functions.

✓ Computerising existing methods is not re-engineering the process, but IT can add value as an **enabler**, rather than the solution.

✓ The **automate**, **informate** and **transformate** framework is very similar to BPR's **automation**, **rationalisation** and **re-engineering**, as is **process innovation**, which focuses on the creation of new processes to achieve business objectives.

✓ Three essential aspects define an organisation: social arrangements, agreed goals and controlled performance. The way organisations are structured has been affected by major environmental changes, such as **globalisation** and **developments in IS**.

✓ A number of writers on organisations and management have recommended the need for **innovation**, **flexibility**, **communication**, **empowerment**, **leveraging of knowledge** and a **network approach to organising resources** both within the organisation and outside its boundaries.

✓ The new approaches to the structuring of organisations will involve **management accountants in providing more information** to more people than previously, for decision making, for control and for reward and motivation.

Quick Quiz

1   In PRINCE2, the continuing viability of a project is established by reference to:

    A   The senior user
    B   The business case
    C   The project board
    D   The most recent end stage assessment

2   Complete the gap in the sentence below using one of the expressions given in brackets.

'In JIT manufacturing, ... is used to ensure that products or components are only produced when needed by the next process.'

(uniform loading, a kanban system, employee involvement, a close relationship with suppliers)

3   Which of the following is not a principle of BPR, according to *Hammer*?

    A   Information gathering should not be separated from information processing
    B   Work people should be self-managing as far as possible
    C   Processes should evolve from current methods
    D   Parallel activities should be linked rather than integrated

4   How does the role of IT differ between BPR and PI?

5   List three of the characteristics of the 'third wave' of economic development.

Answers to Quick Quiz

1   B   A project can only be judged viable by reference to its business case.

2   A kanban system is used for this purpose.

3   C   It is fundamental to BPR that current methods should be examined most critically: the emphasis is always on the desired outcome rather than existing processes.

4   IT is an **enabler** in BPR, but it is often a **change trigger** in PI.

5   Three from:

    • Mass customisation
    • Relationship marketing
    • Disintermediation
    • Network economies
    • Knowledge workers
    • Importance of knowledge

Answers to Questions

10.1 Value-added activity

The correct answer is C.

The other activities are non-value-adding activities

10.2 JIT

The correct answer is B.

Now try this question from the Exam Question Bank

Number	Level	Marks	Time
Q11	Examination	15	27 mins

CHANGE MANAGEMENT

Part C

390

ORGANISATIONAL CHANGE

 Change management is one of the most frequently discussed topics in business strategy. Such discussions may reflect on how important it is for an organisation to change, or may consider an organisation's ability to change.

Change management is therefore an integral and important part of strategic management.

We will begin this chapter by analysing the causes of strategic change, before moving on to look at the process of change (Section 3).

Some models view change as a rational linear process, but in order for a change to be successful, it has to be effectively managed (Section 4).

There will be some stakeholders who support a change while others are likely to resist it. Force field analysis (Section 5) illustrates the driving and resisting forces for any change event.

In order to implement the change, an organisation will have to overcome this resistance to change (Section 6).

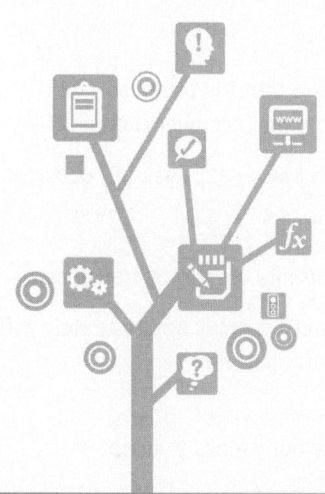

topic list	learning outcomes	syllabus references	ability required
1 Introduction to change management	B1(a)	–	Discuss
2 Triggers for organisational change	B1(a)	B1(i), (iii)	Discuss
3 Stage models of change	B1(a)	B1(ii)	Discuss
4 Other models of managing change	B1(a)	B1(ii)	Discuss
5 Force field analysis	B1(a)	B1(ii)	Discuss
6 Managing resistance to change	B1(b)	B2(iii)	Recommend

1   Introduction to change management

Introduction

It is very hard to ignore the impact of change on contemporary businesses. However, the visibility of change in this way also highlights the importance of understanding and managing the impact of change on businesses and the people who work for them. Change is often an integral part of strategy implementation.

Change management constitutes 20% of the E3 syllabus, and so is likely to be a theme which occurs frequently in exam questions. However, it is very important to be aware that strategic change and change management issues may be implicit in a scenario rather than being the explicit subject of a question requirement. You must be able to recognise the factors that drive change and constrain the ways in which it may be managed.

However, before we start to look at change management theories and models, we will look at some of the practical issues involved by using a case study.

CASE STUDY

McDonald's fast food restaurants

Society's attitudes to fast food have been changing in the last few years, and if the fast food industry is to remain successful it needs to recognise these changing customer needs and respond to them.

Concerns about rising obesity levels and advances in healthcare have highlighted the importance of a healthy diet. Increased access to mass communications (television, internet) have meant that consumers are becoming more informed about issues and are demanding better choices in convenience foods.

Meeting stakeholder needs

Changing **customer needs and requirements** illustrate the more general issue that the business environment is not static, but evolves over time, reflecting changes in the broader social environment.

However, customers are not the only important stakeholder whose interests McDonald's need to consider.

Other stakeholders include:

Business partners – including franchisees and suppliers (McDonald's restaurants are run by franchisees)

Employees – When taken together, McDonald's corporation and its franchisees employ approximately 1.5 million people, with more than 30,000 restaurants spread across about 120 countries.

Opinion leaders – including governments, the media, health professionals and environmental groups. McDonald's is very conscious of its corporate social responsibility, and constantly looks to adapt its operations to increase the positive impact it can have on society.

Responding to customers' needs

McDonald's conducts market research and listens to what its customers what to see on its menu, and also to understand customer opinions about brand image, quality, service, cleanliness and value.

One of the messages which emerged from this research in recent years was that customers wanted more choice, with healthier and lighter food options. Customers also wanted greater visibility in food labelling and more information about what they were eating: for example, how much fat and how much salt their meals contained.

Creating menu changes

McDonalds took a two-fold approach to converting these customer findings into menu changes. On the one hand they improved existing products, on the other they created new ones.

Improving existing products – changes included introducing new cooking oil blends which were low in saturated fat, and reducing the amount of salt used when preparing the meals.

New products – these include new salad and deli choice ranges, which contain low levels of fat.

In addition, McDonalds now provides customers with extensive nutritional labelling, both in-store and on the company website. Packaging includes recommended daily intakes (for example of fats or carbohydrates) so that customers can see how their food choices relate to their overall daily requirements.

However, despite the changes, the new menu options are still consistent with McDonald's brand. The packaging, presentation and service are still recognisably McDonald's.

Communicating the changes

Although making the changes was crucial, it was equally important to communicate the changes to the consumer. To this end, McDonald's developed advertising campaigns which were designed to highlight the new healthier food options, countering public perceptions of McDonald's as only selling unhealthy meals.

McDonald's has made use of a variety of advertising media – print, billboards, television and the internet – and it targets its audience for each media type carefully. For example, website advertising is designed to be appealing to teenagers, so is both interactive and informative, making use of the latest design and technology.

The McDonald's example illustrates how change occurs in a social context. This is an important point to recognise, because change management does not simply involve a choice between technological, organisational or people-oriented solutions. Rather it involves finding solutions which combine these factors to provide integrated strategies which help improve performance and results.

Change management is a crucial part of any project which leads or enables people to accept new processes, technologies, systems, structures and values. Change management consists of the set of activities which help people move from their present way of working to a new, and hopefully improved, way of working.

KEY TERM

We can define CHANGE MANAGEMENT as 'the continuous process of aligning an organisation with its marketplace and doing it more responsively and effectively than competitors'.   *(Berger)*

It is also important to identify the importance of adopting a **contingency approach** to change management. There isn't a single correct way to manage change. Selecting a way to manage a change depends on the **nature** and the **context** of the change, and the **organisation** undergoing the change.

1.1 The need for change

Any organisation that ignores change does so at its own peril, because their inactivity is likely to weaken their ability to manage future scenarios.

The management guru, *Peter Drucker*, argues that a 'winning strategy' will require information about events and conditions outside the organisation, because only once an organisation has that information can it prepare for the new changes and challenges which arise from shifts in the world economy.

This does not, however, mean that implementing a strategic change will necessarily improve an organisation's performance.

CASE STUDY

Marks and Spencer

In 1993, Britain was experiencing a recession, and all the major retailers were suffering as consumers looked to cut back on their spending.

Marks and Spencer's (M&S) chief executive at the time, Richard Greenbury, decided to concentrate on the company's traditional core businesses of clothing and food to steer it through this difficult time.

The strategy appeared to be successful, and M&S's profits rose steadily over the next few years and Greenbury planned to double the number of European stores by the year 2000.

However, the face of high street retail was changing, and a number of new companies such as Monsoon and Gap were emerging. They segmented the market, and offered customers cheaper, more socially aware designs than M&S.

Additionally, Tesco, Sainsbury and Waitrose challenged M&S for some of its core business in the food sector. These companies eroded M&S's competitive advantage by offering products of similar quality at better value, thereby making M&S's product lines look expensive.

M&S's results in 1998 showed that falling sales had caused profits to halve from the previous year.

Luc Vandevelde became CEO in 2000, and he introduced new designers and new product ranges (eg Per Una) and switched to cheaper overseas suppliers to face the increased competition in the clothing market. (M&S had historically only used UK suppliers and had built up strong relationships with its suppliers, using the quality of its produce as a strong source of competitive advantage).

As profits continued to fall, M&S sold off its European operations, and decided to concentrate on its core UK businesses, opening a number of homeware and food only stores.

Celebrity endorsements, such as David Beckham's 'DB07' children's clothing range, were also introduced.

Profits began to rise again in mid 2002 as a result of these activities, and then the top board posts were separated as Mr Vandevelde remained as chairman but handed over the CEO role to Roger Holmes.

By 2004 sales had slowed again, and M&S had to fight to stave off a takeover bid from the retail tycoon, Sir Philip Green. The policy of sourcing products directly from overseas continued, with the Far East and Eastern Europe being the key locations. However, M&S continued to lose market share in its core business areas to competitors such as Asda and Next.

In 2005 M&S reacted to slowing sales by cutting prices to try to put pressure on its rivals.

It also introduced a new promotional brand – Your M&S – which has become the main focus for its advertising and in-store merchandising. The 'Your M&S' brand was designed to portray a more modern and youthful image for M&S. To support this newer image, M&S has also been rolling out a new store format across all its stores – making them brighter and more spacious.

The new look, combined with successful advertising campaigns in 2005-6 (for example the clothing campaign featuring Twiggy, and the food adverts with the slogan "This is not just food, this is M&S food") led to a resurgence in performance in 2006-7.

However, the economic downturn in 2008-9 meant that shoppers once again became more conservative in their spending. Price once more became a key issue, and M&S responded to this in their food stores with their '2 Dine for £10' offers – offering customers a 'restaurant experience' for less. Rather than competing on price with other food retailers, M&S effectively started competing with restaurants: offering customers a main meal, vegetables, and dessert for two, with a bottle of wine, for just £10. In other words, customers could get a restaurant-standard meal for £10, although they had to eat it in their own homes rather than a restaurant.'

1.2 The process of change

In the same way that choosing a business strategy encourages an organisation to assess its current **position**, evaluate its strategic **choices**, and then decide upon a course of action to **implement**, we can also look at change management as a sequence of stages.

For an organisation to respond to the need for change, it needs a way of **planning for**, and **implementing changes**.

Although each situation should be considered individually, we can still identify some general steps which could be followed during a major change initiative.

Change processes usually begin with a change '**trigger**'. The trigger identifies the need or desire for change in a particular area.

Triggers include:

External events

- Changes in the economic cycle (for example, an economic downturn)

- New laws or regulations affecting the industry

- Stiffer competition from rivals or from new entrants

- Arrival of new technology (for example, the impact of faster communications and digital downloads on music and film entertainment)

Internal events

- Arrival of new senior management with different strategies, priorities and styles
- Implementation of new technologies or working practices
- Relocation of the business to different city or country

These triggers will force change. The issue for management is whether to seek to manage the change to get the best outcome, or just to let the change event run its course with uncertain outcomes.

In response to the trigger, some tentative plans about possible changes are prepared. Wherever possible, an organisation should consider a range of alternatives, and consider the advantages and disadvantages of each. **Stakeholders**' probable reactions to the changes should also be considered.

A preferred solution should then be chosen from the range of alternative options, and a **timetable** for implementing the changes should be established. The **speed** at which change is implemented is likely to depend on the nature of the change and people's anticipated reactions to it.

The plan for change then needs to be **communicated** to everyone who will be involved in implementing it, before the actual implementation stage gets underway.

Balogun & Hope Hailey summarise the process of change a change flow chart.

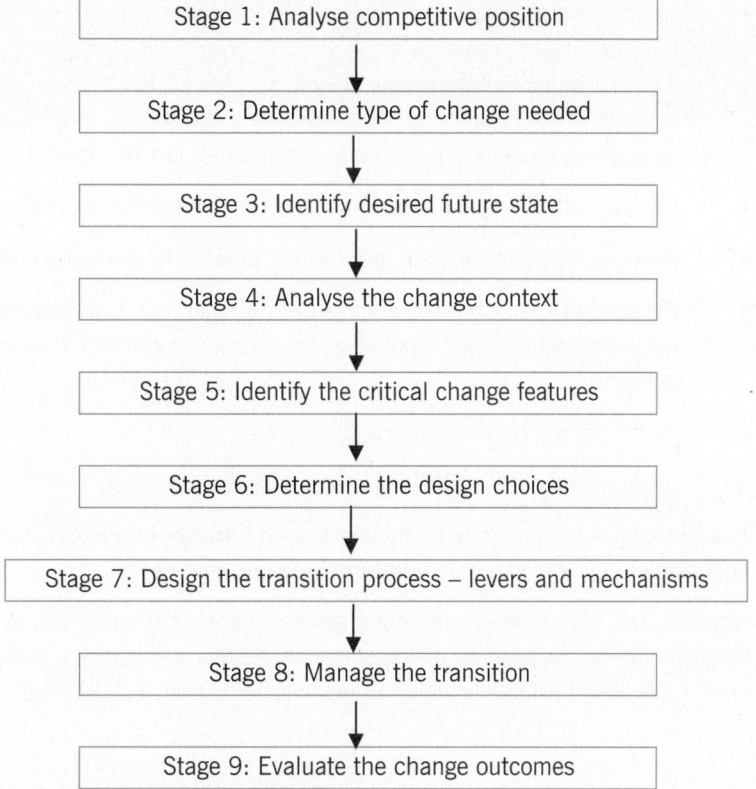

Stage 1: Analyse competitive position

↓

Stage 2: Determine type of change needed

↓

Stage 3: Identify desired future state

↓

Stage 4: Analyse the change context

↓

Stage 5: Identify the critical change features

↓

Stage 6: Determine the design choices

↓

Stage 7: Design the transition process – levers and mechanisms

↓

Stage 8: Manage the transition

↓

Stage 9: Evaluate the change outcomes

Stages 1 & 2 of the flow chart can be summarised as the '**why and what**' of change, while Stages 3-9 can be summarised as the '**how**' of change.

Managing strategic change is a key part of implementing corporate strategy.

Note that both strategic management and change management involve an analysis of current **position**, an evaluation of possible **choices** and a **decision** about the appropriate course of action to take. Therefore the ideas of **suitability, acceptability,** and **feasibility** which we considered in Chapter 7 are also relevant to decisions about strategic change.

Section summary

Organisations need to change and adapt to deal with changes in their environment and to improve their performance and results. The detail of any change management programme will depend on its context, but in general terms change management is likely to require an organisation to assess its current position, evaluate the choices it has for how to change, and then decide upon a course of change action to implement.

Change management can be defined as 'the continuous process of aligning an organisation with its marketplace and doing it more responsively and effectively than competitors.

2 Triggers for organisational change

Introduction

Events which trigger change can either come from outside an organisation (external triggers) or from within it (internal triggers). The E3 syllabus mentions a number of potential change triggers:

- Environmental factors
- Mergers and acquisitions
- Re-organisation and rationalisation

Organisations may need to make strategic changes for lots of different reasons. For example:

- Dealing with changes in the global economy and global markets

- Allowing an organisation to grow, either organically or through mergers or acquisition

- Responding to customer pressures (for example, car manufacturers moving towards producing more environmentally friendly cars in response to consumer concerns about carbon emissions and pollution)

- Re-structuring or re-organising the business

- Implementing new technologies and business processes

The whole change process typically begins with a **trigger for change**, which can be either **external to the organisation** or can come from **within the organisation** itself.

However, it is important to note that changes do not occur solely due to external pressure or events, but they can also be triggered by management perception and choices. Managers respond to events taking place internally or externally which to them signal the need for change.

2.1 Environmental factors

Businesses and managers are faced with highly dynamic and ever more complex operating environments. This dynamism and complexity creates pressure for change.

Industries and products change, along with the markets they serve, and organisations have to change and adapt. Such changes, along with the need to introduce innovations within ever diminishing timescales, places change management towards the top of the core competencies required by an organisation if it is to be successful.

Change triggers can be national or even inter-national. For example, throughout Europe, as countries join the Eurozone or have to conform with directives on working time and working practices, organisations operating within those countries have to adapt to the changing commercial environments they face.

2.1.1 Potential environmental triggers for change

The exact triggers for change will depend on the context of an organisation and its industry, but the following are some of the more common instances where the initial trigger for change comes from outside an organisation:

- Changes in level or intensity of competition (prompting a need to gain or protect market share)
- Changes in economic conditions – either domestically or internationally
- Changes in government legislation
- Changes in customer expectations and tastes
- Change in technology (process or product technology)
- Change in communications media, in particular the growth of e-business
- Changes in supply chain or distribution networks

The PEST framework which was discussed in E2 can be a useful way of identifying factors which may trigger external change. (A brief summary of the PEST framework is provided in the introductory chapter at the start of this Study Text.)

Porter's 'Five Forces' model could also be a useful way of identifying external triggers: for example, new entrants into the market, or the emergence of substitute products, or an increase in inter-firm rivalry leading to price wares or extensive advertising campaign.

Globalisation

Reductions in transportation, information and communication costs, new technologies and e-business, and the growth of new trading blocs such as the 'Tiger' economies of South East Asia mean that the geography of world trade has changed dramatically in the last 20 years.

Organisations (particularly in developed, Western countries) need to plan how to respond to the increasing competitive pressures which result from the growth of rivals based in locations with lower cost bases.

Globalisation also opens up opportunities for organisations to shift production internationally, or to sell to customers in a number of countries. Such changes could have a significant impact on how a company manages its supply chain.

Natural environment

The potential impact of businesses on the natural environment is becoming increasingly recognised. The potential exhaustion of supplies of natural resources; concern about levels of waste and pollution being created; and the threat of climate change and global warming will force organisations to change their behaviour sooner or later.

Organisations are now increasingly keen to show they are responsible corporate citizens, so changes may be introduced so that they can demonstrate their corporate social responsibility.

Changing workplace structures

Historically, the traditional organisation structure has seen businesses staffed by a core, permanent workforce.

However, this model is changing to one where an increasing number of organisations are using a mix of core and peripheral workforces, for example using tele-workers and outsourcing their labour requirements for certain services.

Despite these changes, social and demographic issues will continue to affect the workplace. For example, how will organisations deal with equal opportunities legislation which could affect recruitment decisions on the grounds of gender or age?

Continuing impact of Advanced Communications Technologies (ACT)

Since the 1980's, most of the developed economies in the world have been riding the 'third wave' of an industrial revolution that will bring changes as profound as those that followed the earlier two waves of steam power and the internal combustion engine.

ACT have created new industries, new products, and new lifestyles and have enabled the fragmentation of firms into 'virtual businesses' such that activities that were once all conducted in-house are now being factored out across the globe. The new technologies have also brought new organisational structures, and have led to organisations having enriched information about individuals and groups of customers. These technologies have also raised new concerns about privacy and surveillance.

2.2 Rationalising and cost-cutting

There is often a tendency to see organisational change as a positive step forward – that changes are designed to facilitate growth and development.

However, this is not necessarily the case. Concerns about market conditions and competitiveness may force organisations to downsize, rationalise or cut costs. For example, during times of recession, organisations may reduce the number of new staff they recruit, or may make staff redundant, in an effort to reduce wage costs.

One important point to note here, however, is that organisations should not simply view external triggers as **threats**, because they can also offer **opportunities** for change.

Kanter points out that effective organisations are adept at handling the triggers of change, even when the triggers may appear to be threats.

For example, an unwanted takeover bid may require immediate and dramatic responses. But by managing the situation to **create the environment of a crisis**, the organisation may induce a willingness among all stakeholders to act as one in the defence of the organisation. Therefore the crisis can actually act as a galvanising event, and lead to rapidly agreed responses, within incurring any resistance. (As we will see later in this Text, resistance to change is often a problem in change management processes).

2.3 Mergers and acquisitions

New alliances, acquisitions, mergers and other significant business combinations may require substantial changes in the organisation structure in order to benefit from new synergies, value chain linkages or core competencies.

We looked at mergers and acquisitions as strategic options earlier in this Study Text, and we identified the respective advantages and disadvantages of them as methods of growth. However, in the context of change management it is worth pointing out that there are a number of different reasons why organisations may join together through a merger or an acquisition.

This is important because it means there are a number of different (potential) change management issues depending on the context of the merger or acquisition.

Exam skills

It is quite possible that the examiner could examine change management issues in the context of a strategic option (such as a merger or acquisition, or a diversification strategy). If you get a question like this, make sure you recognise what the organisation is trying to achieve through the strategic option, because this could determine some of the issues it needs to consider when managing the change process.

Let us consider some of the different issues which arise from a range of possible reasons for a merger or acquisition.

Reason for acquisition	Possible issues to consider
Growth	• Senior management team required to deliver a significant change in performance • Likely to be new arrivals in the senior management team • Importance of aligning cultures • Administrative efficiencies; integration in some areas if beneficial to results
Synergy	• Senior management teams need to work closely together on key areas of strategy • Other areas of business left intact
Diversification	• Loosely coupled management teams. • Some administrative efficiencies, but businesses retain separate identities and branding
Integration	• Integrated senior management team • Merged administrative systems; core process tightly coupled • Pooled resources, better services for customers • Single corporate identity. Overcoming cultural problems is key. (Complex 'dual' structures can sometimes result to spare egos)
Defensive measures	• Response to mergers/acquisitions by rivals: may be unexpected by staff • Crisis management techniques may be required • Low performance from staff if they are confused about the process

If the motive behind the deal is simply that there is **pressure on senior management to do a deal**, then potentially many of the issues above may apply.

2.3.1 Post-acquisition issues

After an acquisition, the incoming management will want to integrate the firm they have acquired into the parent company's structure and systems. This will involve visible changes to names and signage, but also deeper changes to organisational structures, culture, job roles, staff numbers and management systems.

However, statistically, 70-80% of acquisitions fail, meaning that they do not create any wealth for the shareholders of the acquiring company.

Key reasons for these failures (and therefore key areas of change which need to be managed) are:

(a) **Poor communication**   In particular, poor communication to staff, resulting in a failure to establish trust and a commitment to a joint future

(b) **Poor structure**   The structure of the new company does not follow the logic of the acquisition

(c) **Cultural differences**   Issues of cultural incompatibility are often cited as problem areas when implementing mergers and acquisitions. Therefore organisations need to consider the compatibility of the respective cultures when considering the suitability of the merger or acquisition.

However, the amount of **cultural integration** required actually depends on the reason for the merger.

If core processes are going to be combined for economies of scale, then integration is important and needs to be given management time and attention. If a company is acquiring a portfolio of diverse businesses, cultural integration may only be necessary at senior management level.

CASE STUDY

Daimler/Chrysler

In 1998, Daimler Benz, the German car manufacturer best known for its Mercedes premium brand, merged with the US company, Chrysler, a volume car manufacturer. The merged company, Daimler Chrysler became the world's largest car manufacturer.

However, although the deal was originally billed as a merger of equals, in practice it was a takeover by Daimler. Interestingly, by March 2001 the share price had fallen to just over 60 percent of what it had been in November 1998.

A number of reasons were identified for the poor performance of the new group:

- US and German **business cultures were different**. Possibly because of cultural problems in the new group, many key Chrysler managers left after the merger.

- Mercedes was a premium brand which had been extended to making smaller cars. Chrysler depended on high volumes, not a premium product. Therefore the distinction between 'premium' and 'volume' businesses got blurred.

- The new group did not properly exploit economies of scale, such as sharing components. There was a degree of technology-sharing among the engineers, and this did result in some success stories, such as the Chrysler 300 model. However, many critics argued that the merger **could not deliver the synergies** which had been expected because the businesses were never successfully integrated. In effect, they seemed to be running two independent product lines: Daimler and Chrysler.

- **Productivity and efficiency** at Chrysler was far lower than industry norms. (In 2000, each vehicle took Chrysler around 40 hours to make, compared to approximately 20 for the American factories of competitors such as Honda and Toyota.) In addition its purchasing was inefficient, and fixed costs were too high for the size of the company. Overall, Chrysler's performance was much weaker than Daimler had realised going into the deal.

Ultimately, the Daimler Chrysler merger failed to produce the trans-Atlantic automotive powerhouse that had been hoped for, and in 2007 Chrysler was sold to a private equity firm that specialises in restructuring troubled companies. In December 2008, Chrysler received a $4bn loan from the US Government to stave off bankruptcy. Nonetheless, Chrysler eventually filed for bankruptcy in April 2009.

While it was by no means the only reason why it failed, the failure to implement change effectively and to integrate the companies after the merger, was a major contributing factor to the failure of the merger.

Impact on the customer

It is very easy for managers to become so focused on a deal that **customers get forgotten**. However, if managers take their eye of the ball, they are in danger of forgetting the main reason for their existence.

Competitors will be looking out for opportunities to exploit any weaknesses arising from a merger or acquisition, and this could be a serious threat if the merged organisations' product offering or customer service standards slip.

2.4 Internal triggers

Although organisational changes often result from external triggers from the outside world, there are also situations where the change trigger is internal to the organisation itself.

Some of these internal triggers may be related to external forces operating in the organisation's environment, but they do not need to be.

The triggers create disequilibrium within the organisation, and for equilibrium to be re-established some element of the organisational system needs to change.

Internal triggers may include:

- Changes in the goals and activities of the organisation which require adaptation and learning (for example in the development of a new product line)

- New senior managers joining the organisation

- A new organisation structure which prompts changes to job responsibilities

- Questioning authority or the accepted way of doing things (the 'status quo')

- The presence of entrepreneurs or innovators within the organisation who act to promote change

- The acquisition of new knowledge or skills, creating both the pressure and the ability to change

Poor performance can be seen as an internal trigger for change, although the wish to improve performance is also likely to be supported by external pressures to become more competitive.

One of the most common internal triggers for change is a change in **business leadership**. When a new CEO or director joins an organisation they often want to make changes, to stamp their authority on the business.

CASE STUDY

Leadership change at General Motors

In the summer of 2009 General Motors (GM) had to accept a $50 billion federal bailout to revive it after bankruptcy, and about 1,900 dealers (a third of its domestic US retail network) had been shut down.

However, as part of its rescue plan, the US government also introduced a new nonexecutive chairman, Edward E. Whitacre Jr, to keep an eye on the company.

Mr Whitacre had a very blunt message for the GM. "We're going to get this company turned around. And if the current leadership can't fix it [the company] we'll find someone who can."

As it turned out, this was a precursor to the incumbent CEO Fritz Henderson leaving the company, as Whitacre and the Board fired him on 1 December 2009. The Board was sceptical that Henderson, who had worked at GM all his life, was radical enough to change the company. Instead, Whitacre – a former telecom executive who had transformed the ailing Baby Bell into a resurgent AT&T – decided that he was the man to fix GM.

One executive who was directly involved in the decision said, 'Fritz [Henderson] was moving to change things, but a lot more needed to be done.'

Within three months of Henderson leaving, Whitacre had eased out four other executives, reassigned 20 more, and brought in seven outsiders to fill top jobs. This came as a shock to GM which had historically been seen as reluctant to change. Vice-chairman Bob Lutz, who became one of the casualties of the regime change said, 'In the past, GM was accused of not enough change. But you have to find the balance between the pace of change and trauma to the organisation'.

However, people close to Whitacre say he would rather cope with trauma than accept the status quo at a company that lost $84.3 million a day in 2008.

(Adapted from an article in Business Week, *Ed Whitacre's Battle to Save GM from Itself*, 29 April 2010)

Internally generated change is likely to be managed more proactively, creatively and effectively than externally generated change.

This is because there is clear ownership of the change, but also because the organisation has a prior knowledge and understanding of the change. Because the trigger for change is internal to the organisation, the organisation can control the nature and timing of the change in a way it cannot do when it has to react to external triggers.

A survey by the Chartered Institute of Personnel and Development (CIPD) in the UK, found that during the 1990s the top 50 UK companies moved from having, on average, one major reorganisation every five years to having one every three years.

Although we mentioned earlier that external market conditions can lead to restructuring through downsizing or cost-cutting, there may also be internal change triggers which force organisations to review their size and structure.

Reorganisation and restructuring can occur as a result of internal triggers aimed at internal improvement:

- efficiency or effectiveness
- centralisation or decentralisation
- flattening of organisational hierarchy

In more general terms, managing strategic change is a key part of implementing corporate strategy, and reorganisation can often come about as part of an organisation's strategy implementation.

- expansion into new markets
- introduction of a new product or service
- change in organisational culture

 When considering the implementation of strategic plans, businesses need to make sure that organisation structures match with business strategy. We looked at organisational structure in Chapter 10.

The relationship between structure and strategy has important implications for change management: if business strategy or organisational structure, or both, are being changed, the new strategy and structure need to fit together for any change to be implemented successfully.

2.5 Internal growth

We mentioned earlier that firms may grow through mergers and acquisitions, but firms may also grow internally through organic growth.

Greiner looked at the way organisations grow, and identified a series of phases through which growing companies tend to pass. Importantly, in the context of change management, Greiner also postulated that this growth was made up of prolonged periods of **evolution** – in which organisational practices remained relatively constant – and periods of **revolution** in which there was substantial turmoil and change in the organisation's life.

In this way, Greiner presented organisational growth as a series of five phases, each of which results in a revolutionary crisis that takes it on to the next phase:

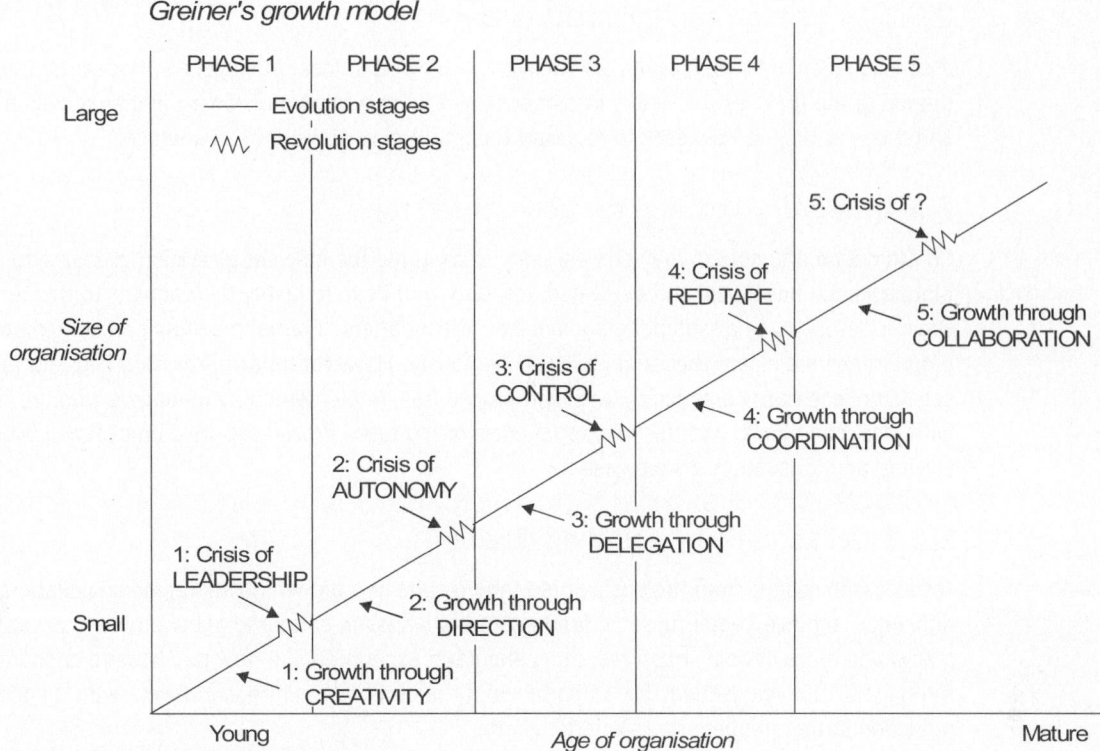

Figure 11.1 Greiner's growth model

Greiner's model suggests that an organisation cannot expect growth and development to be a smooth, evolutionary process. As an organisation grows it reaches critical points at which the existing ways of doing things are no longer efficient or effective. These critical points are the revolutionary periods at which managers need to find a new set of organisational practices which can then form the basis for the next period of evolutionary growth.

2.5.1 Creativity and the crisis of leadership

In the birth stage of an organisation, the emphasis is on creating a product or a market. The culture of the organisation will be essentially entrepreneurial, and communication among staff will be informal. However, as the firm starts to grow, the entrepreneur and the firm will need more sophisticated competencies to cope with increasing volumes of production and a larger workforce. Increased numbers of employees cannot be managed exclusively through informal communication. Investment is likely to be required to continue expansion, which will require further financial control. Therefore, the founding entrepreneurs find themselves burdened with management responsibilities - the crisis of leadership. A solution to this crisis will be to install a strong business manager who can implement a more formal control mechanism and pull the organisation together.

2.5.2 Direction and the crisis of autonomy

However, the control mechanisms and the organisation structure which are put in place as the result of the first crisis become inadequate as the firm continues to grow. Staff are frustrated at bureaucracy, centralised control, and narrowly defined job assignments. They find themselves restricted by a cumbersome and centralised hierarchy and this leads to the crisis of autonomy.

This crisis of autonomy makes it necessary for the firm to start to **delegate** and allow the managers and staff some discretion over decision-making. This delegation accompanies the application of a more decentralised organisational structure. Local managers are given responsibility for running their own plants and markets.

2.5.3 Delegation and the crisis of control

A consequence of the delegation and discretion allowed to local managers is that senior management at the top of the firm begin to feel a loss of control – a crisis of control. Co-ordination across the firm suffers, and those at the top now seek to re-assert their control over the firm as a whole.

2.5.4 Co-ordination and the crisis of red tape

Co-ordination and control may be necessary in ensuring the efficient allocation of scarce resources. Managers still have local and delegated authority, but have to justify their actions to the centre, which Greiner describes as a 'watchdog audience at headquarters.' Formal planning procedures and control programmes are established and reviewed rigorously. However, in turn, the staff begin to resent what they see as unnecessary bureaucracy and rigid procedures, implemented by managers who are not familiar with local conditions, and this leads to a crisis of red tape. Procedures take precedence over problem solving, and innovation is suppressed.

2.5.5 Collaboration – and the crisis of '?'

A successful escape from the crisis of red tape results in a growth of 'interpersonal collaboration'. This is difficult to achieve, requiring some fundamental changes in culture to allow problem solving through teams and more flexible structures. Innovation and experiments in new practice are encouraged throughout the organisation. The importance of the corporate centre is reduced, with a concomitant reduction in the number of headquarters staff.

The final crisis is named by Greiner as 'The ? crisis', one that he could not fully identify back in 1972 (when he published his model). With some foresight, however, he speculated that this crisis would result from increasing stress in the workplace, the 'psychological saturation' of employees who grow emotionally and physically exhausted by the intensity of teamwork and the heavy pressure for innovative solutions.'

2.5.6 General points about Greiner's model

Overall, Greiner's model provides some useful insights into the process of organisational growth, although Greiner himself highlights some of the challenges it presents to managers of growing organisations.

Knowing which stage of development an organisation is at – Management has to recognise when an organisation reaches a 'crisis' point, and to know which crisis point it is at, otherwise they may impose the wrong solution.

Solutions breed new problems – Managers often fail to realise that the solution to one problem eventually becomes the cause of a future problem. For example, the decision to delegate in time causes the crisis of control. This is not to say that the solutions themselves were not appropriate when they were implemented, but it is a reminder that a solution will not remain valid forever. In essence, this suggests that management need to try to predict when the next revolution (or crisis) is imminent so that they can work on a solution to deal with that crisis.

In addition, a general observation about Greiner's model is that it seems to imply that growth is the normal state of affairs for all organisations. However, this is not always the case; and, for example, Greiner's model provides no insight into how to deal with organisational decline.

2.6 Managing decline

So far, we have focused largely on change management in the context of organisational growth, but changes may also be required to help an organisation overcome a decline in performance.

There are a number of factors which may contribute to organisational decline, but some of the more common ones are:

- Decline in demand for products or services, leading to a decline in revenues

- High cost structures, leading to a decline in competitiveness compared to rivals

- Poor financial control, exemplified either by spending not being kept under control, or by management not having suitable information to assess the performance of the business

- Overtrading, leading to excess pressure on the organisation's cash flow

- Too much diversification, causing a business to move away from, and neglect, its core business

In many cases, managers' strategic priorities for reversing the decline will centre on:

- Increasing competitiveness (for example through new product development, or product differentiation) in order to increase revenue, and

- Reducing costs in order to improve efficiency.

However, when looking at ways of reducing costs, it is important that an organisation considers all of its process and structures, and does not only look for a quick fix solution, such as reducing labour costs through redundancies.

Whilst reducing staff numbers can help cut costs, a business needs to think through the implications of making dramatic staff cuts. If, for example, these lead to a reduction in the quality of the products or services offered to customers, they may do long term damage to the business' reputation and its future prospects. Equally, if employee morale is damaged too severely this could have further detrimental consequences for the business, particularly among unionised workforces which may vote for strike action.

2.7 Operational change

Although we have considered change management at a general strategic level, organisations also have to manage changes at a more tactical or operational level. A number of the issues we considered in the previous chapter may be relevant here. For example, business processes may need to be improved through **business process re-engineering** (BPR); or a firm may have a culture of **continuous improvement** and **total quality management** (TQM).

In this context, it is also worth mentioning the Japanese idea of **kaizen** – the continuous improvement of a process or product.

Continuous improvement, by its very nature, involves constant adaptation and change, because it encourages workers to always be looking for better ways of doing things and for innovating processes.

2.8 Links between triggers

Although we have mentioned a number of possible change triggers, it is important to appreciate that triggers do not exist in isolation.

Once a trigger has been 'pulled,' it is likely to set off a chain reaction of interrelated events.

Leavitt's organisational system model expressed this neatly, by considering organisational change as the result of the interaction between four components: task, structure, people and technology.

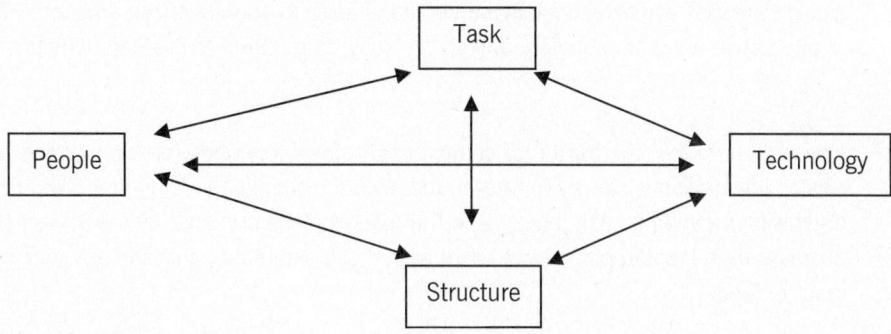

Figure 11.2 Components of change

Whatever the trigger for change, change managers must always consider the impact the change will have on these four interrelated variables, and therefore their organisation as a whole.

Burke and Litwin subsequently expanded this idea to create a model of organisational performance and change in which they suggest 12 variables need to be used to analyse the factors of organisational change.

They are:

- Mission and strategy
- Structure
- Task requirements and individual skills/abilities
- External environment
- Leadership
- Management practices
- Working environment
- Motivation
- Individual and organisational performance
- Organisational culture
- Systems (policies and procedures)
- Individual needs and values

2.9 Problem identification as a precursor to change

The first two boxes in *Balogun & Hope Hailey's* change flow chart which we showed earlier in this chapter illustrate that an organisation needs to analyse its competitive position before determining the type of change required.

We will look in more detail later at the different types of change an organisation can face, but at this point is important to note that regardless of the type of change, it is necessary to **clearly identify the problem or the reason for the change before undertaking** a change programme.

A review of strategy can often highlight the need to address a specific issue relating to the internal or external business environment. So problem identification can act as a trigger for change.

Perhaps more importantly, if there are no problems in the way the business is currently working, it will be difficult to persuade staff of the need to change. Problems with the current strategy, or the results it is delivering, provide one of the forces needed to drive change.

Problem identification can also be used to encourage participation at all levels in an organisation. Although the focus is at an operational level rather than a strategic level, the Japanese approach of *kaizen* involves all workers in problem identification and the quest for continuous improvement.

Exam alert

The question scenario could identify a number of problems which a business is facing, and you could be asked to assess ways the organisation could change to address those problems. There could be a number of alternative ways of changing, and so you may be required to evaluate which is the most appropriate.

However, note that the trigger for change might not always be a problem which has happened or already exists. Organisations can try to foresee the need for change by being proactive. For example, if an organisation can anticipate changes in the market place and identify the impact they might have on its business then it could plan how to deal with those external changes in advance rather than having to react to them.

2.10 Levels of change

At this point, it is also worth pointing out that change can occur at the different levels within an organisation:

- individuals
- structures and systems
- organisational climate

Changing individuals involves changing their skills, values, attitudes and behaviours. Any such individual changes have to support the overall organisational changes required. However, ultimately organisational changes can only be achieved if the individual people working for an organisation change as necessary.

Changing structures and systems involves changing the formal and informal organisational structures in place: for example, changing business processes, or changing roles, responsibilities and relationships.

Changing the organisational climate involves changing the way people relate to each other in an organisation; the management style; and the overall culture of the organisation. For example, this might involve creating a culture of high interpersonal trust and openness between staff.

The presence of these three levels means that a change manager needs to ensure that appropriate methods in order that the desired change is achieved at each level.

Section summary

Change can be triggered by a wide range of factors, some of which are external to an organisation, and some of which are internal to it.

3 Stage models of change   5/10

Introduction

We have identified a number of situations which might act as triggers for change in an organisation. However, it also important that organisations also realise that change is an on-going process and needs to be addressed all the time.

In the modern market economy, change is inherent in society. Not only do technologies change, so too do social norms, tastes and trends, demographic profiles and people's expectations of employment. In fact, almost every aspect of collective human life is subject to constant change.

In this respect it is wrong to think a visionary 'future state' can always be reached through some highly programmed way.

Moreover, successful change management requires more than simply recognising a change trigger and acting on it. Successful exploitation of a change situation requires:

- knowledge of the circumstances surrounding a situation

- understanding of the interactions in that situation

- awareness of the potential impact of the variables associated with the situation (as in the *Leavitt* model highlighting the interaction between task, structure, people and technology)

Nevertheless, many organisations do view change as a highly programmed process which follows a 'formula' and it is useful for us to consider a framework for change:

Recognition – Identify the problem that needs to be rectified

Diagnosis   – Break down the problem into component parts

Solution	–	Analyse possible alternatives
		Select preferred solution
		Apply preferred solution

3.1 Lewin's three stage model (The 'ice cube' model) 3/11, 3/12

Although the essence of change is that it enables a person, department or organisation to move from a current state to a future state, *Lewin* suggested that organisational changes actually have **three steps** (stages): '**unfreeze**', '**move**' and '**freeze**' or '**refreeze**.' (In this Study Text we will refer to the third stage as 'Refreeze' because we think it describes the process more clearly. However, in his original model, *Lewin* actually referred to the stage simply as 'freeze'.)

It is important to note that change involves re-learning: not merely learning something new, but trying to unlearn what it already known and practised in an organisation. This is a key part of the 'unfreeze' stage.

Figure 11.3 The unfreeze-change-refreeze model

 The following website provides some useful practical steps for applying Lewin's model: http://www.consultpivotal.com/lewin%27s.htm

3.1.1 Unfreeze

This first step involves unfreezing the current state of affairs, and creating the motivation to change. This means defining the current state of an organisation, highlighting the forces driving change and those resisting it and picturing a desired end state.

Crucially, the unfreeze stage involves making people within an organisation ready to change: making them aware of the **need (trigger) for change**, and creating a **readiness to change** among the workforce.

A key part of this stage is **weakening the restraining forces** that are resisting change, and **strengthening the driving forces** that are promoting change

Approaches to the unfreeze stage include:

- Physically **removing** individuals from their accustomed routines, sources of information and social relationships, so that old behaviours and attitudes are less likely to be reinforced by familiarity and social influence.

- **Consulting** team members about proposed changes. This will help them to feel less powerless and insecure about the process. It may also involve them in evaluation and problem-solving for more effective change measures – which will create a measure of ownership of the solutions. This in turn may shift resistant attitudes.

- **Confronting** team members' perceptions and emotions about change. Failure to recognise and deal with emotions only leads to later problems. Negative emotions may be submerged, but will affect performance by undermining commitment.

- Positively **reinforcing** demonstrated willingness to change: validating efforts and suggestions with praise, recognition and perhaps added responsibility in the change process.

If the need for change can be 'sold' to the team as immediate, and its benefits highlighted – for example, by securing individuals' jobs for the future - the unfreeze stage will be greatly accelerated.

Either way, effective **communication**, explaining the need for change is essential for the unfreeze process to work successfully.

Note: We have touched on the idea of 'resistance to change' here. We will look in more detail at ways for dealing with resistance to change later in this Study Text.

'Unfreezing' an organisation may sound simple enough in theory, but in practice it can be very difficult because it involves making people ready to change.

Rational argument will not necessarily be sufficient to convince individuals of the need to change, particularly if they stand to lose out from the change, or will have to make significant personal changes as a result of the change.

Sometimes the need for change may be obvious to all employees – for example, the arrival of a new competitor in the market leading to a dramatic reduction in market share.

However, if the need for change is less obvious, then the 'unfreezing' process may need to be 'managed' in some way, to make staff appreciate the need for change.

For example:

- Encourage debate about the appropriateness or effectiveness of the current way of operating (including current management styles)

- Publish information showing how the organisation compares with its competitors in key performance areas

 In Chapter 14 of this Study Text we will look at performance management, and one of the ways organisations can analyse their performance is by benchmarking against competitors' performance. Benchmarking could therefore be useful as part of the unfreeze stage of a change process.

3.1.2 Change (Move)

The change (move) stage involves learning new concepts and new meanings for existing concepts. This is the **transition stage**, by which an organisation moves from its current state to its future state.

It is important that an organisation encourages the **participation** and **involvement** of its staff in this phase so that they do not feel alienated by the change process.

This phase is mainly concerned with identifying the new, desirable behaviours or norms; communicating them clearly and positively; and encouraging individuals and groups to '**buy into**' or '**own**' the new values and behaviours.

Change is facilitated by:

- **Identification:** encouraging individuals to identify with role models from whom they can learn new behaviour patterns. For example, the team leader should adopt the values and behaviours he or she expects the team to follow. Team members who have relevant skills, experience and/or enthusiasm may be encouraged to coach others.

- **Internalisation:** placing individuals in a situation in which new behaviours are required for success, so that they *have* to develop coping behaviours. Pilot schemes or presentation of the changes to others may help in this process.

3.1.3 Refreeze (Freeze)

The refreeze stage involves internalising new concepts and meanings. It focuses on **stabilising (refreezing) the new state of affairs**, by setting policies to embed new behaviours, and establishing new standards.

It is crucial that the **changes are embedded** throughout an organisation to ensure that staff do not lapse back into old patterns of behaviour.

Once new behaviours have been adopted, the refreeze stage is required to consolidate and reinforce them, so that they become integrated into the individual's habits, attitudes and relationship patterns.

- **Habituation effects (**getting accustomed to the new situation) may be achieved over time, through practice, application and repetition.

- **Positive reinforcement** can be used to reward and validate successful change. For example, an element of a staff bonus scheme could be dependent on staff members adopting the new methodology.

3.2 Gemini 4Rs framework for planned strategic change

Although *Lewin's* three stage model of strategic change is probably the best known stage model of change, it is not the only one.

Management consultants *Gouillart and Kelly* describe the process of business transformation (major change) in 4 stages, in a framework known as the **Gemini 4Rs framework**.

For *Gouillart and Kelly*, a transformation process must create a new corporate vision, create new opportunities for an organisation, and introduce new ways of doing things.

According to *Gouillart and Kelly*, such a process needs the four 'Rs' to be present if it is to be successful.

3.2.1 Reframing

Reframing is the process of setting a corporate vision.

It involves asking fundamental questions about what the organisation is and what it is for.

The reframing element of a change process should:

- **Achieve mobilisation**: Create the will and desire to change
- **Create the vision** of where the organisation is going
- **Build a measurement system** that will set and measure progress against those targets

3.2.2 Restructuring

Restructuring is the process of removing elements of an organisation which do not add value. Although it primarily involves looking at the organisation's structure, it may also involve cultural changes.

Restructuring activity should include:

- **Constructing an economic model** to show in detail how **value is created** and where resources should be deployed

- **Aligning the physical infrastructure** with the overall plan

- Redesigning the work architecture so that **processes interact to create value**

 The ideas of value creation here link back to Porter's idea of the value chain, and they also highlight the importance of having a good 'fit' between organisational structure and strategy. (We looked at organisational structure and strategy in Chapter 10 of this Study Text.)

3.2.3 Revitalising

Revitalising is the process of finding **new products and markets**, and ensuring a good fit with the competitive environment.

Revitalising activities will include:

- **Achieving market focus** and identifying new market opportunities
- **Inventing** new businesses or products
- **Changing the rules of competition** by exploiting technology

3.2.4 Renewal

Renewal is the process of developing individuals, to ensure that their skills are aligned to organisational requirements.

Renewal ensures that the people in the organisation support the change process, and acquire the necessary skills to contribute to it.

Renewal activities should include:

- **Creating a reward system** in order to motivate
- **Supporting individual learning** to develop learning as a competence within the organisation

3.3 Evaluation of stage models and Lewin's ideas

Although the three stage model provides a useful outline of the change process, it is not a planning tool for the process.

There is a danger that some managers may view 'unfreeze' as a planning session, before using 'move' as implementation and 'refreeze' as a post-implementation review.

Unfortunately such an approach ignores the fundamental issue that **people will only change if they feel and appreciate the need to do so**. If this need is not properly communicated, the change process will not harness the energy of key players effectively, and will not tackle any potential resistance within an organisation.

Moreover, some critics argue that Lewin's model is based on the simplistic assumption that organisations are stable and static, so change only results from concentrated effort, and even then, the change that results is one-directional. However, the counter argument is that **change is multi-directional and ubiquitous**, and is often a **continuous process**, not the structured process Lewin's model would suggest.

3.3.1 'Biological' models

We should also note that both Lewin's three stage model, and the 4 Rs model imply a structured, planned approach to change in the same way that the rational model views strategic planning as a logical, structured process.

However, in the same way that we can look at emergent processes of strategy development as an alternative approach to the rational model, so we can also suggest **less prescriptive approaches to change management**.

In particular, *Gareth Morgan* presents an alternative approach which considers the organisation as a biological organism which is continually changing. Such an approach seems appropriate given the complexity of modern society and its constant changes.

Morgan suggests that in the same way a living organism continually interacts with its environment, changing it and responding to changes in it, and interacting with other creatures in it, so too does any organisation. Regardless of its industry or sector, an organisation affects its environment (eg by fulfilling the needs of its clients, or by using scarce resources). Equally, an organisation comes into contact with potential collaborators or competitors, and has to respond to changes that occur in the external environment.

In this context, change can be seen as a **dynamic capability** - an organisation understanding how and when to change.

We need to recognise, however, that change involves two complementary factors, and each is essential for an organisation, to derive the fullest benefit from change.

One of these factors is clearly the **readiness** and **ability to change** different aspects of the organisation without wrecking the rest of the entity.

The other factor is the ability to maintain a **sense of continuity** in order for change to be recognisable as a change from one thing to another, rather than just the disappearance of one thing and its replacement. If an organisation changes, then for it to remain that organisation (albeit in a changed form) then some aspect of it has to stay the same.

What this also implies, then, is that the **management of stability** is as important as the **management of difference**, when managing change.

Section summary

Stage models of change suggest a structured process of moving from a current state to a future state. *Lewin's* three stage model (unfreeze, change, refreeze) illustrates this process, although it is important not to overlook the human aspect of change. People will only change their behaviour if they appreciate the need for change.

4   Other models of managing change

Introduction

Although Lewin's stage model of change provides a clear overview of the change process, it doesn't offer any insights into how managers can manage change through the process. Other models draw on project management ideas to suggest how the change process can be managed.

4.1 Bullock and Batten, planned change

A number of approaches to managing the change process draw on the discipline of **project management**. One example of this is *Bullock and Batten's* model.

Bullock and Batten identify four 'steps' to changing an organisation:

Exploration – Verifying the need for change, and acquiring any resources for the change to go ahead (for example, human expertise; IT systems)

Planning – The planning step involves key decision makers and technical experts. A diagnosis of the current position is completed, and actions are arranged into a change plan. This plan is then approved by management, before moving on to the action phase.

Action – Actions are completed according to the plan, with feedback mechanisms which allow some re-planning if activities go off track or get behind schedule.

Integration – The integration phase starts once the action stage has been completed. Integration involves aligning the changes which have been made with other areas of an organisation and formalising the changes, for example, through company policies, and reward systems.

However, while *Bullock and Batten's* model provides a clear sequence of stages, it (like other models derived from project management ideas) assumes that change can be defined and moved towards in a planned way.

The project management approach simplifies the change process by isolating one part of the organisation to make the necessary changes.

Such an approach implies that organisational change is a technical problem which can be solved by using a definable technical solution. This would work well for isolated issues, but less well when organisations face more complex changes – for example, to 'go global'.

4.2 Kotter – Eight-step model

John Kotter analysed a number of organisations going through change, and highlighted eight key lessons which could be learned from this analysis. In 1995, *Professor Kotter* published an article in the Harvard Business Review in which he converted these eight lessons into an eight-step model for managing change.

1. **Establish a sense of urgency** – Discuss the current competitive position and look at potential future scenarios. Increase the 'felt need for change' (in other words, promote the driving forces for change).

2. **Form a powerful guiding coalition** – Assemble a powerful group of people who can work well together to promote the change.

3. **Create a vision** – Build a vision to guide the change effort, together with strategies for achieving it.

4. **Communicate the vision** – The vision, and accompanying strategies and new behaviours, need to be communicated. *Kotter* stresses that effective communication is crucial in change management.

5. **Empower others to act on the vision** – This includes getting rid of obstacles to change such as unhelpful structures or systems. People need to be allowed to experiment.

6. **Plan for and create short-term wins** – Look for, and advertise short-term visible improvements because these will help sustain the driving forces for change. *Kotter* suggests that these short-term wins should be planned into the change programme, and people should be publicly rewarded for making improvements.

7. **Consolidate improvements and produce still more change** – Promote and reward those who are able to promote and work towards the vision. Maintain the energy behind the change process by introducing new projects, resource and change agents.

8. **Institutionalise new approaches** – Ensure that everyone understands that the new behaviours and systems will lead to corporate success.

Kotter's eight-step model is popular with managers, and highlights two key issues – the importance of having a 'felt need' for change in an organisation, and importance of communication throughout the change process.

However, there is a danger that *Kotter's* approach will create an early burst of energy at the start of a change programme followed by a sequence of routine processes. Steps 6, 7 and 8 – 'plan', 'consolidate', 'institutionalise' – seem to suggest a straightforward process which can be embedded into an organisation. But in practice the challenges and excitement of the early stages of a change management project need to be maintained throughout.

4.3 Beer and Nohria – Theory E & Theory O

Beer and Nohria (writing in the Harvard Business Review in 2000) suggest that although each organisation's change is unique, each change is ultimately a variant of two underlying approaches. Beer and Nohria call these underlying approaches 'Theory E' and 'Theory O'.

Theory E starts from the premise that the purpose of change is to **increase economic value**, often expressed as shareholder value. The focus of change is on formal structure and systems, and change is seen as a top-down process, often with extensive help from external consultants. Theory E changes are planned and programmatic, and usually involve the use of economic incentives, drastic layoffs, downsizing and restructuring.

Theory O is concerned with developing an organisation's **human capability** to implement strategy, and to develop corporate culture through **organisational learning**. The focus of change is on culture and cultural adjustment, rather than structure and systems, and the process is participative (rather than being top-down). Consequently, change is emergent rather than planned and programmatic, with an emphasis on feedback and reflection.

Both approaches have drawbacks, however. Theory E approaches ignore the feelings and attitudes of employees, and may lead to a fall in motivation and commitment, and the loss of the creativity needed to sustain competitive advantage. Conversely, by trying to maintain positive relationships with staff, Theory O approaches may mean that organisations avoid taking difficult decisions; for example, decisions about how to reverse a decline in customer numbers or market share.

Moreover, Beer and Nohria argue that, in practice, organisations cannot use only one of these theories alone. Instead, a company should implement both Theory E and Theory O at the same time. However, this then leaves managers with the problem of how to combine the relevant elements from both approaches, and to resolve the tension between Theories E and O in a way that obtains the benefits of each while minimising the negative consequences.

Yet at the same time, Beer and Nohria argue that this 'problem' should also be the objective of managers leading change. Their objective should be to integrate E and O in a way that resolves the tension between the two, allowing organisations to satisfy their shareholders and yet also have the capacity and capabilities to adapt and survive as viable institution in the long run.

For example, an organisation should look to make changes to the corporate structure and systems at the same time as making changes to the dynamic of the corporate workplace and its culture. In other words, it needs to combine elements of 'hard' change and 'soft' change (which we look at in more detail in the next chapter). Equally, consultants should be used to get managers and staff to think about, and not just act blindly on, a set of procedures. Often the presence of consultants can make managers abdicate any sense of leadership; however, managers should be encouraged to use consultants as a tool to help them make better decisions and become better leaders, not to replace them as leaders.

 The contrast between Theory E and Theory O mirrors the contrast between a prescriptive, rational model approach to strategy and emergent approaches to strategy, which we looked at in Chapter 1 of this Study Text.

 Section summary

One of the criticisms of Lewin's stage model is that it doesn't give any insights into how change should be managed. Change managers can draw on project management ideas to help them here. Communication is also crucial throughout the change process.

5 Force field analysis

Introduction

In the 'unfreeze' stage of the three stage model, we highlighted the interaction of driving forces promoting change, and resisting forces preventing it. *Lewin* recognised the importance of this interaction, and so alongside the three stage model, he also introduced the idea of force field analysis.

Force field analysis assists change management by examining and evaluating – in a summary form – the forces 'for' and 'against' the change.

Force field analysis consists of identifying the factors that promote or hinder change. In order for change to be successfully implemented, promoting forces need to be exploited and the effect of hindering forces need to be reduced, such that the driving forces for change outweigh those forces resisting change.

It is traditional to represent these forces by **arrows** whose individual dimensions correspond to their perceived strengths. Promoting and hindering forces are then shown pointing from opposite sides to a vertical line. This representation is useful for purposes such as brainstorming and staff briefings, but two lists in order of magnitude are just as useful for purposes of analysis.

The example below concerns a public sector organisation that is introducing performance review.

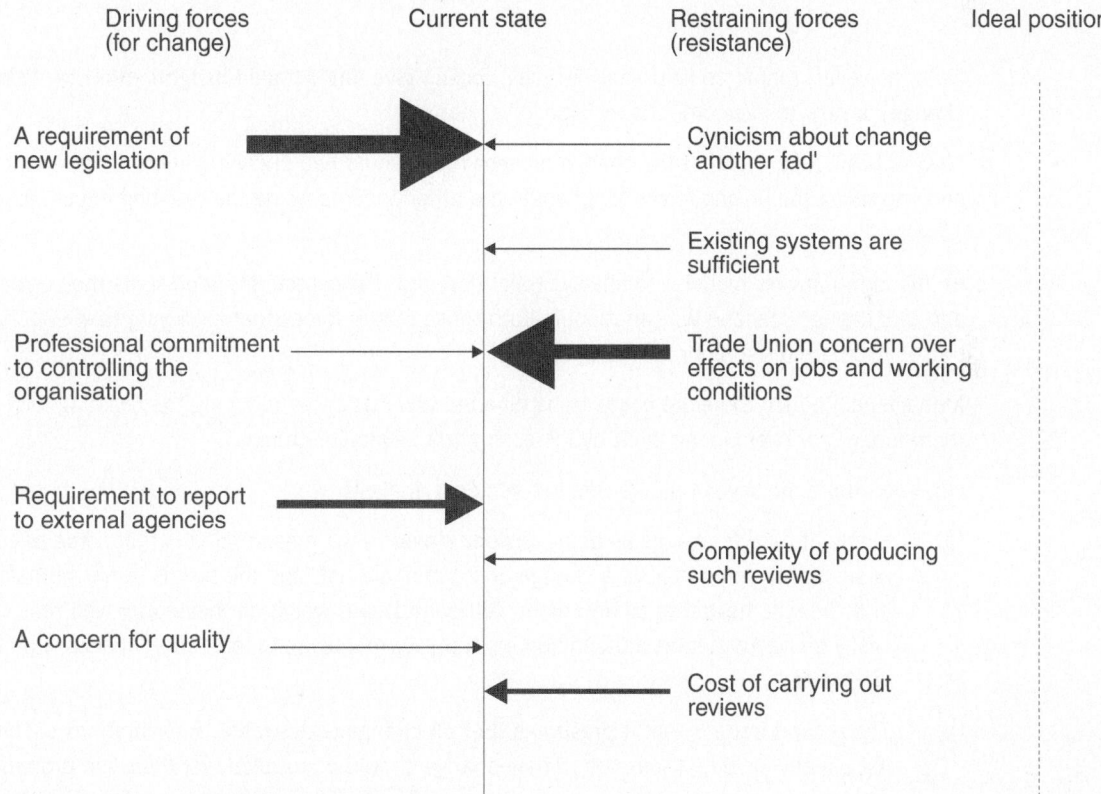

Figure 11.4: Example of force field analysis

Senior (drawing on the advice of *Carnall* and *Huczyuski and Buchanan*) suggests a practical route to applying the force field analysis idea.

(a)   Define the problem in terms of the current situation and the desired future state.

(b)   List the forces supporting and opposing the desired change and assess both the strength and the importance of each one.

(c)   Draw the force field diagram.

(d)   Decide how to strengthen or weaken the more important forces as appropriate and agree with those concerned. Weakening might be achieved by persuasion, participation, coercion or bargaining, while strengthening might be achieved by a marketing or education campaign, including the use of personal advocacy.

(e)   Identify the resources needed.

(f)   Make an action plan including event timing, milestones and responsibilities.

Elements of the culture of an organisation may also emerge as important forces promoting or hindering changes. So the **cultural web** can also be used alongside force field analysis as a diagnostic tool in looking at the forces driving and resisting change.

We will look at culture and the cultural web in Chapter 12, but make a mental note that it could potentially be useful here.

Exam alert

Note the possible link between force field analysis and stakeholder analysis. In a question scenario, you may need to identify who the key stakeholders are, and then identify whether they will be driving forces for change or whether they will resist change.

You may also need to recommend ways in which various stakeholders could be managed to overcome their resistance to change.

Note, however, that force field analysis itself **doesn't give any detailed insights into how to manage change**, or how to overcome the resistance to change.

Lewin's basic idea was that the change process represented two opposing fields of force, one encompassing the driving forces for change, the other encompassing the resisting forces (as in Figure 11.4).

In this form, Lewin's model is relatively straightforward: the central line represents the current situation, and in a change scenario we can identify both those sets of forces that are trying to effect change and those which are resisting or providing barriers.

Management action therefore needs to be directed towards either reducing the resisting forces, turning them around, or overcoming them by increasing the drivers for change.

However, there are several drawbacks to force field analysis.

(a)   Firstly, it depicts change as being '**insider' driven** – the presumption is that some people in the business are committed to a change and others are not, and the task is to tilt the balance in favour of those who have that commitment. Although Lewin would not have approved of it, this can easily be interpreted as a technique for enabling managers to force their decisions on an unwilling workforce.

(b)   The second issue is that it **presumes that all change is desirable**. Presentations of this model do not usually include discussion of how change should be resisted, yet there are probably as many occasions when a proposal is undesirable or unworkable as there are ones where it is to be encouraged.

(c)   The Lewin image as it is generally presented depicts all driving forces as operating in the same direction, and all resisting forces as running in the opposite direction. In practice the key influences in a situation – usually the more powerful stakeholders – are pointing in varying directions, rather like Figure 11.5 below.

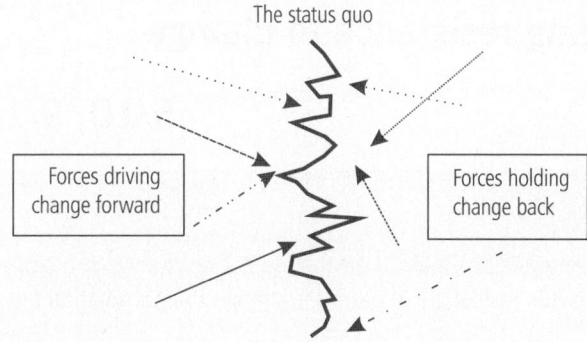

Figure 11.5: The 'real' Lewin context

The point of Figure 11.5 is that it reflects the complexity of the force fields in a change scenario more accurately than the simple illustration we showed in Figure 11.4 earlier. For example, people may resist change for different reasons and so different solutions will be needed to manage their resistance to change.

Figure 11.5 also highlights not only the different strengths of the forces either driving or resisting change, but also how far they are opposed. A resisting force that is almost vertical is easier to turnaround to support the change, than a resistance which is horizontally opposed to the change.

Resisting forces are central to Lewin's approach to change management. It is therefore important both to identify these resisting forces and then also to think of ways to deal with them. (Before doing this, though, bear in mind a point made earlier, that not all change is desirable.)

Sources of resistance are generally linked to human interests – hygiene factors mostly, to use *Herzberg's* concept. *Senior* has set out the following as the main sources of individual resistance.

- Fear of the unknown
- Dislike of uncertainty
- Potential loss of power
- Potential loss of rewards
- Potential lack of or loss of skills

These sources of resistance spring from direct human concerns. Interestingly, *Senior* also identifies a number of organisational resistances, such as resource constraints, or inertias resulting from the interlocked nature of the different features and processes of the organisation. But for the most part organisational resistances feed back to human concerns. Where they do not, there is unlikely to be a strategic change problem, but perhaps a technical problem of issues such as co-ordination or process design.

Section summary

Force field analysis illustrates a summary of the forces promoting change and the forces resisting change.

6 Managing resistance to change

5/10, 9/10, 5/11, 11/11, 5/12

Introduction

Force field analysis has introduced the idea of resistance to change, and identified that organisations need to overcome this resistance in order for change to be implemented successfully.

We will now look at ways of managing resistance to change in more detail.

While some people within an organisation may accept, co-operate with, or even support a change programme, it is likely that others will resist it.

In the simplest terms, when management is faced with resistance to change, they have two underlying choices for how to deal with that resistance:

(a) **Overcoming resistance** through strengthening the driving forces for change, for example increasing management pressure, enhancing fears of dismissal and so forth

(b) **Reducing resistance** by weakening the forces that currently hold down output, for example through job redesign, or through the adoption of a more people-centred management style

The essential characteristic of **overcoming resistance** as a strategy for change is that increasing any of the 'push' factors driving change will prompt an opposite reaction on the other side of the force field equilibrium. Management seemingly gets what it wants – for example, an increase in production – but at the cost of more tension, conflict, suspicion and hostility.

On the other hand, by **reducing resistance**, the same objective is accomplished – again, for example, production is increased – but there is a much lower level of resistance.

So, at the simplest level, force field analysis suggests that there are two ways of managing this resistance to change:

- Strengthening your own side
- Weakening the opposing forces

However, this still leaves a number of questions unanswered. In particular, how much coercion should be used to make people change, or how much should people be encouraged to participate in the change process and help identify solutions themselves.

How much **coercion** should be used?

(a) Some element of coercion may ultimately be necessary. However, it helps, for example if a supposedly neutral consultant can be persuaded to suggest measures supported by the proponents of the innovation.

(b) Involving people in diagnosing problem situations (eg in quality circles) wins over 'hearts and minds'.

6.1 Resistance to change

Leaders and managers of change sometimes cannot understand why individuals or groups of individuals do not embrace the changes that are being introduced. This failure to embrace change is often labelled as resistance to change.

No matter how much an organisation overall welcomes change, it will still face a degree of resistance from employees, suppliers, customers, distributors or other stakeholders.

One of the key issues here is that people resist change because they feel comfortable with what they know, but fear the unknown and the uncertainty which goes with it.

Why do people of groups of people fear change?

- They do not understand the nature of the change and/or the reasons for it
- They do not trust the people leading the change, and/or their motives for change
- It can result in organisational redesign – changes of jobs, and possibly even job losses
- It may present technological challenges
- It confronts apathy – people will have to move outside their 'comfort zone'
- It reduces stability – the continuity of products or services, processes and staff leads to a stable operating environment.

Change is often a difficult process for the individuals involved, and so resistance to a change programme should always be expected.

Potential areas of resistance need to be identified. Then appropriate tactics need to be agreed to overcome the resistance anticipated among different stakeholders.

Schein adopts a similar approach to force field analysis when looking at resistance to change. He argues that there are two forces acting on every individual undergoing change:

Learning anxiety: The anxiety associated with learning something new. Will I be able to deal with the new situation? Will I fail? Will gaps in my knowledge or skills be exposed?

Survival anxiety: This concerns the pressure to change. What if I don't change? Will I be left behind?

Used in conjunction with force field analysis, we can see survival anxiety as a driving force for change, and learning anxiety as a restraining force.

Schein suggests that there are two principles to enable change to work:

- First, survival anxiety must be greater than learning anxiety
- Second, learning anxiety needs to be reduced, rather than survival anxiety being increased.

Schein suggests increasing people's **sense of psychological safety** is crucial in reducing learning anxiety, and therefore in managing change.

He suggests a number of ways this can be done:

- presenting a compelling vision of the future
- training
- involving the learner in discussions about the change
- establishing support groups (for example, mentors or counsellors)
- using consistent systems and structures across the change

6.2 Kotter & Schlesinger's approaches to resistance

Kotter & Schlesinger also highlighted that overcoming resistance to change is a critical aspect of managing the change process.

They identified six approaches to dealing with resistance to change, with a key underlying theme being that **communication is critical** in overcoming resistance to change.

Approach	Comment
Education and communication	This approach assumes that resistance is caused by ignorance. Communicating the reasons for the change and the outcomes will undermine resistance to the change. Communicating the 'vision' for change, and the potential benefits of the change may also help overcome negative perceptions. In effect, this approach involves 'selling' the change to those people who are currently resisting it.
Participation and involvement	Get people involved in the change process. If staff are involved in the change process and feel they have contributed to the design of the changes they are less likely to resist them. Getting people involved may also help reduce concerns about the impact of change and their ability to cope. Those potentially affected can help to: • Identify problem situations • Define the problem and its causes • Define solutions • Develop strategies for implementation
Facilitation and support	There are a number of ways to facilitate and support people facing change. These could include counselling services for those experiencing difficulties or stress, or else simply the availability of a line manager for staff to talk to about their concerns. Support could also include training for those staff who need new technical or business skills to deal with changes to their jobs. If the change involves making people redundant, they should also be supported, and this support can include outplacement counselling and/or generous redundancy packages.
Negotiation and agreement	Negotiation is often necessary where there are strong unions, so changes to working practices may be considered in exchange for extra pay. For example, according to *The Economist* (20 September 2003), long before the economic slowdown of 2008-9 the United Auto Workers Union (representing US car workers) gained some modest pay rises and protection of medical healthcare in return for agreeing to management's closure of plants. General Motors and Ford were competing with non-unionised Japanese subsidiaries, and needed to increase productivity. Negotiation involves discussion with employees to resolve areas of dispute about the changes – for example, remuneration, hours of work, or changes to terms and conditions. The negotiations may involve offering incentives to workers to encourage them to accept changes – for example, offering them additional payments to take on more demanding duties.

Approach	Comment
Manipulation and co-optation	In this case, resistance is undermined in a more covert manner, perhaps by the way information is presented or by a political process. For example, the company can manipulate the debate (eg by invoking public opinion).
	However, if individuals feel they are being manipulated this could increase the resistance to change.
	It is also important to consider whether there are any ethical issues at stake here. Given the ethical principal of integrity, how ethical is it to manipulate (or even deceive) people into accepting change?
Coercion, implicit and explicit	Where management have power, this appears the easiest way - sometimes it is the only way.
	Individuals are forced to accept change, for example by being threatened with redundancy if they do not.
	This sort of tactic can often be successful if rapid change is required.
	However, such aggressive tactics are not always desirable because people resent them, even if their resistance is overcome.

Each approach will be suited to different circumstances, based on the respective power of each party, and the type of change being experienced.

Kotter & Schlesinger's approaches to change management illustrate there are a variety of ways of managing chance and resistance to change, so it is important that change leaders select an appropriate method for managing change.

The appropriateness of different methods will depend, in part, on the degree of collaboration or conflict which is expected from staff.

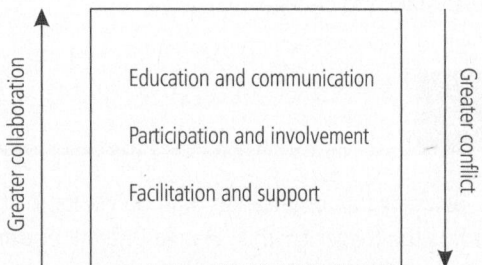

Figure 11.6: Kotter and Schlesinger's scale of change management approaches

Kotter & Schlesinger's work is important because, as well as identifying ways of managing resistance they also make the link between triggers of resistance and ways of managing change.

We looked earlier at Kotter's eight step model, and a number of the steps in this model of change management could also be seen as ways of overcoming resistance to change.

Section summary

Organisations need to **overcome resistance to change** in order for change to be successfully implemented. The methods used to deal with resistance will vary according to the change context, and the degree of collaboration or conflict which may be expected from staff. Kotter & Schlesinger identified six approaches for dealing with resistance to change.

Chapter Roundup

✓ Organisations need to change and adapt to deal with changes in their environment and to improve their performance and results. The detail of any change management programme will depend on its context, but in general terms change management is likely to require an organisation to assess its current position, evaluate the choices it has for how to change, and then decide upon a course of change action to implement.

✓ Change management can be defined as 'the continuous process of aligning an organisation with its marketplace and doing it more responsively and effectively than competitors'.

✓ Change can be triggered by a wide range of factors, some of which are external to an organisation, and some of which are internal to it.

✓ **Stage models of change** suggest a structured process of moving from a current state to a future state. *Lewin*'s three stage model (unfreeze, change, refreeze) illustrates this process, although it is important not to overlook the human aspect of change. People will only change their behaviour if they appreciate the need for change.

✓ One of the criticisms of Lewin's stage model is that it doesn't give any insights into how change should be managed. Change managers can draw on project management ideas to help them here. Communication is also crucial throughout the change process.

✓ **Force field analysis** shows a summary of the forces promoting change and the forces resisting change.

✓ Organisations need to **overcome resistance to change** in order for change to be successfully implemented. The methods used to deal with resistance will vary according to the change context, and the degree of collaboration or conflict which may be expected from staff. Kotter & Schlesinger identified six approaches for dealing with resistance to change.

Quick Quiz

1 A new CEO has just joined an orgnisation, and he wants to change the organisation structure to make it more streamlined. Is the trigger for this change internal or external?

2 Leavitt considered organisational change as the result of interaction between four components. What are they?

3 An organisation which is currently enjoying good profitability should not consider change. True or False?

4 What are the three stages of Lewin's stage model?

5 Who suggested the model of an organisation as a biological organism which is constantly changing?

    A Schein
    B Morgan
    C Carnall
    D Kotter

6 Reducing resistance to change involves strengthening the driving forces for change. True or false?

7 What is force field analysis?

8 What are Kotter & Schlesinger's six approaches for dealing with resistance to change?

Answers to Quick Quiz

1   Internal. Although the CEO has only recently joined from outside the organisation, he is promoting the changes in his role of CEO.

2   Task, structure, people, technology.

3   False. Organisations should embrace change, and not wait until the obsolescence of their current practices leads to a fall in profitability or a time of crisis.

4   Unfreeze, move (change), refreeze (freeze).

5   Gareth Morgan considers an organisation as a biological organism which is constantly changing.

6   False. Reducing resistance to change involves weakening the forces that are resisting change. Overcoming resistance involves strengthening the driving forces for change.

7   Force field analysis shows the driving and restraining forces which promote or hinder any change process.

8   (i)   Education and communication
     (ii)   Participation and involvement
     (iii) Facilitation and support
     (iv)   Negotiation and agreement
     (v)   Manipulation and co-optation
     (vi)   Coercion

Now try this question from the Exam Question Bank

Number	Level	Marks	Time
Q12	Intermediate	15	27 mins

424 | 11: Organisational change

PART C CHANGE MANAGEMENT

IMPLEMENTING CHANGE

The dynamics of the external environment mean that organisations' strategies will inevitably change and evolve.

The key questions for an organisation then become how rapid and how extensive that change will be, and how it manages the change process.

Change management is therefore an integral and important part of strategic management (Section 11).

We will begin this chapter by looking at the types of change which may be required (Section 1). We will then explore the organisational context and the cultural influences involved in change (Sections 2 and 3).

In Section 4, we will look at the different styles which can be used to manage the change process. This section also highlights the importance of communication in the change process.

Leadership is another important factor in a change programme. Organisations need leaders to have the vision to identify changes, and then deliver them (Section 7).

However, it is important that any changes are ethical and respect the concerns of staff concerned (Sections 8 and 9).

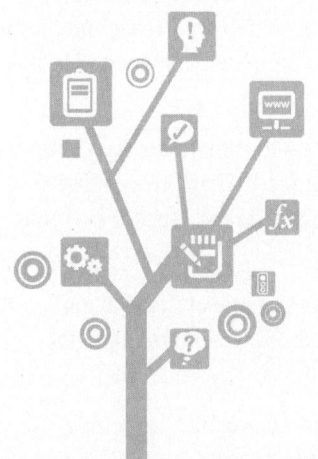

topic list	learning outcomes	syllabus references	ability required
1 Types of change	B1(a), B2(b)	B2(i), B2(iv)	Discuss
2 The context of change	B1(a), B2(b)	B1(iv), B2(ii)	Evaluate
3 Culture and change	B1(a)	B1(iv)	Discuss
4 Styles of change management	B2(a), B2(c)	B2(iii), B3(ii)	Evaluate
5 Why change succeeds or fails	B2(a)	B2(iii)	Evaluate
6 Change and the individual	B2(a)	B2(iii)	Evaluate
7 Leading change	B2(d)	B2(v)	Evaluate
8 Group formation and its impact on change	–	B3(iii)	Evaluate
9 Business ethics and change management	B3(b)	B3(iv)	Evaluate
10 Change in practice	–	–	–
11 Change management and strategy implementation	B3(a)	B3(i)	Evaluate

1 Types of change

Introduction

A wide range of stimuli may lead an organisation's managers to recognise the need for strategic change (change triggers). Consideration of the broader contexts of the **environment** and the organisation's **strategic capability** may show that large scale developments are necessary. The need to put strategy into action may call for more detailed but no less far-reaching adjustment of processes, relationships, technologies and so on. In any event, the management of change starts with an understanding of **two main considerations**.

(a) The **type** of change required
(b) The **wider context** of the change

Importantly, these considerations mean that the particular management challenges involved in initiating and implementing change can vary considerably from one scenario to another.

When faced with a potential change situation, an organisation has to analyse the nature of the change, in order to identify the most appropriate way of managing the change.

Change can be classified in relation to the **extent** of the change required and the **speed** with which that change needs to be achieved.

Speed – Change can range from an all-at-once, 'big bang' change to a series of step-by-step, incremental changes.

Extent – The extent of change can range from an overall **transformation** of an organisation's central assumptions, culture and beliefs to a **realignment** of its existing assumptions. Although a realignment may affect the way an organisation operates at a practical level it will not lead to an underlying change in the organisation's culture.

In their book 'Exploring Strategic Change', *Balogun and Hope Hailey* illustrate that there are four main types of change, based on differences in the speed and extent of change required. They present these types of change in a matrix, with the two axes being the **nature** of the change required (speed) and the **scope** of the change required (extent).

The measure of the scope of change is whether or not the methods and assumptions of the existing **paradigm** must be replaced. (The paradigm is the set of assumptions and beliefs which are taken for granted in an organisation and define that organisation and its culture).

The **nature** of change may be incremental and built on existing methods and approaches, or it may require a 'big bang' approach if rapid response is required, as in times of crisis.

Nature of change	Scope of change	
	Realignment	**Transformation**
Incremental	Adaptation	Evolution
'Big bang'	Reconstruction	Revolution

(a) **Adaptation** is the most common type of change. An adaptive change realigns the way an organisation operates, but does not require the development of a new paradigm. It proceeds step by step.

(b) **Reconstruction** can also be undertaken within an existing paradigm but requires rapid and extensive action. It is a common response to a long-term decline in performance, or to a changing competitive context.

(c)   **Evolution** is an incremental process that leads to a new paradigm. It may arise from careful analysis and planning or may be the result of **learning processes**. Evolutionary change is often undertaken in anticipation of the need for future change. Its transformational nature may not be obvious while it is taking place

(d)   **Revolution** is a rapid and wide ranging response to extreme pressures for change, and can often be triggered by changes in the competitive conditions an organisation is facing. Because revolution is both wide-ranging and fast-paced, it is likely to involve a number of simultaneous initiatives, dealing with different aspects of a business. Revolution will be very obvious and is likely to affect most aspects of both what the organisation does and how it does them.

You may notice the overlap between Balogun & Hailey's ideas and Greiner's growth model which we discussed in the last chapter. Greiner also talked of evolution and revolution, suggesting that an important aspect of successful change management is understanding the **nature of the change required**.

While *Balogun & Hope Hailey* talk about realignment and transformation, *Johnson, Scholes and Whittington* categorise types of strategic change as being either **incremental** or **transformational**.

Again, however, a matrix can be used; change is either **incremental** or **transformational**, and the approach to managing change is described as being either **reactive** or **proactive**.

Incremental change is characterised by a series of small steps, and does not challenge existing organisational assumptions or culture. It is a gradual process, and can be seen as an extension of the past. Management will feel that they are in control of the change process. There is also a feeling that incremental change is reversible. If the change does not work out as planned, the organisation can revert to its old ways of doing things.

Transformational change is characterised by major, significant change being introduced relatively quickly. The existing organisational structures and the organisational culture are changed. Transformational change is likely to be a top-down process, initiated, and possibly imposed, by senior management. However, unlike incremental change it requires new ways of thinking and behaving, and leads to discontinuities with the past. Consequently it is likely to be irreversible.

Transformational change may come about because:

*   The organisation is faced with **major external events** that demand large-scale changes in response

*   The organisation **anticipates major changes** in the environment and initiates action to make shifts in its own strategy to cope with them

*   Strategic drift has led to deteriorating performance and so leaves the organisation now requiring **significant changes to improve performance**.

Johnson, Scholes and Whittington's change matrix reflects these different change categories, but also highlights how management's response differs according to the different change categories.

Nature of change

		Incremental	Transformation
Management role	Proactive	Tuning	Planned
	Reactive	Adaptation	Forced

The importance of **proactive management** is that it implies that organisational change may be undertaken **before** it is imposed by events. It may, in fact, result from the process of forecasting and be a response to expected developments.

Forced change (for example, where an orgnisation has to make significant and rapid change due to changes in the external environment) is likely to be both painful and risky for an organisation.

Although these change matrices are a useful summary of types of change, we also need to recognise that the degree of change varies so in practice there is a **continuum** between **adaptive** changes and **transformation**.

BPP
LEARNING MEDIA

Also, the **severity** of the change depends on **where** it is experienced, or by whom. Redundancies may be an **adaptive** response to changed product market conditions for an organisation, and will preserve the future of the organisation. However, for the people experiencing them, they are likely to be **transformational changes.**

1.1 Hard or soft change

The relative physical and organisational impacts of a change should also affect the way it is implemented. In this respect, change can be classified as either **hard** (mechanistic) or **soft** (people based). Is the change a purely technical, systems-oriented one, or will it also affect people?

The aspect of the business undergoing change should influence the way change is implemented.

If the change is relatively routine and technical in nature (for example, the machines in a factory are being upgraded) then existing knowledge can be applied in a mechanistic manner to implement the change.

A 'hard' model of change is similar to the 'rational' model of decision making. In short, there is a **description** of the current situation, **options** for change are evaluated, and the change is **implemented**. The process is logically in a sequence and is linear. Feedback comes at the end of the process.

Hard models of change can be looked at as following three sequential phases:

- **Define**: clarify objectives; perform systems diagnostics and systems analysis
- **Design**: determine options; evaluate solutions
- **Implement**: implement solution; appraise and monitor performance

However, purely 'mechanistic' changes are uncommon, and most changes have a degree of impact of people orientation.

Consequently approaches to change implementation need to take account of **personal interrelationships** and **emotional responses**. Also, they have to reflect the volatile and dynamic nature of the change environment.

Paton & McCalman in their book *'Change management'* contrast the characteristics of hard and soft change situations, which can summarised as follows:

Hard	Soft
Objectives, constraints and performance indicators are predominantly quantifiable	Objectives are likely to be subjective, interrelated and hard to quantify
Environmental forces are relatively static	The environment is likely to be volatile and complex
Timescales known with reasonable certainty	Timescales will be uncertain
The change environment is clearly defined and has minimal interaction with external forces	The change environment is unbounded, and characterised by having many internal and external interactions
The problem being addressed by the change can be clearly and concisely defined	It is difficult to define problem characteristics
May be defined in systems/ technological terms	The problem is likely to be defined in interpersonal and social terms
The resources required to achieve a solution are reasonably well known	Resource requirements are likely to be uncertain
The number of viable potential solutions is limited, and the organisation has knowledge of them	There will be a wide range of solutions, all of which may appear relevant and interconnected

Hard	Soft
Structured approaches will produce good results	No clear solution methodology is visible
Consensus about the best way forward can be reached easily	There is a lack of consensus about the way forward, arising from a lack of common perception of the problem

1.1.1 Illustration of hard versus soft changes

Senior illustrates the differences between the hard and soft models of change by looking at how they could be applied to improving performance in a call centre.

Hard changes

Stages	Tasks	Example
1 *Situation analysis*	Formally identify need for change, and obtain agreement that change is needed.	'Response times at our call centre are too slow'.
2 *Identify objectives and constraints*	An objective is a desired outcome; a constraint is something that inhibits it achieving the outcome.	Objective – response times must be better than a competitor's response times. Constraint – there are not enough people and/or recruiting more is too expensive.
3 *Identify performance measures*	This will show if the change has been successful once it is implemented.	90% of calls to be answered within three rings.
4 *Generate options*	These could be many possible ways of reaching objectives, all of which can be considered.	For example: • Change processes to reduce the length of each call, thereby freeing up time to answer more. • Relocate call centre to a lower-cost environment such as India. • Abandon the call centre and go for Internet-only ordering – but this is outside the scope of the problem definition.
5 *Develop promising options*	Some ideas may be more promising than others. However, for the promising options, a review of who is involved and how it will work is essential. This could involve detailed plans and budgets, computer simulations and so on.	The practicalities of each option are looked at (eg how easy is it to develop a call centre in India?)
6 *Evaluate options against performance measures*	Each option is evaluated in terms of the performance criteria in Stage 3. Will it deliver the desired result? It is important that any model used does represent the system accurately.	It is important to consider risk here.

Stages	Tasks	Example
7 *Develop implementation strategies*	The preferred option is selected.	This may involve informing staff, training them, reassuring them, pilot or dual running and so on. It could involve redundancy, if the relocation option is chosen.
8 *Carry out the change*	The changes are put in place from a certain date.	For example, new procedures become live – or the new call centre operational.

The **hard system** model is most suitable where 'difficulties' can be easily identified. However, it is less suitable in situations where it is harder to define the problem, obtain information or come to conclusions. Senior classifies these situations as 'messes' and suggests that soft models of change should be applied to '**messes**' while hard models should be applied to '**difficulties**'.

In this respect, soft models of change could be seen more like **emergent strategies**, and hard models of change more like rational, **prescriptive strategies**.

1.1.2 Soft models of change

Three different approaches can be taken to dealing with change situations

Resolve the problem	A satisfactory solution can be employed based on what worked in the past in a similar situation – this is referred to as **satisficing**. It lacks analytical rigour. In our call centre example above, a knee-jerk reaction might be to increase the number of staff, if that has improved service standards in the past: but note that other options have not been considered.
Solve the problem	This is like the hard systems model. Problem solvers try to quantify messes and, so to speak, turn them into quantifiable 'difficulties'. However, a mess is series of interlocking problems, and attempts to quantify it and break it down may destroy the holistic nature of the problem. Poor call centre service standards may be the result of poor training. However, high staff turnover may mean that call operators are not experienced, and the training department cannot cope. High staff turnover may be caused by boredom in the job, lack of good pay, an inappropriate management style and so on.
Dissolve the problem	This is to change the nature of the problem. In the call centre example above, one 'option' to deal with the problem was to abolish the call centre completely and change over to Internet-only ordering: here the problem has been redefined as a customer access problem. However, a problem cannot be simply defined away. Changes to the organisation structure and the wider system may be needed to deal with the problem finally. Most 'messes' require systems to be redefined at many levels. For example, co-ordination problems can be solved by formal mechanisms such as changing people's jobs.

Section summary

When considering a strategic change, managers need to analyse the speed and extent of the change required. They also need to assess whether management's role is proactive or reactive, and whether the change is hard (systems based) or soft (people based). All of these factors will affect the way the change is implemented.

2 The context of change

Introduction

Many organisations have a poor track record of bringing about strategic change.

This is often because they fail to grasp that it is the *implementation* of the change, rather than the *formulation* of it, that is the hard part of the process. For strategic change to become reality, it is necessary to change the way in which the individuals within an organisation behave.

This means that there is a personal and cultural dimension to change management, and it is not simply an exercise in mechanical restructuring or the introduction of new systems.

The context of change is provided by the **organisational setting**; this has many aspects and can therefore be very complex. A change agent faces a wide range of choices about how change should be implemented in the specific context of his or her organisation.

We can look at the context of change by reference to what *Balogun and Hope Hailey* call the **change kaleidoscope**.

The kaleidoscope was created to help managers design a **change management approach which is appropriate** to their organisation, and it offers eight headings for the **context** in which change occurs (**contextual features**).

One of the eight contextual features is **scope** which we have discussed in relation to the type of change. The rest of the contextual features are discussed below.

In relation to scope, a change manager also needs to consider how much of an organisation is going to be affected by the change. A single division or department, or the whole organisation?

The headings represent a wide range of influences and the specific considerations affecting the impact of each may vary from organisation to organisation. For example, the first on the list, **time available**, may be largely determined by stakeholder sentiment in one organisation and by anticipated political change in another, with different aspects of the market situation influencing both.

2.1 Aspects of context

(a) The **time available** may vary dramatically, but can often be quite limited when responding to competitive or regulatory pressure. Organisations in crisis have little time, but those looking at longer term strategic development normally have more time to change.

(b) The **preservation** of some organisational characteristics and resources may be required. Do certain ways of working need to be maintained? Do particular groups of staff need to be retained? Do specific organisational competencies need to be preserved?

(c) **Diversity** of general experience, opinion and practice is likely to ease the change process: homogeneity in these factors is unlikely to do so.

(d) The **capability** to manage and implement change is obviously important. To a great extent, this depends on past experience of change projects, both among managers and among lower-level staff.

Capability can be analysed at three levels:

- **Individual**: are individuals able to cope with the transition they will have to undertake?

- **Managerial**: do managers have the ability to help their staff through the transition process?

- **Organisational**: does the organisation as a whole have sufficient resources with the knowledge and ability required to manage the types of change required?

(e) **Capacity** to undertake change depends on the availability of resources, particularly **finance**, **IS/IT**, and management time and skill. We have looked at the importance of IS/IT to strategy earlier in this Study Text, but it is important to note that unrealisable or out-dated systems could become a blockage in the change process.

(f) The degree of workforce **readiness** for change will affect its success. Are staff aware of the need for change, and are they committed to making the personal changes required of them?

Readiness may be contrasted with **resistance** to change, which can exist at varying levels of intensity and may be widespread or confined to pockets.

(g) The **power** to effect change may not be sufficient to overcome determined resistance among important **stakeholder groups**. This can apply even at the strategic apex, where, for example, major shareholders, trustees or government ministers may constrain managers' freedom of action.

Stakeholder analysis is very important because stakeholders can affect an organisation's capacity to change, so an organisation needs to ensure that its proposed changes are acceptable to key stakeholder groups.

For example, in 1995 Shell announced plans to dispose its Brent Spar oil storage platform in deep waters in the Atlantic Ocean. The environmental group Greenpeace organised a high-profile international campaign to prevent this. The campaign prompted significant public and political opposition to Shell across Europe, including a widespread boycott of Shell service stations. As a result, Shell abandoned its plans to dispose Brent Spar at sea.

An examination of context leads to four questions.

(a) Is the organisation able to **achieve** the change required?

(b) Does the context affect the **means** by which change should be achieved?

(c) Should the context itself be **restructured** as a preliminary to strategic change?

(d) Will constraints present in the context make it necessary to proceed in **stages** rather implementing the changes all at once?

Exam skills

The change kaleidoscope, and references to the context of change, reinforce the importance of making sure a proposed change is appropriate to its context. This will also be the case in your E3 exam. If you need to evaluate a change an orgnisation is proposing to make, you must consider the change specifically in the context highlighted by the case study scenario.

2.2 Design choices

As well as the eight contextual features, the change kaleidoscope also identifies six design choices which affect change implementation itself.

Once a change agent has considered the context of the change process, he or she can then select a change approach from the menu of design choices.

Change path – The change path refers to the type of change (the nature and scope of change) that needs to be undertaken for the required outcome to be achieved.

Change start point – The change start point is the point where change is initiated and developed. For example, is the change **top-down** or **bottom-up**? Will the change initially be applied to a **pilot site** and then extended to the whole organisation, or will it immediately be rolled out across the whole organisation?

Change style – The change style is the management style of the implementation. We will look at change management styles later, but it is important to realise there is range of possible styles for managing change – ranging from highly **collaborative**, to **directive** and then **coercive**. However, there is no one single 'correct' style of management. Style needs to be appropriate to the change context.

Change target – Deciding which organisational level to intervene at is an important design choice. For example, does a change process try to change employees' values, or focus on behavioural change, or does it instead try to change the performance objectives and outputs of employees?

Change interventions – The change interventions are the levers and mechanisms which need to be deployed to implement the change. They include:

- technical interventions (structures and systems)
- political interventions
- cultural interventions (changing the culture in the organisations)
- interpersonal interventions (education, communication, training, personal development)

Change roles – This determines who is responsible for leading and implementing the changes. These roles may include:

- leadership (for example, the individual responsibility which lies with a senior manager such as the MD or the CEO)

- external consultants who facilitate the process

- change action team

2.2.1 Comments on the kaleidoscope

Balogun and Hope Hailey stress that the kaleidoscope is not intended to prescribe formulaic design choices for particular contexts.

In the same way as a real kaleidoscope continuously rearranges the same small pieces of coloured glass to produce different images, to the eight contextual features in the model are constantly reconfigured to produce different scenarios for each change situation.

As a result, the change designs also vary according to individual situations.

Also, the importance of the eight contextual features on the design choices does not come from the impact of isolated, individual features, but from the impact of all of them together.

2.3 Top down or bottom up change

Balogun and Hope Hailey's kaleidoscope highlights the importance of context in change management, and their change matrix highlights the potential variety in the scope and nature of the change which an organisation could face.

However, we also need to recognise that the starting point for change (top down or bottom up) can in itself affect the change.

BPP
LEARNING MEDIA

2.3.1 Top down change

In a top down change, the direction, control and initiation of the change comes from the **strategic apex** of the organisation

Top down change usually involves a programme of change **determined** and implemented by the **senior management** or their representatives.

Top down change may need to be **imposed** on an organisation. In a crisis or turnaround situation, there may be no alternative but to impose change on the organisation.

2.3.2 Bottom up change

The logic behind emergent, or bottom up change, is that the responsibility for change should not rest solely with senior management.

Whilst top down change offers the benefits of speed and clarity it is unlikely to **encourage ownership or commitment** to the required changes.

By contrast, bottom up change involves consultation with staff so that employees contribute to the themes and ideas in the changes.

This collaborative approach to change gives the employees a sense of ownership of the change process.

However, there are some limitations to a bottom up approach:

- Because it involves consultation and emerges from the organisation, it can be **slower to implement** than a top down approach.

- Bottom up change can produce much more **unpredictable consequences** than top down change because it is subject to interpretation and negotiation by the staff who put the change in place.

- Senior management have less control over the change process, because it has to be participative and collaborative.

- A top-down, or directive approach to change (as would be necessary for a reconstruction or a revolution) leads to a cultural web developed by one person (usually the CEO) or a small group of people (senior management). By contrast, a bottom-up, collaborative approach leads to a wider range of employees being involved in the process of vision and cultural web development.

2.4 Adaptation and continuous change

The change matrices illustrating the nature and scope of change have highlighted that while some changes can be rapid, one-off events (revolutions or reconstructions), other changes take place much more gradually.

Although 'adaptation' is less dramatic than a 'revolution' it can be equally important for an organisation. In essence, adaptive change is about making organisations more efficient, or better, at what they already do.

Adaptive change occurs when an organisation's environment changes slowly, and is change in little stages. One of the advantages of this is that it **minimises the resistance faced** at any time.

Also, although many models and approaches to change present a 'change event' as a one-off occurrence, this is not always the case.

We have already mentioned that many organisations view change as a means of reaching a visionary future state. However, this ignores the fact that for some organisations change management is most realistically about what *Buchanan & McCalman* call a '**perpetual transition management**'.

In this case, a key aspect of successful change management is managers' ability to deal with **constant change**.

For *Buchanan* & *McCalman* change is not simply a stage process. Instead they suggest that **four interlocking management processes** or layers need to be in place to implement and sustain major organisational changes.

(a)   **Trigger layer**: Identification of needs and opportunities for major change

(b)   **Vision layer**: Establishing the future development of the organisation by articulating a vision of the future and communicating this effectively.

(c)   **Conversion layer**: Mobilise support in the organisation for the new vision as being the most appropriate way of dealing with the triggers of change.

This has important implications for management: everyone involved in making change work has to feel part of the change, and has to accept the logic behind not. If are not involved, they are liable to the 'you've introduced this without consulting us' syndrome, which could lead to them resisting the changes, and therefore reducing their effectiveness.

(d)   **Maintenance and renewal layer**: Identifying ways in the changes are sustained and enhanced through alterations in attitudes, values and behaviours, thereby avoiding regression back to 'old' ways of doing things.

Many change initiatives fail to achieve the results which had been hoped for. And the reason for this is often that there are inherent tendencies in an organisation to preserve the status quo.

Therefore approaches to change management which focus on planning and vision (at the start of the change process) are in danger of overlooking the vital importance of **sustaining and renewing organisational change**: that is, recognising that change is an on-going process.

2.5 Continuous and discontinuous change

The 'scope of change' axis on Balogun & Hope Hailey's change matrix illustrates that change can either take place within the existing organisational paradigm or else can lead to the creation of a new paradigm.

Continuous change comprises small scale incremental changes, which do not alter the organisational paradigm. *Tushman* call this type of change '**convergent**' reflecting the fact that changes do not alter the underlying strategy of the organisation.

Discontinuous change results in a radical change in the firm's environment or operations. This change can be a sudden one-off change, or can be the result of a series of incremental changes. Discontinuous change is sometimes also described as '**frame-breaking**'.

The existence of discontinuous change is very significant in the unfreeze process.

Characteristics of discontinuous change

(a)   **Magnitude of change**: Discontinuous change means doing things in fundamentally different ways from the way there were previously done. The whole nature of the business is reshaped.

(b)   **Organisational fit**: Because the new strategic imperatives are inconsistent with the old ways of doing business, the old organisational structure is unlikely to fit with the new business model. This can lead to new organisational structures.

(c)   **Strategic vision**: Discontinuous change is nearly always linked to a reshaping of the overall corporate strategy.

(d)   **Multiple changes**: The magnitude of the change means that discontinuous change often affects several aspects of an organisational simultaneously – for example, strategy, structure, staffing and systems.

(e)   **Unclear future state**: At the outset, it is impossible to know precisely where discontinuous change will lead. Because discontinuous change involves the movement to a **new paradigm**, it is impossible to predict the detail of that paradigm in advance.

(f) **Leadership**: The leadership of discontinuous change cannot be delegated: because of the magnitude of the change, the CEO and other top executives must be involved with the change.

(g) **Speed of change**: Discontinuous change often involves rapid implementation, particularly if the change is a response to an external crisis.

The environment where frame-breaking change is necessary can be highly volatile, suggesting that unless an organisation changes quickly to meet the changed circumstances it may go out of business. In such a situation, there is a risk attached to any delay in the change process.

2.5.1 Dangers of simplistic classification

Before we leave this section, it is again worth considering that there is a danger of simply categorising change into two distinct categories – essentially either some kind of change or a kind of corporate earthquake.

This distinction is too simplistic, and we need to acknowledge a middle ground between convergent change and frame-breaking change. We could see this middle ground as 'frame-stretching' rather than 'frame-breaking.'

Frame-stretching change might involve the following features:

- Parts of the corporate mission may be revised but the whole is not replaced.

- Some elements of the power structure at the top of an organisation may change but not the whole management team.

- Some modifications may be needed around the whole business, though they do not require wholesale redesign of every major process.

- Some aspects of the organisational structure might be changed in some, but the basic elements and the overall balance of size and shape will remain largely the same.

2.6 Uncertainty and change

Earlier in this Study Text, we suggested that the rational model of strategic planning underplays the level of uncertainty and complexity in strategy development. In that context, we introduced Stacey's ideas of chaos and complexity.

These ideas of chaos and complexity also have important implications for organisational change.

The interaction between a system and its environment has the potential for significant disruption. And if a system (in this case, an organisation) is operating in a chaotic and complex environment, the potential for disruption is increased still further.

Stacey argues that the complexity and instability of the business environment mean that organisations are operating in **unpredictable circumstances**. Consequently, there is no value in setting a prescriptive strategy. The reality is so complex that the **linear assumptions** between **cause** and **effect** cannot be justified.

Instead strategy should be allowed to emerge and adapt to the changes in the environment.

The importance of this for business strategists is that because organisations are operating in an unpredictable environment, **strategy becomes virtually impossible to model** because the future can not be known with any certainty.

For example, could strategists looking at three or five year plans in 2006 have predicted the global economic downturn and crisis in the financial markets in 2008/9?

One other characteristic of chaotic systems is that they oscillate between **steady states** and **states of flux**; and at the end of a period of turbulence a new order will emerge. *Strebel* makes an important point here when he refers to the way **changes in technology** lead to '**breakpoints**' in the development of an organisation. For example, look how the development of the internet has triggered changes through new e-commerce opportunities. Could these have been anticipated 20 or more years ago?

Another important consequence of these ideas about chaos is that it **challenges the way organisations manage change**.

The traditional rational model would suggest that change is somehow internally generated and an organisation can, to some extent, control the change. However, the chaos theory approach suggests that organisations **cannot ultimately predict or control the change** in the longer term, however well they have planned for the future.

Instead, change management becomes a means of **responding to**, and **coping with**, the uncertainties created by an unpredictable environment.

2.6.1 Thriving on chaos

The management guru Tom Peters has argued that in this age of rapidly changing information technology, 'chaos' and constant change are now integral parts of companies' success. Peters argues that constant change is something that companies should pursue, rather than discourage.

In his book 'Thriving on Chaos', Peters argues that companies have to adapt by creating open information societies and knowledge-sharing, encouraging employees to be responsible and adaptable, and by flattening hierarchical organisational structures.

Peters suggests that successful companies will embrace a policy of **constant innovation** , and will understand the value of **speed in responding to the opportunities** created by the volatility and dynamism in the external environment. (Developments in information technologies are one of the key drivers of this.) Conversely, companies need to rid themselves of 'the evils of bureaucracy,' which Peters suggests will prevent them from being able to introduce change quickly and successfully.

Section summary

When facing a strategic change, an organisation needs to consider the **context of the change**, and the change kaleidoscope illustrates the contextual features it should consider. It is also important to note that change could be **continuous**, rather simply a one-off, **discontinuous** event.

Equally, the organisation needs to consider whether change needs to be **imposed** by senior management or whether it can **emerge** from within the organisation.

3 Culture and change

Introduction

In the same way that we can look at the way individuals 'feel' and 'behave' we can also look at the way organisations do. Also, like individuals, organisations can adapt to their surroundings – changing their appearance, beliefs and behaviours.

Nevertheless, organisational culture has a very important impact on the management of change. Every organisation will have its own cultural blueprint which dictates how it interacts with its environment and manages its people.

Understanding the relationships between an organisation's culture and its (changing) environment greatly assist the organisation in managing change.

In their text, *Exploring Corporate Strategy*, Johnson, Scholes and Whittington argue that 'Strategic developments can only be successful if they recognise and address the cultural aspects of the change at hand.'

In other words, change cannot be isolated from the organisation overall, and therefore change needs to be linked to the culture of the organisation.

Two important characteristics of successful strategic change initiatives highlight this:

Alignment – ensuring that all the components of the change plan form an integrated whole. This means they are consistent within themselves, but are also linked into the whole organisational system.

Attunement – mirroring the preferred organisation culture, and ensuring that all aspects of the change are carried out in line with organisational values, and with sufficient attention to the human side of change.

If you think about the change kaleidoscope and the elements of context outlined above, you can see that they are all affected to some extent by **cultural considerations**. For example, even the adequacy or otherwise of the time available may be affected by culturally-influenced attitudes to speed of action, caution and risk.

Johnson, Scholes & Whittington bring these ideas of culture and change together to create what they call the **cultural web**. The web helps an organisation analyse its current culture and identify which aspects of this culture need to be changed in order for the organisation to be able to achieve its strategic goals.

3.1 The cultural web

The cultural aspects which need to be considered when managing change can be illustrated in the cultural web:

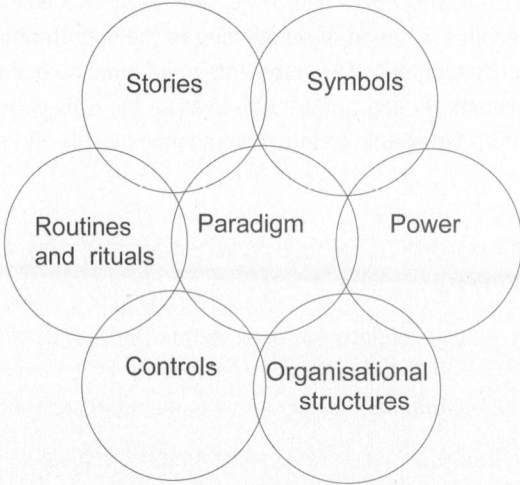

Figure 12.1: The Cultural Web (Johnson, Scholes & Whittington)

The web comprises six physical manifestations of culture:

(a)   **Stories** – The past events and people talked about inside and outside the company. Who and what are talked about most in these stories can illustrate the behaviour and organisation encourages, and the sorts of things it values.

(b)   **Rituals and Routines** – The daily behaviour and actions of people that signal what is considered acceptable. This determines what is expected to happen in given situations, and what is valued by management.

(c)   **Symbols** – The visual representations of an organisation including logos, premises and dress can illustrate the nature of that organisation. Also, verbal representations like language and titles can also act as symbols of the nature of an organisation.

(d) **Organisational Structure** – This includes both the formal structure defined by the organisation chart, and the unwritten lines of power and influence that indicate whose contributions are most valued. Structure is likely to reflect power.

(e) **Control Systems** – The ways that the organisation is controlled. These include financial systems, quality systems, and rewards (including the way they are measured and distributed within the organisation.) Looking at the areas which are controlled most closely can indicate what is seen as most important to an organisation, and where most attention is focused.

(f) **Power Structures** – The pockets of real power in the company. This may involve one or two key senior executives, a whole group of executives, or even a department. The key is that these people have the greatest amount of influence on decisions, operations, and strategic direction.

These cultural elements all combine to underpin **the paradigm**. The paradigm signifies the **basic assumptions and beliefs** that an organisation's decision-makers **hold in common** and **take for granted**.

Note that the paradigm is a slightly different concept from **culture**. The paradigm represents **collective experience** and is used to make sense of a given situation. It is thus essentially conservative and inhibiting to innovation, while an innovative **culture** is entirely feasible.

3.1.1 Challenging the paradigm

The entrenched assumptions and habits of mind which represent the **paradigm** constitute an important obstacle to strategic change. Therefore, if change is to be achieved, the existing organisational paradigm has to be challenged. A key part of the 'unfreeze' aspect of change management may need to be changing organisational behaviours and the paradigm.

Changing routines

Routines are the **habitual behaviours** that members of the organisation display both internally and externally. They are *not* procedures or processes but the **wider ways of doing things** that are typical of the organisation.

The problem of routines is that they can subvert change efforts. For example, it is unlikely that simply explaining required new processes and procedures will lead to their effective adoption: existing routines will mould the way they are put into operation.

When a **top-down change programme** requires the introduction of new methods, the detail of implementation can be driven by the careful identification of **critical success factors** and the **competences** they demand.

When change is to be introduced in a **less directed** way, change agents may focus on routines, **extending** existing ways of doing things toward what is required and then '**bending** the rules of the game' when sufficient stakeholder support has been created.

Symbolic processes

The importance of symbolic processes in the context of change is that they can often be used as levers of change. However, it is important to understand that the significance of a given symbol may vary from person to person; this makes their use as a tool of management difficult.

(a) New **rituals** can be introduced and old ones abolished in order to communicate and implement change. For example, the replacement of a strictly hierarchical approach to management with a culture of coaching and empowerment can be signalled and reinforced by the introduction of social occasions such as office parties that will allow staff to meet relatively informally.

(b) Formal **systems and processes** can have symbolic aspects, typically when they signal status and power relationships, but also when they direct attention to new concerns, such as customer service.

(c)   Changes to **physical aspects** of the workplace can have strong symbolic effect, as, for instance, when open-plan offices or hot-desking are introduced.

(d)   The **behaviour** of leaders and change agents has very powerful symbolic effect and must reflect intended change if the intention is not to be undermined: staff will respond far better to example than to edict.

(e)   **Language** can have symbolic significance beyond the bald meaning of the words used. Well chosen words can inspire and motivate change; similarly, the use of badly chosen words can undermine their inherent meaning.

(f)   **Stories** have an important symbolic role, but are not easy to exploit since much corporate communication is automatically dismissed as mere marketing puff.

Power and politics

Politics is about the exercise of **power** and the use of **influence**. Managers and other important individual stakeholders establish and exploit **power structures** and **networks of influence** that are intertwined with both formal hierarchies and the informal aspects of the organisation's life. The implementation of strategy is inevitably influenced by the operation of these structures and networks. Change management is also, therefore, subject to political influence and change managers should take due account of political processes.

Change managers can use political activity to achieve the following goals:

- Building the **power base**
- Overcoming **resistance**
- Achieving **compliance**

3.1.2 Example of the cultural web

The example below shows some of the questions which the cultural web asks about an organisation. It also illustrates some of the expressions of culture that could be generated by the web, based on an example of a car repair workshop.

Culture web	Examples (based on a car repair workshop)
Stories	
What stories do people tell about the organisation? What do these stories say about the values of the organisation?	They're always the cheapest on the market; they do things the cheapest way they can.
What reputation is communicated among customers and other stakeholders?	They are known for having high numbers of customer complaints, and for doing shoddy work.
What do employees talk about when they think of the history of the organisation?	The founder started the company with a $10,000 loan from a friend.
Rituals and routines	
What do employees expect when they come to work?	Employees have their time sheets examined by the boss
What do customers expect when they walk in?	Customers expect to hear the radio playing and to be given a mug of coffee while they wait for their cars
What would be immediately obvious if it changed?	Workshop repainted and new machinery installed
What behaviour do the routines encourage?	Lots of talk about money, and especially how to cut costs

Culture web	Examples (based on a car repair workshop)
Symbols	
What language and jargon is used? Is it well know and usable by all?	Mechanics use jargon which customers don't understand to describe parts and problems
What aspects of strategy are highlighted in publicity?	Adverts and leaflets say they won't be beaten on price
Are there any status symbols?	No, the boss wears an overall, like the staff
Organisational structure	
Is the structure formal or informal? Flat or hierarchical?	Flat structure: Owner, Mechanics, Receptionist.
What are the formal lines of authority?	Mechanics report to the owner (who is also a mechanic)
Are there any informal lines of authority?	The receptionist is the owner's wife so she discusses customer complains directly with him
Do structures encourage cooperation and collaboration?	Each mechanic looks after himself. There is no sharing of tools or jobs.
Control systems	
What process has the strongest controls?	Costs are high controlled. Customers are billed for all parts used
What process has the weakest controls?	Quality is not seen as important. Getting work done as cheaply as possible is emphasised ahead of quality
Is emphasis on rewarding good work or penalising poor work?	Employees pay is deducted if actual costs on a job exceed quotes by more than 10%
Power structures	
Who has the real power in the organisation?	The owner
How strongly held are the beliefs of the people with power?	The owner believes strongly in a low cost model, and is prepared to lose repeat customers in order to keep costs down
How is power used or abused?	The threat of having their pay docked keeps mechanics working to this low cost model
What are the main blockages to change?	The owner insists that his low cost model is the best way to run the business and won't invest in any new equipment if it will cost lots of money

3.1.3 The cultural web, business strategy and change

The importance of the cultural web for business strategy is that it provides a means of looking at cultural assumptions and practices, to make sure that **organisational elements are aligned with one another, and with an organisation's strategy**.

If an organisation is not delivering the results its management wants, management can use the web to help diagnose whether the organisation's **culture is contributing to the underperformance**.

The cultural web may be used as a tool to establish specific implications of the desired overall strategic change by facilitating comparison between the current position and the desired future outcome.

For example, consideration of power structures may make it clear that there should be a move away from some aspects of uncontrolled devolution of power and towards a clearer definition of responsibility.

Similarly, it might be decided that dress is a powerful symbol and that providing all customer-facing staff with a corporate uniform will give them a greater sense of pride and identity in their work.

3.2 McKinsey 7 S model

Like the cultural web, the **McKinsey 7 'S' model** is a useful way of looking at organisations facing organisational change.

The model represents the organisation as a set of interconnected and interdependent sub-systems, some of which are seen as 'hard' (quantifiable or easily defined) and some of which are 'soft' (more subjective and less easily defined).

Although the model was designed to show how the various aspects of a business relate to one another, it can also illustrate how change will affect both the organisation as a whole, and individual people and functions within it.

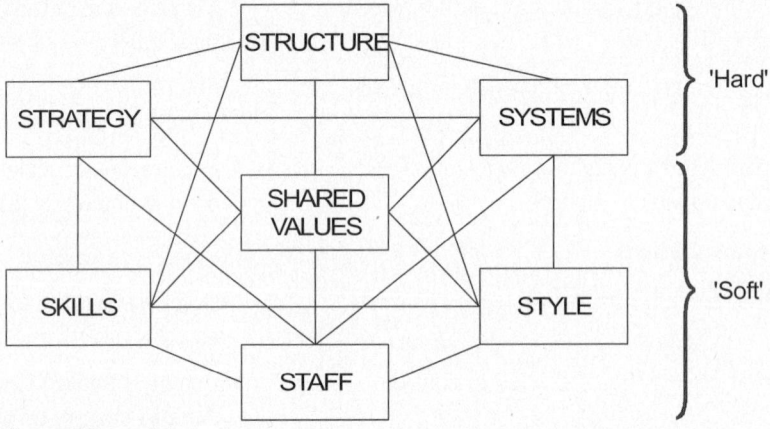

Figure 12.2 McKinsey 7S model

The organisation's **structure** determines the division of tasks in the organisation and the hierarchy of authority from the most senior to junior.

Strategy is way in which the organisation plans to outperform its competitors, or how it intends to achieve its objectives. **Systems** include the technical systems of accounting, personnel, management information and so forth.

These 'hard' elements are easily quantified or defined, and deal with facts and rules. However, certain 'soft' elements are equally important.

Staff are the people in the organisation (who have their own complex concerns and priorities) and **skills** are those things that the organisation does well. **Shared values** are the guiding beliefs of people in the organisation about why it exists, while **style** includes the shared assumptions, ways of working and attitudes of management (especially senior management).

Shared values thus approximate closely to the 'paradigm', underpinning management beliefs.

3.3 Culture and mergers/acquisitions

Issues of cultural incompatibility have often been cited as problem areas when implementing a merger or acquisition, and are often considered to be an important reason why mergers fail.

Signs of a culture clash might be:

- people talk in terms of 'them' and 'us'
- people glorify the past, talking of the 'good old days'
- newcomers are not integrated into the team
- there is obvious conflict – arguments between staff members, refusal to share information; formation of cliques and coalitions.

However, rather than running the risk of cultural issues disrupting a merger or acquisition, it would be sensible for managers to examine the existing cultures of the two organisations at the start of the integration process, while looking at the suitability of the deal.

3.4 Change and national cultures

As well as considering change in the context of organisational culture, we also need to consider how different **national cultures** can affect the way organisations change.

Differences between national cultures can be stronger than between different organisations.

(a) **Organisational culture** is something we learn afresh each time we join a different workforce, and is therefore easy to pick up and put down as appropriate.

(b) **National culture** is something we are born into, and therefore is generally non-negotiable; it is something inherent to all of us.

This point lends is often used to explain why management approaches developed in Japan that have been successful there, such as TQM, and *kaizen*, may not work in Western companies because the national cultures are so different. Of course it might be added that Japanese approaches may not work even in other Asian countries, such as South Korea, because their cultures are sufficiently different from Japan's. However, the underlying point is clear: business practices cannot be divorced from their social context.

This has important implications for managing change, particularly major transformational change, because it suggests change managers need to pay attention to **national cultural characteristics**.

Section summary

Many aspects of change will be affected to some extent by cultural considerations. Therefore it is important to establish the impact of a strategic change by comparing the current cultural position with that of the desired future position.

4 Styles of change management

Introduction

In the previous chapter, we saw that there are three basic stages to a change implementation process: (unfreeze, move, refreeze) and we highlighted the role of change 'triggers' in initiating the process of change.

However, in order to implement a change, a change manager needs to use a number of levers to actually unfreeze and move an organisation, and then sustain the changes that have been put in place.

4.1 Change and communication

Interestingly, people are often not as averse to change as some managers think. Although we have looked at ways of managing resistance to change, staff will often **accept change when they know it is necessary**. However, **resistance to change** can often be caused where the reasons and triggers for change have not been properly communicated.

This again highlights the importance of **communication as a change lever.**

However, communication can be a double-edged sword. Poor communication can damage a change process just as much as effective communication can help it.

For example, employees will resent hearing about changes which affect them from sources other than management, for example, the press. If staff members feel that managers are not being open and honest with them, resistance to change will be increased.

Honesty – even it means admitting that all the details have not yet been finalised – is better than cover-ups.

The table below summarises the role of communication in the change process:

Change phase	Communication purpose
Unfreeze	Creating readiness for change; spread understanding of the need for change
Move	Provide individuals with the explanation about the changes; reduce uncertainty about the impact of the changes.
	Enable staff to make any changes required of them
Refreeze	Keep staff informed of the progress of the change process.

4.2 Communication channels

There are a wide variety of communication channels available:

- Conferences, or videoconferences
- Seminars and workshops
- Briefings and departmental meetings
- One-to-one meetings with managers
- Memos
- Manuals and information packs
- Newsletters (electronic or in hard copy)
- Announcements on notice boards (on intranet as well as hard copy)
- E-mail
- Websites

This variety of possible channels available means it is important to select a channel which is appropriate to the message being delivered and the audience.

In general, complex, non-routine change situations are best delivered through rich forms of communication – usually face-to-face interactions. Face-to-face communication – especially in small groups – allows the people the opportunity to ask questions and raise concerns they may have.

Less rich forms of communication – such as written and electronic means – are usually better suited to routine, less-complex changes.

4.2.1 Dangers of communication by e-mail

Email is a useful mechanism for distributing a standard message to a large number of people at one time. However, e-mail can be impersonal and 'soulless' so it is usually not appropriate for delivering messages of an emotional nature, particularly ones which convey bad news (eg redundancy).

Communication efforts should include clear and plentiful opportunities and routes for **feedback**, so that omissions, poorly constructed messages, misunderstandings and anxiety can be dealt with.

Care must be taken with **emotional aspects** of communication so that appropriate media, language and symbols are used.

4.2.2 Timing

The time at which actions are taken can be selected for tactical effectiveness.

(a)   A **crisis** can be used to justify extensive change, so monitoring a mounting crisis and delaying action until it is ripe may enhance acceptance.

(b)   **Windows of opportunity** may occur, as, for example, when a takeover occurs.

(c)   **Messages** about timing must be coherent so that, for example, rapid action is not undermined by the retention of procedures that enforce long time frames.

(d)   Fear and anxiety about change may be reduced if unpleasant consequences can be **decoupled in time** from the main change programme. An example would be a programme of redundancy that does not commence until other change objectives such as the outcomes of product and market reviews have been implemented.

4.2.3 Job losses

The threat of job losses associated with change is likely to be bad for morale and to provoke resistance. Redundancy programmes must be managed with care.

(a)   A single, rapid and extensive round of cuts is preferable to a long drawn out programme of smaller reductions: the former can be stressful but the latter creates **long-term uncertainty and anxiety**.

(b)   Where **delayering** is required, it may be possible to concentrate the job losses among managers identified as being opposed to change: these are likely to be more senior figures.

(c)   Those who lose their jobs should be dealt with as **sympathetically and compassionately** as possible; the provision of services such as outplacement, counselling and retraining may help.

4.2.4 Quick success

Momentum for change can be created by putting simple but highly visible improvements into successful operation. Even where the overall position is difficult and requires a complex solution, such **quick wins** are often available: it is common for them to emerge in the form of suggestions from the lower echelons of the organisation.

Even where there are no obvious easy options, it may be possible to create some by **concentrating the available resources** on specific problems rather than spreading them too thinly.

4.3 Stakeholders and communication channels

Stakeholder	Their needs	What they want to know	How to communicate
Shareholders	Reassurance	That there is well thought-through strategy. How the strategy will benefit them	The press Financial statements AGM Website
Suppliers	Information	How the changes will affect their working relationship	Face-to-face meetings with major suppliers Letters/ e-mail to small suppliers
Customers	Motivation	That they will still be able to buy the products they want That the service they receive will continue uninterrupted	The press Advertisements
Senior managers	Acknowledgement and involvement	How they will be involved and opportunities in the new structure. Reassurance over employment positions	One-to-one meetings
Staff	Reassurance Help to adapt	Training and support Job security	Briefings One-to-one with line manager

Stakeholder	Their needs	What they want to know	How to communicate
Line managers	Reassurance Involvement	Opportunities to be involved and opportunities to learn Job security	Briefings One-to-one with senior manager/HR
The press	A good story	What is happening, the rationale, and whether the changes are under control	Briefings

Although this table illustrates that change will need to be communicated to a range of external as well as internal stakeholders, we will focus here on the internal stakeholders, and how change is managed within an organisation.

Balogun & Hope Hailey's change kaleidoscope shows that one of the design choices in a change project is choosing which change intervention to use.

Successful change implementation ultimately requires an organisation to deploy a range of levers to change all the relevant organisational subsystems shown in the cultural web.

Levers will need to be designed to remove the barriers to change in the existing web, and to create new structures, systems, routines and so on, as defined by the new cultural web.

The number of levers required is likely to depend on the scope of the project. The greater the extent of the change, the more change initiatives that are likely to be required.

Communication, education, training and **personal development** initiatives (including possibly coaching and counselling) are all likely to be required to help individuals undertake the changes required of them.

However, managers will also need to ensure that changes across an organisation are **mutually supportive**.

For example, if there is a focus on improved teamwork, then the rewards system needs to reflect this and not simply reward individual performance. If the rewards system rewards individual performance then the behaviour it encourages could undermine the rhetoric of the change.

4.4 Five styles for managing change

We have already mentioned the importance of communicating appropriately and effectively in managing change effectively. However, it is also important that the overall style in which the change is managed is appropriate to the context. (You may notice some similarities between these styles for managing change and *Kotter & Schlesinger's* styles for overcoming resistance to change, which we looked at earlier.)

Johnson, Scholes and Whittington identify five styles of change management:

- Education and communication
- Collaboration/participation
- Intervention
- Direction
- Coercion/edict

4.4.1 Education and communication

Education and communication is an approach based on persuasion: the reasons for change and the means by which it will be achieved are explained in detail to those affected by it. This style is appropriate when change is **incremental**.

This style is **time-consuming**, but can be useful if there has been misinformation in the past. However, it is a top-down approach and depends on a **willingness to accept management's plans** as appropriate. This may not, in fact, be present.

If the willingness to change is initially missing, managers may also need to have a **negotiation strategy.**

In other words, they may need to negotiate with staff to resolve any issues, overcome any resistance and avoid any future conflicts. However, the negotiation process is likely to be a lengthy, time-consuming one.

4.4.2 Collaboration/participation

Collaboration, or **participation**, brings those affected by strategic change into the change management process. For example, this may include drawing them into issue identification, prioritisation and the creation of new routines to implement newly established strategy. This approach may improve decision quality by bringing wider experience and knowledge to bear.

However, it may be time-consuming and it will be **subject to the influence of the existing culture and paradigm**, which may limit its potential effectiveness. This approach is both **ethical**, in basic deontological terms, and advantageous in practice, since it can nurture a positive attitude, thus building both **readiness** and **capability** for change. It is suited to incremental change.

4.4.3 Intervention

Intervention is undertaken by a **change agent** who delegates some aspects of the change process to teams or individuals, while providing guidance and retaining overall control. Delegated aspects can include both design and implementation activities. Final responsibility for achieving the necessary change remains with the change agent, but this kind of participation can build **commitment** and a **sense of ownership**. This style is appropriate for incremental change.

4.4.4 Direction

Direction is a top-down style in which **managerial authority** is used to establish and implement a change programme based on a clear future strategy. It is thus suited to **transformational change**.

It has the potential advantages of speed and clarity, but may lead to **resistance**. Its success depends in part on the adequacy of the proposed strategy: if this is inappropriate, the best managed of change programmes will still not result in wider strategic success.

4.4.5 Coercion

Coercion is an **extreme form of direction**, being based on the use of power to impose change. It is likely to provoke opposition due to the lack of participation or consultation, but it may be the best approach in **times of confusion or crisis**. At such times there may simply not be time to consult, because decisions need to be taken quickly.

4.5 Using change management styles

Although we have looked at five change management styles in isolation, there may be advantages to making use of more than one of the change management styles at any one time.

4.5.1 Context

Specific aspects of the organisational context will influence the use that can be made of the five styles. Clear and appropriate **direction** can be a strong motivating force and may enhance **readiness** to change, while **collaboration/participation** and **intervention** may help to build **capability** to change.

4.5.2 Scope and nature

Using *Balogun and Hope Hailey's* change matrix (scope and nature of change) we might suggest that progression down the list of change management styles corresponds reasonably well with progression from top left to bottom right of the matrix.

In **adaptation**, where time is not critical and the extent of the change required is small, styles from the collaborative-communicative end of the spectrum may be appropriate.

Revolution, on the other hand will require a great element of **direction** and even of **coercion**.

The intermediate cases are likely to require a combination of **participation** and **direction**, with the emphasis on the former in **evolution** and on the latter in **reconstruction**.

As with all change processes, the likely success of different change management strategies is context-specific: what works in one context will not necessarily work in another.

Again, the change kaleidoscope could be a useful tool here. Key **contextual features** will affect the decision about which styles of management might be appropriate.

For example, an organisation with little time to deliver change, and a low readiness for change may need to use dramatic and directive means of unfreezing their current position. But an organisation with more time to deliver change could afford more communication and discussion with staff.

4.5.3 Power structures

In many cases, it will be appropriate to **echo an organisation's normal power structure** when managing change. Direction or intervention are likely to be more suitable in a firmly hierarchical organisation than they would be in a network or learning organisation, except in time of crisis, for example.

4.5.4 Personality type

Management style is a tool. Good managers will be capable of using a **style appropriate to the conditions** they have to work in. However, many managers' personality types will incline them to the **style with which they are most comfortable**. But this style may not be appropriate to the context of the change.

4.5.5 Combining styles

It will often be appropriate to use a combination of styles in a change programme, **taking different approaches with different stakeholders**. Providers of capital are likely to respond better to **education and communication** than to **direction**, for example, while something approaching **coercion** may be necessary in some internal areas simply because of the pressure of time.

Most of the time, a **mixed approach between coercive change and adaptive change** is suitable. Adaptive change may be too slow, whereas coercive change is often resented and may not be 'refrozen' into the organisation's future state.

4.6 Context-sensitive change

The strategic change needed to implement a new corporate strategy often involves a need to change an organisation's skills, style and operating culture.

Pettigrew & *Whipp's* research identified that there are five interrelated factors which need to be considered in order to manage strategic change successfully.

(a)   **Environmental assessment**. Strategy constantly emerges from a review of the environment and competitors' actions.

(b)   **Leadership style**. Leaders are constrained by the actual situation of their organisation.

(c)   **Linking strategic and operational change**. The strategy will allow for evolution over time, as issues become apparent in its implementation.

(d)   **Manage human resources** – It is important to manage the knowledge, skills and attitudes of the organisation as a whole. Long-term learning and development are crucial for an organisation to develop its full potential.

(e)   **Coherence** – This is the most complex of the five factors. It attempts to combine the other four into a consistent whole, which is reinforced by a set of complimentary support mechanisms:

- Consistency – the goals of the organisation must not conflict with each other

- Consonance – the whole process must respond well to its environment

- Competitive advantage – the change must deliver competitive advantage to the organisation

- Feasibility – the strategy must be feasible given the resources the organisation has available to it.

Exam skills

Note the similarity here between evaluating strategic change and evaluating a strategic option. The ideas of 'suitability, feasibility and acceptability' could therefore be useful in evaluating a strategic change.

The organisation needs to develop a balanced approach to change that is internally efficient whilst also adapting successfully to external changes.

Potentially, organisations may wish to pursue emergent strategic change in favour of prescriptive change because it is less disruptive.

However, emergent models of change take a long-term approach and so may have limited usefulness when the organisation faces a short-term strategic crisis.

Consequently, there may be occasions when strategic circumstances force prescriptive change.

Ultimately, the choice of which strategy to use to manage change – and therefore also to manage corporate strategy – depends on the situation facing the organisation at the time.

Section summary

It is important to use an appropriate management style for the type of change being managed. Management styles and types of change form a spectrum: the education and communication style works best for an adaptive change, while direction or coercion work best for revolutionary change.

5 Why change succeeds or fails

Introduction

We have highlighted the importance of context in change management and the different management styles which can be used in the change process. We will now look at some of the specific factors which can contribute to the success of a change management programme.

5.1 What makes change go well?

Studies carried out by Prosci Research (www.prosci.com) have identified that there are a number of common factors which contribute to the success of change management projects:

(a)   **Effective support from senior management:** active, visible support, ongoing support throughout the life of the initiative, acting as role models and ambassadors for the change

(b)   **Buy-in from front-line managers and employees** which got the change moving and maintained momentum through the project

(c)   **Continuous and targeted communication** throughout the project, tailored for different interested parties

(d) **An experienced and credible change management team** who maintained good internal working relationships

(e) **A well-planned and well-organised approach** which is suited to the type of change being managed

However, one very interesting conclusion this research highlighted is that in order to buy into the change, employees need to **hear about change from two people**:

(i) the most senior person involved in the change and

(ii) their line manager

The senior official – possibly even if the CEO – should communicate the general business message around the change to the orgnisation as a whole, while the line manage should communicate more personal messages, such as the impact the change might have on an individual's roles and responsibilities.

5.2 Why does change fail?

By contrast to the research looking at the ways that make change management successful, *Professor John Kotter*, one of the leading authors on change, picked out eight key aspects of the change process which could a cause change initiative to fail if they were not managed correctly.

Reason for failure	Possible antidotes
Not enough sense of urgency	**Establish a sense of urgency by:** • examining market or competitive pressures; • identifying potential crises or major opportunities • ensure levels of dissatisfaction with current position or perception of future threat are sufficient to kick-start the change and maintain momentum
Failure to create a powerful support base	**Form a powerful guiding coalition by:** • assembling a group with enough power to **lead the change effort**. (Without an effective change management team, any change management project is likely to fail.) • encouraging the group to work together as a team • ensure that key stakeholders are engaged
Vision not clearly developed	**Create a vision by:** • having a clear understanding of what the change needs to achieve • developing clear strategies for achieving the vision
Vision poorly communicated	**Communicate the vision by:** • using a variety of media to communicate the new vision and strategies. Within this, it will also be important to **highlight the benefits** of the changes • teaching new behaviours by the example of the guiding coalition senior management • ensuring people have a shared understanding and commitment to the direction of the change
Obstacles block the vision	**Empower people to act on the vision:** • senior management demonstrably tackling obstacles to change • ensure that all the people who are needed to make the change happen have the necessary resources and authority to achieve their goals

Reason for failure	Possible antidotes
Failing to create short-term wins	**Plan for and create short-term wins by:** • planning for visible performance improvements • identifying smaller goals along the way to the ultimate target so that success can be demonstrated. Being able to demonstrate success will maintain momentum • recognising and rewarding employees involved in improvements
Systems, policies and skills not aligned	**Consolidate improvements and produce more change by:** • changing systems, structures and policies that don't fit the vision • hiring, promoting and developing employees who can implement the vision • building on improvements in the organisation as and when they occur to continue to move the change forward
Failing to anchor changes in the corporate culture (not refreezing)	**Institutionalise new behaviours by:** • explaining how the new behaviours will deliver corporate success • developing the means to ensure leadership development and succession • ensuring knowledge about the new approaches is captured and shared

Source: adapted from *Cameron & Green*, 'Making sense of change management' and based originally on an article by *Kotter* in the Harvard Business Review

One additional factor which could jeopardise the successful of a change management project is a **lack of change management/implementation expertise** and skills within an organisation's senior management team. Change does not just happen on its own; management need to define the change programme, ensure the necessary resources are allocated to it, and drive it forward. However, for example, if the senior management team do not have any previous experience of change programmes, and do not allocate sufficient resources to a change programme this could jeopardise its success.

5.2.1 IT in change management

Although *Kotter* doesn't mention it, we should also consider the role of IT in the potential success or failure of any change programme.

Businesses have become increasingly dependent on effective IT systems, and this often creates tensions between the IT department and operational departments in organisations

Despite the best of intentions, IT and operational departments end up clashing and blaming each other for problems which emerge during projects.

However, effective change relies on an integrated shift of people, systems and processes – supported by IT. For example, if a business wants to introduce a new e-commerce strategy, for that strategy to be successful it will need an IT infrastructure which can support online transactions etc.

Therefore a lack of confidence and trust between the IT and operational teams which are critical to the success of a change is unlikely to lead to a successful project.

Section summary

There are a number of factors which contribute to the success of change management projects, but having a clear vision for a project and communicating effectively are particularly important.

6 Change and the individual

Introduction

So far we have looked at change as something which affects organisations. However, it is also important to appreciate that change affects individual people as well, and their reactions and response to change have to be appreciated.

One of the more common themes in modern business management is that 'people are a firm's best asset' and in the context of change management, this may be particularly true.

All changes are ultimately made by people, and the success of a change project is achieved by people, even if their role is in planning or designing systems and processes.

Yet the critical role of people in the change process also highlights a crucial risk in change management. A **key part of change management is about dealing with people**, and unfortunately people are not always rational or logical.

Therefore, as well as possibly being a firm's best asset, people can also potentially be its biggest liability.

If organisations do not understand their people, and their reactions to potential changes, the risk of change programmes failing increases.

Therefore, although our main focus is on organisational change, we also need to recognise that, in order for an organisation to change, the individuals within it are also likely to have to change to some degree.

Therefore when managing change, a change agent will have to consider how to change individuals' behaviours to support the change programme.

6.1 Approaches to managing change

There are a number of approaches to managing individual change.

6.1.1 Behavioural approach to change

This approach focuses on how one individual can change another's individual behaviour through reward and punishment in order to achieve intended results.

The implications for business are an organisation needs to get its **reward strategies** right, and reward people for following change.

6.1.2 Cognitive approach to change

This approach is founded on the idea that people's emotions and problems are a result of the way they think. Individuals react in the way they do because of the way they appraise the situation in which they find themselves. In the context of change, individuals need to look at the way they limit themselves through sticking to old ways of thinking, and replace that with new ways of being.

However, there are some drawbacks to this approach.

In particular, there may be a lack of recognition of the inner emotional world of the individual, and the positive and negative impact that this can have when attempting to manage change. Some obstacles to change need to be worked through, and cannot simply be made all right by reframing or positive talk.

6.1.3 Psychodynamic approach to change

The word 'psychodynamic' is based on the idea that, when facing change in their external world, an individual can experience a variety of **internal psychological states**. Although this approach has now been applied to the workplace, the original research by *Elizabeth Kubler-Ross* involved observing the way terminally ill patients come to terms with being informed about their conditions.

Kubler-Ross realised that patients go through five stages as they come to terms with their diagnosis.

Denial – the initial reaction is one of disbelief; trying not to accept the news, pretending that it did not happen.

Anger – Once people acknowledge what is happening, disbelief gives way to anger. For example, people want to know 'Why me?' or 'How could such a thing happen to me?'

Bargaining – Instead of continuing angry, the patient now desperately tries to find a way of remedying the situation.

Depression – When it becomes apparent that bargaining is not going to provide any escape from the situation, the scale and impact of the situation becomes realised, and patients recognise that they will be losing their life as they knew it. They experience a sense of grief and depression for that loss.

Acceptance – The patients have now come to terms with the reality and inevitability of their situation. While they are not necessarily happy about it, they are nonetheless prepared for it.

Adam, Hayes & Hopson developed Kubler-Ross's ideas to apply them to business, and have added the concepts of 'experimentation', 'discovery' and 'integration' after the acceptance stage in the original model.

Experimentation – Staff begin to think that some of the changes 'out there' might be worth thinking about.

Discovery – As staff enter the 'new world' that has changed they may actually discover that things are not as bad as they had imagined. Perhaps the organisation was telling the truth after all, when it said the changes would provide new opportunities and a better way of working. In which case, they then begin to **integrate** this 'new world' into their own.

The complexity of this psychodynamic approach has important implications for business. When introducing change, businesses to need to **treat people as individuals** and understand their emotional states when responding to change. Change cannot simply be forced through.

6.1.4 Humanistic psychology approach to change

For many years, we have been led to believe that organisations are ruled by the **rational mind**. However, humanistic psychology moves away from this rational approach and argues that managers need to have an emotional apathy with a situation and to be present emotionally in the situation in order to be fully effective.

This approach also emphasises the importance of development and growth, and maximising the potential of staff.

Section summary

In any change programme it is vital to consider the impact change will have on an organisation's staff as individuals. People respond to change in different ways, and develop their own ways of copying with change. In this way, change cannot simply be considered as a mechanical process.

7 Leading change 5/10

Introduction

Effective leadership is crucial in times of change. A leader will not only have to identify the vision for change but also communicate that to the organisation. The challenge leaders face in any change situation will depend on the scale, timeframe and possible implications of the change.

Change management is a comprehensive effort to lead an organisation through transformation. However, to be successful the transformation effort must be actively led and managed, with a clear set of objectives and an agreed plan for achieving these objectives.

A crucial problem organisations have to address is how they can **manage change** in the fast-moving environment of contemporary business, whilst also **maintaining control** and their **core competencies**.

Designing, evaluating and implementing successful change strategies depends to a significant extent on the quality of the senior management team, and in particular that team's ability to design organisation in a way to facilitate the change process.

7.1 Who leads change?

Although a CEO plays an important role in leading change, leading change is not only the responsibility of the CEO.

Whetten and Cameron have pointed out:

'...the most important leadership demonstrated in organisations usually occurs in departments, divisions, and with teams and with individuals who take it upon themselves to enter a temporary state of leadership...'

Inevitably, though, leading change will also require competencies in influencing and conflict handling, because people may need to be persuaded of the value and benefits of change.

Change may create conflict between individuals and their environment – and, often, within individuals themselves.

We have already noted that change can make people uncomfortable, which is why so many people resist it. Organisational change also creates potential conflict between management (who may be identified as the causes or agents of change) and employees (who often feel like the 'victims' of it).

Managing change is in essence a process of facilitating internal and external conflict resolution.

So change leaders have to play a dual role of not only leading a business forward, but also resolving any conflicts which are created during the course of the change process.

Whetten and Cameron suggest 5 key steps as to how a leader can encourage those involved with change to be positive about that change.

(a)   **Establishing a climate of positivity**: This is about focusing on the positive, rather than dwelling on negative aspects of the change. To do this requires identifying 'positive energizers', people who are optimistic and enthusiastic about the change and then enable them to have opportunities to interact with others and influence them. Leaders also need to display compassion in dealing with people experiencing change – supporting staff, providing positive feedback and recognising that mistakes may occur if staff are faced with new challenges. Another part of establishing a positive climate is to focus on people's strengths and successes.

(b)   **Create 'readiness' for change**: this is about helping people understand the reasons for change and its importance and urgency. One suggestion made by Whetten and Cameron is to use benchmarking to show areas for achieving higher levels of performance, showing that higher standards are achievable by looking at relevant comparators. They link this to the idea of 'unfreezing', getting people to let go of the past and identify a better future.

(c)   **Articulating a vision**: developing and communicating a vision of the future, which illustrates the benefits of the change. *Whetten and Cameron* comment:

'Positive change seldom occurs without a leader articulating a vision of abundance...by abundance we mean a vision of a positive future, a flourishing condition, and a legacy about which people care passionately.'

(d)   **Generating commitment to the vision**: Once the vision has been articulated, the next step is to get people to sign up to and adopt the vision.

(e)   **Institutionalising the change**: this final change is about making the new change part of everyday working life. This involves continually reinforcing the new ways and finding ways to communicate, celebrate and reward achievement.

7.2 Change roles

We can identify a number of key players in the change process.

Change leader: The success of the change programme is based on a key, pivotal figure. This leader may be the CEO, the MD, or another senior manager acting as an internal change agent.

Change advocate: who proposes the change

Change sponsor: who legitimises the change

Change agent: who implements the change. Change agents seek to initiate and manage a planned change process.

Change targets/recipients: although they do not lead the change, it is important in any change programme to remember the change targets – these are the people who undergo the change.

Other changes roles to consider are:

External facilitators: External consultants may be appointed to help coordinate the change process

Change action team: A team of people within the organisation may be appointed to lead the changes. This team may take the form of a steering committee. If the team does not include any influential senior managers it will need the backing of more powerful individuals to support any major change efforts.

Functional delegation: The responsibility for managing change may be assigned to a particular function – often the HR department. This approach is probably most suitable when the skills needed to manage the change reside within a particular department. However, unless the department head is a powerful authority figure, he or she will need the backing of a more powerful figure to spearhead major change efforts.

7.3 Change agents   11/10, 9/11, 3/12

For change to be effective, it needs to be effectively implemented. Many organisations seek to use changes agents to facilitate change.

A CHANGE AGENT is an individual or group that helps to bring about strategic change in an organisation.

Although a change agent might be a single person (sometimes called a **champion of change,** or a **change master**), change agency could equally be spread among the members of a group, such as a project team or the management team more generally. Outsiders, such as consultants, may share in change agency and have the responsibility for driving and 'selling' the change.

The role of the change agent varies depending on the brief they are given. It may include:

*   Defining the problem
*   Examining what causes the problem and considering how this can be overcome
*   Suggesting possible solutions
*   Selecting an appropriate solution
*   Implementing the change
*   Communicating information about the change throughout the organisation

The change agent must possess the skills to manage the transition process, but must also have the determination to see the change through.

Rosabeth Moss Kanter suggests that a change agent needs to have the following attributes:

- Needs to encourage those who are to be affected by change to participate and get involved in the management of the change. This helps stimulate interest and commitment to the change, and minimise fears, thereby reducing opposition to change

- Needs to reduce uncertainty associated with the change situation and encourage position action

- Questions the past and challenge old assumptions and beliefs

- Leaps from operational and process issues to the strategic picture; and has an understanding of the relevant processes

- Thinks creatively and avoids becoming bogged down in the detail of 'how to…'

- Can manipulate and exploit triggers for change

The following additional skills and attributes might also be important for a change agent:

- Communication skills – and the ability to communicate effectively with people at all levels within an organisation

- Networking skills to establish and maintain contacts, both within and outside an organisation

- Negotiation and 'selling' skills – negotiating with stakeholders in the business to obtain resources for a project, or to resolve conflict; selling the vision of change to key stakeholders to increase support for a change programme. Alongside this, a change agent also needs to have influencing skills, to be able to convince potential sceptics about the benefits of a change programme, and thereby to overcome their resistance to it.

- An awareness of organisational 'politics'

- Sensitivity to the impact changes will have on different stakeholders, and sensitivity in dealing with different stakeholders

- An understanding of the relevant processes

- Financial analysis skills: to assess the financial impacts of proposed changes, or to be able to look at how changes to operations and systems can deliver a desired financial goal

- Flexibility to be able to respond to shifts in project goals or objectives; or to adapt in response to internal or external factors which affect the change process.

An important point that *Kanter* highlights is that a change agent needs to be able to adapt to cope with the complexities of modern organisations.

In particular, a change agent needs to:

- Be able to work across a range of business units and functions and across a network of different stakeholders

- Be an effective collaborator, able to work in ways that enhance collaboration across different functions and divisions.

Importantly though, a change agent should not be selected just because they have good general project management skills. The change agent must be **directly involved in the change process**, and must see clear linkages between their future success in an organisation and the effective implementation of the change.

7.3.1 The champion of change model

The **champion of change model** recognises the importance of change being led by a **change agent.**

 Senior management are the change strategists, and decide in broad terms what is to be done. There is a need for powerful advocacy for change at the strategic apex. This will only occur if senior management are themselves agreed on the need for change. This is a role requiring a clear vision of what the change is to achieve.

 Senior management appoint a change agent to drive change through. Senior management has three roles:

- Supporting the change agent, if the change provokes conflict between the agent and interest groups in the organisation

- Reviewing and monitoring the progress of the change

- Endorsing and approving the changes, and ensuring that they are publicised

 The change agent has to win the support of functional and operational managers, who have to introduce and enforce the changes in their own departments. The champion of change has to provide advice and information, as well as evidence that the old ways are no longer acceptable.

 The change agent galvanises managers into action and gives them any necessary support. The managers ensure that the changes are implemented operationally, in the field. Where changes involve, say, a new approach to customer care, it is the workers who are responsible for ensuring the effectiveness of the change process.

It is important to realise that **successful change is not something exclusively imposed from above**. There is a sense in which middle and junior managers are **change recipients** in that they are required to implement new approaches and methods. However, they are themselves also **change agents** within their own spheres of responsibility. They must be committed parts of the change process if it is to succeed.

7.3.2 External change agents

Although a change agent can be selected from within the organisation which is experiencing change, many organisations choose to use external consultants as change agents.

The advantages of using an external change agent include:

Expertise – An external agent may need to be brought in because the organisation doesn't have the capabilities or skills required internally.

Best practice - Additionally, an external agent can recommend '**best practice**' approaches, drawing on their experience from working with other organisations.

Collaboration – An external agent who has expertise and experience in managing change can collaborate with people from the organisation, and together they can make sense of the change situation and what needs to be done. The external agent can work with members of the organisation to facilitate the change process, and in doing so the organisation's leaders and managers can gather expertise from the agent.

Resources – An external agent may be required simply because an organisation doesn't have the capacity to dedicate an existing member of their internal staff to the role. In particular, an external change agent may be able to devote themselves to the change process on a full time basis; something which internal members of staff may not be able to do.

Fresh perspective – Even if an organisation has the skills and resources necessary to manage change internally, it can still be useful to bring in someone with a fresh perspective, who can take an **independent view** of the change required. This fresh perspective may enable them to see things that people familiar with the organisations had stopped noticing, or had chosen to stop noticing due to internal politics within the organisation.

Section summary

A **change agent** is an individual or group that helps to bring about strategic change in an organisation.

For change to be effective, it needs to be effectively implemented. For this reason, many organisations seek to use change agents to facilitate change.

8 Group formation within organisations, and its impact on change processes

Introduction

In most organisations, staff do not work in isolation from their colleagues, but they work as part of a team, or a group.

Therefore, when considering change management, we need to consider not only how individuals react to change, but also how groups do.

One of the key issues in successfully implementing change is obtaining a shared perception among those affected, of the issues and implication associated with the change.

8.1 How groups respond to organisational change

In an organisation, the employees and management are used to working in a particular way. They develop or establish a set of relationships with the work environment.

A change process inevitably leads some kind of **shift in the work environment**, the routine or the composition of the group.

The members of a group in an organisation may respond in different way to this the change. In other words, some may support the change, while others may oppose it.

If those people who oppose the change are very influential in the group, they can influence the responses of the other people in the group, such that the change will not be successfully implemented.

Equally, if the influential members of the group support the change, they can influence the other members of the group to help ensure the change is successfully implemented.

In both situations, there are likely to be some people who are neutral, and will accept whatever decision is finally taken by the employee and management.

In a way, the group dynamic could be seen as similar to a force field: some members of the group will be driving forces for change, while others will resist change.

For the change to be successfully implemented, the driving forces need to be stronger than the resisting forces.

Group resistance to change is often manifest through strike action. For example, if management propose changes which workers don't like, in extreme cases, the workers respond by taking strike action. In particular, this may be the case with **unionised workforces**, where trades unions will support their members in a dispute with management. The strike action can only be resolved by the workers accepting management's proposal, or by management backing down and heeding to the workers' grievances about the changes.

8.2 Stakeholder analysis and change

When considering a change exercise, a stakeholder analysis could be a useful starting point because it can help analyse what each of the **interested parties will stand to gain or lose from the change process**. In this way, it could highlight the potential benefits of the process which management can use to help rally support for the process.

It could also instruct management that they need to find ways to compensate or compromise those who feel that they stand to lose more than they gain from the change. If such people are influential members of a group they might otherwise persuade other members of the group to resist the change.

8.3 The role of groups in change

Peter Senge in his analysis of the learning organisation argues that **teams**, not single individuals, are the key to successful organisations in the future, and individuals have to 'learn how to learn' in the context of the team.

In this respect, teams and groups can also be useful to the process of change:

Often they can be used as a **source of support** during the change process; members can support and counsel each other during the changes.

Sensitivity training, undertaken in groups or established teams can help people involved in change talk openly about issues that they find difficult to discuss any other way. Often groups of this nature will have a facilitator, but the facilitator is not a leader and so leaves the group to discuss a topic by themselves.

During periods of change and uncertainty, these discussions will often concentrate on group members fears and concerns about the change. However, by discussing their concerns with their peers, group members can often gain reassurance that they are not alone in facing the change and this can help them feel more positive about the change.

We have discussed the concept of learning organisations in Chapter 9 earlier in this Study Text. However, learning organisations are also interesting to consider in the context of change management. Learning organisations learn from their external environments and adapt to them. Change, for learning organisations, becomes natural and on-going, and not something which only occurs in times of crisis or pressure.

8.4 Building teams after change

Change programmes often lead to changes in the composition of work teams. Therefore, the new teams which are created after a change programme need to re-establish themselves to ensure they operate as effectively as possibly.

Tuckman's ideas of team formation (forming, norming, storming, performing) are relevant here. These are covered in paper E2.

Section summary

In many organisations, staff do not work in isolation from their colleagues, but as part of a group. Therefore, management need to consider not only how individual people might respond to change, but how groups as a whole may react.

9 Business ethics in change management and the implementation of strategic plans

Introduction

The process of change often raises serious questions of ethics and value: for example where people are encouraged or even forced to take on new roles, or even more acutely when structural changes in an organisation may lead to people being made redundant.

We have mentioned many times in this text already that all organisational changes affect people, and so it is therefore important that the potential ethical implications if any change programme are assessed before that programme is undertaken.

For example, organisational change can often lead to:

- Loss of individual roles and jobs
- New individual roles and jobs
- New organisational or departmental strategy

It is important that any people affected by these changes are treated fairly and are not unnecessarily disadvantaged by them.

9.1 Consultation processes

In this respect, we should highlight the importance of having a consultation process in advance of any planned change programme.

The consultation process should be taken in such areas as:

- Establishing whether change is necessary and if so to what extent
- Identifying options for change
- Evaluating options for change
- Taking the strategic decision as to what kind of change to implement
- Designing and then putting into practice the implementation plan

The question of consultation is important because:

(a) it is often seen as ethically worthwhile in its own right, empowering and enabling people who otherwise might see their individual rights over-ridden.

(b) it can be argued that many of the areas where conflicts of value and ethics occur come about due to inadequate consultation processes.

A well known model of consultation is provided by *Tannenbaum and Schmidt* who depict it in relation to the power that is implicitly available to parties to the consultation process.

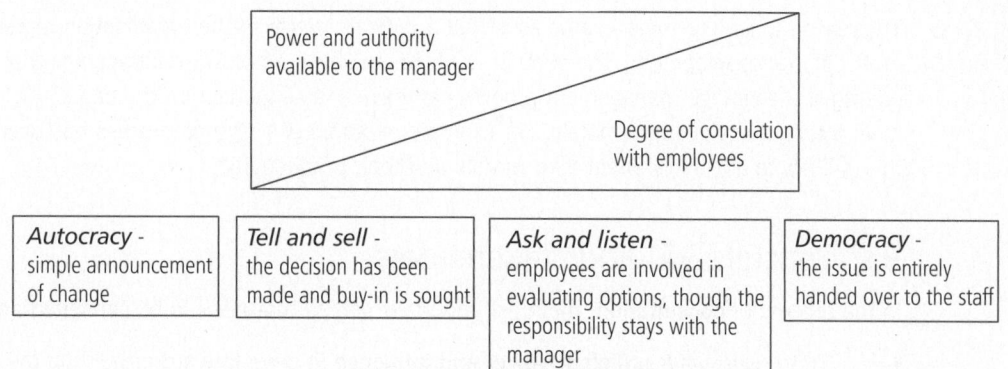

Figure 12.3: The Tannenbaum-Schmidt model of consultation and power

The idea behind the model is that the degree of consultation that a manager engages in amounts to a passing across of her or his power and authority. The more that a manager (genuinely) consults with employees (and we could add here other stakeholders as well) the more they are giving some of the responsibility for the change to those who are consulted.

(a)   At one extreme, a manager retains all power by identifying and analysing a change autonomously, generating options and deciding between them, formulating how to put the change into practice and then right at the end just telling others what will happen.

(b)   At the other a manager decides that the issue would be best resolved by giving it to the staff to deal with, and they are allowed full authority to do what they believe is best. And in between there are progressive stages moving partially from one extreme to the other.

Certain assumptions are built in to this model, of which an important one is whether or not the consultation process is genuine. Many managers, for a variety of reasons, may misrepresent what they are doing when they engage in a dialogue with staff. A few examples of how this may happen are given below.

Type of misrepresentation	Example
Unintentional misrepresentation	A manager may be carrying on an activity that they see as 'tell and sell' where they have already made up their mind about the change but want to lead the staff through their thought processes in order to achieve the degree of commitment they require. So they ask the employees to consider how to solve a certain problem. The employees, on the other hand, may feel that they are being given the opportunity to contribute to the formulation of the solution.
Deliberate misrepresentation	A manager may feel that if the choice they have already made is made public then there will be a concerted attempt by the workforce to resist or subvert it. So rather than act with overt secretiveness they pretend that they are consulting more openly than is actually the case.
Self-deception	Nowadays, consultation is often regarded as good management practice. Most managers will want to think of themselves as good managers. As a result they may fail to realise that they have a distinct bottom line, and go ahead with a consultative process even though subconsciously they have no intention of following it through.
Weakness of position	Often a manager may feel unable to contest a strongly held opinion concerning change – perhaps a forceful major investor has a strong view about what kind of change is appropriate. So they conceal this from the workforce as it would erode their authority.

The reason to go into these examples is that a radical change to the organisation represents a major event in its cultural development. The good or harm to employee-employer relationships that results from the quality of the change management process can have a lasting effect on the capacity of the business to meet future changes appropriately. For example, if staff feel a change process has been managed poorly, this is likely to adversely affect their morale and their productivity.

9.2 Consultation and stakeholders

In the process of **consultation**, the most important parties that need to be consulted are:

- Those who have **sufficient power and influence** to drive forward or hold up the change process
- Those who are **most vulnerable** to any potential changes

In practice, the same group is usually the main target of consultation – namely the workforce, as they have a great deal of potential power to prevent a change happening (or at least to make a quite different kind of change emerge from the process) and they are often the people at most risk, for example because of the possibility of losing their jobs.

Depending on the scale of the change, it may be that other parties are also consulted – for something that might affect the capital structure of the company then the majority shareholders will be asked their views, for a change that might result in relocation of premises local residents might (in certain specific circumstances) and local government town planning departments might be consulted (in many countries this would happen by law).

When considering any change process, it is important to remember the differences in power which different people in the process have. Senior management have the power to shape the process whereas workers in their organisation may feel vulnerable to change.

In this context, there could be ethical questions as to whether management are introducing changes in the best interests of their organisation as a whole, or to benefit their self-interest.

Johnson and Scholes provide a useful matrix that helps us understand the position of stakeholders in a change scenario.

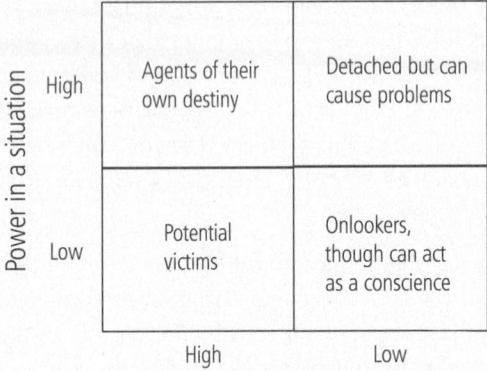

Figure 12.4: The position of stakeholders in change contexts

The most ethically important quadrant is probably the low power- high vulnerability one. People in this quadrant have to rely on others for their protection. For example, a retired person living close to the factory cannot directly influence what happens but has to hope that others will not subject him or her to unnecessary risks of toxic pollution.

In contrast the 'high power –high vulnerability' quadrant (usually employees and managers) is often the one which is most directly affected by change. People in this quadrant are vulnerable to what happens but have a chance to act on the situation with some reasonable degree of impact.

9.3 Potential ethical issues arising from change situations

Exam skills

In the E3 exam you should always be alert to any ethical issues which may be implied in the case study scenario. Equally you should ensure that any courses of action you recommend to an organisation upheld ethical practices in line with the CIMA Code of Ethics for Professional Accountants.

The indicative syllabus content – reference B3(iv) – indicates that you need to be able to apply the CIMA Code of Ethics for Professional Accountants (Parts A and B) in the context of the implementation of strategic plans. Please make sure you are familiar with the contents of the Code before you sit your exam, so that you can identify any ethical issues which may arise in change management scenarios, and can make appropriate recommendations in your answers about how to deal with those issues.

As you read through the scenarios in your exam questions, think whether they raise any issues in relation to the five fundamental principles of the CIMA Code of Ethics, or whether they pose any potential threats to complying with them.

The five fundamental principles are:

- Integrity
- Objectivity
- Professional competence and due care
- Confidentiality
- Professional behaviour

The Code of Ethics makes clear that the professional accountant must react and respond if he or she uncovers a threat to compliance with the fundamental principles. You should be prepared to advise on the alternative courses of action an accountant should take if they discover any such potential threat. An appropriate response may be to discuss the matter with a line manager and then subsequently with the internal audit department or the audit committee.

Alternatively, if the matter cannot be resolved internally, the accountant should consider taking advice from CIMA's ethics helpline, and possibly even seeking legal advice. If the accountant still cannot resolve the dilemma between their responsibility to their employee and their obligations to the ethical code they may ultimately have to resign from the organisation they currently work for.

Note also that the **TOPCIMA (T4)** exam offers 10 marks in total for highlighting and discussing ethical issues so you should get into the habit of looking to identify these in case study scenarios.

The precise nature of any ethical issues arising from a scenario will be determined by the nature of the scenario but here are some possible issues to be aware of:

- If an organisation is looking to hire new employees, have they followed a fair and equitable recruitment policy? Is there any evidence of discrimination?

- If an organisation is looking to reduce its head count, has it imposed any compulsory redundancies on its staff or has it tried to manage the process through natural wastage and by consulting with its staff? Could the organisation be guilty to a charge of unfair dismissal? Equally, has the organisation treated all its employees fairly, or is there any evidence of discrimination (eg by age, gender, or race)?

- Has an organisation intimidated its staff to support a particular course of action? For example, by threatening them with redundancy if they do not support proposed changes?

- Are staff being manipulated to support change?

- Are the accountant staff being pressurised to produce reports which materiality misrepresent the facts of a case?

- If an organisation is negotiating new contracts does it have any vested interests in the contract being awarded to a particular company?

- Are staff misinformed about the nature / extent of change being considered?

- Are schemes designed to increase profit / reduce costs putting profit before (customer) safety?

- Do any proposed schemes contravene regulations, technical or professional standards?

- Is process automation putting jobs at risk?

- Skills obsolescence – The value of workers skills may decrease due to changes in production technology or the production process. Job-specific skills obsolescence can occur when job requirements change, because workers existing skills do not fully equip them to do their new job. In this context, does an organisation provide its workers with training to do their new job? Does it allow them flexibility to move into different roles within the organisation? Or does it simply make them redundant?

- Age discrimination – If businesses are looking to expand or recruit new staff, they cannot discriminate against applicants on grounds of age. Researchers have found that many businesses inherently prefer to take on younger workers ahead of older ones, but if a candidate is rejected on the grounds of age alone this is not only unethical, but also illegal in many countries.

However, in any scenarios, we need to remember than an organisation has a duty of responsibility to its owners as well as its employees. There may be times when it is necessary to reduce staff costs in order to safeguard the future of the business. In such a situation, we cannot simply say it is unethical to make people redundant.

The list above is by no means exhaustive, and hopefully you can think of other examples, but it should give you some pointers as to the sorts of things you should be looking out for in case studies about change.

 Section summary

Strategic changes may often raise ethical issues, and change managers need to consider the ethical implications of a change when assessing the suitability and acceptability of that change.

10 Change in practice

 Introduction

We will now bring together a number of the change management issues we have considered to look at an example where organisational change is required.

For this, we will look at the case of a **turnaround,** where a business is in severe decline and faces either closure or takeover.

Although change management is often linked to expansion and growth, this is not always the case. Change management skills could equally be needed if an organisation needs to change its business strategy in response to falling revenues or profits.

Such a situation could possibly lead to the **divestment** of a business unit or part of an organisation, or its **liquidation**. Alternatively, the organisation could try to address its decline by means of a **turnaround**.

10.1 Turnaround

When a business is in terminal decline and faces closure or takeover, there is a need for rapid and extensive change in order to achieve cost reduction and revenue generation. This is a **turnaround strategy**. We can identify **seven elements of such a strategy**.

10.1.1 Crisis stabilisation

The emphasis is on reducing costs and increasing revenues. An emphasis on reducing direct costs and improving productivity is more likely to be effective than efforts to reduce overheads.

(a)   **Measures to increase revenue**

- Tailor marketing mix to key market segments
- Review pricing policies to maximise revenue
- Focus activities on target market segments
- Exploit revenue opportunities if related to target segments
- Invest in growth areas

(b)   **Measures to reduce costs**

- Cut costs of labour and senior management
- Improve productivity
- Ensure clear marketing focus on target market segments
- Financial controls
- Strict cash management controls
- Reduce inventory
- Cut unprofitable products and services

Severe cost cutting is a common response to crisis but it is unlikely to be enough by itself. The **wider causes of decline** must be addressed.

10.1.2 Management changes

It is likely that new managers will be required, especially at the strategic apex. There are four reasons for this.

(a)   The old management allowed the situation to deteriorate and **may be held responsible by key stakeholders**.

(b)   **Experience of turnaround management** may be required.

(c)   Managers brought in from outside will not be **prisoners of the old paradigm**.

(d)   A **directive approach** to change management will probably be required.

10.1.3 Communication with stakeholders

The support of key stakeholder groups – groups with both a high level of power and a high degree of interest in an organisation – such as the workforce and providers of finance, is likely to be very important in a turnaround; it is equally likely that stakeholders did not receive full information during the period of deterioration. A **stakeholder analysis** (discussed earlier in this Study Text) should be carried out so that the various stakeholder groups can be informed and managed appropriately.

10.1.4 Attention to target markets

A **clear focus on appropriate target market segments** is essential; indeed a lack of such focus is a common cause of decline. The organisation must become customer-oriented and ensure that it has good flows of marketing information.

10.1.5 Concentration of effort

Resources should be concentrated on the best opportunities to create value. It will almost certainly be appropriate to **review products and the market segments** currently served and eliminate any distractions and poor performers. A similar review of internal activities would also be likely to show up several candidates for **outsourcing**.

10.1.6 Financial restructuring

Some form of **financial restructuring** is likely to be required. In the worst case, this may involve trading out of insolvency. Even where the business is more or less solvent, capital restructuring may be required, both to provide cash for investment and to reduce cash outflows in the shorter term.

10.1.7 Prioritisation

The eventual success of a turnaround strategy depends in part on management's ability to **prioritise necessary activities**, such as those noted above.

11   Change management and strategy implementation

Introduction

We will end our review of change management by revisiting its role in business strategy, to highlight why change management is so important in implementing business strategy.

The key role of change management in strategy implementation can be illustrated by looking at the key elements of strategic management. The diagram below illustrates these:

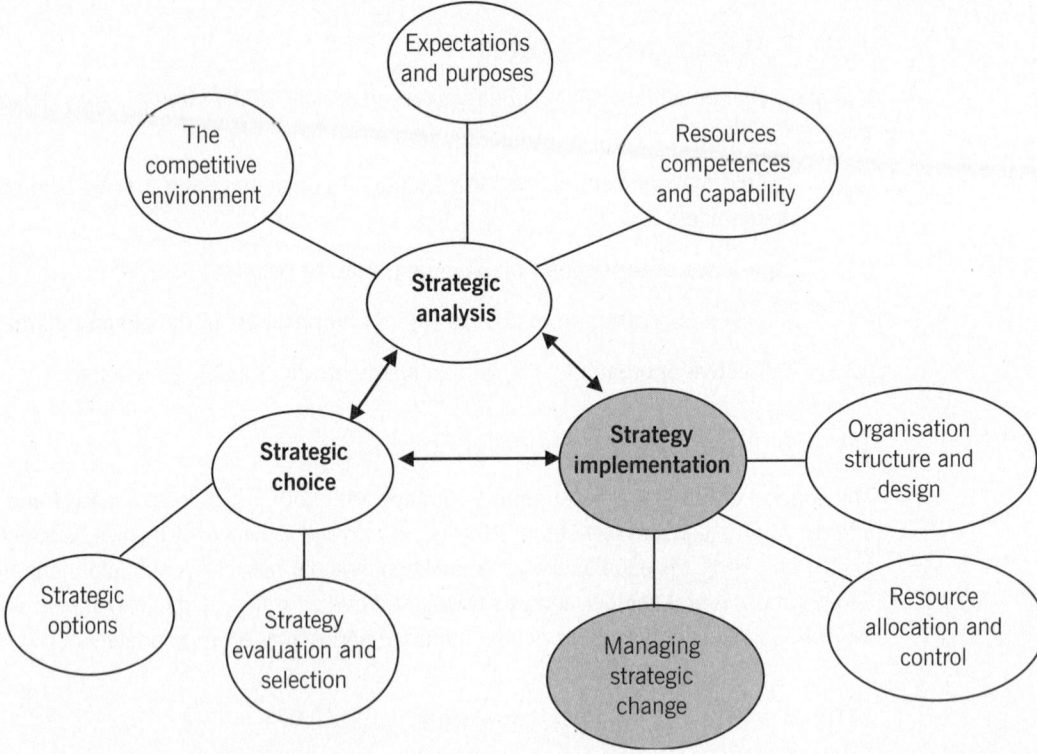

Figure 12.5: A summary model of the elements of strategic management
(Diagram adapted from *Johnson, Scholes & Whittington*: 'Exploring Corporate Strategy')

KEY TERM

STRATEGIC CHANGE is 'the proactive management of change in organisations to achieve clearly defined strategic objectives or to allow the organisation to experiment in areas where it is not possible to define strategic objectives previsely'.   (*Lynch*, Strategic Management.)

This definition – particularly the first half of it –clearly identifies the central role which change management plays in strategic implementation. Managing strategic change is one of the key components of strategy implementation.

We can also illustrate how change can affect all the aspects of an organisation, but also in turn how a strategy implementation could require changes in all the aspects of an organisation.

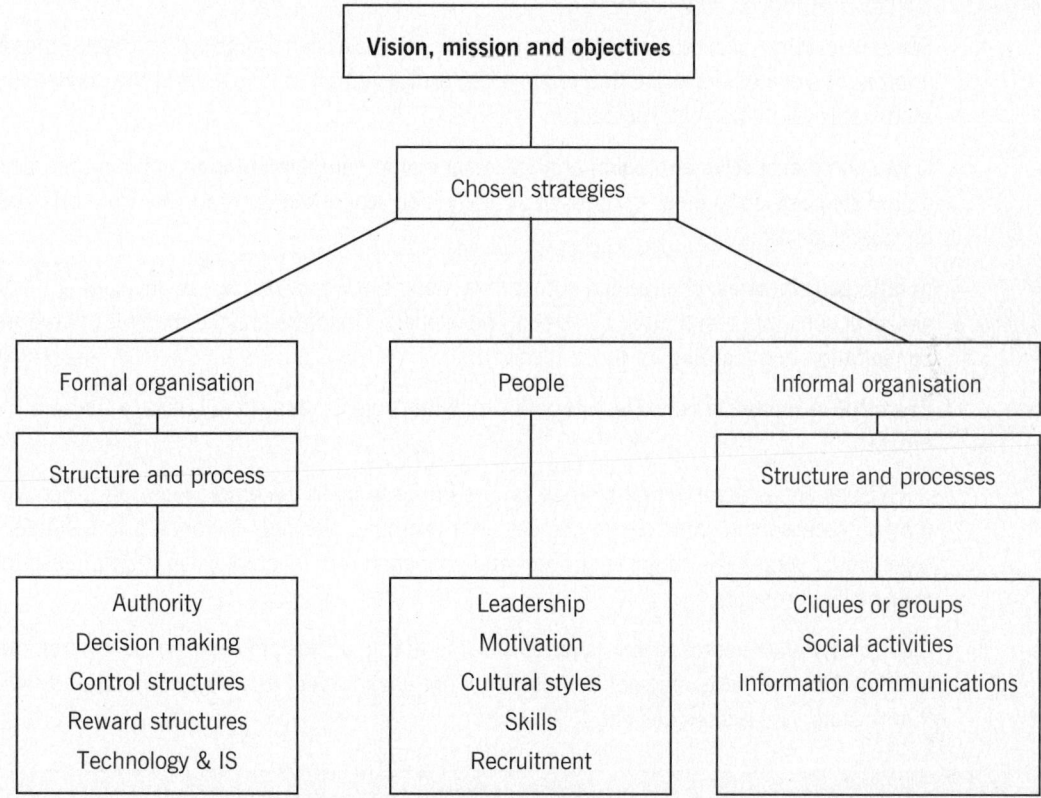

Figure 12.6: Aspects of an organisation affected by change

However, in the same way that some strategists favour a prescriptive view of corporate strategy and others favour an emergent approach, so there are diverse viewpoints on how best to manage change.

11.1 Strategy and change management

Change is inevitable in any progressive organisation. Any business that wants to thrive in an ever-changing world needs to adapt to its environment.

One of the key responsibilities for an organisation's management is to detect trends inside and outside the organisation to identify changes that are needed and then to initiate a change management process to introduce those change.

The change management process can be summarised in three steps:

(a) **Strategic planning and design:** form a change management team, define the vision and strategy, design a programme from which to manage the change and determine the tools needed for implementation

(b) **Strategy implementation:** communicate the vision and implementation to staff, manage staff responses and lead them through the change; maintain momentum

(c) **Evaluation and readjustment:** look at the results, track performance against targets, modify structure if necessary, plan for the future but continue to monitor performance

However, in the same way that corporate strategy can be either **prescriptive** or **emergent**, so can strategic change and change management.

Some researchers view the management of change as clear and largely predictable (the prescriptive approach) while others argue that change has a momentum of its own and the consequences are less predictable (the emergent approach).

Under the **prescriptive approach**, change is seen as the **implementation actions** that result from the deliberate decision to pursue a chosen strategy, and where the way to move from one state to another can be clearly identified.

In **emergent theories**, change can sometimes mean the whole process of developing the strategy, as well as the actions that result after it has been developed. Therefore change many involve **experimentation**, **consultation** and **learning** for those involved.

Prescriptive models tend to treat people simply as 'objects' and do not involve them in the change process.

Such approaches assume that change can be imposed upon the employees concerned. Imposing change may be necessary in some circumstances – for example, closing a factory – but in situations where the organisation needs the on-going support and cooperation of its employees such a prescriptive approach may be inappropriate.

Also, prescriptive approaches to change assume that it is possible to move clearly from one state to another. However, this may not be possible if the environment itself is turbulent, and therefore the desired 'future state' is therefore unclear.

Section summary

It will be unusual for an organisation's strategy to remain unchanged for any length of time as environmental developments mean that strategies will change and evolve. The management of change is therefore an integral and important part of strategic management.

Further reading

Although this Study Text is designed to provide you will all the coverage you need for your E3 exam, if you wish to do any further reading around change management issues the following texts offer some very useful material:

Balogun, J. & Hope Hailey, V. (2008) *Exploring Strategic Change,* (3rd ed.), Harlow, Essex: Pearson Education

Cameron, E. & Green, M. (2012) *Making Sense of Change Management* (3rd ed.) London: Kogan Page

Whetten, D. & Cameron, K. (2011) *Developing Management Skills* (8th ed.), Harlow, Essex: Pearson Education

Chapter Roundup

✓   When considering a strategic change, managers need to analyse the speed and extent of the change required. They also need to assess whether management's role is proactive or reactive, and whether the change is hard (systems based) or soft (people based). All of these factors will affect the way the change is implemented

✓   When facing a strategic change, an organisation needs to consider the **context of the change**, and the change kaleidoscope illustrates the contextual features it should consider. It is also important to note that change could be **continuous,** rather than simply a one-off, **discontinuous** event. Equally, the organisation needs to consider whether change needs to be **imposed** by senior management or whether it can **emerge** from within the organisation.

✓   Many aspects of change will be affected to some extent by cultural considerations. Therefore it is important to establish the impact of a strategic change by comparing the current cultural position with that of the desired future position.

✓   It is important to use an appropriate management style for the type of change being managed. Management styles and types of change form a spectrum: the education and communication style works best for an adaptive change, while direction or coercion work best for revolutionary change.

✓   There are a number of factors which contribute to the success of change management projects, but having a clear vision for a project and communicating effectively are particularly important.

✓   In any change programme it is vital to consider the impact change will have on an organisation's staff as individuals. People respond to change in different ways, and develop their own ways of copying with change. In this way, change cannot simply be considered as a mechanical process.

✓   A **change agent** is an individual or group that helps to bring about strategic change in an organisation.

✓   For change to be effective, it needs to be effectively implemented. For this reason, many organisations seek to use change agents to facilitate change.

✓   In many organisations, staff do not work in isolation from their colleagues, but as part of a group. Therefore, management need to consider not only how individual people might respond to change, but how groups as a whole may react.

✓   Strategic changes may often raise ethical issues, and change managers need to consider the ethical implications of a change when assessing the suitability and acceptability of that change.

✓   It will be unusual for an organisation's strategy to remain unchanged for any length of time as environmental developments mean that strategies will change and evolve. The management of change is therefore an integral and important part of strategic management.

Quick Quiz

1   What is meant by the scope of change?

2   Which styles of management are required to effect revolution?

3   What is a change agent?

4   What are the main differences between 'hard' change and 'soft' change?

5   What are the objectives of political activity that may be sought by change managers?

6   How can change managers create opportunities for early success?

Answers to Quick Quiz

1   The scope of change is the degree of change required – whether it can be transformational or whether a more fundamental realignment is required.

2   Direction and, probably, coercion

3   A change agent is an individual or group that helps to bring about strategic change in an organisation

4   Hard changes tend to be mechanistic, technical, and systems-oriented, and have quantifiable outcomes.

    Soft changes tend to be people-based and subjective, and have outcomes which are harder to quantify.

5   Building a powerbase; overcoming resistance; achieving compliance

6   By concentrating resources on potentially solvable problems rather than spreading them thinly.

Now try these questions from the Exam Question Bank

Number	Level	Marks	Time
Q13	Examination	20	36 mins
Q14	Examination	12	22 mins

IMPLEMENTING STRATEGIC PLANS

Part D

STRATEGIC CONTROL

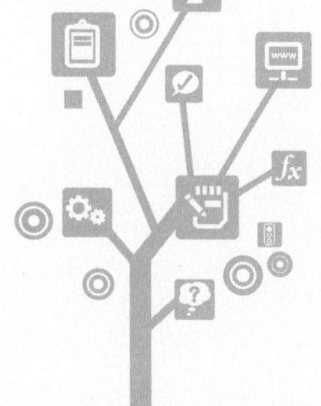

In this chapter we review the performance of investment decisions and we also look at contribution analysis and variance analysis (Sections 2 and 3). This should be mostly revision for you. In Sections 4-5 we discuss appraisal of particular business units and divisions, and we look at the relationships between them (Section 7). We then consider some more themes in controlling performance with the ultimate aim of increasing shareholder value (Section 8). Many large firms are organised into strategic business units, and multinational firms in particular have specific management problems in relation to setting objectives and performance assessment (Section 9).

Transfer prices (Section 10) are a way of promoting divisional autonomy, but the transfer price needs to be fair, neutral and administratively simple. Otherwise, prices may be set in such a way as to improve the results of one subsidiary at the expense of another.

In Section 11 we look at rewarding managerial performance itself, where we describe agency theory. A typical public company has a large number of owners (or principals) who have no real idea what their agents (the directors/managers) are doing.

Rewarding managers for their performance is a method of control in the sense that the reward will provide managers with an incentive to achieve the organisation's objectives.

We conclude the chapter by considering the various ways in which the strategic apex may elect to exert control.

topic list	learning outcomes	syllabus references	ability required
1 Planning and control	D1(a)	D1(vi)	Evaluate
2 Inflation and NPVs	D1(b), D1(c)	D1(vi)	Evaluate
3 Using contribution margin as a measure of performance	D1(b), D1(c)	D1(vi)	Evaluate
4 Divisional performance: return on investment (ROI)	D1(b), D1(c)	D1(vi)	Evaluate
5 Divisional performance: residual income (RI)	D1(b), D1(c)	D1(vi)	Evaluate
6 Comparing profit centre performance	D1(b), D1(c)	D1(vi)	Evaluate
7 Interfirm comparisons and performance ratios	D1(b), D1(c)	D1(vi)	Evaluate
8 Achieving success for the shareholder	D1(b), D1(c)	D1(vi)	Evaluate
9 International subsidiaries	D1(b), D1(c)	D1(vi)	Evaluate

10 Transfer pricing	D1(b)	D1(vi)	Recommend
11 Managerial performance: agency theory and reward systems	D1(a)	D1(vi)	Recommend
12 Strategic management styles	D1(a)	D1(vi)	Recommend

1 Planning and control

Introduction

In order for a business to achieve its goals and objectives, it will need to ensure that what is meant to happen actually happens. Control is essential to ensure that a desired course of action is implemented.

Control is a process of ensuring that an organisation's goals are achieved, that procedures are adhered to, and that an organisation responds appropriately to changes in its environment.

In effect, control means establishing what an organisation wants to do and then ensuring that what is supposed to happen, actually happens.

In order to know 'what is supposed to happen', organisations also need to make plans. Therefore, we should consider planning and control as being closely linked.

1.1 Levels of control   9/10

When we looked at strategic information in Chapter 9 in this Study Text, we introduced the *Anthony* hierarchy:

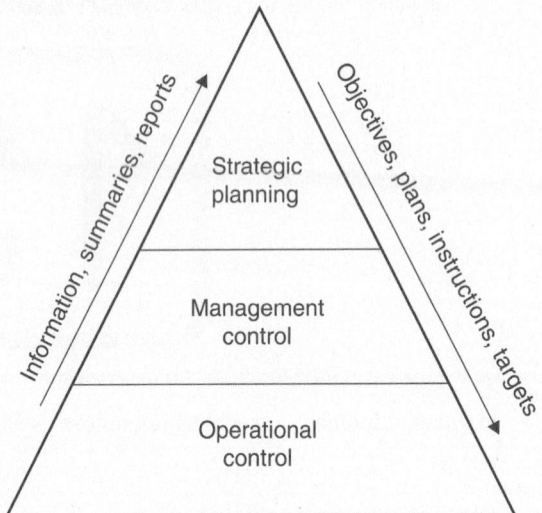

This hierarchy is also important here, because it illustrates that there are three primary types of organisational control:

(a) **Strategic control** - setting the long term goals and objectives of an organisation and ensuring they are achieved. For *Anthony*, strategic planning and strategic control are inextricably linked, so although his model shows 'strategic planning' you should treat this as strategic **planning and control**.

(b) **Management control.** Management control is an intermediate level of control, and focuses on the various sub-strategies which will be required to achieve the overall strategy. For example, are quality control objectives being met? Operating budgets are also an important part of management control.

(c)   **Operational control.** Operational control is the lowest level of control, and involves ensuring that specific tasks are being carried out effectively and efficiently. Operational controls are used by departmental supervisors to control the day-to-day operations of their department or division. For example, are individual sales targets being met?

An important distinction between management and operational control is that in management control, there is an equal focus on planning as well as execution, whereas in operational control, the focus is primarily on execution.

As we work through this chapter, we will look at a number of issues relating to the way organisations manage and control their financial performance, and then in the next chapter we will look at non-financial measures as well as financial ones.

However, as you work through these chapters, remember that the various control mechanisms can be applied at different levels throughout an organisation.

Also, remember that the way controls are applied could be different in a **unitary organisation** (one operating from a single location and usually with a single product range) compared to a **multidivisional organisation** (with a range of different business units, often in different locations, and therefore exposed to diverse environmental conditions.)

Finally, it is also important to remember that alongside the specific financial (or non-financial) controls that organisations can use to try to ensure they achieve their goals, there are also more generic processes which organisations can employ. For example, an organisation should ensure that its infrastructure and culture are designed to produce the behaviour it thinks will best help it achieve its goals.

Section summary

Control can be described as the management of an organisation's activities in accordance with strategic plans and objectives. Three levels of control can be identified: strategic, managerial and operational.

2   Inflation and NPVs

Introduction

Inflation makes it harder to compare performance over time, as it affects accounting values, and hence measures of performance. It affects base line and comparative figures.

Discounted cash flows can be used to assess the performance of capital investment projects, by comparing anticipated and actual cash flows, discounted in an appropriate way. It is probably a lot harder, although not impossible, to apply these to profit centres.

2.1 Inflation and strategy

When an organisation prepares its strategic plans, it will probably build some assumptions about the rate of inflation into the plan itself.

2.1.1 The consequences of inflation

The problem for performance measurement is to decide what the actual effect of inflation has been, how this compares with the plan, and what significance this might have for performance measures and control action.

(a)   If a company operates in a competitive market, where customers resist price increases, it may be unable to pass on all its cost increases to the customer. Inflation would reduce its profitability.

(b)   If a company exports goods overseas, domestic price inflation will push up the cost of its goods to foreign buyers unless the exchange rate were to fall to compensate for the rate of inflation.

2.1.2 Controlling inflation

Inflationary pressures on costs should be kept as much under control as possible.

- Given anticipated material cost increases is there scope through exercising 'buyer power' over suppliers to keep them below the rate of inflation?
- Is the material being effectively used?
- Labour pay agreements should be competitive but kept as low as possible.
- Labour efficiency must match the competition.
- Expenses should be rigorously controlled.
- The timing of price increases should be monitored carefully.

2.1.3 Performance measurement and inflation

You should already know the argument that a major problem with the historical cost convention is that it can report that an organisation is making a profit, when it has in fact suffered a fall in its operating capacity. In other words, inflation can conceal poor performance.

There are five consequences of historical cost accounting which, because of price inflation, reduce the reliability of the information given in company accounts.

- Non-current asset values and depreciation.
- Cost of sales.
- Increase in working capital needed to support normal trading operations.
- Borrowing benefits.
- Comparability of figures from year to year (and also between one company and another).

2.1.4 Trends: comparability of figures over time

One method of measuring performance is to look at trends over a period of time. For example, the trend over a number of years in dividend per share, EPS, and sales volume (in £s). An estimate of whether there has been 'real' growth in dividends, earnings or sales can be made simply by 'taking away' an estimate of the inflationary element in the growth. For example, given the following figures:

| | Year | | |
	1	2	3
Earnings per share	40p	45p	55p
Retail price index	100	105	112

The rate of 'real' growth in EPS could be estimated approximately as follows.

(a)   Year 2 compared with Year 1

  (i)   Total increase $\dfrac{45p}{40p}$ = 1.125

  (ii)   Increase in RPI $\dfrac{105}{100}$ = 1.05

  (iii)   'Real' increase $\dfrac{1.125}{1.05}$ = 1.071 ie 7.1%

(b) Year 3 compared with Year 2

(i) Total increase $\dfrac{55p}{45p}$ = 1.222

(ii) Increase in RPI $\dfrac{112}{105}$ = 1.067

(iii) 'Real' increase $\dfrac{1.222}{1.067}$ = 1.145 ie 14.5%

2.1.5 Ratios for control

When ratio measurements are used as targets for control, they may be unaffected by inflation, because both sides of the ratio might be equally inflated.

(a) Accounting return on capital employed, ie:

$$\frac{Profit}{Capital\ employed}$$

If both profit and capital employed are equally affected by inflationary increases, the ROI ratio would be unaffected. However, if capital employed is not subject to the same inflationary increases as profit, trends in ROI would be misleading.

(b) Similarly, the profit/sales ratio would be unaffected as a control measure by inflation, provided that profits and sales were equally boosted by inflationary increases.

(c) The same argument would apply to a number of other ratios, such as asset turnover, average receivables payment period, inventory turnover, gearing ratio, and the current ratio etc.

2.2 Using NPVs to control strategic investments

The easiest form of strategic decision to control relates to **capital expenditure**, such as investment in machinery.

2.2.1 The control of capital expenditure

KEY TERM

CAPITAL PROJECTS involve 'any long term commitments of funds undertaken now in anticipation of a potential inflow of funds at some time in the future.' *(Hartley)*

Once a project is given the go-ahead, with a budget of £x, the progress of the project should be monitored. Although **direct expenditure** can be monitored, it is not always easy to identify **additional indirect expenditures** and extra **working capital investment** as a direct cause of the project.

Assume a firm has a level of sales of £1,000,000 pa. It has a choice of two investments. Both involve saving costs, but neither will have an effect on sales revenue. Project A involves developing an exclusive distribution system, and has a positive NPV of £50,000. Project B involves investing in new production equipment and has an NPV of £100,000. Normally project B would be chosen, as it has the higher NPV, but if you were told that:

(a) A new competitor had entered the market, threatening sales revenue by an undefined amount

(b) Project A would raise barriers to entry

you might prefer Project A, as it has additional benefits in **protecting revenue**.

With long-term planning, capital expenditure decisions should be based on an evaluation of future cash flows, discounted at an appropriate cost of capital to an NPV.

2.2.2 Cash flows and NPVs for strategic control: shareholder wealth

Control at a strategic level should be based on measurements of **cash flows**, ie actual cash flows for the period just ended and revised forecasts of future cash flows. Since the objective of a company might be to maximise the wealth of its shareholders, a control technique based on the measurement of cash flows and their NPV could be a very useful technique to apply.

A numerical example might help to illustrate this point.

Suppose that ABC Ltd agrees to a strategic plan from 1 January 20X1 as follows.

Year	20X1	20X2	20X3	20X4	20X5	Total
Planned net cash inflow (£'000)	200	300	300	400	500	1,700
NPV at cost of capital 15%	174	227	197	229	249	1,076

Now suppose that ABC Ltd reviews its position one year later.

(a)   It can measure its actual total cash flow in 20X1 – roughly speaking, this will be the funds generated from operations minus tax paid and minus expenditure on fixed assets and plus/minus changes in working capital.

(b)   It can revise its forecast for the next few years.

We will assume that there has been no change in the cost of capital. Control information at the end of 20X1 might be as follows.

Year	20X1 (actual)	20X2 (forecast)	20X3	20X4	20X5	Total
Net cash inflow (£'000)	180	260	280	400	540	1,600
NPV at cost of capital 15%	180	226	212	263	309	1,190

A control summary comparing the situation at the start of 20X1 and the situation one year later would now be as follows.

	£'000
Expected NPV as at 1.1.20X1	1,076
Uplift by cost of capital 15%	161
	1,237
Expected NPV as at 1.1.20X2	1,190
Variance	47 (Adverse)

The control information shows that by the end of 20X1, ABC Ltd shows signs of not achieving the strategic targets it set itself at the start of 20X1. This is partly because actual cash flows in 20X1 fell short of target by (200-180) £20,000, but also because the revised forecast for the future is not as good now either. In total, the company has a lower NPV by £47,000.

Notice the link here to the ideas we identified earlier in gap analysis: forecasts are falling below original targets.

The reasons for the failure to achieve target should be investigated. Possible reasons include the following.

•   A higher-than-expected pay award to employees, which will have repercussions for the future as well as in 20X1

•   An increase in the rate of tax on profits

•   A serious delay in the implementation of some major new projects

•   The slower-than-expected growth of an important new market

Exam skills

Do not be surprised if calculations are required in the exam. However, if calculations are required you will inevitably have to use or comment on them in support of an argument. Do not simply do the calculations and then ignore them in the result of your answer.

NPV calculations rely on obtaining information about actual and forecast cash flows. In practice, it is not often easy to identify the attributable cash flows for individual capital projects or individual profit centres, and so other financial measures of performance have to be applied.

Section summary

Inflation affects base line and comparative figures making it difficult to compare performance over time. Organisations generally build assumptions about the rate of inflation into their strategic plans.

Capital expenditure decisions should be based on an evaluation of future cash flows, discounted at an appropriate cost of capital to an NPV.

3 Using contribution margin as a measure of performance

Introduction

The basic concept of **contribution** can be used strategically if questions about strategic factors are examined in its light. It is also appropriate for SBU performance measurement.

KEY TERM

CONTRIBUTION MARGIN can be defined as 'the difference between sales volume and the variable cost of those sales, expressed either in absolute terms or as a contribution per unit.'

The contribution per unit is 'often related to a key or limiting factor to give a sum required to cover fixed overhead and profit, such as contribution per machine hour, per direct labour hour or per kilo of scarce raw material.'

(a)   A **contribution centre** is a profit centre where expenditure is calculated on a marginal cost basis.

(b)   **Contribution per unit of limiting factor** is a measurement for optimising the use of scarce resources.

Contribution margins are also used for measuring performance in terms of **breakeven analysis**.

3.1 Contribution and strategic decisions

3.1.1 Product market issues

Consider, for example, a situation where a car manufacturer wishes to launch a new model, the success of which is crucial to corporate survival. Fixed costs are the capital required to develop the vehicle and tool up, which will appear in the breakeven equation as depreciation, development costs and operational fixed costs. Variable costs will have been identified and reliable sales forecasts will have been obtained. From this data, two figures can be computed.

(a)   The number of vehicles required to **break even**.

(b)   The number of vehicles required to generate **adequate returns** over the life of the model or the investment, and, significantly, what this represents in terms of market penetration and market share.

Johnson, Scholes and Whittington argue that breakeven analysis has a useful role in appraising and controlling strategy. Questions can be asked based on the breakeven model.

- What is the **probability** of achieving the desired levels of market penetration?

- Do the **conditions in the market** lend themselves to achieving that desired penetration?

- Will the **competitors** allow a profitable entry?

- Are the **cost and quality** assumptions feasible?

- Are the **funds available**, not just to complete the development but to establish the production capacity and skilled manpower to achieve the desired penetration?

3.1.2 Exit

Firms with high exit barriers may use contribution as the main tool for decision making. *Ward* cites the example of a coal mine, as to the type of decisions taken. High exit barriers result from:

- The actual costs of closure, redundancy and so on
- The cost of re-opening the mine, if demand for coal and prices picks up
- Costs which will not be avoided by the closure

3.2 Applying contribution margin accounting to divisional performance measurement

A danger with contribution margin analysis is that firms in a competitive industry might be tempted to sell at prices which cover marginal costs, but fail to earn an adequate return on **sunk fixed costs**.

Applying the principle that managers should only be accountable for costs and revenues which they can control directly, it follows that short-term controls for profit centres should focus on contribution margins. This is because only revenues and variable costs are **controllable** in the short run.

However, some directly attributable fixed costs might also be controllable, or at least avoidable, in the short term if the scale of business operations was significantly reduced. Fixed costs can therefore be classified as follows.

(a)   Costs which are **directly attributable** to a particular activity, and which tend to rise or fall in steps as the scale of activities is increased or lowered.

(b)   **Unavoidable costs**. Many fixed costs are committed, or not directly attributable to any particular activity.

One way of measuring profit for an investment centre or a profit centre is as follows.

	£
Sales revenue	X
less Variable cost of sales	(X)
equals Contribution	X
less Directly attributable fixed	
costs (avoidable/controllable)	(X)
equals Gross profit	X
less Share of unavoidable	
(committed*/uncontrollable*)	
fixed costs	(X)
equals Net profit	X

(* in the short term. In the long term, all fixed cost items should be controllable and 'variable'.)

Section summary

Contribution margins can be used for measuring performance and as a tool for decision making.

4 Divisional performance: return on investment (ROI)   3/11

Introduction

Profit centre organisation reflects the structure of authority in the organisation, and managers are made accountable and rewarded on the basis of profit centre results.

Return on investment (ROI) is a convenient measure, which ties in easily with the firm's accounts. However, there are measurement and valuation problems, especially in relation to non-current assets. These can encourage managers to take decisions which are not in the firm's best long-term interest. ROI does not easily account for risk.

ROI is based on **organisation structure**, not business processes, and is only suitable to products at the mature phase of the life cycle.

Many large firms are organised into **strategic business units** (SBUs).

KEY TERM

A STRATEGIC BUSINESS UNIT (SBU) is a 'section, usually a division, within a larger business organisation, that has a significant degree of autonomy, typically being responsible for developing and marketing its own products or services'.   (CIMA *Official Terminology*)

A typical SBU is a division of the organisation 'where managers have control over their own resources, and discretion overt the deployment of resources within specified boundaries'.   *(Ward)*

The performance of these business units is complicated by the degree of autonomy their managers enjoy.

We have covered DCF and contribution margin accounting first for these reasons.

(a)   Both techniques are in theory applicable to controlling and assessing strategies and can be applied to **divisional performance measurement**

(b)   DCF addresses the issue in terms of **cash flows**

In practice, many firms use more 'traditional' accounting based measures, such as return on investment (ROI). First some definitions.

KEY TERMS

RETURN ON CAPITAL EMPLOYED (ROCE)

$$\frac{\text{Profit before interest and tax} \times 100}{\text{Average capital employed}}$$

ROCE indicates the productivity of capital employed. The denominator is normally calculated as the average of the capital employed at the beginning and end of the year. Problems of seasonality, new capital introduced or other factors may necessitate taking the average of a number of periods within the year.

RETURN ON INVESTMENT (ROI)

$$\frac{\text{Profit before interest and tax} \times 100}{\text{Operations management capital employed}}$$

ROI is often used to assess managers' performance. Managers are responsible for all assets (normally defined as non-current assets plus net current assets).   (CIMA *Official Terminology*)

ROI is normally used to apply to investment centres or profit centres. These normally reflect the existing organisation structure of the business.

ROI shows how much profit in accounting terms has been made in relation to the amount of capital invested. For example, suppose that a company has two investment centres A and B, which show results for the year as follows:

	A	B
Profit after depreciation, before tax and interest	£60,000	£30,000
Assets generating income	£400,000	£120,000
ROI	15%	25%

Investment centre A has made double the profits of investment centre B, and in terms of profits alone has therefore been more 'successful'. However, B has earned a much higher ROI. This suggests that B has been a more successful investment than A.

The main reasons for the widespread use of ROI as a performance indicator are:

(a) **Financial reporting**. It ties in directly with the accounting process, and is identifiable from the profit and loss account and the balance sheet, the firm's most important communications media with investors. Therefore it is easy to investors to understand.

(b) **Aggregation**. ROI is a very convenient method of measuring the performance for a division or company as an entire unit.

(c) It can be used to **compare divisions**. Because ROI provides a percentage figure rather than an absolute amount, it can be used to compare performance in divisions of different sizes.

4.1 Measurement problems: non-current assets

The problems with ROI relate to accurate measurement.

4.1.1 Net assets

It is probably most common to use **return on net assets**. There are two main problems.

(a) If an investment centre maintains the same annual profit, and keeps the same assets without a policy of regular non-current asset replacement, its ROI will increase year by year as the assets get older. This can give a false impression of improving 'real' performance over time.

The dangers of this are twofold:

(i) Managers will avoid buying new assets (even though they may be needed to improve performance)

(ii) Management might wrongly think the divisions with the newest assets are the worst performing, leading them to be shut down.

(b) It is not easy to **compare fairly** the performance of one investment centre with another. Non-current assets may be of different ages or may be depreciated in different ways.

4.1.2 Return on gross assets

(a) **Advantage**. Ignoring depreciation removes the problem of ROI increasing over time as non-current assets get older and get depreciated.

(b) **Disadvantages**

(i) Measuring ROI as return on gross assets ignores the **age factor**. Older non-current assets usually cost more to repair and maintain. An investment centre with old assets may therefore have its profitability reduced by repair costs.

(ii) **Inflation and technological change** alter the cost of non-current assets. If one investment centre has non-current assets bought ten years ago with a gross cost of £1 million, and another investment centre, in the same area of business operations, has non-current assets bought very recently for £1 million, the quantity and technological character of the non-current assets of the two investment centres are likely to be very different.

4.1.3 ROI: replacement cost

The view that ROI should be measured in terms of **replacement cost** (either net or gross) is connected to the arguments in favour of **current cost accounting**. In a period of price inflation, ROI based on historical costs is difficult to interpret because it will become higher as assets get older, as profits will be measured in current-year money.

4.1.4 Measurement problems: what are 'assets' anyway?

Prudence and other accounting principles require items such as R&D to only be carried forward as an investment in special circumstances.

Many 'costs' enhance the long-term revenue-earning capacity of the business, **brands** for example. Many firms have capitalised brands for this reason. For decision-making and control purposes, brand expenditure might be better treated as an investment.

4.1.5 The target return for a group of companies

If a group of companies sets a target return for the group as a whole, or if a company sets a target return for each SBU, it might be company policy that no investment project should go ahead in any subsidiary or investment centre unless the project promises to earn at least the target return. For example, it might be group policy that:

(a)   There should be no new investment by any subsidiary in the group unless it is expected to earn at least a 15% return.

(b)   Similarly, no non-current asset should be disposed of if the asset is currently earning a return in excess of 15% of its disposal value.

(c)   Investments which promise a return of 15% or more ought to be undertaken.

Problems with such a policy are these.

(a)   Investments are appraised by DCF whereas actual performance will probably be measured on the basis of ROI.

(b)   The target return makes no allowance for the different risk of each investment centre.

(c)   In a conglomerate an identical target return may be unsuitable to many businesses in a group. The financial returns and investment costs of a division will vary according to its location, the type of business it engages in, and the stage it is at in its product life cycle. A company needs to remember this when assessing the performance of different divisions.

(d)   Managers **may reject profitable investment opportunities**, and thereby not act in the best interests of their shareholders. For example, assume a division currently earns an ROI of 12%, the estimated ROI on a new project is 10%, but the company's cost of capital is 8%.

The project's estimated ROI is greater than the cost of capital and so it should be accepted because it will increase shareholder wealth. However, a divisional manager whose performance is measured in terms of ROI will reject the project because its expected return (10%) is less than the 12% the division is currently generating.

4.2 Example: the problem with setting a target ROI

Suppose an investment in a non-current asset would cost £100,000 and make a profit of £11,000 pa after depreciation. The asset would be depreciated by £25,000 pa for four years. It is group policy that investments must show a minimum return of 15%.

The DCF net present value of this investment would just about be positive, and so the investment ought to be approved if group policy is adhered to.

Year	Cash flow (profit before dep'n) £	Discount factor 15%	Present value £
0	(100,000)	1.000	(100,000)
1	36,000	0.870	31,320
2	36,000	0.756	27,216
3	36,000	0.658	23,688
4	36,000	0.572	20,592
		NPV	2,816

However, if the investment is measured year by year according to the accounting ROI it has earned, we find that its return is less than 15% in year 1, but more than 15% in years 2, 3 and 4.

Year	Profit £	Net book value of equipment (mid-year value) £	ROCE
1	11,000	87,500	12.6%
2	11,000	62,500	17.6%
3	11,000	37,500	29.3%
4	11,000	12,500	88.0%

In view of the low accounting ROI in year 1, should the investment be undertaken or not?

(a) Strictly speaking, investment decisions should be based on IRR, and should not be guided by short term accounting ROI.

(b) Even if accounting ROI is used as a guideline for investment decisions, ROI should be looked at over the full life of the investment, not just in the short term. In the short term (in the first year or so of a project's life) the accounting ROI is likely to be low because the net book value of the asset will still be high.

In our example, it is conceivable that the group's management might disapprove of the project because of its low accounting ROI in year 1. This approach is short-termist, but it nevertheless can make some sense to a company or group of companies which has to show a satisfactory profit and ROI in its published accounts each year, to keep its shareholders satisfied with performance.

4.3 Possible behavioural implications of ROI: short-termism and lack of goal congruence

Managers are judged on the ROI earned by their centre each year. This motivates them into taking decisions increase their centre's short-term ROI. An investment desirable to the group might not be so appealing to the individual investment centre. This demonstrates a lack of **goal congruence**.

In the short term, a desire to increase ROI might lead to projects being taken on without due regard to their risk.

Any decisions which benefit the company in the long term but which reduce the ROI in the immediate short term would reflect badly on the manager's reported performance.

We have already suggested that using ROI as a performance measure may prevent managers buying new assets. This is an example of short-sighted decision making. The manager's decision is being based on the affect it will have on ROI in the short term, rather than the longer term benefits to the business which may accrue from having the new assets.

However, we need to remember that ROI is a measure of historic performance – it describes performance in the past year. But this may not be an accurate guide as to what future earnings may be, and ultimately, shareholders will be interested in the future earnings which a company can deliver.

Question 13.1   Manipulation

Learning outcome D1(b)

Describe any methods you can think of (and their implications) which managers would use to manipulate the return on investment figures, if ROI was calculated as:

$$\text{Return on total assets} = \frac{\text{Profit before interest, tax, depreciation}}{\text{Gross non-current assets} + \text{total current assets}}$$

4.4 ROI, strategy and product-market issues

4.4.1 ROI reflects organisation structure, not business processes

ROI is based on the existing organisation structure of a business.

(a)   Business process re-engineering suggests that many organisation structures are badly designed in themselves.

(b)   The use of ROI in a responsibility accounting framework perpetuates the bad effects of the existing organisation structure.

(c)   All investment projects may involve the co-operation of many departments in a business, along the whole extent of the value chain.

4.4.2 Product life cycle: ROI is not suitable to all phases

Product-market issues are also relevant. ROI is suited to the **mature phase**, when the market is established. ROI is also best suited to cash cows on the BCG matrix.

4.4.3 ROI aggregates all products in a portfolio

We have seen that many firms have a **portfolio of products** in different stages of the life cycle – in fact this is necessary for the firm's long term survival. ROI does not suggest the right strategic action to be taken with regard to new products or declining products (rising stars, question marks or dogs).

Section summary

Return on investment (ROI) is based on organisational structure, not business processes, and is best suited to products at the mature phase of the life cycle. The problems with ROI relate to accurate measurement.

5   Divisional performance: residual income (RI)

Introduction

Residual income (RI) gets around some of the problems of ROI, by deducting an imputed interest charge for the use of assets from profits.

An alternative way of measuring the performance of an investment centre, instead of using ROI, is residual income (RI).

KEY TERM

RESIDUAL INCOME is 'profit minus a charge for capital employed in the period'.

(CIMA *Official Terminology*)

RI is calculated as 'Earnings before interest and tax – (invested capital x imputed rate).'

The imputed cost of capital might be the organisation's cost of borrowing or its weighted average cost of capital. Alternatively, the cost of capital can be adjusted to allow for the risk characteristics of each investment centre, with a higher imputed interest rate being applied to higher risk centres.

5.1 The advantages and weaknesses of RI compared with ROI

The advantages of using RI are as follows.

(a)   Residual income will increase when:

(i)   Investments earning above the cost of capital are undertaken
(ii)   Investments earning below the cost of capital are eliminated

(b)   Residual income is more flexible since a different cost of capital can be applied to investments with different risk characteristics.

(c)   The cost of financing a division or an investment is highlighted to division managers through the use of the cost of capital figure.

The weakness of RI is that it does not facilitate comparisons between investment or organisations of different sizes, because it uses an absolute figure rather than a percentage.

5.1.1 RI versus ROI: marginally profitable investments

Residual income increases if a new investment is undertaken which earns a profit in excess of the imputed interest charge on the value of the asset acquired. When a manager is judged by ROI, a marginally profitable investment would be less likely to be undertaken because it would reduce the average ROI earned by the centre as a whole.

Residual income does not always point to the right decision, because notional interest on accounting capital employed is not the same as IRR on cash investment. However, residual income is more likely than ROI to improve when managers make correct investment/divestment decisions, and so is probably a 'safer' basis than ROI on which to measure performance.

5.2 Example: ROI versus RI

Suppose that Department H has the following profit, assets employed and an imputed interest charge of 12% on operating assets.

	Department H £	£
Operating profit	30,000	
Operating assets		100,000
Imputed interest (12%)	12,000	
Return on investment		30%
Residual income	18,000	

Suppose now that an additional investment of £10,000 is proposed, which will increase operating income in Department H by £1,400. The effect of the investment would be:

	£	£
Total operating income	31,400	
Total operating assets		110,000
Imputed interest (12%)	13,00	
Return on investment		28.5%
Residual income	18,200	

If the Department H manager is made responsible for the department's performance, he would resist the new investment if he were to be judged on ROI, but would welcome the investment if he were judged according to RI, since there would be a marginal increase of £200 in residual income from the investment, but a fall of 1.5% in ROI.

The marginal investment offers a return of 14% (£1,400 on an investment of £10,000) which is above the 'cut-off rate' of 12%. Since the original return on investment was 30%, the marginal investment will reduce the overall divisional performance. Indeed, any marginal investment offering an accounting rate of return of less than 30% in the year would reduce the overall performance.

Residual income should not be used as a means of making asset purchasing decisions; nevertheless, it may be a useful alternative to ROI where there is a conflict between purchase decisions indicated by a positive NPV in discounted cash flow, and the resulting reduction in divisional ROI which 'reflects badly' on management performance.

5.3 General issues with RI

Some of the disadvantages we identified in relation to using ROI as a performance measure also apply to RI:

- It can lead to short-termist decision making by discouraging managers from replacing non-current assets which would increase the cost of their capital assets.

- The financial returns and investment costs of a division will vary according to its location, the type of business it engages in, and the stage it is at in the product life cycle. A company needs to remember this when assessing the performance of different divisions.

- RI (like ROI) is a measure of historic performance, but it does not give an indication of what future earnings may be, despite this being an important consideration for shareholders.

Section summary

An alternative to ROI for measuring the performance of an investment centre is **residual income** (RI). This avoids some of the problems with ROI by deducting from profit an interest charge for the use of assets. However, RI does not facilitate comparison between investment centres, nor does it relate the size of a centre's income to the size of the investment.

6 Comparing profit centre performance

Introduction

Profit centres are often compared. Problems arise when managers are judged on matters they cannot control. A variety of measures involving **contribution** are used to isolate controllable costs.

Problems in measuring **divisional performance** include allocation of head office costs, and different asset valuations.

When departments within an organisation are set up as profit centres, their performance will be judged on the profit they earn. This performance might be compared on the basis of profit/sales ratios, contribution earned per unit of scarce resource, or profit growth rates.

6.1 Dysfunctional decisions and goal congruence

A profit centre manager might take decisions that will improve his own centre's performance at the expense of other parts of the business.

- Profit centre managers tend to put their own profit performance above everything else.
- Profit centres are not isolated entities, but related divisions within a single organisation.

Question 13.2   Head office

Learning outcome D1(ii)

What are the likely behavioural consequences of a head office continually imposing its own decisions on divisions?

6.2 Comparing profit centre performance

Shillinglaw suggested that four profit concepts could be used to measure and report divisional profit internally within a company. Each has its own purpose.

(a)   **Contribution**

(b)   **'Controllable profit'** – contribution minus all the division's fixed costs controllable by the manager.

(c)   **Controllable margin** – controllable profit minus all other costs directly traceable to the division.

(d)   **Net profit or net contribution**, less a share of service centre costs and general management overhead. However, 'net profit' is the least useful of the four, because the allocation of general overhead costs must inevitably be largely arbitrary.

6.2.1 Contribution

A principle of responsibility accounting is that profit centre managers should only be held accountable for those revenues and costs that they are in a position to control. Increases in production volume, within the relevant range of output, will raise profit by the amount of increase in contribution.

A divisional performance statement based on contribution might appear as follows.

	Division A	Division B	Total
	£'000	£'000	£'000
Sales	80	100	180
Less variable costs	60	50	110
Contribution	20	50	70
Less fixed costs			50
Profit			20

(a)   Divisional performance can be improved by increasing the sales price, or volume of sales, or reducing the unit variable cost.

(b)   The relative profitability of divisions A and B could be compared by means of their C/S ratios (in this example, 25% and 50% respectively).

(c)   If there is a production limiting factor, performance could also be measured in terms of contribution per unit of limiting factor. In our example, if there is a shortage of cash for working capital acting as a restriction on output, and if divisions A and B use £2,500 and £8,000 in working capital respectively, the contribution per £1 of working capital employed would be £8 for division A and £6.25 for division B (so that a transfer of some production resources from B to A might be profitable under these circumstances).

6.2.2 Controllable profit

One drawback to using contribution alone as a measure of divisional performance is that although it indicates the short-term controllable results of the division, it gives no indication as **to longer-term underlying profitability**.

In the following example, closure of division X might be justified, since there would be a net saving in annual running costs of £5,000.

	Division X £'000	Division Y £'000	Total £'000
Sales	70	120	190
Less variable costs	50	80	130
Contribution	20	40	60
Less directly attributable fixed costs	25	25	50
Profit of the division	(5)	15	10
Less fixed costs (general)			8
Company profit			2

6.2.3 Controllable margin

A further refinement of this approach to profit centre accounting is to make a distinction between fixed costs over which the centre manager has short-run discretionary control, for example advertising costs and sales promotion expenditures, and fixed costs over which the manager has no personal control, such as his own salary, or depreciation of assets.

		Division X £'000	Division Y £'000	Total £'000
	Sales	70	120	190
	Less variable costs	50	80	130
(1)	Contribution	20	40	60
	Less fixed costs directly attributable to manager's discretionary control	8	20	28
(2)	Profit attributable to the manager	12	20	32
	Less fixed costs directly attributable the profit centre, outside the manager's control	17	5	22
(3)	Profit attributable to the profit centre	(5)	15	10
	Shared fixed costs			8
	Company profit			2

6.2.4 Net profit: after charging a proportion of shared fixed costs

An argument against measuring profit on the basis of contribution less directly attributable fixed costs is that no one is made responsible for earning a sufficiently large profit to ensure that shared fixed costs are covered, and that the organisation as a whole is profitable.

6.2.5 The problems of absorption costing

Absorption costing systems are perhaps the 'traditional' method of accounting for divisional performance, but they have some serious drawbacks.

(a) **They are not a method of responsibility accounting**, in that managers cannot control the general fixed costs charged to their division, and are not properly responsible for them.

(b) **The method of apportioning fixed costs can vary**, according to the basis chosen.

Residual income and interdepartmental comparisons.

With a residual income method of reporting divisional profits, four different 'profit' figures can be identified, as follows. It is quite possible that divisions will do better or worse, in comparative terms, according to which measure is used.

	£'000	Division A £'000
Sales: external		310
internal transfers		210
		520
Variable costs of goods sold internally and externally	220	
Variable divisional expenses	20	
		240
(1) **Controllable contribution**		280
Controllable divisional overhead		90
(2) **Controllable profit**		190
Depreciation and other expenses on controllable fixed assets (eg lease costs)	50	
Interest on controllable fixed assets	15	
		65
(3) **Controllable residual income**		125
Depreciation and other expenses on non-controllable fixed assets	20	
Allocated central expenses	40	
Interest on non-controllable fixed assets	10	
		70
(4) **Net residual income**		55

6.3 Head office as a profit centre or investment centre: charging for services

One way of improving the responsibility accounting system might be to establish head office as a profit centre or investment centre in its own right.

6.4 Service departments

The same cost distinctions should be made for service department costs.

(a)   The department might incur costs that are variable with the volume of activity. Variable costs should be identified, and control reporting should compare actual costs with a flexed budget.

(b)   The department's directly attributable fixed costs should be identified, because these are the running costs that would be saved if the department were to be closed down.

6.5 Making non-current assets controllable

Non-current assets are 'controllable' by divisional managers if they have the authority to purchase or dispose of assets. A temporary surplus of non-current assets will reduce the division's short term ROI or RI as the assets are 'controllable'. The manager could dispose of the assets to prevent this, but they may be needed in the future and so disposal might be inappropriate. A way around this is to establish a head office 'pool' of non-current assets from which non-current assets can be obtained when required, and returned to when they become surplus to requirements.

6.6 Added value

KEY TERM

Although added value can be measured in different ways, the broad concept is that ADDED VALUE equals sales minus the costs of materials and bought-in services.

Managers are then made responsible for the following.

(a)   Total value added earned.

(b)   The way in which value added is divided between labour costs, non-current asset depreciation, profit.

(c)   Value added earned per unit of key resource (per machine hour, say, or direct labour hour).

Division B

	£'000	£'000
Sales		400
Materials	160	
Bought-in services	80	
		240
Value added		160
Direct labour	70	
Indirect labour	50	
Depreciation	30	
		150
Profit		10

Section summary

When comparing **profit centres**, managers should only be held accountable for those revenues and costs that they are in a position to control. Controllable costs can be isolated using a variety of methods involving **contribution**.

7   Interfirm comparisons and performance ratios

Introduction

As well as comparing profit centres within a group, comparisons are also made between **companies in an industry**. Problems include a lack of information and different accounting policies. As well as monitoring performance from the investor's point of view, such schemes can be used in **competitive analysis**. **Ratio analysis** might be useful in this context.

Interfirm comparisons are comparisons of the performance of different companies, subsidiaries or investment centres.

7.1 The purpose of interfirm comparisons

(a)   One company can compare its performance against another, as part of **competitive analysis or benchmarking**.

(b)   **Senior management** can compare the performance of different subsidiary companies within their group.

(c)   **Investors** can compare different firms in an industry.

(d)   A company's **status** as a potential takeover target, or as a potential takeover threat, can be evaluated.

A financial comparison between rival public limited companies might cover:

*   The best profits record (ROI, growth in profits and EPS)
*   The best financial structure (financial gearing, debt ratio, interest cover)
*   The 'best quality' profits or best growth prospects (P/E ratio comparison)
*   The best cash flow position

7.2 Which firms should be compared with each other?

It is unrealistic to assume that all firms ought to be able to earn comparable ROI.

- Some industries are more profitable than others
- Some companies need a big investment in non-current assets

There are a number of basic requirements for an interfirm comparison to be successful.

(a)   The companies compared must all belong to a **similar industry** to enable comparison.

(b)   Reports might be given in the form of lists of **ratios**. If ratios are to be helpful for control purposes, comparisons should be limited to companies of roughly the same size.

(c)   The results of each of the participants must be adjusted so that, as far as possible, the same **accounting policies** are used for each.

7.3 Performance ratios

Ratios are useful in that they provide a means of comparison of actual results:

- With a budget, or desired target
- With ratios of previous years' results, in order to detect trends
- With ratios of other companies or divisions
- With industry or governmental indices.

7.3.1 Ratios from financial statements

You should be familiar with the statement of financial position (balance sheet) and income statement (profit and loss account) ratios.

(a)   **Income statement ratios** include profit margin (profit/sales) which can be analysed as follows, in a hierarchy of subsidiary ratios.

(i) $\dfrac{\text{Production cost of sales}}{\text{Sales}}$ which can be broken down into:

(1) $\dfrac{\text{Material costs}}{\text{sales value of production}}$ or $\dfrac{\text{Material costs}}{\text{total costs of production}}$

(2) $\dfrac{\text{Works labour cost}}{\text{sales value of production}}$ or $\dfrac{\text{Labour costs}}{\text{total cost of production}}$

(3) $\dfrac{\text{Production overheads}}{\text{sales value of production}}$ or $\dfrac{\text{Production overheads}}{\text{total costs of production}}$

(ii) $\dfrac{\text{Distribution and marketing costs}}{\text{Sales}}$

(iii) $\dfrac{\text{Administrative costs}}{\text{Sales}}$

(b)   **Statement of financial position ratios** include the following, broken down further.

(i)   **Asset turnover** (sales/capital employed), which can be analysed by class of asset (eg sales/non-current assets).

(ii)   **Working capital ratios** covering liquidity (eg current ratio, current assets/current liabilities) and turnover periods for receivables, payables and inventory (eg credit period taken by credit customers).

(iii)   Gearing ratios covering borrowings.

Question 13.3	Strategic significance

Learning outcome D1(ii)

What might be the strategic significance of the following, when compared to the industry average?

(a)   A high non-current asset turnover.
(b)   High gearing
(c)   Far higher non-current assets but lower labour costs.

Question 13.4	Subsidiaries

Learning outcome D1(b)

Calculate and compare the ROI, asset utilisation and profitability of the two subsidiaries whose results are shown below.

	A Ltd	B Ltd
	£	£
Capital employed	300,000	800,000
Net profit	60,000	120,000
Sales	1,250,000	2,400,000

7.4 The calculation of return on investment in interfirm comparisons

There are several issues to consider when deciding how to measure both the return and the capital employed.

7.4.1 Return

Definition of return. Return might be taken as profit after tax. However, when interfirm comparisons are being made, this would be unsuitable, for two reasons.

(a)   The **tax rate** applicable to one company's profits may be different from the tax rate applicable to another's.

(b)   One company might be financed largely by borrowing, receiving tax relief on interest payments. Another company might be entirely equity financed.

Measuring return (profit). When there is a comparison between the results of subsidiaries within the same group or the results of investment centres within a single company, there may be a problem with **transfer prices.**

7.4.2 Capital employed/investment

Should assets be valued on the basis of historical cost, replacement cost, disposal value, current value or some other similar inflation-adjusted basis?

(a)   Historical cost has the severe drawback that in a period of inflation, the balance sheet value of older non-current assets can fall below their 'realistic' current value, and so the measurement of ROI will give a misleading (excessively high) percentage return.

(b)   Depreciation charges against non-current assets might also fail to reflect the loss of value from using the assets during the period, when historical cost accounting is used.

(c)   Replacement cost or current cost might be difficult to estimate whereas historical cost is a readily-known value.

(d)   Disposal value is only useful when the non-current assets are readily marketable (eg property) but in such cases a target return on disposal value represents an opportunity cost of the investment.

7.4.3 The accounting policies of different companies

Typical differences in accounting policies and asset acquisition methods between one firm and another are these.

* The assumed life of non-current assets
* The method of depreciation used
* Accounting for intangible non-current assets, such as development costs and goodwill
* Inventory valuation methods
* Renting accommodation instead of buying the freehold or leasehold
* Purchasing operating non-current assets or leasing/renting them

Section summary

Interfirm comparisons are comparisons of the performance of different companies, subsidiaries or investment centres. Ratios are useful in that they provide a means of comparison of actual results.

8   Achieving success for the shareholder

Introduction

A management team is required by an **organisation's shareholders** to **maximise the value of their investment** in the organisation and a plethora of performance indicators is used to assess whether or not the management team is fulfilling this duty.

8.1 Shareholder value

Shareholders require managers to **maximise the value of their investment** in the organisation. Performance indicators assess how well this duty is carried out.

Most of these **performance measures** are based on information from the organisation's published accounts. Not only do these indicators often give **conflicting messages**, they can be easily **manipulated** and often provide **misleading** information. Earnings per share, for example, is reduced by capital-building investments in research and development and in marketing.

What is more, the **financial statements** themselves **do not provide a clear picture of whether or not shareholder value is being created.** The income statement (profit and loss account), for example, indicates the **quantity** but not the **quality** of earnings, and it does not distinguish between earnings derived from operating assets as opposed to non-operating assets. Moreover, **it ignores the cost of equity financing** and only takes into account the costs of debt financing, thereby penalising organisations which choose a mix of debt and equity finance.

The statement of cash flows (**cashflow statement**) also fails to provide appropriate information as large, positive cashflows are possible when organisations underspend on maintenance, or undertake little capital investment, to increase short-term profits at the expense of long-term success. On the other hand, an organisation can have large negative cashflows for several years and still be profitable.

A **shareholder value approach** to performance measurement involves moving the focus away from short-term profits to a **longer-term view of value creation**, the motivation being that it will help the business stay ahead in an increasingly competitive world.

Individual shareholders have different definitions of shareholder value as different shareholders value different aspects of performance.

- Financial returns in the short-term
- Short-term capital gains
- Long-term returns or capital gains
- Stability and security
- Achievements in products produced or services provided
- Ethical standards

(It is unlikely that the last two alone make a company valuable to an investor.)

These factors and others will all be reflected in a company's share price, but stock markets are notoriously fickle and tend to have a short-term outlook.

8.1.1 Shareholder value analysis

Wider share ownership and more knowledgeable investors are forcing companies to understand the techniques by which their companies are being judged. The terminology **shareholder value** is used widely to describe a range of shareholder focussed performance indicators developed by various consultancies.

One approach is **shareholder value analysis (SVA)**, devised by *Alfred Rappaport* (*Creating Shareholder Value,* 1986).

KEY TERM

SHAREHOLDER VALUE is the 'total return to the shareholders in terms of both dividends and share price growth, calculated as the present value of future free cash flows of the business discounted at the weighted average cost of the capital of the business less the market value of its debt'.

(CIMA *Official Terminology*)

Shareholder value = (corporate value – debt)

Where business value is calculated as the PV of free cashflows from operations plus the value of any marketable assets held.

The value of a corporation can be established by developing a future **cash flow forecast** and converting it into a present value. The total value of the business is then found by taking away the value of any debt and adding any value from external investments. Dividing the result by the number of shares gives the **shareholder value per share**. This technique has been used extensively in acquisition situations and is often known as **cash flow return on investment (CFROI)**.

8.1.2 Drivers of shareholder value

Rappaport proposes that this **single figure value** for a business be calculated by **reference to seven 'value drivers'**, which drive the generation of **cash.**

(a) **Sales growth rate**: an increase in profitable sales should increase free cash flow.

(b) **Operating profit margin**: the higher the margin on sales, the better. Margins can be increased either by increasing prices, or reducing costs.

The return on capital generated by a business depends on the combination of profit margins relative to turnover (margin) and the ability to generate turnover from capital invested (efficiency). In order to improve return on capital, a business needs an improvement in the combination of margin and efficiency.

(c) **Cash taxation rate**: the higher the tax, the more of the shareholders' value the government takes.

(d)   **Fixed capital investment rate**: cash invested in non-current assets reduces free cash flows even though it may lead to growth.

(e)   **Working capital investment rate**: a similar principle applies.

(f)   **Life of the business (or project)**: the further into the future a firm can reasonably forecast its cash flows, the greater the PV and hence the business value.

(g)   **Cost of capital**: PV obviously depends on the discount rate employed (WACC).

According to *Johnson, Scholes & Whittington*, applying shareholder value analysis requires a whole new mindset, termed **value based management**. Central to this way of thinking is the identification of the cash generators of the business, or **value drivers**, such as those identified by Rappaport. These will be both external and internal. For example, **competitive rivalry** is a major external value driver because of its direct impact on margins.

8.2 Value based management

KEY TERM

VALUE BASED MANAGEMENT is 'a managerial process which effectively links strategy, measurement and operational processes to the end of creating shareholder value'.

(CIMA Official Terminology)

Value based management (VBM) consists of three elements:

(a)   **Strategy for value creation** – ways to increase or generate the maximum future value for an organisation

(b)   **Metrics** – for measuring value

(c)   **Management** – managing for value, encompassing governance, remuneration, organisation structure, culture and stakeholder relationships

Value based management highlights that management decisions designed to lead to higher profits do not necessarily create value for shareholders. Often, management are under pressure to meet short term profit targets, and they are prepared to sacrifice long term value in order to achieve these short term targets. For example, management might avoid initiating a project with a positive net present value if that project leads to their organisation falling short of expected profit targets in the current period.

Profit-based performance measures may therefore obscure the true state of a business. By contrast, value based management seeks to ensure that analytical techniques and management processes are all aligned to help an organisation maximise its value. VBM does this by focusing management decision-making on the key drivers of value, and making management more accountable for growing an organisation's intrinsic value.

Therefore, whereas profit-based performance measures look at what has happened in the past, VBM seeks to maximise returns on new investments. What matters to the shareholders of a company is that they earn an acceptable return on their capital. They are not only interested in how a company has performed in the past, but also how it is likely to perform in the future.

8.2.1 Creating shareholder value

Although it is easy to identify the logic that companies ought to be managed for shareholder value, it is much harder to specify how this can be achieved. For example, a strategy to increase market share may not actually increase shareholder value.

Good quality information is essential in a VBM system, so that management can identify where value is being created – or destroyed – in a business. For example, continuing the previous example, there is no value in increasing market share in a market if that market is not profitable.

An organisation will need to identify its value drivers, and then put strategies in place for each of them. When identifying its value drivers, an organisation may also find that its organisational structure needs reorganising, to ensure that it is aligned with the processes which create value.

8.2.2 Measurement

VBM will lead to a change in the performance metrics used in a company. Instead of focusing solely on historical returns, companies also need to look at more forward-looking contributions to value: for example, growth and sustainability. The performance measures used in VBM are often non-financial.

8.2.3 Managing value

In today's companies, the intellectual capital provided by employees plays a key role in generating value. VBM attempts to align the interests of the employees who generate value and the shareholders they create value for. Otherwise VBM could drive a wedge between those who deliver economic performance (employees) and those who harvest its benefits (shareholders). In practice, this equate to remuneration structures which include some form of share-based payments.

Successfully implementing VBM will also involve cultural change in an organisation. The employees in the organisation will need to commit to creating shareholder value. Value is created throughout the company not just by senior management, so employees all need to appreciate how their roles add value.

Nonetheless, visible leadership and strong commitment from senior management will be essential for a shift to VBM to be successful.

However, as with any change programme, implementing VBM could be expensive and potentially disruptive, particularly if extensive restructuring is required.

8.2.4 Elements of VBM

A comprehensive VBM programme should consider the following:

- **Strategic planning** – strategies should be evaluated to establish whether they will maximise shareholder value

- **Capital allocation** – funds should be allocated to the strategies and divisions that will create most shareholder value

- **Operating budgets** – budgets should reflect the strategies the organisation is using to create value

- **Performance measurement** – the economic performance of the organisation needs to lead to increases in share prices, because these promote the creation of shareholder wealth

- **Management remuneration** – rewards should be linked to the value drivers, and how well value-based targets are achieved

- **Internal communication** – the background to the programme and how VBM will benefit the business need to be explained to staff

- **External communication** – management decisions, and how they are designed to achieve value, must be communicated to the market. The market's reaction to these decisions will help determine movements in the organisation's share price.

All the consultants who have followed *Rappaport's* ideas work from the same principles.

- **Profit** has become discredited as a performance measure.

- The traditional cost of capital used in the income statement interest figure is inadequate. A composite measure taking into account the complex **capital structure** of a business is needed.

- What really needs to be measured is **how well the business is performing for the shareholders.**

8.3 How does business strategy promote increased shareholder value?

A diagram helps to show how strategy drives the business towards increased shareholder value, which for many businesses is the primary objective of strategy.

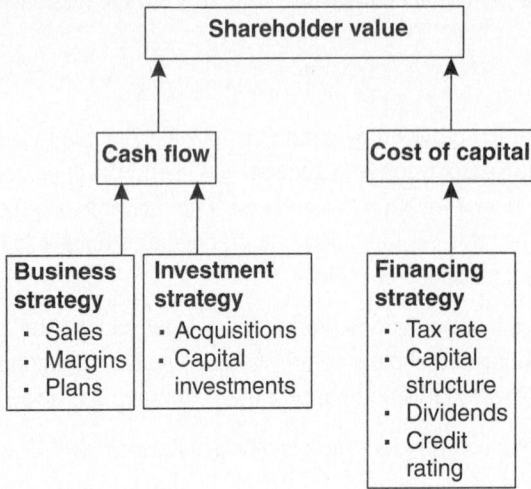

(Adapted from *CIMA Insider*, March 2001)

Adopting a value based approach to managing an enterprise has wide-ranging implications.

Culture: shareholder value must be accepted as the organisation's purpose. This may have greatest impact at the **strategic apex**, whose members may have had different ideas on this subject. However, the importance of creating shareholder value must be emphasised in all parts of the business.

Nevertheless it is crucial that management do not overlook underlying business processes in the quest for value based metrics. Core business processes (for example, quality management, innovation, and customer service) should still be monitored alongside value based metrics.

Relations with the market: shareholder value should be reflected in share price. The company's senior managers must **communicate effectively with the market** so that their value-creating policies are incorporated into the share price. However, they must not be tempted to manipulate the market. This may be a difficult area to manage as executive rewards should reflect the share price. One way in which management can communicate performance to the market is through performance indicators. These metrics should then, in turn, form the basis of the performance targets for divisional managers to achieve.

Strategic choices: the maximisation of shareholder value must be the object of all strategic choices. This will affect such matters as **resource allocation** and HR policies and will have particular relevance to the evaluation of expensive projects such as acquisitions and major new product development.

CASE STUDY

Demergers and shareholder value

In March 2010, telecoms groups Cable & Wireless and Carphone Warehouse both underwent demerger deals. And the management of both companies argued that splitting up their groups into two clearly defined businesses would help unlock shareholder value.

However, some investors are concerned that companies do not rush to demerge simply because demergers have become the flavour of the month in a sluggish market where bankers are looking for new sources of fees.

The sentiment among investors remains that a deal – whether it is a merger or a demerger – must only be done because it creates value for shareholders.

However, research carried out into demerged European companies, suggests that demerger activity does usually create shareholder value. A report published by UBS in March 2010, showed that 75 European companies demerged since 2000 outperformed Europe's top-300 groups by 16% a year.

As if to reinforce this, when the newly demerged retail and telecoms arms of Carphone Warehouse made their stock market debut, the combined market capitalisations of the demerged companies was 10% higher than the old Carphone group.

The author of the UBS report anticipates there will be a 'flurry' of spin-offs in the near future. However, he points out that not all demergers do well. While the share price of AstraZeneca has soared since it was split from its parent, ICI, the demerger of Mondi from AngloAmerican has seen the parent outperform the spin-off.

Nevertheless, the spin-off part of the business often performs better than the larger parent, and one reason for this is the demerger throws light upon parts of the business that were hidden to investors beforehand.

The demerger of the former British Gas business illustrates how a successful demerger can unlock shareholder value, as the value of shares has risen almost 10-fold since the group's demerger (in 1997) into Centrica, BG Group and National Grid. However, as one long-standing Centrica executive commented, management have to be mature to deliver value on the demerger. 'To give shareholder value, management have to make sure the right components go with the right business, and not be steered by various factions with the business".

(Adapted from FT.com article 'Spin-offs show demergers are staging comeback' 29 March, 2010)

8.4 Economic value management

Economic value management hinges in the idea of an **economic profit,** which is derived after adjusting traditional accounting profits for the write offs that are made for **value building expenditures** such as training and advertising. By adding such expenditures back to accounting profit, better comparison can be made between companies.

KEY TERM

ECONOMIC VALUE ADDED (EVA)^{TM} 'A measure which approximates a company's profit. Traditional financial statements are translated into EVA statements by reversing distortions in operating performance created by accounting rules and by charging operating profit for all of the capital employed. For example, written-off goodwill is capitalised, as are extraordinary losses and the present value of operating leases. Extraordinary gains reduce capital.'   *Stern Stewart*

EVA = Adjusted operating profits* after tax – (Adjusted invested capital × Imputed rate of interest)

* Stern Stewart calls this net operating profit after tax (NOPAT).

Economic value management hinges on the calculation of **economic profit (EP).** A comparison of economic profit with required return results in a figure for **economic value added or destroyed.** The calculation of EP requires several **adjustments** to be made to traditionally-reported accounting profits. These adjustments are made to **avoid the immediate write-off of value-building expenditure** such as research and development expenditure, advertising expenditure or the purchase of goodwill.

The adjustments are intended to produce a figure for capital employed which is a more accurate reflection of the **base upon which shareholders expect their returns to accrue** and to provide a profit after tax figure which is a more realistic measure of the **actual cash yield generated** for shareholders from recurring business activities.

EVA theory says that in order to add economic value, a project or business unit must deliver more net operating profit, after all taxes and costs, than it costs to have access to the total capital used to generate that profit.

8.4.1 Principles of EVA

The principles of EVA, devised by the US consultants *Stern Stewart*, are:

- Investment leads to assets regardless of accounting treatments
- Assets once created cannot be diminished by accounting action

Such an approach contrasts favourably with information based on traditional accounting concepts and conventions. The prudence concept, for example, requires revenue expenditure (such as maintenance expenditure on plant and machinery) to be written off to the income statement in the accounting period in which it is incurred. This is to reflect the fact that such expenditure may have no long-term benefits. It is therefore not very surprising that if management are assessed using performance measures calculated using traditional accounting policies, they are unwilling to invest in or spend money on activities which immediately reduce current year's profit.

It is claimed that EP provides the basis for a useful management performance appraisal measure because **while EP increases, so does the market value added (MVA) for a company and shareholder value**.

8.4.2 Benefits of economic value added

(a) **Net present value**

EVA focuses on the **long-term net present value of a company.** Managerial performance will be improved by investing in positive NPV projects, not investing in negative NPV projects and lowering the cost of capital.

(b) **Financing**

By including a financing element, the **cost of capital** is emphasised, and so managers must have regard for **careful investment** and **control of working capital.** If managers choose negative NPV projects, the imputed capital charge will ultimately be greater than earnings.

(c) **Cash flows**

The adjustments within the model mean that EVA should be based on **cash flows** rather than accounting data so may be **less distorted** by the **accounting policies** chosen.

(d) **Clarity of measure**

EVA is a **monetary figure** (rather than a ratio) that can be easily **linked to financial objectives.**

8.4.3 Drawbacks of economic value added

(a) **Failure to measure short-term position**

EVA does **not measure NPV** in the short-term. Projects with good long-term NPV, but large initial cash investments or poor initial returns, may be rejected by managers who are being judged on their **short-term performance.**

(b) **Use of historical accounts**

EVA is based on historical accounts which may be of **limited use** as a guide to the future. Also, influences of accounting policies on the starting profit figure may not be completely negated by the adjustments made to it in the EVA model.

(c) **Other value drivers**

Other value drivers such as non-capitalised goodwill may be important despite being **excluded from the accounts**.

(d) **Adjustments**

Making the necessary adjustments can be **problematic** as sometimes a large number of adjustments are required.

(e) **Cost of capital**

The cost of capital used is calculated by the **capital asset pricing model,** and is therefore based upon the **assumptions** of that model such as **no change in risk.**

(f) **Inter-company comparisons**

Companies which are larger in size may have larger economic value added figures for this reason. Allowance for relative size must be made when inter-company comparisons are performed.

8.5 Example on EVA

Recommend which plc, X or Y, to invest funds in. Justify your decision.

Profit and loss account for the previous year (£m's)

	X	Y
	£	£
Sales	26.0	62.0
Cost of sales	18.0	47.0
Gross profit	8.0	15.0
Production overheads	1.2	2.4
Advertising	0.6	2.0
Depreciation	1.1	1.6
Training	0.1	1.8
R & D	0.6	2.0
Bad debt expense	0.2	0.3
PBIT	4.2	4.9
Investment base	26.5	40.3

Solution

Traditional ROI techniques would give X plc 15.8% and Y plc 12.1%, and therefore choose X plc for investment. However this ignores the fact that Y is more heavily involved in developing the long term future of its company by spending on training, advertising and R & D. These items, under EVA, would be added back to obtain a comparison using operational expenses.

	X	Y
Adjusted ROI		
Original profit	4.2	4.9
Training	0.1	1.8
Advertising	0.6	2.0
R & D	0.6	2.0
New profit	5.5	10.7
New ROI	20.8%	26.4%

There is still a lack of information here to make a final decision, although the original analysis and decision to invest in X plc has been considerably refined. Business risk, market dynamics, previous year's results, competitor comparisons, and investment portfolio issues will all affect the analysis.

'**Economic value added** is the best indicator of business performance. When it is projected for future years and discounted to the present value, it represents the net present value of all past and future investments and cash flows. Therefore, by making increases in EP a priority, the economic value added of a company will increase, which will, in turn, lead to increases in a company's market value (and therefore its share price).'

(John Mayfield, 'Economic value management: the route to shareholder value', *Management Accounting,* September 1997)

8.6 EVA and strategy

As well as considering how EVA is calculated, it is also worth thinking how the elements of EVA might affect a firm's strategy.

For example, possible ways of increasing net operating profit might be:

Increased revenues:

- Higher sales volumes: market penetration; product development; innovation (new products in early stages of product life cycle); build barriers to entry (eg patent protection)

- Higher prices: branding; product differentiation; quality of product / service

- Cross-selling and customer retention: customer relationship management

- Customer profitability

Reduced operating costs:

- Cost reduction programmes, and target costing of products

- Productivity and efficiency initiatives (eg review of staffing levels)

- Outsourcing of non-core areas

- Vertical integration (to gain access to materials and markets), and to generate greater economies of scale

- Relocation – to benefit from cheaper rents, labour costs etc. (International relocation could also have the benefit of reducing tax).

8.7 Market value added (MVA)

Market value added (MVA) is the difference between the market value of a company and the economic book value of capital employed.

This might be thought of as being related to EVA, being the net present value created for shareholders over the life of the company. The difference is that EVA is essentially **historic**, while MVA is assumed (under the efficient market hypothesis) to be the market's assessment of the firm's ability to add value **in the future**. It is similar to Rappaport's idea of business value and his list of **value drivers** is relevant. The idea of market valuation, however, brings into play all the variables that affect market expectations, such as the firm's ability to win the trust of investors and investors' understanding of the business.

KEY TERM

MARKET VALUE ADDED is 'the difference between a company's market value (derived from share price) and its economic book value (the amount of capital that shareholders and debt holders have committed to the firm throughout its existence, including any retained earnings)'.   (CIMA *Official Terminology*)

Put another way, MVA is 'the difference between what investors put into the company as capital and what they could get out by selling at today's market price' (*Al Ehrbar*). In theory, **MVA is the present value of all future EVAs**. However, **market sentiment** will always affect the share price too.

The difficulty with this measure is that while capital employed (monies invested by shareholders in the company) represents investments made in the **past**, market value is the present value of **future** cash flows. So what does MVA (ie, the difference between these two) really represent? In addition, shareholders are buying and selling shares all the time. There must be as many measures of MVA for a company as there are individual shareholders.

8.8 Total shareholder return (TSR)

Total shareholder return (TSR) is the total percentage return to shareholders over a given period.

Total shareholder return is defined as the **total percentage return to shareholders over a period** using the formula:

$$\frac{\text{Dividend per share} + \text{Movement in share price}}{\text{Share price at the start of the period}}$$

This measure is very simple to calculate, and can be used to compare performance of similar companies. As with MVA, however, it is not immune to market sentiment.

CASE STUDY

Total shareholder value

BP's annual report for 2009 revealed that the chief executive, Tony Hayward, received a 41 per cent rise in his total pay, in spite of total shareholder returns since 2007 that ranked fourth out of five in the company's peer group. The chairman of the remuneration committee argued that Mr Hayward and his team had produced "excellent results" in "a volatile year for the world economy".

Mr Hayward was paid a total of £4m for 2009, including basic pay of £1.045m, a bonus of £2.09m – nearly the maximum possible award – and shares under a long-term incentive plan worth £852,000.

Interestingly, BP's performance in terms of shareholder return during 2007-09 implied that no share award should have been given, but the remuneration committee took other factors into account.

A year earlier, at Royal Dutch Shell, when the remuneration committee exercised their judgement and approved a share award, this contributed to an investor revolt that forced the company to revise its pay policies.

However, one large investor in BP said that shareholders had been told about the planned award at BPP, and discussed the reasons for it, and they considered that it was justified.

During 2007-09, BP's total shareholder return has been fourth out of its peer group of five, which includes Total of France as well as Shell, Exxon and Chevron.

However, the remuneration committee determined it was "very close to third place" and, as it scored highly on many other metrics, decided to award half of the shares under the incentive plan that would have been paid out had BP come third.

Since Mr Hayward took over in May 2007, BP has been closing the gap on its competitors and has come first in its peer group for earnings per share growth, increase in return on capital, production growth and several other scores.

(Adapted from an article on FT.com *'BP's Hayward given 41% increase'* 5th March, 2010)

Section summary

Shareholders require managers to **maximise the value of their investment** in the organisation. Performance indicators assess how well this is carried out.

Economic value management hinges in the idea of an economic profit, which is derived after adjusting traditional accounting profits for the write offs that are made for **value building expenditures** such as training and advertising. By adding such expenditures back to accounting profit, better comparison can be made between companies.

Market value added is the difference between the market value of a company and the economic book value of capital employed.

Total shareholder return is the total percentage return to shareholders over a given period.

9   International subsidiaries

Introduction

The task of setting objectives within a **multinational** is complex, and several problems must be resolved

The task of setting objectives within a **multinational** is complex, and several problems must be resolved. For example, setting up systems of **performance measurement** will need to consider:

- realistic **standards** country to country
- **controllability** of cash flows
- **currency conversion**

Exam skills

A question may require consideration of particular difficulties with performance measurement when plant and marketing operations are in various parts of the world. Make sure you think about the specific difficulties which are relevant to the scenario: don't just discuss general issues.

(a) **Capital structure**. Where foreign subsidiaries are financed partly by loans, the differing rates of interest in each country might affect the relative profitability of subsidiaries.

(b) **Cost structure**. Overseas subsidiaries may have a different operational gearing.

(c) **Accounting policies**. In each country, the subsidiary may adopt a different rate of depreciation so that profits and asset values are not comparable. Profits can be transformed into losses by accounting policies.

(d) **Government policy**. There will be differences in the levels of grants or concessions from the national government and in the rate of taxation and interest.

(e) **Transfer prices** for goods and services between the subsidiaries may be set in such a way as to improve the results of one subsidiary (or head office) at the expense of another (eg if goods are transferred from a subsidiary to head office at cost, the subsidiary will get no profit and the head office will obtain the goods at a low price).

(f) **Workforce**. A justification for expanding into developing countries is to take advantage of lower wages. However, an organisation also needs to recognise **cultural differences** between countries.

(g) **Exchange rate fluctuations** may turn profits into losses and vice versa.

(h) **Risk**. Some overseas operations may be a greater risk than others so that higher returns may be required from them.

(i) **Life cycle**. The same product may be at different stages in its product life cycle in each country.

(j) **Transport**. If a subsidiary in, say, the United Kingdom is performing much worse, and incurring higher unit costs of production than a comparable subsidiary in, say, Germany, it may still be uneconomic to switch production from the United Kingdom to Germany because the extra costs of transport to the UK may exceed the savings in the costs of production.

(k) **Domestic competition**. The market of the overseas subsidiary may face a unique configuration of Porter's five forces.

(l) **Different economic conditions**.

Increasing demands that larger companies adopt the principles of **corporate social responsibility** complicate the problem of controlling the activities of foreign subsidiaries. The corporate **mission statement** can be useful here, if it incorporates the aspirations and standards promoted by all stakeholder groups, not just those of shareholders. Such a mission statement can be incorporated into divisional

performance measurement schemes that can also reflect the particular national and industrial circumstances of each division.

9.1 International comparisons

If the firms or subsidiaries being compared operate in different countries there will be certain problems for performance measurement.

(a)   **Realistic standards.** It may be difficult to establish realistic standards for each different country. Performance standards should take account of local conditions, considering local opportunities as well as any restrictions on the activities of an operating unit in a particular country.

(b)   **Controllable cash flows**. Care must be taken to determine which cash flows are controllable and to separate these from those outside the control of local management. In particular the distortions caused by local taxation laws should be eliminated.

(c)   **Currency conversion.** Considerable friction and difficulty in measuring performance can be caused by the use of inappropriate currency conversion rates.

(d)   **Basis for comparison.** Following on from the problem of setting realistic standards of performance, central management must exercise care when attempting to compare performance between the different countries.

Normal procedures may have to be adjusted.

(a)   **Reports**

   (i)   **Standardised** to allow comparative analysis between subsidiaries
   (ii)   Use an agreed **common language** and currency
   (iii)   **Frequent** as necessary to allow proper management
   (iv)   Cover all the **information needs** of headquarters

(b)   **Meetings**

   Meetings between HQ executives and subsidiary management allow for more intensive information exchange and monitoring, and minimise misunderstandings. They do however take up time and resources, and are generally not as regular as reports.

(c)   **Information technology**

   The transmission speed of mail and Internet communications makes close monitoring of marketing and financial performance much easier. Video conference meetings allow both financial and time savings to be made.

(d)   **Control of intermediaries**

   The problem with controlling 'outsiders' is that there is no control by **ownership**. In the final analysis **negative controls** such as legal pressures or threats to discontinue relationships can be used, resulting perhaps in loss of business. The best control is through good selection and by making it clear to intermediaries that their interests and the company's coincide.

9.2 Exchange rates and transfer pricing

The most obvious problem is the exchange rate, but *Ward* argues that this may not be serious.

(a)   A firm which makes an investment in a factory intends to use the factory, not sell it. So whilst changes in exchange rates alter the value of the original investment this does not matter so much in the long term, providing that the subsidiary is making a profit at the same rate, in local terms.

(b)   This might seem a rather dangerous assertion but it is sometimes asserted that long-term differences in rates of exchange result from inflation.

10 Transfer pricing

Introduction

Transfer pricing is used to encourage optimal performance by keeping track of costs incurred throughout a business. Ideally, prices should be set by reference to the **external market**, but where this is not possible transfer prices will have to be **negotiated,** or head office might **impose** a transfer price.

KEY TERM

TRANSFER PRICE is the 'price at which goods or services are transferred between different units in the same company. May be set on a number of bases, such as marginal cost, full cost, market price or negotiation. For the transfer of goods between units in different countries, tax implications mean that the respective governments have to accept the method used. They are likely to insist on *arm's-length transfer prices*.'   (CIMA *Official Terminology*)

Where there are **transfers of goods or services between divisions**, the transfers could be made 'free' to the division receiving the benefit. For example, if a garage and car showroom has two divisions, one for car repairs and servicing and the other for sales, the servicing division will be required to service cars before they are sold. The servicing division could do its work for the car sales division without making any record of the work done. However, unless the cost or value of such work is recorded, management cannot keep a check on the amount of resources (such as labour time) being used up on new car servicing. It is necessary for control purposes that some record of the inter-divisional services should be kept. Inter-divisional work can be given a cost or charge: a **transfer price**.

Transfer prices are a way of promoting **divisional autonomy**, ideally without prejudicing the measurement of **divisional performance** or discouraging overall **corporate profit maximisation**. The management accountant must devise a method of transfer pricing which meets three criteria.

- **Equity** (provides a fair measure of divisional performance)
- **Neutrality** (avoids the distortion of business decision making)
- **Administrative simplicity**

The transfer price should provide an **'artificial' selling price** that enables the transferring division to earn a return for its efforts, and the receiving division to incur a cost for benefits received, and should be set at a level that enables profit centre performance to be measured 'commercially'. This means that the transfer price should be a **fair commercial price**.

10.1 Transfer pricing with constant unit variable costs and sales prices

An ideal transfer price should reflect **opportunity cost.** Where a **perfect external market price exists** and unit variable costs and sales prices are constant, the opportunity cost of transfer will be one or other of the following

- External market price
- External market price less savings in selling costs

10.2 Example: transferring goods at market price

A company has two profit centres, A and B. Centre A sells half of its output on the open market and transfers the other half to B. Costs and external revenues in a period are as follows.

	A	B	Total
	£	£	£
External sales	8,000	24,000	32,000
Costs of production	12,000	10,000	22,000
Company profit			10,000

Required

What are the consequences of setting a transfer price at market price?

If the transfer price is at market price, A would be happy to sell the output to B for £8,000, which is what A would get by selling it externally.

	A £	A £	B £	B £	Total £
Market sales		8,000		24,000	32,000
Transfer sales		8,000		–	
		16,000		24,000	
Transfer costs			8,000		
Own costs	12,000		10,000		22,000
		12,000		18,000	
Profit		4,000		6,000	10,000

The consequences are as follows.

(a)	**A earns the same profit** on transfers as on external sales. B must pay a commercial price for transferred goods.

(b)	A will be indifferent about selling externally or transferring goods to B because the profit is the same on both types of transaction. B can therefore ask for and obtain as many units as it wants from A.

10.3 Adjusted market price

Internal transfers in practice are often cheaper than external sales, with savings in selling and administration costs, bad debt risks and possibly transport/delivery costs. It would seem reasonable for the buying division to expect a **discount** on the external market price.

If profit centres are established, however, and unit variable costs and sales prices are constant, there are two possibilities.

(a)	Where the supplying division has spare capacity the ideal transfer price will simply be the **standard variable cost of production.**

(b)	When there is a scarce production resource, the ideal transfer price will be the variable cost of production plus the contribution forgone by using the scarce resource instead of putting it to its most profitable alternative use.

10.4 Cost-based approaches to transfer pricing

Cost-based approaches to transfer pricing are often used in practice, where there is no external market for the product being transferred, or the external market is imperfect due to limited external demand.

10.4.1 Transfer prices based on full cost

Under this approach the full standard cost (including fixed overheads absorbed) incurred by the supplying division in making the product is charged to the receiving division. If a **full cost plus** approach is used, a profit margin is also included in this transfer price.

A company has 2 profit centres, A and B. Centre A can only sell half of its maximum output externally because of limited demand. It transfers the other half of its output to B which also faces limited demand. Costs and revenues in a period are as follows.

	A £	B £	Total £
External sales	8,000	24,000	32,000
Costs of production in the division	12,000	10,000	22,000
(Loss)/ profit	(4,000)	14,000	10,000

If the transfer price is at full cost, A in our example would have 'sales' to B of £6,000 (ie half of its total costs of production). This would be a cost to B, as follows:

	A		B		Total
	£	£	£	£	£
Open market sales		8,000		24,000	32,000
Transfer sales		6,000		–	
Total sales, inc transfers		14,000		24,000	
Transfer costs			6,000		
Own costs	12,000		10,000		22,000
Total costs, inc transfers		12,000		16,000	
Profit		2,000		8,000	10,000

The transfer sales of A are self-cancelling with the transfer costs of B so that total profits are unaffected. The transfer price simply spreads the total profit of £10,000 between A and B. Division A makes no profit on its work and using this method, would prefer to sell its output on the open market if it could.

10.4.2 Transfer prices based on full cost plus

If the transfers are at cost plus a margin of, say, 25%, A's sales to B would be £7,500.

	A		B		Total
	£	£	£	£	£
Open market sales		8,000		24,000	32,000
Transfer sales		7,500		–	
		15,500		24,000	
Transfer costs			7,500		
Own costs	12,000		10,000		22,000
		12,000		17,500	
Profit		3,500		6,500	10,000

Compared to a transfer price at cost, A gains some profit at the expense of B. However, A makes a bigger profit on external sales in this case because the profit mark-up of 25% is less than the profit mark-up on open market sales, which is (£8,000 – 6,000)/£6,000 = 33%. The transfer price does not give A fair revenue or charge B a reasonable cost, and so their profit performance is distorted. It would seem to give A an incentive to sell more goods externally and transfer less to B. This may or may not be in the best interests of the company as a whole.

Division A's total costs of £12,000 will include an element of fixed costs. Half of division A's total costs are transferred to division B. However from the point of view of division B the cost is entirely variable.

Suppose that the cost per unit to A is £15 and that this includes a fixed element of £6, while division B's own costs are £25 per unit, including a fixed element of £10. The total variable cost is really £9 + £15 = £24, but from division B's point of view the variable cost is £15 + £15 = £30. This means that division B will be unwilling to sell the final product for less than £30, whereas any price above £24 would make a contribution.

10.4.3 Transfer prices based on variable cost

A variable cost approach entails charging the variable cost that has been incurred by the supplying division to the receiving division. As above, we shall suppose that A's cost per unit is £15, of which £6 is fixed and £9 variable.

	A		B		Company as a whole	
	£	£	£	£	£	£
Market sales		8,000		24,000		32,000
Transfer sales at variable cost		3,600		–		
($£9/£15 \times 6,000$)						
		11,600		24,000		
Transfer costs			3,600			
Own variable costs	7,200		6,000		13,200	
Own fixed costs	4,800		4,000		8,000	
Total costs and transfers		12,000		13,600		22,000
(Loss)/Profit		(400)		10,400		10,000

The problem is that with a transfer price at variable cost the supplying division does not cover its fixed costs.

10.5 Transfer prices based on opportunity costs

It has been suggested that transfer prices can be set using the following rule.

Transfer price per unit = **standard variable cost** in the producing division plus the opportunity cost to the organisation of supplying the unit internally.

The opportunity cost will be one of the following.

(a) The maximum **contribution foregone** by the supplying division in transferring internally rather than selling externally

(b) The **contribution foregone** by not using the same facilities in the producing division for their next best alternative use

(c) If there is no external market for the item being transferred, and no alternative uses for the division's facilities, the transfer price = standard variable cost of production.

(d) If there is an external market for the item being transferred and no alternative use for the facilities, the transfer price = the market price.

10.6 Transfer pricing when unit variable costs and sales prices are not constant

When unit variable costs and/or unit selling prices are not constant there will be a profit-maximising level of output and the ideal transfer price will only be found by careful analysis and sensible negotiation.

(a) The starting point should be to establish the output and sales quantities that will optimise the profits of the company or group as a whole.

(b) The next step is to establish the transfer price at which both profit centres, the supply division and the buying division, would maximise their profits at this company-optimising output level.

(c) There may be a range of prices within which both profit centres can agree on the output level that would maximise their individual profits and the profits of the company as a whole. Any price within the range would then be 'ideal'.

10.7 Problems in transfer pricing

(a) If transfer prices are set at **full cost** the transferring division makes no profit.

(b) If **full cost plus** is used the problem is how to set the margin at a level that all parties perceive as being fair.

(c) If **variable cost** is used the transferring division does not cover its fixed costs but two-part prices (the variable cost transfer price plus a fixed annual fee) might be used to overcome this.

(d) Transfer prices based on **standard cost** are fairer than transfer prices based on actual costs because if actual costs are used the transferring division has no incentive to control its costs: it can pass on its inefficiencies to the receiving division.

(e) On the other hand, standards may become out of date so it is advisable to have an agreement to revise them periodically.

10.8 Negotiated transfer prices

When authority is decentralised to the extent that divisional managers negotiate transfer prices with each other, the agreed price may be finalised from a mixture of accounting arithmetic, politics and compromise.

Inter-departmental disputes about transfer prices are likely to arise and these may need the intervention of head office to settle the problem.

(a)   **Head office imposition**. Head office management may impose a price which maximises the profit of the company as a whole.

(b)   On the other hand, head office management might restrict its intervention to the task of **keeping negotiations in progress** until a transfer price is eventually settled.

Where **negotiation** is necessary there should be an understanding of the 'risk/return' profile. *Tomkins* suggests the following methodology, which head office can apply when mediating in disputes.

(a)   **Identify the outer bounds of the transfer price**. In other words, at what transfer price does the buying division end up earning the entire group profit, and at what transfer price does the selling division earn the entire group profit?

(b)   **Variability**. At each transfer price, compare each division's expected profits and the variability of the profits.

(c)   Incorporate **risk attitudes** in a fair transfer price, so that the profit-share between divisions takes the riskiness of the project into consideration.

10.9 International transfer prices

When firms transfer goods and services *internally*, but also *internationally*, the transfer price mechanism allows them to **move value from one country to another** without actually engaging in trade. Bearing in mind the difficulty discussed above of establishing the level at which a transfer price should be set, we may say that a 'low' price effectively moves value into the receiving country, while a 'high' one moves it into the transferring country.

10.9.1 Using transfer prices

This ability to decide in which country value (and particularly *profit*) is created is extremely useful.

(a)   It can be used to **manage taxation**.

(i)   Profit can be minimised in states with high profits taxes.

(ii)   Selling prices can be minimised in states with high levels of irrecoverable VAT (and similar taxes).

(iii) The value imported into countries with high tariff levels can be minimised.

(b)   It can be used to **move profits to the home country** from states with restrictions on repatriation of profits or on currency exchange.

(c)   It can be used strategically.

(i)   It can **disguise the attractiveness** of an operation to competitors by reducing profits.

(ii)   It can enable a **low-price strategy aimed at driving out competition** without arousing the suspicions of the local tax authorities by declaring a very low level of profit. However, this course of action is likely to lead to accusations of dumping.

10.9.2 Centrally determined transfer prices and strategy

These considerations produce pressure for multinational companies to set their transfer prices centrally. There are, however, other important strategic considerations relating to this approach.

(a)   **Autonomy**. Centrally determined transfer prices can seriously affect the ability of national managers to **influence the performance of their divisions**. This can affect their overall motivation, encourage them to seek ways around the restrictions imposed and make it more difficult to assess their overall performance.

(b)   **Transaction cost economics**. Transaction cost theory is dealt with in Paper E2 but it is also relevant to Paper E3. In terms of transaction cost economics, a centrally determined, non-market based transfer price makes an implicit assumption that the **hierarchy solution** is the best one. However, there may not have been any actual consideration of the market alternative. A resource or competence based approach to strategy would immediately challenge this and call for detailed consideration of the benefit a market based approach. The crucial question is whether the business should actually be operating any given national subsidiary at all, or whether its services should be bought in.

10.10 The Eccles matrix

R J Eccles suggested that the method of setting transfer prices should reflect the organisation's **degree of diversification** and its **degree of vertical integration**.

(a)   Where both diversification and integration are low, as, for example, in the relationship between two shops in a retail chain, a transfer price may not even be required, but if it is, it can be set collaboratively.

(b)   Where diversification is low, but vertical integration is high, as in the relationship between two different stages of product assembly, co-operation is important, so the transfer price should be negotiated: it should probably be set at full cost so that resource allocation is appropriate and the supplying division's costs are covered.

(c)   Where diversification is high and integration is low, as in the now unfashionable diversified conglomerate, transfers are likely to be uncommon and should be at market price, as is the rest of each subsidiary's trade.

(d)   Nevertheless, where diversification and integration are both high, as may be the case when there is extensive trade along a supply chain combined with similarly extensive market-based exchanges, once again, the transfer price should be set collaboratively.

Section summary

Transfer prices are a way of promoting **divisional autonomy**, ideally without prejudging the measurement of **divisional performance** or discouraging overall **corporate profit maximisation**.

An ideal transfer price should reflect **opportunity cost**.

Cost-based approaches to transfer pricing are often used in practice, where there is no external market for the product being transferred, or the external market is imperfect due to limited external demand.

11 Divisional performance and control

Introduction

Many organisations are split into different business units, with authority and responsibility being devolved to managers with specific areas of responsibility. However, this raises potential problems as to how to appraise the performance of these managers, if aspects of the performance of their business units depends on factors which they cannot control.

When measuring the performance of a business unit or a division, one of the key issues is distinguishing which items the manager of that business unit can control (and therefore they should be held accountable for) and those items over which they have no control (and therefore they should not be held accountable for).

The principle of **controllability** dictates that **managers should only be made accountable for those aspects of performance they can control**. In this respect, the controllability principle suggests that uncontrollable items (such as, for example, reapportioned head office costs) should either be eliminated from any reports which are used to measures manager's performance, or that the effects of these uncontrollable items are calculated and then the relevant reports should distinguish between controllable and uncontrollable items.

In practice, the controllability principle can be very difficult to apply, because many **areas do not fit neatly into controllable and uncontrollable categories**. For example, if a competitor lowers their prices, this may be seen as an uncontrollable action. However, a manager could respond to the competitor's action by changing the company's own prices, which could then reduce the adverse effect of the competitor's actions. So, in effect, there are both controllable and uncontrollable actions here.

Similarly, if a supplier increases the price of their product, this may be seen as an uncontrollable action. However, a manager could respond by looking to change supplier or by using a different product in order to reduce the adverse impact of the supplier's actions. Again, there are potentially both controllable and uncontrollable actions here.

Accordingly, any analysis of performance would need to consider the impact of the competitor or supplier's actions as one element, and then the impact of manager's response as a second element.

11.1 Controllable costs

Controllability can also be a particular issue when looking at costs within companies.

Consider the following example:

A company has three operating divisions and a head office. The divisional managers think it is unfair that a share of indirect costs – such as central Finance, HR, Legal and Administration costs – are included in their divisional results because the divisional managers cannot control these costs.

Importantly, however, there is a distinction here between considering the divisional **manager's** performance and the **division's performance** as a whole.

Horngren provides a good illustration of this:

'The most **skilful divisional manager is often put in charge of the sickest division in an attempt to change its fortunes**. Such an attempt may take years, not months. Furthermore the manager's efforts may merely result in bringing the division up to a minimum acceptable ROI. The division may continue to be a poor profit performer in comparison with other divisions. If top management relied solely on the absolute ROI to judge management, the skilful manager would be foolish to accept such a trouble-shooting assignment.'

In order to evaluate the **performance of the divisional manager**, then only those items which are directly controllable by the manager should be included in the performance measures. So, in our mini example,

the share of indirect costs re-apportioned from the head office should not be included. These costs can only be controlled where they are incurred. Therefore the relevant head office managers should be held accountable for them. As the divisional managers have suggested, it would be unfair to judge them for this aspect of performance.

However, in order for the head office to evaluate the **division's overall performance** for decision-making purposes (for example, in relation to growth, or divestment) it is appropriate to include a share of the head office costs. If divisional performance is measured only on those amounts the divisional manager can control, this will overstate the economic performance of the division. If the divisions were independent companies, they would have to incur the costs of those services which are currently provided by the head office (for example, finance and HR costs). Therefore, in order to measure the economic performance of the division these central costs, plus any interest expenses and taxes, should included within the measure of the division's performance.

Impact on information requirements

The potential requirements to measure different aspects of performance (eg, manager's performance; divisional performance) could have important implications for a management accounting system. The system will need to be able to produce the different types of report required, or distinguish between controllable and non-controllable costs as necessary. If the management accountant cannot produce the reports required, then any performance measurement based on those reports also cannot be undertaken.

11.2 Rewarding managers

Rewarding managers for their performance is a method of **control**, although money is not the only type of reward they may seek. Managers may also look for power, status and responsibility.

Rewarding managers for their performance is a method of control in the sense that it is **assumed that attempts will be made to achieve the organisation's objectives in return for rewards.** This, in turn, **derives from motivation theory,** which suggests that people have wants or desired outcomes and modify their behaviour accordingly.

11.2.1 What type of reward?

Money is not the only type of reward that managers might seek. Vancil categorised rewards into three types.

- The **pleasure** that is derived from **managing one's own entity**
- The **power and status** that accompanies the position of being manager
- Rewards in the form of **money** or with **a monetary value**

11.2.2 How to link performance and rewards

A good reward system should have the following characteristics.

(a)   It should **offer real incentives**, sufficiently high after tax to make extraordinary effort worthwhile.

(b)   It should **relate payments to criteria over which the individual has control** (otherwise he will feel helpless to ensure his reward, and the expectancy element in motivation will be lacking).

(c)   It should **make clear the basis on which payments are calculated**, and all the conditions that apply, so that individuals can make the calculation of whether the reward is worth the extra level of effort.

(d)   It should be **flexible** enough to reward different levels of achievement in proportion, and with provision for regular review and adaptation to the changing needs of the organisation.

(e)   It should be **cost effective** for the organisation.

11.2.3 Common types of scheme

There are three common types of scheme.

(a)   Under a **profit-related pay scheme**, pay (or part of it) is related to results achieved (performance to defined standards in key tasks, according to plan). A form of **management by objectives** will probably be applied.

(b)   **Profit-sharing schemes** offer managers bonuses, perhaps in the form of shares in the company, related directly to profits.

(c)   **Group incentive schemes** typically offer a bonus for a group (equally, or proportionately to the earnings or status of individuals) which achieves or exceeds specified targets.

Incentive and recognition schemes are **increasingly focused not on cash**, but on non-cash awards, such as gifts and travel vouchers. These are cheaper for the organisation, especially as they are regarded as 'won' rather than deserved by right.

Schemes should of course be **tailored to suit the circumstances**. A bonus scheme for part-time non-executive directors remunerated by fees under contract for a fixed term of years should ensure that they take a longer-term view of the organisation in the interests of shareholders.

11.3 Problems with incentive schemes

One of the major dangers of incentive schemes is that they may lead to sub-optimisation, particularly in relation to incentive schemes for divisional managers. Sub-optimisation refers to actions or strategies that appear to be beneficial but aren't. Examples of sub-optimisation might be:

Short-termism – actions taken to achieve short-run performance targets at the expense of the long run performance.

Dysfunctionality – actions taken because they benefit one division although they may not benefit the organisation overall.

Risk of manipulation – excessive pressure to hit results (in order to quality for an inventive) may result in a culture where it is considered acceptable to use 'creative accounting' to improve the reported figures.

11.3.1 Short-termism

Although the usual argument is that strategic decisions should look at the long term and should avoid short-termism, there are still some problems associated with performance measures and incentives specifically designed to avoid short-termism.

(a)   The link between current expenditure or savings and long-term effect may not be clear.

(b)   There is a danger that investment for the future may have such an adverse impact on present performance that the future envisaged is impossible to achieve. In the worst case, if current performance deteriorates too far, an organisation may not actually have a future.

(c)   Incentive schemes for long-term achievements may not motivate, since effort and reward are too distant in time from each other (or managers may not think that they will be around that long!).

A short-term approach may be appropriate in certain circumstances:

•   In **highly uncertain and changeable situations**, for example in the fashion industry

•   When a short-term approach is **consistent with long-term goals** (for instance a business may make do with old, inefficient plant, awaiting the availability of a new technology)

•   When **stakeholders also take a short-term view**

•   When **competitors** do likewise

•   Under **financial constraints** or difficulties such as workflow problems or insolvency

- Some organisations have **duties to maintain a certain financial position**

11.3.2 Problems of motivation

Incentive schemes will only work if **rewards** seem both **desirable and achievable.**

(a) **Money is not the only motivator** – different individuals value different types of reward. Some people may be in a job because it offers **'job for life'** security and a pension; although current working practices have made this less common it is still true in areas of the public sector and large 'institutionalised' companies. **Personal objectives** may also be important; public sector nurses or teachers may feel they are following a vocation regardless of the rewards offered.

(b) When an individual's work performance is dependent on work done by other people (and much work involves co-operation and interdependence with others), an **individual bonus scheme is not always effective**, since **individual performance can be impaired by what other people have done.**

(c) There is evidence that the **effectiveness** of incentive schemes **wears off over time**, as acceptable 'norms' of working are re-established.

(d) The **value of a reward may be affected by factors beyond the organisation's control.** For example a reward such as a company car (associated with achieving a certain status) may be so highly taxed that managers do not consider the effort of achieving the reward to be worthwhile.

11.4 Problems with performance measures

One of the main problems of poorly designed performance management systems is that they can send the wrong signals to managers, and can encourage dysfunctional behaviour.

Berry, Broadbent and Otley have identified the following problems which could accompany the use of performance measures.

(a) **Tunnel vision** (undue focus on performance measures to the detriment of other areas). For example, if a performance measure for an accountancy firm is the staff utilisation ratio in terms of chargeable hours as a proportion of total hours, this may lead to an insufficient amount of time being spent on staff development or training.

(b) **Sub-optimisation** (focus on some objectives so that others are not achieved). For example, if an audit partner focuses too much on winning new clients, this may lead to inadequate time being given to managing relationships with existing clients and supervising the work being done on the audits of those clients.

(c) **Myopia** (short-sightedness leading to the neglect of longer-term objectives). For example, the audit firm might be focussed on maximising client revenues rather than investing in the technology to provide automated audit software which will generate efficiency savings in the future.

(d) **Measure fixation** (measures and behaviour in order to achieve specific performance indicators which may not be effective). For example, if the audit firm's primary objective is to reduce costs on its audits, this may lead it to use staff who are too junior for the complexity of the work involved at particular clients. This may lead to client dissatisfaction (and loss of clients) or extra costs when a more senior member of staff has to re-do work which is unsatisfactory or incomplete.

(e) **Misrepresentation** ('creative' reporting to suggest that a result is acceptable). For example, the audit firm may produce a report saying that 90% of its clients have expressed complete satisfaction with the service they have received. But if the firm only sent its client satisfaction survey to a carefully selected number of clients, rather than all its client, the satisfaction score is misleading.

(f) **Misinterpretation** (failure to recognise the complexity of the environment in which the organisation operates). Within the accountancy firm, one partner might be focused on winning new business from large, national clients, another might be focused on winning new business from small, local

clients, while a third might be focused on selling additional services to existing clients. In this scenario, the motives of the different partners creates a complex environment in which the objectives of the firm's key players may conflict.

(g)   **Gaming** (deliberate distortion of a measure to secure some strategic advantage). This might include deliberate under-performance in the current period to avoid higher targets being set in future periods. For example, assume an audit manager spots an opportunity to sell some additional services to a client, but knows the audit firm is already on target to exceed budgeted profit for the current period. The manager may suggest that the consultancy work begins in the next period, with the hope that the additional services help create a favourable performance to budget in that period as well.

(h)   **Ossification** (an unwillingness to change the performance measure scheme once it has been set up). For example, the questions in the audit firm's questionnaire may be poorly designed and don't give clients the opportunity to comment on some aspects of the firm's offering. However, because the firm gets good responses from the questionnaire in its current form, it may be unwilling to change the questionnaire.

As a general point, these problems also highlight the issue of **congruence between the goals of individuals** and the **goals of the organisation.**

Section summary

Results measures work most effectively when the individuals whose performance is being measured are able to control and influence the results. **Managerial performance** should be assessed on those items that are directly controlled by the manager in question.

If **controllable factors** cannot be separated from **uncontrollable factors** then the results control measures are unlikely to provide any useful information for evaluating the actions taken by individuals.

Moreover, if the outcomes of desirable behaviours are offset by the impact of uncontrollable factors, then results measures will lose any motivational impact, and will create the impression that they are unfair.

12   Strategic management styles

Introduction

Goold and Campbell identified three major approaches to running divisionalised conglomerates: **strategic planning, strategic control** and **financial control.**

The **role of the corporate centre** in a divisionalised company has been the subject of much theory and research. Indeed, the diversified conglomerate itself has itself been challenged as a form of economic organisation. There are **three generally accepted possible roles for the centre**.

*   Determination of overall strategy and the allocation of resources
*   Controlling divisional performance
*   Provision of central services

All three of these roles have been subject to debate.

Centralised determination of strategy has been challenged as inappropriate in a diversified conglomerate. Similarly, **resource allocation**, it has been suggested, is the proper role of **capital markets**; and the rigour of the vetting carried out by central staff has been questioned.

Controlling divisional performance is subject to all the arguments for and against decentralisation already discussed. The ability of the centre to prevent **strategic drift** has been questioned, though the radical market alternative can only work in drastic ways, such as takeover.

Centralised provision of certain **services**, such as legal and HR departments, is promoted as enhancing efficiency through the attainment of economies of scale. However, it is also suggested that many of these services can be contracted for locally at no greater cost and with the advantage of precluding any tendency to empire-building at the centre.

12.1 Research

Goold and Campbell researched the role of the centre in 16 British-based conglomerates. They concentrated on the first two roles summarised above, which they referred to as **planning influence** and **control influence**. The variation in these roles allowed the identification of eight distinct **strategic management styles**.

Planning influence was exercised in a variety of ways, but a fairly smooth spectrum of styles was observable, ranging from minimal, where the centre is little more than a holding company, to highly centralised, where the managers in the business units have responsibility only for operational decisions.

Control influence was exercised by the agreement of **objectives**, the monitoring of **results** and the deployment of **pressures and incentives**. This gave rise to three distinct categories of control influence: **flexible strategic**, **tight strategic** and **tight financial**.

Of the eight strategic management styles they defined, Goold and Campbell found that three of them were particularly common; each was associated with one of the three **control influence** categories mentioned above and with a different degree of **planning influence**.

12.2 Strategic management styles

12.2.1 Strategic planning

The strategic planning management style is associated with a fairly high degree of central planning influence, but less control influence. The centre does not impose rigid targets and constraints over the divisions. The strategic planning process is the main mechanism for the corporate centre's control over the divisions.

The **centre establishes extensive planning processes** through which it works with business unit managers to make substantial contributions to strategic thinking, often with a unifying overall corporate strategy. The strategic planning process involves a lot of dialogue between the corporate centre and each division. Performance targets are set in broad terms, with an **emphasis on longer-term strategic objectives**, which arise from the planning process. The corporate centre also allocates resources to different divisions according to its view of the group's need to secure competitive advantage in certain divisions.

Business units tend to follow bold strategies and often achieve above industry average **growth** and **profitability**.

12.2.2 Strategic control

The strategic control management style involves a **fairly low degree of planning influence** but uses **tight strategic control**. The centre prefers to leave the planning initiative to the business unit managers, though it will **review** their plans for acceptability. **Firm targets are set** for a range of performance indicators and performance is judged against them. However, within this framework of group objectives and goals (laid down by the corporate centre) divisions are allowed to pursue their own business strategies. The centre allocates resources to the divisions according to long-term strategic considerations, but it only does so in response to requests from the divisions for resources.

The centre concentrates on rationalising the portfolio. Such companies achieve **good profits** but are **less successful at achieving growth**.

12.2.3 Financial control

The centre exercises influence almost entirely through the budget process. It takes little interest in business unit strategy, and divisions make their own strategic decisions. Financial control companies do not have formal long-term strategies; instead any strategic decisions revolve around the annual budgeting process.

The centre exercises control through financial targets (eg, ROCE, profit). Careers are at stake if budgets are missed, and managerial rewards and progression are based on meeting budget targets. Strategies are **cautious** and rarely global. Business unit managers tend to sacrifice market share to achieve high profits. As a result, these companies produce **excellent profits**, but **growth comes mainly from acquisitions**.

In general, the corporate centre allocates resources and funds requested by the divisions, provided that the centre is convinced by the competence of divisional management. However, the centre will manage the acquisition or disposal of any subsidiaries or major assets.

Exam skills

Note that the strategic planning style identified by *Goold and Campbell* is a specific term used in relation to management styles. Do not confuse this with the concept of strategic planning in general – for example, the ideas of the rational model and strategic options.

Question 13.6

Head office

Learning outcome D1(v)

XYZ has over 500 profit centres (covering a wide range or products and services) and it earns revenues of £7bn. Head office staff amount to 47. Each profit centre must provide the following:

(a) The *annual profit plan*. This is agreed in detail every year, after close negotiation. It is regarded as a commitment to a preordained level of performance.

(b) A *monthly management report*, which is extremely detailed (17 pages). Working capital is outlined in detail. Provisions (the easiest way to manipulate accounts) are highlighted.

Does XYZ have a strategic planning, a strategic control or financial control management style?

12.2.4 Influences on the choice of planning organisation

(a) Highly diversified groups are much more difficult to control from the centre, and a **financial controller** system would probably be suitable.

(b) When **big capital investments** are planned, head office should be involved in the decision.

(c) When **cash flow** is tight, other strategies must be sacrificed to the paramount concern for short term survival and attention to cash flow.

(d) Organisations in a single industry which is fairly stable would perhaps be more efficiently managed by a hierarchical, centralised management system, structured perhaps on a functional basis (production, marketing etc).

(e) Top management might prefer one approach.

Section summary

Goold and Campbell identified three different strategic management styles which the corporate centre uses when dealing with its business units. These styles (strategic planning, strategic control and financial control) reflect differences in the level of planning influence and control influence the centre has over its division.

Chapter Roundup

✓ Control can be described as the management of an organisation's activities in accordance with strategic plans and objectives. Three levels of control can be identified: strategic, managerial and operational.

✓ **Inflation** affects base line and comparative figures, making it difficult to compare performance over time. Organisations generally build assumptions about the rate of inflation into their strategic plans.

✓ Capital expenditure decisions should be based on an evaluation of future cash flows, discounted at an appropriate cost of capital to an NPV.

✓ Contribution margins can be used for measuring performance and as a tool for decision making.

✓ **Return on investment (ROI)** is based on organisational structure, not business processes, and is only suitable to products at the mature phase of the life cycle. The problems with ROI relate to accurate measurement.

✓ An alternative to ROI for measuring the performance of an investment centre is **residual income** (RI). This avoids some of the problems of ROI, by deducting from profit an imputed interest charge for the use of assets. However, RI does not facilitate comparisons between investment centres, nor does it relate the size of a centre's income to the size of the investment.

✓ When comparing **profit centres,** managers should only be held accountable for those revenues and costs that they are in a position to control. Controllable costs can be isolated using a variety of measures involving **contribution**.

✓ Interfirm comparisons are comparisons of the performance of different companies, subsidiaries or investment centres. Ratios are useful in that they provide a means of comparison of actual results.

✓ **Shareholders** require managers to **maximise the value of their investment** in the organisation. Performance indicators assess how well this duty is carried out.

✓ **Economic value** management hinges in the idea of an economic profit, which is derived after adjusting traditional accounting profits for the write offs that are made for **value building expenditures** such as training and advertising. By adding such expenditures back to accounting profit, better comparison can be made between companies.

✓ Market value added is the difference between the market value of a company and the economic book value of capital employed.

✓ Total shareholder return is the total percentage return to shareholders over a given period.

✓ Objective setting for multinationals is complex. Problems can arise with performance measurement due to realistic standards country to country, controllability of cash flows and currency conversion. Normal procedures may have to be adjusted. The most obvious problem is the exchange rate. Levels of control and staffing can also be problems when managing overseas subsidiaries.

✓ Transfer prices are a way of promoting **divisional autonomy**, ideally without prejudging the measurement of **divisional performance** or discouraging overall **corporate profit maximisation**.

✓ An ideal transfer price should reflect **opportunity cost**.

✓ **Cost-based approaches to transfer pricing** are often used in practice, where there is no external market for the product being transferred, or the external market is imperfect due to limited external demand.

✓ Results measures work most effectively when the individuals whose performance is being measured are able to control and influence the results. **Managerial performance** should be assessed on those items that are directly controlled by the manager in question.

✓ If **controllable factors** cannot be separate from **uncontrollable factors** then the results control measures are unlikely to provide any useful information for evaluating the actions taken by individuals.

✓   Moreover, if the outcomes of desirable behaviours are offset by the impact of uncontrollable factors, then results measures will lose any motivational impact, and will create the impression that they are unfair.

✓   *Goold and Campbell* identified three different strategic management styles which the corporate centre uses when dealing with its business units. These styles (strategic planning, strategic control and financial control) reflect differences in the level of planning influence and control influence the centre has over its division.

Quick Quiz

1   Control of a strategic level should be based on measurements of ....

2   Define 'contribution margin'.

3   What is the main problem associated with ROI as a performance measure?

4   ROI is a form of ROCE.

         ☐   True

         ☐   False

5   Residual income (RI) is a measure of the centre's profits after deducting a notional or imputed .... cost.

6   What do you understand by the term 'divisional autonomy'?

7   What are 'controllable profit' and 'controllable margin'?

8   Give a broad definition of 'added value'.

9   In what way can inflation conceal poor performance?

10   What are the three main strategic management styles identified by Goold and Campbell?

Answers to Quick Quiz

1   Cash flows

2   Contribution margin can be defined as 'the difference between sales volume and the variable cost of those sales, expressed either in absolute terms or as a contribution per unit.'

3   It is mainly to do with the problem of accurate measurement of the value of the assets used to produce the return. For example, it is probably most common to use return on net assets. Inflation and technological change alter the cost of fixed assets, so that it becomes difficult to compare the performance of different divisions.

4   True

5   Interest

6   The term refers to the right of a division to govern itself, that is, the freedom to make decisions without consulting a higher authority first and without interference from a higher body.

7   Controllable profit – contribution minus all the division's fixed costs controllable by the manager.

         Controllable margin – controllable profit minus all other costs directly traceable to the division.

8   Added value equals sales minus the costs of materials and bought-in-services

9   An organisation may be making a profit, but have suffered a fall in its operating capacity. Using the historical cost accounting convention, a company might have assets in its balance sheet valued on the basis of costs dating back 5, 10, 20, 30, or even 40 years or more. The costs of these assets would not be comparable with each other, partly because of technological developments over time, but largely because of inflation.

10   Strategic planning style
      Strategic control system
      Financial control style

Answers to Questions

13.1 Manipulation

(a)   Keep gross assets to a minimum

     (i)   Avoid capital expenditure

     (ii)   Acquire all assets on operating leases

(b)   Manipulate current assets

     (i)   Factor debtors (ie sell the debts)

     (ii)   Introduce over-generous settlement discounts, set not by the prevailing interest rate (the true cost) but by divisional ROI targets to encourage early payment.

     (iii)   Sell all inventories before the balance sheet date and repurchase them immediately after.

     (iv)   Refuse credit.

(c)   Manipulate the return by investing in projects with higher long-term risk even if they offered better short-term profits.

Compare these measures to the balanced scorecard: clearly they cause dysfunctional behaviour in customer relations and in internal processes (eg inventory management). Too much effort is devoted to manipulating the figures, not improving the business.

(Note. This exercise is based on an example cited by Ward in *Strategic Management Accounting*.)

13.2 Head office

Decentralisation recognises that those closest to a job are the best equipped to say how it should be done and that people tend to perform to a higher standard if they are given responsibility. Centrally imposed decisions are likely to make managers feel that they do not really have any authority and therefore that they cannot be held responsible for performance. They will therefore make less effort to perform well.

13.3 Strategic significance

(a)   The firm is using capital efficiently – or is operating at high capacity.

(b)   The firm has to reach a high profit level to pay its lenders – it might have less flexibility in pricing than competitors.

(c)   This might imply that the firm is more capital-intensive, in other words that perhaps it has invested in technology rather than labour. Given the high level of fixed costs which can be deduced from this, the firm might have to price aggressively to maintain market share.

13.4 Subsidiaries

	A Ltd £	B Ltd £
ROI	$\dfrac{£60,000}{£300,000} \times 100\% = 20\%$	$\dfrac{£120,000}{£800,000} \times 100\% = 20\%$
Asset turnover	$\dfrac{£1,250,000}{£300,000} = 4.17 \text{ times}$	$\dfrac{£2,400,000}{£800,000} = 3 \text{ times}$
Profit/sales ratio	$\dfrac{£60,000}{£1,250,000} \times 100\% = 4.8\%$	$\dfrac{£120,000}{£2,400,000} \times 100\% = 5\%$

A Ltd has a higher ROI than B Ltd. This is because, although it earned a lower net profit per £1 of sales (4.8p compared with 5p) its capital employed generated more sales turnover, and its asset turnover was nearly 40% higher, at 4.17 times compared with 3 times for B Ltd.

13.5 Overcapacity

(a)

(i)   Pflatte sources from the UK (£1 = 20 ZAR)

	£	*Pflatte* ZAR	Yen equivalent
Selling price	–	2,000	28,000
Sourcing cost from UK	75 × 20	(1,500)	(21,000)
Transport from UK	10 × 20	(200)	(2,800)
Gross profit margin		300	4,200
Margin			15%

(ii)   Pflatte sourcing from the UK (£1 = 15 ZAR)

	£	ZAR	Yen
Selling price (ZAR)	–	2,000	28,000
Sourcing cost from UK	75 × 15	(1,125)	(15,750)
Transport from UK	10 × 15	(150)	(2,100)
Gross profit margin		725	10,150
Margin			36.2%

(b)

	£	ZAR	Yen
Revenue	–	2,000	28,000
Cost (UK)	(75)	–	15,000
Transport	(10)	–	2,000
Profit/(loss)	(85)	2,000	11,200

Tutorial note

Further permutations can be tried. For example the relative exchange rates between £ and Yen, and ZAR and Yen would also affect the decision. So, even though greater Yen profit is made by Pflatte, the differences in production costs can, at *some* rates of exchange, make it easier for Pflatte merely to sell andantes imported from Sharp. In option (b), no currency changes hands between Pflatte and Sharp, but at prevailing rates of exchange, it is still better for Pflatte to sell andantes made at Sharp than to make them itself.

13.6 Head office

Financial control.

Now try these questions from the Exam Question Bank

Number	Level	Marks	Time
Q15	Examination	25	45 mins
Q16	Examination	25	45 mins

ENTERPRISE PERFORMANCE MANAGEMENT

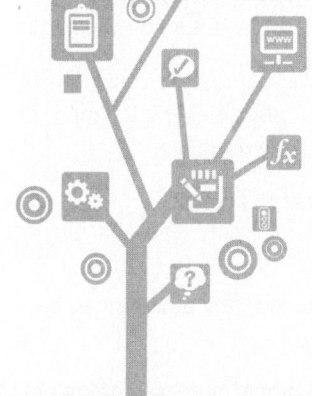

However well designed they are, the ultimate test of strategies is their impact on organisational performance. Therefore, it is very important that managers measure performance effectively, to assess how well an organisation is performing against its objectives.

Historically, organisations have relied purely on financial measures, but this created some problems, particularly in relating the short term to the long term.

Performance measurement is all about **communicating the objectives** of an organisation and concentrating efforts towards them. **Strategic control** (Section 2) indicates the need for a review of strategic performance over a whole host of measures, as opposed to just the numbers, although many organisations still use the traditional **budgetary**

control process as the main basis for measuring performance (Section 3).

The aim of strategic control is to review **long term** indicators of the business. The **balanced scorecard** (Section 5) is one way by which **financial and non-financial** (strategic) performance can be measured. Other multidimensional models of performance, chiefly the **performance pyramid,** are described in Section 6.

At **operational level,** some useful indicators of performance are given for both service and manufacturing businesses (Sections 7 and 8).

Finally, this chapter considers the impact of both legal and voluntary **regulation** on corporate performance. Corporate codes, for example on ethical issues, are becoming an increasingly important feature of business strategy.

topic list	learning outcomes	syllabus references	ability required
1 Control and performance measurement	D1(a)	D1(ii)	Recommend
2 Strategic control and critical success factors	D1(a)	D1(ii)	Recommend
3 Budgetary control systems	D1(a)	D1(ii)	Recommend
4 Performance measures: financial and non-financial	D1(a), D1(b)	D1(i), D1(vii)	Evaluate
5 The balanced scorecard	D1(b), D1(c)	D1(i), D1(vii)	Evaluate
6 Developing a performance measurement system	D1(c)	D1(vii), D1(ix)	Recommend
7 Other multidimensional measures of performance	D1(b), D1(c)	D1(i), D1(vii)	Evaluate
8 Performance: service departments and firms	–	D1(vii)	Recommend
9 Performance: manufacturing	–	D1(vii)	Recommend
10 Regulation and performance	–	D1(vii)	Recommend

1   Control and performance measurement

1.1 Control systems

Introduction

All systems of control can be analysed using the **cybernetic model**. The essence of this model is the **feedback** of control action to the controlled process: the control action itself being generated from the comparison of actual results with what was planned.

You should be familiar with the way that control systems work from your studies for E2 (or P5 if you studied under the old syllabus). However, we will revise the essentials here as a preparation for the material we cover in this chapter.

1.1.1 Cybernetic control

To some extent, planning and controlling are two sides of a single coin, since a plan is of little value if it is not put into action, while a system of control can only be effective if the people running it know what it is they are trying to achieve.

In the cybernetic system, an objective is established: for the organisation, this might be the current year's budget. Actual achievement is measured, perhaps by means of monthly reports, and a process of comparison takes place. In the organisation, managers fulfil this role by comparing budget and actual figures. They then take control action to make up for any failure to achieve the plan. This control action feeds back into the activity of the organisation and its effects should become apparent in the next monthly report. This **feedback loop** is the essence of any control system, though sometimes it may be difficult to discern its existence and operation.

KEY TERMS

FEEDBACK occurs when the results (outputs) of a system are used to control it, by adjusting the input or behaviour of the system. Businesses use feedback information to control their performance.

SINGLE LOOP FEEDBACK results in the system's behaviour being altered to meet the plan.

DOUBLE LOOP FEEDBACK can result in changes to the plan itself.

Emmanuel et al describe **four necessary conditions that must be satisfied before any process can be said to be controlled.** These will help us to put control into a wider context still.

(a)   **Objectives** for the process being controlled must exist, for without an aim or purpose control has no meaning.

(b)   The **output of** the process must be **measurable** in terms of the dimensions defined by the objectives.

(c)   A **predictive model** of the process being controlled is required so that causes for the non-attainment of objectives can be determined and proposed corrective actions evaluated.

(d)   There must be a **capability of taking action** so that deviations of attainment from objectives can be reduced.

It is important to understand that this concept of control involves more than just measuring results and taking corrective action. Control in the broad sense embraces the formulation of objectives – deciding what the things that need to be done are – as well as monitoring their attainment by way of feedback. Management accountants working in senior management will be major contributors to the objective-setting process for two reasons.

(a)   As *Drucker* pointed out, the most crucial aspect of management performance in business is economic success; that is, **financial targets are the vital ones**.

(b)   Targets are only useful if performance can be **measured**: performance measurement is a major aspect of management accountancy.

1.1.2 Control strategies

William Ouchi identified three types of control strategy for organisations. They are all capable of analysis as cybernetic control systems.

*   **Market** control
*   **Bureaucratic** control
*   **Clan** control

To these we add **personal centralised** control, described by *Child.* This is the type of control that is based on hierarchical relationships, where decisions are taken by superiors who then supervise their implementation.

Market control

Market control is the use of the **price mechanism and related performance measures** internally and externally, to control organisational behaviour. It is used in loose organisational firms such as consortia and alliances and in the construction industry when sub-contractors are employed.

At **divisional level**, market control can also be used, although this is sometimes problematic. It is only relevant if there are separate divisions, which are established as **profit centres, or investment centres**.

Such control systems are only effective where it is possible to price the output of a division effectively and where there is **external competition as a reference**.

Bureaucratic control

Bureaucratic control uses rules and reports to maintain control. Control is based on the principles of scientific management – specialisation of work, simplification of work methods, and standardisation of procedures.

Four main mechanisms are used: standard operating procedures, statistical reports, budgets, and appraisal.

Clan control

Clan control is based on **corporate culture** and depends on three principal organisational characteristics.

(a)   Shared **values and traditions**.

(b)   It is assumed that those who are hired are committed to the organisation and its customers. In other words, they share the same **assumptions** as management.

(c)   Creating a sense of **common purpose**. Employees develop a strong personal identification with the goals of the organisation.

1.2 Performance measurement

Performance measurement aims to assess how well something or somebody is doing in relation to previous or expected activity, or in comparison with other processes or people.

KEY TERM

PERFORMANCE MEASUREMENT is the 'process of assessing the proficiency with which a reporting entity succeeds, by the economic acquisition of resources and their efficient and effective development, in achieving its objectives. Performance measures may be based on non-financial as well as on financial information.'

(CIMA *Official Terminology*)

1.2.1 The purpose of performance measurement

Performance measurement has become such an accepted part of business life that sometimes we lose sight of its purpose.

(a) Performance measurement is part of the overall cybernetic (or feedback) control system, providing the essential **feedback** spur to any necessary control action.

(b) It is a major input into communications to **stakeholder groups**, including the widening field of corporate reporting.

(c) It is intimately linked to **incentives** and **performance management** systems, providing evidence of results against agreed objectives.

(d) Motivation may be enhanced since managers will seek to achieve satisfactory performance in areas that are measured.

Neely summarised the purpose of performance measurement in his '**Four CPs of Performance Measurement**':

(a) **Check position** – how well are we doing? (This should look at both financial and non-financial factors)

(b) **Communicate position** – to stakeholders so that they know how the business is performing

(c) **Confirm priorities** – setting targeted for business and developing action plans to help achieve them

(d) **Compel progress** – measuring performance is a strong driver for change, especially if it is linked to reward.

1.2.2 Approaches to performance measurement

An important aspect of the management accountant's role is to help implement and control strategies through performance measurement.

There are a number of key areas to consider when determining the approach to adopt towards performance evaluation in a given set of circumstances.

Area to consider	Comments
What is evaluated?	Some approaches concentrate on the performance of the organisation as a whole, while others look at strategic business units, divisions, functions or the individual.
Who wants the evaluation?	Some approaches are based on the viewpoint of a single interest group such as investors. Others take in the views of various interest groups (for example employees).
What are the objectives of the organisation?	Is there a single goal or many goals? Are the goals short or long term?

Area to consider	Comments
Are quantitative measures or qualitative measures appropriate?	Quantitative measures (eg ROI or number of rejects) may not seem relevant but qualitative measures (eg customer satisfaction) are sometimes perceived to be too subjective.
What targets are used to assess performance?	Measures are meaningless unless they are compared against something. Common sources of comparison are historic figures, standards/budgets, similar external activities, similar internal activities, indices and trends over time.

Question 14.1   Product leadership

Learning outcome D1(vii)

How could product leadership be measured, besides considering market share?

Section summary

Controls are vital for an organisation to assess how well it is performing against its strategic plans. However, plans and controls need to be reviewed together. A plan is of little use if it is not put into action, while a system of control can only be effective if the people overseeing it know what they are trying to achieve.

2 Strategic control and critical success factors

Introduction

In Chapter 2 earlier in this Study Text, we looked at strategic planning, and we identified the way organisations need to translate their mission into strategic objectives and goals.

In turn, if an organisation is going to achieve its goals, it will have to ensure it performs well in key areas.

These key areas can be identified as **critical success factors**.

KEY TERM

A CRITICAL SUCCESS FACTOR (CSF) is 'An element of the organisational activity which is central to its future success. Critical success factors (CSFs) may change over time, and may include items such as product, quality, employee attitudes, manufacturing flexibility and brand awareness'.   (*CIMA Official Terminology*)

Johnson, Scholes and Whittington define CSFs as: 'those components of strategy where the organisation must excel to outperform competition. These are underpinned by competences which ensure this success.'

The importance of this definition is that it links to the idea of performance. If an organisation has identified the components of its strategy where it needs to outperform the competition, is also needs some way of being able to measure its performance in those areas.

These key performance measures – **key performance indicators (KPIs)** – are a key part of the control system for reviewing how successfully a strategy has been implemented and how well an organisation is performing.

However, note that the definitions of CSFs highlights that, in order to be successful, organisations have to perform well across a range of key processes. Therefore CSFs and KPIs should focus on key operational processes, and **should not focus only on financial performance**.

Michael Goold and *John J Quinn* write: 'Most companies take pride in fostering a performance-driven culture that emphasises profitability as the key goal for business management ... [but] ... too much emphasis on budgetary control and short-term profit can disguise strategic problems.'

2.1 Gaps and false alarms

Many firms have spent time measuring the wrong things – the trick is to remove 'false alarms' from performance measures and replace them with measures that fill gaps in coverage. **Gaps** (important areas which are neglected) include:

- New product introduction
- Customer satisfaction
- Employee involvement

However, a number of problems could emerge if firms concentrate on measuring gaps, and then looking for ways of filling them.

- Short-term measures predominate over long-term measures
- Financial proxies (eg EPS) predominate over reality
- Efficiency takes precedence over effectiveness
- Economy takes precedence over efficiency
- Individual department performance measures take precedence over how departments are linked together to satisfy the customers

2.2 Strategic control systems

Formal systems of strategic control are still relatively rare, although more companies are adopting them.

(a)   The formal process begins with a **strategy review**, perhaps each year. The key assumptions on which the strategy is based must be monitored.

(b)   **Milestones of performance** both of a quantitative and qualitative nature are developed.

(c)   **Strategic budgets** indicate the resources to be spent on strategic targets.

Informal systems of strategic control. Many companies do not 'define explicit strategic objectives or milestones that are regularly and formally monitored as part of the ongoing management control process'.

- Informality promotes flexibility
- Formal systems can become over-bureaucratic
- Openness of communication is necessary
- A narrow focus on individual strategic objectives can blind managers to wider issues

The characteristics of strategic control systems can be measured on two axes: how formal is the process and how many milestones are identified for performance? *Goold and Quinn* recommend the following guidelines.

(a)   **Linkages**. If there are important linkages among business units, the formality of the process should be low, to avoid undermining co-operation.

(b)   **Diversity**. If there is a great deal of diversity, it is doubtful whether any overall strategic control system is appropriate.

(c)   **Risk**. Firms whose strategic stance depends on high risk decisions which could destroy the company as a whole need strategic control systems which have a large number of performance criteria so that problems will be easily detected.

(d)   **Change**. Fashion-goods manufacturers must respond to relatively high levels of environmental turbulence, and have to react quickly.

(e)   **Competitive advantage**. For control purposes, it is useful to distinguish between two types of business.

     (i)   Businesses with few sources of competitive advantage. In this case, perhaps market share or quality is the source of success.

     (ii)   Businesses with many sources of advantage. In this case, success over a wider number of areas is necessary. The greatest dangers in this sort of business are misdirected effort and high cost.

The introduction of a formal or semi-formal strategic control system to monitor a firm's strategic position has certain advantages.

- Realism in planning
- The encouragement of higher performance standards
- More motivation for business units
- More timely intervention by senior management

2.3 Critical success factors and key performance indicators 5/10, 5/11

Critical success factors (CSFs) are those actions that must be performed well in order for the goals and objectives established by an organisation to be met successfully.

However, having identified which areas an organisation needs to perform well in, its performance in those areas also needs to be measured. Therefore, one or more **key performance indicators** (KPIs) have to be established for each CSF. The purpose of KPIs is to enable management to measure and control progress in each of the CSFs.

For example, in relation to a customer perspective, a CSF could be quality; and in turn KPIs could be number of complaints (or lack of them), or customer satisfaction ratings.

The KPIs need to cover both **financial and non-financial criteria**. Some possible KPIs are outlined below.

Sphere of activity	Key performance indicators
Marketing	Sales volume Market share Gross margins
Production	Capacity utilisation Level of defects
Logistics	Capacity utilisation % of deliveries on time

Some criteria which are regularly used in choosing between alternative plans for specific elements of the marketing mix are outlined below.

Activity	Key performance indicators
New product development	Trial rate Repurchase rate
Sales programmes	Contribution by region, salesperson Controllable margin as percentage of sales Number of new accounts Travel costs
Advertising programmes	Awareness levels Attribute ratings Cost levels

Activity	Key performance indicators
Pricing programmes	Price relative to industry average
	Price elasticity of demand
Distribution programmes	Number of distributors carrying the product

Exam skills

It is important to appreciate the relationship between, and the difference between, objectives, CSFs and KPIs.

It could be useful to think of them as a flowchart in which objectives determine CSFs which, in turn, determine KPIs.

CSFs represent '**what**' must be done to enable the organisation to be successful and to achieve its objectives. **KPIs** are the **measures** of whether or not the CSFs are being achieved.

If a question asks you to recommend performance indicators, make sure you recommend KPIs rather than CSFs. For example, 'ensuring high quality' is a CSF because it is what a company want to achieve. By contrast, 'the number of complaints' or 'the number of defects' would be KPIs, because they are measurable.

2.4 The product life cycle and control systems

We have already seen that the product life cycle has implications for an organisation's product mix and its marketing mix. *Ward* suggests that the product life cycle is also relevant to the design and operation of control systems and performance measurement.

	Introduction	Growth	Maturity	Decline
Information needed	The environment Potential market size and buyer value	Market growth Market share Marketing effectiveness Competitor information and effectiveness of marketing	Competitors' costs Limiting factor	Rate of decline When to exit Realisable asset values
Critical success factors	Time to develop and launch	Growth in share Sustainable competitive advantage	Contribution per unit of limiting factor Customer retention rates	None
Performance measures	Evaluate using DCF of life-cycle cash flows Lead indicators of market success, eg advertising effectiveness, distributor acceptance	DCF evaluation of marketing costs Specific marketing objectives Market share	ROI Profit margin Operating cash flow Market share	Free cash flow compared with opportunity costs of assets used

Note *Ward's* emphasis on external measures relating to customers and competitors and the way that conventional financial measures such as ROI do not appear until the maturity phase.

2.5 Stakeholder interest performance measures

Shareholders (as the owners of the company) have a keen interest in a company's performance.

However, we need to remember that shareholders are not the only stakeholders who are interested how a company is performing. Therefore, performance measures need to include measures which are relevant to all key stakeholders.

Also, remember that not-for-profit organisations, charities or government bodies may have different performance measures to commercial organisations.

Section summary

Strategic control is bound up with measurement of performance, which often tends to be based on financial criteria. Techniques for strategic control suggest that companies develop strategic milestones (eg for market share) to monitor the achievement of strategic objectives, as a counterweight to purely financial issues.

Critical success factors are the few key areas where things must go right for the organisation to flourish.

3 Budgetary control systems   11/10

Introduction

Budgetary control systems are used by many companies to compel planning, co-ordinate activities and motivate employees, as well as to evaluate performance. Deviations from the plan are corrected via **control action**.

KEY TERM

BUDGETARY CONTROL is the process whereby the 'master budget, devolved to responsibility centres, allows continuous monitoring of actual results versus budget, either to secure by individual action the budget objectives or to provide a basis for budget revision'.   (CIMA *Official Terminology*)

A budget is a **plan expressed in monetary terms.** It is prepared and approved prior to the budget period and may show income, expenditure and capital to be employed.

Purpose of budgets

- To compel planning
- To co-ordinate activities
- To communicate ideas
- To provide a framework for responsibility accounting
- To motivate employees and management
- To evaluate performance

Negative effects of budgets include

- No incentive as the budget is unrealistic
- A manager may add 10% to his expenditure budget to ensure that he can meet the figure
- Manager achieves target but does no more
- A manager may go on a 'spending spree'
- Draws attention away from the longer term consequences

Problems with budgetary control

- The managers who set the budgets are often not responsible for attaining them.
- The goals of the organisation as a whole, expressed in the budget, may not coincide with the personal aspirations of the individual managers.
- Control is applied at different stages by different people.

How to improve behavioural aspects of budgetary control

- Develop a working relationship with operational managers
- Keeping accounting jargon to a minimum
- Making reports clear and to the point
- Providing control and information with a minimum of delay
- Ensuring actual costs are recorded accurately
- Allow for participation in the budgetary process

Limitations to the effectiveness of participation

- Some people prefer tough management
- A manager may build slack into his won budget
- Management feels that they have little scope to influence the final outcome

3.1 Criticisms of traditional budgeting

According to an article in *CIMA Insider* in February 2001, 'traditional budgets hold companies back, restrict staff creativity and prevent them from responding to customers'. The authors of the article, *Jeremy Hope and Robin Fraser*, quoted a 1998 survey which found that 88% of respondents were dissatisfied with the budgeting model. They also quoted research which came up with some surprising statistics.

(a)   78% of companies do not change their budget during the annual cycle. Managers tend to 'manage around' their budgets.

(b)   60% do not link strategy and budgeting.

(c)   85% of management teams spend less than one hour a month discussing strategy.

Budgets tend to focus upon financial outputs rather than quantitative performance measures, and are not linked to employee performance. *Hope and Fraser* believe that organisational and behavioural changes are required, and they link these with the new business environment to suggest 'a management model that really supports strategy'. We summarise this in the table below:

Change in environment	How to succeed?	Key success factors	'Budget barriers'
• **Rising uncertainty**	• Cope with uncertainty by adapting quickly	• Devolve authority • Fast information • Strategy an adaptive process	• Too many rules • Restricted information flows • Fixed cycles are difficult to change
• **Importance of intellectual capital**	• Find (and retain) good people	• Recruit and develop good staff and set up a fair reward system	• Budgets tend to ignore people and lead to 'management by fear' and a cost-cutting mentality
• **Increasing pace of innovation**	• Create an innovative climate	• Share knowledge • See the business as a series of investments, not just components of a	• Central planning and bureaucracy encourage short-termism, and stifle creativity

Change in environment	How to succeed?	Key success factors	'Budget barriers'
		budget	
• **Falling prices and costs**	• Operate with low costs	• Adopt a low cost network structure • Challenge costs • Align resources and costs with strategy	• Budgets prevent costs being challenged, they simply become 'entitlements'
• **Declining customer loyalty**	• Attract and keep the right customers	• Set up strong customer relationships • Establish a customer-facing strategy	• Budgeted sales targets and product focus tends to ignore customer needs
• **More demanding shareholders**	• Create consistent shareholder value	• Take a long term view of value creation • Base controls on performance	• Budgets tend to focus on the short term, with no future view

CASE STUDY

According to *Hope and Fraser*, 'giving managers control of their actions and using a few simple measures, based on key value drivers and geared to beating the competition, is all that most cases require'.

Challenging costs is inevitably part of such a process. Hope and Fraser identified Swedish bank Svenska Handelsbanken as a key exponent. Its low costs are the product of several factors:

(a)   Small head office staff, and a flat, simple hierarchy

(b)   People in regions and branches are self sufficient and well-trained and are measured by competitive results, which has produced an attitude keen to weed out unwarranted expenses

(c)   Lower credit losses because front line staff feel more concerned to make sure that the information on which they base lending decisions is correct

(d)   Central services and costs are negotiated rather than allocated

(e)   Internet technology is used to reduce costs, with the benefit accruing to the customer's own branch

The European Vice President of Svenska Handelsbanken believes that 'devolving responsibility for results, turning cost centres into profit centres; squeezing central costs, using technology and ... eradicating the budgeting "cost entitlement" mentality are just some of the actions we have taken to place costs under constant pressure'.

Another criticism of the annual budgeting and planning process is that it does not add value. Instead, it uses a large amount of senior managers', budget holders' and finance team's time, but creates an output which can be almost meaningless in times of rapid change.

Establishing a rolling quarterly forecast may actually be more appropriate in times of rapid change, and these forecasts should also be linked to CSFs rather than simply be a summary of financial targets.

4 Performance measures: financial and non-financial 11/10,11/11

Introduction

Performance measures must be relevant to both a clear objective and to operational methods, and their production must be cost-effective.

4.1 Deciding what measures to use

Clearly different measures are appropriate for different businesses. Determining which measures are used in a particular case will require **preliminary investigations** along the following lines.

(a) The **objectives/mission** of the organisation must be **clearly formulated** so that when the factors critical to the success of the mission have been identified they can be translated into performance indicators.

(b) **Measures** must be **relevant** to the way the organisation operates. Managers themselves must believe the indicators are useful.

(c) **The costs and benefits of providing resources** (people, equipment and time to collect and analyse information) to produce a performance indicator must be carefully **weighed up**.

4.2 Financial modelling and performance measurement

Financial modelling might assist in performance evaluation in the following ways.

(a) **Identifying the variables** involved in performing tasks and the relationships between them. This is necessary so that the model can be built in the first place. Model building therefore shows what should be measured, helps to explain how a particular level of performance can be achieved, and identifies factors in performance that the organisation cannot expect to control.

(b) **Setting targets for future performance**. The most obvious example of this is the budgetary control system described above.

(c) **Monitoring actual performance**. A flexible budget is a good example of a financial model that is used in this way.

(d) **Co-ordinating long-term strategic plans with short term operational actions.** Modelling can reflect the dynamic nature of the real world and evaluate how likely it is that short-term actions will achieve the longer-term plan, given new conditions.

4.3 Profitability, activity and productivity

In general, there are three possible **points of reference for measurement**.

(a) **Profitability**

Profit has two components: **cost and income**. All parts of an organisation and all activities within it incur costs, and so their success needs to be judged in relation to cost. Only some parts of an organisation receive income, and their success should be judged in terms of both cost and income.

(b) **Activity**

All parts of an organisation are also engaged in activities (activities cause costs). Activity measures could include the following.

(i) Number of orders received from customers, a measure of the effectiveness of marketing
(ii) Number of machine breakdowns attended to by the repairs and maintenance department

Each of these items could be measured in terms of **physical numbers**, **monetary value**, or **time spent**.

(c)   **Productivity**

This is the quantity of the product or service produced in relation to the resources put in, for example so many units produced per hour or per employee. It defines how efficiently resources are being used.

The **dividing line between productivity and activity is thin**, because every activity could be said to have some 'product', or if not can be measured in terms of lost units of product or service.

Question 14.2	Invoicing

Learning outcome D1(vii)

An invoicing assistant works in a department with three colleagues. She is paid £16,000 per annum. The department typically handles 10,000 invoices per week.

One morning she spends half an hour on the phone to her grandfather, who lives in Australia, at the company's expense. The cost of the call proves to be £32.

Required

From this scenario identify as many different performance measures as possible, explaining what each is intended to measure. Make any further assumptions you wish.

4.4 Financial performance measures

Financial measures (or **monetary measures**) are very familiar to you. Here are some examples, accompanied by comments from a single page of the *Financial Times.*

Measure	Comment
Profit	The commonest measure of all. Profit maximisation is usually cited as the main objective of most business organisations: 'ICI increased pre-tax profits to £233m'; 'General Motors... yesterday reported better-than-expected first-quarter net income of $513 (£333m) ...
Revenue	'The UK businesses contributed £113.9m of total group turnover of £409m'.
Costs	'Sterling's fall benefited pre-tax profits by about £50m while savings from the cost-cutting programme were running at around £100m a quarter'; 'The group interest charge rose from £48m to £61m'.
Share price	'The group's shares rose 31p to 1278p despite the market's fall'.
Cash flow	'Cash flow was also continuing to improve, with cash and marketable securities totalling $8.4bn on March 31, up from $8bn at December 31'.

The important point to note here is that the monetary amounts stated **are only given meaning in relation to something else**. Profits are higher than last year's; cashflow has improved compared with last quarter's.

We can generalise the above and give a list of yard-sticks against which financial results are usually placed so as to become measures.

- **Budgeted** sales, costs and profits
- **Standards** in a standard costing system
- The **trend** over time (last year/this year, say)
- The **results of other parts** of the business
- The **results of other businesses**
- The **economy** in general
- **Future potential** (eg a new business in terms of nearness to breaking even)

4.5 The profit measure

Profit has both advantages and disadvantages as a measure of performance.

Measure	Comment
Single criterion	Easier to manage, as the sole concern is the effect on the bottom line
Analysis has a clear objective: ie the effect on future profits.	Easier than cost/benefit analysis, for example
A broad performance measure that incorporates all other measures	'If it does not affect profit it can be ignored.'
Enables decentralisation	Managers have the delegated powers to achieve divisional (and therefore group) profit.
Profitability measures (eg ROI) can compare all profit-making operations even if they are not alike.	This ignores the balance between risk and return.
Encourages **short-termism** and focus on the annual cycle, at the expense of long term performance	Examples: cutting discretionary revenue investments, manipulating of accounting rules, building up inventories
Profit differs from **economic income.**	
A firm has to satisfy **stakeholders** other than shareholders, such as the government and the local community.	This may include environmental/ethical performance measures.
Liquidity is at least as important as profit.	Most business failures derive from liquidity crises.
Profit should be related to **risk**, not just capital employed.	Rarely done
Profits can **fluctuate** in times of rapid change.	For example, as a result of exchange rate volatility
Profit measures cannot easily be used to motivate **cost centre** managers.	They do not control profit.
Not useful for new businesses	Most startups will be unprofitable for at least two years.
Easily manipulated	Especially over a single period: think back to your cost accounting studies and the effect of stock changes on profit under absorption costing, for example
Pure profit based measures do not consider **capital spending**.	Growth in asset levels can be uncontrolled; alternatively, productive capacity may be allowed to decline.

4.5.1 Ratios

Ratios are a **useful** way of measuring performance for a number of reasons.

(a)   It is easier to look at **changes over time** by comparing ratios in one time period with the corresponding ratios for periods in the past.

(b)   Ratios are often **easier to understand** than absolute measures of physical quantities or money values. For example, it is easier to understand that 'productivity in March was 94%' than 'there was an adverse labour efficiency variance in March of $3,600'.

(c)   Ratios relate one item to another, and so help to **put performance into context**. For example the profit/sales ratio sets profit in the context of how much has been earned per $1 of sales, and so shows how wide or narrow profit margins are.

(d)   Ratios can be **used as targets**. In particular, targets can be set for ROI, profit/sales, asset turnover, capacity fill and productivity. Managers will then take decisions which will enable them to achieve their targets.

(e)   Ratios provide a way of **summarising an organisation's results**, and **comparing them with similar organisations**.

4.5.2 Percentages

A percentage expresses one number as a proportion of another and gives meaning to absolute numbers.

Measure	Comment
Market share	A company may aim to achieve a 25% share of the total market for its product, and measure both its marketing department and the quality of the product against this.
Capacity levels	These are usually measured in percentages. 'Factory A is working at 20% below full capacity' is an example which indicates relative inefficiency.
Wastage	This is sometimes expressed in percentage terms. 'Normal loss' may be 10%, a measure of inefficiency.
Staff turnover	This is often measured in this way. In the catering industry for example, staff turnover is typically greater than 100%, and so a hotel with a lower percentage could take this as an indicator both of the experience of its staff and of how well it is treating them.

4.6 Quantitative and qualitative performance measures

It is possible to distinguish between **quantitative information**, which is **capable of being expressed in numbers**, and **qualitative information**, which **can only be expressed in numerical terms with difficulty**.

An example of a quantitative performance measure is 'You have been late for work twice this week and it's only Tuesday!'. An example of a qualitative performance measure is 'My bed is very comfortable'.

The first measure is likely to find its way into a staff appraisal report. The second would feature in a bed manufacturer's customer satisfaction survey. Both are indicators of whether their subjects are doing as good a job as they are required to do.

Qualitative measures are by nature **subjective and judgmental** but this does not mean that they are not valuable. They are especially valuable when they are derived from several different sources because then they can be expressed in a mixture of quantitative and qualitative terms which is more meaningful overall: 'seven out of ten customers think our beds are very comfortable' is a quantitative measure of customer satisfaction as well as a **qualitative** measure of the perceived performance of the beds.

4.7 Measuring performance in the new business environment

As well as arguing that organisations need to rethink the basis on which they prepare budgets, *Hope and Fraser* have also argued that if organisations are serious about gaining real benefits from decentralisation and empowerment, they need to **change the way in which they set targets, measure performance and design reward systems.** (The emphasis and heading are BPP's.)

Targets and responsibilities

'The SBU [strategic business unit] manager is once again asked for a **'stretch target'.** However, under this management model [suggested by *Hope and Fraser*] she knows that 'stretch' really means her best shot with **full support** from the centre (including investment funds and improvement programmes) and a sympathetic hearing should she fail to get all of the way. Moreover, she alone carries the **responsibility** for achieving these targets. There is neither any micro-management from above, nor any monthly 'actual versus budget' reports.

Targets are both strategic and financial, and they are underpinned by clear action plans that cascade down the organisation, building **ownership and commitment at every level**. Monthly reports comprise a **balanced scorecard set** of graphs, charts and trends that track progress (eg financial, customer satisfaction, speed, quality, service, and employee satisfaction) **compared with** last year and with other **SBUs within the group** and, where possible, with **competitors**. Quarterly **rolling forecasts** (broad-brush numbers only) are also prepared to help manage production scheduling and cash requirements but they are not part of the measurement and reward process.

Performance review

Of course, if there is a significant blip in performance (and the fast/open information system would flag this immediately), then a performance review would be signalled. Such reviews focus on the effectiveness of action plans and what further improvements need to be made and maybe even whether the targets (and measures) themselves are still appropriate.'

There are a number of reasons why this approach is **successful**.

(a)   Managers are not punished for failing to reach the full target.

(b)   The use of the balanced scorecard ensures that all key perspectives are considered.

(c)   Because managers set their own targets and plan the changes needed to achieve them, real ownership and commitment are built. Feedback and learning takes place as a result of the tracking of action plans. (Contrast this with numerical variances that tell managers nothing about what to do differently in the future).

(d)   Beating internal and external competitors is a constant spur to better performance.

(e)   Managers share in a bonus pool that is based on share price or long-term performance against a basket of competitors. Resource and knowledge sharing is therefore encouraged.

4.8 Non-financial performance measures

It is worth remembering that performance measures can be both financial and non financial.

KEY TERM

NON-FINANCIAL PERFORMANCE MEASURES are 'measures of performance based on non-financial information which may originate in and be used by operating departments to monitor and control their activities without any accounting input. Non-financial performance measures may give a more timely indication of the levels of performance achieved than financial measures do, and may be less susceptible to distortion by factors such as uncontrollable variations in the effect of market forces on operations.'

(CIMA *Official Terminology*)

Here are some examples of non-financial performance measures.

Areas assessed	Performance measure
Service quality	Number of complaints Proportion of repeat bookings Customer waiting time On-time deliveries
Production performance	Set-up times Number of suppliers Days' inventory in hand Output per employee Material yield percentage Schedule adherence Proportion of output requiring rework Manufacturing lead times
Marketing effectiveness	Trend in market share Sales volume growth Customer visits per salesperson Client contact hours per salesperson Sales volume forecast versus actual Number of customers Customer survey response information
Personnel	Number of complaints received Staff turnover Days lost through absenteeism Days lost through accidents/sickness Training time per employee

Question 14.3   Hotel

Learning outcome D1(vii)

Draw up a list of performance criteria for a hotel.

The beauty of non-financial performance measures is that **anything can be compared if it is meaningful to do so**. The measures should be tailored to the circumstances so that, for example, the number of coffee breaks you take for every hour you study indicate to you how hard you are studying!

4.8.1 The advantages and disadvantages of non-financial measures

Unlike traditional variance reports, they can be provided **quickly** for managers, per shift or on a daily or hourly basis as required. They are likely to be **easy to calculate**, and **easier for non-financial managers to understand** and therefore to use effectively.

There are problems associated with choosing the measures and there is a danger that **too many such measures could be reported**, overloading managers with information that is not truly useful, or that sends conflicting signals. There is clearly a need for the information provider to work more closely with the managers who will be using the information to make sure that their needs are properly understood.

Research on more than 3,000 companies in Europe and North America has shown that the strongest drivers of competitive achievement are the intangible factors, especially **intellectual property, innovation** and **quality.** Non-financial measures have been at the forefront of an increasing trend towards **customer focus** (such as TQM), **process re-engineering** programmes and the creation of **internal markets** within organisations.

Arguably, non-financial measures are **less likely to be manipulated** than traditional profit-related measures and they should, therefore, **offer a means of counteracting short-termism**, since short-term profit at any expense is rarely an advisable goal.

Remember, the ultimate goal of commercial organisations in the long run is likely to remain the maximisation of profit, and so the **financial aspect cannot be ignored**.

A further danger is that they might lead managers to pursue detailed operational goals and become blind to the overall strategy in which those goals are set. A combination of financial and non– financial measures is likely to be most successful.

4.8.2 The performance measurement manifesto

Eccles argues that financial measures alone are inadequate for monitoring the progress of business strategies based on creating customer value, satisfaction and quality, partly because they are **historical** in nature and partly they cannot measure current progress with such strategies directly. He also notes the impulse to **short-termism** given by such measures.

There is a need for a performance measurement system that includes both financial and non-financial measures. The measures chosen must be **integrated**, so that the potential for discarding non-financial measures that conflict with the financial ones is limited. *Eccles* argues that too often firms prioritise financial measures above non-financial ones, and if the two clash the financial priorities take priority. However, *Eccles* points out that **non-financial measures** such as quality, customer satisfaction and market are now equally important as purely financial measures.

Eccles says that the development of a good system of performance measurement requires activity in five areas.

(a) The **information architecture** must be developed. This requires the identification of performance measures that relate to strategy and the gradual, iterative development of systems to capture the required data.

(b) An appropriate **information technology strategy** must be established.

(c) The company's **incentives system** must be aligned with its performance measures. Eccles proposes that qualitative factors should be addressed by the incentive system.

(d) **External influences** must be acknowledged and used. For example, benchmarking against other organisations may be used, while providers of capital should be persuaded to accept the validity of non-financial measures.

(e) **Manage the implementation** of the four areas above by appointing a person to be responsible overall as well as department agents.

4.9 Value for money (VFM) audits

Value for money audits can be seen as being of particular relevance in not-for-profit organisations. Such an audit focuses on **economy, efficiency** and **effectiveness.** These measures may be in conflict with each other. To take the example of higher education, larger class sizes may be **economical** in their use of teaching resources, but are not necessarily **effective** in creating the best learning environment.

Section summary

Performance measures can be both financial and non-financial. A growing dissatisfaction with financial performance measures has led to non-financial measures being developed, based on operational performance.

Nonetheless, commercial organisations need to remember that maximising profit is likely to remain one of their key goals, so they cannot ignore the financial aspect of performance.

5 The balanced scorecard   9/10, 9/11, 5/12

Introduction

The balanced scorecard tries to integrate the different measures of performance by highlighting the linkages between operating and financial performance. This scorecard offers four perspectives on performance:

- Financial
- Customer
- Innovation and learning
- Internal business

A theme so far has been that financial measurements do not capture all the strategic realities of the business, but it is equally important that financial measurements are not overlooked. A failure to attend to the 'numbers' can rapidly lead to a failure of the business.

Nonetheless, financial measurements do not capture all the strategic realities of a business so businesses need to look at both financial and non-financial measures. A technique which has been developed to integrate the various features (financial and non-financial) of corporate success and to make organisations more strategy-focused is *Kaplan and Norton's* **balanced scorecard**.

CASE STUDY

Business failures

The global recession in 2008-9 has meant that there have been stories about business failures almost every day in the newspapers. These articles often mention the reason given for the failure, and the state of economy is often seen as the number one cause.

However, this tends to obscure a rather more painful truth. The reason for the business failure is usually the business itself.

An article in a local newspaper in Tupelo, Mississippi illustrated this point. The article looked at three food outlets in the town which had failed in 2009, and noted the owners' reasons for the failure. The reasons given were "poor timing and the economy".

However, customers who had been to the businesses noted that all three had three things in common: high prices, poor service and mediocre food.

One in particular - a sandwich shop - stood out. It had an ordering process that involved standing in line to order, and then moving to another station and standing in line to repeat your order and pay for it. The total wait for an expensive and really poor take out sandwich was over 45 minutes. The shop was located in a mall, and four units away from a Mexican restaurant that was not only surviving but positively thriving. So it seems the economy was not the main reason for business failure after all!

The more pertinent point is that businesses – and particularly small businesses – are often launched and operated without the resources needed to succeed. To be successful, a business needs to supply a cost effective solution to customer needs.

If business don't understand their markets, their customers or their competition, and if they don't have a clear vision or direction which is executed by management they are likely to fail.

(Adapted from article, *'Who's to blame for most business failures'* on www.articlesbase.com, 19 January, 2010)

KEY TERM

The BALANCED SCORECARD approach is 'an approach to the provision of information to management to assist strategic policy formulation and achievement. It emphasises the need to provide the user with a set of information which addresses all relevant areas of performance in an objective and unbiased fashion. The information provided may include both financial and non-financial elements, and cover areas such as profitability, customer satisfaction, internal efficiency and innovation.' (CIMA *Official Terminology*)

The balanced scorecard seeks to translate **mission** and **strategy** into **objectives** and measures, and focuses on **four different perspectives**. For each of the four perspectives, the scorecard aims to articulate the **outcomes** an organisation desires, and the **drivers** of those outcomes.

Financial Perspective

How should we create value for our shareholders to succeed financially?

(covers traditional measures such as growth, profitability and shareholder value, with measures set through talking directly to the shareholders)

Internal Business Process

What business processes what must we excel at to achieve financial and customer objectives?

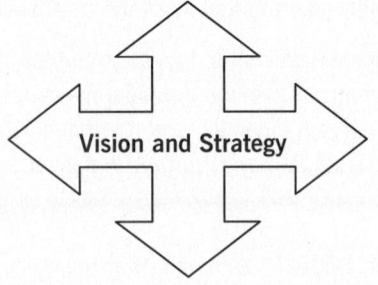
Vision and Strategy

Customer Perspective

To achieve our vision, how should we appear to our customers?
What do new and existing customers value from us?
(cost, quality, reliability etc)

Innovation and Learning Perspective

How can we continue to create value and maintain the company's competitive position through improvement and change?
(acquisition of new skills; development of new products)

Performance targets are set once the key areas for improvement have been identified, and the balanced scorecard is the **main monthly report**.

The scorecard is **balanced** in the sense that managers are required to think in terms of all four perspectives, to **prevent improvements being made in one area at the expense of another.**

Broadbent and Cullen identify the following **important features** of this approach.

- It looks at both **internal and external matters** concerning the organisation
- It is related to the key elements of a company's strategy
- Financial and non-financial measures are linked together

Kaplan and *Norton* have found that organisations are using the balanced scorecard to:

- Identify and align strategic initiatives
- Link budgets with strategy
- Align the organisation (structure and processes) with strategy
- Conduct periodic strategic performance reviews with the aim of learning more about, and improving, strategy

Kaplan & Norton suggest that using the Balanced Scorecard can also help an organisation improve its strategic performance:

- The process of identifying key outcomes and drivers should help individuals and divisions become more aware of how their work fits in with the organisation's strategy

- Giving individuals and divisions regular reports on their performance against key measures will help them monitor their own performance, and identify areas for improvement

- The scorecard as a whole should provide senior management with regular information on how their organisation is performing against key measures, and therefore how well strategies are being implemented

5.1 Problems

As with all techniques, problems can arise when the balanced scorecard is applied.

Problem	Explanation
Conflicting measures	Some measures in the scorecard such as research funding and cost reduction may naturally conflict. It is often difficult to determine the balance which will achieve the best results.
Selecting measures	Not only do appropriate measures have to be devised but the number of measures used must be agreed. Care must be taken that the impact of the results is not lost in a sea of information. The innovation and learning perspective is, perhaps, the most difficult to measure directly, since much development of human capital will not feed directly into such crude measures as rate of new product launches or even training hours undertaken. It will, rather, improve economy and effectiveness and support the achievement of customer perspective measures. When selecting measures it is important to measure those which actually add value to an organisation, not just those that are easy to measure.
Expertise	Measurement is only useful if it initiates appropriate action. Non-financial managers may have difficulty with the usual profit measures. With more measures to consider this problem will be compounded. Measures need to be developed by someone who understands the business processes concerned.
Interpretation	Even a financially-trained manager may have difficulty in putting the figures into an overall perspective.
Management commitment	The BSC can only be effective if senior managers commit to it. If they revert to focusing solely on the financial measures they are used to, then the value of introducing additional measures will be reduced. In this context, do not overlook the **cost** of the BSC. There will be costs involved in data-gathering and in measuring the performance of additional processes.

It may also be worth considering the following issues in relation to using the balanced scorecard:

- It doesn't provide a single aggregate summary performance measure; for example, part of the popularity of ROI or ROCE comes from the fact they provide a convenient summary of how well a business is performing.

- In comparison to measures like EVA, there is no direct link between the scorecard and shareholder value.

- Culture: Introducing the scorecard may require a shift in corporate culture; for example, in understanding an organisation as a set of processes rather as departments.

  Equally, implementing the scorecard will require an organisation to move away from looking solely at short-term financial measures, and focus on longer-term strategic measures instead.

The scorecard should be used **flexibly.** The process of deciding **what to measure** forces a business to clarify its strategy. For example, a manufacturing company may find that 50% – 60% of costs are represented by bought-in components, so measurements relating to suppliers could usefully be added to the scorecard. These could include payment terms, lead times, or quality considerations.

5.2 Linkages

Disappointing results might result from a **failure to view all the measures as a whole**. For example, increasing productivity means that fewer employees are needed for a given level of output. Excess capacity can be created by quality improvements. However these improvements have to be exploited (eg by increasing sales). The **financial element** of the balanced scorecard 'reminds executives that improved quality, response time, productivity or new products, benefit the company only when they are translated into improved financial results', or if they enable the firm to obtain a sustainable competitive advantage.

5.3 Implementing the balanced scorecard

The introduction and practical use of the balanced scorecard is likely to be subject to all the problems associated with balancing long-term strategic progress against the management of short-term tactical imperatives. Kaplan and Norton recognise this and recommend an iterative, four-stage approach to the practical problems involved.

(a) **Translating the vision**: the organisation's mission must be expressed in a way that has to be clear operational meaning for each employee.

(b) **Communicating and linking**: the next stage is to link the vision or mission to departmental and individual objectives, including those that transcend traditional short-term financial goals. This stage highlights an important feature of the scorecard: that it translates strategy into day-to-day operations.

(c) **Business planning**: the scorecard is used to prioritise objectives and allocate resources in order to make the best progress towards strategic goals.

(d) **Feedback and learning**: the organisation learns to use feedback on performance to promote progress against all four perspectives.

5.3.1 Strategy maps

As an extension to the balanced scorecard, Kaplan and Norton also developed the idea of strategy maps, which could be used to help implement the scorecard more successfully.

Strategy maps identify six stages:

(a) Identify **objective**. Identify the key objectives of the organisation

(b) **Value creation**. In the light of the key objectives, determine the main ways the organisation creates value

(c) **Financial perspective**: Identify financial strategies to support the overall objective and strategy

(d)   **Customer perspective**. Clarify customer-orientated strategies to support the overall strategy

(e)   **Internal processes**. Identify how internal processes support the strategy and help to create value

(f)   **Innovation and learning**. Identify the skills and competencies needed to support the overall strategy and achieve the objectives.

The 'map' illustrates that the four perspectives in the Scorecard are clearly linked, but, perhaps more importantly, the **sequence of the stages** illustrates that there is a **hierarchy among the perspectives**. The financial perspective is the highest level perspective, meaning that the measures and goals an organisation seeks to achieve in relation to the other perspectives should, in turn, help that organisation achieve its financial goals.

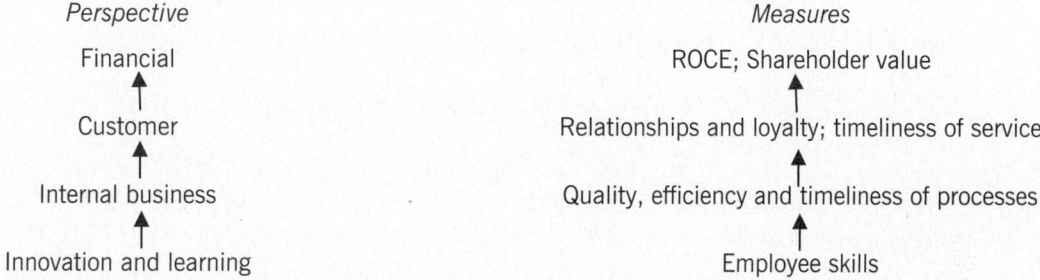

Perspective	*Measures*
Financial	ROCE; Shareholder value
↑	↑
Customer	Relationships and loyalty; timeliness of service
↑	↑
Internal business	Quality, efficiency and timeliness of processes
↑	↑
Innovation and learning	Employee skills

In this way, the strategy map highlights how the four perspectives of the scorecard help create value, with the overall aim of helping an organisation achieve its objectives. It can also help staff appreciate the way that different elements of performance management are linked to an organisation's overall strategy.

However, it is also important to recognise that the **balanced scorecard only measures performance. It does not indicate that the strategy an organisation is employing is the right one.** 'A failure to convert improved operational performance into improved financial performance should send executives back to their drawing boards to rethink the company's strategy or its implementation plans.'

Practical steps in developing a scorecard

As with any other projects or changes, if an organisation is going to implement a scorecard successfully, it will need to think carefully about the steps involved in developing a scorecard:

Identify key outcomes – Identify the key outcomes critical to the success of the organisation (this is similar to identifying the organisation's critical success factors)

Key processes – Identify the processes that lead to those outcomes

KPIs – Develop key performance indicators for those processes

Data capture – Develop systems for capturing the data necessary to measure those key performance indicators

Reporting – Develop a mechanism for communicating or reporting the indicators to staff (for example, through charts, graphs or on a dashboard)

Performance improvement – Develop improvement programmes to ensure that performance improves as necessary

5.4 Examples of indicators

Exam skills

You may be asked to recommend some indicators organisations can use to measure performance. If you are, do not just give generic measures, but tailor them specifically to the organisation and the situation described in the question scenario.

The exact measures an organisation uses will depend on its context, but the indicators below suggest some possible measures for each scorecard category:

Financial perspective
Increase monthly turnover
Increase monthly operating profit (by division)
Improve asset utilisation
Increase market share
Increase ROI
Increase cash flow
Customer perspective
Increase market share
Number of new customers attracted
Extend product range
Customer satisfaction rating
Number of recommendations or referrals
Customer retention rates
Level of returns/refunds
On-time delivery
Percentage of sales from new products (introduced in the last two years)
Internal business processes
Reduce inventory levels
Reduce lead times
Minimise wastage / errors
Actual delivery dates of new products / services in line with plan
Reliability and usability (for websites in online business)
Security of transactions and credit card handling

Innovation and learning perspective (learning and growth)
Develop new products
Time to market (time taken for new product ideas to become 'live')
Percentage of sales from new products (introduced in the last two years)
Number of new products introduced (< 2years) compared to competitors
Ideas from employees
Adaptability and flexibility of staff
Reward and recognition structure for staff

5.5 Using the balanced scorecard

(a)   Like all performance measurement schemes, the balanced scorecard can influence behaviour among managers to conform to that required by the strategy. Because of its comprehensive nature, it can be used as a wide-ranging driver of organisational change.

(b)   The scorecard emphasises **processes** rather than **departments**. It can support a competence-based approach to strategy, but this can be confusing for managers and may make it difficult to gain their support.

(c)   Deciding just what to measure can be especially difficult, especially since the scorecard **vertical vector** lays emphasis on customer reaction. This is not to discount the importance of meeting customer expectations, purely to emphasise the difficulty of establishing what they are.

5.5.1 A word of warning

Kaplan and Norton never intended the balanced scorecard to replace all other performance measurement systems a business may use. They acknowledge that financial measures and financial results remain important, but suggest business can use the BSC to help deliver strategic goals.

Kaplan and Norton have also acknowledged that the BSC needs to recognise the linkages between **strategic**, **tactical** (management) and **operational levels** in organisations. In this context, they recognise that indicators measured in the scorecard often focus on the strategic level, rather than looking on the practical, day-to-day operational levels.

Increasingly, organisations are looking to be able to identify the linkages between these levels, and to be able to drill down and identify the sources and root causes behind the under-performance at a strategic level.

KEY POINT

The scorecard can be used both by profit and not-for-profit organisations because it acknowledges the fact that both financial and non-financial performance indicators are important in achieving strategic objectives.

5.6 The Balance Scorecard and Enterprise Management solutions

Strategic Enterprise Management (SEM) refers to the methods of management, and the related tools, that businesses can use when making high-level strategic decisions.

SEM focuses primarily on strategic management rather than operational management, with a view to allowing organisations to improve their business processes and procedures, and their business decision-making, in order to sustain a competitive advantage in a competitive business environment.

SEM can be seen as an extension of the BSC approach, because it encourages senior managers to combine financial and strategic measures when formulating business decisions.

SEM software provides organisations with the capability to support financial consolidation and to manage strategy and performance through a single piece of software (such as SAP Strategic Enterprise Management; *SAP SEM.*)

SAP's SEM software supports:

- **Financial reporting** – it can generate financial and management account information to allow managers to monitor the financial performance of business units and divisions

- **Planning, budgeting, and forecasting**

- **Corporate performance management and scorecards** – the software allows managers to develop KPIs that support balanced scorecards and economic value-added scorecard methodologies. The software allows managers to link both operational and strategic plans and to develop scorecards and performance measures based on both financial and non-financial data.

- **Risk management** – the software helps managers identify, quantify, and analyse business risks within their business units and thereby to identify risk-reducing activities.

5.7 Strategic scorecards vs balanced scorecards

Strategic scorecards are similar to balanced scorecards because they consist of summary report of financial and non-financial information to provide a summary of the organisation's progress towards its strategic goals.

However they are an advance on balanced scorecards because:

- They normally include information on external factors that could affect the strategy
- They explicitly consider risk factors
- They are not confined to quantitative metrics
- They are explicitly strategic whereas many balanced scorecards focus on operational performance

The CIMA Strategic Scorecard™

CIMA has worked with The International Federation of Accountants (IFC) to develop a strategic scorecard as the centre-piece of a framework of enterprise governance.

Strategic position List all key issues eg • competitor activity • legislative developments	**Strategic options** List all options eg • divestment • outsourcing • new products • new markets
Strategic implementation List all key initiatives underway eg progress of IT project recent launch	**Strategic risks** All major process issues & risks eg • risk appetite • risk management • capabilities

Adapted from CIMA Strategic Scorecard- executive summary (2007)

1   **Strategic position**: information to allow assessment of current and likely future position.

This should include *internal* data such as competences and resources and *external* data such as economic, market and competitive developments.

Tools that may be used for internal assessment may be mapping the firm's position against the Critical Success Factors for the industry, benchmarking against resources and competences of rivals. External assessment may include environmental analysis, scenario planning, SWOT analysis and stakeholder mapping. 'Headlights' information on long-term currents in the industry and market could also be included to stimulate discussion.

The scorecard may also record process issues under this heading such as how well this data is presently being collected, the quality of the data being included under this heading, and whether there have been any unexpected external events that the board had not been alerted to.

2   **Strategic options***: a list of current options under consideration or previously discussed but not yet active.

This provides assurance to the board that management are identifying new options on a continuous basis rather than resting on the firm's laurels, and also provides a concise summary of options to enable the Board to act as a strategic parent and to discuss at meetings.

Tools that can assist in categorising these are the Boston Portfolio matrix, Ansoff's product/market growth vector diagram and evaluation models such as the Suitability, Acceptability and Feasibility framework of Johnson, Scholes and Whittington.

The scorecard may also record process issues under this heading such as whether there are processes in the divisions to carry out innovation, the quality of information gathering on developments in the industry, and the availability of resources and incentives to innovate. Data on effectiveness such whether others have grasped opportunities that the firm missed could be included.

3   **Strategic implementation***: key milestones for the board and to monitor implementation of the agreed strategy.

All strategic initiatives that are undertaken should include attainable milestones and timelines as well as the critical success factors that must be achieved if the strategy is to succeed. These should be summarised in this section and progress against them recorded.

Tools here could include attainment against the steps in recognised project management approaches (eg PRINCE2 or PERT), quality and process improvement systems (eg Six Sigma) or the perspectives of the balanced scorecard.

The scorecard may also record process issues under this heading such as whether there are project and change management methodologies in use, whether the firm has an SEM solution configured to track strategic implementation, and whether there are weaknesses in these such as whether any strategic initiatives have gone off-the-rails.

4   **Strategic risks** *(or strategy for risks)*: major risks that affect the achievement of the firm's strategic goals and key issues such as its risk appetite.

The Enterprise Risk Management (ERM) approach recognises that risk management needs to encompass all the firm's risks such as operational, financial, compliance, regulatory and strategic because these can impact on shareholder value significantly.

Strategic risk management requires that the board monitors three components:

Risk appetite: how willing it and its investors are to take risks.

Strategic risks facing the organisation as a consequence of external events as well as in consequence of the strategies and actions management have followed.

Risk treatment processes: how risks are identified and management within the organisation.

Section summary

The balanced scorecard is a performance measurement scheme which translates mission and strategy into objectives and measures under four perspectives. These combine both financial and non-financial aspects, being:

- Financial perspective
- Customer perspective
- Internal business processes
- Innovation and learning perspective

6 Developing a performance measurement system

Introduction

KPIs and the balanced scorecard highlight the importance of developing appropriate internal measures for monitoring the performance of a business or process.

However, it is important that an organisation selects what it is going to measure carefully so that it is controlling the outputs and processes which contribute to its CSFs.

Understanding, measuring and managing CSFs is increasingly important to ensuring the prosperity of organisations. CSFs, and the performance measures within them, need to link daily activities to the organisation's strategies.

In this respect the following factors are important in developing a performance measurement system:

- Identify the key outputs required from an activity

- Identify the key processes in providing the output

- Identify the interfaces of the activity with other parts of the firm, or with other processes in the value chain

- Develop KPIs for key processes

- Identify data sources for KPI information

The data required will vary considerably depending on what is being measured. The table below illustrates some of the aspects that could be measured.

Aspect of performance	Data sources For KPIs
Physical efficiency	Time to output Staff – customer ratios Chargeable time vs slack time
Perceptions and attitudes	Customer satisfaction surveys Customer retention/client turnover Staff turnover Peer group rating
Compliance	Key deadlines met Accuracy of documentation Data security – number of security breaches
Competence	Quality and training of staff in key positions Ability of management in controlling the process

Aspect of performance	Data sources For KPIs
Comparators	Benchmarking: Historical (year on year) Compared to best practice

- Develop reporting system

  Note that the desire to measure these performance indicators may highlight to an organisation that its information systems cannot provide the information they want from them.

  In this context, the desire to report on CSFs and performance indicators may prompt changes to an organisation's information systems.

Section summary

CSFs, and the performance measures within them, link daily activities to an organisation's strategies. If an organisation does not know its CSFs, performance measurement can become a random process creating a range of reports which do not measure an organisation's progress against its intended strategic direction.

7 Other multidimensional measures of performance

Introduction

The **performance pyramid** derives from the idea that an organisation operates at different levels, each of which has different (but supporting) concerns.

7.1 Performance across a range of dimensions

There have been a number of ideas concerning the measurement of performance across a range of dimensions. For example, as long ago as 1952 General Electric undertook a measurements project which concluded that there were eight key results areas (or critical success factors).

- Profitability
- Market position
- Productivity
- Product leadership
- Personnel development
- Employee attitudes
- Public responsibility
- Short v long term balance

7.2 The performance pyramid

The **performance pyramid** (developed by Lynch and Cross) stems from an acknowledgement that traditional performance measures which focused on financial indicators such as profitability, cash flow and return on capital employed did not address the driving forces that guide an organisation's ability to achieve its strategic objectives.

Instead of focusing purely on financial objectives, the pyramid focuses on a range of **objectives** for both **external effectiveness** (related to customer satisfaction) and **internal efficiency** (related to flexibility and productivity), which Lynch and Cross propose are the driving forces upon which company objectives are based. The status of these driving forces can then be monitored and measured by the indicators at the lower levels in the pyramid – measures of quality, delivery, cycle time and waste.

However, a crucial point behind the presentation of the model as a pyramid is that, although the organisation operates at different levels, each of which has a different focus, it is vital that each different level supports each other. In this way, the pyramid explicitly makes the link between **corporate level strategy** and the **day-to-day operations** of an organisation.

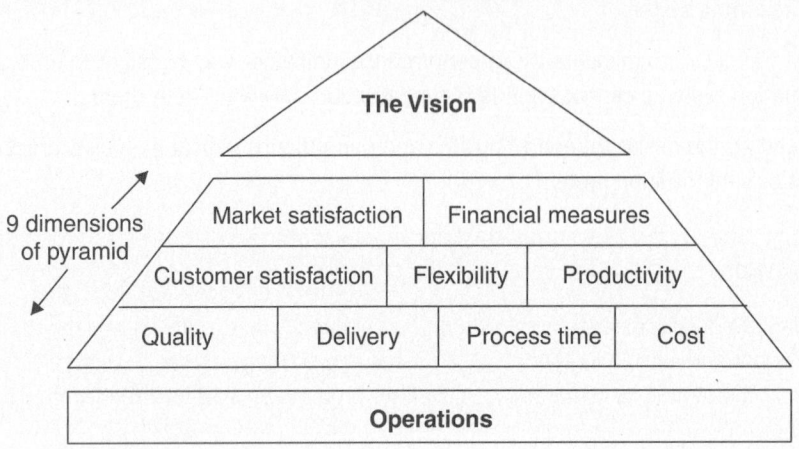

Note: When looking at any appraisal of costs it is crucial to understand the **processes driving** the costs rather then simply looking at them as figures in the management accounts.

(a) At **corporate level** the vision is developed and **financial** and **market objectives** are set in accordance with it.

(b) At **strategic business unit** level, strategies are developed to achieve these financial and market objectives.

   (i) **Customer satisfaction** is defined as meeting customer expectations

   (ii) **Flexibility** indicates responsiveness of the business operating system as a whole

   (iii) **Productivity** refers to the management of resources such as labour and time

(c) These in turn are supported by more specific **operational** criteria.

   (i) **Quality** of the product or service, consistency of product and fit for the purpose

   (ii) **Delivery** of the product or service, ie the method of distribution, its speed and ease of management

   (iii) **Cycle time** of all processes from cash collection to order processing to recruitment

   (iv) **Cost** (or waste) meaning the elimination of all non value added activities

The pyramid highlights the **links** running between the **vision for the company** and **functional objectives**. For example, a reduction in process time should lead to increased productivity and hence improved financial performance. The links within the pyramid help to ensure not only **goal congruence** but also a **consistency of performance** across all business areas, and a balanced approach.

7.3 Strengths and weaknesses of the performance pyramid

The performance pyramid clearly links the performance measures at the different hierarchical levels of the organisation, and encourages operational performance measures to be linked to strategic goals.

Individual departments need to be aware of the extent to which they are contributing to strategic aims, and their performance measures should link operational goals to strategic goals. This in itself is a strength, but perhaps the key strength of the model is the fact that it links this **hierarchical view** of performance measurement with an appreciation of **business processes** and the need to focus all business

activities on the **requirements of the customer.** (In this respect, the model contains echoes of Porter's Value Chain which highlights the importance of business processes creating **value** for the customer.)

The model also makes clear the measures that are of interest to **external** parties (such as customer satisfaction, quality and delivery) and those that the business focuses on **internally** such as (productivity, cycle time and waste.)

However, critics argue that the performance pyramid tends to concentrate on two main groups of stakeholders: shareholders and customers. However, it could also be necessary to look at measures which relate to other stakeholders (such as employees or suppliers).

Moreover, as with the Balanced Scorecard, critics have pointed to some practical problems that apply to the performance pyramid.

- Applying it may significantly increase the **cost** of organisational control

- **Management effort**, which could otherwise be devoted to running the business, could be used in devising performance measures and responding to reports

- Measures may **conflict**. This could demotivate managers who feel they are in a 'no win' situation

- Staff turnover may increase if staff feel they are being checked upon on all the time or have to spend lots of time inputting data

Section summary

The performance pyramid is an alternative performance measure to the BSC, and looks at how different performance measures will be required at different levels of an organisation.

8 Performance: service departments and firms

Introduction

Performance is more difficult to measure where there is no physical product. Services are intangible, they are consumed at the same time as they are produced and they cannot be stored. This leads to measures of performance based on output productivity and effectiveness.

8.1 Service departments

Measuring performance in a service department will focus management attention on matters such as the following.

- How the service department is using up resources of the organisation
- What its resources are costing
- Whether the department should be capable of improved efficiency and lower costs

The principles of control theory still apply, so that a system of performance evaluation for service departments or selling activities needs:

(a) A **budget, standard or target** for the department to work towards

(b) A system of **measuring actual performance** and comparing it against the budget, standard or target

(c) A system for deciding when **control action** ought to be considered

8.1.1 Setting a standard, budget or target

A standard, budget or target can be set for a service department in a number of ways.

(a)   There might be a budgeted expenditure limit for the department.

(b)   **Standard performance measures** might be established as targets for efficiency. Standard performance measures are possible where the department carries out routine activities for much of its work.

(c)   Targets or standards might be set for the **quality of the service**.

   (i)   To provide training to employees up to a quantifiable standard
   (ii)   To respond to requests for help within a specified number of minutes, hours or days
   (iii)   To respond to materials requisitions within a specified period of time

(d)   To perform a **targeted quantity of work** with a budgeted number of staff.

(e)   **To meet schedules for completing certain work**.

   (i)   Scheduled dates for completion of each stage in a product development project in the R&D department

   (ii)   Scheduled dates for the DP department to complete each stage of a new computer project

(f)   **To make a profit**. A service department might be designated as a profit centre. It would charge other departments for the services it provides at a 'commercial' transfer price rate, and it would be expected to earn a 'profit' on the work it does.

8.1.2 Standards for cost or efficiency

Two methods of setting a standard measure of performance in a service department are:

*   Standard cost per unit of activity
*   Standard quantity of 'output' per unit of resource used up

With both methods, there has to be a measurable quantity or volume of activity in the department. Both types of standard can be employed within a control system, and they are not mutually exclusive.

Examples of standard measures of performance in service departments might be as follows.

(a)   In the accounts receivable section of an accounts department, for example, the volume of activity could be measured by:

   (i)   Number or value of invoices issued
   (ii)   Number or value of payments received
   (iii)   The number or value of bad debts

   A budget for the section could then establish a standard cost per invoice issued, or a standard cost per £1 received or receivable, or a standard % of bad debts. In addition, there could be standards for the number or value of invoices issued per man/day.

(b)   In a sales department, activity could be measured by the number and value of orders taken, the number of customer visits, or the number of miles travelled by sales representatives. There could be a standard cost per customer visit, a standard cost per £1 of sales, and so on. Alternatively, standards could be set for the amount of work done per unit of resource consumed, and in a sales department, such standards include:

   (i)   Standard number of customer visits per salesperson per day
   (ii)   Standard number and value of sales per customer visit
   (iii)   Standard number of miles travelled per £1 of sales

(c)   In a transport department, activity could be measured in tonne/miles (tonnes of goods delivered and miles travelled) and standards could be established for:

   (i)   Cost per tonne/mile
   (ii)   Drivers' hours per tonne/mile
   (iii)   Miles per gallon consumed

8.1.3 Measuring and evaluating performance

Once a target, budget or standard has been set, we have a basis for evaluating performance, by comparing actual results against the target.

8.1.4 Indices of 'output' in a service department

Standards for work done in a service department could be expressed as an index. For example, suppose that in a sales department, there is a standard target for sales representatives to make 25 customer visits per month each. The budget for May 20X9 might be for ten sales representatives to make 250 customer visits in total. Actual results in May might be that nine sales representatives made 234 visits in total.

Performance could then be measured as:

Budget   100   (Standard = index 100)

Actual 104 $\left(\dfrac{234}{9\times25}\times100\right)$

This shows that 'productivity' per sales representative was actually 4% over budget.

Advantages of indices are as follows.

(a)   They are easily understood.

(b)   Once established, they can be used to evaluate:

   (i)   Actual results in a period against the standard
   (ii)   Trends in productivity over time

(c)   They can incorporate a 'basket' of different types of job. In the example of customer visits by sales representatives, not all customer visits are the same. Travelling time to some customers will be longer than to others, and some customers will take longer to deal with than others. With indexing, weightings can be given to different types of visit.

KEY POINT

Service departments vary between organisations, and in your examination you might be required to suggest standards of performance and methods of measuring and evaluating actual performance for a particular department in a particular type of organisation.

8.1.5 Selecting measures of performance

Key item(s) of performance to be measured should be identified. Examples include return, growth, productivity, market share, and cost control.

(a)   Return can be measured as ROI, RI, profit and so on.

(b)   Growth can be measured by sales growth, profit growth, investment spending, capacity fill and so on.

(c)   Productivity measures can be applied to machinery as well as labour.

(d)   Market position and status, or quality of product/service, could be measured by market research, or through customer responses and complaints.

(e)   Cost control involves identifying the nature of the costs that ought to be controlled and comparing actual spending with budget.

This can be applied to the finance function.

(a) **Define the boundaries** of the finance function. Does it include data processing, for example, or inventory control or treasury management?

(b) **Define formal objectives** for the function as a whole, and then for each main section, for supervisory and managerial staff and for the operation of systems (for example payroll).

(c) Ascertain what **activities** each section does (or should do) to achieve its objectives.

(d) **Identify appropriate measures**, on the basis of the objectives and activities identified. The 'pyramid' approach should be used, with successively more detailed information for successively junior levels of staff.

(e) Select suitable **bases of comparison**. Possibilities are time, budgets, standards or targets, intra-group comparison, or intra-organisational comparison, if verifiably comparable data is available.

8.2 Types of service organisation

Lin Fitzgerald et al, identify three different types of service organisation, as follows.

(a) **Professional services**, for example a management consultancy. Such services are characterised as being highly adaptable to individual customer needs, dependent upon staff/customer contact, people-based and relying on short chains of command and highly autonomous employees.

(b) **Mass services**, for example rail travel. These involve little customisation and limited customer contact, they are predominantly equipment-based and require defined tasks and set procedures to be performed with little exercise of judgement.

(c) **Service shops**, for example, a bank. These fall between the above extremes in terms of customisation, customer contact, people/equipment and levels of staff discretion.

8.3 Measuring performance in service businesses

The building block model

Fitzgerald & Moon developed the '**building block model**' as an attempt to overcome the perceived problems associated with performance measurement in service businesses.

Performance measurement in service businesses has often been perceived as difficult due to the nature of services compared to products (for example, their intangibility, the lack of any transfer of ownership, and the inherent variability in them: eg the quality of haircuts that customers might receive from two hairdressers within the same firm could be very different).

However, Fitzgerald & Moon provide building blocks – **dimensions**, **standards** and **rewards** – which can be used for designing performance measurement systems in service businesses.

Dimensions are the areas of performance which yield the specific performance metric for a company. These dimensions are then split into **results** and **determinants** (the factors which shape the results). And the logic is that controlling and improving performance in relation to the determinant should then lead to improvements in the results.

(a) **Results**

   (i) **Competitive performance**, focusing on factors such as sales growth and market share.

   (ii) **Financial performance**, concentrating on profitability, liquidity, capital structure and market ratios.

(b)   **Determinants** (of those results)

    (i)   **Quality of service** looks at matters like reliability, responsiveness, courtesy, competence and availability/accessibility. These can be measured by customer satisfaction surveys.

    (ii)   **Flexibility** is an apt heading for assessing the organisation's ability to deliver at the right speed, to respond to precise customer specifications, and to cope with fluctuations in demand.

    (iii)   **Resource utilisation** considers how efficiently resources are being utilised. This can be problematic because of the complexity of the inputs to a service and the outputs from it and because some of the inputs are supplied by the customer.

    (iv)   **Innovation** is assessed in terms of both the innovation process and the success of individual innovations. Individual innovations should be measured in terms of whether they have led to improvements in the other five 'dimensions'.

(c)   **Standards**

Standards are the measures used to monitor an organisation's performance in each of the dimensions chosen. In order for the standards to be effective, employees must view them as **fair** and **achievable**, and must take **ownership** of them.

    (i)   To ensure that employees take **ownership** of standards, they need to **participate** in the budget and standard-setting processes. They are then more likely to **accept** the standards, feel more **motivated** as they perceive the standards to be achievable and **morale** is improved. The disadvantage to participation is that it offers the opportunity for the introduction of **budgetary slack**.

    (ii)   **Achievability** - Standards need to be set **high enough** to ensure that there is some **sense of achievement** in attaining them, but **not so high** that there is a **demotivating** effect because they are felt to be unachievable. It is management's task to find a **balance** between what the organisation perceives as achievable and what employees perceive as achievable.

    (iii)   **Fairness** - It is vital that equity is seen to occur when applying standards for performance measurement purposes. The performance of different business units should not be measured against the same standards if some units have an inherent advantage unconnected with their own efforts. For example, divisions operating in different countries should not be assessed against the same standards.

(d)   **Rewards**

Rewards are the motivators which encourage employees to work towards the standards set.

Three issues need to be considered if the performance measurement system is to operate successfully: **clarity**, **motivation** and **controllability**.

    (i)   **Clarity**. The organisation's objectives need to be **clearly understood** by those whose performance is being appraised; that is, they need to know what goals they are working towards.

    (ii)   Individuals should be **motivated** to work in pursuit of the organisation's strategic objectives. Goal clarity and participation have been shown to contribute to higher levels of motivation to achieve targets, providing managers accept those targets. Bonuses can be used to motivate.

    (iii)   Managers should have a certain level of **controllability** for their areas of responsibility. For example they should not be held responsible for costs over which they have no control.

Dimension	Type	Example measures
Competitive performance	Competitor focused	Market share Prices Product features
	Customer focused	Customer retention Customer numbers
Financial performance	Profitability	Profit Working capital cycle
	Liquidity	Bad debts
Quality of service	Reliability	Punctuality Dependability of service and staff
	Responsiveness	Response times Number of phone lines Delivery speed (for goods ordered online or by phone)
	Courtesy	Politeness Respect to customers
	Competence	Staff skill Expertise Knowledge Diligence
	Availability	Product availability Product range
	Accessibility	Ease of finding site
Flexibility	Delivery speed	Customer waiting time Time from customer enquiry to job completion
	Coping with demand	Spare capacity to deal with peak times Overtime worked
	Response to customer specification	Customer feedback surveys (degree to which advice or assistance is tailored to customer needs) Range of staff and skills
Resource utilisation	Productivity	Labour hours worked Skill levels of work performed by staff grade
	Premises	% of area used for value-adding services, or customer-facing services
Innovation	Cost	Development cost per new service line
	Speed	Time taken from concept being devised to service being offered to customers

Section summary

It can be more difficult to measure performance in organisations which do not produce a physical product. However, the building block model offers a useful range of performance measures for measuring service performance.

9 Performance: manufacturing

Introduction

A wide range of measures exists for measuring manufacturing performance. They range from simple cost/output efficiency measures to more complex ideas relating to quality and innovation.

A number of performance indicators can be used to assess operations. They are particularly relevant to the internal business and customer perspectives of the balanced scorecard.

- Quality
- Number of customer complaints and warranty claims
- Lead times
- Rework
- Delivery to time
- Non-productive hours
- System (machine) down time

These indicators can also be expressed in the form of ratios or percentages for comparative purposes. Like physical measures, they can be produced quickly and trends can be identified and acted upon rapidly. Examples of useful ratios might be as follows.

(a) **Machine down time: total machine hours**. This ratio could be used to monitor machine availability and can provide a measure of machine usage and efficiency.

(b) **Component rejects: component purchases**. This ratio could be used to control the quality of components purchased from an external supplier. This measure can be used to monitor the performance of new suppliers.

(c) **Deliveries late: deliveries on schedule**. This ratio could be applied to sales made to customers as well as to receipts from suppliers.

(d) **Customer rejects/returns: total sales**. This ratio helps to monitor customer satisfaction, providing a check on the efficiency of quality control procedures.

(e) **Value added time: production cycle time**. Value added time is the direct production time during which the product is being made and value is therefore being added.

9.1 Advanced manufacturing technology

The advent of **advanced manufacturing technology (AMT)** has meant that many organisations will need to modify their performance measures so that the information they provide will be useful in controlling operations in the new manufacturing environment.

9.2 Performance measurement for manufacturing

Performance measurement in manufacturing is increasingly using non-financial measures. Malcolm Smith identifies four over-arching measures for manufacturing environments.

- **Cost**: cost behaviour
- **Quality**: factors inhibiting performance
- **Time**: bottlenecks, inertia
- **Innovation**: new product flexibility

9.2.1 Cost

Possible non-financial or part-financial indicators are as follows.

Area	Measure
Quantity of raw material inputs	Actual v target number
Equipment productivity	Actual v standard units
Maintenance efforts	No. of production units lost through maintenance No. of production units lost through failure No. of failures prior to schedule
Overtime costs	Overtime hours/total hours
Product complexity	No. of component parts
Quantity of output	Actual v target completion
Product obsolescence	% shrinkage
Employees	% staff turnover
Employee productivity	direct labour hours per unit
Customer focus	% service calls; % claims

9.2.2 Quality

Integrating quality into a performance measurement system suggests attention to the following items.

Area	Measure
Quality of purchased components	Zero defects
Equipment failure	Downtime/total time
Maintenance effort	Breakdown maintenance/total maintenance
Waste	% defects; % scrap; % rework
Quality of output	% yield
Safety	Serious industrial injury rate
Reliability	% warranty claims
Quality commitment	% dependence on post-inspection % conformance to quality standards
Employee morale	% absenteeism
Leadership impact	% cancelled meetings
Customer awareness	% repeat orders; number of complaints

KEY TERM

TOTAL QUALITY MANAGEMENT (TQM) is an 'integrated and comprehensive system of planning and controlling all business functions so that products or services are produced which meet or exceed customer expectations. TQM is a philosophy of business behaviour, embracing principles such as employee involvement, continuous improvement at all levels and customer focus, as well as being a collection of related techniques aimed at improving quality such as full documentation of activities, clear goal-setting and performance measurement from the customer perspective.   *(CIMA Official Terminology)*

9.2.3 Time

A truly just-in-time system is an ideal to which many manufacturing firms are striving. Time-based competition is also important for new product development, deliveries etc. The management accounting focus might be on throughput, bottlenecks, customer feedback and distribution.

Area	Measure
Equipment failure	Time between failures
Maintenance effort	Time spent on repeat work
Throughput	Processing time/total time per unit
Production flexibility	Set-up time
Availability	% stockouts
Labour effectiveness	Standard hours achieved / total hours worked
Customer impact	No. of overdue deliveries Mean delivery delay

9.2.4 Innovation

Performance indicators for innovation can support the 'innovation and learning' perspective on the balanced scorecard. Some possible suggestions are outlined below.

Area	Measure
The ability to introduce new products	% product obsolescence Number of new products launched Number of patents secured Time to launch new products
Flexibility to accommodate change	Number of new processes implemented Number of new process modifications
Reputation for innovation	Media recognition for leadership Expert assessment of competence Demonstrable competitive advantage

9.3 Activity based measures of performance

Many writers have seen the potential of the activity-based approach to management accounting to provide new performance indicators. For example, if the number of purchase requisitions is a cost driver for a number of purchasing, receiving and accounting activities then it would be possible to compare the resources which ought to be employed to process a given number of requisitions with the resources actually employed.

9.4 Use of experience curves

Experience curves can also be used in strategic control of costs. Experience curves suggest that as output increases, the cost per unit of output falls. This fall in cost results from:

(a)   **Economies of scale** – in other words an increased volume of production leads to lower unit costs, as the firm approaches full capacity.

(b)   A genuine **'learning effect'** as the workforce becomes familiar with the job and learns to carry out the task more efficiently. As a process is repeated, it is likely that costs will reduce due to **efficiency, discounts** and **reduced waste**.

(c)   **Technological improvements**.

9.5 Target costing

This brings us on to **target costing**, an approach used in Japan. This is based on the principle that a product must have a target price that will succeed in winning a target share of the market.

When a product is first manufactured, the **target cost** will usually be well below the current cost, which is determined by current technology and processes, and experience effects. Management then sets benchmarks for improvement towards the target costs, by improving technologies and processes.

Target costing is thus in effect a process of establishing what the cost of the product should be over the entire **product life cycle**.

(a)   In the short run, because of development costs and the learning time needed, costs are likely to exceed price.

(b)   In the longer term, costs should come down (eg because of the experience curve) to their target level.

Section summary

A range of financial and non-financial measures will also be useful for measuring manufacturing performance. These range from simple cost and output efficiency measures to more complex ideas relating to quality and innovation.

10 Regulation and performance

Introduction

Modern society is very concerned to define for itself what is and what is not 'acceptable'. Businesses are taking this concern on board, and both **legal** and **voluntary** regulations will affect company performance.

10.1 Organisational guidelines and corporate codes

Corporate governance, controls and ethics are covered in much more detail in Paper P3 – Performance strategy.

The relevance to E3, though, is that alongside operational performance measures, organisations are also increasingly measuring how well they fulfil their wider social obligations. Equally, performance management will increasingly relate to social and ethical aspects of performance rather than more narrowly defined financial or commercial ones.

Organisations are coming under increasing pressure from a number of **sources** to behave more ethically.

- **Government**
- UK and European **legislation**
- **Treaty obligations** (such as the *Kyoto protocol*)
- **Consumers**
- **Employers**
- **Pressure groups**

These sources of pressure expect an ethical attitude towards the following.

- **Stakeholders** (employees, customers, competitors, suppliers and society at large)
- **Animals**
- **Green issues** (such as pollution and the need for recycling)
- **The disadvantaged**
- Dealings with **unethical companies or countries**

10.2 Corporate codes and corporate culture

In Chapter 2 of this Study Text we looked at ethics, but many commentators would argue that the introduction of a code of ethics as a means of improving behaviour is **inadequate** on its own. To be effective, a code needs to be accompanied by **positive attempts to foster guiding values, aspirations and patterns of thinking that support ethically sound behaviour** – in short a **change of culture**.

10.2.1 Company code of conduct

A corporate code typically contains a series of statements setting out the company's values and explaining how it sees its responsibilities towards stakeholders.

CASE STUDY

Codes of conduct - Henkel

The German-based home care, cosmestics and adhesive technologies group, Henkel, publishes a series of behavioural guidelines that determine how all its staff should act every day. These guidelines are based on the company's 'Vision and Values' and include a Code of Conduct, a Code of Teamwork & Leadership, and a Code of Corporate Sustainability.

These Codes provide all Henkel staff with a set of practical guidelines for their relationships with customers as well as with their co-workers.

The Code of Conduct reminds staff:

'Henkel's image and reputation, as a company that operates in an ethically and legally appropriate manner, is inseparable from the conduct of each of us as we perform our work, everyday. We, the employees of Henkel, are expected to respect laws and regulations, avoid conflicts of interest, protect the Company's assets, and show consideration and appreciation for the local customs, traditions and social *mores* of the various countries and cultures in which Henkel conducts business. In fulfilling our responsibilities within Henkel, we do not take ethical shortcuts. Improper conduct will never be in Henkel's interest.

If you have any questions, or if you are uncomfortable with a decision or a course of action being undertaken, take the issue to a higher level within the Henkel organisation. Make sure you get good advice. But what is most important: Observe our Code of Conduct and never accept that others will violate it. We should be aware that our values define us to the world. Therefore, Henkel's image and reputation rests in each of our hands, everyday.'

10.2.2 The impact of a corporate code

A code of conduct can set out the company's expectations, and in principle a code such as that outlined above addresses many of the problems that the organisations may experience. However, **merely issuing a code is not enough**.

(a)   The **commitment of senior management** to the code needs to be real, and it needs to be very clearly communicated to all staff. Staff need to be persuaded that expectations really have changed.

(b)   Measures need to be taken to **discourage previous behaviours** that conflict with the code.

(c)   **Staff need to understand** that it is in the **organisation's best interests** to change behaviour, and become committed to the same ideals.

(d)   Some employees – including very able ones – may find it very difficult to buy into a code that they **perceive may limit their own earnings** and/or restrict their freedom to do their job.

(e)   In addition to a general statement of ethical conduct, **more detailed statements** (codes of practice) will be needed to set out formal procedures that must be followed.

10.3 Green and social issues and the management accountant

As green and social issues surrounding sustainability become more important to businesses, management accountants will also need to consider how such issues might affect financial performance.

Martin Bennett and Peter James (in an article in *Management Accounting* in November 1998) looked at the **ways in which a company's concern for the environment can impact on its performance.**

(a)   **Short-term savings** through waste minimisation and energy efficiency schemes can be substantial.

(b)   **Pressures on businesses** for environmental action are increasing.

(c)   Companies with poor environmental performance may face **increased cost of capital** because investors and lenders demand a higher risk premium.

(d)   There are a growing number of **energy and environmental taxes**, such as the UK's landfill tax.

(e)   Accidents and long-term environmental effects can result in **large financial liabilities**.

(f)   **Pressure group campaigns** can cause damage to reputation and/or additional costs.

(g)   Environmental legislation may cause the **'sunsetting'** of products and opportunities for **'sunrise' replacements**.

(h)   The cost of processing input which becomes **waste** is equivalent to 5-10% of some organisation's turnover.

(i)   The phasing out of CFCs has led to markets for alternative products.

Bennett & James go on to suggest six main ways in which business and environmental benefits can be achieved.

(a)   **Integrating the environment into capital expenditure decisions** (by considering environmental opposition to projects which could affect cash flows, for example)

(b)   **Understanding and managing environmental costs**. Environmental costs are often 'hidden' in overheads and environmental and energy costs are often not allocated to the relevant budgets.

(c)   **Introducing waste minimisation schemes**

(d)   **Understanding and managing life cycle costs.** For many products, the greatest environmental impact occurs upstream (such as mining raw materials) or downstream from production (such as energy to operate equipment). This has led to producers being made responsible for dealing with the disposal of products such as cars, and government and third party measures to influence raw material choices. Organisations therefore need to identify, control and make provision for environmental life cycle costs and work with suppliers and customers to identify environmental cost reduction opportunities.

(e)   **Measuring environmental performance.** Business is under increasing pressure to measure all aspects of environmental performance, both for statutory disclosure reasons and due to demands for more environmental data from customers.

(f)   **Involving management accountants in a strategic approach to environment-related management accounting and performance evaluation.** A 'green accounting team' incorporating the key functions

should analyse the strategic picture and identify opportunities for practical initiatives. It should analyse the short-, medium– and long-term impact of possible changes in the following.

(i)   **Government policies**, such as on transport
(ii)   Legislation and regulation
(iii)   Supply conditions, such as fewer landfill sites
(iv)   Market conditions, such as changing customer views
(v)   Social attitudes, such as to factory farming
(vi)   Competitor strategies

Possible action includes the following.

(i)   Designating an **'environmental champion'** within the strategic planning or accounting function to ensure that environmental considerations are fully considered.

(ii)   Assessing whether **new data sources** are needed to collect more and better data

(iii)   Making **comparisons** between sites/offices to highlight poor performance and generate peer pressure for action

(iv)   Developing **checklists** for internal auditors

Such analysis and action should help organisations to better understand present and future environmental costs and benefits.

KEY TERM

CORPORATE SOCIAL ACCOUNTING is the 'reporting of the social and environmental impact of an entity's activities upon those who are directly associated with the entity (for instance, employees, customers, suppliers) or those who are in any way affected by the activities of the entity, as well as an assessment of the cost of compliance with relevant regulations in this area'.   (CIMA *Official Terminology*)

Lynne Paine (writing in the *Harvard Business Review*, March-April 1994) suggests that ethical decisions are becoming more important, as penalties, in the US at least, for companies which break the law are become tougher. Paine suggests that there are two approaches to the management of ethics in organisations:

(a)   A **compliance-based** approach is primarily designed to ensure that the company and its personnel act within the letter of the law. Mere compliance is not an adequate means for addressing the full range of ethical issues that arise every day. This is especially the case in the UK, where **voluntary codes** of conduct and self-regulating institutes are perhaps more prevalent than the US.

(b)   An **integrity-based approach** combines a concern for the law with an emphasis on managerial responsibility for ethical behaviour … . When integrated into the day-to-day operations of an organisation, such strategies can help prevent damaging ethical lapses.   .

Section summary

In addition to operational performance measures, organisations also need to monitor how well they fulfil their wider ethical and CSR obligations. Green issues and sustainability are becoming increasingly important in this respect.

Chapter Roundup

✓   Controls are vital for an organisation to assess how well it is performing against its strategic plans. However, plans and controls need to be reviewed together. A plan is of little use if it is not put into action, while a system of control can only be effective if the propel overseeing it know what they are trying to achieve.

✓   **Strategic control** is bound up with measurement of performance, which often tends to be based on financial criteria. Techniques for strategic control suggest that companies develop strategic milestones (eg for market share) to monitor the achievement of strategic objectives, as a counterweight to purely financial issues.

✓   **Critical success factors** are the few key areas where things must go right for the organisation to flourish.

✓   Performance measures can be both financial and non-financial. A growing dissatisfaction with financial performance measures has led to non-financial measures being developed based on operational performance.

✓   Nonetheless, commercial organisations need to remember that maximising profit is likely to remain one of their key goals, so they cannot ignore the financial aspect of performance.

✓   The balanced scorecard is a performance measurement scheme which translates mission and strategy into objectives and measures under four perspectives. There combine both financial and non-financial aspects, being:

- financial perspective
- customer perspective
- internal business processes
- innovation and learning perspective

✓   CSFs, and the performance measures within them, link daily activities to an organisation's strategies. If an organisation does not know its CSFs, performance measurement can become a random process creating a range of reports which do not measure an organisation's progress against its intended strategic direction.

✓   The performance pyramid is an alternative performance measure to the BSC, and looks at how different performance measures will be required at different levels of an organisation.

✓   It can be more difficult to measure performance in organisations which do not produce a physical product. However, the building block model offers a useful range of performance measures for measuring service performance.

✓   A range of financial and non-financial measures will also be useful for measuring manufacturing performance. These range from simple cost and output efficiency measures to more complex ideas relating to quality and innovation.

✓   In addition to operational performance measures, organisations also need to monitor how well they fulfil their wider ethical and CSR obligations. Green issues and sustainability are becoming increasingly important in this respect.

Quick Quiz

1   **Fill in the blanks** in the statements below, using the words in the box.

The aims of performance measurement are as follows

• (1) .... the (2) .... of the company

• Concentrating (3) .... towards objectives

• Part of the (4) .... process where (5) .... is compared with the (6) ....

• plan	• objectives	• control
• feedback	• efforts	• communicating

2   What is an example of a critical success factor for the production function?

3   Which of the following is a perceived disadvantage of zero based budgeting (ZBB)?

A   There are no incentives as the budget is often unrealistic
B   The managers who set the budgets are not responsible for attaining them
C   Too many people are involved
D   It may emphasise short term benefits rather than long term goals

4   'In general, there are three possible points of reference for measurement'. What are they?

....

....

....

5   Give some examples of non-financial performance measures that can be applied to an assessment of marketing effectiveness.

6   What are the four perspectives on the balanced scorecard?

....

....

....

....

7   What are the specific operational criteria contained in the performance pyramid?

8   What have been seen as the four 'over-arching' measures for manufacturing environments?

9   **Fill in the blanks** in the statements below, using the words in the box.

A corporate (1) ....   typically contains   a series of (2) .... setting out the company's (3) .... and explaining how it sees its (4) .... towards (5) ....

• stakeholders	• code	• statements
• responsibilities	• values	

10   What are some of the disadvantages of using profit as a performance measure?

Answers to Quick Quiz

1   (1) Communicating (2) objectives (3) efforts (4) control (5) feedback (6) plan

2   Quality standards / capacity utilisation

3   D

4   Profitability
        Activity
        Productivity

5   Trend in market share   Sales volume growth
        Customer visits per salesperson   Client contact hours per salesperson
        Sales volume forecast v actual   Number of customers
        Customer survey response information

6   Financial
        Customer
        Internal business processes
        Innovation/learning

7   Quality   Delivery
        Process time   Cost

8   Cost   Quality
        Time   Innovation

9   (1) code (2) statements (3) values (4) responsibilities (5) stakeholders

10   Encourages short-termism and focus on the annual cycle, at the expense of long term performance

        Profit differs from economic income

        A firm has to satisfy stakeholders other than shareholders, such as the government and the local community

        Liquidity is at least as important as profit

        Profit should be related to risk, not just capital employed

        Profits can fluctuate in times of rapid change, eg exchange rates

        Profits measures cannot easily be used to motivate cost centre managers

Answers to Questions

14.1 Product leadership

Qualitative measures ought to be available in the form of reviews by consumer magazines, newspapers, and trade press, awards, endorsement by public figures, and direct comment from customers.

14.2 Invoicing

Invoices per employee per week: 10,000/4 = 2,500 (activity)

Staff cost per invoice: £0.12 (cost/profitability) 16,000/(2,500 × 52)

Invoices per hour: 2,500/(7 × 5) = 71.4 (productivity). (Assume employee works 5 days a week, 7 hours per day.)

Cost of idle time: £32 + £4.28 = £36.28 (cost/profitability). (Cost of phone call + ½ hour lost productivity (½ × £0.12 × 71.4)

You may have thought of other measures and probably have slight rounding differences.

14.3 Hotel

Financial performance: profit and loss per department, variance analysis (eg expenditure on wages, power, catering, bedrooms and so on).

Competitive performance: market share (room occupied on a total percentage of rooms available locally); competitor occupancy; competitor prices; bookings; vacant rooms as a proportion of the total attitudes of particular market segments.

Resource utilisation: rooms occupied/rooms available service quality measure: complaints, room checks.

Quality of service: Complaints, results of questionnaires

Now try these questions from the Exam Question Bank	Number	Level	Marks	Time
	Q17	Examination	25	45 mins
	Q18	Examination	50	90 mins

Question 18 does not relate specifically to Chapter 14. Instead it is a longer case study question to revisit some of the ideas we have covered in this Text as a whole.

Exam skills

The 50 mark Section A question in your exam will comprise a pre-seen scenario (released about six weeks before the exam) supplemented by additional unseen material you will receive when you sit the exam.

We have included a sample Section A question, including the pre-seen and unseen material, after the Exam Question Bank in this Study Text.

You should attempt this question now as well.

However, please note the pre-seen scenario included here is NOT the scenario you will be given for your exam.

BPP produces a Strategic Case Study Kit based on the pre-seen scenarios for each exam, and these Kits are available to purchase separately during the six weeks before the exam.

EXAM QUESTION AND ANSWER BANK

What the examiner means

The table below has been prepared by CIMA to help you interpret exam questions.

Learning objectives	Verbs used	Definition
1 Knowledge What are you expected to know	• List • State • Define	• Make a list of • Express, fully or clearly, the details of/facts of • Give the exact meaning of
2 Comprehension What you are expected to understand	• Describe • Distinguish • Explain • Identify • Illustrate	• Communicate the key features of • Highlight the differences between • Make clear or intelligible/state the meaning of • Recognise, establish or select after consideration • Use an example to describe or explain something
3 Application How you are expected to apply your knowledge	• Apply • Calculate/ compute • Demonstrate • Prepare • Reconcile • Solve • Tabulate	• Put to practical use • Ascertain or reckon mathematically • Prove with certainty or to exhibit by practical means • Make or get ready for use • Make or prove consistent/compatible • Find an answer to • Arrange in a table
4 Analysis How you are expected to analyse the detail of what you have learned	• Analyse • Categorise • Compare and contrast • Construct • Discuss • Interpret • Prioritise • Produce	• Examine in detail the structure of • Place into a defined class or division • Show the similarities and/or differences between • Build up or compile • Examine in detail by argument • Translate into intelligible or familiar terms • Place in order of priority or sequence for action • Create or bring into existence
5 Evaluation How you are expected to use your learning to evaluate, make decisions or recommendations	• Advise • Evaluate • Recommend	• Counsel, inform or notify • Appraise or assess the value of • Propose a course of action

This list is very important, and the guidance in our Practice and Revision Kit focuses on verbs.

1 IT Four Star Products

Learning outcome C-1(ii)

Four Star Products plc is a major manufacturing organisation with a range of consumer products. Founded over seventy years ago and run for many years by the founder and his family, the company was rather traditional in its strategy, tending to stick to the hardware and other household goods that it understood. A formal system of strategic planning was introduced in 1962 and remains in place today, with a 47 person strong planning department reporting to a Planning Director.

Since a financial crisis in 1994, the dominance of the founding family has been diluted by banker power and the appointment from outside of a new CEO, a new CFO and three non-executive directors. The CEO has a reputation for turning companies around and his strategy has been to move into the IT and telecommunications sectors in force. He has made little use of the work of the planning department, preferring to commission research externally. Unfortunately, the recent collapse of the Internet bubble and fall in interest in IT and telecomms shares has led to Four Star suffering significant losses and a fall in its share price. One of the CEO's plans for cost reduction is to abolish the planning department.

Required

(a)   In the light of the CEO's attitude towards the planning department, discuss whether or not having a planning department is valuable for Four Star products.

(b)   Explain how the formal planning process is intended to deal with events such as the collapse of the Internet business model.

Approaching the question

You must learn to read question settings critically. Look for hints and keywords and ask questions of the information given to you. This is illustrated here.

Four Star Products plc is a major manufacturing organisation with a range of consumer

products. Founded over seventy years ago and run for many years by the founder and his

> How quickly does the market move? Is rapid introduction of new

family, the company was rather traditional in its strategy, tending to stick to the hardware and

> Culture? Flexibility? Innovation?

other household goods that it understood. A formal system of strategic planning was

introduced in 1962 and remains in place today, with a 47 person strong planning department

> Rational model

reporting to a Planning Director.

> That is a lot of people and likely to be a major overhead

Since a financial crisis in 1994, the dominance of the founding family has been diluted by

> Concern for financial performance

banker power and the appointment from outside of a new CEO, a new CFO and three non-

executive directors. The CEO has a reputation for turning companies around and his strategy

> Change of sector – how practical?

has been to move into the IT and telecommunications sectors in force. He has made little use

of the work of the planning department, preferring to commission research externally.

> Why?

Unfortunately, the recent collapse of the Internet bubble and fall in interest in IT and telecomms

shares has led to Four Star suffering significant losses and a fall in its share price. One of the

CEO's plans for cost reduction is to abolish the planning department.

> Requirement for cost reduction

BPP
LEARNING MEDIA

2 Management and social responsibility

45 mins

Learning outcome A-1(ii)

In what respects may the need to exercise social responsibility shape the relationship of management to stakeholders?

(25 marks)

Approaching the answer

This is a difficult question, mainly because it seems very short, and possibly even a bit vague, and you may wonder how you can plan and write for 45 minutes on this topic. Thinking about the requirement should throw up several issues for you to consider. Let's look at it again.

In what respects may the need to exercise social responsibility shape the relationship of management to stakeholders?

> Who are the stakeholders likely to be affected?
>
> Not just talking about shareholders!

> Why is there ever a need to exercise social responsibility?

> What is social responsibility? A minefield! Different stakeholders define it in different terms. (But have a definition in your mind)

> What is the usual relationship between managers and stakeholders? Why are such relationships important?

Answer plan

Organise the things that you have noticed and your points arising into a coherent answer plan. Not all of the points may need to go into your answer, so spend some time thinking them through and prioritising them.

Definition of social responsibility – not just environmentalism, but also social issues. Organisation must be aware of wider society. This will sometimes have to override commercial pressures. There are costs and benefits.

Where are the limits? The world as a whole? Argument that businesses discharge some responsibility simply by creating wealth and paying taxes.

Pressures come from stakeholders – managers don't do it under their own steam.

Stakeholder analysis (for each one, describe the relationship, and their particular interest in social responsibility)

(a)   **Employees** – paid workers, but also members of society. Legal regulations such as health and safety

(b)   **Customers** – paying for goods and services. Can put pressure on products to set new standards eg 'dolphin friendly' tuna fishing

(c)   **Suppliers** – may impose restrictions

(d)   **Professional bodies** – ethical standards for management to follow

(e)   **Elected authorities** – can affect management in a number of ways (legislation, public opinion, influence over commercial organisations)

(f)   **Shareholders** – profit! Might not appreciate resources being used on worthy projects that earn no money.

Management issues – they need to weigh up the conflicting demands

(a)   Monitoring the expectations people have of the organisation

(b)   Achieving good publicity

(c)   Selecting socially responsible activities.

(i)   Ensuring core activities are conducted in a socially responsible way

(ii)   Supporting activities which are for public welfare (eg charitable donations)

(d)   Clearly knowing the minimum acceptable standards. Is it worth going further?

3 Development agencies   36 mins

Learning outcome C-1(ii)

A leading manufacturer of personal computers has set up its manufacturing operation in a region of the country which has seen a decline of its traditional industries, lower prosperity and higher unemployment than the rest of the country. Its decision was seen as a success for the Regional Development Agency, which had been hoping to attract such companies to the region.

Required

(a)   Identify the objectives of a Regional Development Agency (RDA), and how might its objectives and those of a manufacturer of high technology items might be expected to coincide in the matter of choosing a location for the European manufacturing base?   **(8 marks)**

(b)   Describe the environmental factors which you think might be influential in encouraging a high-tech manufacturer to locate its operations in an under-developed or declining region, and how the RDA might have tried to exploit these influences.   **(12 marks)**

(Total = 20 marks)

4 Toroidal Tooling   45 mins

Learning outcome C-2(iii)

Toroidal Tooling manufactures a range of highly specialised cutting tools for the engineering industry. It also acts as exclusive UK selling agent for three complementary product ranges manufactured overseas. Toroidal tooling has been in the machine tool industry for 107 years and is still largely family owned. Perhaps as a result, it is rather sleepy and vulnerable to competition from the major global players. Recently, Toroidal has seen its annual turnover stagnate at about £27M and is aware that its competitors are cutting deep into its market. Profitability is falling.

Toroidal has never had a very sophisticated accounting system, so its knowledge of its costs is rudimentary. However, its salespeople have good knowledge of the market and they suggest that prices are not the most important consideration among customers. Delivery, after sales service and product reliability seem to be more important. Toroidal's product reliability is generally good, but it is often late with deliveries and customers complain that they can rarely obtain accurate information on the progress of their orders. The sales force also note that the overall product range contains several important gaps that are not compensated for by overlaps elsewhere. The overlaps are caused by Toroidal's well-established agency policy of accepting their overseas principals' complete product ranges. There are four basic sales categories: buffing and polishing wheels; grinding wheels; taps and dies; and high speed steel cutting tools. Within each of these main categories, however, there are up to seven distinct product groups and five brand names.

Required

The Managing Director of Toroidal has asked your advice about two principal areas of concern.

(a)   With regard to the company's product portfolio, explain a technique that could be used to assess the commercial value of the various product groups.

(b)   With regard to the company's business systems, explain a technique that could be used to provide a broad overview of the way it operates.

5 GHK restaurants

18 mins

Learning outcome C-1(iv)

> **Note**: This question is taken from the Specimen Paper provided by CIMA for the 2010 Syllabus.

GHK is a restaurant chain consisting of eight restaurants in an attractive part of a European country which is popular with tourists. GHK has been owned by the same family for the previous 15 years and has always traded at a profit. However, a number of factors have meant that GHK is now in danger of making a trading loss. There has been a substantial drop in the number of tourists visiting the region whilst, at the same time, the prices of many of the foodstuffs and drinks used in its restaurants has increased. Added to this, the local economy has shrunk with several large employers reducing the size of their workforce.

The owners of GHK commissioned a restaurant consultant to give them an independent view of their business. The consultant observed that the eight restaurants were all very different in appearance. They also served menus that were very different, for example, one restaurant which was located on a barge in a coastal town specialised in fish dishes, whereas another restaurant 20 miles away had a good reputation as a steak house. The prices varied greatly amongst the restaurants; one restaurant in a historic country house offered 'fine dining' and was extremely expensive; yet another located near a busy railway station served mainly fast food and claimed that its prices were 'the cheapest in town'. Three of GHK's restaurants offered a 'middle of the road' dining experience with conventional menus and average prices. Some of the restaurants had licences which enabled them to serve alcohol with their meals but three restaurants did not have such licences. One restaurant had a good trade in children's birthday parties whereas the restaurant in the historic country house did not admit diners under the age of 18.

The consultant recommended that GHK should examine these differences but did not suggest how. The owners responded that the chain had grown organically over a number of years and that the location, style and pricing decisions made in each restaurant had all been made at different times and depended on trends current at that time.

Required

Advise the owners of GHK how the application of Porter's Three Generic Strategies Model could assist them in maintaining or improving the profitability of their restaurants.

Note: You are not required to suggest individual generic strategies for each of GHK's restaurants.

(10 marks)

6 Packit Co

27 mins

Learning outcome C–1 (iii)

Len Wills, Managing Director of Packit Co, a medium sized manufacturing company based in a European country, has been faced with an interesting dilemma.

Packit Co has produced a unique, easy opening packaging process which had found a ready market with large multinational food companies in Europe. Packit's packaging process had a significant competitive advantage over its rivals, and the company ensured its technological superiority was protected by patents.

However, as its dealings with global customers have increased, Packit has come under increasing pressure to become a global supplier with some form of presence in America and the Far East. Having a global presence would help secure its technological leadership, and its increased size would help prevent its American and Asian competitors moving into the European market.

Packit has been considering the various strategic options which are open to it. Acquiring a similar packaging company in an appropriate location seems unlikely, as few companies are for sale. Furthermore, Packit's technological advantage meant that a joint venture was not a realistic short term possibility.

Eventually the decision was taken to pursue some form of internal or organic growth. Packit has looked at three alternative options. One is to achieve this growth either by opening company sales office in a number of key markets. The second is to establish foreign manufacturing operations handling the final stages of the manufacturing process and buying semi-finished material from the parent company. The third is to appoint agents or distributors to look after Packit's interests in the key American and Asian markets.

Len has asked for your assistance in evaluating the risk and benefits associated with these alternative ways of expanding its international operations.

Required

Analyse the advantages and disadvantages of the three stated organic options open to Packit Co in its move to become a global company. **(15 marks)**

7 Product market strategy   45 mins

Learning outcome C-1(iv)

It has been stated that an industry or a market segment within an industry goes through four basic phases of development. These four phases – introduction, growth, maturity and decline – each has an implication for an organisation's development of growth and divestment strategies.

The following brief profiles relate to four commercial organisations, each of which operate in different industries.

- **Company A.** Established in the last year and manufactures state of the art door locks which replace the need for a key with computer image recognition of fingerprint patterns.

- **Company B.** A biotechnological product manufacturer established for three years and engaged in the rapidly expanding animal feedstuffs market.

- **Company C.** A confectionery manufacturer which has been established for many years and is now experiencing low sales growth but high market share in a long established industry.

- **Company D.** A retailing organisation which has been very profitable but is now experiencing a loss of market share with a consequent overall reduction in turnover.

Required

(a)   Explain

  (i)   The concept of the industry life cycle, and

  (ii)   The phase of development in which each of the industries served by the four companies is positioned. **(7 marks)**

(b)   Discuss how Ansoff's product market growth vector matrix may be applied by the firms in developing their growth and divestment strategies. **(18 marks)**

(Total = 25 marks)

8 U plc

45 mins

Learning outcome C-2(v)

The management accountant of U plc has evaluated the activities of two of its important competitors. Within their industry the three firms together share some 60% of the market supplying public authorities. It is suggested that the three firms' financial results can be represented as follows.

	Variable costs turnover	Operating profit turnover	Operating profit turnover
A Limited	40%	10%	22½%
U plc	30%	7½%	15%
Z plc	25%	15%	20%

A Limited is thought to enjoy a 25% share of the market, Z plc some 20% and U plc 15%. It is also significant that U plc's price/earnings ratio is reported as 10.4 whereas shares in Z plc are fetching 17.3 times current earnings. This confirms the directors' belief that U plc's attempts to improve market share by promotional advertising and exhibition activity have been less effective than had been hoped for.

Senior sales personnel have argued that buyers' search costs are such that once a satisfactory vendor rating has been arrived at, it is difficult to persuade authorities to change their suppliers. It has also become apparent that several customers are merely using U plc's fine pricing to prise additional discounts from their regular supplier. This has had the effect of reducing competitors' return on capital employed below what would otherwise be regarded as reasonable.

Alternative marketing strategies have been proposed – one is that U plc should increase its prices in line with competition so that at least 12½% is earned on turnover. If, as is believed, customers will not readily change their suppliers, it is assumed that improved returns will become available to U plc. This would also bring U plc's variable costs' ratio more into line with those of Z plc.

An alternative argument is that U plc is out-of-date in its production procedures and that the difficulties arise mainly because its capital equipment cannot be adapted to product development sufficiently quickly. A Limited may use less capital-intensive production methods but it compensates for this by being able to adapt more readily to changes required by its customers.

Required

(a)   Evaluate U plc's existing and the two proposed marketing strategies in terms of the likely effects on the company's financial results. **(9 marks)**

(b)   Recommend whether an offer by U plc of three of its shares for every two held in Z plc would be in the interest of the present shareholders of U plc. **(8 marks)**

(c)   Explain what further growth could be reasonably expected by U plc's shareholders were the merger to come about. **(8 marks)**

(Total = 25 marks)

9 Marketing orientation

Learning outcome A-1(iv)

(a)   Organisations which claim to be 'market orientated' attempt to define the nature of the business in which they are operating. Discuss the relevance of such a definition to an organisation which has its objective stated other than in profit terms. **(13 marks)**

(b)   In what ways does organisational buyer behaviour differ from consumer buyer behaviour?

(12 marks)

(Total = 25 marks)

10 GHK restaurants

27 mins

Learning outcome D-1 (viii)

> Note: This question is taken from the Specimen Paper provided by CIMA for the 2010 Syllabus.
>
> Part (a) of this question forms Question 5 of this Question Bank. Part (b) of this Question should be attempted now as Question 10 of this Question Bank. However, if you have not already answered Question 5, you should answer both parts of the Question now.

GHK is a restaurant chain consisting of eight restaurants in an attractive part of a European country which is popular with tourists. GHK has been owned by the same family for the previous 15 years and has always traded at a profit. However, a number of factors have meant that GHK is now in danger of making a trading loss. There has been a substantial drop in the number of tourists visiting the region whilst, at the same time, the prices of many of the foodstuffs and drinks used in its restaurants has increased. Added to this, the local economy has shrunk with several large employers reducing the size of their workforce.

The owners of GHK commissioned a restaurant consultant to give them an independent view of their business. The consultant observed that the eight restaurants were all very different in appearance. They also served menus that were very different, for example, one restaurant which was located on a barge in a coastal town specialised in fish dishes, whereas another restaurant 20 miles away had a good reputation as a steak house. The prices varied greatly amongst the restaurants; one restaurant in a historic country house offered 'fine dining' and was extremely expensive; yet another located near a busy railway station served mainly fast food and claimed that its prices were 'the cheapest in town'. Three of GHK's restaurants offered a 'middle of the road' dining experience with conventional menus and average prices. Some of the restaurants had licences which enabled them to serve alcohol with their meals but three restaurants did not have such licences. One restaurant had a good trade in children's birthday parties whereas the restaurant in the historic country house did not admit diners under the age of 18.

The consultant recommended that GHK should examine these differences but did not suggest how. The owners responded that the chain had grown organically over a number of years and that the location, style and pricing decisions made in each restaurant had all been made at different times and depended on trends current at that time.

Required

(a) Advise the owners of GHK how the application of Porter's Three Generic Strategies Model could assist them in maintaining or improving the profitability of their restaurants.

Note: You are not required to suggest individual generic strategies for each of GHK's restaurants.

(10 marks)

(b) Advise how GHK could employ a range of organisational information systems to support whichever generic strategy it chooses to adopt.

(15 marks)

(Total = 25 marks)

11 Organisation structure

27 mins

Learning outcome D-1 (iv)

Don Wilson is the managing director of XYZ Technology, a medium-sized high-tech company which operates in several different countries.

XYZ Technology provides software and instrumentation, mainly for military projects, but it also does have some civilian (non-military) customers. It currently has four key projects:

(1)   A new artillery command, communication and control system
(2)   A programme for updating the electronic systems in fighter aircraft
(3)   An air traffic control system for a regional airport in XYZ's own country
(4)   Radar installations for harbour authorities in the Middle East.

All these projects were expected to have a life expectancy of at least five years before completion. However, Don Wilson is worried because they are all increasingly falling behind schedule and the contracts have late delivery penalties.

Don Wilson is convinced that a significant cause of the problem is the way that the company is organised. He believes a firm can generate a competitive advantage by the way it organises and performs its activities.

XYZ Technology is currently structured on a functional basis, which does not seem to work well with complex technologies when operating in dynamic markets. The functional structure appears to result in a lack of integration of key activities, reduced loyalties and an absence of team work.

Don Wilson has contemplated moving towards a divisionalised structure, organised either by product or by market so as to provide some element of focus, but his experience has suggested that such a structure might create internal rivalries and competition which could adversely affect the performance of the company. Furthermore there is a risk that such a structure may lead to an over-emphasis on either the technology or the market conditions. He is seeking a structure that will encourage both integration and efficiency.

Mr Wilson is concerned that a tendency towards decentralisation – whilst encouraging initiative and generating motivation – may result in a failure to pursue a cohesive strategy, whereas a move towards centralisation could reduce flexibility and responsiveness.

XYZ Technology is already relatively lean and so any move towards delayering, resulting in a flatter organisation is likely to be resisted. Furthermore the nature of the market – the need for high technical specifications and confidentiality – is likely to preclude outsourcing as a means of achieving both efficiency and rapidity of response.

Required

Discuss an alternative organisational structure for XYZ Technology, and analyse the benefits and problems which such a structure might bring.   **(15 marks)**

12 Steyn Steel Co   27 mins

Learning outcome B-1 (ii)

Steyn Steel Co has recently appointed a new Chief Executive Officer (CEO), and the new CEO is intent on making the company more competitive.

The CEO has made it clear than he considers the current operational performance to be below acceptable levels. He feels that a number of managers who have worked for Steyn Steel for a long time have become complacent about the company's performance, and this is having a detrimental effect on its competitiveness. The CEO has publicly stated, 'Costs are too high and productivity is too low.'

Global demand for steel is still growing, particularly in countries in the Pacific Rim which Steyn Steel exports to. The CEO believes Steyn should capitalise on this. However, to do so, he believes some changes in the working conditions at Steyn will be necessary. A reduction in import duty in some of the proposed export markets will also be necessary for Steyn to trade profitably with them.

The majority of the steel workers at Steyn belong to a trade union. Their union is well-organised and has promised the workers it will defend their wages levels and working conditions in the face of any changes.

Required

(a)   Analyse the forces for changes and the causes of resistance in the Steyn Steel company.

(10 marks)

(b)   Using an appropriate stage model of change, recommend how the newly-appointed CEO at Steyn might manage the process of change he wants to implement in the company.   (5 marks)

(Total = 15 marks)

13 Simon Clark   36 mins

Learning outcomes B-2(iii), B-2(v)

Simon Clark is Head of the Department of Business at a local public sector college which provides professional training on a part-time basis for students who are already in employment. The students are mainly studying for professional qualifications in either accountancy, marketing or personnel. A number of students are also studying for general management qualifications. Increasingly this college is experiencing competition from a newly established private sector organisation. This private sector organisation is able to deliver programmes more efficiently and effectively than the older established college because of its more flexible work contracts and working practices. The traditional method of tuition has been on a part-time day release basis (one day or one half-day a week) away from work, studying within the college. With local companies becoming more reluctant to give their staff time off on a regular basis to study, Simon is proposing that more of the training should be carried out on a distance-learning basis, often being supplemented by taught weekend programmes. This will involve the staff in writing study materials and working weekends.

Simon's college has a teaching staff who, in recent years, have had to adapt to new situations including organisational structure changes and syllabus changes. However they are most unhappy about the current proposals which could result in their conditions of service worsening. They are reluctant to work on a weekend basis without additional payments. This would make the college uncompetitive. The private sector college, although it employs high quality staff, is able to absorb the high costs by employing lecturers on a freelance basis and by having larger class sizes, the students being drawn from a larger catchment area. Simon is becoming frustrated by his staff's apparent opposition to accept the proposed changes, and he is contemplating what to do next.

Required

Simon has arranged a meeting with his staff to discuss weekend working and study material production.

(a)   Identify and discuss the different tactics which Simon could make use of in dealing with this conflict.   (10 marks)

(b)   Discuss how Simon might encourage his staff to be more supportive of the proposed change in work practice.   (10 marks)

(Total = 20 marks)

14 Auto Direct   22 mins

Learning outcome B-2(iii)

Mark Howe, Managing Director of Auto Direct, is a victim of his own success. Mark has created an innovative way of selling cars to the public which takes advantage of the greater freedom given to independent car distributors to market cars more aggressively within the European Union. This reduces the traditional control and interference of the automobile manufacturers, some of whom own their distributors. He has opened a number of showrooms in the London region and by 2004 Auto Direct had 20 outlets in and around London. The concept is deceptively simple; Mark buys cars from wherever he can source them most cheaply and has access to all of the leading volume car models. He then

concentrates on selling the cars to the public, leaving servicing and repair work to other specialist garages. He offers a classic high volume/low margin business model.

Mark now wants to develop this business model onto a national and eventually an international basis. His immediate plans are to grow the number of outlets by 50% each year for the next three years. Such growth will place considerable strain on the existing organisation and staff. Each showroom has its own management team, sales personnel and administration. Currently the 20 showrooms are grouped into a Northern and Southern Sales Division with a small head office team for each division. Auto Direct now employs 250 people.

Required

Using appropriate strategies for managing change, produce a brief report for Mark describing how he should pursue his proposed growth plans. **(12 marks)**

15 Nominee holdings   45 mins

Learning outcomes D(ii), D(vi)

Nominee Holdings plc, an investment conglomerate, co-ordinates the capital expenditure proposals of its subsidiaries by:

(a)   Allowing each company to pledge its asset base as loan security where value is likely to be added to the equity provided the parent's resources are in no way jeopardised (eg by having to give any form of guarantee)

(b)   Ranking applications from subsidiaries for reinvestment of operating profits according to the premium available over the group's average cost of capital and their accord with its medium-term strategy.

Outline investment plans have been submitted for approval as follows.

	Dairy-P Ltd	*Keen Casements*	*Flexi-Carbon Ltd*
Project cost *	£150,000	£65,000	£125,000
(standard deviation)	£41,000	0 (ie firm)	£15,000
Profitability index (using DCF 19.5%)	1.41	1.28	1.35
Current Asset ratio (of project proposal)	1.70	0.65	1.21
Mortgage debentures outstanding	£200,000	nil	£150,000
Rate of interest	10%	–	15%
Second mortgage debentures outstanding	£50,000	nil	nil
Rate of interest	17%	–	–
Fixed assets at current valuation	£400,000	£15,000	£250,000

* mean of pessimistic, most likely and optimistic

The subsidiary companies are not aware of the parent company's directors' unhappiness about the future of Dairy-P Ltd. The parent board expects the European Union to continue inflating the cost of that company's inputs and is investigating the feasibility of moving the processing facilities to Greece as that country integrates its economy into the European Union. Nominee Holdings plc's cash and short-term deposits earn on average only 5% pa and amount to some 20% of the company's net worth according to its management accounts, which price non-monetary assets at replacement cost.

Required

(a)   Prepare appropriate recommendations for Nominee Holdings plc's directors to consider.

(15 marks)

(b)   Explain how divisional performance should be measured in the interest of the group's shareholders.

(5 marks)

(c)   Advise the means of charge-out that would be appropriate for the parent company to debit subsidiaries for their capital employed. **(5 marks)**

(Total = 25 marks)

16 Grier and Box plc

45 mins

Learning outcomes D(ii), D(vi)

Grier and Box plc is a manufacturing company that has emerged from economic recession to earn a profit before interest and tax of £14.8 million last year. The company has six operating divisions, and the results for last year were as follows.

	Electrical equipment £m	Fluid controls £m	Metals £m	Division Industrial services £m	Bathroom accessories £m	Tubes £m	Total £m
Sales	40.0	25.2	17.1	33.7	7.0	6.0	129.0
Cost of sales							
Materials	34.7	20.3	8.0	14.7	4.5	1.5	83.7
Salaries and wages	1.2	1.8	2.1	3.0	1.0	2.4	11.5
Other costs	2.1	1.9	4.0	8.0	1.0	2.0	19.0
	38.0	24.0	14.1	25.7	6.5	5.9	114.2
Profit before interest and tax	2.0	1.2	3.0	8.0	0.5	0.1	14.8
Market share	40%	27%	30%	25%	8%	3%	

The company's summarised balance sheet as at the end of last year was:

	£m	£m
Non-current assets		65.0
Current assets	35.0	
Current liabilities	20.0	
Net current assets		15.0
		80.0
Loan capital		48.0
		32.0
Share capital		10.0
Reserves		22.0
		32.0

Required

You are asked to comment on each of the following matters that have been raised by the company's managing director.

(a)   He believes that some of the product divisions manufacture too many low value-added items which require huge working capital investments.

From the data given, identify which product divisions these are, and what are the implications of low value-added items for financial returns and profitability?   **(8 marks)**

(b)   He wishes to make a strategic decision about the long-term viability of both the bathroom accessories division and the tubes division.

(i)   The bathroom accessories division produces bathroom fittings, which are sold to a manufacturer of bathroom ceramics (baths and washbasins etc). The division is still profitable, but there are indications that the manufacturers of bathroom ceramics are beginning to produce their own bathroom accessories, and market a total 'package' to their own customers.

(ii)   The tubes division is barely profitable and would need considerable capital expenditure to improve efficiency and make it more competitive.

What are the arguments for selling off these divisions now, even though both are profitable?   **(6 marks)**

BPP
LEARNING MEDIA

(c) The company needs to reduce its financial gearing, which is too high. However, the company also needs to spend large sums of capital for equipment replacement and modernisation programmes, investments in new projects and new product developments. All capital investment projects should have a target payback period.

   (i) Discuss the factors which should influence how long the payback period should be for:

      (1) equipment replacement programmes
      (2) new development projects

   (ii) Discuss the relative importance of the strategic aim of reducing gearing and the aim to continue to invest in modernisation programmes. **(5 marks)**

(d) The company is about to introduce a decentralisation programme, in which decision making is pushed as far down the line as possible and head office staff is cut from 56 in number to just 20. The managing director believes that control can be exercised from head office by having a regular reporting system. 'There is much more attention in my mind to looking at ratios and questioning deviations from budget.'

Explain the main dangers of relying on ratio analysis and budgetary control for co-ordination and control of the group. **(6 marks)**

(Total = 25 marks)

17 Management accounting information   45 mins

Learning outcome D(viii)

It has been said that management accounting has traditionally been concerned with providing information for decision making and controlling costs. It has often been criticised for not providing sufficient relevant information to management because it tends to impose general techniques as a solutions in situations which demand custom-designed (directly applicable) methods and specific information.

Required

(a) Discuss the validity of this criticism of management accounting. **(13 marks)**

To be relevant to the needs of the organisation, management accounting systems need to be designed to accommodate its specific requirements taking account of the circumstances of its particular business environment. One such circumstance may be the change in traditional working patterns. For example, it can no longer be assumed that all employees will be located on the organisation's premises in carrying out their duties. Some are likely to provide their services from remote locations.

(b) Compare the approach to providing relevant management accounting information for strategic decision making purposes in

   (i) a manufacturing organisation which employs staff on site, with

   (ii) a service organisation which employs contractors. The contractors mainly work from home to provide technical solutions for customers engaged in large scale building projects. **(12 marks)**

(Total = 25 marks)

18 The S group

90 mins

Learning outcome D(iii); C-1(iii)

Company development

The headquarters of the S Group is located in K, a country which has experienced rapid economic growth in recent years.

S itself has been established for over 100 years. Two brothers first started trading in K and developed the group, which is now a highly profitable international conglomerate company. Its diverse business activities range from capital goods manufacture, through materials handling to operation of airlines and banking. Some of its activities involve the transfer of partly completed goods between manufacturing and assembly plants located in different countries. The group operates a divisional structure.

Economic circumstances

Over the last three years the region of the world in which K is located has been subject to serious economic difficulties. K itself has not been affected as much as some of its neighbours, owing to the fact that its independent currency is pegged to the US dollar.

There has been much activity and intervention by the monetary authorities in K to protect the value of the currency, and this has proved to be largely successful, despite the intense pressure exerted by foreign speculators. Nevertheless, the effects of the regional economic difficulties are being felt. This is exemplified by the recent emergence of unemployment after a period of 30 years of full employment and a dramatic fall in property prices.

Organisational economic objectives

Fifty five per cent of S's holding company shares are held within the families of the original founders. The remaining forty five per cent of the shares are mainly held by international banks and other financial institutions located all over the world. These institutional shareholders maintain constant pressure on the directors to improve earnings per share and increase dividend payments. The directors have stated that their main objective is to increase shareholder value. In satisfying the requirements of the shareholders the directors are conscious of the need for improved efficiency in the group's operations. Consequently, the holding company's board of directors carefully scrutinises the activities of the constituent subsidiary companies within the group.

Divisional performance measurement

S has always applied a traditional form of measurement to assess the performance of the group's subsidiaries. It uses return on capital employed (ROCE) and defines this as:

$$\frac{\text{Profit before interest and tax}}{\text{Average capital employed}} \times 100$$

(The capital employed value is the average of that shown at the beginning and end of the year.)

The performance of the divisional managers is strictly monitored on this basis and their remuneration increases if they achieve growth in their ROCE, which is measured annually. Inevitably, the divisional managers strive to improve their performance as measured by this method.

The Agricultural Equipment (AE) Division

The AE division, which is not located in K, assembles components into a single product. It receives the components from other subsidiaries in the group which are situated in other countries. The group as a whole has been able to benefit from economies of scale, as a result of other subsidiary divisions, which have long experience in manufacturing, supplying AE. Following assembly, AE ships the product to various customers throughout the world. The geographical location of the country in which AE is situated enables the product to be easily exported, but the division is subject to high levels of corporation tax.

The transfer prices of the components transferred to AE are set centrally by group head office located in K. The divisional manager of AE has no influence over them at all. The group head office may vary the transfer prices during the financial year.

Comparative results for the AE division over the last two years (translated into K's currency) are as follows:

	Last year		Previous year	
	K$m	K$m	K$m	K$m
Sales		800		750
Components	600		400	
Assembly costs	100		75	
		700		475
Gross profit		100		275
AE Division Head Office (all fixed)		75		75
Net profit before interest and tax		25		200
Average capital employed		2,020		2,000

Selling prices over the two years remained stable.

It may be assumed that the variable costs of the supplying division, relating to the transferred components, were neutral in respect of AE division's profitability over the two years.

The budgeted and actual selling price per unit was K$50,000 in each of the two years. The budgeted production and sales level for each year was 18,000 units. it can be assumed that there were no opening and closing inventories of finished goods or work in progress in either of the years.

The budgeted cost per unit for each of the last two years was as follows:

	Last year	Previous year
	K$	K$
Assembly	6,000	5,000
Components transferred	35,000	25,000
	41,000	30,000

It can be assumed that there was no change in the currency exchange rate between the AE division's host country and K$ in the last two years. There have been discussions at S Group headquarters regarding the deteriorating performance of AE and there is growing pressure to close it down. The AE divisional manager believes there is little he can do in the circumstances, where he only controls a small proportion of the total costs of the division.

Potential for growth in AE division

Despite the reduced profitability in the last financial year, the divisional manager of AE believes there is potential for growth. He has put forward plans to group headquarters to take over a competitor company in the country in which the division is situated. This would result in an increase for the division in world wide market share and provide the capacity to increase the range of agricultural equipment supplied in accordance with the divisional manager's perception of demand. To do this AE will need to obtain funds which will be secured against group assets.

Required

(a) Identify the sources from which the board of directors of S may obtain information relating to the group's business environment and how it might use that information for strategic management purposes. Explain how the board of directors might assure itself of the quality of that information for strategic management purposes. (You are not required to consider the ecological environment in answering this question.) **(12 marks)**

(b) Making use of the information contained in the case, produce a critical appraisal of the method applied by S Group's directors to assess the performance of the AE division. **(16 marks)**

(c) Discuss the factors which should be taken into consideration by the directors of S in deciding whether the strategic development proposals put forward by AE's divisional manager should be pursued. **(10 marks)**

(d) Assume that the AE division makes the acquisition as proposed by its divisional manager. Recommend how S Group's directors should improve the methods of measuring the performance of the AE division in order to assess its contribution to the group's strategic requirement to increase shareholder value. **(12 marks)**

(Total = 50 marks)

Approaching the answer

You should read through the requirement before working through and annotating the question as we have, so that you are aware of what things you are looking for. We have also prepared a précis of the case, which follows this annotated version, summarising the key issues.

Company development

> Turbulent environment? Unstable? Good infrastructure? Or boom then bust?

The headquarters of the S Group is located in K, a country which has experienced rapid economic growth in recent years.

> Long established indicates a certain stability

S itself has been established for over 100 years. Two brothers first started trading in K and

> Big numbers, although an unfashionable business model now

developed the group, which is now a highly profitable international conglomerate company. Its diverse business activities range from capital goods manufacture, through materials handling

> Products and services – marketing/ branding issues?

to operation of airlines and banking. Some of its activities involve the transfer of partly completed goods between manufacturing and assembly plants located in different countries.

The group operates a divisional structure.

> Performance assessment

> Transfer pricing issues

Economic circumstances

> Will foreign exchange policy become an issue?

Over the last three years the region of the world in which K is located has been subject to serious economic difficulties. K itself has not been affected as much as some of its neighbours, owing to the fact that its independent currency is pegged to the US dollar.

> Economic environment could become unfavourable

There has been much activity and intervention by the monetary authorities in K to protect the value of the currency, and this has proved to be largely successful, despite the intense pressure exerted by foreign speculators. Nevertheless, the effects of the regional economic difficulties are being felt.

This is exemplified by the recent emergence of unemployment after a period of 30 years of full employment and a dramatic fall in property prices.

Organisational economic objectives

> Could this imply conservative management and resistance to change?

> Global profile

> Stakeholder analysis – short term interests?

> As would generally be expected).

Fifty five per cent of S's holding company shares are held within the families of the original founders. The remaining forty five per cent of the shares are mainly held by international banks and other financial institutions located all over the world. These institutional shareholders maintain constant pressure on the directors to improve earnings per share and increase dividend payments. The directors have stated that their main objective is to increase shareholder value. In satisfying the requirements of the shareholders the directors are conscious of the need for improved efficiency in the group's operations. Consequently, the holding company's board of directors carefully scrutinises the activities of the constituent subsidiary companies within the group.

> Tight central control?

> What does 'efficiency' mean? Cost control?

Divisional performance measurement

> Advantages and disadvantages of this as a measure

S has always applied a traditional form of measurement to assess the performance of the group's subsidiaries. It uses return on capital employed (ROCE) and defines this as:

$$\frac{\text{Profit before interest and tax}}{\text{Average capital employed}} \times 100$$

> Note this for your calculations!

> Possible disadvantages here – disincentive to invest and thereby increase capital employed, for example

(The capital employed value is the average of that shown at the beginning and end of the year.)

The performance of the divisional managers is strictly monitored on this basis and their remuneration increases if they achieve growth in their ROCE, which is measured annually. Inevitably, the divisional managers strive to improve their performance as measured by this method.

The Agricultural Equipment (AE) Division

> Interest from the tax authorities in the transfer pricing, as a method of reducing profits?

The AE division, which is not located in K, assembles components into a single product. It receives the components from other subsidiaries in the group which are situated in other countries. The group as a whole has been able to benefit from economies of scale, as a result of other subsidiary divisions, which have long experience in manufacturing, supplying AE. Following assembly, AE ships the product to various customers throughout the world. The geographical location of the country in which AE is situated enables the product to be easily exported, but the division is subject to high levels of corporation tax.

The transfer prices of the components transferred to AE are set centrally by group head office located in K. The divisional manager of AE has no influence over them at all. The group head office may vary the transfer prices during the financial year.

> No incentive to manage his costs as he does not control them, yet he is judged on them via ROCE!

Comparative results for the AE division over the last two years (translated into K's currency) are as follows:

> These numbers are vital for answering part (b)

	Last year		Previous year	
	K$m	K$m	K$m	K$m
Sales		800		750
Components	600		400	
Assembly costs	100		75	
		700		475
Gross profit		100		275
AE Division Head Office (all fixed)		75		75
Net profit before interest and tax		25		200
Average capital employed		2,020		2,000

Selling prices over the two years remained stable.

It may be assumed that the variable costs of the supplying division, relating to the transferred components, were neutral in respect of AE division's profitability over the two years.

> What does this mean? Basically that the big increase in costs is not due to higher costs of the supplying division being passed on, but rather due to higher transfer prices. Is using ROCE in such circumstances a fair performance measure? There must be a better one!

The budgeted and actual selling price per unit was K$50,000 in each of the two years. The budgeted production and sales level for each year was 18,000 units. It can be assumed that there were no opening and closing stocks for finished goods or work in progress in either of the years.

The budgeted cost per unit for each of the last two years was as follows:

	Last year	Previous year
	K$	K$
Assembly	6,000	5,000
Components transferred	35,000	25,000
	41,000	30,000

It can be assumed that there was no change in the currency exchange rate between the AE division's host country and K$ in the last two years. There have been discussions at S Group headquarters regarding the deteriorating performance of AE and there is growing pressure to close it down. The AE divisional manager believes there is little he can do in the circumstances, where he only controls a small proportion of the total costs of the division.

> Is it really deteriorating?

Potential for growth in AE division

Despite the reduced profitability in the last financial year, the divisional manager of AE believes there is potential for growth. He has put forward plans to group headquarters to take over a

> Increased sales, profits, contribution to shareholder value

> Cost of those funds?

> But is this perception Realistic

competitor company in the country in which the division is situated. This would result in an increase for the division in world wide market share and provide the capacity to increase the range of agricultural equipment supplied, in accordance with the divisional manager's perception of demand. To do this, AE will need to obtain funds which will be secured against group assets.

Overall précis of the case

S Group, **highly profitable international conglomerate**, established for over 100 years. Located in K, a country which has experienced rapid economic growth (currency pegged to the US$), although the region it is in has been subject to difficulties recently: unemployment and falling property prices.

Business activities: capital goods manufacture, materials handling, operation of airlines, banking. Some **transfer of goods** between plants in different countries. The group operates a **divisional structure**.

Shareholders: 55% families of the original founders, 45% held by worldwide financial institutions who press for improved **EPS** and increased **dividends**. Main **objective** of group is to **increase shareholder value**. Subsidiaries' activities closely scrutinised by centre.

Uses **ROCE** for performance measurement and for influencing manager remuneration, defined as:

$$\frac{\text{Profit before interest and tax}}{\text{Average capital employed}} \times 100$$

The **AE division** (not located in K) assembles components which it receives from other subsidiaries in other countries, and then ships the completed capital goods to customers. Group benefits from economies of scale. AE is subject to high levels of corporation tax.

Transfer prices of the components are set **centrally**. Divisional manager of AE has no influence.

(**Results** for the AE division are as in the tables above).

There have been discussions at head office regarding the **deteriorating performance** of AE, with pressure to close it down. AE divisional manager only controls a small proportion of his total costs, but remains committed – has put forward plans for **acquisition** of a domestic competitor to increase both AE's **global market share** and its **product range**, to be **financed** by funds secured against group assets.

> What information do they really need about the business environment?

> What are the likely sources?

> Don't make things up! Use the information that you are given - the numbers are vital.

Required

(a)   State the sources from which the board of directors of S may obtain information relating to the group's business environment and how it might use that information for strategic management purposes. Explain how the board of directors might assure itself of the quality of that information for strategic management purposes. (You are not required to consider the ecological environment in answering this question.)

> Quality issues an unusual angle – internal checking, external verification?

> Why does strategic management need information?

Is ROCE a good method to apply, in the specific circumstances of the question?

Critical appraisal means 'analyse its good and bad points'.

(b)   Making use of the information contained in the case, produce a critical appraisal of the method applied by S Group's directors to assess the performance of the AE division.

No need to make any recommendations yourself!

(c)   Discuss the factors which should be taken into consideration by the directors of S in deciding whether the strategic development proposals put forward by AE's divisional manager should be pursued.

Discuss – this is easiest if you categorise the factors. Which ones are more important?

Financial and non-financial is a useful basis upon which to structure your discussion

It is irrelevant if you think it is a bad idea!

(d)   Assume that the AE division makes the acquisition as proposed by its divisional manager. Recommend how S Group's directors should improve the methods of measuring the performance of the AE division in order to assess its contribution to the group's strategic requirement to increase shareholder value.

Indicate how appropriate your recommendation is to the need to monitor contributions towards shareholder value: ease of measurement, validity of calculations, fairness to the division...

Recommend new divisional performance assessment methods – and give reasons.

Define shareholder value.

Answer plan

Think about the points you want to make, and prioritise them.

Importance of understanding the environment/trends – define strategic intelligence

(**Maintain a database** – financial/non-financial indicators).

(a)   *Sources of environmental information*

(i)   **Internal sources** – staff, stakeholders

Importance of management information system – info on sales, costs, market share

(ii)   **External sources** – media, consultants, academic/trade journals, trade bodies, Internet, government, public databases, stockbrokers

Using the information

Needs to be coherently organised and presented, as there will be a lot of it.

Strategy planning process – involve divisional managers, who will have their own awareness of the environment

Quality of the information

Information must be accurate/reliable: **why** is it being collected, and **what** will it be used for?

Comparing information from various sources: more sources, and more checks, as time goes on.

ROCE is a **historical measure** – no guide to future performance. Manager could consider only those decisions which increase AE's short term ROCE (at expense of group): lack of **goal congruence**.

(b) **ROCE calculations** and analysis.

Fair comparison between divisions based on ROCE is difficult.

Analysis of **sales and profitability**, concentrating on **transfer pricing policy** (75% of sales value last year/53% in previous year).

Conclusion that the performance of AE is being assessed on factors beyond its control, using an unsatisfactory measure.

(c) Key objective: **increase shareholder value.** Does acquisition fit in with the overall **strategic direction** of the group? Must understand reasons for it – do they balance the level of **risk**?

Possible problems/issues to consider:

(i)   Costs
(ii)   Customers reaction/ market research
(iii)   Incompatibilities
(iv)   Lack of information

Refer to the analysis in part (b) – AE is actually profitable, so should it risk that with this venture?

Non financial factors too – such as problems of implementation /human resources issues.

(d) **Performance measurement** should become more **forward looking.** Balance long v. short term.

Shareholder value analysis – definition

Factors to focus on re the AE division (Rappaport's value drivers):

(i)   **Market share** forecasts and trends
(ii)   Investment in **working capital**
(iii)   **Cash flows**
(iv)   **Corporation tax planning**
(v)   **Cost of funding** (incremental value of the acquisition must exceed the cost of capital)

Economic value management – definition

Applied to the AE division – adjust for the transfer price.

EXAM ANSWER BANK

598

1 Four Star Products

Part (a)

> **Top tips.** This is a relatively simple question to start this subject with. It will give you good practice at marshalling your knowledge and presenting it in a way that is related to the scenario, both of which are essential skills for this subject.
>
> Do not worry if you reach a different conclusion from the one in the suggested solution, or even no conclusion at all. It is very important to understand that there are few absolutely correct answers to questions in strategic management. Success does not just depend on learning. You must be familiar with the material, certainly, but you must also be able to apply it to an infinite variety of problems.
>
> What is important in questions of this type is that you offer reasoning that is both theoretically sound and relevant to the setting.

Answer plan

NB Q not so much about the planning department as about what it does. Therefore answer requires critique of formal planning approach.

Against

- Difficulty of forecasting discontinuities
- Linear approach – annual cycle
- Isolation of planners from operations
- Politics
- Implementation
- Learning

For

- Systematic approach
- Sets targets
- Co-ordination of objectives, departments, activities
- Organised attention to environment

Criticisms of the rational model concern both the theory behind it and how it has worked in practice. Empirical studies have not proved that formal planning processes contribute to success.

Planning theory assumes that the development of the business environment can be forecast, and to some extent controlled. In conditions of stability, forecasting and extrapolation make sense. But forecasting cannot cope with sudden **discontinuities** and **shocks**, such as the change from mainframe computing to PCs, which nearly destroyed IBM.

Part of the problem is the **linear approach** sometimes adopted, using an annual cycle. Unfortunately, strategically significant events outside the organisation are rarely synchronised with the annual planning cycle. Four Star's financial crisis in the early 1990s is, perhaps, an example.

Another problem is that formal planning can **discourage strategic thinking** among operational managers. Once a plan is locked in place, people are unwilling to question it. The internal significance of the chosen performance indicators leads managers to focus on fulfilling the plan rather than concentrating on developments in the environment. Strategy becomes something for specialists.

A complementary problem arises when the planners are separated from the operational managers; the implication is that the planners do not really need day-to-day knowledge of the product or market. However, small-scale developments can have important strategic influence and should not be ignored.

The rational model by definition assumes that an **objective approach** prevails. Unfortunately, no account is taken of the essentially political processes that determine many plans. There also problems of implementation. Managers are not all-knowing, and there are limits to the extent to which they can

control the actual behaviour of the organisation. This places limits upon what can be achieved. Discovering strengths and weaknesses is a learning process. Implementing a strategy is necessary for learning – to see if it works.

On the other hand, we can discern an important role for **formal planning activities**. Apart from anything else, a desire to do things in a systematic way naturally leads to rational planning; deciding what to do, and when and how it should be done. Such an approach can make management control more effective by developing detailed and explicit targets. This shows managers at all levels where they fit in and forces them to confront the company's expectations of them

The development of a plan for a large organisation such as Four Star includes an important element of **co-ordination**. Long-term, medium-term and short-term objectives, plans and controls must be made consistent with one another. Similarly, the activities of the different business functions must be directed towards a common goal.

Also, companies cannot remain static: they have to cope with and exploit changes in the **environment**. It is clear from the CEO's use of external agencies and his new strategy for Four Star that he understands this. We may speculate that he is not so much an enemy of strategic planning as much as he is unimpressed with the performance of the Four Star planning department.

Part (b)

Top tip. This part of the question is fairly unusual in that there is pretty much a single correct approach to a good answer; that is, this question is about the environmental analysis aspect of the rational planning model and not very much else will do. However, notice that a good answer will point out the weakness of the forecasting process: the future is essentially unknowable and the danger of detailed research is that we forget this and come to believe that we do indeed know just what is going to happen.

Answer plan

- Nature of environmental analysis
- The environment – divisions
- Desk research
- Market research
- Informal research
- Technical nature of Internet boom
- Importance of judgement
- Relationship of formal planning to strategic decision making-support

Environmental analysis is a fundamental part of strategic business management. The aim of the analysis is to identify opportunities and threats and to assess their significance. The environment itself may be divided both according to its proximity to the organisation and according to its inherent features. Thus, the task environment, dealing with suppliers, customers, competitors and so on, may be differentiated from the wider, general environment and, indeed, from the global physical environment. The general, or macro, environment is often analysed under such headings as political, economic, social and technological.

The work of analysis can be carried on to a great extent by **desk research**. This may be quite adequate for keeping abreast of the more general aspects of the macro environment, and even for some parts of the task environment, such as changing labour costs and the fortunes of competitors. However, more complex and expensive methods, such as market research surveys may be required for some aspects of the task environment, and more intuitive ones, such as personal contact between senior managers for others.

In the case of the Internet business model, which was given enormous publicity, it should have been easy to obtain a full understanding of both principle and technique by the methods outlined above. The problem with the collapse of confidence in the model was that foretelling was very much a matter of **judgement**. Extremely large sums of money were invested on quite rational grounds and very few commentators took a pessimistic view.

This is not a failure of the formal planning process as such, but rather a failure of strategic judgement at the highest levels of the organisations concerned. Planning techniques cannot foretell exactly what the future holds, let alone control it. Their purpose is to support those who must take strategic decisions, not to replace them.

2 Management and social responsibility

> Start off with a definition, and try to come up with an example

Social responsibility is a hard term to define, but many would say it means acting with regard to social welfare. No organisation would ever admit to be socially irresponsible. Organisations claim to act responsibly on social issues, whether this means using social issues in a marketing campaign (such as 'Computers for Schools' vouchers handed out by supermarkets), or the widespread claims of **environmentalism** (claimed by many organisations, from petrol companies to 'dolphin-friendly' tuna fleets).

> As we said, this area is a minefield! Try not to be too controversial with opinions or political allegiances. Refer instead to the obvious difficulties faced by an organisation charged with corporate social responsibility

In brief, for an organisation to act with social responsibility, it should align its goals with those of the wider society in which it is a part. However, the **purpose and direction of society**, not to mention its goals, are generally political decisions, rather than obviously commercial ones. Any company these days has to overcome an almost inbuilt public distrust and cynicism about corporate objectives. Many simply will not believe that a company is operating other than purely for the benefit of its shareholders and senior managers. Recent scandals such as Enron have not helped.

Moreover, is the wider society limited to the national economy or the world as a whole? The consequences of a **global corporation** acting with 'social responsibility' in one society may cause it to act without social responsibility in another (eg shipping hazardous waste from a country with tough environmental legislation, to one with few controls).

So we can see that in multinational corporations, the exercise of social responsibility is distributed over several countries, but again, management will only let it override commercial objectives if it either is part of the inbuilt culture of the firm, or if the voice of public opinion in the market is strong. An example is the use of rainforest hardwoods: some consumer organisations are suggesting boycotting these products.

A business almost certainly has objectives, which, in the long term, it can claim will enhance social welfare – the creation of wealth as a result of business activities is felt to be of benefit to society as a whole.

> Refer to the specifics of the manager's role, as this is what the question is asking. It is pressure from stakeholders that we are really concerned with

The managers of organisations which seek to be socially responsible rarely start off with a theoretical notion of social responsibility which they then seek to implement. Rather, organisations which act responsibly do so in response to **pressures from their various stakeholders**. Some of these pressures are outlined below.

Employees

> Make sure that you know who the relevant stakeholders are!

Employees are stakeholders. Their relationship is twofold. Firstly, it is their labour which keeps the organisation in operational existence, despite the impact of technology. Secondly, as citizens they are members of the wider society in which the organisation operates.

> What are their concerns?

Employees value certainty and regularity of wages, in other words that the employing organisation will honour the contract of employment. Secondly, to act with social responsibility implies a concern and respect for safety in the workplace, whether this be equipment, buildings, or hours worked. (It is believed that repetitive strain injury arises from too much uninterrupted time at the word processor.)

Social responsibility towards workers can also include a coherent career and training structure so that people can better themselves. It is believed that an economy's productivity is affected by the level of workforce skill, and so training is both beneficial for the trainee and for the company as a whole.

Other aspects include adapting to other pressures on employee's lifestyles. Workplace crèches, for example, are of great assistance to great numbers of working women, but employers are unlikely to introduce them if there is no commercial benefit.

> Show some awareness of current workplace issues – social changes and the law are fruitful areas for discussion. (You do not need detailed knowledge of employment legislation)

BPP
LEARNING MEDIA

Management has a certain amount of discretion, but this is circumscribed by law. Health and safety for example is subject of regulation, as it was felt that commercial imperatives would not justify the expense, and that employers are not necessarily altruistic. Other benefits are won as the result of the relationship between management and organised labour.

So, the exercise of social responsibility towards the workforce is constrained by the law, by organised labour, and in some instances by the recognition that social responsibility can be of benefit in encouraging employee loyalty and skill.

Customers

For each stakeholder that you note in your answer, explain the relevance of social responsibility for them. Give examples where you can

Customers are stakeholders in that they pay for the organisation's output of goods and services. They generally want quality products for as low a price as possible, but it can get more complex than that. In some consumer goods sectors, public attitudes – with some direction from government and lobby groups – have made the environmental impact of an organisation's activities open to public comment. This has led suppliers to reduce CFCs in aerosol cans, and to introduce ranges of goods which are supposed to be friendly to the environment.

Suppliers

Social responsibility towards suppliers may include the simple procedure of paying them on time. Many small businesses fail, and people lose their jobs, because of liquidity issues connected with late payment by business customers.

A supplier may also make restrictions on the end-use of products a condition of sale. For example, a supplier of high-technology items may require that these are not re-exported to the enemies of the nation where the supplier is based.

Professional bodies

Control is exercised over certain members of management by their membership of professional bodies, which have standards of ethics and conduct

Elected authorities

Society's elected political representatives can affect management in a number of ways, by legislation as has already been mentioned, by influencing the climate of public opinion, or by trying to persuade commercial organisations to follow a particular line or policy. An example is business sponsorship of the arts in the UK. The tenor of government policy was to reduce government funding and to encourage commercial organisations to avail themselves of the marketing opportunities thereby provided.

For example, if a firm bids for a contract from a local authority, contract compliance (by which the contract is only awarded to a firm which operates an equal opportunities policy) could affect the actions of management.

Elected authorities can also compel social authority by legislation (eg anti-pollution legislation), 'contract compliance' rules, or even taxation. Company reporting requirements might include a 'social audit'.

Shareholders

The main interest of shareholders is profit, and they might have objections to money being spent on projects which are socially responsible, as such profits reduce the return on the investment. As many shareholders are large institutions like pension funds, their duties can be adversely affected by the use of organisational resources on activities which do not make a profit.

It is possible that some shareholders, and other commentators, would assert that the creation of wealth is the only desirable social objective, and anything which intervenes in this objective is damaging in the long run.

Now go back to considerations of management – there are costs and benefits to be weighed up

Management options

Social responsibility has costs and benefits for an organisation, and management have to weigh up the **conflicting demands** of different stakeholders. With this must be balanced the duty of

managing the business so that the most **effective use is made of the resources** allocated for the purpose. In the context of social responsibility, this can involve the following initiatives.

(a) Monitoring the **expectations** people have of the organisation, as an enterprise which trumpets its environmental friendliness will be expected to live up to its claims in all areas.

(b) Achieving maximum **good publicity** for any project.

(c) Selecting appropriate socially responsible activities.

  (i) Ensuring that the firm's **core activities** are conducted in a socially responsible way

  (ii) **Subsidising, supporting or sponsoring** those activities which are for public welfare (eg charitable donations)

(d) Clearly distinguishing between what are the **minimum acceptable standards** in a particular situation, and what are **additional** to them.

(e) Reporting the **social audit** has been suggested as a means to monitor the wider record of companies and their responsibilities (eg number of industrial accidents).

3 Development agencies

Top tips. This is a tricky question on the environment, which concentrates on the "P" of the PEST framework (the political/legal environment). A variety of incentives, funded by national governments, exist for locating capacity in a particular area. Think of the reasons why this might be, and do not let the specific language of the question (the Acronym 'RDA', for example) put you off providing a sensible answer. There are clues in the question scenario as to the issues involved.

In part (a) set out the objectives of the RDA, then those of the computer manufacturer, followed by your analysis of how they may be expected to coincide.

For part (b) we have offered six influential environmental factors, which would be enough to earn the 15 marks on offer, provided there is adequate explanation of the points given and they are not merely listed. Think of the important supporting factors for a business when setting up anywhere. They can be grouped into the following broad areas:

- Customers and markets
- Suppliers
- Competitors
- Labour and physical resources
- Finance

(a) The objective of a Regional Development Agency is to promote industrial and commercial growth and development in an underdeveloped or declining region, with a view to bringing more employment and economic wealth to relatively underdeveloped areas of the country.

The objective of the computer manufacturer would be primarily a financial one, to seek certain financial returns for its shareholders. The strategic decision to set up a computer manufacturing operation in Europe would seem to indicate the following about the manufacturer.

- Expects increasing sales in Europe

- Wishes to locate a manufacturing plant close to its European markets

The objective of the RDA and the objective of the computer manufacturer would coincide if a location in the region is the best location commercially for the manufacturer. The RDA should therefore have done its best to achieve the following.

- Bring the commercial advantages of the region to the manufacturer's attention
- Offer some commercial incentive itself, if possible
- Offer assistance to the manufacturer in identifying suitable sites

(b) The environmental factors might have been as follows.

    (i) **The availability of components supplies**

    A computer manufacturer will want supplies of components from external suppliers, and is likely to want the bulk of its supplies to be provided from local sources. Many components will be custom made for the specific manufacturer.

    The RDA should have been able to:

    (1) Obtain a list of the components that the manufacturer would want to buy locally

    (2) Arrange local suppliers able to supply the components and who would provide price quotations for them

    (3) Provide this supplier and price information to the manufacturer.

    (ii) **Other high-tech manufacturers in the area**

    The existence of other high-tech manufacturers in the region would be an indication that there are good component suppliers in the region and that other environmental factors might be conducive to small computer manufacture in the area.

    (iii) **Proximity to markets**

    A manufacturing base should be fairly close to its major markets, so as to minimise distribution costs (provided, of course, that manufacturing costs are not so high in the area as to outweigh the advantages of proximity to markets). Geographical distance need not be a problem if there are efficient transport links.

    (iv) **Productivity**

    An important factor in keeping down manufacturing costs is productivity, especially amongst skilled workers. A reputation in high-tech industries for highly productive staff and good labour relations would be an advantage for the region.

    (v) **The availability of a good site**

    The site wanted by the computer manufacturer would presumably be close to a good transport system and a prestige location, to suit the corporate image of a major computer manufacturer. One of the key tasks of the RDA would be to help the manufacturer to locate such a site.

    (vi) **Financial incentives**

    The government (through the RDA) could offer certain financial incentives to encourage a manufacturer to set up operations in the region. The most obvious of these would be a cash grant, in the form perhaps of a regional development grant and selective regional assistance.

    Financial incentives will therefore be a 'sweetener' for the computer manufacturer.

4 Toroidal Tooling

Top tips. We have used the BCG matrix in part (a) as it is the simplest and possibly the most useful of the portfolio analysis matrices. It is certainly one you should be completely familiar with. We mention other approaches in our suggested solution.

In part (b), we use the value chain. There are certainly other approaches that the company could use to improve its systems, such as business process re-engineering, but the value chain is an ideal route to the overview the question asks for. In fact, the value chain is widely applicable in the exam as a framework for answering many questions, because it offers a comprehensive framework for analysing business problems.

Part (a)

Portfolio analysis examines the current status of the organisation's products and their markets. A variety of techniques may be used, including the product lifecycle concept, the GE business screen and the Shell matrix. One of the best established is the BCG matrix

The Boston Consulting Group (BCG) developed a matrix based on empirical research that assesses a company's products in terms of potential cash generation and cash expenditure requirements. Products (or even complete product divisions) are categorised in terms of market growth rate and relative market share.

(a) Assessing rate of market growth as high or low depends on the conditions in the market. No single percentage rate can be set, since new markets may grow explosively while mature ones grow hardly at all. Toroidal's sales force seems to be well informed about its market and its collective judgement will be useful here.

(b) Relative market share is assessed as a ratio: it is market share compared with the market share of the largest competitor. Thus a relative market share greater than unity indicates that the product or SBU is the market leader. It has been established empirically that market leaders tend to be more profitable than their competitors. This is felt to be due largely to economies of scale. Obtaining this information requires Toroidal to do some desk research in industry publications: their marketing staff are probably best placed to do this.

The matrix offers guidance as to appropriate strategy for each category of product.

Four major strategies can be pursued with respect to products, market segments and, indeed, SBUs.

(a) **Build**. A build strategy forgoes short term earnings and profits in order to increase market share.

(b) **Hold**. A hold strategy seeks to maintain the current position.

(c) **Harvest**. A harvesting strategy seeks short-term earning and profits at the expense of long-term development.

(d) **Divest**. Divestment reduces negative cash flow and releases resources for use elsewhere.

		Relative market share	
		High	Low
Market growth	High	Stars	Question marks
	Low	Cash cows	Dogs

(a) **Stars**. In the sort term, these require capital expenditure in excess of the cash they generate, in order to maintain their market position, but promise high returns in the future. Strategy: build.

(b) In due course, stars will become **cash cows**. Cash cows need very little capital expenditure and generate high levels of cash income. Cash cows can be used to finance the stars. Strategy: hold or harvest if weak.

(c) **Question marks**. Do the products justify considerable capital expenditure in the hope of increasing their market share, or should they be allowed to die quietly as they are squeezed out of the expanding market by rival products? Strategy: build or harvest.

(d) **Dogs** may be ex-cash cows that have now fallen on hard times. Although they will show only a modest net cash outflow, or even a modest net cash inflow, they are cash traps which tie up funds and provide a poor return on investment. However, they may have a useful role, either to complete a product range or to keep competitors out. Strategy: divest or hold.

Toroidal has a wide range of products and product groups. It may be advisable to preface the portfolio analysis exercise with an assessment of the appropriateness of the existing classification. This might save a great deal of work in those areas where brand ranges overlap.

Part (b)

The value chain model of corporate activities, developed by Michael Porter, offers a bird's eye view of the firm and what it does. Competitive advantage, says Porter, arises out of the way in which firms organise and perform value activities. These are the means by which a firm creates value in its products

Activities incur costs, and, in combination with other activities, provide a product or service which earns revenue.

Porter grouped the various activities of an organisation into what he calls a value chain, which is illustrated below.

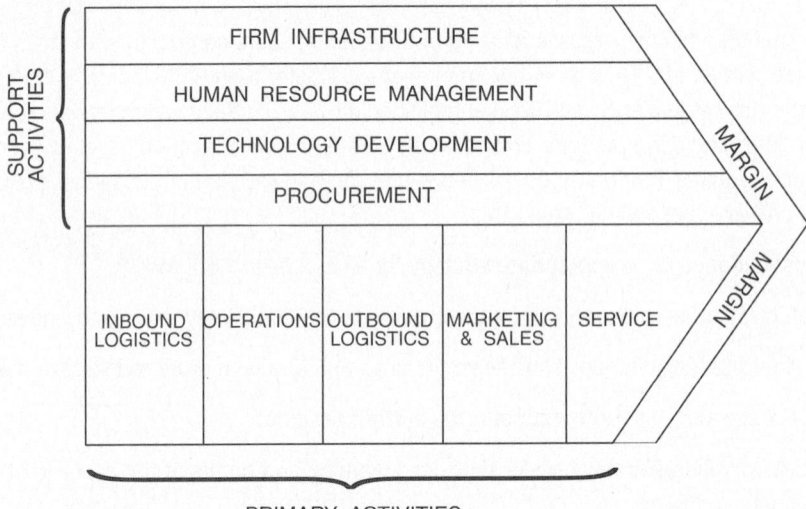

PRIMARY ACTIVITIES

The margin is the excess the customer is prepared to pay over the cost to the firm of obtaining resource inputs and providing value activities. It represents the value created by the value activities themselves and by the management of the linkages between them.

Primary activities are directly related to production, sales, marketing, delivery and service.

(a) Inbound logistics includes receiving, handling and storing inputs to the production system: warehousing, transport, stock control and so on. Toroidal's apparent poor performance in meeting orders promptly is a weakness that would be highlighted here.

(b) Operations convert resource inputs into a final product. Resource inputs are not only materials. People are a resource especially in service industries. Toroidal has two kind of operations: manufacturing its own products and dealing those produced by its agency principals. This area will therefore bear close examination in case the two types of operation come into conflict, for example over stock holding and packing (which take us into the next activity).

(c) Outbound logistics includes storing the product and its distribution to customers: packaging, testing, delivery and so on.

(d) Marketing and sales activities include informing customers about the product, persuading them to buy it, and enabling them to do so: advertising, promotion and so on. There is much scope for thought here, concerning the multiplicity of brands that Toroidal deals in.

(e) After sales service includes installing products, repairing them, upgrading them, providing spare parts and so forth. Clearly, Toroidal has problems in this area.

Support activities provide purchased inputs, human resources, technology and infrastructural functions to support the primary activities.

(a)   Procurement acquires the resource inputs to the primary activities (eg purchase of materials, subcomponents equipment).

(b)   Technology development includes such activities as product design, improving processes and resource utilisation.

(c)   Human resource management activities include recruiting, training, developing and rewarding people.

(d)   Management planning activities include planning, finance and quality control. Porter believes that these activities are crucially important to an organisation's strategic capability in all primary activities.

Linkages connect the activities of the value chain.

(a)   Activities in the value chain affect one another. For example, more costly product design or better quality production might reduce the need for after-sales service.

(b)   Linkages require co-ordination. For example, Just In Time requires smooth functioning of operations, outbound logistics and service activities such as installation.

The variety of Toroidal's products, brands and business relationships may make the management of linkages a fruitful area for investigation.

5 GHK restaurants

Top tips. The scenario identifies that the restaurants in the GHK group seem to have a variety of different generic strategies: some are cost leaders, some are following differentiation strategies, some have focus strategies, but some are stuck in the middle. So make sure you link the ideas of Porter's model directly to the scenario. How can they help GHK's owners maintain or improve profitability?

At an individual restaurant level, Porter's generic strategies could be used to help achieve a competitive advantage for the restaurants stuck in the middle. However, it is also worth considering whether this variety in strategies between the restaurants means that the group overall risks being stuck in the middle if it tries to use a single brand across the different restaurants.

Choosing a competitive strategy – Porter's logic behind his Three Generic Strategies Model is that a firm should follow only one of the strategies in order to achieve **competitive advantage**. If firms try to combine more than one of the strategies they risk becoming '**stuck in the middle**' and losing their competitive advantage.

Applying these ideas could help the owners of GHK assess whether their restaurants are following a coherent competitive strategy – either individually or as group - or whether they are becoming 'stuck in the middle.' If they are becoming 'stuck' in this way, the lack of a clear strategy might be contributing to the **decline in GHK's profits**.

Generic strategies – Porter suggests firms should choose between three generic strategies: cost leadership, differentiation and focus.

Cost leadership - If GHK chooses to become a cost leader, it must ensure it has the lowest costs in the industry as a whole. By having a lower cost base than its competitors, GHK could achieve a greater profit than them, even if its prices were the same as theirs.

Although this aspect of Porter's strategy focuses primarily on cost rather than price, it appears that GHK's **restaurant near the railway** is pursuing this kind of strategy, since it claims to be 'the cheapest in town.' However, to maintain its profitability, it must ensure it can continue to keep its cost base lower than any of its competitors' cost bases.

Differentiation – If GHK chooses a strategy of differentiation, it must deliver a product or service which the industry as a whole believes to be unique. As a result of this uniqueness, GHK will be able charge its customers a **premium price**.

It appears that the extremely expensive '**fine dining' restaurant** in the historic country house is charging a premium price in this way. However, to maintain its profitability, the restaurant must ensure it maintains its distinguishing features – be they the quality of the menu; the service, or the ambience. These features are what differentiates the restaurant from others in the industry and they make attractive to customers, even though it is charging a premium price.

Focus – A focus strategy will involve segmenting the industry, such that GHK would then pursue a strategy of cost leadership or differentiation within a single segment of the restaurant industry.

Three of GHK's restaurant seem to following this type of strategy and tailoring their offering to a specific **market niche**: the barge restaurant specialising in **fish dishes**; the **steak house**; and the restaurant catering for **children's birthday parties**.

Stuck in the middle – GHK has eight restaurants in total. We have identified five of them as following one or other of Porter's generic strategies, but this means the other three - with conventional menus and average prices - are stuck in the middle.

In this respect, GHK need to look urgently at finding a way of establishing a competitive advantage for these three restaurants. This should allow them to improve their profitability.

Strategy and marketing – We do not know whether all the restaurants in the chain are branded unilaterally as GHK restaurants, or whether they have retained their own names as well as their own styles and prices. If GHK is trying to run the restaurants as a single group, under a single brand name, then the analysis of the restaurants' current position, indicates that the **group as a whole is at risk of being 'stuck in the middle'** due to the diversity of its strategies.

In this respect, Porter's generic strategies model suggests that GHK would be best advised to run the restaurants as separate business units, and to develop marketing strategies which support their individual characteristics.

However, if GHK chooses to do this, it still needs to consider whether the restaurants' current strategies can deliver a **sustainable competitive advantage**. For example, the prices of foodstuffs and drinks are rising in GHK's country, which will increase its cost base. So, how sustainable is a cost leadership strategy, particularly as there is little evidence of specific technologies or processes which will allow GHK to sustain a lower cost base than any of its competitors?

Given the overall economic context in which GHK is operating, GHK's owners might decide that Porter's **focus strategies** (either cost-focus, or differentiation-focus) offer them the most practical way of maintaining or improving the profitability of their restaurants.

6 Packit Co

Top tips. Do not ignore the explicit reference in both the scenario and the question to organic options. The firm has ruled out global expansion using either merger and acquisition or joint venture. Therefore answers which set out to describe the advantages and disadvantages of merger/acquisition and joint ventures would not score any marks.

Part (a)

Companies can grow **organically** (via internal development), building up their own products and developing their own market. This is the primary method of growth for many companies. Some form of organic growth needs to be chosen by Packit Co: the choice will depend upon the prevailing attitude to **risk**, the **timescale** available, and the **opportunities** for growth that each option creates. The preferred strategy should reflect the **long-term goals** of the company. Furthermore, each option will affect the

structure and processes within the company, and will have its own implications for staffing and management control.

Overseas sales office

Advantages

Setting up a sales office in an international location probably involves **low risk** and **low cost** with respect to changing manufacturing and technological processes.

The company already is based in Europe and so already has operations in Europe. Its experience of selling to the European market (outside its home country) may be transferable to other markets.

Packit Co will need to consider whether it sells to its customers directly, or through a local distributor, after developing its brand sufficiently. Having a localised sales office will allow Packit to get a better understanding of customer requirements in those markets.

Disadvantages

Opening an overseas sales office will not prevent Packit being subject to any tariff barriers.

Local sales staff could act independently from head office. Management at head office will have to devote time to controlling the sales office.

Packit may find it difficult to recruit suitable local staff.

Manufacturing operation

Advantages

A manufacturing plant may be the only option in some countries, where governments might be looking for **inward investment and job creation**. Governments may impose **prohibitive tariffs** on imported products to protect local products and jobs.

Producing overseas may also **lower production costs** if resource costs (especially wages) are cheaper than in Packit's home country.

Disadvantages

A manufacturing facility involves **more commitment of finance and other resources**, and a significant alteration to the **value chain**. The required investment may in some cases be prohibitively expensive, and it may be difficult to find enough suitable local staff if there is no local partner in the operation.

In Packit's case, the **logistics** of getting the semi-finished product to the overseas manufacturing base will also need some thought. The plant may actually end up acting independently, which will affect the **level of control** that can be exercised by Packit, and may end up increasing the **business risk**.

Quality control will be of importance. Involving another plant may add considerably to quality risks.

Agents and distributors

Advantages

Agents will have already **established business networks** and local expertise which Packit can take advantage of.

There will be no capital costs incurred for setting up overseas manufacturing bases, and there will be no changes to the current manufacturing process.

Disadvantages

Gaining the **motivation** and **full commitment** of local agents and distributors could be a major problem. They might be carrying the products of several firms, and will be tempted to commit themselves to those products that earn the best return. The question of **exclusivity** therefore becomes important, and this may be able to be negotiated by Packit Co.

The provision of attractive **commission and other financial incentives** will help the relationship. However, if the commissions the agents demand become too high, the operation will not be economic for Packit.

Controlling agents and distributors can be difficult, so it is important for Packit to set out realistic performance expectations, and contracts should be clear to all parties involved.

7 Product market strategy

Top tips. This question requires practical application of two syllabus models to various companies in different industries, and as such it is typical of questions at this level. You must be able to analyse the information presented, in this case identifying the phase of development reached by each industry, then applying Ansoff's matrix. You may have been distracted by the phrase 'industry' life cycle, but this is no different in principle to the product life cycle with which you should be familiar. Being able to tie the industries in question to the respective life cycle phases in part (a) should cause few problems, and indeed is not worth too many marks.

Part (b) is more challenging. We have opened our answer with a diagram to link the narrative to, as it makes the answer easier to follow. You may have done the same, as it helps to focus the mind!

In summary, our conclusions for part (b) were broadly as follows

Key feature	*Option*	
• Company A	Innovation	Product development
• Company B penetration	Growing market	Product development and/or market
• Company C	Mature market	Market development
• Company D fighting on where possible	Weak position, with sales down	Divestment to free resources before

(a)　(i)　The **industry life cycle** reflects the fact that the profitability and sales of an industry can be expected to change over time. It is an attempt to recognise distinct stages in an industry's sales history. The classic **life cycle pattern** is commonly described by a curve as follows.

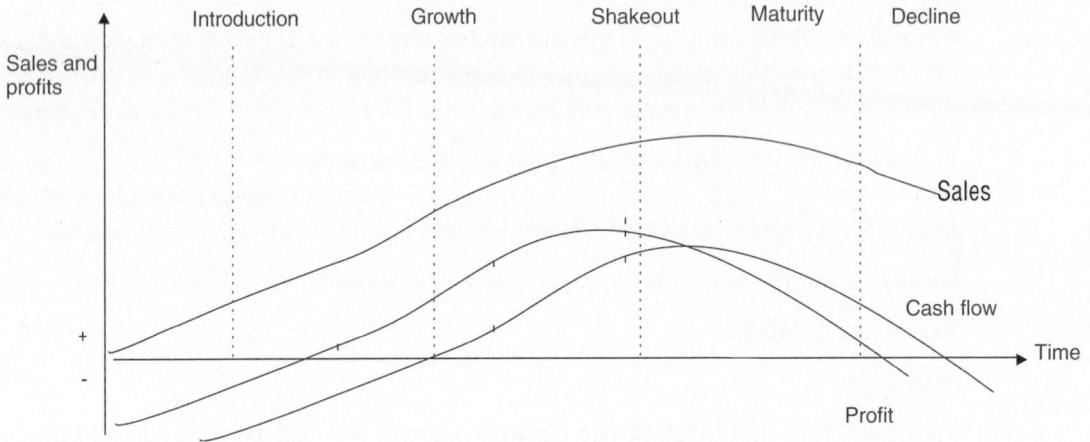

Introduction

(1)　A new industry product takes time to find acceptance by would-be purchasers and there is a slow growth in sales. Unit costs are high because of low output and expensive sales promotion.

(2)　There may be early teething troubles with technology.

(3)　The industry for the time being is a loss-maker.

Growth

(1)   With market acceptance, sales will eventually rise more sharply, and profits will rise.

(2)   Competitors are attracted. As sales and production rise, unit costs fall.

Maturity

(1)   The rate of sales growth slows down and the industry reaches a period of maturity which is probably the longest period of a successful industry's life. Innovation may have slowed down by this stage.

(2)   Most products on the market will be at the mature stage of their life. Profits are good.

Decline

(1)   Sales will begin to decline so that there is over-capacity of production in the industry. Severe competition occurs, profits fall and some producers leave the market.

(2)   The remaining producers seek means of prolonging product life by modification and searching for new market segments. Many producers are reluctant to leave the market, although some inevitably do because of market fragmentation and falling profits.

(ii)   The industries in which each of the companies appear to be operating are as follows.

(1)   **Company A**. This is operating in the introductory phase of what is a very new innovation, but this innovation is located within a very old industry.

(2)   **Company B**. This is positioned in a rapidly expanding and relatively young industry, experiencing a growth phase.

(3)   **Company C**. This company is in a mature industry, as witnessed by the low growth but high market share. Profits are likely to be good.

(4)   **Company D**. While the retailing industry itself is not in decline, this company appears to be, as it is losing ground to competitors in what is a highly competitive industry. The competitors may be larger companies able to compete more effectively on marketing mix issues such as price.

(b)   **Ansoff** drew up a **growth vector matrix**, describing a combination of a firm's activities in current and new markets, with existing and new products. The matrix can be represented diagrammatically as follows.

		Product	
		Present	*New*
Market	*Present*	Market penetration; (for growth) or consolidation (to maintain position)	Product development
	New	Market development	Diversification

Company A is involved with launching a very **innovative** product to revolutionise an existing market (home security). Such product development forces competitors to innovate and may provide initial barriers to entry, with newcomers to the industry being discouraged. This will give Company A the chance to build up rapid **market penetration**, but as competitors enter the market, it must make sure that it keeps household and commercial customers interested via constant

innovation. The drawback to this is the related **expense and risk**. Company A must also make sure that it has enough resources to satisfy demand so that competitors cannot poach market share.

Product improvements will be necessary to sustain the market, so Company A must make sure that enough resources are given to **research and development** of new technologies (and hence new products) in its field, as well as to maintaining sufficient production capacity to satisfy current demand.

Company B is engaged in a rapidly expanding market that is likely to attract many **competitors** keen for their own share of the market and profits. The growth strategy is limited to the current agricultural market, so referring to the Ansoff matrix above, the company is going to be mainly concerned with **market penetration** and **product development**, with an emphasis on the latter to make life more difficult for new competitors. By investing in product development, the company will see a necessary expansion in its R&D facility. To keep the new products and the company itself in the public eye, it may need to invest more in **marketing** and **promotion.**

With **market penetration**, the company will aim to achieve the following.

- Maintain or increase its **share** of the current market with its current products, for example through competitive pricing, advertising, sales promotion and quality control

- Secure **dominance** of the market and drive out competitors

- Increase **usage by existing and new customers**. The customer base is likely to be expanding

Company C is in the **mature phase** of its life cycle. As the current market is mature, the company can achieve growth via the investigation of **new markets**. Referring to the Ansoff matrix, this means pursuing a strategy of **market development.** Seeing as the current market is mature, with satisfied customers and little innovation, there is small scope for market development, unless it is via short term aggressive tactics such as cuts in prices.

Selling current products to new markets is likely to be more successful, and may include one or more of the following strategies.

- New **geographical areas** and export markets

- **Different package sizes** for food and other domestic items

- **New distribution channels** to attract new customers

- **Differential pricing policies** to attract different types of customer and create new market segments

- **Mass marketing techniques** that encourage customers to switch brands

The company may also investigate the possibility of developing **new products** to make up for those that are in the **decline phase** of the life cycle. This may lead to the creation of more **cash cows**.

Company D is in a difficult position, with a weak position in a well established market. It needs to undertake some rigorous **analysis of costs**. A strategy of **divestment** may be advised to enable it to reduce costs and concentrate on more profitable areas of activity. **Resource limitations** mean that less profitable outlets or products may have to be abandoned. This could involve analysis of individual contributions, perhaps using **direct product profitability** techniques.

The market has become less attractive and Company D needs to assess its image and profitability. It is likely that customers have become more discerning on price, as has happened in the UK retailing sector in the past few years. When some product areas have been divested, the company may find that it has the **resources** to pursue strategies of **market penetration** for some products and **new product development** to improve its image with customers.

A strategy of **total withdrawal**, and **diversification** into wholly new industries is not seen as appropriate for any of the companies described in the question. It could not be recommended because of the attendant **risks**.

Company D does need to be careful, and it is facing the most difficult situation of all the companies that have been described. It is one thing to eliminate unprofitable products, but will there be sufficient growth potential among the products that remain in the product range?

In addition, new products require some initial **capital expenditure**. Retained profits are by far the most significant source of new funds for companies. A company investing in the medium to long term which does not have enough **current income from existing products** will go into liquidation, in spite of its future prospects.

8 U plc

Top tips. The answer to part (a) examines the three strategies in turn.

(i)   Existing promotional advertising and exhibitions
(ii)   Raise prices
(iii) Adapting production procedures

It looks at the potential risks and benefits of each, keeping in mind the objective of increasing market share, turnover and margins, and comes up with a conclusion.

Other points to note are

- The reaction of A Ltd and Z plc to any strategy change of U plc
- The cost of the different options for U plc
- The timescale needed to introduce major changes
- The high investment risk in a major spending programme
- Balancing long-term and short-term benefits for U plc

It is not clear from the question whether the 'alternative' marketing strategies are mutually exclusive, or whether they should be considered in combination. This solution tries to adopt the view that the strategies could be considered either in isolation or in combination.

Part (b) concludes that the offer described would not be good enough for acceptance by Z. Simple manipulation of the figures given in the question, with a basic assumption about turnover levels, shows that Z is a far stronger company. The question does ask whether it would be in the interest of U plc shareholders, so make sure that your answer includes reference to this (even though such a deal would be highly unlikely to take place!)

In part (c) do not forget to mention the benefits of operating synergy (in addition to increased turnover, profit and ROCE). Marketing and production operations, for example, could be combined.

(a)   **Existing strategy**

The existing strategy of attempting to **boost market share** by **promotional** advertising and exhibitions has not shown any success to date. It is difficult to relate advertising expenditure directly to higher sales, and it is possible that U plc's market share will improve in the course of time if advertising and exhibition displays are continued.

On the other hand, there may be a weakness in the nature of the advertising campaign – ie what is the objective of the campaign? – and the product might not be one which can be exhibited with any great success. The **reluctance of customers to switch** to a new supplier indicates that advertising might not be an effective marketing strategy at all.

Unless the promotional advertising and exhibitions can be expected to increase sales, or prevent a fall in sales, the expenditure involved in the current strategy will result in a lower **profit/turnover ratio** and lower **profit/capital employed ratio** than would otherwise be achievable.

Strategy to raise prices

The strategy to raise prices so as to achieve a minimum profit/sales ratio of 12½%, compared with the current 7½%, implies **price rises** of at least 5%. If the strategy were successful, profits would be about two-thirds higher, and so the profit/capital employed figure would also rise by about two-thirds to 25%. With an unchanged P/E ratio the **share price** of U plc shares would also rise by two-thirds.

Another advantage of this strategy, compared with the current one, is that the company would make savings in advertising and promotion costs.

The major drawback to this strategy is that U plc's current **low price strategy**, whilst not winning any new customers because of the reluctance of customers to change supplier, could mean that higher prices will result in some loss of business. If the demand for U plc's product is **inelastic**, the financial benefits of a price rise would exceed the drawback of some loss of market share. However, if demand at higher prices shows a **high elasticity**, (which is sometimes the case in oligopoly markets) the loss of sales and market share could be considerable, in which case the higher-price strategy would **fail to achieve the objective** of a 12½% profit/sales ratio.

Adopting production procedures

The third marketing strategy of adapting **production procedures** so as to become more flexible, **responsive to customer demands** and capable of faster **product development**, would presumably have the objective of increasing market share. A Ltd, which has the greatest flexibility of the three companies, has the biggest market share but also the highest variable costs. This strategy, were it successful, might eventually succeed in improving U plc's results so as to become comparable to A Ltd's. However, it is not clear how easily U plc could switch to a strategy of greater flexibility, and what this might involve in terms of scrapping existing capital equipment and converting to a less capital-intensive system of operating.

The third strategy would take longer to implement than the other two, and so its benefits would be longer in coming. It would also be the highest-risk strategy of the three, if a large amount of **capital expenditure** were involved.

The choice of strategy must also take account of **competitors'** reactions. Presumably they have already reacted to the current strategy. A price increase by U plc should not be a direct threat to the others. A change in production methods, though, would be more threatening, and Z plc and A Ltd might take counter-measures of some kind.

Of the three strategies, a strategy of increasing prices might seem to offer the best immediate prospects of improved financial results, but the consequences of higher prices on sales volume ought to be investigated closely before such a strategy is adopted. The strategy of adapting production procedures might offer the best long-term prospects, but it is a high-risk strategy, especially if competitors take successful counter-measures.

(b)　It is assumed that the three companies specialise in the single market and that their financial results do not include results from any other trading activities.

A 'takeover' of Z plc by U plc would then appear to be an unusual suggestion, and one that would be most unlikely to succeed.

Suppose, for the purpose of illustration, that the total market were worth £10 million in sales turnover. The results of U plc and Z plc could then be compared as follows:

	Turnover £m		Profit £		Capital employed £	P/E ratio	Market capitalisation £m
U plc	1.5	(7.5%)	112,500	(÷ 15%)	750,000	10.4	1.17
Z plc	2.0	(15%)	300,000	(÷ 20%)	1,500,000	17.3	5.19
			412,500		2,250,000		

On the basis of the figures, it would seem that Z plc has twice the **capital employed** of U plc and over four times the current **market capitalisation**. An offer of only three shares in U plc for two shares in Z plc would be impossibly low.

The offer would be in the interests of U plc shareholders, were it to succeed, because the **ROCE** of the new company would be higher (about 18.3% on the basis of the figures above). Since U plc would be offering three of its shares (currently priced on a P/E of 10.4) for two shares in Z plc (currently on a P/E of 17.3) there would also be a small improvement in the **EPS** for U plc shareholders. This in turn would result in a higher share price, even if the P/E ratio of the new company remained at 10.4.

In order to afford the takeover, U plc would almost certainly have to **issue new shares**, and **control** of the company would be affected. This might not be in the interest of existing shareholders, especially any major shareholder in the company.

As indicated earlier, however, this is not an offer that Z's board of directors or shareholders should wish to accept.

(c)   The growth that might be expected would be as follows:

    (i)   Without synergy and without growth, the combined company's **profits and ROCE** would be higher than for U plc on its own.

    (ii)   The combined **market share** of the merged company would start at 35%. If the sales turnover of the total market is rising annually, the company's **turnover** would also increase. This should result in a higher total **contribution** and **operating profit**, a higher **profit/sales ratio** and a higher **ROCE**.

    (iii)   The combined company might hope to succeed in improving its results through **synergy**.

        (1)   **Marketing operations** could be combined, with some savings in costs. There would also be the possibility of more effective sales and promotional activities, resulting in new clients and a bigger market share.

        (2)   **Production operations** might be rationalised with some savings in **capital equipment**. This would improve the profit/capital employed ratio and the ROCE.

        (3)   There might be some synergy with **R&D activities**, enabling the combined company to develop **new products** more successfully, thus rivalling A Ltd in this respect and so perhaps winning some customers from A Ltd.

9 Marketing orientation

> **Top tips.** The essence of a market orientation is to find out what the customer needs and attempt to satisfy those needs, rather than to devise a product or service and then offer it for use.
>
> A non-profit organisation will have 'customers' too. Our answer to part (a) indicates that a bit of re-thinking can help any organisation to focus its effort on its customers. We include three examples. You may have thought of others.
>
> Part (b) is a straightforward examination of the differences between consumer and industrial marketing. It is worth learning these differences, but the concept of the DMU is the most important element to mention.

(a)   Marketing orientation' is a management philosophy which holds that the key task of an organisation is to identify the needs and wants of **customers** in a **target market**, and to adapt the organisation to satisfying them **effectively and efficiently**. An organisation whose objective is to make profits would be market-oriented in order to satisfy customers and thereby be more profitable than it could by means of any other policy.

An organisation which does not have a profit objective may be a charity, an organisation formed to promote a cause (for example a political party) or an organisation which is established to provide a certain non-commercial service (for example a club or a government department). These organisations still have 'target markets' and 'customers' with needs to satisfy, and therefore a market-oriented approach by the management of the organisation is a feasible proposition.

An initial **definition of the nature of the business** in which an organisation operates is useful because it helps the business to focus on the interests of the consumer. For example, as profit-making organisations, Hollywood film companies eventually realised that they were not film-makers but firms in the entertainment market. As a result, instead of competing unsuccessfully with television, they switched profitably into the production of television programmes.

A similar exercise might help **non-profit-motivated organisations** to re-assess their future. For example, the fire department of a local authority might redefine its purpose from fighting fires to 'being in the business of minimising injury and damage through fire or other accidents'. This redefinition, if it is in keeping with the needs of customers, would extend the activities of the department to fire prevention, rescuing victims from accidents etc.

Another example might be a public swimming pool, which defines its business, not as providing a facility for swimming but as swimming for general recreation and life protection. In this way, the pool's management might extend its activities into swimming classes, life-saving classes, opening a swimming club for sports competition etc.

As a final example, a charitable organisation might define itself, not in terms of raising funds and providing food to help a starving population in an overseas country, (product or service orientation) but in terms of the business of providing for the health and security of the population in the short term and for the improvement of the population's well-being in the longer term (ie market orientation). In this way the charity's management might actively seek ways, not only of providing food and medical supplies, but also of providing funds for education and investment in agricultural machinery, or even an infrastructure of roads and communications for the country concerned.

(b)   An understanding of who buys your product, how they buy it and what influences the buying process is fundamental to establishing marketing strategy for both **consumer** and **industrial** marketing managers. There is, however, general agreement that there are certain features in **organisational buying** that are not found in consumer markets and that these features have implications for sales strategy. These are as follows.

(i)   **Fewer potential organisational buyers**. Often 80% of output is sold to relatively few organisations. In consumer selling, the presence of intermediaries (ie wholesalers/retailers) can mean there are relatively few direct buyers, although the ultimate number of end consumers can amount to millions.

(ii)   **Organisational buyers are more rational.** Although people buying for organisations are only human and may, as individuals, prefer the colour of a particular product, on the whole the buying behaviour is more rational. Economic criteria tend to be used. Also, the buying decision has to be justified to other parts of the organisation.

(iii)   **Organisational buying may be to satisfy specific requirements.** Often buyers determine product specifications and so the seller must tailor the product to meet them. In consumer marketing, products are rarely geared to individual customers.

(iv)   **Reciprocal buying may be important.** For example, a company supplying business documentation (eg invoices) to a chain of garages may only get the business if they have all their company cars serviced there.

(v)   **Organisational buying can be more risky.** Often the contract is agreed before the product is made. Technical problems could arise later which could make the product uneconomic to produce. In addition, very large sums of money are often involved, such as with the purchase of a new computer system.

(vi) **Organisational buying is usually more complex than consumer buying.** Many people could potentially get involved – engineers, directors, marketing people. It may therefore be necessary to sell as a team. The main way in which the decision making process varies is that a **group** of people, rather than an individual consumer, will normally be involved. This is known as the Decision Making Unit (DMU). The DMU is usually made up of:

- Users (often initiators, for example production)
- Deciders (those with authority, for example directors)
- Influencers (marketing, research and development, other managers)
- Buyers (who execute the purchase)
- Gatekeepers (for example, secretaries, receptionists)

(vii) **Organisational buying has a different buying motive** or need. Consumer buying is usually for personal consumption whereas industrial buying is not. The development of formal specifications and the review of potential supplier proposals, together with the development of an order routine, make the process more formal and tangible.

10 GHK restaurants

(a)

The answer for part (a) is shown as Question 5 above.

(b)

Top tips. Although the question refers to 'a range of organisational information systems' you could usefully consider these systems at two different levels: systems which provide strategic information, and systems which provide operational information.

Also, try to think of the range of information which it would be useful for GHK's owners to find out about: the external competitive environment and market information; customer details and marketing information; and restaurant usage, costs and revenues.

Make sure you show how the systems can directly help GHK rather than simply talking about information systems in general though.

Market research – In order to decide look at the suitability of any potential strategies for its restaurants, GHK needs to have detailed **market** and **demographic information** to see whether the proposed strategies are suitable. For example, if GHK wants to pursue a strategy of differentiation, it will need to assess whether there are sufficient people who are willing to pay premium prices to eat in the restaurant in order for the restaurant to be profitable.

Market research could also identify **new opportunities**, especially if there is market demand which is currently not being met. This could allow GHK to adapt its strategy (particularly in the restaurants which are currently 'stuck in the middle') to cater for this latent demand. For example, market research might identify that customers want a restaurant which serves locally-sourced, organic food, and they would be prepared to pay a premium for this food. In this way, the findings from the market research could support a focus differentiation strategy.

Market share analysis - GHK should also try to get overall market revenue figures for the various market segments in which it operates, and compare its own performance against these overall market figures. This will indicate whether its market share is increasing or decreasing, and therefore will give some indication of how successful GHK's strategies are proving.

Customer Information – We do not know whether customers need to book in advance to eat at GHK's restaurants, but it is likely they do for the 'fine dining' restaurant and for the birthday parties, at least.

BPP
LEARNING MEDIA

Website – If GHK develops a website which customers can use for booking this will allow GHK to build up a **database of contacts**. If customers give an e-mail address when they book, GHK can use these addresses for future e-marketing campaigns.

GHK could also introduce a **loyalty card programme** as a way of getting a database of customers, finding out which of its restaurants they use, and how frequently they use them.

Such information could have two different uses:

*   **Customer relationship management** - On the one hand, it can be useful for customer relationship management – for example, GHK could send reminder emails to lapsed customers who have not been to one of its restaurants recently, or it could inform customers of any special offers they might be interested in at restaurants they have visited recently. Given that the local economy has shrunk recently, **maintaining customer numbers** is likely to be an important issue for GHK.

*   **Trend analysis** - On the other hand, the database could be analysed to highlight patterns and trends in customer usage at the different restaurants. Understanding these trends could, in turn, be useful for marketing campaigns or operational decisions for example working out staffing levels.

Management Information Systems – GHK's owners are clearly concerned about the performance of their business. Therefore it will be important that they have timely and reliable management information which they can use to see how the restaurants are performing. For example, the owners might find it useful to have summary reports which provide them daily or weekly snapshots of restaurant revenues and customer numbers, and the gross profit margins at each of the restaurants.

Operational information systems – In order to provide this summary information, GHK will need a way of capturing detailed operational information. If the waiters and waitresses in all the restaurants recorded customer orders on **hand-held personal digital assistants** (PDA's) the information from these could be captured, and ultimately transmitted back to a **central data warehouse**. The PDA's could capture, for example, customer numbers, the days and times of orders, and the dishes being ordered. Analysing this information could highlight, for example, whether some items on the menu more popular than others, or whether some times of day busier than other.

This information could then be used to help the owners make decisions such as whether the **menus need changing**, or whether the opening hours need revising. For example, if there are some items on the menu which do not sell well, they should be removed or replaced. If they were removed, and the menus were shortened, this would mean that GHK needed to hold fewer ingredients in stock, which would be beneficial in a period of rising food prices. Equally, if there are times of day where customer numbers are low, the owners may decide not to open all day, or to introduce some **special offers** to attract customers during those off-peak periods.

In addition to the hand-held PDA's, the **tills in the restaurants** should also be linked to the central data warehouse, so that the management information system can update figures for **sales receipts** and **cash takings** on a real time basis. Given that GHK is now in danger of making a loss for the first time, it will be important to be able to monitor sales figures closely, to see what impact any new strategies have on sales.

Performance information – There is no indication that GHK has any key performance indicators (KPIs) for its restaurants. However, the information available from the operational information systems could be used in **KPIs**. The management accountant could report how well the restaurants are performing in certain key areas, for example, spend per customer head, or spend per waiter. These again can provide useful headline information to the owners to enable them to see how the business is performing in areas which are critical to its success.

11 Organisation structure

Top tips. A common problem for candidates is the **application** of their theoretical knowledge to question scenarios. In this answer we show in *italics* those parts that constitute application of theory to the specific problems represented by the scenario.

Easy marks. The setting for this question points you fairly clearly towards the matrix and project team approaches. When you get a question that gives you this kind of steer, accept it gratefully and don't waste time trying to think of something different, even if you think you can. However, relevant comment on suitability and potential problems is clearly called for.

Matrix structure

*XYZ Technology might consider a **matrix** form of organisation structure.* This provides control of activities that overlap functional boundaries, while at the same time maintaining functional departmentation.

Senior managers are appointed to oversee activities that span functional boundaries. Lateral lines of communication and authority are thus superimposed on the functional departmental structure. A common example is the appointment of marketing managers with responsibility for all aspects of the marketing of a particular product group. *In XYZ, for instance, a manager might be appointed to draw together all the design, manufacturing, financial and promotion efforts relating to the new electronic systems for the fighter aircraft business.*

Project team structure

A related approach is **project team** organisation. This is very similar to matrix management, but is based on *ad hoc* cross-functional teams with responsibility for a defined project. *This might be more appropriate for YXZ, since the company is effectively working on specific projects with a defined life cycle rather than steady-state production.*

Project team organisation allows for the co-ordination of interdisciplinary effort, with experts in different functions appointed to the team while retaining membership and status within their own functional department.

Advantages of a cross-disciplinary structure

(a)   It offers greater **flexibility**. This applies both to **people,** as employees adapt more quickly to a new challenge or new task, and develop an attitude which is geared to accepting change; and to **task and structure**, as the matrix may be short-term (as with project teams) or readily amended (eg a new product manager can be introduced by superimposing his tasks on those of the existing functional managers). *Flexibility should facilitate efficient operations at XYZ by helping it to cope with the complexity of the technology it is deploying and the dynamism of the markets in which it operates.*

(b)   It provides for **inter-disciplinary co-operation** and a mixing of skills and expertise. This should improve **communication** within the organisation and give XYZ the **multiple orientation** it needs to integrate its key activities and keep functional specialists from becoming wrapped up in their own concerns.

(c)   It provides a **structure for allocating responsibility to managers for end-results**. A product manager is responsible for product profitability, and a project leader is responsible for ensuring that the task is completed. *This also will promote the integration of effort that XYZ needs.*

Disadvantages of a cross-disciplinary structure

(a)   Dual authority threatens a **conflict** between managers. It is important that the authority of superiors should not overlap and areas of responsibility must be clearly defined. *Don Wilson must ensure that subordinates know to which of their superiors they are responsible for each aspect of their duties.*

(b)   One individual with two or more bosses is more likely to suffer **role stress** at work. *This is another problem for senior management at XYZ to monitor.*

(c)   It is likely to be more **costly**, since additional managers are appointed that would not be required in a simple structure of functional departmentation. *XYZ is already quite lean, so it may be able to absorb these costs without great difficulty.*

(d)   It may be difficult for managers **to accept**. It is possible that managers will feel that their authority is being eroded. Similarly, it requires consensus and agreement which may **slow down** decision-making. *Don Wilson must monitor managerial attitudes to ensure that managerial conservatism does not seize opportunities to make any new approach fail.*

12 Steyn Steel Co

> **Top tips.**
>
> (a)   In effect, this question is asking you to work out the forces which need to be considered in a force field analysis at Steyn Steel. However, the question asks you to analyse them, so need to discuss them. Do not be tempted to draw a force field analysis diagram.
>
> (b)   Although the question does not specify any specific model, Lewin's three stage model is a useful model to use here. The CEO will need to unfreeze existing behaviours, make the changes he believes are necessary, and then refreeze the new behaviours he wants to establish.

Part (a)

Forces for change

Internal

New CEO – A new CEO has recently joined Steyn Steel and he has identified areas where the company's performance needs to be improved. More importantly, he has also made it clear he intends to address these directly in order to improve Steyn's competitiveness.

As an 'outsider' joining the company, the CEO is likely to look more objectively at performance issues than managers and staff who have worked for the company for a long time.

Poor operational performance – The CEO is only having to act because Steyn's current operational performance does not appear to be competitive. These performance issues are characterised by costs being too high and productivity being too low, and may reflect the perceived complacency among the staff.

External

High export demand – It seems that the scope to increase sales is greater in export markets than in Steyn's domestic market. However, the CEO has suggested that Steyn will need to change some of its working practices in order to capitalise on these export opportunities.

The fact that the CEO is clearly focussing on exports as the main source of revenue opportunities suggests that he doesn't see any real growth opportunities in Steyn's domestic market. This again reinforces the need to change working practices in order to be competitive in the international market.

Forces resisting change

Internal

Long-serving managers – The managers who have worked at Steyn for a long time appear do not appear to be worried about the company's performance and so may not appreciate the company need for change. In this case, they are unlikely to support any proposals for change.

Alternatively, it may be that the long-standing staff members have become familiar and comfortable with the current practices and so do not want these to change. Change will bring uncertainty into their routines, and may involve them having to learn new skills or adapt to less favourable working practices.

Trade union - The trade union has promised the workers it will defend their wage levels and working conditions, and so this could lead them into direct conflict with the CEO if he tries to make changes.

If the pay and conditions which the workers (particularly the long-serving workers) receive are more favourable than the industry standard, this may be another reason for them to resist changes. If the CEO's proposals are aimed at bringing them more in line with industry standards, this may be disadvantageous to the workers.

External

Import duties – Steyn's ability to increase its sales into export markets appears constrained by the high import duties it has to pay in some of these markets. Given the strategic importance of increasing export sales, the on-going presence of these duties could be a significant problem for the company.

Part (b)

In his work on force field analysis and stage models of change, Lewin suggested that, after the forces for change and the forces resisting change have been established, efforts need to be made to break down the forces resisting change and also to reinforce the influence of those supporting it.

Unfreeze – 'Unfreezing' current working practices and attitudes is the first phase of Lewin's stage model of change.

The CEO will have to set up a programme of education and support for the complacent managers and enter into negotiations with the trade union. Given his concern's about Steyn's performance, the CEO may well be advise to emphasise the financial problems which the company could face if action is not taken to improve its competitiveness.

Communication will be vital here, and the CEO needs to explain to the staff not only what his plans for the future are, but why they are required.

Change –The second phase of the change programme will require action to change employees' behaviours: establishing new patterns of behaviour and reinforcing them.

Communication will again be important, but staff may also need training and development programmes to help them adapt to the new behaviours required.

Refreeze - For the change programme to be successful, the CEO will need to ensure that staff continue to embrace the new culture and behaviours rather than slipping back into their old ways. It is likely there will need to be a mixture of rewards to recognise good performance and also sanctions against staff who lapse back into their old habits. In extreme cases, staff who persistently refuse to adapt to the change may even be made redundant, although Steyn will be aware of the union presence and so will have to handle any such decisions with great care.

13 Simon Clark

Part (a)

> **Top tips**. As always, knowing the theory is not enough for success in the E3 exam. You must relate your knowledge to the setting, as we relate it in our answer below.
>
> You could use Lewin's models to approach this question and you would be awarded appropriate marks so long as you demonstrated the pressures and influences on Simon Clark and integrated your answers with the case scenario.

Simon has a range of possible responses to his problem of potential conflict with his staff.

Deny problem exists

Some essentially trivial problems blow over without particular management effort. This type of problem can be ignored. If Simon feels that this is the case here, he can effectively deny that a problem exists and withdraw from considering it further. However, the proposed changes would require very important changes to working practices at the college and conditions of service and the staff are 'most unhappy'. It seems unlikely that denial and withdrawal would be a satisfactory response, since teaching as an occupation is particularly demanding of individual motivation.

Smoothing over disputes

A more active policy would be to suppress the problem by smoothing over any overt disputes, if possible, in order to preserve working relationships. This approach is unlikely to produce the changes evidently required at the College, so Simon may have to combine it with a certain amount of coercion, imposing necessary changes unilaterally. This is a recipe for continuing dispute and the lingering hostility of 'win-lose' situations. The effect on motivation is likely to be even more dire than a policy of denial and withdrawal. Indeed, the teaching staff may retaliate by withdrawing their co-operation and working to rule.

Compromise and negotiation

A more positive approach for Simon to take would involve a willingness to make compromises *via* a process of bargaining, negotiation and conciliation. It is likely that there is some room for manoeuvre in the matter of weekend working, perhaps by offering time off *in lieu*. The staff are no doubt well aware of the potential threat to their interests from the private college and may be prepared to adjust their initial position.

Integration and collaboration

This approach may, perhaps, be extended into a more sophisticated process of integration and collaboration, in which a continuing dialogue can establish both common ground and general agreement as to what is necessary for the achievement of the overall task. To achieve this, Simon must overcome his frustration and attempt to bring the staff into full participation in the changes that affect them.

Part (b)

> **Top tips**. Generating support is an important aspect of change management generally. This question is about one department in quite a small organisation, so more complex change management strategies, such as the Gemini 4Rs, are probably too complex. We are concerned here with management techniques that would be useful to the head of a single department in such an organization.
>
> This is essentially a problem of practical leadership. Some aspects of the solution, such as providing resources, are easy both to specify and to implement. Other, less concrete, measures related to human behaviour, such as the importance of communication are less easy to describe and, indeed, to perform. Do not shy away from these less material things and do cover them in as precise a way as you can. It is very easy to be vague and woolly about such matters. Try to be definite. For example, don't just say 'communicate' say 'hold a meeting' as well.

It seems likely from the staff's initial reaction to Simon's proposals that he has not given sufficient thought to enlisting their support. This may reflect his managerial technique, or lack of it. If he is to succeed with his plan to change the way things are done, he will have to improve the way he deals with his staff in both material and intangible ways.

Improve communications

The highest priority is to improve his overall relations with the staff. He must make more effective communication a continuing personal target in order to improve motivation and mutual understanding. He must ensure that the staff see him as approachable and sympathetic to their concerns, within the limitations set by reality.

Improve understanding

Simon Clark should ensure that his staff understand that his proposals are a response to a serious commercial threat that affects them all and not an arbitrary decision. He should point out the potential effects upon them of failing to respond to the commercial competition and the opportunities and rewards that success will bring. He should encourage the staff to think for themselves about the situation the college is in, invite them to debate it among themselves and make alternative proposals if they can. Such participation, even if it does not produce any feasible new ideas, will make whatever solution is eventually decided upon more acceptable.

However, Simon must not abdicate responsibility. It is his role to make the final decision and to implement it. There are several measures he can take to promote acceptance of change.

Promote acceptance of change

He may be able to **enlist the support of more senior staff** who have the respect of their peers as change agents. Their role would be to lend their credibility to the new arrangements, to assist with its planning and implementation and to provide practical day-to-day leadership in the context of change.

He should **support positive responses** to change with praise and reward and deal firmly with negative behaviour such as murmuring and absenteeism.

The need for change has been forced upon the College and the Department and it may be that time and resources are limited. However, Simon's aim should be to introduce change at a measured pace and avoid the rush and panic that is sure to upset the staff and provoke hostility.

Similarly, he should make a case for the provision of resources to the change process, so that for instance, some promotions might result, or working conditions be improved. Quite small enhancements such as decorating the staff common room or providing a new photocopier would help to present the change in a positive light.

14 Auto direct

> **Top tip**. You must think hard about the wording of this question. Superficially, it asks you for a summary of change management strategies in a particular context, which would be a large job to do properly, but offers only twelve marks. The implication is that you must not descend into too much detail about any particular model or approach.

Managing Director, Auto Direct

Date

Report: Change management strategies and methods

The change that you are contemplating, while extensive, is incremental and does not involve the transformation of your organisation. It therefore falls into the category of **adaptation**, which implies that you may proceed step by step and leave your basic assumptions and approach unchanged.

It would be a very worthwhile exercise to consider some of the factors that might affect the success of your programme of change. Chief among these are likely to be the various human factors present in your staff.

Presumably you will include some element of promotion and cross-posting of your existing workforce in order to provide a basis of experience at your new sites, so you should consider the degree of **readiness** (or willingness) of your staff to undertake the development you plan.

You should also consider your company's managerial **capability** and **capacity** in terms of resources to undertake change. The former depends largely on past experience

While good **project management** of a programme of change is very important, it is the **human aspects of the change management process** that are crucial. This is because change will not happen unless people make it happen. A number of strategies are proposed for dealing with this aspect of change management.

Participation in decision-making is sometimes recommended as a way of improving motivation generally and may be useful in the context of change. It is probably advantageous to involve staff in decisions affecting them, their conditions and their work processes and at least hear what they have to say. However, participation is not a universal panacea and can be very **time consuming**. Also, the normal **management style and culture** of the organisation must be considered. It is probably inappropriate to promote participation exclusively in the context of change if staff are not used to it: their main reaction may be one of suspicious cynicism.

An **autocratic** approach, imposing change by means of **coercion** can work reasonably well in some circumstances, especially where the staff expect nothing else. It has the benefit of saving time and is probably the **best approach in times of crisis**. However, it does have the weakness of ignoring the experience and knowledge that staff may be able to offer.

In any event, **communication** with staff about the proposed change is commonly regarded as an essential process. Ideally, information will be provided as early as possible, explaining why change is necessary and the course that will be followed. Anxiety, particularly over job security, is common during change and a programme of communication and education can go a long way to allay it.

Sometimes neither participation nor coercion can resolve all problems and **negotiation** may be required. This is often the case when the labour force is strongly organised and when there is disagreement between management factions as to the best course to follow.

This has been a brief overview of some approaches to change management. You will no doubt be in a position to decide which are most appropriate to the circumstances of Auto Direct.

15 Nominee holdings

Top tips. This is a question which includes elements of financial management and management accounting (DCF, performance measurement). Indeed, the DCF rate of return or 'charge out' rate for capital is relevant to quantifying a company's long-term objectives.

The need to balance risk and return is an idea strongly suggested by the data in the question, and this touches on the overall objectives of the group. Sources of finance and gearing have to be considered, and these are problems of financial strategy as well as financial management.

The possible closure of a subsidiary is also a feature of the question, with emphasis on the strategic planning considerations.

It is necessary for some assumptions to be made.

It is not clear whether the project cost is the cost of the initial fixed asset expenditure, or whether it also includes the required investment in working capital.

It is also not clear what is meant by a 'current asset ratio'. If the question intended this to be the current ratio – ie the ratio of current assets to current liabilities, a current ratio of over 1 would indicate that some investment in working capital would be needed in addition to the fixed asset expenditure. A current ratio of less than 1 would indicate that current liabilities would help to finance the fixed assets.

(a)   To: directors of Nominee Holdings

Recommendations to consider

(i)   Three subsidiaries have submitted capital expenditure proposals, all of which would probably add value to the holding company's equity. The nature of the projects should be studied, to ensure that each project is in accord with the group's medium-term strategy. In the case of the Dairy-P project, this might not be so, since the group's strategy might favour a move of processing facilities to Greece. Clearly, if it is the group's intention to close down Dairy-P, the Dairy-P project should not be approved.

(ii)   The holding company's cash and short-term deposits amount to some 20% of its net worth, which is a very high proportion. The company is cash rich. However, its return on its cash

and short-term deposits is exceedingly low, at 5%. This poor return compares most unfavourably with the company's average cost of capital (19.5%) and mortgage debenture nominal rates of interest (10% – 17%).

The holding company ought to investigate its cash management, with a view to:

(1) Improving the return to much more than 5%.

(2) Using some cash to finance investments by subsidiaries. It is an unsatisfactory situation when the holding company employs its assets to earn 5% whilst subsidiaries are having to borrow at 10% – 17% gross (6.5% – 11% net of tax relief, taking the rate of corporation tax to be 35%) to finance new projects.

(3) Using some surplus cash to buy back and cancel some ordinary shares in the company. Authority for the company to purchase its own shares would have to be obtained from the shareholders in general meeting.

(iii) Subsidiaries are required to justify projects financially, using DCF and the group's weighted average cost of capital, on the grounds that each project holds prospects of a positive NPV. The group should re-assess whether the weighted average cost of capital ought to be used. (Further recommendations about this are given in part (c)).

(iv) **Dairy-P Ltd project**

This is a risky project. The estimated PV of benefits is (£150,000 × 1.41) = £211,500 and the NPV is £61,500. However, the project cost of £150,000 has a standard deviation of £41,000 and so if the actual project cost turns out to be 1.5 standard deviations above the mean, the project's NPV would be negative.

Assuming a normal distribution for project costs, the probability of a negative NPV would be (0.5 – 0.4332) = 0.0668, or 6.68%.

Dairy-P's fixed assets are currently valued at £400,000, and it is not stated how many of these assets provide the security for the first and second mortgage debentures, totalling £250,000. If the project were to go ahead, costing £150,000 in fixed assets plus the need for some working capital investment, Dairy-P might not be able to raise the finance by borrowing without a guarantee being given to the lender from Nominee Holdings. This appears to be unacceptable to the group. Dairy-P would therefore need finance from the cash resources of the holding company.

In view of the uncertain future of Dairy-P anyway, this project appears to be too risky, and incapable of attracting suitable finance at an acceptable rate of interest. Unless the group decides not to switch operations to Greece, and to risk some of its own cash in the project, the Dairy-P Ltd proposal should be turned down.

(v) **Keen Casements project**

This is a fairly small project, which promises to earn an NPV of (0.28 × £65,000) £18,200 on an investment of £65,000.

There is a problem, however, with financing the project. The subsidiary has no loan capital outstanding, but if it had to finance the project by borrowing, it is unlikely that fixed assets worth £15,000 plus the fixed assets bought for the project (up to £65,000) would provide adequate security. Indeed, if the subsidiary has a bank overdraft as part of its negative net current assets (current ratio = 0.65) the bank might already have a fixed and floating charge over the existing assets.

It is assumed that the management of Keen Casements has the ability to invest successfully in a project costing over 400% more than the value of its entire fixed assets at current valuation.

(vi) **Flexi-Carbon project**

This project involves some risk. The estimated NPV is $(0.35 \times £125,000)$ £43,750. The standard deviation of the project cost is £15,000, and so the actual cost would have to be 2.92 standard deviations above the mean before the NPV became negative. The probability that this would occur is negligible - $(0.5 - 0.4983) = 0.0017$ or 0.17%, assuming that the potential project cost is normally distributed.

Flexi-Carbon's gearing level is already quite high. It has fixed assets currently valued at £250,000, a fairly low current ratio (1.21 for the proposed project) and yet mortgage debenture borrowings of £150,000. Further borrowing from external lenders would be difficult, and as with the Keen Casements project, it is doubtful whether the subsidiary could raise the finance unless the holding company itself provided the funds, or at least a guarantee for further borrowing.

(vii) In conclusion, it is recommended that the holding company should finance all (or most) of the Keen Casements and Flexi-Carbon projects, provided that they are in accord with the group's medium-term strategy.

In contrast, the Dairy-P project is more risky, and Dairy-P's future is uncertain. The expectation of higher input costs and the possibility of moving operations to Greece are two aspects of the same problem. If the Dairy-P project is rejected, the group's directors should perhaps initiate discussions with the subsidiary's board about Dairy-P's problems and future.

(b) **Divisional performance** should be measured in such a way as to indicate what sort of return each subsidiary is making on the **shareholders'** investment. Shareholders themselves are likely to be interested in the performance of the group as a whole, measured in terms of return on shareholders' capital, earnings per share, dividend yield, and growth in earnings and dividends.

These performance ratios cannot be used for subsidiaries in the group, and so an alternative measure has to be selected, which compares the return from the subsidiary with the value of the investment in the subsidiary.

Two performance measures could be used which provide a suitable indication of performance from the point of view of the group's shareholders.

(i) **Return on capital employed**, which from the shareholders' point of view would be:

$$\frac{\text{profit after interest}}{\text{net assets at current valuation minus long - term liabilities (eg long - term borrowings)}}$$

(ii) Alternatively, **residual income** could be used. This can be measured as:

profit before interest (controllable by the subsidiary's management)

minus

a notional interest charge on the controllable investments of the subsidiary

equals

residual income

Each subsidiary would be able to increase its residual income if it earned an **incremental profit in excess of the notional interest charge on its incremental investments** – ie in effect, if it added to the value of the group's equity.

(c) It is assumed that the rate of charge-out should apply to the reinvestment of operating profits of the group.

It seems that at the moment the subsidiaries are expected to earn a return on their investments in excess of the group's weighted average cost of capital (WACC), in other words the return that the market expects (currently 19.5%). This is not satisfactory, for two separate reasons.

(i) The WACC is not the group's marginal cost of extra capital. Decisions ought to be made on an **incremental** principle, so that if the incremental return from a project exceeds its incremental costs, allowing for the incremental cost of the capital needed to finance it, the project should go ahead. In the case of Nominee Holdings, a cash rich company, the marginal cost of capital at the moment would appear to be the opportunity cost of the cash and short-term investments, which is only 5%.

(ii) Each subsidiary is likely to have different **risk characteristics**. Investments in some subsidiaries will be more risky than investments in others. Investments that are more risky should be expected to promise a higher return, if the principle of the Capital Asset Pricing Model is applied, and arguably, each subsidiary ought to be set its own **target rate** of **return** to allow for its particular risk characteristics.

If the 'risk free' rate of return is taken as 5% – ie the return earned by the group's cash resources, a suitable premium over this rate might be worked out for each subsidiary.

16 Grier and Box plc

> **Top tips.** This is a 'bitty' question that needs to be approached stage by stage.
>
> In part (a), given that 'value added' is a simple measure of the value earned by a company from selling a product, over and above the direct material costs of production, some simple analysis will show us the worst performing divisions. Low value added items drag down profitability, and it is often difficult to turn their performance around because if materials costs are high (no matter how efficient you are), then the only way to achieve better profitability is to obtain cheaper supplies if you can.
>
> Part (b) is concerned with the rationale for a divestment. We have referred to the threat from competitors and small market shares to conclude that a significant investment would be needed to establish these divisions more firmly in their markets. Note here that you are not asked to recommend whether or not to sell the divisions. The question almost assumes that such a decision has already been made, by asking you **why** they *should* be sold off.
>
> When answering part (c) (i) the key factor to consider is the relative risk of the two types of investment. For part (ii) make use of the numbers given and take note of the need to balance the aims of reducing gearing and continuing to modernise. Which option represents the better use of cash resources? We show in our answer that both options are valid, but Grier and Box should certainly reduce their gearing to improve their interest cover.
>
> Part (d) is a more general question on performance control using traditional methods of ratio analysis and budgetary control. Such systems must provide regular and up-to-date information if they are to be effective. Annual budgets are becoming notorious for their inflexibility and many companies now prepare revised forecasts every quarter.

(a) **Value added** is 'the increase in realisable value resulting from an alteration in form, location or availability of a product or service, excluding the cost of purchased materials or services' (CIMA). In a simplified definition, value added is measured as **sales minus materials costs**.

Division	Value added £m	Value added/sales ratio
Electrical equipment	5.3	13.25%
Fluid controls	4.9	19.44%
Metals	9.1	53.22%
Industrial services	19.0	56.38%
Bathroom accessories	2.5	35.71%
Tubes	4.5	75.00%

The MD would appear to be referring to the electrical equipment and fluid controls divisions, whose value added is only about 13% and 19% of sales value respectively. The implications of making and selling low value added items are the following.

(i) **Profit/sales ratios** will be small because materials costs are a large proportion of total sales value. For electrical equipment, this was 5% last year, ignoring interest on capital, and for fluid controls, it was 4.8%.

(ii) Attempts to **improve efficiency and reduce labour costs** will therefore have only a small effect on profit/sales ratios.

(iii) Improving **profitability** will rely largely on reducing materials costs or increasing sales.

(iv) A very **large increase in sales** would be needed to earn a sizeable increase in profits.

(v) The **working capital investment** in the products will be high, because of the high materials cost of production.

(vi) For reasons (i) and (v), **ROCE** will be low.

(b) The fundamental question in both cases is whether each business can make an effective **contribution** to the company in the future. Both divisions are currently earning profits, but if they are unlikely to contribute significantly to the group in future the following will occur.

(i) Any capital invested in the division will be tied up, earning relatively low returns.

(ii) It is therefore be more appropriate to sell the businesses now, to obtain a reasonable price whilst they are profitable, and to use the revenue earned from the sales to invest in projects that would earn a better return.

The bathroom accessories division faces the prospect of having to compete in its market with companies which are currently its customers. The threat of backward vertical integration by manufacturers of bathroom ceramics suggests that the division:

(i) Might struggle to retain its market share
(ii) Might even lose market share

The long-term prospects for profit and sales growth are therefore poor.

The tubes division has a very small share of its market. It is doubtful whether the capital investment needed to improve efficiency would be justified (although a DCF evaluation should be made) and in view of the very small market share, the long term prospects for the product are probably poor.

In terms of **BCG classification**, tubes and bathroom accessories are probably **'dog'** products for the company and should be sold off.

(c) (i) **Capital expenditure on replacement equipment** to manufacture well-established products should have a **short payback period**, because the products ought to be earning good profits and cash inflows. A payback period of about 2 – 3 years might be suitable.

Capital expenditure on new development projects will be **high risk spending** and so should perhaps be evaluated at a higher DCF cost of capital. However, new projects take time to become established, and so their payback period will be longer than for equipment replacement projects.

A suitable payback period would depend on the nature of the business and the 'normal' time for new projects to become established in the marketplace.

(ii)   If the company wishes to **reduce its gearing**, which is currently high at 60%, a suitable balance should be made in the company's strategic plans between using cash inflows to **reduce borrowing** and using cash inflows to **invest** in modernisation programmes.

Manufacturing companies must remain efficient to be competitive and profitable, and effective modernisation programmes should be an essential feature of their strategic plans. There is no reason why Grier and Box plc cannot use its earnings partly to repay debt and partly for new investments.

The need to reduce gearing from 60% is a valid **strategic aim**. Taking the company's average interest cost of debt is 10%, then the current level of debt would be £4.8m per annum which gives the company an interest cover of only (14.8 ÷ 4.8) 3.1 times.

(d)   There are several main **dangers**.

(i)   The **reporting system**, using performance ratios and budget variances, might be inadequate. It must be capable of providing regular and up-to-date reports which:

(1)   Report key performance measures
(2)   Draw management attention to significant divergences between actual and plan.

(ii)   The **budget** itself might be built on incorrect assumptions and so budget **variances** might be misleading and incorrect.

(iii)   Budgets get **out of date**. There would probably need to be an additional system whereby revised forecasts are prepared, perhaps every three months, and actual results compared against the revised forecast in reports to head office.

(iv)   There has to be a **retained authority** for head office staff to insist on control measures being taken by line managers, when they consider that actual performance indicates a need for **control action**.

17 Management accounting information

Top tip. The question is broken down into two parts. The first requires an analysis of the validity of the criticism that management accounting information is irrelevant for decision making. The second part asks you to think about the provision of management accounting information in two different types of organisation.

Our answer to the first part takes the stance that while new techniques are available, many firms do not sufficiently tailor their information collection to specific decisions, and need to develop systems to make sure that they are able to undertake financial analysis, planning and control. No one solution will suit all businesses.

Our answer to the second part considers issues of financial v non-financial information, organisational structure and performance measurement. These will vary between the two organisations concerned.

(a)   In the 1980s and 1990s critics began to question management accounting's relevance to decision making. Seeing the challenge facing management accountants as being one of providing more relevant information for decision making, critics argued that traditional management accounting systems may not always provide this. Management accounting information is often biased towards the **past** rather than the future, and management accounting systems do not always detect **strategic issues**.

Decision making is a **forward** and **outward** looking process, and management accounting information has been too inward looking and directed largely towards **financial reporting**. Historical

costs are necessary to report to shareholders, but the classifications of transactions for reporting purposes are not necessarily relevant to decision making.

Internal vs external focus

Much management accounting information is devised for **internal consumption**. However, strategic management involves looking at the **external environment**, and strategy is pursued in relation to **competitors**. Their actions need to be understood and quantified to be able to devise appropriate response activity.

Some management accounting techniques such as **variance analysis** are seen as too simplistic and largely irrelevant for decision making in a 21st century business. Modern business is embracing new ways of working, including **outsourcing** and **homeworking**, and there is constant pressure to improve quality and service and reduce costs. Some techniques such as **activity based costing** have been developed which are designed to take specific business processes and cost drivers into account when measuring profitability and performance. Techniques such as **customer account profitability and direct product profitability** attempt to replace general analysis with specifics, but in general many firms continue to use old costing systems which are too general in their application to be able to support specific strategic decisions.

It could be argued, that the production of more relevant costs does not necessarily make the management accountant a strategic partner for the chief executive overnight. Management accountants do however need to tackle this issue of the relevance of the information they provide for **strategy formulation** and **control decisions** at higher levels in the organisation. Strategic plans may cover a long period into the future, and often involve big changes and new ventures. How can the management accountant support such developments?

CIMA has defined **'strategic management accounting'** as 'a form of management accounting in which emphasis is placed on information which relates to factors external to the firm, as well as to non-financial information and internally generated information.' Ward suggests that the role of the strategic management accountant can be analysed as being split between **financial analysis, financial planning** and **financial control**. These roles encompass the current **position** of the business, its **goals** and **objectives** and its **feedback** mechanisms, which compare planned with actual performance. They may involve obtaining information from other **functions** in the organisation, such as production, distribution or marketing.

Contingency theory is a theory that has been developed which states that there is no universally applicable best practice in the design of control systems such as management accounting systems. Specific **business** and **environmental** factors will influence the operation of the system, such as organisational structure, technology and the market. The management accountant needs to analyse and present information which takes these specifics into account.

(b)   Both types of organisation are going to be interested in the provision of a range of both **financial** and **non-financial information.** On the financial side, both organisations will be interested in measures such as cost control, contribution, profits, return on investment, cash flow measures, liquidity, competitiveness and market share. Non-financial measures will include issues such as product or service quality, levels of innovation, customer satisfaction and flexibility in meeting customer needs quickly.

The main distinction between the two companies is in **organisational structure**. One of the companies operates from one site. Usual methods of cost collection, reporting and profitability analysis will be able to be employed. The other is highly fragmented and so information collection may require more detailed systems and closer monitoring of the operatives working from home.

Performance appraisal of staff will be easier for the manufacturing company, and it may be that the staff identify with the company more strongly and are more motivated to achieve **company objectives**, both because they are contracted employees in the traditional sense and because they work together at one site each day. The homeworking contractors may have less sense of such

loyalty and could be motivated mainly by considerations such as adding to their own stock of experience and their hourly rate.

The homeworkers are also likely to be working on their own individual projects or tasks, and could all be facing different problems and issues in the effective performance of their work. The standard management accounting system will not necessarily recognise this. It is also possible that they are being paid at different rates according to their experience (this is less likely to be sustainable in a one-site company), making comparisons of individual profitability more complex.

Many organisations operate with off-site employees, and it is becoming increasingly common to employ **outworkers** as traditional working methods are replaced. Standard reports on activities and profitability, both historical and future, are still capable of being produced despite the fact that off-site employees are now more common. The **collection** of such information may be more complicated, but advances in **technology** and computer links should enable information to be logged from remote sites all over the world if necessary.

This scenario provides an example of how management accounting systems need to be **adapted** to organisational realities. Some techniques may be consistently applied in all organisations (measuring employee productivity, for example) while others will be adapted. The one-site company may find it easier than the fragmented one to establish, define (and therefore control) meaningful **cost centres**. Individual **contract profitability** should be easily measurable by both companies, regardless of staff location, although comparing the costs of off-site employees may need to take pay rate differentials into account, as mentioned above.

Measures such as **return on investment** will be more easily defined in the manufacturing company because it is likely to have significant investment in plant and equipment. For the service company on the other hand, the chief asset is its body of professional staff, which may have a high turnover and which is less capable of being assessed in this way. As ROI is normally used to apply to investment centres or profit centres it generally reflects the **organisation structure** of the business. As mentioned previously, such centres are more likely to be a feature of the site-based company.

18 The S group

(a)   A key task in the strategic management of any company is a willingness and an ability to understand the environment and anticipate future trends. Information will be required at both strategic and operational level. This is known as strategic intelligence, which can be defined as what a company needs to know about its business environment in order to be able to anticipate change and come up with appropriate strategies for the future.

There are many sources of environmental information.

Internal sources, or sources relatively close to the company, may include the sales force. It deals with the customers and so is in a position to obtain customer and competitor information. Stakeholders in the business such as employees, management and shareholders will influence the business and so are also a good source of internal information. It will be appropriate to set up a **database** for this information, containing both financial and non-financial indicators.

The **management information system** may generate information about the environment as well as information on sales, costs, market share and profitability.

External sources of information are various. The media (newspapers, periodicals and television) offer many types of environmental information covering all kinds of environmental issues: social, political, economic and technological. Export consultants might specialise in dealing with particular countries (possibly relevant to a multinational like the S Group thinking about new markets), and academic or trade journals will give information about a wide variety of relevant issues to a particular industry. The S Group is likely to subscribe to some of these. As a large multinational, it may be represented on a trade body (an example is the British Retail Consortium in the UK) where

it can meet competitors and discuss issues of interest. The **Internet** is also a fruitful source of information.

The **government** and public **databases** can be a source of statistical data, maybe relating to the money supply, the trade balance and so forth. Stockbrokers provide investment reports which often contain detailed analysis of industries and countries, and specialist consultancy firms can provide information. Universities and academic journals publish research results, with projects often being sponsored by large companies like the S Group.

Using the information

The information can be used in **devising appropriate strategies** for the future direction of the business environment. It is easy to be overwhelmed by the volume of relevant environmental information on offer and the variety of data that could be used, so S must make sure that the information it collects is collated and presented in a **coherent** fashion. This will enable the directors of S to assess the current position of the company and decide upon future strategies appropriate to the business environment.

Assuming that a company the size of S has some kind of **strategic planning function**, then it must make sure that the strategy planning process involves the divisional managers, who will be able to see that the business environment (of which they will be keenly aware) is being taken account of in strategy formulation.

Quality of the information

To be relevant and useful for decision making, the information gathered by S, both internal and external, must be **accurate** and **reliable**. A key priority is an understanding of **why** the information is being collected, and **what** it will be used for. This will indicate the level of detail required.

To be sure of the reliability and accuracy of internal information, **specialists** from the relevant company departments may be required to give assurances on the accuracy of information provided by their systems. Staff 'on the ground', such as the sales staff mentioned earlier, will have a far better knowledge of individual markets and competition activity than strategy setters higher up in the organisation.

Databases must be used with care as they can rapidly go out of date and must be regularly maintained. S should assure itself of the quality of data from both its internal and external databases. Comparing information from various sources can provide checks as to accuracy. As time goes on and S develops more and more **information sources**, it is likely that these sources will fluctuate in number as the less reliable sources are replaced with more accurate ones, and new methods of collecting information are devised.

(b) **ROCE**

By using return on capital employed (ROCE) as a performance measure, S is using an **historical measure** which is no guide to future performance and shows a lack of a forward looking perspective. **Past results** are not necessarily an indication of **future profitability**. Since the manager of AE is judged on this basis, he may be tempted into decisions which increase AE's short term ROCE. An investment might be desirable from the group's point of view, but would not be in the individual manager's interest to undertake. Thus there is a lack of **goal congruence**. A desire to increase ROCE might lead to projects being taken on without due regard to their **risk.**

If we look at ROCE for the AE division for last year and the previous year, we can see that it has decreased from 10% to 1.24%. This has very little to do with an increase in average capital employed (which has only increased by 1.1% over the year) and everything to do with an erosion in gross profit from 36.7% to 12.5% (see below).

The tiny increase in capital employed probably reflects the fact that there is little incentive for the manager to invest (assuming the investment decision is his to take) because any decisions which reduce ROCE in the short term will reflect badly on his reported performance. It is difficult to

comment further on this small increase in capital employed, as no information is given in the scenario.

A **fair comparison** between different divisions using ROCE is not easily achieved. Fixed assets may be of different ages or may be depreciated in different ways. If a division maintains the same annual profit, and keeps the same assets without a policy of replacement, its ROCE will increase year by year as the assets get older. This can give a false impression of improving 'real' performance over time.

Sales and profitability

AE has suffered a reduction in gross profit from $275m to $100m, a decrease of 64%. Head office fixed costs remained constant, but budgeted costs per unit increased from 63% of sales value to 87.5%. This can be attributed to **transfer pricing policy** (see below).

Despite this, it can be demonstrated that the performance of the division last year was an improvement on the previous

	Last year	Previous year
Budgeted sales	K$900m	K$900m
Actual sales	K$800m	K$750m
Increase on previous year	6.67%	–
Actual volumes	16,000 units	15,000 units
% short of revenue target	11.1%	16.7%
Contribution volume variance	K$18m (A)	K$60m (A)

Assembly costs increased by 33.3% across the year, which is surprising given the much smaller increase in sales revenue, and the fact that the budgeted increase was 20%. No more information is given on assembly costs to enable further comment, although the divisional manager should certainly examine these costs as they fall under his control.

The **contribution volume variance** is calculated by multiplying the shortfall in unit sales volume from budget by the budgeted contribution per unit. Performance by this measure appears to be much better than the previous year, but it is probably unwise to read too much into this figure as the unit cost structures in both years are so different, with the budgeted contribution being dramatically reduced last year (from $20,000 to $9,000) after the rise in components transfer costs (which are in any case beyond the control of the divisional manager).

Transfer pricing policy

This is the area of prime concern as regards impact on AE division profitability. Transfer costs have risen to 75% of sales value last year, which compares with 53% in the previous year. They were budgeted at 70% of selling price (50% in the previous year). Total components costs have increased by 50% over the year, with sales up only around 7%.

Questions need to be asked about how the transfer price is being set. If the transferring division is inefficient, it is transferring those inefficiencies to AE, and AE's profitability is being severely affected. Alternatively the head office of S, under pressure to increase returns to its shareholders, may be deliberately imposing a large transfer price in order to cut AE division profits and **minimise its tax** bill in what is a high rate regime. This is likely to be investigated by tax authorities, especially since there has been a big year-on-year increase.

Either way, the performance of AE is being assessed on factors beyond its control. From the figures given in the question, the transfer pricing policy has contributed to 86% of the division's unit costs and is therefore a highly significant factor in assessing its performance. The board must consider AE's longer term potential for adding to shareholder value. Assessing its performance using ROCE alone, especially when that return is rendered artificially low by high transfer prices, will be to ignore its future profit potential.

(c)   The key objective of the board of S is to **increase shareholder value** and it must ensure that the AE divisional manager's plans fit in with the overall **strategic direction** of the group. Some acquisitions

are driven by the personal goals of the acquiring company's managers. Again, the issue of **goal congruence** needs to be addressed. If it is true that the acquisition will enable AE division to increase market share then the board should give the proposal serious consideration.

It is important for the company to understand its reasons for acquisition, and that these reasons should be valid in terms of its strategic plan. The acquisition may give the AE division a new product range, heightened market presence and enable it to consolidate its distribution process, for example. However, the board of S must consider the level of **risk** involved. Acquiring companies in overseas markets is risky.

The divisional manager of AE is likely to believe, seeing as his division is under threat of closure, that the opportunities offered by the acquisition cannot be found within AE itself. However, acquisitions do have associated problems and the board of S may have to consider the following issues.

(i) **Cost.** The deal may be too expensive, or resisted by the target company. The necessary funds may have to be diverted from other group operations. Advice fees (bankers, corporate financiers) may be high.

(ii) The **customers** of the target company may go elsewhere and the promised market share fail to materialise. Has enough **market research** been carried out?

(iii) **Incompatibility**. In general, the problems of assimilating new products, customers, suppliers, markets, employees and different management systems might create problems of 'overload' for AE.

(iv) **Lack of information**. Will the improvements in market share really be achieved? How strong is the competition? Does the AE division have the skills and experience to see the plan through? It has failed to achieve its own turnover targets, so can it manage those of an entirely new company?

Following the analysis presented in part (b), it should be clear to the directors of S that the AE division is improving its performance, despite the transfer pricing policy. This profitability may be jeopardised by the acquisition.

Aside from financial factors such as **expected costs and revenues** (which S must be fully satisfied on if it is to commit funds which could, after all, be deployed elsewhere in the group), the group should bear in mind **non-financial factors** regarding the takeover.

Some major problems of **implementation** may arise relating to human resources and personnel issues, such as morale, performance assessment and culture. If key managers or personnel leave, the business will suffer and future development of the new entity (maybe into more new markets) may be compromised.

This acquisition may well be an opportunity not to be missed, but S must make sure that this is indeed the case and that **market development** is likely to flow from it.

(d) **Performance measurement** should become more **forward looking** than merely placing a reliance on historical measures such as ROCE. In this way the future of the AE division can be planned with more clarity, and its contribution to increasing shareholder value will be considered over the longer term, although this may clash with some investors who are looking for a **short term return.**

As an increase in shareholder value is a key objective of the business, performance indicators will be required to assess whether or not the management team is fulfilling this duty. The use of what is known as a **shareholder value approach** to performance measurement involves moving the focus of attention away from simply looking at short term profits to a longer term view of **value creation**, the motivation being that it will help the business stay ahead in an increasingly competitive market. The success (or otherwise) of the new AE division will contribute to the determination of shareholder value.

Shareholder value analysis

This is defined as 'an approach to financial management which focuses on the creation of economic value for shareholders, as measured by share price performance and flow of dividends'. The main premise is that a business is worth the net present value of its **future cash flows**, and these are driven by the following factors: sales growth, operating margin, fixed capital investment, working capital investment, cash taxes, the planning period and the cost of capital.

It follows that these are therefore the factors that the directors of S need to focus on when measuring the performance of the AE division.

When looking at future sales growth and margin, the directors will want to see whether the divisional manager's forecasts of increased **market share** have been realised, but will also need to extrapolate **forecast trends** in the market. This may include a consideration of new products.

Investment in both fixed and working capital will be required if growth is to be **sustained**. Forecast cash flows may need to be revised if growth and return to shareholders is to be achieved. Additional funding may be required.

The level of **corporation tax** borne by the AE division has been high in the past. S has sought to mitigate its effects via its transfer pricing policy, but this may not be viable in the longer term (the policy is onerous, as we saw in part (b)) and S may need to look again at **tax planning** for the division.

The cost of funding the project is fundamental to its success in increasing shareholder value. If the **incremental value** of the acquisition is in excess of the **cost of capital**, then **shareholder value** will be added. The cost of capital should be minimised, and any changes to it reflected in revised NPV calculations.

Economic value management

This is another form of strategic value analysis and hinges on the calculation of **economic profit (EP).** The calculation of EP requires several **adjustments** to be made to **traditionally reported accounting profits**. These are intended to produce a figure for capital employed which is a more accurate reflection of the base upon which shareholders except their returns to accrue, and to provide a figure which is a more realistic measure of the **actual cash generated** for shareholders from recurring business activities.

In the case of the AE division, adjustments could be made to take the transfer price items out of the calculation and apply a **notional cost of capital** to the adjusted profit. This would eliminate the somewhat artificial (and high) transfer price from the consideration of the **economic value added** by the division. The figures would read as follows.

		Last year K$m	Previous year K$m
Sales		800	750
Division costs	– assembly	(100)	(75)
	– head office	(75)	(75)
Cost of capital (say 12%)		(242)	(240)
EVA		383	360

This analysis can be carried further and presented in terms of future expectations for the new division. This will enable future performance to be planned and any action taken that may be necessary to ensure that the acquisition continues to deliver acceptable results.

SAMPLE PRE-SEEN QUESTION

Question 1

Pre-seen case study

Introduction

M plc is a long established publisher of newspapers and provider of web media. It is based in London and has had a full listing on the London Stock Exchange since 1983. The company has three operating divisions which are managed from the United Kingdom (UK). These are the Newspapers Division, the Web Division and the Advertising Division.

Newspapers Division

The Newspapers Division publishes three daily newspapers and one Sunday newspaper in the UK. The Division has three offices and two printing sites. Between them the three offices edit the three daily newspapers and the Sunday newspaper. The Newspaper Division has two subsidiary publishing companies, FR and N. FR is based in France within the Eurozone and N in an Eastern European country which is outside the Eurozone. Printing for all the Division's publications, except those produced by FR and N, is undertaken at the two printing sites. FR and N have their own printing sites.

Web Division

The Web Division maintains and develops 200 websites which it owns. Some of these websites are much more popular in terms of the number of "hits" they receive than others. Web material is an increasing part of M plc's business. In the last ten years, the Web Division has developed an online version of all the newspapers produced by the Newspapers Division.

Advertising Division

The sale of advertising space is undertaken for the whole of M plc by the Advertising Division. Therefore, advertisements which appear in the print media and on the web pages produced by the Newspapers Division (including that produced by FR and N) and the Web Division respectively are all handled by the Advertising Division.

Group Headquarters

In addition to the three operating divisions, M plc also has a head office, based in the UK, which is the group's corporate headquarters where the Board of Directors is located. The main role of M plc's headquarters is to develop and administer its policies and procedures as well as to deal with its group corporate affairs.

Mission statement

M plc established a simple mission statement in 2005. This drove the initiative to acquire FR in 2008 and remains a driving force for the company. M plc's mission is "to be the best news media organisation in Europe, providing quality reporting and information on European and world-wide events".

Strategic objectives

Four main strategic objectives were established in 2005 by M plc's Board of Directors. These are to:

1. Meet the needs of readers for reliable and well informed news.

2. Expand the geographical spread of M plc's output to reach as many potential newspaper and website readers as possible.

3. Publish some newspapers which help meet the needs of native English speakers who live in countries which do not have English as their first language.

4. Increase advertising income so that the group moves towards offering as many news titles as possible free of charge to the public.

Financial objectives

In meeting these strategic objectives, M plc has developed the following financial objectives:

i. To ensure that revenue and operating profit grow by an average of 4% per year.

ii. To achieve steady growth in dividend per share.

iii. To maintain gearing below 40%, where gearing is calculated as debt/(debt plus equity) based on the market value of equity and the book value of debt.

Forecast revenue and operating profit

M plc's forecast revenue and net operating profit for the year ending 31 March 2012 are £280 million and £73 million respectively.

Extracts from M plc's forecast income statement for the year ending 31 March 2012 and forecast statement of financial position as at 31 March 2012 are shown in the appendix.

Comparative divisional performance and headquarters financial information

The following information is provided showing the revenue generated, the operating profit achieved and the capital employed for each division and the operating costs incurred and capital employed in M plc's headquarters. This information covers the last two years and also gives a forecast for the year ending 31 March 2012. All M plc's revenue is earned by the three divisions.

Newspapers Division

	Year ended 31.3.2010 £million	Year ended 31.3.2011 £million	Forecast for year ending 31.3.2012 £million
Revenue external	91	94	94
Revenue internal transfers	90	91	96
Net operating profit	45	46	48
Non-current assets	420	490	548
Net current assets	4	8	(10)

Web Division

	Year ended 31.3.2010 £million	Year ended 31.3.2011 £million	Forecast for year ending 31.3.2012 £million
Revenue internal transfers	55	60	66
Net operating profit	10	13	16
Non-current assets	37	40	43
Net current assets	1	1	(2)

Advertising Division

	Year ended 31.3.2010 £million	Year ended 31.3.2011 £million	Forecast for year ending 31.3.2012 £million
Revenue external	162	180	186
Internal transfers	(145)	(151)	(162)
Net operating profit	10	18	19
Non-current assets	3	6	7
Net current assets	1	1	(2)

Headquarters

	Year ended 31.3.2010 £million	Year ended 31.3.2011 £million	Forecast for year ending 31.3.2012 £million
Operating costs	8	9	10
Non-current assets	37	39	43
Net current assets	1	1	(1)

Notes:

1. The Advertising Division remits advertising revenue to both the Newspapers and Web Divisions after deducting its own commission.

2. The Web Division's entire revenue is generated from advertising.

3. The revenues and operating profits shown for the Newspapers Division include those earned by FR and N. The converted revenue and operating profit from N are forecast to be £20 million and £4 million respectively for the year ending 31 March 2012. FR is forecast to make a small operating profit in the year ending 31 March 2012. The Board of M plc is disappointed with the profit FR has achieved.

Additional information on each of M plc's divisions

Newspapers Division

FR is wholly owned and was acquired in 2008. Its financial statements are translated into British pounds and consolidated into M plc's group accounts and included within the Newspaper Division's results for internal reporting purposes.

Shortly after it was acquired by M plc, FR launched a pan-European weekly newspaper. This newspaper, which is written in English, is produced in France and then distributed throughout Europe. M plc's board thought that this newspaper would become very popular because it provides a snapshot of the week's news, focused particularly on European issues but viewed from a British perspective. Sales have, however, been disappointing.

N, which publishes local newspapers in its home Eastern European country, is also treated as part of the Newspapers Division. M plc acquired 80% of its equity in 2010. At that time, M plc's board thought that Eastern Europe was a growing market for newspapers. The subsidiary has proved to be profitable mainly because local production costs are lower than those in the UK relative to the selling prices.

The Newspapers Division's journalists incur a high level of expenses in order to carry out their duties. The overall level of expenses claimed by the journalists has been ignored by M plc in previous years because it has been viewed as a necessary cost of running the business. However, these expenses have risen significantly in recent years and have attracted the attention of M plc's internal audit department.

There has been significant capital investment in the Newspapers Division since 2009/10. The printing press facilities at each of the two printing sites have been modernised. These modernisations have improved the quality of output and have enabled improved levels of efficiency to be achieved in order to meet the increasing workloads demanded in the last two years. Surveys carried out before and after the modernisation have indicated higher levels of customer satisfaction with the improved quality of printing.

The increased mechanisation and efficiency has reduced costs and led to a reduction in the number of employees required to operate the printing presses. This has led to some dis-satisfaction among the divisional staff. Staff in the other divisions have been unaffected by the discontent in the Newspapers Division. Staff turnover has been relatively static across the three divisions, with the exception of the department which operates the printing presses in the Newspapers Division where some redundancies have occurred due to fewer staff being required since the modernisation.

Web Division

The web versions of the newspapers are shorter versions of the printed ones. There is currently no charge for access to the web versions of the newspapers. Revenues are generated from sales by the Advertising Division of advertising space on the web pages. Some of the websites permit unsolicited comments from the public to be posted on them and they have proved to be very popular. The Web Division is undertaking a review of all its costs, particularly those relating to energy, employees and website development.

The Web Division's management accounting is not sophisticated: for example, although it reports monthly on the Division's revenue and profitability, it cannot disaggregate costs so as to produce monthly results for each of the 200 websites. The Division is at a similar disadvantage as regards strategic management accounting as it lacks information about the websites' market share and growth rates. This has not mattered in the past as M plc was content that the Web Division has always been profitable. However, one of M plc's directors, the Business Development Director (see below under The Board of Directors and group shareholding) thinks that the Web Division could increase its profitability considerably and wants to undertake a review of its 200 websites.

Advertising Division

The Advertising Division remits advertising revenue to both the Newspapers and Web Divisions after deducting its own commission. In addition, the Advertising Division offers an advertising service to corporate clients. Such services include television and radio advertising and poster campaigns on bill boards. Advertisements are also placed in newspapers and magazines which are not produced by M plc, if the client so wishes. An increasing element of the work undertaken by the Advertising Division is in providing pop-up advertisements on websites.

Planning process

Each division carries out its own planning process. The Newspapers Division operates a rational model and prepares annual plans which it presents to M plc's board for approval. The Web Division takes advantage of opportunities as they arise and is operating in a growth market, unlike the other two divisions. Its planning approach might best be described as one of logical incrementalism. Increased capital expenditure in 2010/11 helped the Advertising Division to achieve an 11% increase in revenue in that year. The Divisional Managers of both the Web Division and the Advertising Division are keen to develop their businesses and are considering growth options including converting their businesses into outsource service providers to M plc.

The Board of Directors and group shareholding

M plc's Board of Directors comprises six executive directors and six non-executive directors, one of whom is the Non-executive Chairman. The executive directors are the Chief Executive, and the Directors of Strategy, Corporate Affairs, Finance, Human Resources and Business Development. The Business Development Director did not work for M plc in 2005 and so had no part in drafting the strategic objectives. She thinks that objective number four has become out-dated as it does not reflect current day practice. The Business Development Director has a great deal of experience working with subscription-based websites and this was one of the main reasons M plc recruited her in March 2011. Her previous experience also incorporated the management of product portfolios including product development and portfolio rationalisation.

There are divisional managing directors for each of the three divisions who are not board members but report directly to the Chief Executive.

One of M plc's non-executive directors was appointed at the insistence of the bank which holds 10% of M plc's shares. Another was appointed by a private charity which owns a further 10% of the shares in M plc. The charity represents the interests of print workers and provides long-term care to retired print workers and their dependents. Two other non-executive directors were appointed by a financial institution which owns 20% of the shares in M plc. The remaining 60% of shares are held by private investors. The board members between them hold 5% of the shares in issue. None of the other private investors holds more than 70,000 of the total 140 million shares in issue.

It has become clear that there is some tension between the board members. Four of the non-executive directors, those appointed by the bank, the charity and the financial institution, have had disagreements with the other board members. They are dissatisfied with the rate of growth and profitability of the company and wish to see more positive action to secure M plc's financial objectives.

Some board members feel that the newspapers market is declining because fewer people can make time to read printed publications. Some of the non-executive directors think that many people are more likely to watch a television news channel than read a newspaper.

Editorial policy

M plc's board applies a policy of editorial freedom provided that the published material is within the law and is accurate. The editors of each of the publications printed in the UK and France and of the websites have complete autonomy over what is published. They are also responsible for adhering to regulatory constraints and voluntary industry codes of practice relating to articles and photographs which might be considered offensive by some readers.

There is less scrutiny of the accuracy of the reporting in N's home country than in other countries. The Eastern European country in which N is situated has become politically unstable in the last two years. Much of this unrest is fuelled by the public distaste for the perceived blatant corruption and bribery which is endemic within the country's Government and business community. It is well known that journalists have accepted bribes to present only the Government's version of events, rather than a balanced view. There is also widespread plagiarism of published material by the country's newspapers and copyright laws are simply ignored.

Corporate Social Responsibility

A policy is in place throughout M plc in order to eliminate bribery and corruption among staff especially those who have front line responsibility for obtaining business. This policy was established 15 years ago. All new employees are made aware of the policy and other staff policies and procedures during their induction. The Director of Human Resources has confidence in the procedures applied by his staff at induction and is proud that no action has ever been brought against an employee of M plc for breach of the bribery and corruption policy.

M plc is trying to reduce its carbon footprint and is in the process of developing policies to limit its energy consumption, reduce the mileage travelled by its staff and source environmentally friendly supplies of paper for its printing presses. The Newspapers Division purchases the paper it uses for printing newspapers from a supplier in a Scandinavian country. This paper is purchased because it provides a satisfactory level of quality at a relatively cheap price. The Scandinavian country from which the paper is sourced is not the same country in which N is situated.

Strategic Development

The Board of Directors is now reviewing M plc's competitive position. The Board of Directors is under pressure from the non-executive directors appointed by the bank, the charity and the financial institution (which between them own 40% of the shares in M plc), to devise a strategic plan before June 2012 which is aimed at achieving M plc's stated financial objectives.

Extracts from M plc's forecast group income statement and forecast statement of financial position

Forecast income statement for the group for the year ending 31 March 2012

	Notes	£ million (GBP million)
Revenue		280
Operating costs		(207)
Net operating profit		73
Interest income		1
Finance costs		(11)
Corporate income tax	1	(19)
FORECAST PROFIT FOR THE YEAR		44

Forecast statement of the group financial position as at 31 March 2012

	£ million (GBP million)
ASSETS	
Non-current assets	641
Current assets	
Inventories	2
Trade and other receivables	27
Cash and cash equivalents	2
Total current assets	31
Total assets	672
EQUITY AND LIABILITIES	
Equity	
Share capital	140
Share premium	35
Retained earnings	185
Non-controlling interest	16
Total equity	376
Non-current liabilities	
Long term borrowings	250
Current liabilities	
Trade and other payables	46
Total liabilities	296
Total equity and liabilities	672

Note the Share capital row references Note 2 and Long term borrowings references Note 3.

Notes:

1. The corporate income tax rate can be assumed to be 30%.

2. There are 140 million £1 shares currently in issue.

3. The long-term borrowings include £83 million of loan capital which is due for repayment on 1 April 2013 and the remainder is due for repayment on 1 April 2019.

End of pre-seen material

Unseen material for Case Study

Trading performance

In response to the pressure from the non-executive directors, the executive directors on the Board are concerned about how M can increase its revenues and operating profits. However, there is disagreement among the directors about how M should do this.

Development of mobile applications

The Chief Executive believes that M needs to make use of technology and develop mobile applications (mobile apps)* for its three main daily newspapers and its main Sunday newspaper, to allow users to download key news stories onto their hand-held devices.

[*: Mobile applications (mobile apps) are pieces of computer software which allow users to download and view online content on hand-held devices such as smart phones, tablet computers, portable media players, and personal digital assistants.]

The Chief Executive has pointed out that a number of other newspapers and agencies have already introduced rival applications to the market, and if M does not follow suit then it risks losing market share.

By contrast, the Director of Strategy raised concerns about the quality of the apps. He acknowledged that the application may be useful for some users, but argued that M would be better served by developing mobile websites**, because these will provide users with much better coverage of the important stories.

[**: Mobile websites are internet applications which users can access from mobile devices such as smart phones or tablet computers, rather than having to access the internet via fixed-line services.]

In addition, the Director of Strategy pointed out that although the market for mobile apps is still relatively young, it is quite crowded. A number of national and regional newspapers, broadcasters, news agencies and magazines have already introduced mobile apps.

The Director of Finance said that he supported the idea of using technology to increase revenues, but questioned how much revenue the mobile apps would generate for M. He said he believed some of the news apps offered by competitor organisations are currently free, and he suggested that M should follow this model in order to be competitive. Consequently, any revenue and profit growth from the apps would need to be generated through the sale of associated advertising space.

However, the Director of Strategy highlighted a concern he had about this approach, pointing out that customer feedback on the apps of several leading newspapers indicated that the advertising displayed at the bottom of the screen is deemed to be a very annoying aspect of the service.

The Chief Executive acknowledged this point, but stressed that the idea of free apps and free content is consistent with M's strategic objectives. In addition, he said he remained convinced that M could earn substantial revenues from the advertising associated with the apps.

The Director of Human Resources (HR) also urged caution when deciding whether or not to launch the mobile apps service. He said he felt that launching such service represented a significant change to what he felt was still M's core business: publishing newspapers. He said that he felt launching the apps could have a significant and negative impact on the newspaper business. The Director of HR also queried what impact the change would have on the journalists. He said that customers would expect to be able to download the key news stories almost as soon as they happen, rather than in the next scheduled edition of their newspaper as has historically been the case.

The Chief Executive said he thought the Director of Human Resources was being too negative and cautious here. In the Chief Executive's view, the apps are merely extensions of M's existing online presence, providing additional channels through which customers can access existing information.

Financial analysis

At the last Board meeting, the Chief Executive decided that the option to introduce mobile apps should be evaluated in more detail, and he has asked the Managing Director (MD) of the Web Division to prepare some revenue and cost projections, looking at two different models:

(i)   Where the apps and content are free to download and view, but the images have advertising displayed at the bottom

(ii)   Where customers pay a subscription of £3 per month to download and view content, but with no advertising displays along the bottom of the screen.

The Finance Director has indicated that an important part of the analysis of the proposals will be looking at the respective revenues and profits they are likely to generate.

The Managing Director (MD) of the Web Division has now assembled the following estimates about the introduction of mobile applications services, for the three daily newspapers and the Sunday newspaper currently produced by the Newspapers Division, under both models. The two models are not mutually exclusive.

Free Service

The expected cumulative total numbers of people who download and view the free apps are:

Year 1	1,420,000
Year 2	1,775,000
Year 3	2,130,000

The MD's market research indicates that only 30% of the total number of people who have downloaded the free apps use them regularly (at least once a month).

The MD's preliminary discussions with advertisers have indicated clearly that the advertising commission rates will vary according to the number of regularly active users (RAU's) – those who view the apps at least once a month. Based on his discussions with prospective advertisers, the MD has estimated that commissions will generate a flat rate of £1 per year per RAU if the number of RAU's is less than 500,000 per year, but this commission income will increase to a flat rate of £1.50 per year per RAU if the number of RAU's is greater than 500,000 per year.

The development cost of developing the four apps are estimated at £20,000 each, and these development costs are to be written off over 3 years.

Operating costs directly related to the apps are estimated to be £200,000 in the first year, increasing 5% each year thereafter. The majority of the cost relates to the cost of time spent by web editors, updating stories provided by M's journalists to feed into the apps.

Paid for Service

The average numbers of people who are expected to subscribe each month are:

Average monthly subscribers in Year 1	44,375
Average monthly subscribers in Year 2	50,000
Average monthly subscribers in Year 3	53,250

The development cost of and operating costs for the paid for service are not expected to be significantly different than the costs for the free service.

Business newspapers

The Executive Directors have also asked the Managing Director (MD) of the Newspapers Division to suggest ways of improving the performance of his division. In particular, they have asked the MD to look at ways of improving sales for FR's pan-European weekly newspaper.

At the last Board meeting, the MD presented a proposal to transform the newspaper into a high-end tabloid format, aimed at the European business community. The MD pointed out that he believed the idea of a pan-European newspaper was viable, but that at the same time it needed to focus on a more specific market niche.

The MD stressed that he believed the paper's focus needed to be on "European issues from a business perspective" rather than taking a British perspective as was currently the case. The MD noted that nearly 60% of the paper's current readers were British, and he said he believed paper's overtly British perspective was the main reason which limited its appeal to other European readers.

Strategic development and strategic planning

The Business Development Director has also indicated she is concerned about the newspaper division's approach to strategic planning. She believes that nowadays all businesses need to respond quickly to the opportunities and threats they face, and so it is no longer appropriate to operate a rational model of strategic planning. Consequently, she has proposed that the newspapers division should follow the web division's approach of logical incrementalism.

In a private conversation with the Chief Executive, the Business Development Director also raised her concerns about what the differences in strategic planning approaches across the divisions. She said she felt that the Group would benefit from having a common strategic management style which it applied across all the divisions, and that a Strategic Control style would be the most appropriate for M to adopt.

Required

(a) **Evaluate** the proposals to introduce mobile applications (apps), and **recommend**, with reasons, whether M should introduce the apps. Your evaluation and recommendations should take account of both strategic and financial analysis.

Note: Up to 9 marks are available for calculations. Ignore the time value of money.

(24 marks)

(b) (i) Briefly **explain** the use of Ansoff's product market scope matrix in strategic planning

(4 marks)

(ii) **Categorise**, using Ansoff's product market scope matrix, the proposal to develop mobile applications and the proposal to transform the European newspaper, and **explain** your categorisation for each proposal.

Note: Ansoff's model is also described as the growth vector matrix.

(5 marks)

(c) In the light of the HR Director's comments, **discuss** the scope and nature of the changes which are likely to be required by M plc if it decides to adopt the proposal to develop mobile applications.

(5 marks)

(d) In the light of the Business Development Director's comments, **advise**:

(i) Whether it is appropriate for the Newspapers division to continue to use the traditional rational model for its strategic planning

(6 marks)

(ii) Whether it is appropriate for M plc to introduce a Strategic Control management style in relation to all the divisions.

(6 marks)

(Total marks for question = 50 marks)

Suggested Solution

Marking scheme

Marks

Requirement (a)
Calculations:
Calculating active users (under Free model) — 1
Advertising income (in Free model) — 2
Calculation of annual subscription income (in Subscription model) — 2
Calculation of annual amortisation charge and operating costs – 1 mark each — 2
Calculation of annual profits under each model – 1 mark each — 2
— 9

Evaluation:
Suitability of apps proposals (Up to 2 marks for each valid point) — Up to 6
Acceptability of apps proposals (Up to 2 marks for each valid point) — Up to 6
Feasibility (Up to 2 marks for each valid point) — Up to 6
Maximum marks available for evaluation — Max 12
(To score all the marks available, both options must be included in the evaluation; and the evaluation must address financial and strategic objectives.)

Recommendation: Clear and justified recommendation: Up to 3 marks — Max 3
MAXIMUM FOR REQUIREMENT — 24

Requirement (b) (i)
Brief explanation of each of the four strategic options in Ansoff's matrix – 1 mark each
(There is no requirement to draw the matrix, so marks can still be obtained without doing so). — Up to 4
MAXIMUM FOR REQUIREMENT — 4

Requirement b (ii)
Categorisation of each option – ½ mark each — 1
Explanation of categorisation of apps – 1 mark — 1
Explanation of categorisation of newspaper – Up to 1½ marks for explanation of product; Up to 1½ marks for explanation of market — Up to 3
MAXIMUM FOR REQUIREMENT — 5

Requirement (c)
Up to 3 marks for discussion of scope of change — Max 3
Up to 3 marks for discussion of nature of change — Max 3
MAXIMUM FOR REQUIREMENT — 5

Requirement (d) (i)
Explanation of traditional rational planning model vs less formal models — 1
For any relevant reason why it is appropriate (or is not appropriate) for the Newspapers Division to continue to use the rational model – Up to 2 marks each — Max 6
MAXIMUM FOR REQUIREMENT — 6

Requirement (d) (ii)
Explanation of Strategic Control management style (Goold & Campbell) — 1
For any relevant reason why the Strategic Control management style is (or is not appropriate) – Up to 2 marks each. (Reasons must be linked to the scenario to score the full 2 marks each. Any general points about strategic management styles – max ½ mark). — Max 6
MAXIMUM FOR REQUIREMENT — 6
TOTAL FOR QUESTION — 50

Suggested solution

(a) There are a number of valid points you could have made in part (a), and the marking guide illustrates this. Consequently, you may have made different points to the ones we have in this solution. Provided, your points were relevant, you would earn marks for them.

However, it is important that you make a recommendation at the end of your answer. The scenario states that the two models are not mutually exclusive, so M could introduce both and then leave the customers to choose which version they wanted. This is the option we have recommended in our solution, but you did not need to do this.

Financial analysis of the two proposals

Free apps

	Year 1	Year 2	Year 3	Total (£)
Subscribers	1,420,000	1,775,000	2,130,000	
% regular	30%	30%	30%	
Regularly active users	426,000	532,500	639,000	
Advertising revenue	**426,000**	**798,750**	**958,500**	**2,183,250**

(£1 per unique user <500,000; £1.50 per unique visitor if total visitors > 500,000)

	Year 1	Year 2	Year 3	Total (£)
Development cost: £80,000 (£20,000 per app) Amortised over 3 years	26,667	26,667	26,667	
Direct operating costs (£200,000 in year 1; increasing 5% per year)	200,000	210,000	220,500	
Profit	**199,333**	**562,083**	**711,333**	**1,472,750**

Subscription model

	Year 1	Year 2	Year 3	Total (£)
Average monthly subscribers (*Monthly* subscription £3 per month)	44,375	50,000	53,250	
Annual Revenue	**1,597,500**	**1,800,000**	**1,917,000**	**5,314,500**
Amortisation costs	26,667	26,667	26,667	
Direct operating costs	200,000	210,000	220,500	
Profit	**1,370,833**	**1,563,333**	**1,669,833**	**4,604,000**

Evaluation of the proposals

Suitability

Product portfolio - As a number of M's competitors have already introduced mobile apps, there is a risk that M will lose customers (and therefore market share) if it does not offer its customers equivalent products and service. Therefore, developing its own apps will allow M to address this perceived weakness in its product portfolio, particularly given the feelings among some board members that the market for printed newspapers is declining.

Using existing resources and competences – The Web division already has an online version of the newspapers, so, as the Chief Executive has suggested, providing content for downloads seems to be a logical extension of this existing online presence. It should also make use of the web division's experience at converting the material produced by the journalists and the newspapers division into online content.

Fit with mission and objectives – One possible issue of concern how is whether the subscription model contradicts M's objective of moving towards offering as many news titles as possible free of charge. In this respect, the free app seems to be more suitable, and fits with M's current model of not charging for access to the web versions of its newspapers.

However, it is important to note that the current strategic objectives were set six years ago, and the Business Development Director has now challenged the validity of the objective of offering as many titles as possible free. If the Business Development Director can convince the other directors that it is out-dated – and can get the objective changed – then there will no longer be a conflict between the subscription model and the objectives.

Another possible concern with the apps proposal overall is how well it fits with M's mission statement. Part of M's mission is to provide 'quality reporting and information', but there is a suggestion that M could provide better coverage of important stories by developing **mobile websites** rather than apps.

> *Possible additional point:*
>
> **Cannibalising existing markets** - It is not clear from the MD's figures whether the potential app users are new 'customers' or whether they are existing customers of M. If some of them currently buy the printed newspapers, they may simply switch from the printed copy to the app. In such cases, the apps will not generate any extra revenue for the Group overall, in fact revenue will be lost because the monthly subscription will be lower than the revenue from the printed papers.

Acceptability

Revenue and profit growth – The non-executive directors appear dissatisfied with M's rate of growth and profitability. In this respect, **both models should be acceptable** because they generate additional revenue and operating profit.
However, based on the MD's projections, the subscription model is forecast to generate significantly more additional profit over the three year period than the free apps model, which suggests it may be more acceptable from a purely financial perspective.

Interestingly, however, the rate of growth in years 2 and 3 is higher in the free model, reflecting the fact that M earned the higher rate of commission charges in those two years.

Free titles – Moreover, although simple financial analysis would suggest that the subscription model appears to be the more profitable one, it does not seem to fit with M's strategic objectives. As we have already noted, the subscription model seems to conflict with the objective of offering as many titles as possible free of charge.

However, the free app may also fit better with the sentiment of Strategic Objective 2 'to reach as many potential ... readers as possible.' The number of regular active users of the free app is forecast to be around 10 times that of the number of monthly subscribers.

Acceptability to customers – This disparity between the user numbers might also be seen as an indicator that the subscription service might be less acceptable to customers than a free service.

In this respect, M might consider whether it is possible to offer both models, so that customers who want a free service can get one, while those who are prepared to pay can have an advert-free service. However, in order to evaluate this additional scenario, the MD would need to do some further research to assess the potential impact on user numbers in each model if M offered its customers a choice of options.

Feasibility

Resources and content – The MD's forecasts suggest that there will not be any significant additional staff required to support the apps. However, Director of HR's concerns in this respect do appear to be valid. App users will want to be able to download stories almost instantly, rather than waiting to read about them in the scheduled edition of their paper. In this respect, it appears the **MD may have understated the level of resources required** to prepare content for the apps.

Nonetheless, the level of resources and content required should still be feasible for M, even if they mean that the apps are less profitable than the MD's original forecast suggest.

Money – The scenario suggests that the only development costs involved are developing the applications software, and this costs £20,000 per app. Therefore there should not be any problems with the feasibility of the project from this perspective.

Technology – The scenario does not mention any technology requirements or constraints in relation to introducing mobile apps. It seems reasonable to assume that since M already produces online newspapers, it should have the technological capability to produce the related mobile applications as well.

Time – Again, it is not clear from the scenario what the intended timetable is for developing and introducing the apps, but it seems unlikely that there will be any externally-imposed deadlines. Equally, the amount of development work required to prepare the develops should not be particularly extensive. Therefore, the timescales involved should not prevent the project being feasible.

Recommendation

Opportunity for growth – Overall the idea to introduce apps looks as if it will generate additional revenues and profits for M, and on this basis, M should introduce them.

Model to use – Based solely on the financial analysis, it would look as if M should use the subscription model, because this offers higher overall revenues and profits. However, the free apps model seems to fit better with M's current strategic objectives. Consequently, M should consider whether it can adopt a hybrid approach, and offer customers the option of either free apps (with adverts) or a subscription service (with no adverts).

However, if M is considering this hybrid approach, then it needs to do gather some additional information on how this approach would affect the costs, revenues and profits involved in introducing the apps.

(b)

(i)

Ansoff's growth vector matrix identifies a range of strategic options which firms can use to try to achieve growth. The matrix identifies four product-market strategies:

Market penetration – a firm continues to sell its existing products or services to existing markets, but it gets existing customers to buy more of those products or services.

Market development – a firm continues to sell its existing products or services, but expands sales into new markets.

Product development – a firm launches new products but sells them to existing markets.

Diversification – a firm launches new products, and sells them to new markets.

(ii)

> The question asks you to 'categorise', so you must do allocate each proposal to a category, but depending on how you interpret the concepts of 'product' and 'market' in relation to the European newspaper your categorisation may differ from that in our solution below. Nonetheless, provided you present a relevant and valid explanation for your categorisation you would still earn the marks available.

Developing mobile applications

Product development – The mobile applications would be a **new addition to M's product portfolio**. However, it seems likely that M will offer the apps alongside its existing products (printed newspapers, online newspapers) in its **existing markets**, rather than selling them to new markets.

European newspaper

Product format – Although the MD has proposed changing the format of the paper, the product remains a printed newspaper. Therefore the extent to which M is launches a new product is debatable. However, the change to a high-end tabloid format, in conjunction with the change in the paper's focus, suggests that the relaunched paper can be treated as a **new product**.

Market focus – Again, it is debatable whether M is changing the market for the newspaper or not. The paper has always been aimed at the pan-European market, and this will continue to be the case. However, the re-launched paper seems to be aimed specifically at the business community, and the MD's suggestion that the paper needs a more specific market niche suggests he envisages that business readers as a different market from the paper's existing market. To this end, we can suggest that M is expanding into a **new market**.

On the basis that the re-launched paper is a new product, being sold into a new market, then the proposal represents a **diversification strategy**.

(c)

Scope of change

Building on existing business and capabilities – The web division already produces online news content, and so the proposal to develop mobile apps seem likely to be an extension of the existing business rather than creating an entirely new business.

Realignment – The development of the apps may have some impact on the way M operates at a practical level. For example, as the Director of HR has suggested stories may need to be reported and published more quickly than they historically have been. This may require additional systems or processes being added to M's existing operations. However, such changes are only likely to affect M at an operational level, rather than leading to any underlying change in the culture or central beliefs of the organisation.

In this respect, the change can be seen as a realignment of M's existing strategy, and a way of helping it to reinforce its pre-existing mission 'to be the best news media organisation in Europe.'

Nature of change

Incremental change – As we have already suggested, the change is likely to build on the existing capabilities and processes within the web division. Therefore, it is likely to be manifest in a series of step-by-step, incremental changes, rather than a sudden one-off change.

External triggers - However, given that a number of other newspapers and news agencies have already introduced mobile apps, and M doesn't want to lose its share of the news market to them, this suggests the change will need to be **more rapid** than might otherwise be the case with an incremental change.

(d)

(i)

Stability vs uncertainty – The traditional rational model provides a structure and order to strategic planning, which less formal approaches to strategic planning do not. This suggests that the traditional rational model is appropriate to a stable and predictable environment, whereas the less formal approaches may be more appropriate in a context of rapid change and uncertainty.

Context – The Web division and Newspapers division appear to be operating in different market environments. While the Web division is operating in a growth market, the Newspaper division is operating in a more mature

market. The Web division is only able to pursue its more opportunist strategy because opportunities arise which it can take advantage of. By contrast, the opportunities available to the Newspaper division are likely to be much more limited, and its slow revenue growth seems to reinforce this. In this respect, it does seem appropriate for the Newspaper division to continue to use a rational model approach to strategic planning.

Control and co-ordination – The traditional rational model is also appropriate for large organisations, where detailed forecasting and planning are needed to co-ordinate activities. The Newspapers division is the largest division within M, which again suggests that a formal planning approach which allows control and co-ordination to be maintained over the division is appropriate. Again, this control aspect is also appropriate in the context of a mature market, where controlling costs and margins will be important in helping the Newspapers division to maintain its profitability.

Established strategic objectives – M's four main strategic objectives were established six years ago (in 2005), and have not been updated since. This suggests that the overall approach to strategic planning, and the corporate culture, is relatively formal rather than flexible. Again, this suggests that the Newspaper Division's rational model approach is consistent with the Group's perspective at the moment.

However, the Business Development Director's concern that strategic objective number four no longer reflects current day practice is an important reminder of one of the disadvantages of the rational model: it is not appropriate to environments in which strategic plans need to be regularly revised. Overall, it is appropriate for the Newspapers Division to continue to use the traditional rational model at the current time. However, this may cease to be the case if there are any significant changes to M's market environment or its objectives.

(ii)

Strategic control – The Strategic Control management style means a corporate centre that has little involvement in the strategic planning of its divisions but imposes tighter controls over their performance. The corporate centre sets financial and non-financial targets for the divisions, but it leaves the divisions to choose their own strategies to meet those targets. However, the centre will then review the divisions' plans for acceptability.

Divisional autonomy – It appears that the Web Division and the Advertising Division currently have quite high degrees of autonomy, making them appropriate for the strategic control style. For example, neither of them appears to have a formalised budget which is approved by the Board. Furthermore, it seems that because M plc are content that the Web Division is profitable, the corporate centre has not looked at the Division's results or performance in any detail. Instead, the Web division has undertaken its own review of all its costs.

However, the Newspaper Division does have a formalised budget, which is submitted to the Board for authorisation.

Appropriateness of strategic control management style – In this respect, the Strategic Control management style could be appropriate, because it will allow the divisions to retain their autonomy over how they run their own businesses. If this autonomy were significantly reduced it is likely that this would create unrest among the managers in the Web and Advertising Divisions.

Working towards objectives – The Strategic Control management style would also be appropriate because it will require the corporate centre M plc to establish a framework of objectives (both financial and non-financial) for them to work towards. Given that there could be increasing pressure from the Non-Executive Directors to improve performance, establishing such a framework of objectives would help ensure that the division's performance objectives are directly aligned to the Group's.

Newspapers Division – One potential area of concern, however, about introducing a Strategic Control style could be the impact it has on the management team in the Newspaper Division. The Newspaper Division currently prepares annual plans which it present to the Group board for approval. Depending on the level of the Group's involvement in developing these plans, it is possible that the Newspaper Division is currently being managed under a **Strategic Planning style** rather than a Strategic Control style. Therefore the change to a new style (the Strategic Control style) may lead to resentment and a fall in motivation among the Division's management team.

As was the case with the rational planning model compared to less formal models, it may be the case that the newspapers division is actually better suited to a different management style than the other divisions.

INDEX

Note: **Key Terms** and their references are given in **bold**.

Notes

Notes

LEARNING MEDIA

Notes

Notes

Notes

Review Form – Paper E3 Enterprise Strategy (6/12)

Please help us to ensure that the CIMA learning materials we produce remain as accurate and user-friendly as possible. We cannot promise to answer every submission we receive, but we do promise that it will be read and taken into account when we up-date this Study Text.

Name: _____   Address: _____

_____

_____

How have you used this Study Text?
(Tick one box only)

☐ Home study (book only)

☐ On a course: college _____

☐ With 'correspondence' package

☐ Other _____

Why did you decide to purchase this Study Text? *(Tick one box only)*

☐ Have used BPP Texts in the past

☐ Recommendation by friend/colleague

☐ Recommendation by a lecturer at college

☐ Saw information on BPP website

☐ Saw advertising

☐ Other _____

During the past six months do you recall seeing/receiving any of the following?
(Tick as many boxes as are relevant)

☐ Our advertisement in *Financial Management*

☐ Our advertisement in *Pass*

☐ Our advertisement in *PQ*

☐ Our brochure with a letter through the post

☐ Our website www.bpp.com

Which (if any) aspects of our advertising do you find useful?
(Tick as many boxes as are relevant)

☐ Prices and publication dates of new editions

☐ Information on Text content

☐ Facility to order books off-the-page

☐ None of the above

Which BPP products have you used?

Text	☑	*Success CD*	☐
Kit	☐	*i-Pass*	☐
Passcard	☐	*Interactive Passcard*	☐

Your ratings, comments and suggestions would be appreciated on the following areas.

	Very useful	Useful	Not useful
Introductory section	☐	☐	☐
Chapter introductions	☐	☐	☐
Key terms	☐	☐	☐
Quality of explanations	☐	☐	☐
Case studies and other examples	☐	☐	☐
Exam skills and alerts	☐	☐	☐
Questions and answers in each chapter	☐	☐	☐
Fast forwards and chapter roundups	☐	☐	☐
Quick quizzes	☐	☐	☐
Question Bank	☐	☐	☐
Answer Bank	☐	☐	☐
OT Bank	☐	☐	☐
Index	☐	☐	☐

	Excellent	Good	Adeqate	Poor
Overall opinion of this Study Text	☐	☐	☐	☐

Do you intend to continue using BPP products?   Yes ☐   No ☐

On the reverse of this page is space for you to write your comments about our Study Text We welcome your feedback. The BPP Learning Media author of this edition can be e-mailed at: adrianthomas@bpp.com

Please return this form to: Stephen Osborne, CIMA Publishing Manager, BPP Learning Media Ltd, FREEPOST, London, W12 8BR

TELL US WHAT YOU THINK

Please note any further comments and suggestions/errors below. For example, was the text accurate, readable, concise, user-friendly and comprehensive?